FOR ORGANS, PIANOS & ELECTRONIC KEYBOARDS

E-Z PLAY® TODAY

82

THE BIG BOOK OF FOLK POP ROCK

ISBN 978-1-4234-8080-8

HAL•LEONARD®
CORPORATION
7777 W. BLUEMOUND RD. P.O. BOX 13819 MILWAUKEE, WI 53213

For all works contained herein:
Unauthorized copying, arranging, adapting, recording, Internet posting, public performance,
or other distribution of the printed music in this publication is an infringement of copyright.
Infringers are liable under the law.

E-Z Play® Today Music Notation © 1975 by HAL LEONARD CORPORATION

E-Z PLAY and EASY ELECTRONIC KEYBOARD MUSIC are registered trademarks of HAL LEONARD CORPORATION.

4	**ALL I KNOW**	ART GARFUNKEL
8	**AMERICAN PIE**	DON MCLEAN
20	**AMERICAN TUNE**	PAUL SIMON
24	**ANNIE'S SONG**	JOHN DENVER
28	**ANTICIPATION**	CARLY SIMON
32	**AT SEVENTEEN**	JANIS IAN
36	**BEST OF MY LOVE**	EAGLES
38	**BLACKBIRD**	THE BEATLES
40	**CONSTANT CRAVING**	K.D. LANG
44	**COTTON FIELDS**	THE HIGHWAYMEN
17	**DO YOU BELIEVE IN MAGIC**	THE LOVIN' SPOONFUL
46	**DON'T LET THE RAIN COME DOWN**	SERENDIPITY PLAYERS
54	**DUST IN THE WIND**	KANSAS
56	**EVERYBODY'S TALKIN'**	HARRY NILSSON
49	**EVERYTHING I OWN**	BREAD
58	**FAST CAR**	TRACY CHAPMAN
65	**GET CLOSER**	SEALS & CROFTS
70	**HAPPY TOGETHER**	THE TURTLES
72	**HELLO, IT'S ME**	TODD RUNDGREN
82	**HELP ME MAKE IT THROUGH THE NIGHT**	KRIS KRISTOFFERSON
75	**HER TOWN TOO**	JAMES TAYLOR
84	**I FEEL THE EARTH MOVE**	CAROLE KING
92	**I'LL HAVE TO SAY I LOVE YOU IN A SONG**	JIM CROCE
94	**IF I WERE A CARPENTER**	BOBBY DARIN
87	**LAST GOODBYE**	JEFF BUCKLEY
96	**LEAVING ON A JET PLANE**	JOHN DENVER

99	**LEMON TREE**	PETER, PAUL & MARY
102	**LONGER**	DAN FOGELBERG
104	**LOVE THE ONE YOU'RE WITH**	CROSBY, STILLS & NASH
114	**MAKE IT WITH YOU**	BREAD
118	**ME AND BOBBY MCGEE**	JANIS JOPLIN
122	**MONDAY, MONDAY**	THE MAMA & THE PAPAS
109	**MRS. ROBINSON**	SIMON & GARFUNKEL
124	**NIGHTS IN WHITE SATIN**	THE MOODY BLUES
127	**NORWEGIAN WOOD**	THE BEATLES
130	**OPERATOR (THAT'S NOT THE WAY IT FEELS)**	JIM CROCE
132	**PUFF THE MAGIC DRAGON**	PETER, PAUL & MARY
134	**SAME OLD LANG SYNE**	DAN FOGELBERG
140	**SAN FRANCISCO**	SCOTT MCKENZIE
137	**SARA SMILE**	DARYL HALL & JOHN OATES
142	**SCOTCH AND SODA**	THE KINGSTON TRIO
144	**SENTIMENTAL LADY**	BOB WELCH
147	**SOMEBODY TO LOVE**	JEFFERSON AIRPLANE
152	**SUNSHINE (GO AWAY TODAY)**	JONATHAN EDWARDS
155	**SUNSHINE SUPERMAN**	DONOVAN
158	**THIS LAND IS YOUR LAND**	THE NEW CHRISTY MINSTRELS
160	**THOSE WERE THE DAYS**	MARY HOPKIN
162	**TIME IN A BOTTLE**	JIM CROCE
164	**VINCENT (STARRY STARRY NIGHT)**	DON MCLEAN
168	**WE JUST DISAGREE**	DAVE MASON
176	**WHERE HAVE ALL THE FLOWERS GONE?**	THE KINGSTON TRIO
171	**YOU'RE ONLY LONELY**	J.D. SOUTHER
178	**YOU'VE GOT A FRIEND**	JAMES TAYLOR

All I Know

Registration 1
Rhythm: Country Pop or 4/4 Ballad

Words and Music by
Jimmy Webb

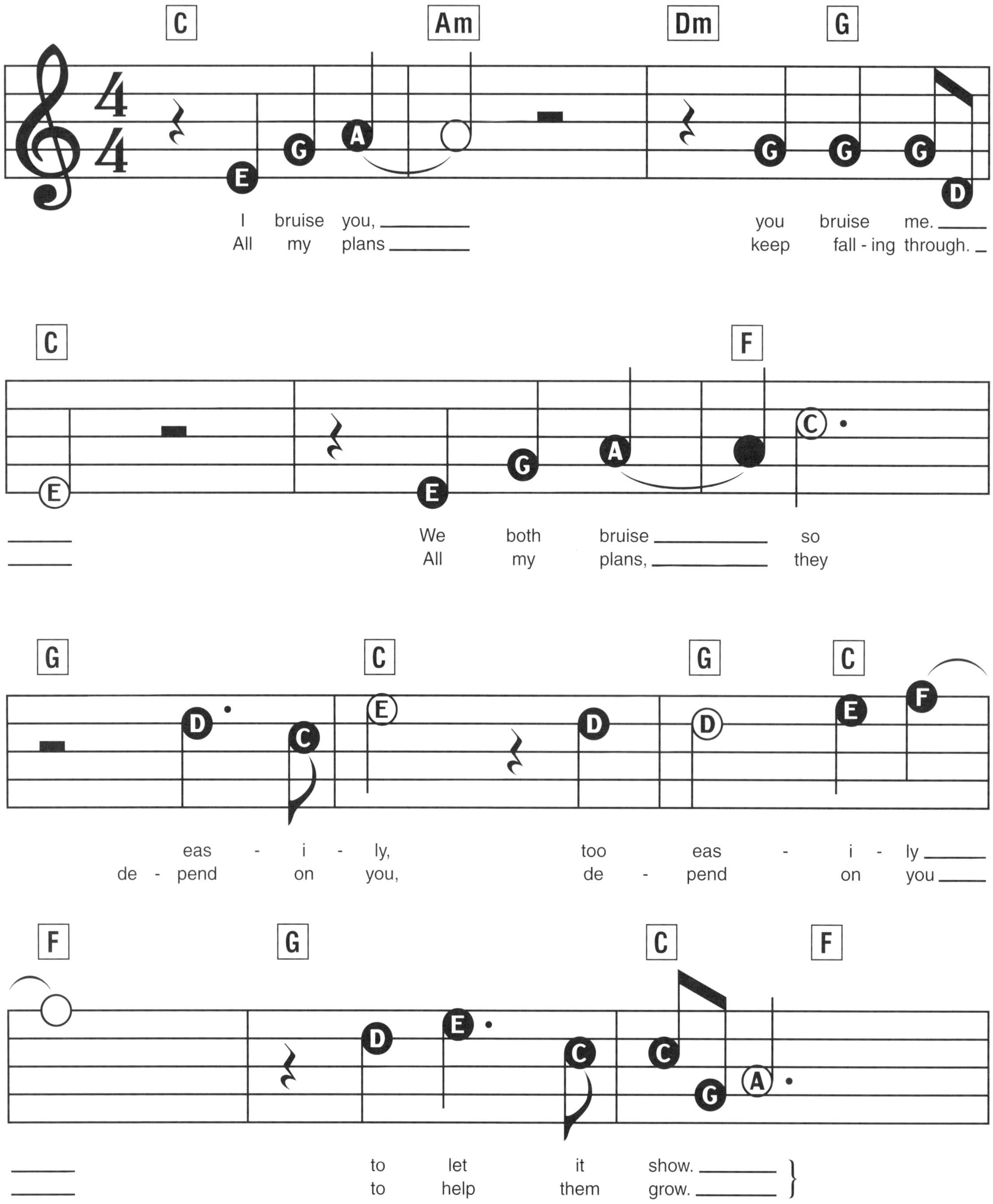

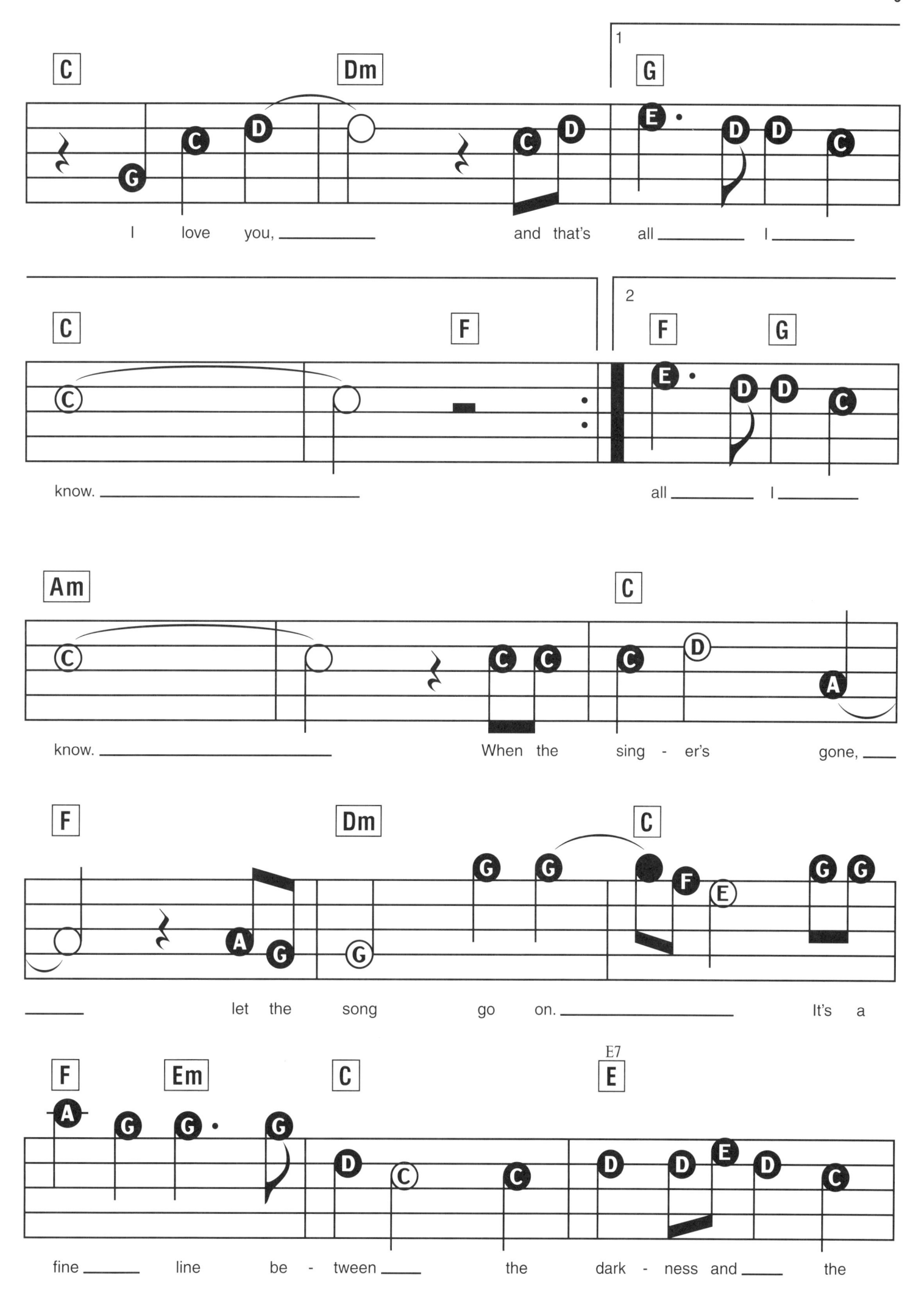

I love you, and that's all I know. all I know. When the singer's gone, let the song go on. It's a fine line be-tween the dark-ness and the

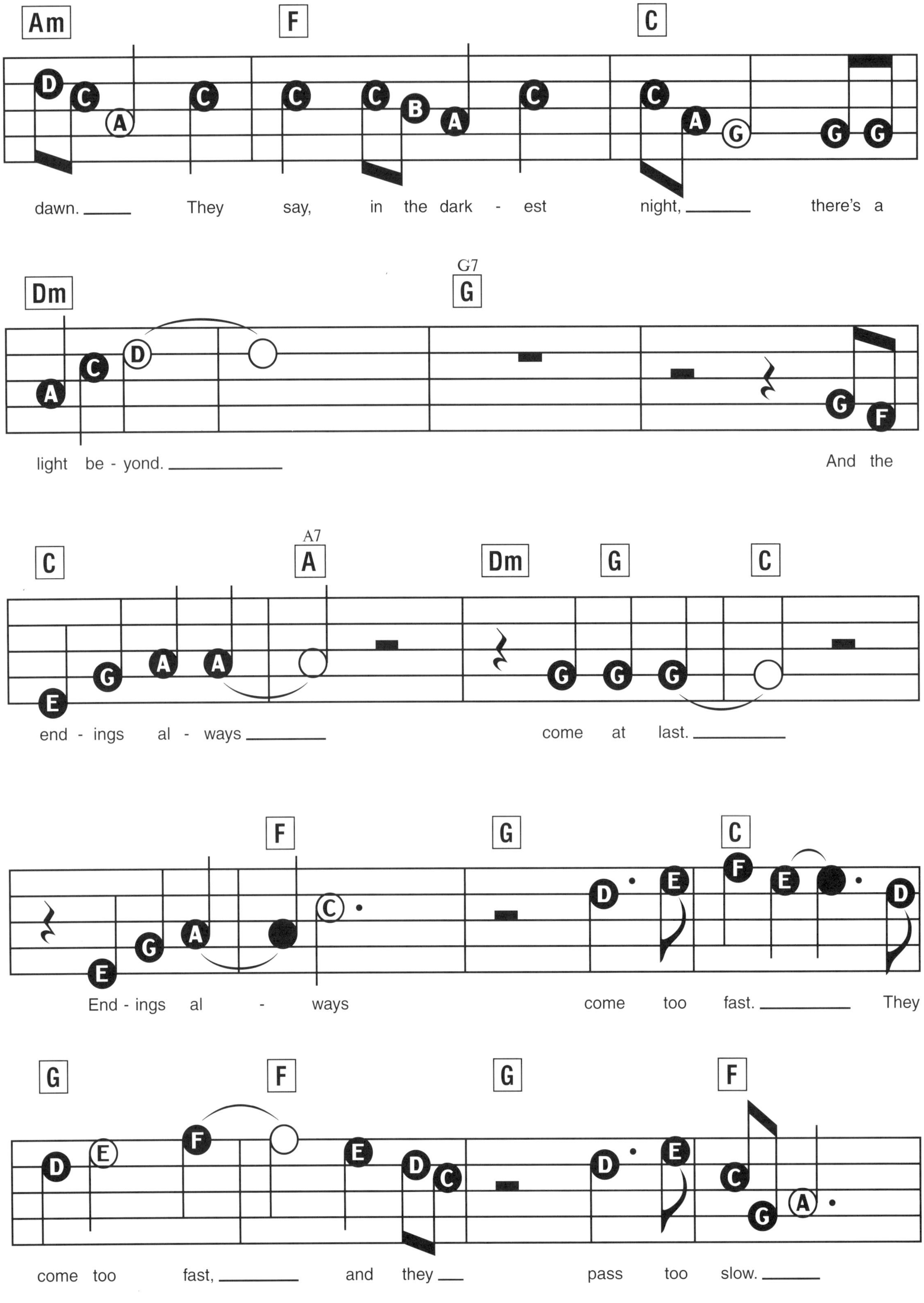
Am F C
dawn. They say, in the dark - est night, there's a
Dm G7 G
light be - yond. And the
C A7 A Dm G C
end - ings al - ways come at last.
F G C
End - ings al - ways come too fast. They
G F G F
come too fast, and they pass too slow.

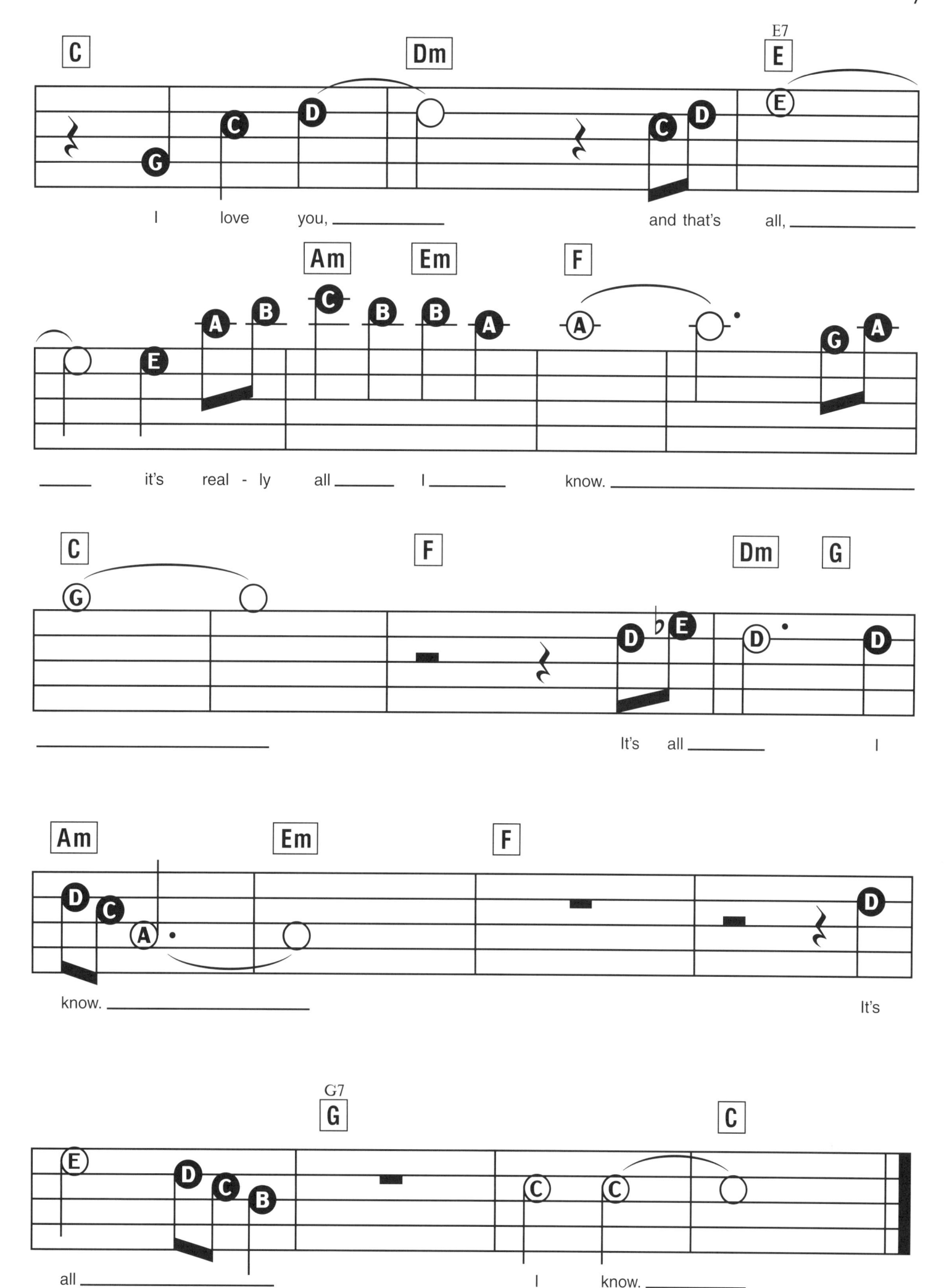

I love you, _____ and that's all, _____ it's real-ly all _____ I _____ know. _____ It's all _____ I know. _____ It's all _____ I know. _____

American Pie

Registration 2
Rhythm: Rock

Words and Music by
Don McLean

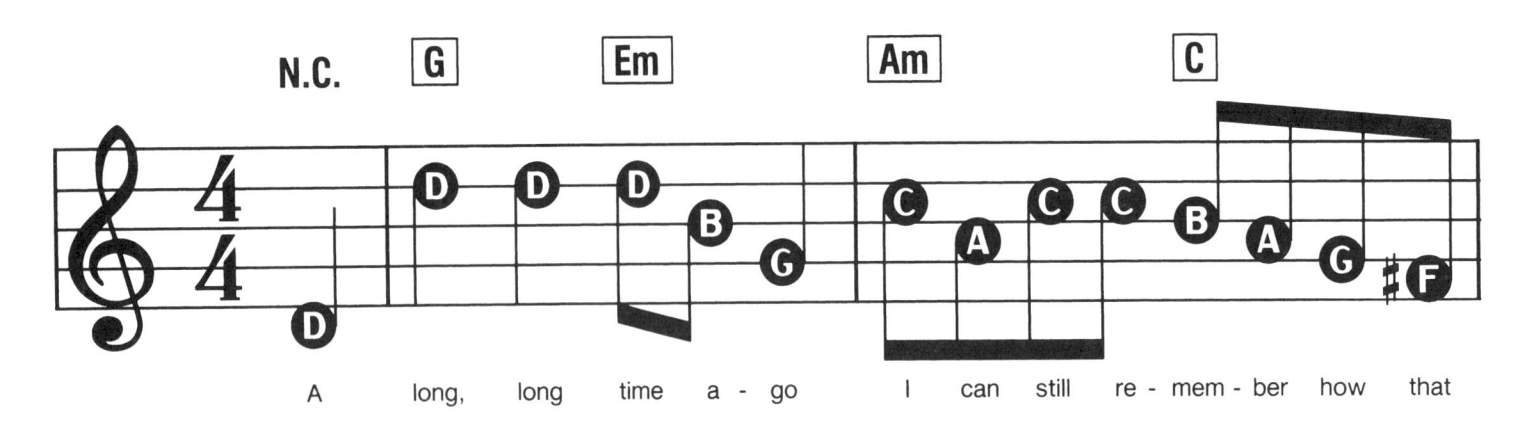

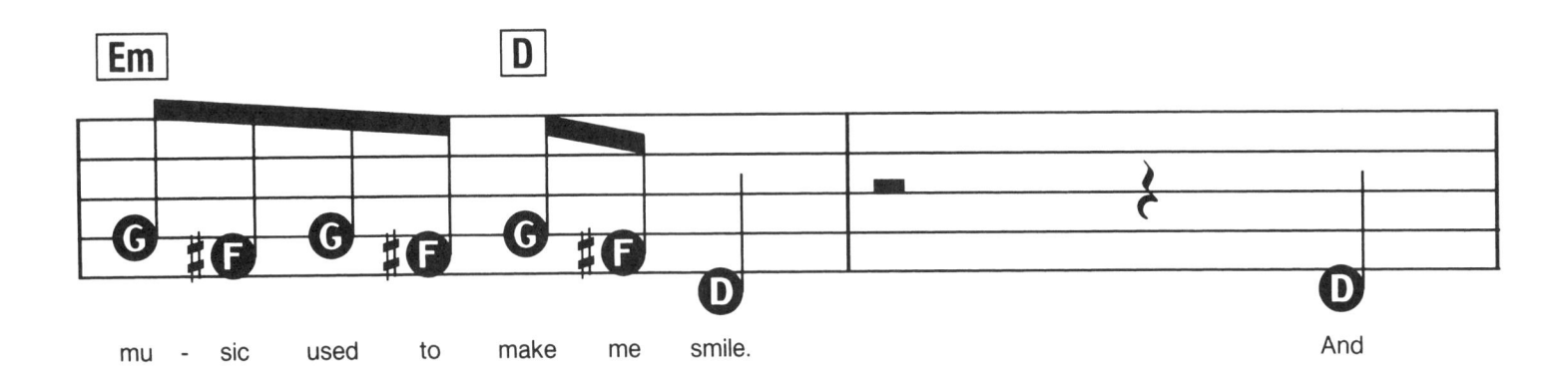

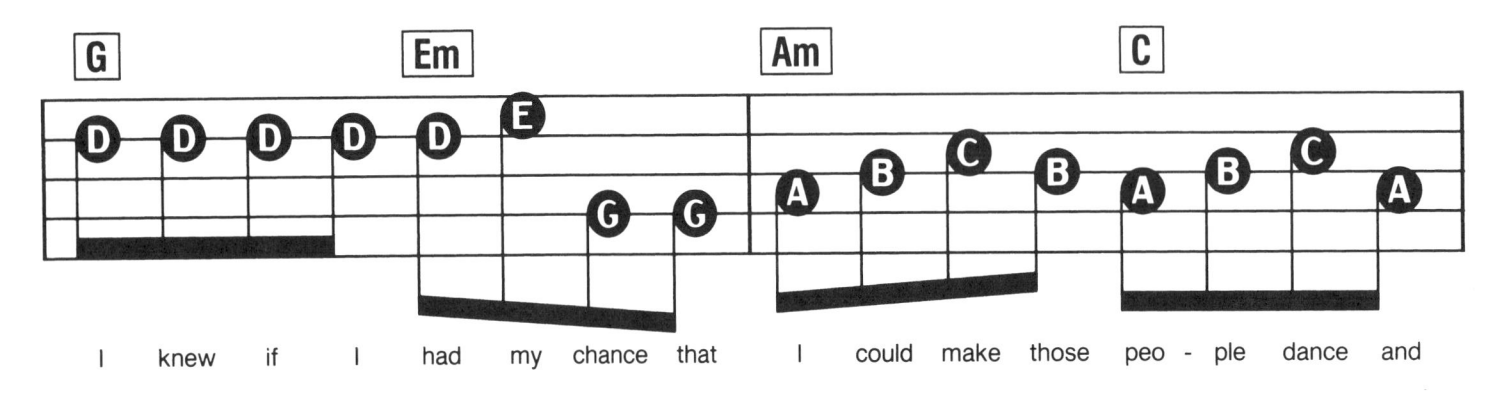

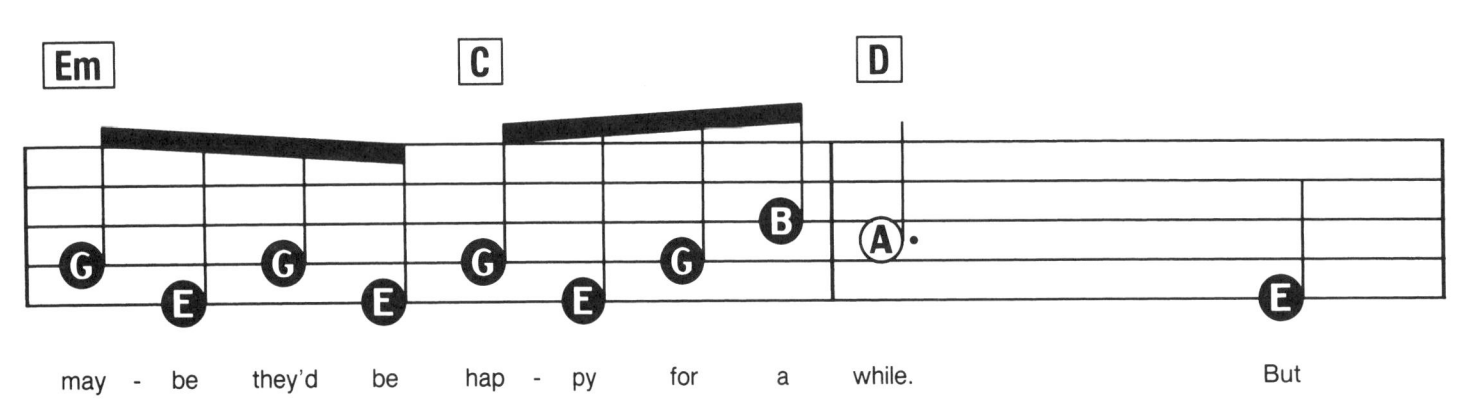

A long, long time ago I can still re-mem-ber how that mu-sic used to make me smile. And I knew if I had my chance that I could make those peo-ple dance and may-be they'd be hap-py for a while. But

Copyright © 1971, 1972 BENNY BIRD CO., INC.
Copyright Renewed
All Rights Controlled and Administered by SONGS OF UNIVERSAL, INC.
All Rights Reserved   Used by Permission

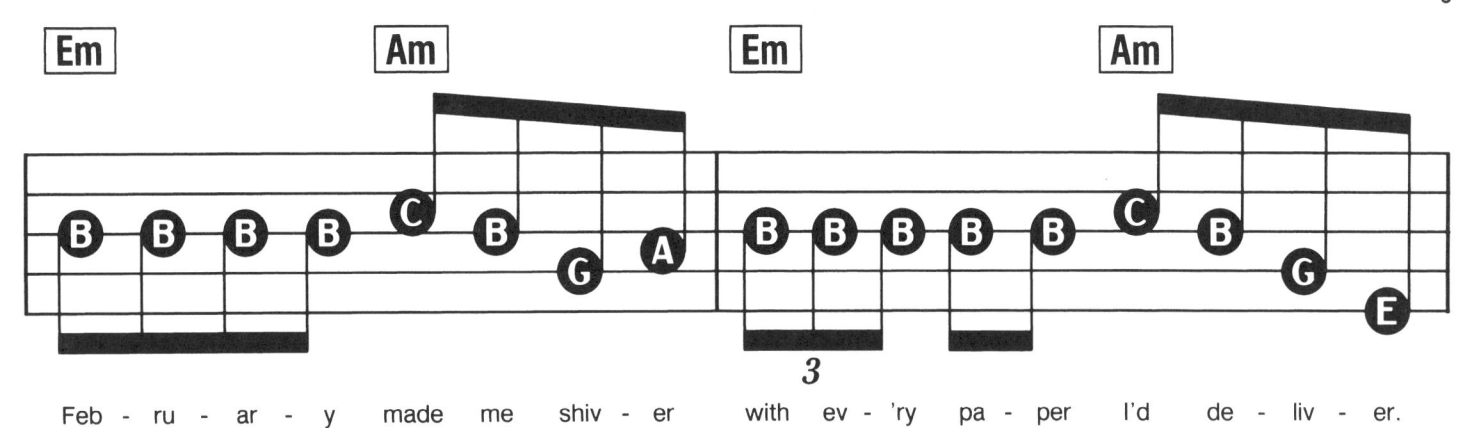

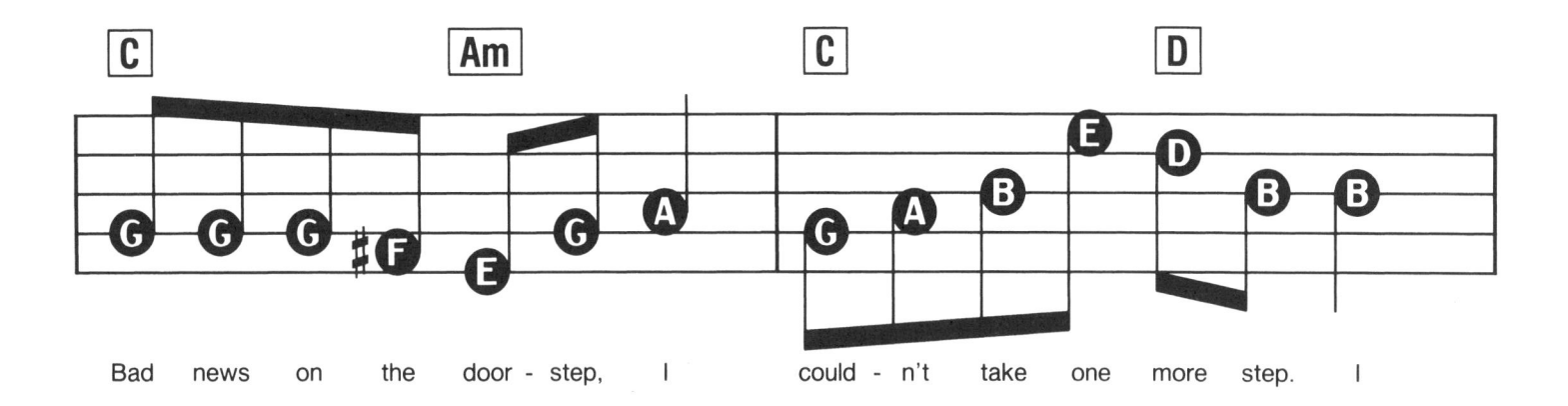

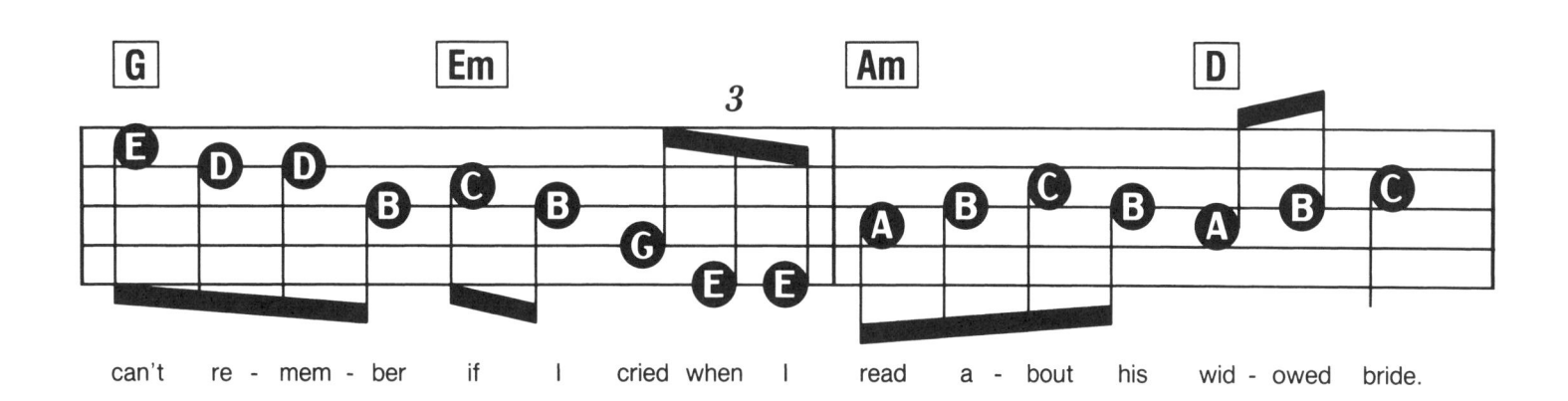

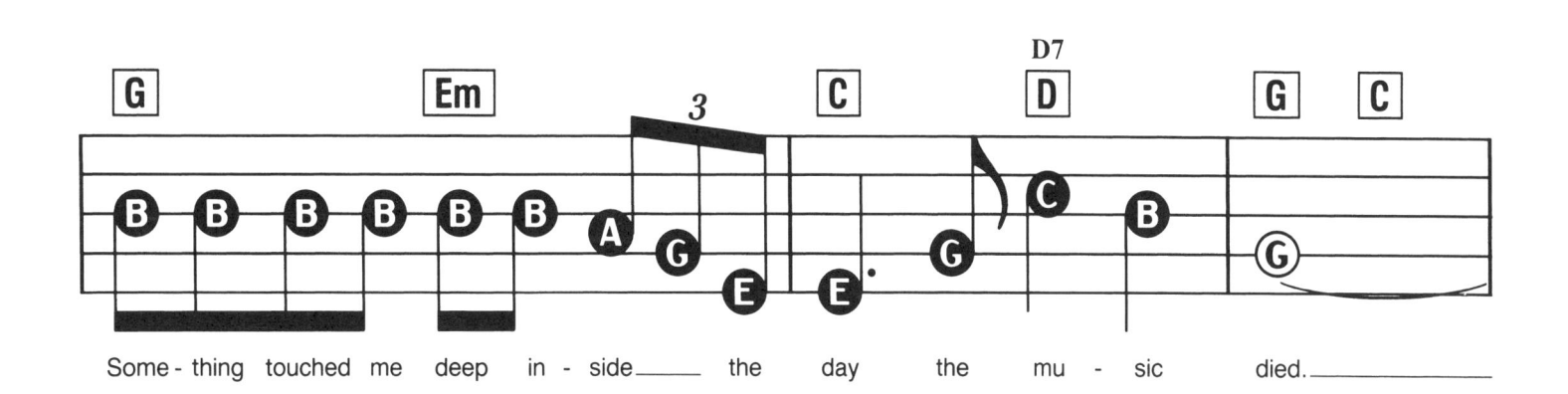

| Em | Am | Em | Am |

February made me shiver with ev-'ry pa-per I'd de-liv-er.

| C | Am | C | D |

Bad news on the door-step, I could-n't take one more step. I

| G | Em | Am | D |

can't re-mem-ber if I cried when I read a-bout his wid-owed bride.

| G | Em | C | D (D7) | G | C |

Some-thing touched me deep in-side____ the day the mu-sic died.____

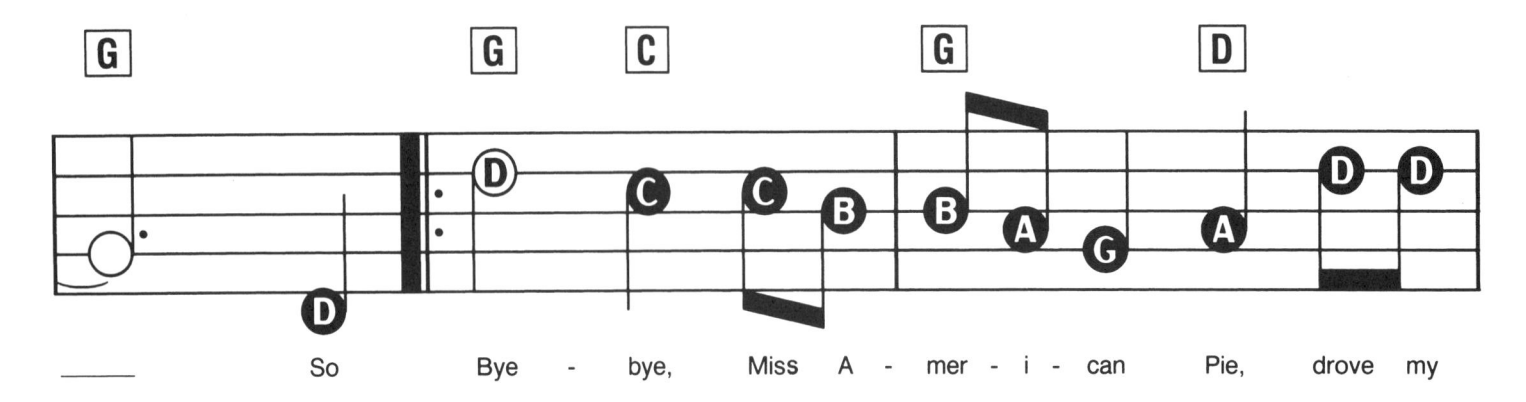

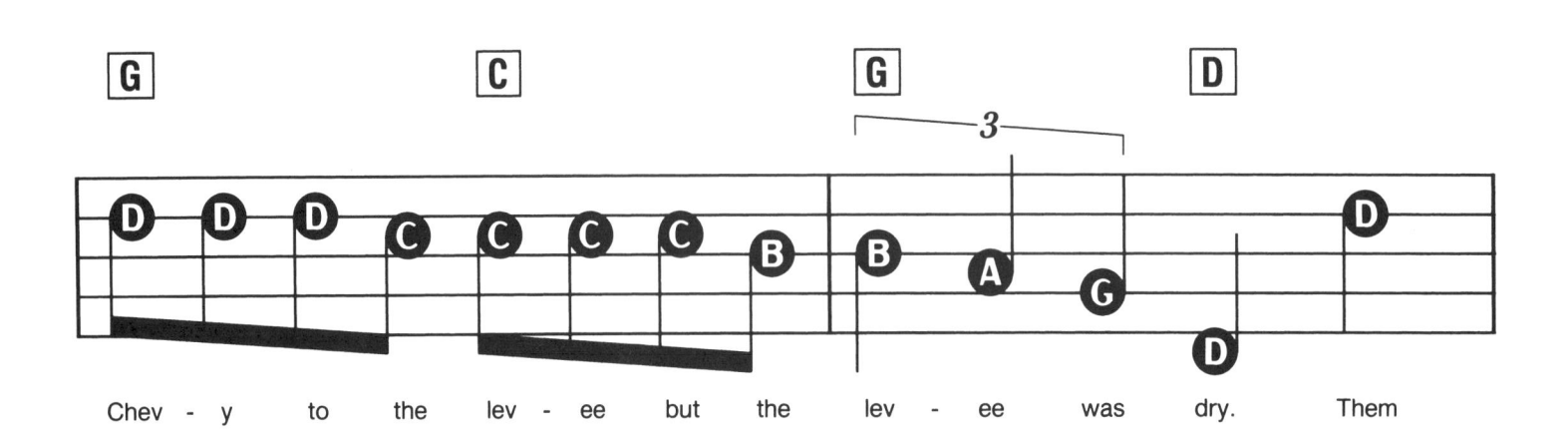

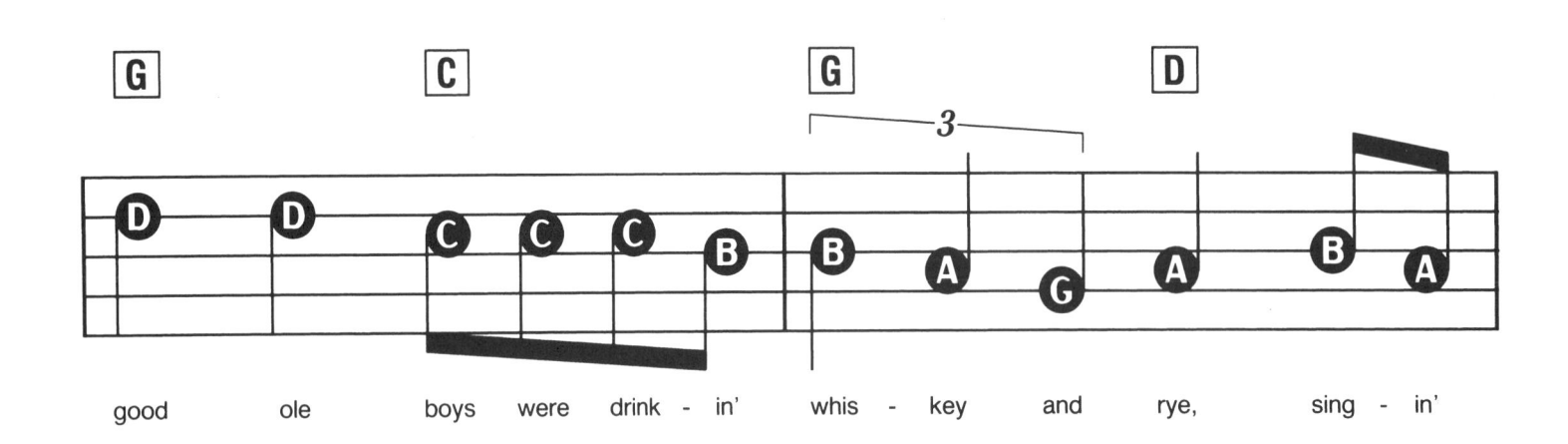

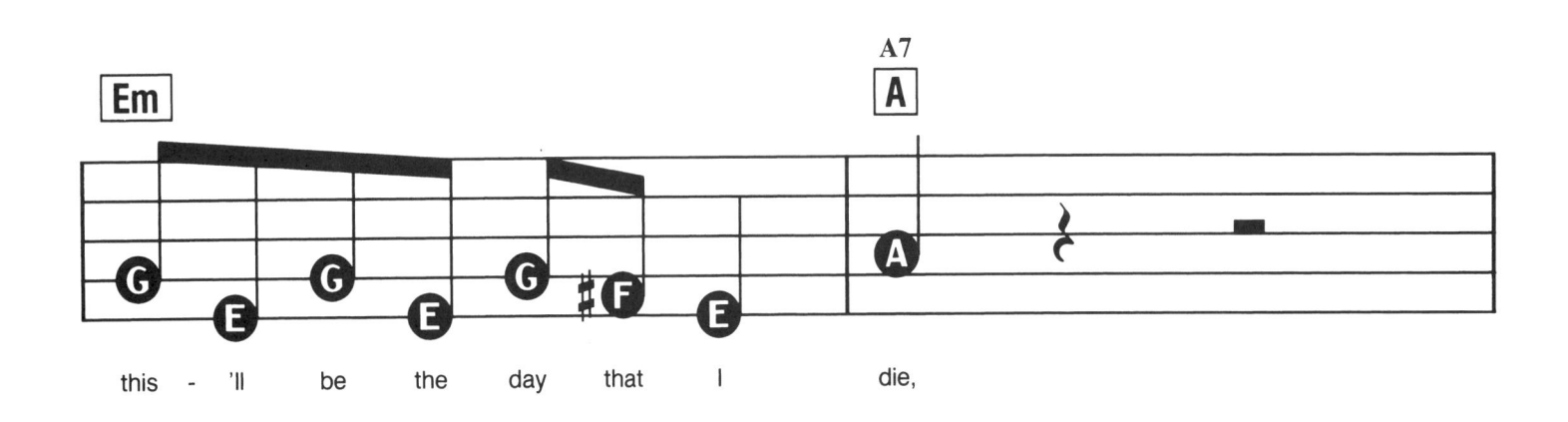

| G | G | C | G | D |

So Bye - bye, Miss A - mer - i - can Pie, drove my

| G | C | G | D |

Chev - y to the lev - ee but the lev - ee was dry. Them

| G | C | G | D |

good ole boys were drink - in' whis - key and rye, sing - in'

| Em | A (A7) |

this - 'll be the day that I die,

11

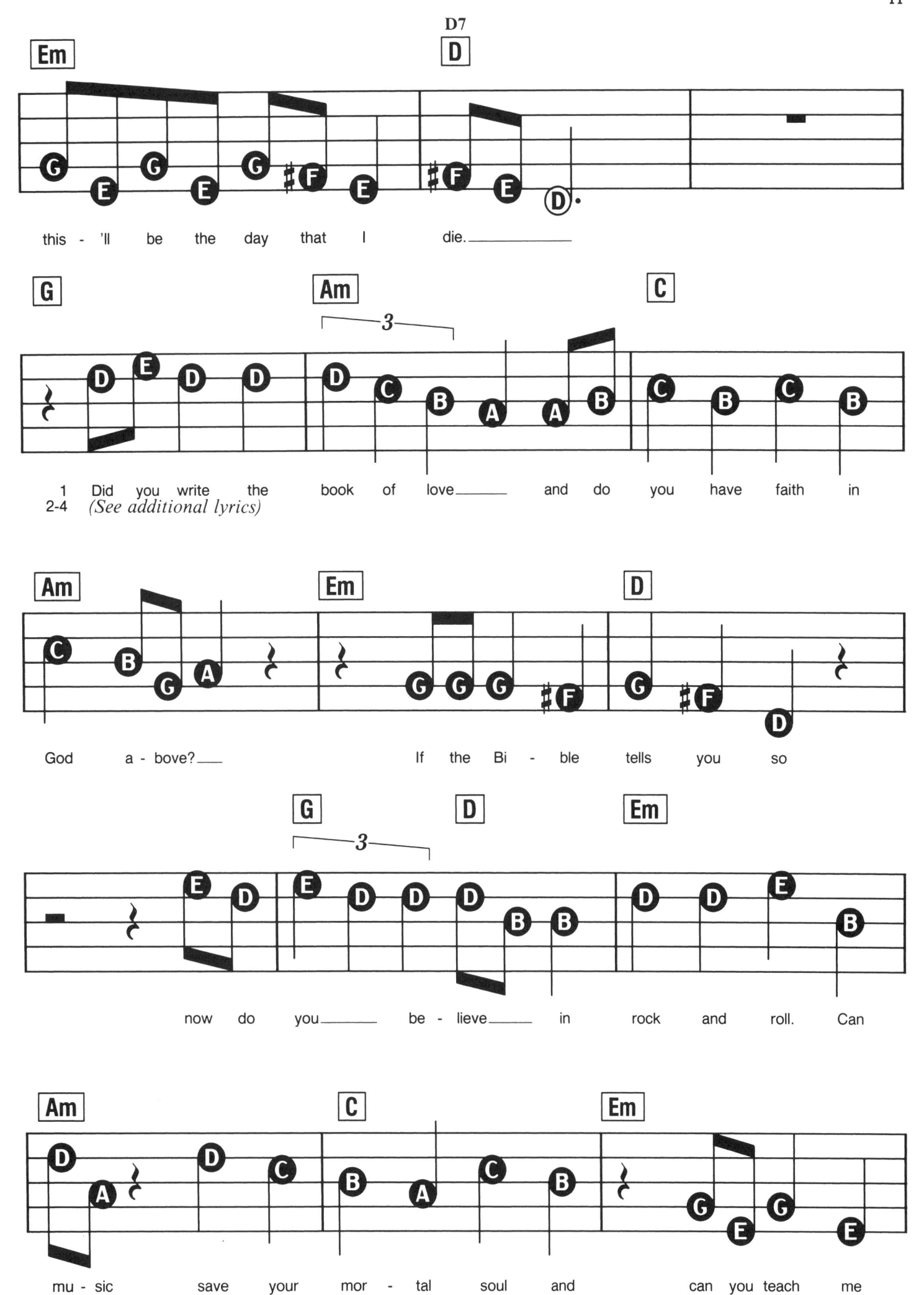

12

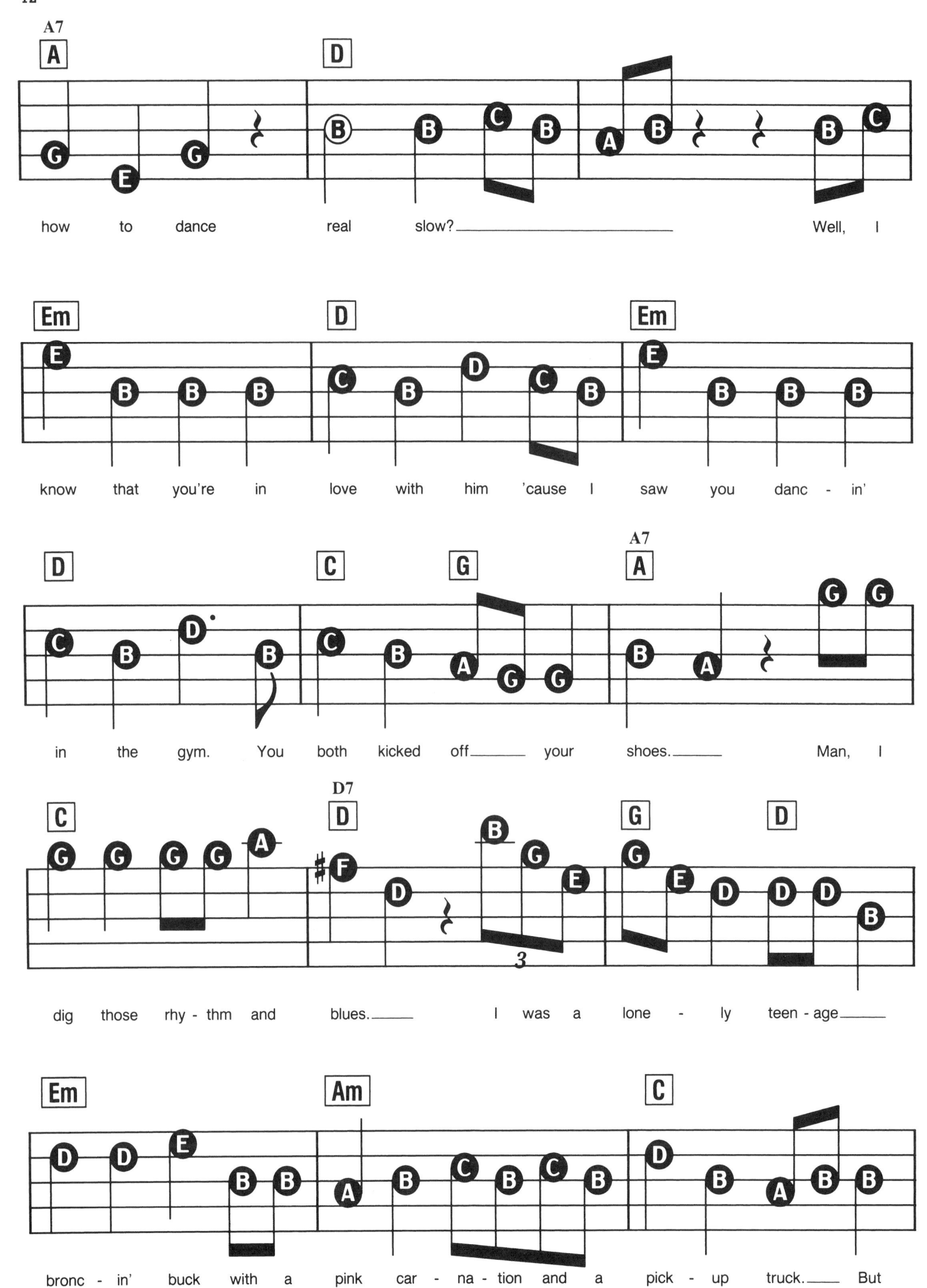

how to dance real slow? _____ Well, I know that you're in love with him 'cause I saw you dancin' in the gym. You both kicked off ___ your shoes. ___ Man, I dig those rhy-thm and blues. ___ I was a lone-ly teen-age ___ bronc-in' buck with a pink car-na-tion and a pick-up truck. ___ But

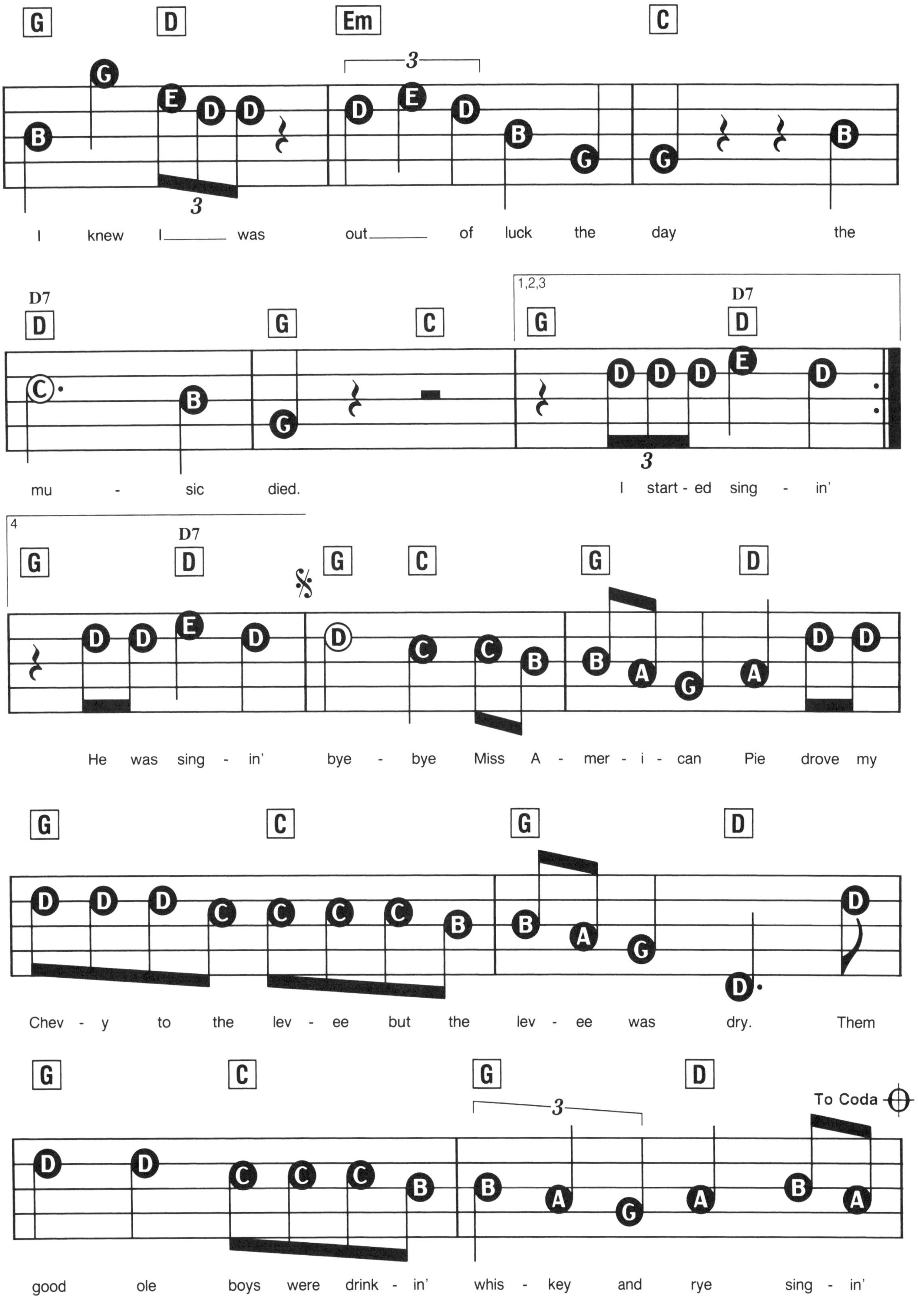
G D Em C
I knew I___ was out___ of luck the day the
D7
D G C
1,2,3
G
D7
D
mu - sic died.
I start - ed sing - in'
4
G
D7
D
G C G D
He was sing - in' bye - bye Miss A - mer - i - can Pie drove my
G C G D
Chev - y to the lev - ee but the lev - ee was dry. Them
G C G D
To Coda
good ole boys were drink - in' whis - key and rye sing - in'

14

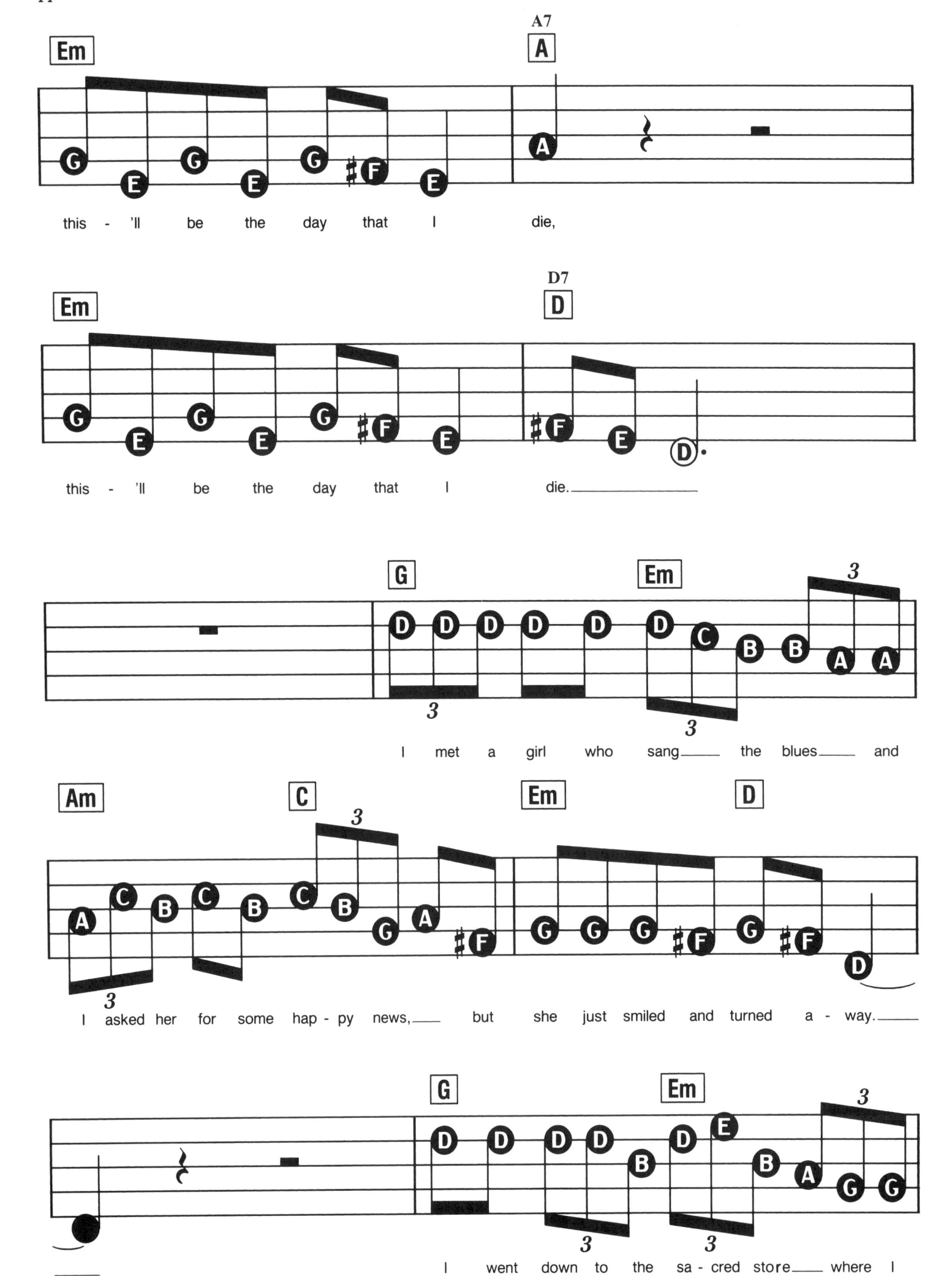

Em | **A7 / A**

G E G E G F♯ E | A

this-'ll be the day that I die,

Em | **D7 / D**

G E G E G F♯ E | F♯ E D.

this-'ll be the day that I die.

G | **Em**

D D D D D D C B B A A

I met a girl who sang the blues and

Am | **C** | **Em** | **D**

A C B C B C B G A | G G G F♯ G F♯ D

I asked her for some hap-py news, but she just smiled and turned a-way.

G | **Em**

D D D D D E B B A G G

I went down to the sa-cred store where I

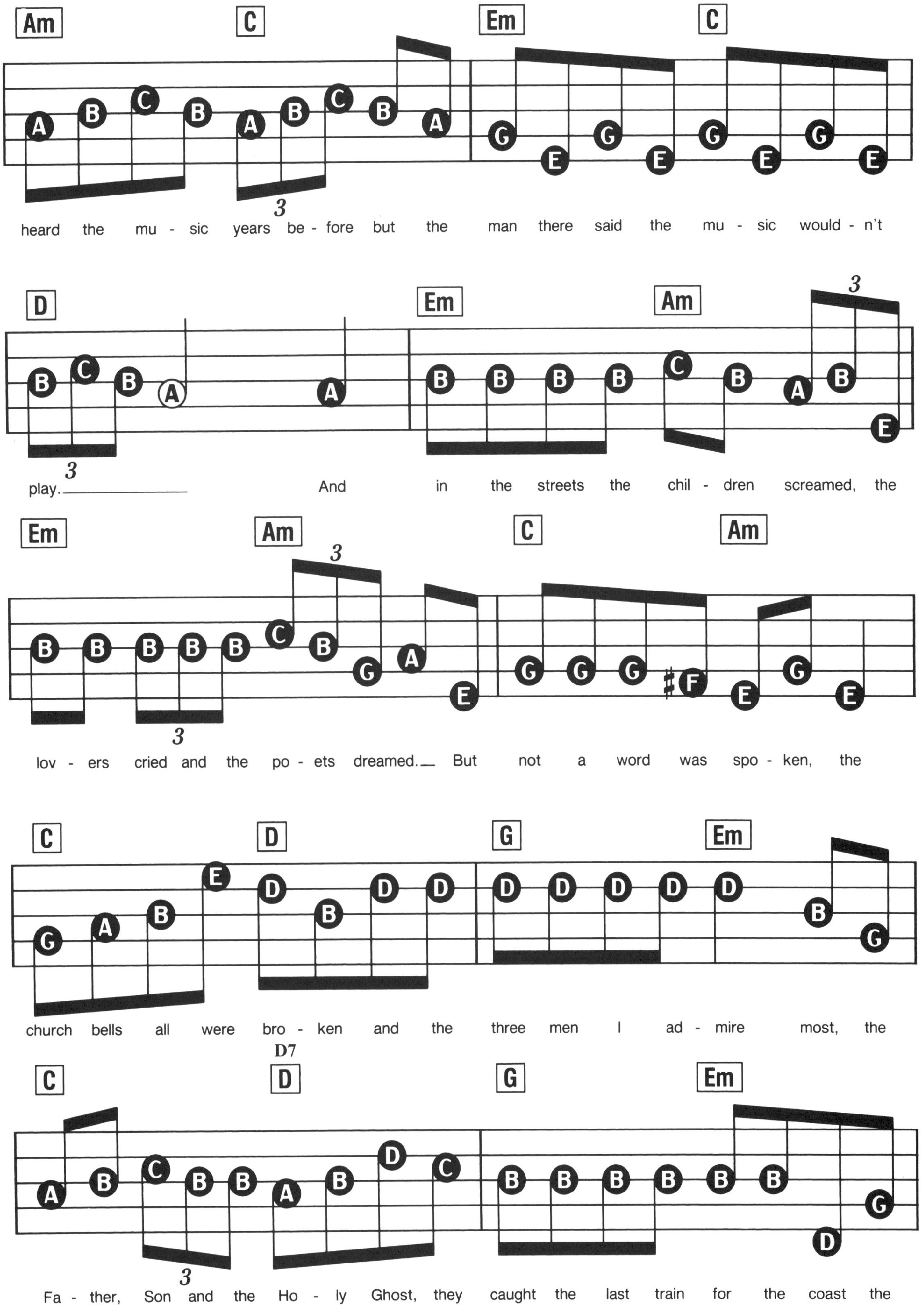
Am C Em C
heard the mu - sic years be - fore but the man there said the mu - sic would - n't
3
D Em Am
3
play. And in the streets the chil - dren screamed, the
Em Am C Am
3
3
lov - ers cried and the po - ets dreamed. But not a word was spo - ken, the
C D G Em
church bells all were bro - ken and the three men I ad - mire most, the
D7
C D G Em
3
Fa - ther, Son and the Ho - ly Ghost, they caught the last train for the coast the

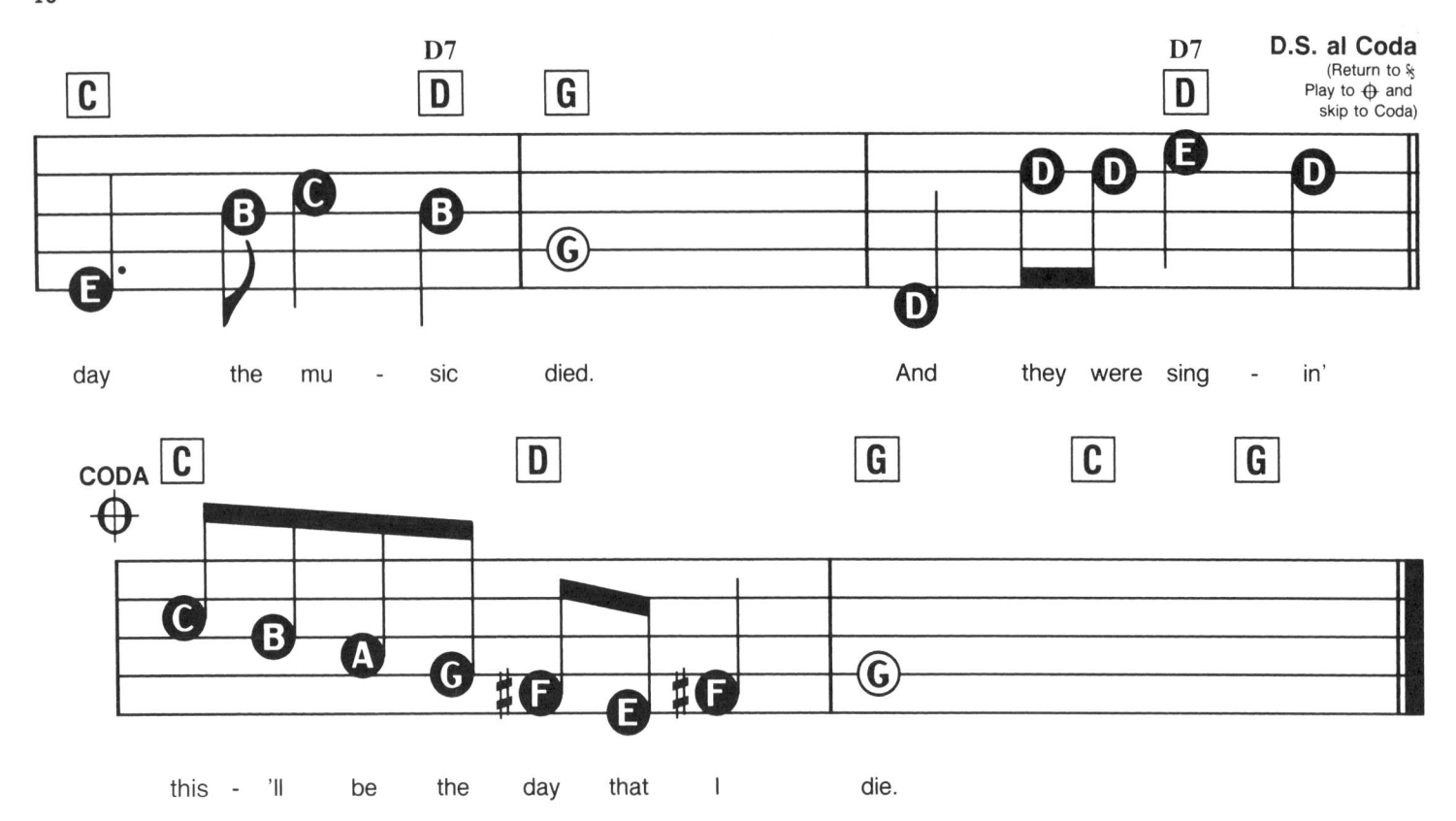

Additional Lyrics

2. Now for ten years we've been on our own, and moss grows fat on a rollin' stone
   But that's not how it used to be when the jester sang for the king and queen
   In a coat he borrowed from James Dean and a voice that came from you and me
   Oh and while the king was looking down, the jester stole his thorny crown
   The courtroom was adjourned, no verdict was returned
   And while Lenin read a book on Marx the quartet practiced in the park
   And we sang dirges in the dark
   The day the music died
   We were singin'... bye-bye..., *etc.*

3. Helter-skelter in the summer swelter the birds flew off with a fallout shelter
   Eight miles high and fallin' fast, it landed foul on the grass
   The players tried for a forward pass, with the jester on the sidelines in a cast
   Now the half-time air was sweet perfume while the sergeants played a marching tune
   We all got up to dance but we never got the chance
   'Cause the players tried to take the field, the marching band refused to yield
   Do you recall what was revealed
   The day the music died
   We started singin'... bye-bye..., *etc.*

4. And there we were all in one place, a generation lost in space
   With no time left to start again
   So come on, Jack be nimble, Jack be quick, Jack Flash sat on a candlestick
   'Cause fire is the devil's only friend
   And as I watched him on the stage my hands were clenched in fists of rage
   No angel born in hell could break that Satan's spell
   And as the flames climbed high into the night to light the sacrificial rite
   I saw Satan laughing with delight the day the music died.
   He was singin'... bye-bye..., *etc.*

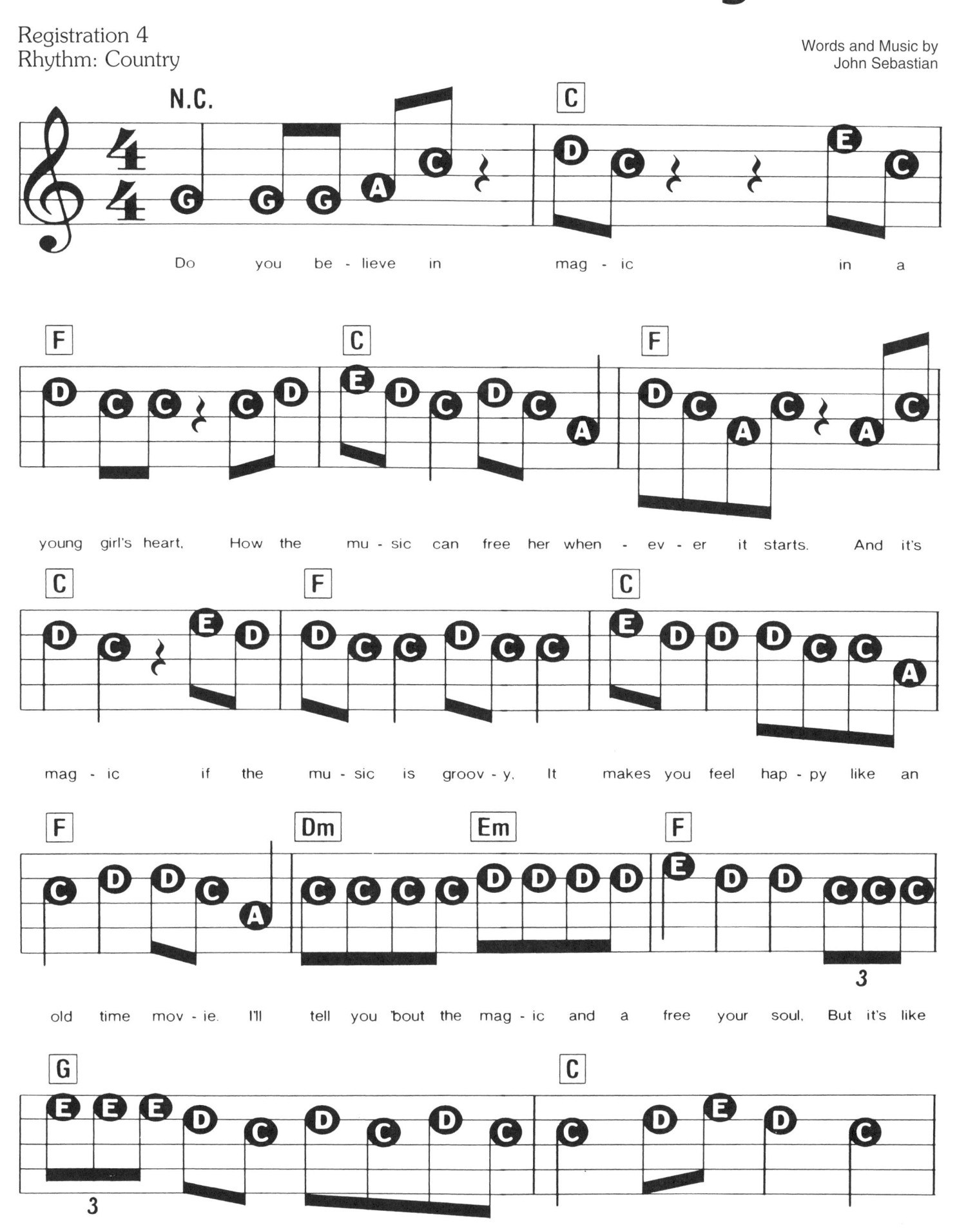

Do You Believe in Magic

Registration 4
Rhythm: Country

Words and Music by
John Sebastian

Do you be-lieve in mag-ic in a young girl's heart, How the mu-sic can free her when-ev-er it starts. And it's mag-ic if the mu-sic is groov-y, It makes you feel hap-py like an old time mov-ie. I'll tell you 'bout the mag-ic and a free your soul, But it's like try-in' to tell a stran-ger 'bout a rock and roll.___

Copyright © 1965 by Alley Music Corp. and Bug Music-Trio Music Company
Copyright Renewed
International Copyright Secured   All Rights Reserved
Used by Permission

18

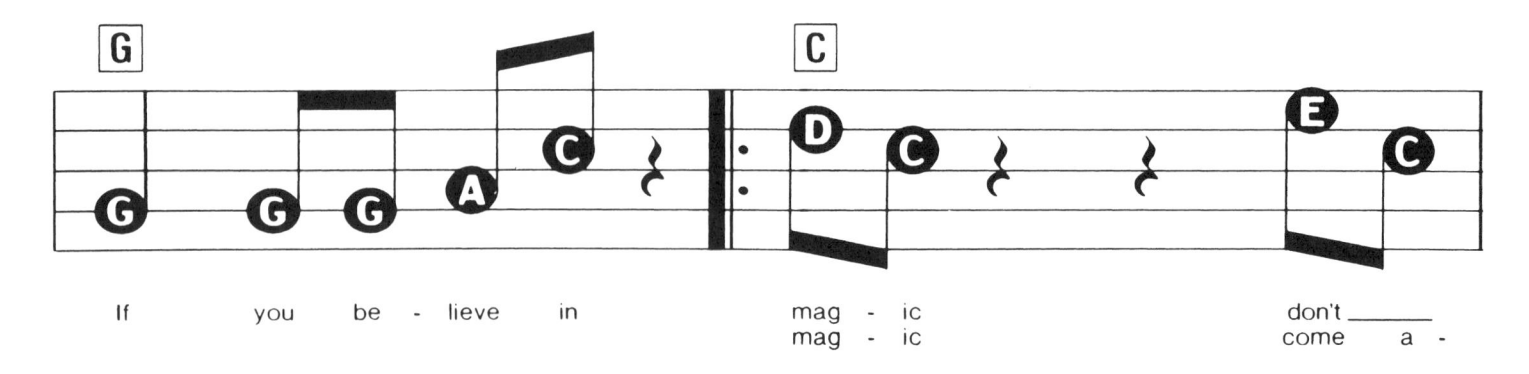

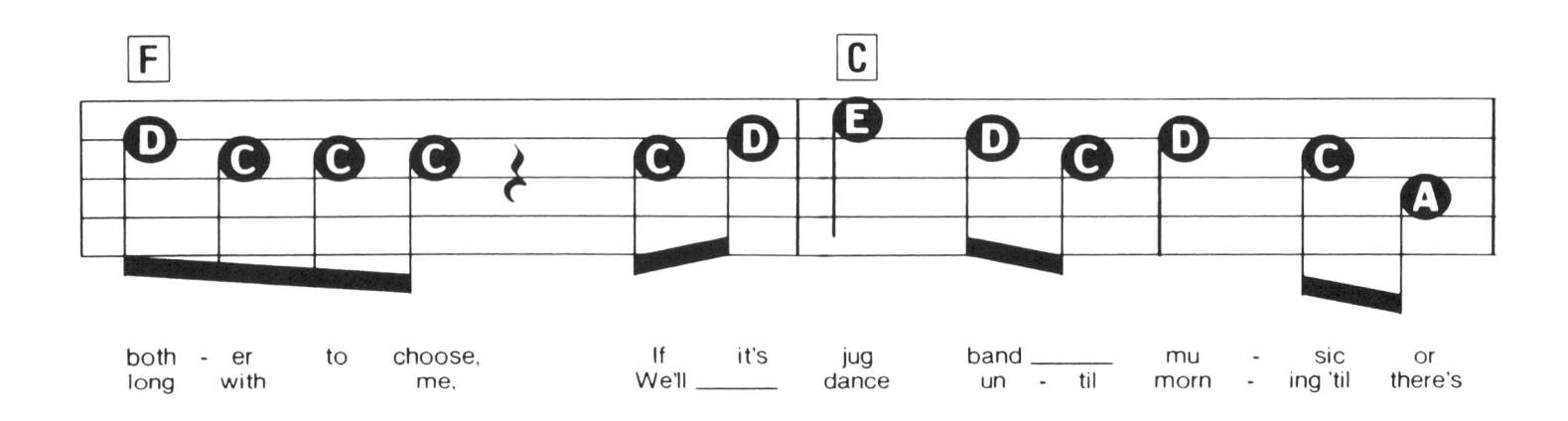

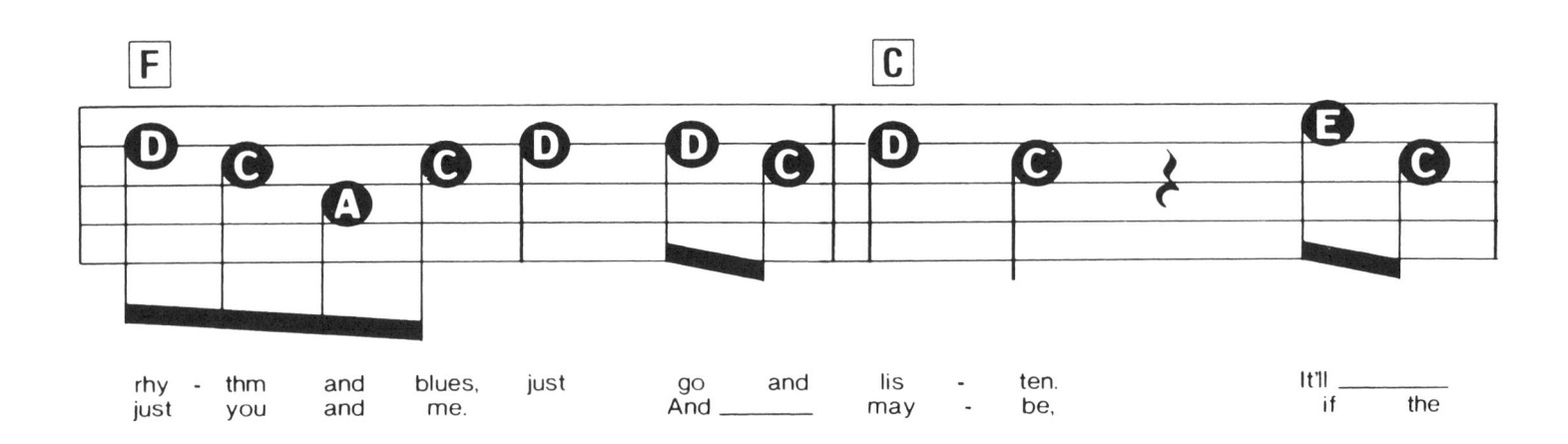

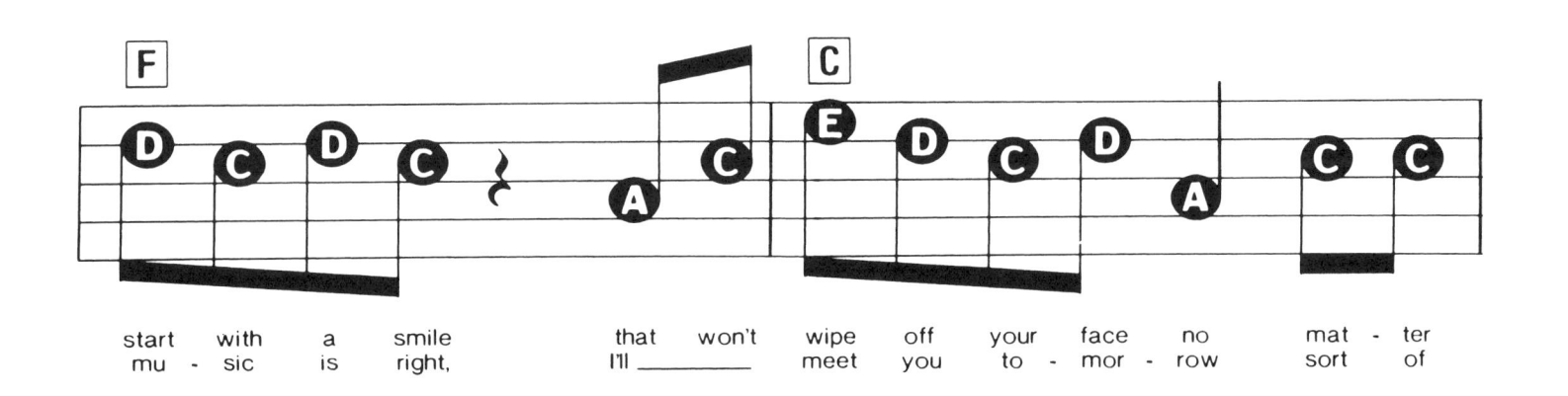

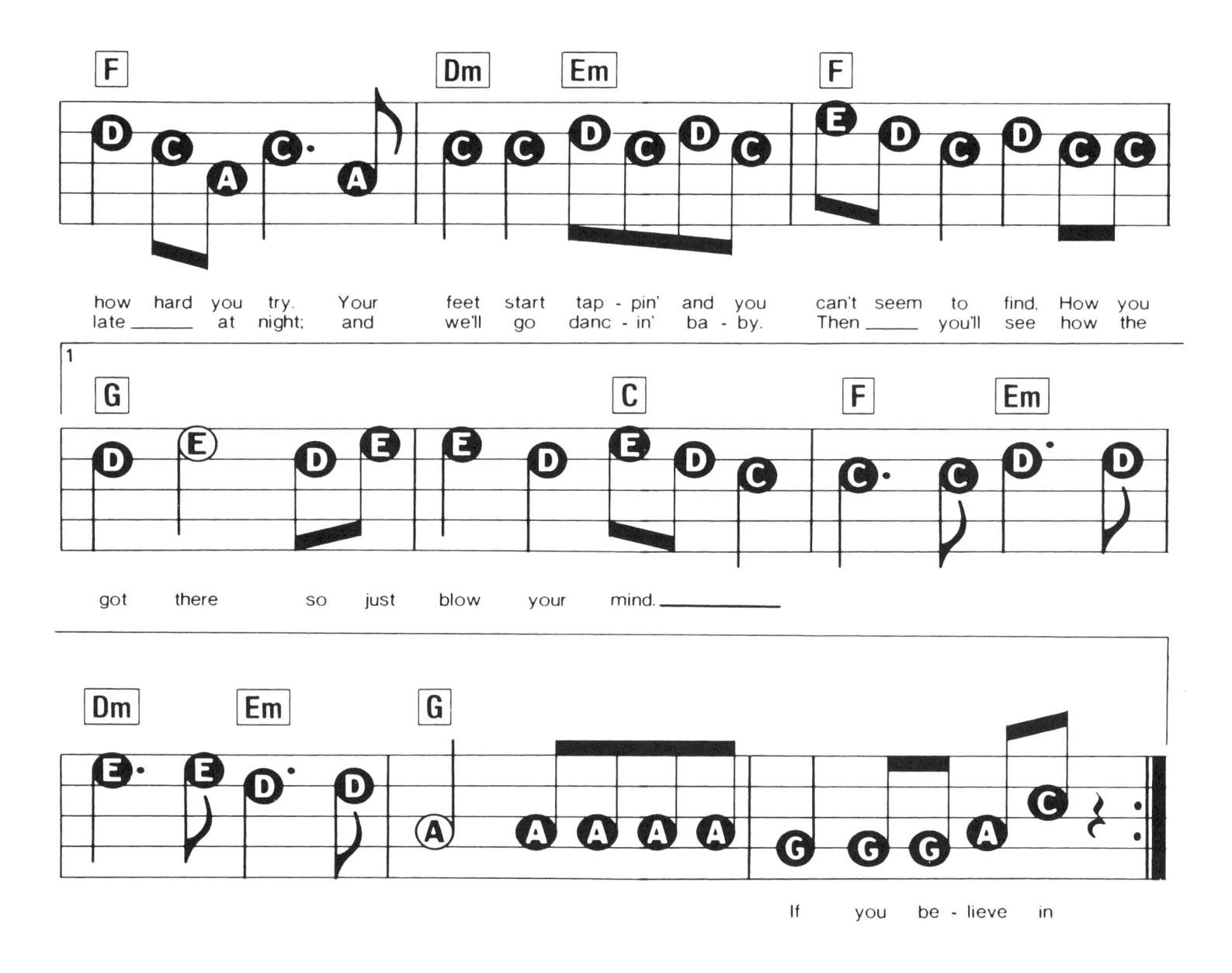

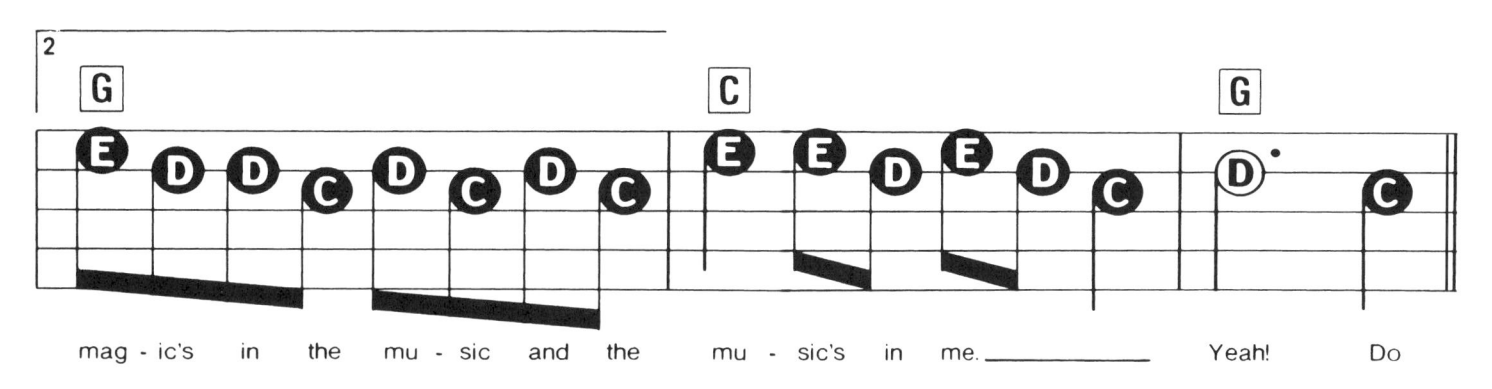

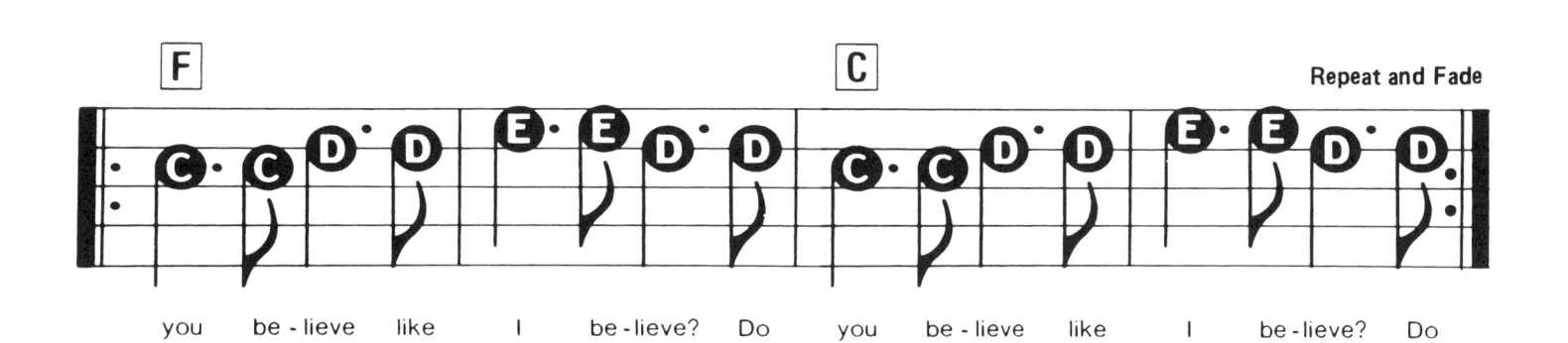

19

how hard you try. Your feet start tap-pin' and you can't seem to find, How you
late _____ at night; and we'll go danc-in' ba - by. Then _____ you'll see how the

got there so just blow your mind. _____

If you be-lieve in

mag-ic's in the mu - sic and the mu - sic's in me. _____ Yeah! Do

Repeat and Fade

you be-lieve like I be-lieve? Do you be-lieve like I be-lieve? Do

American Tune

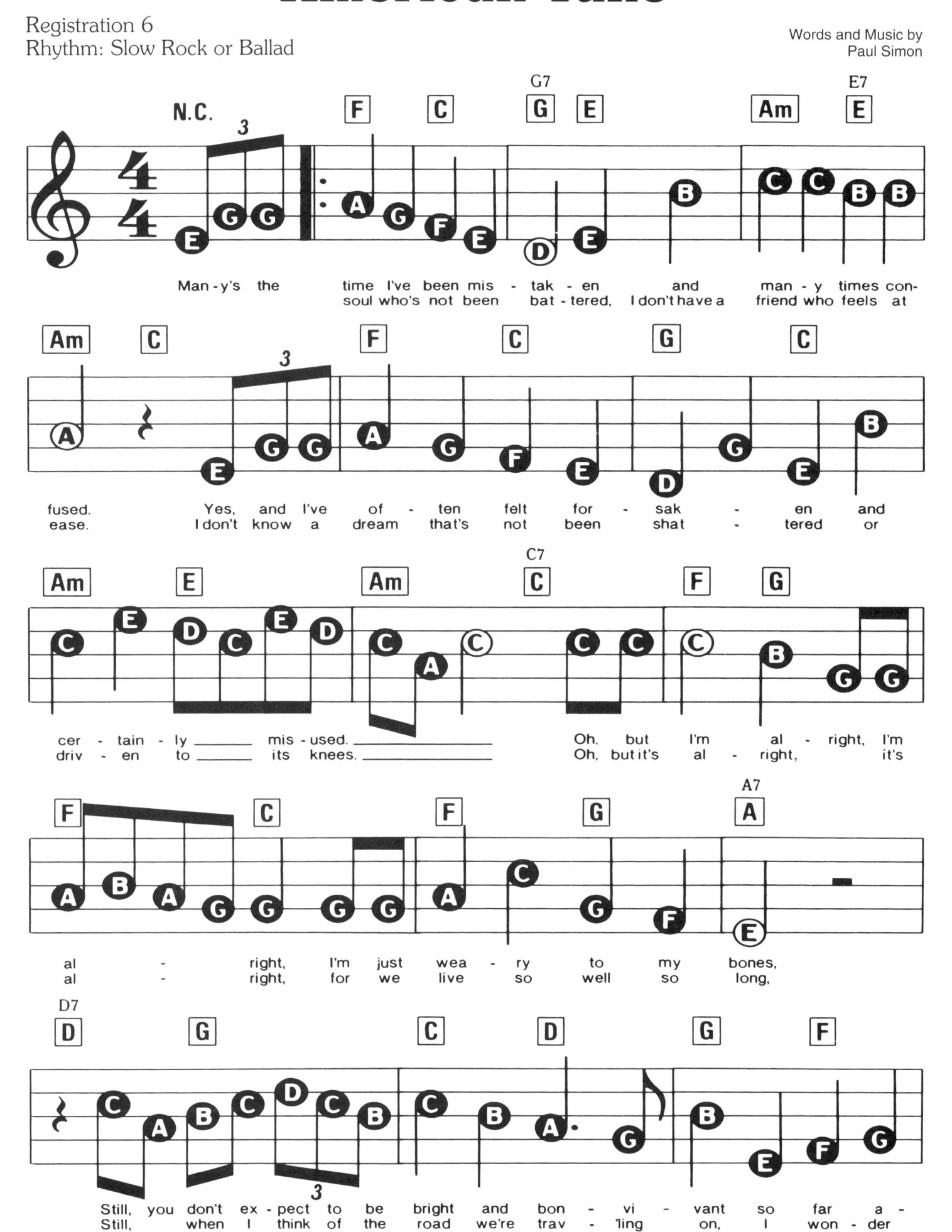

Registration 6
Rhythm: Slow Rock or Ballad

Words and Music by
Paul Simon

Man-y's the time I've been mis-tak-en, and man-y times con-
soul who's not been bat-tered, I don't have a friend who feels at

fused. Yes, and I've of-ten felt for-sak - en and
ease. I don't know a dream that's not been shat - tered or

cer - tain - ly ___ mis-used. ___ Oh, but I'm al - right, I'm
driv - en to ___ its knees. ___ Oh, but it's al - right, it's

al - right, I'm just wea - ry to my bones,
al - right, for we live so well so long,

Still, you don't ex - pect to be bright and bon - vi - vant so far a -
Still, when I think of the road we're trav - 'ling on, I won - der

Copyright © 1973 by Paul Simon Music (BMI)
Copyright Renewed
International Copyright Secured   All Rights Reserved
Reprinted by Permission of Music Sales Corporation

21

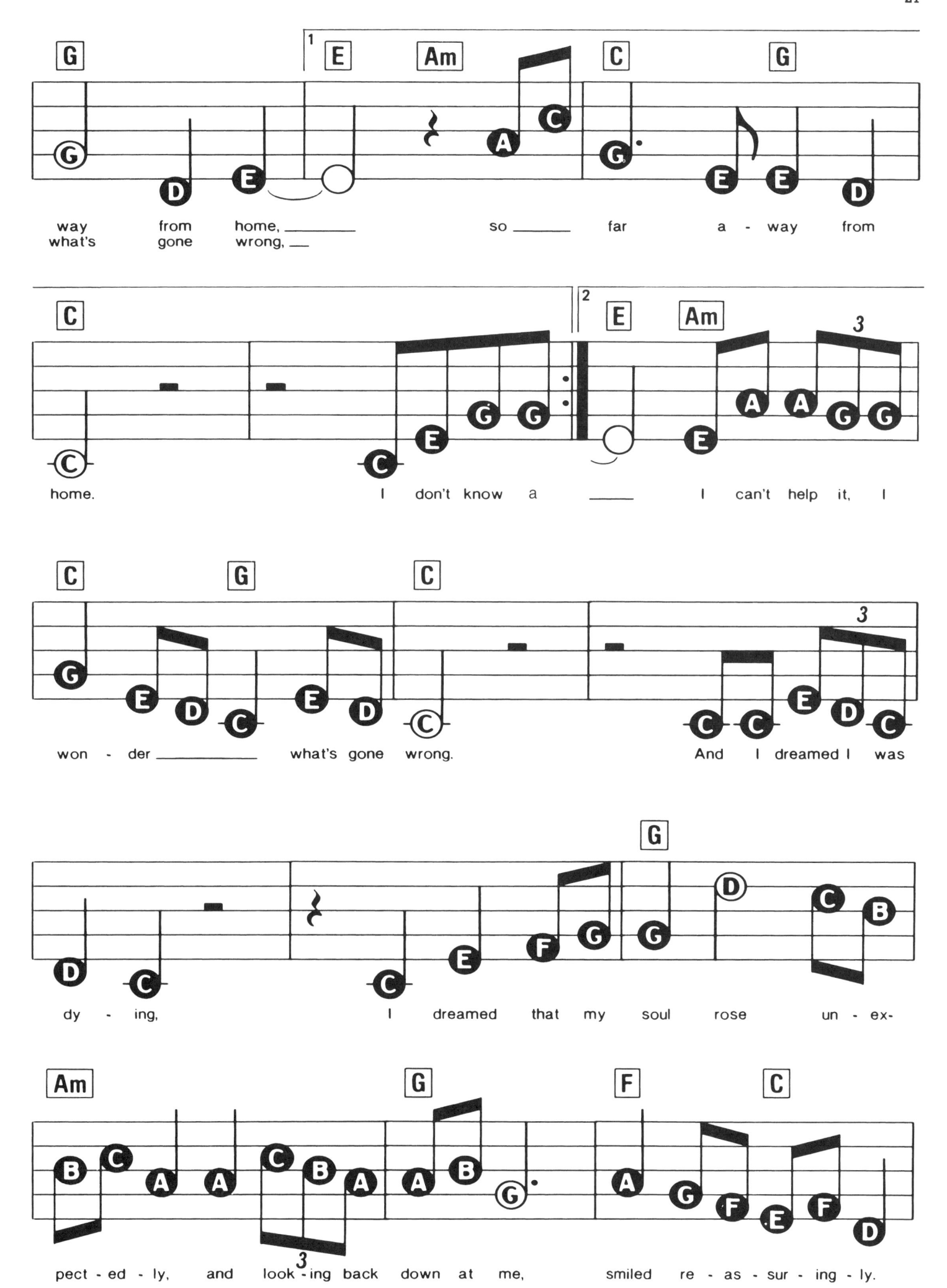

way from home, _____ so _____ far a-way from
what's gone wrong, _____

home. I don't know a _____ I can't help it, I

won - der _____ what's gone wrong. And I dreamed I was

dy - ing, I dreamed that my soul rose un-ex-

pect-ed-ly, and look-ing back down at me, smiled re-as-sur-ing-ly.

22

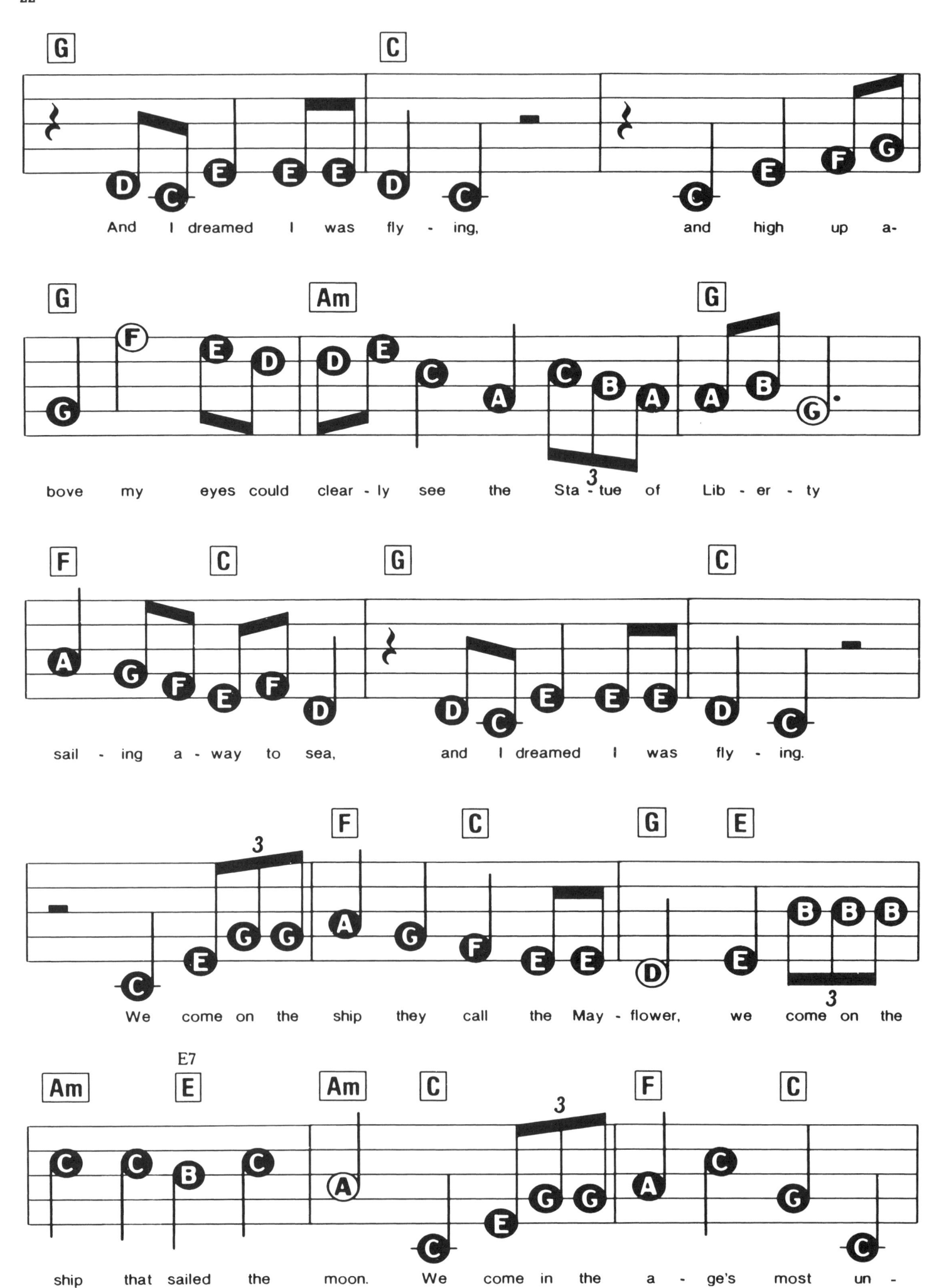

And I dreamed I was fly - ing, and high up a-bove my eyes could clear - ly see the Sta - tue of Lib - er - ty sail - ing a - way to sea, and I dreamed I was fly - ing. We come on the ship they call the May - flower, we come on the ship that sailed the moon. We come in the a - ge's most un -

23

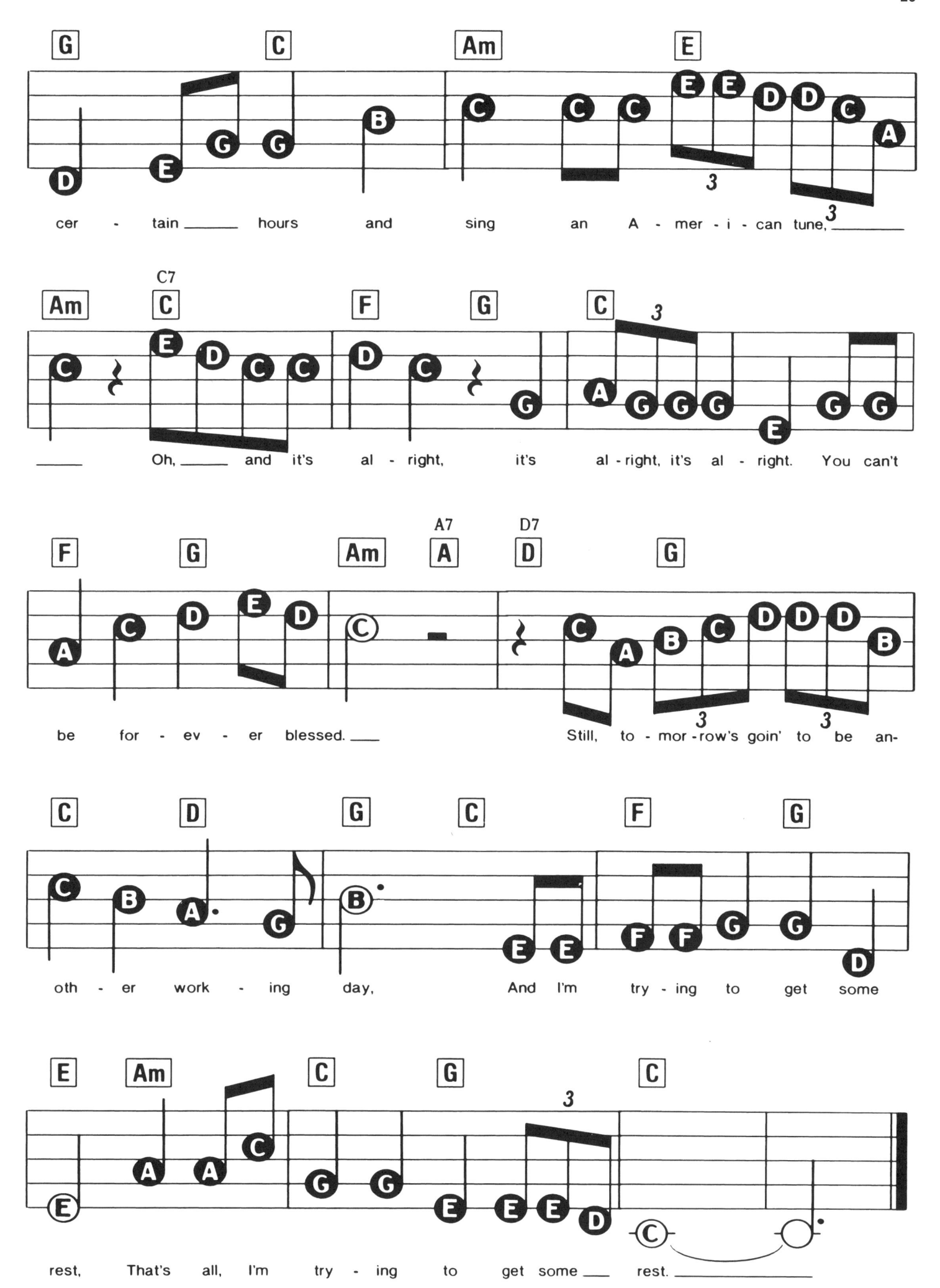

Annie's Song

Registration 1
Rhythm: Waltz

Words and Music by
John Denver

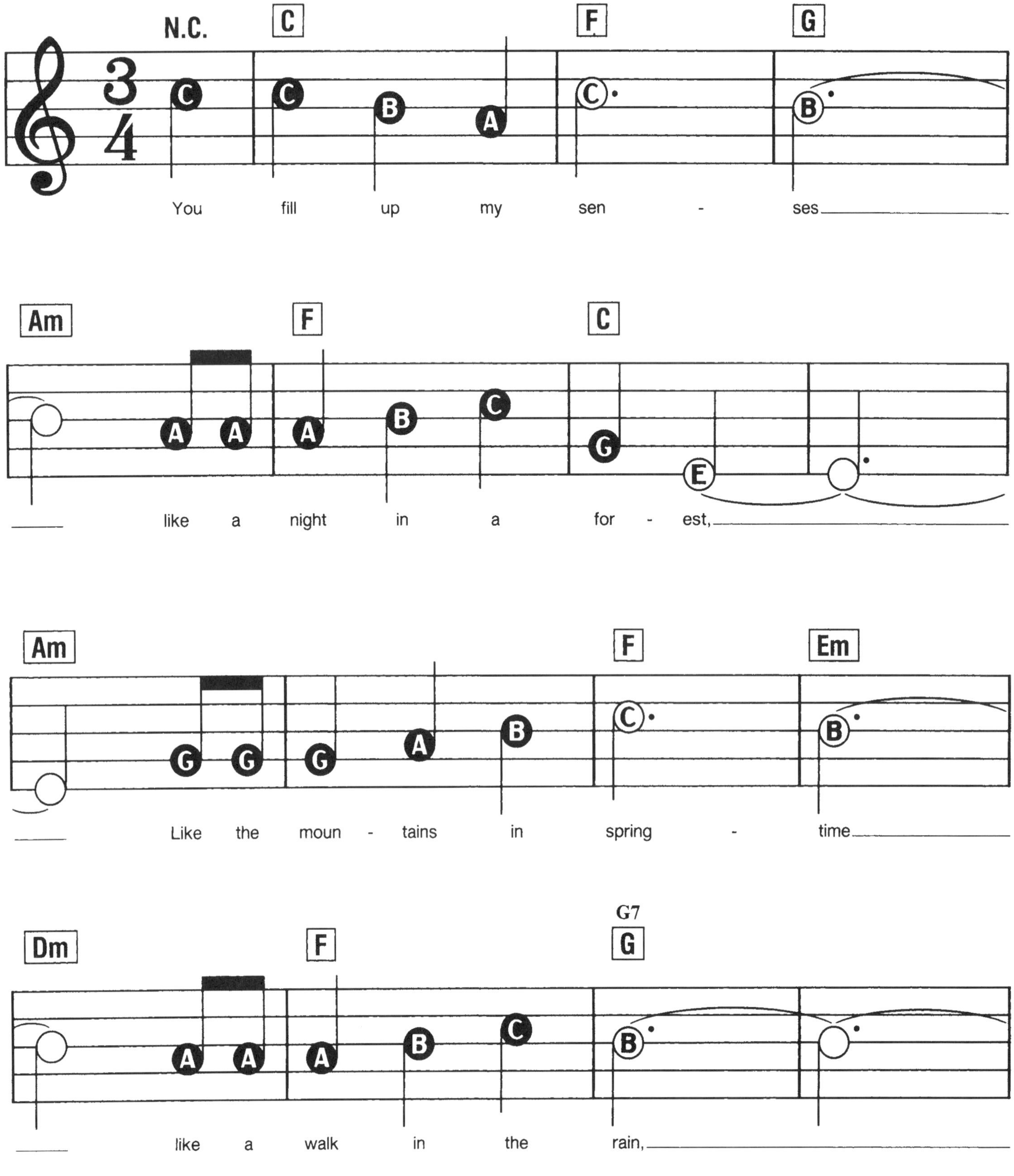

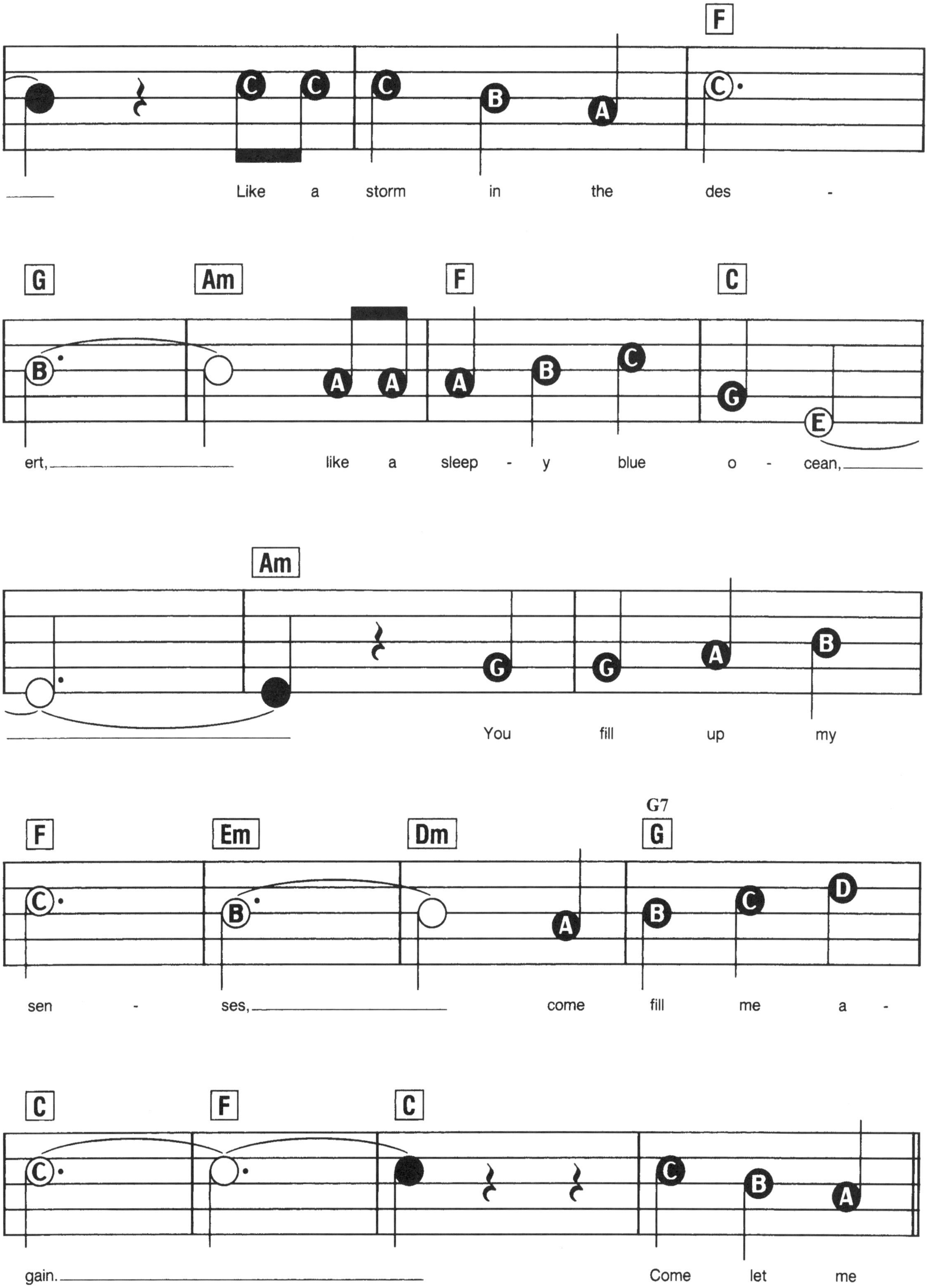
F
Like a storm in the des -
G Am F C
ert, like a sleep - y blue o - cean,
Am
You fill up my
F Em Dm G7 G
sen - ses, come fill me a -
C F C
gain. Come let me

love you,____ let me give my life
sen - ses____ like a night in a

to you,____ Let me
for - est,____ Like the

drown in your laugh - ter,____ let me
moun - tains in spring - time,____ like a

die in your arms.____ Let me
walk in the rain.____ Like a

lay down be - side you,____ let me
storm in the des - ert,____ like a

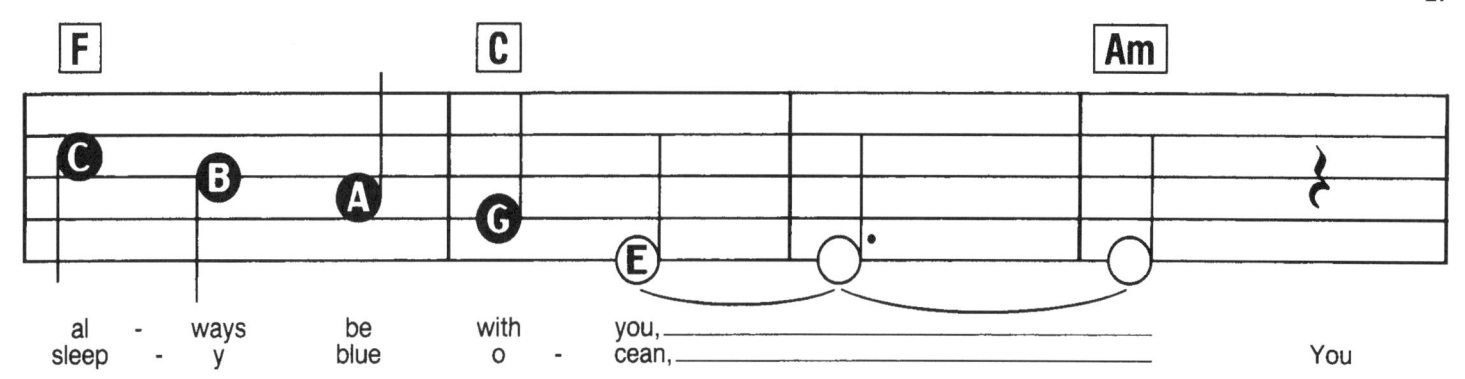

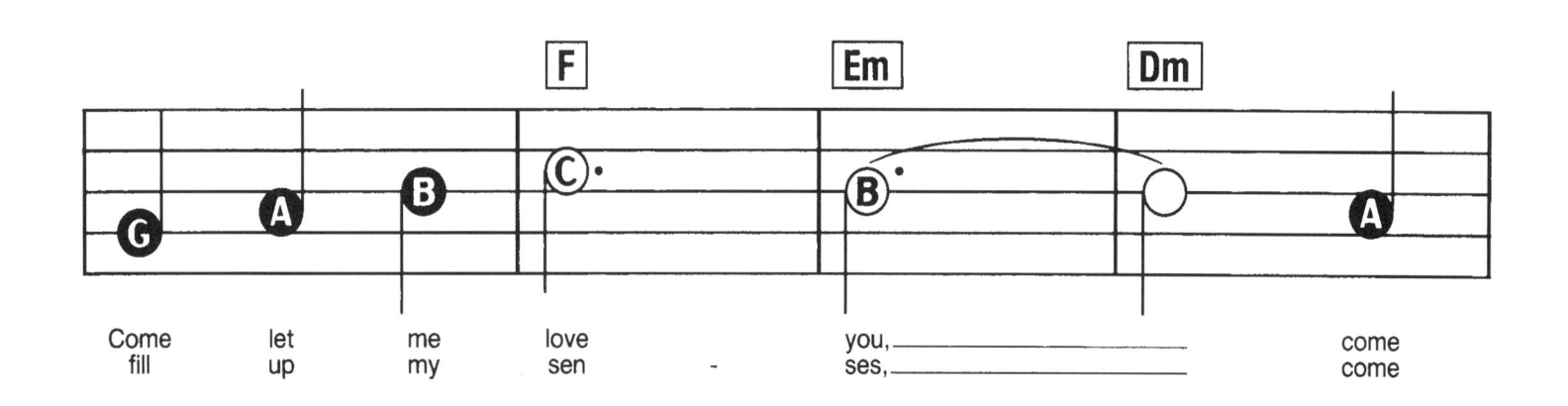

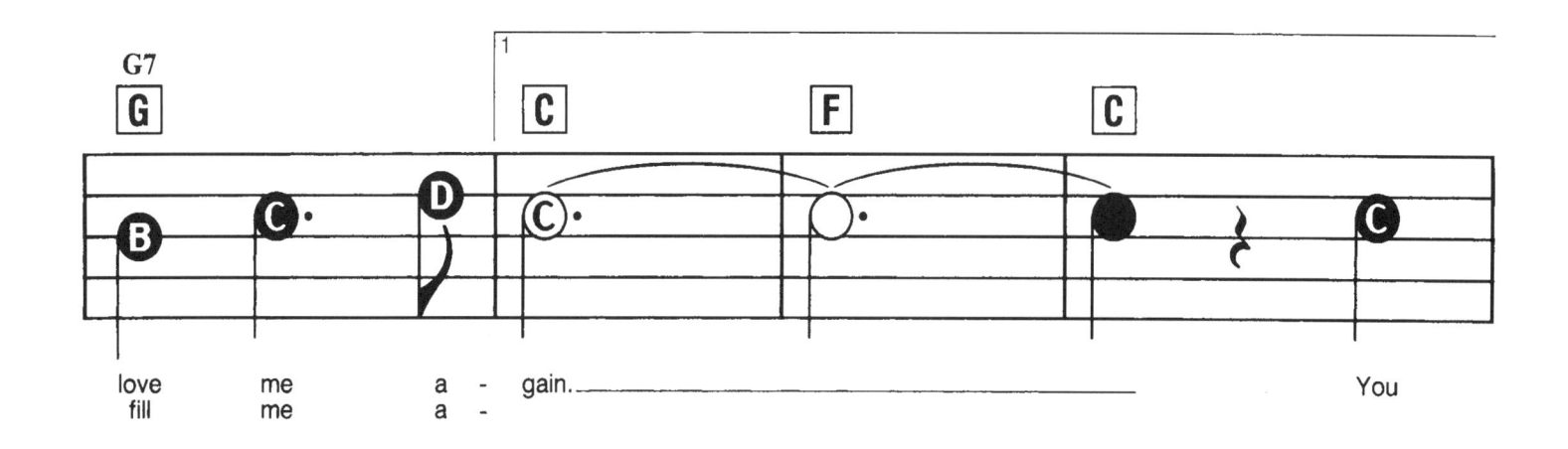

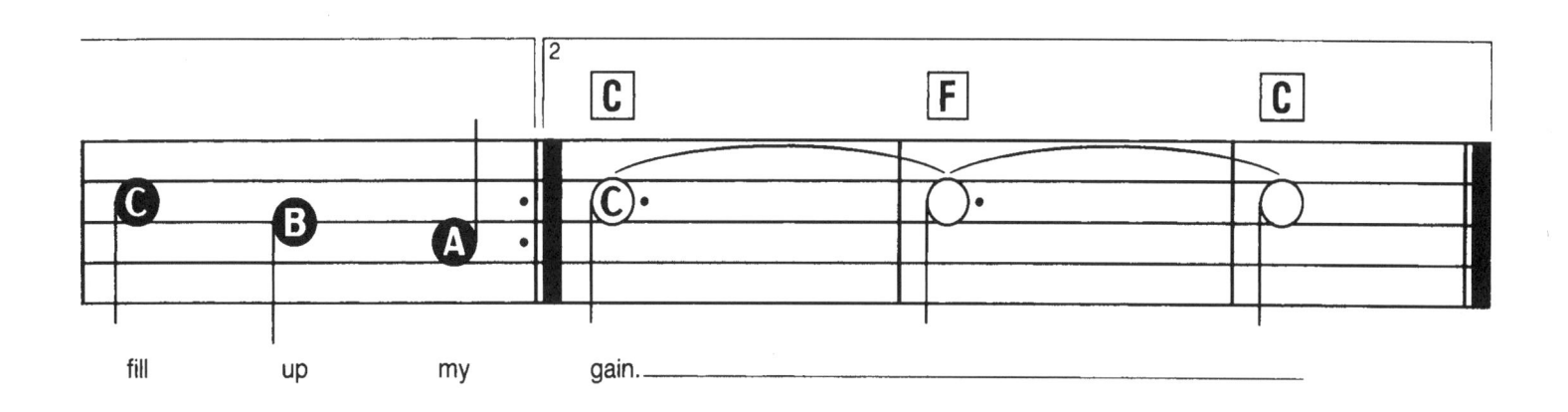

al - ways be with you,
sleep - y blue o - cean, You

Come let me love you, come
fill up my sen - ses, come

love me a - gain. You
fill me a -

fill up my gain.

Anticipation

Registration 4
Rhythm: Rock or Jazz Rock

Words and Music by
Carly Simon

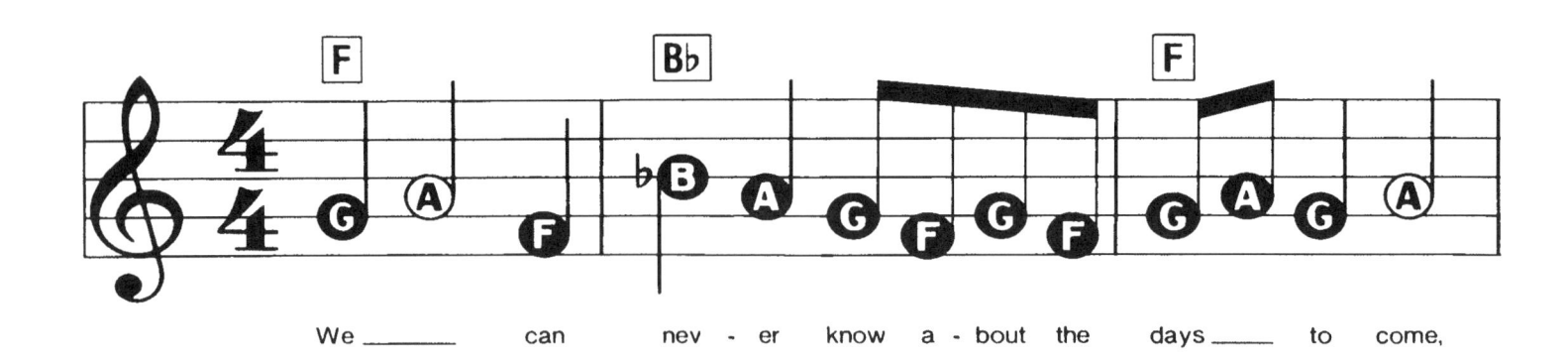

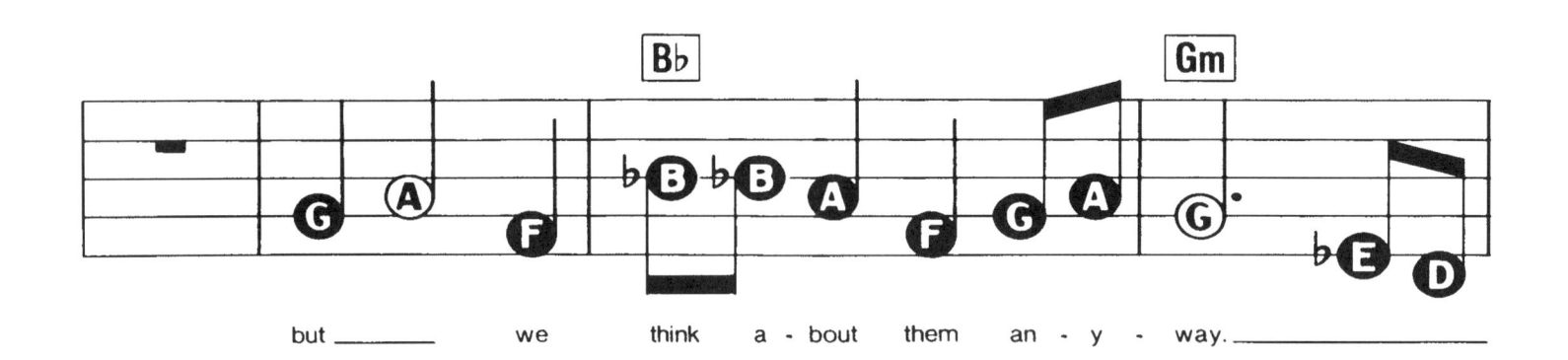

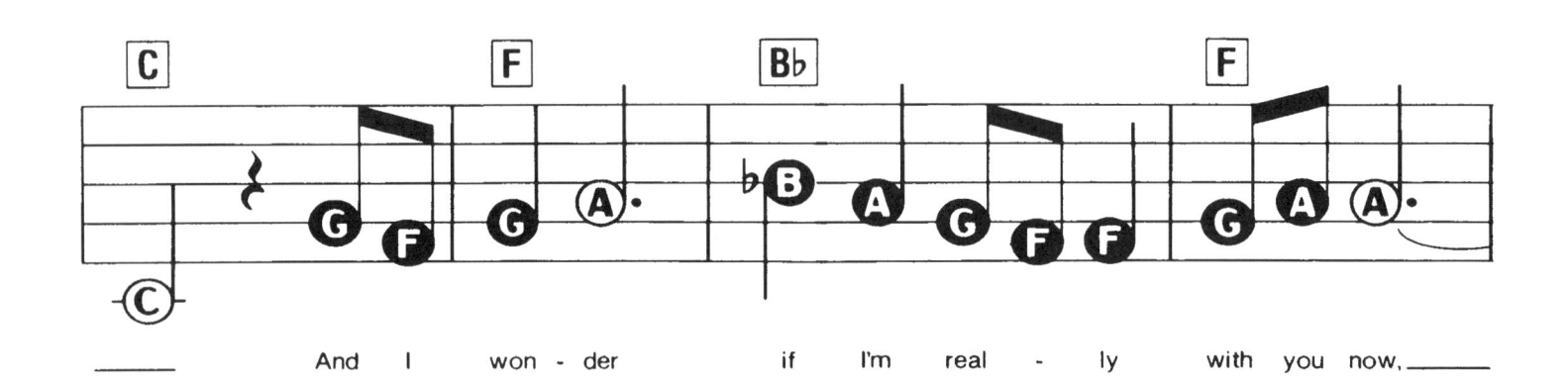

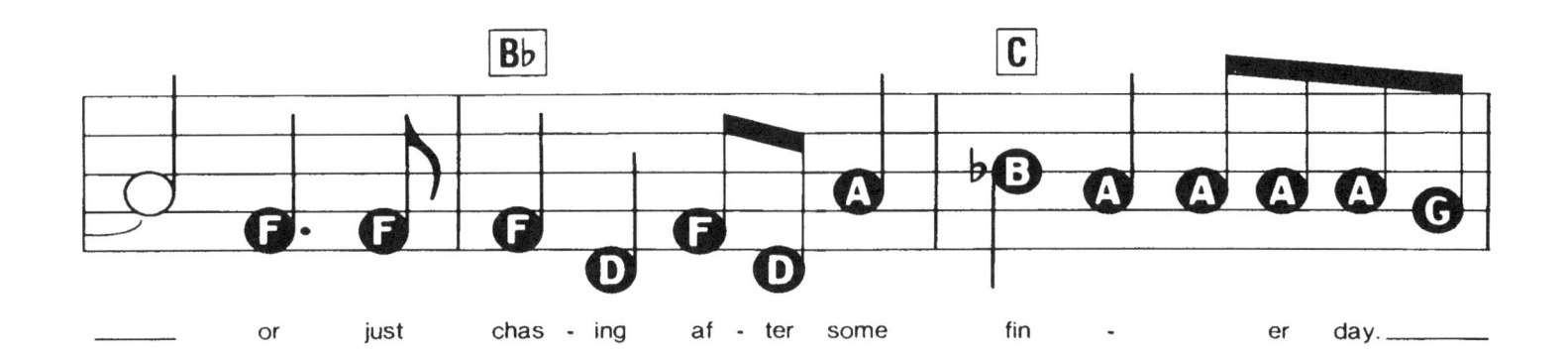

We can nev-er know a-bout the days to come,

but we think a-bout them an-y-way.

And I won-der if I'm real-ly with you now,

or just chas-ing af-ter some fin-er day.

Copyright © 1971 Quackenbush Music Ltd.
Copyright Renewed
All Rights Reserved Used by Permission

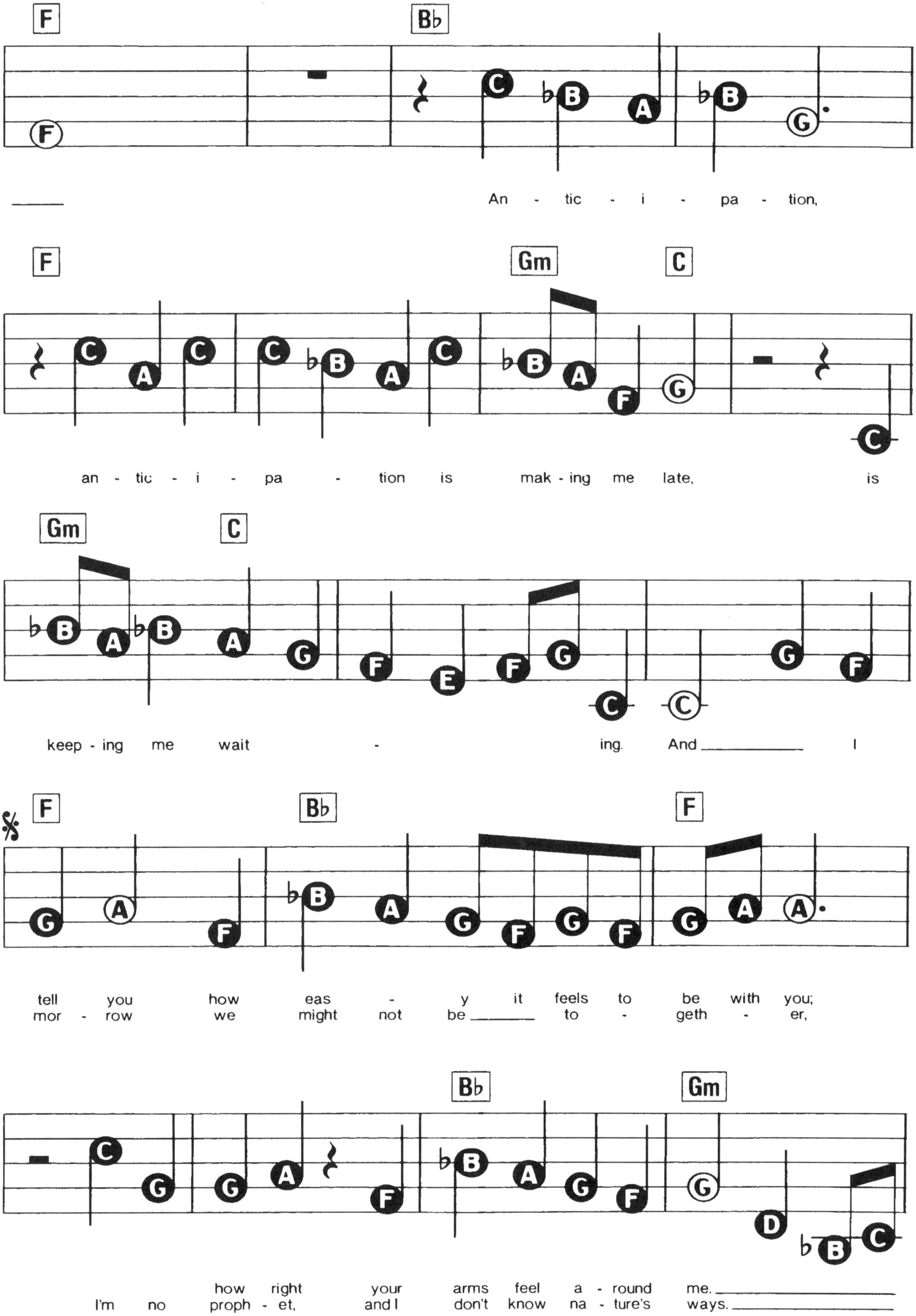
F
B♭
An - tic - i - pa - tion,
F
Gm
C
an - tic - i - pa - tion is mak - ing me late, is
Gm
C
keep - ing me wait - ing. And I
F
B♭
F
tell you how eas - y it feels to be with you;
mor - row we might not be to - geth - er,
B♭
Gm
how right your arms feel a - round me.
I'm no proph - et, and I don't know na - ture's ways.

30

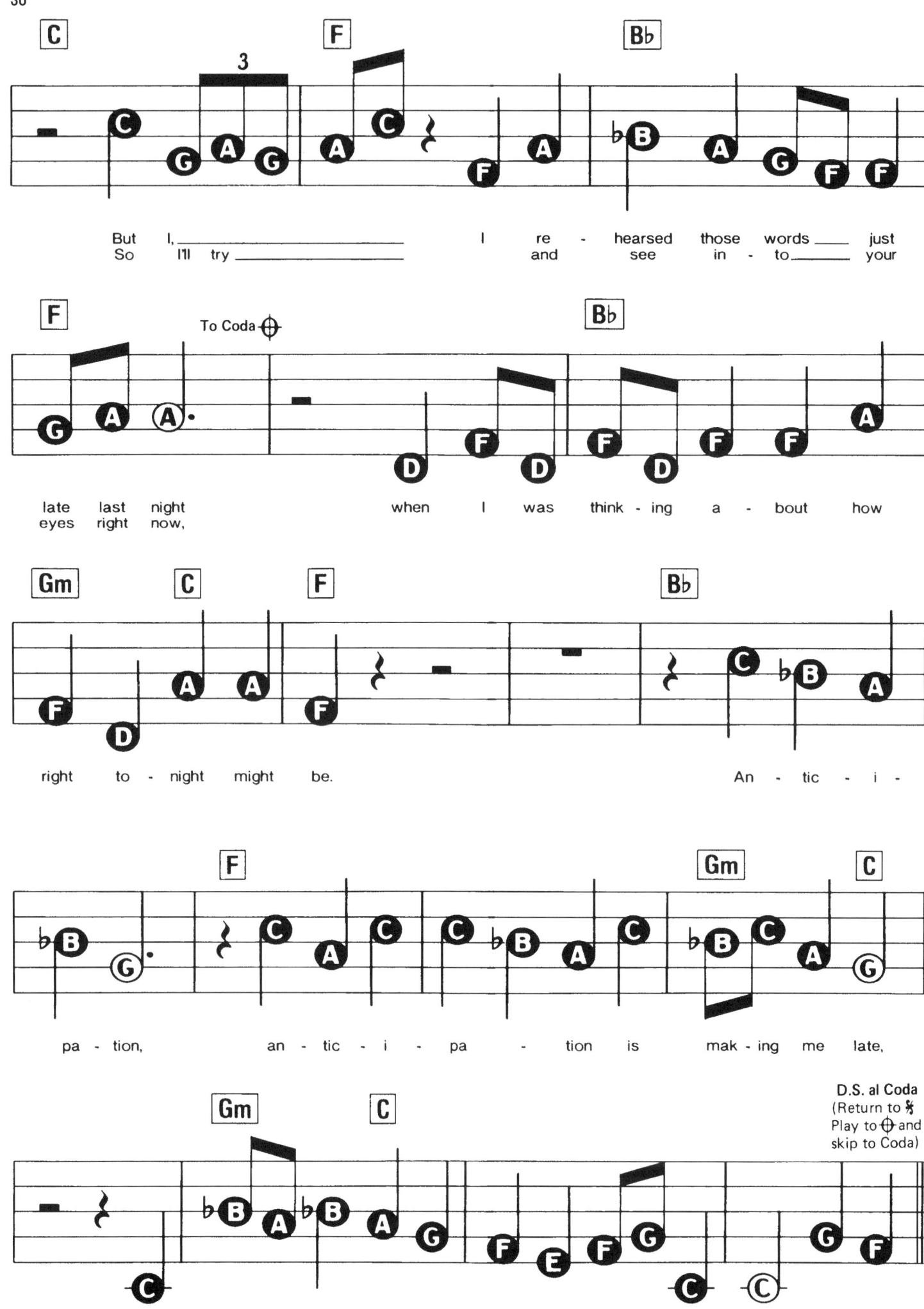

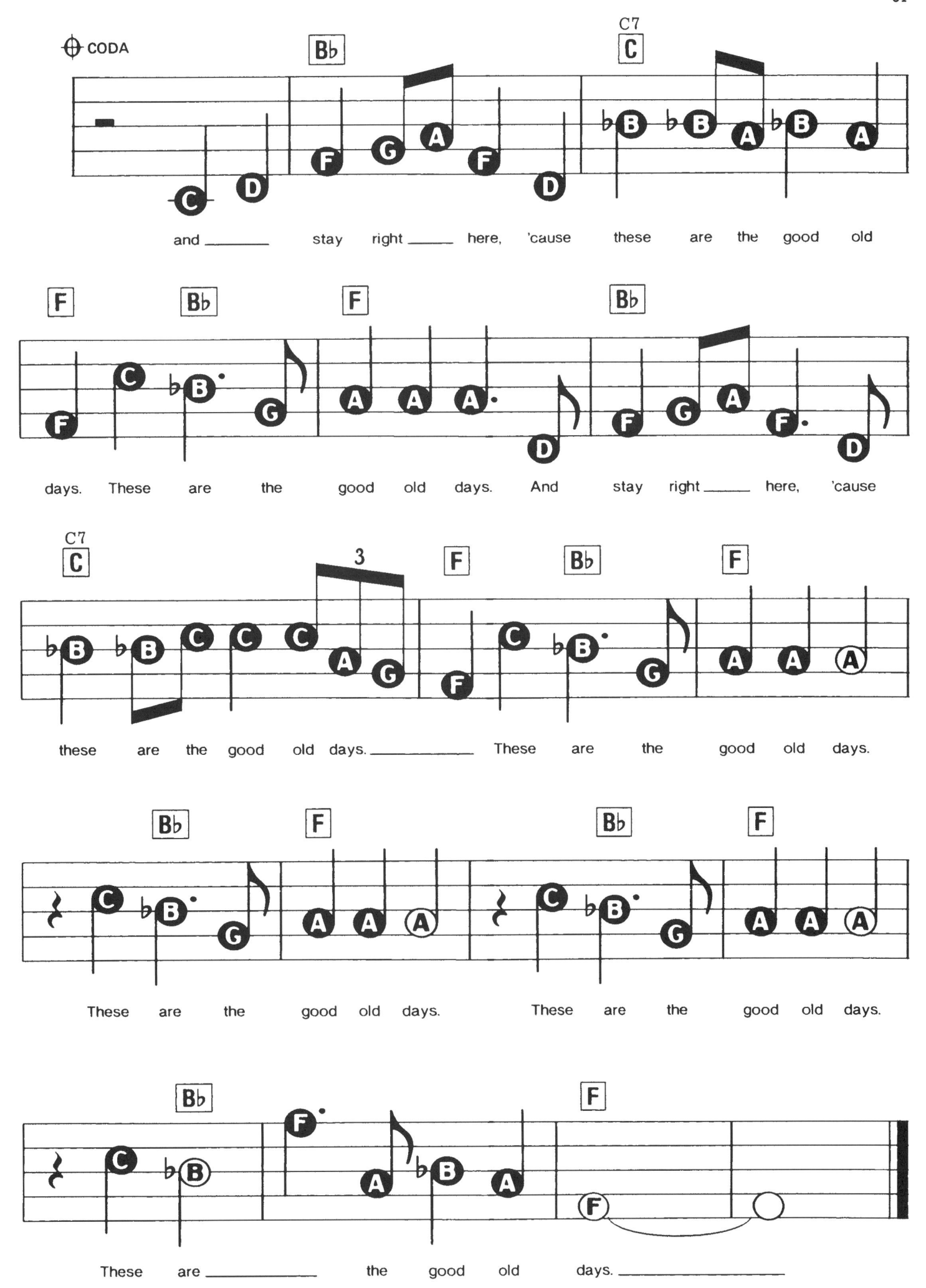

and ____ stay right ____ here, 'cause these are the good old days. These are the good old days. And stay right ____ here, 'cause these are the good old days. ____ These are the good old days. These are the good old days. These are the good old days. These are ____ the good old days. ____

At Seventeen

Registration 4
Rhythm: Rock or 8 Beat

Words and Music by
Janis Ian

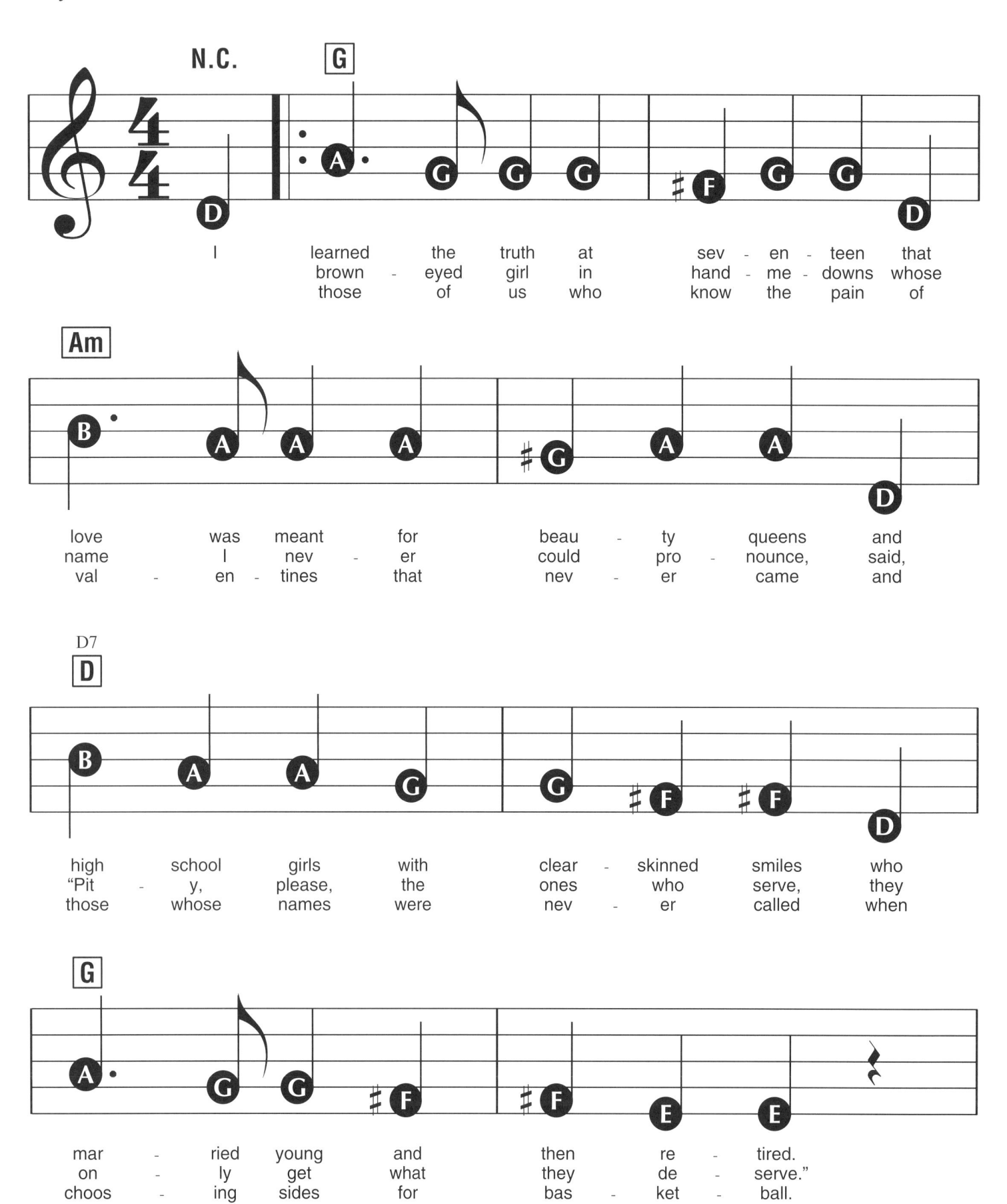

I learned the truth at sev-en-teen that
brown - eyed girl in hand-me-downs whose
those of us who know the pain of

love was meant for beau - ty queens and
name I nev - er could pro - nounce, said,
val - en - tines that nev - er came and

high school girls with clear - skinned smiles who
"Pit - y, please, the ones who serve, they
those whose names were nev - er called when

mar - ried young and then re - tired.
on - ly get what they de - serve."
choos - ing sides for bas - ket - ball.

© 1975 (Renewed 2003) MINE MUSIC LTD.
All Rights for the U.S.A. and Canada Controlled and Administered by EMI APRIL MUSIC INC.
All Rights Reserved   International Copyright Secured   Used by Permission

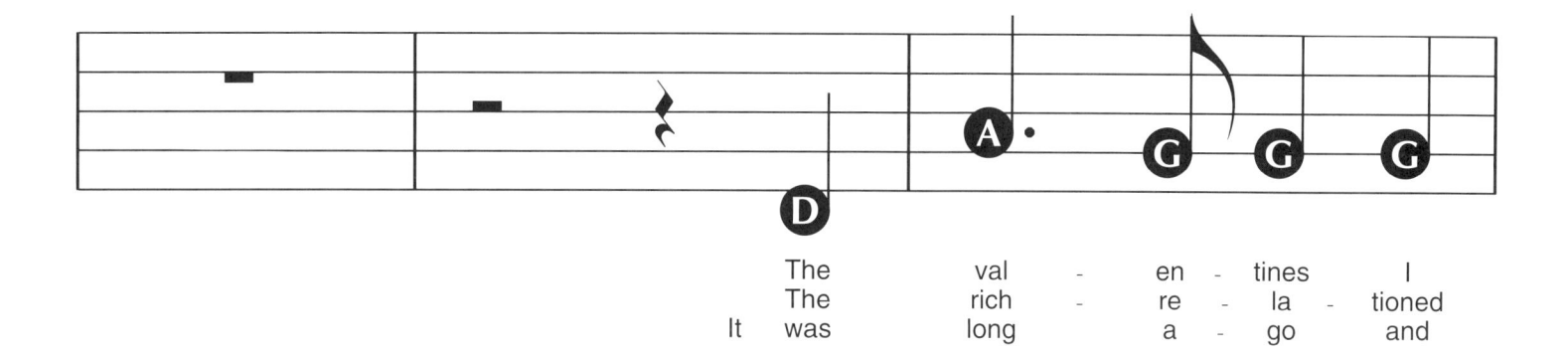

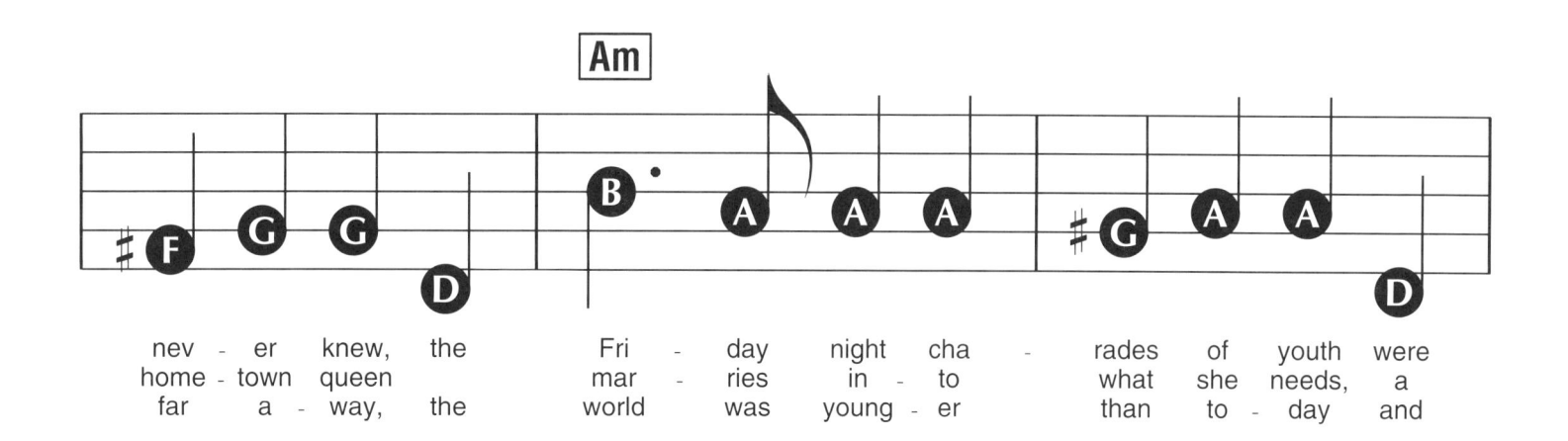

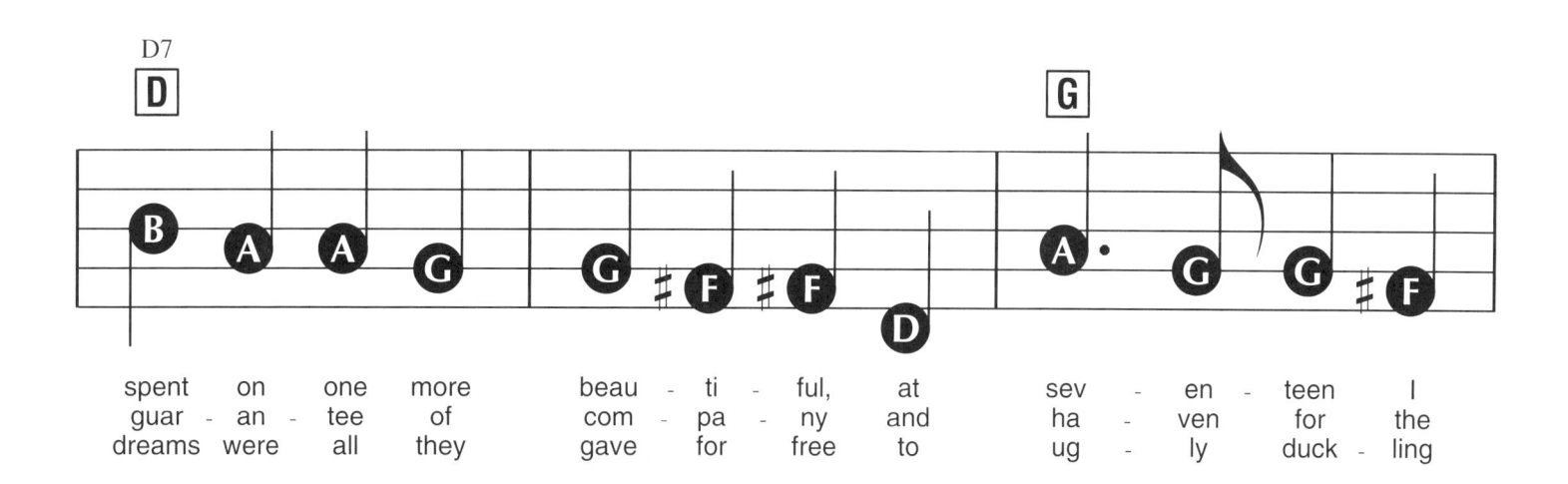

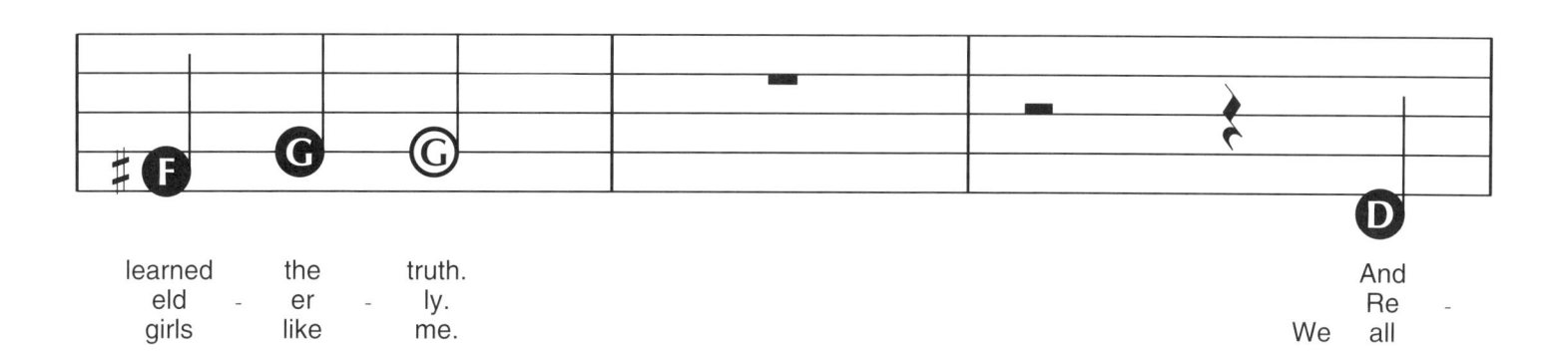

The val - en - tines I
The rich - re - la - tioned
It was long a - go and

nev - er knew, the Fri - day night cha - rades of youth were
home - town queen mar - ries in - to what she needs, a
far a - way, the world was young - er than to - day and

spent on one more beau - ti - ful, at sev - en - teen I
guar - an - tee of com - pa - ny and ha - ven for the
dreams were all they gave for free to ug - ly duck - ling

learned the truth. And
eld - er - ly. Re -
girls like me. We all

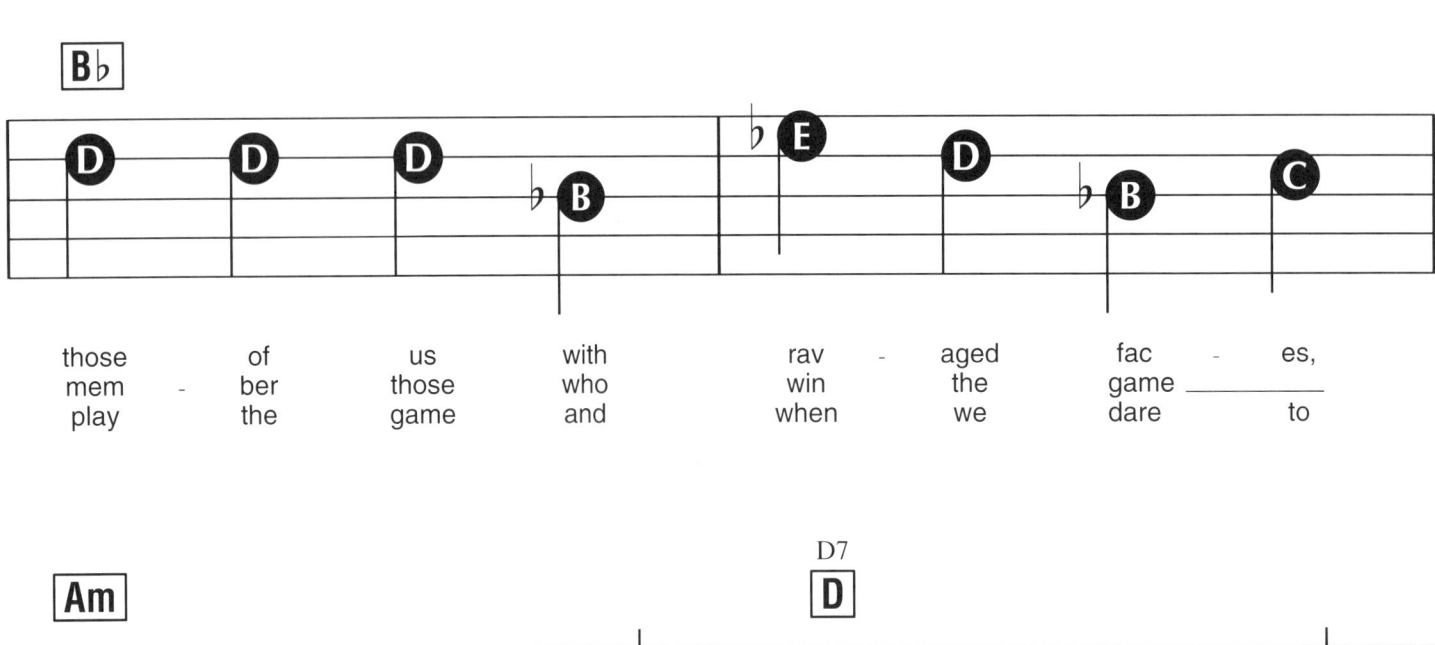

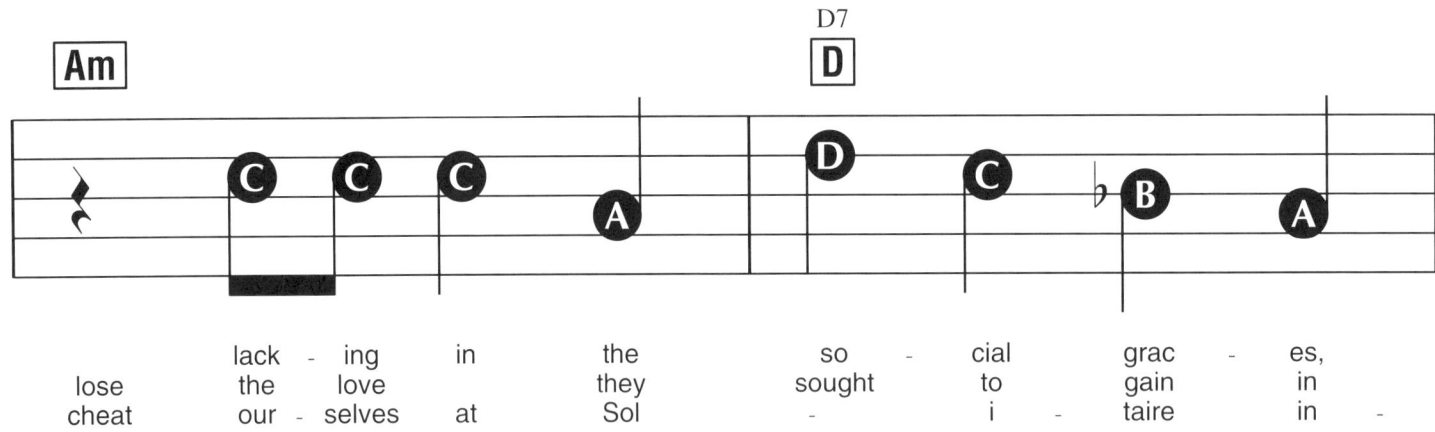

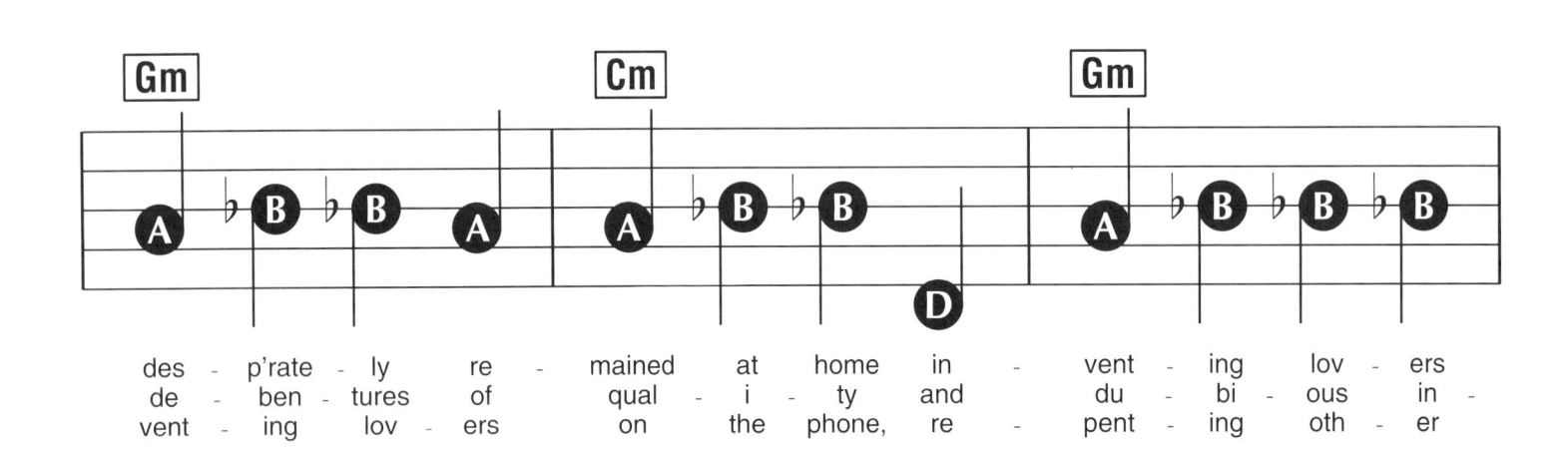

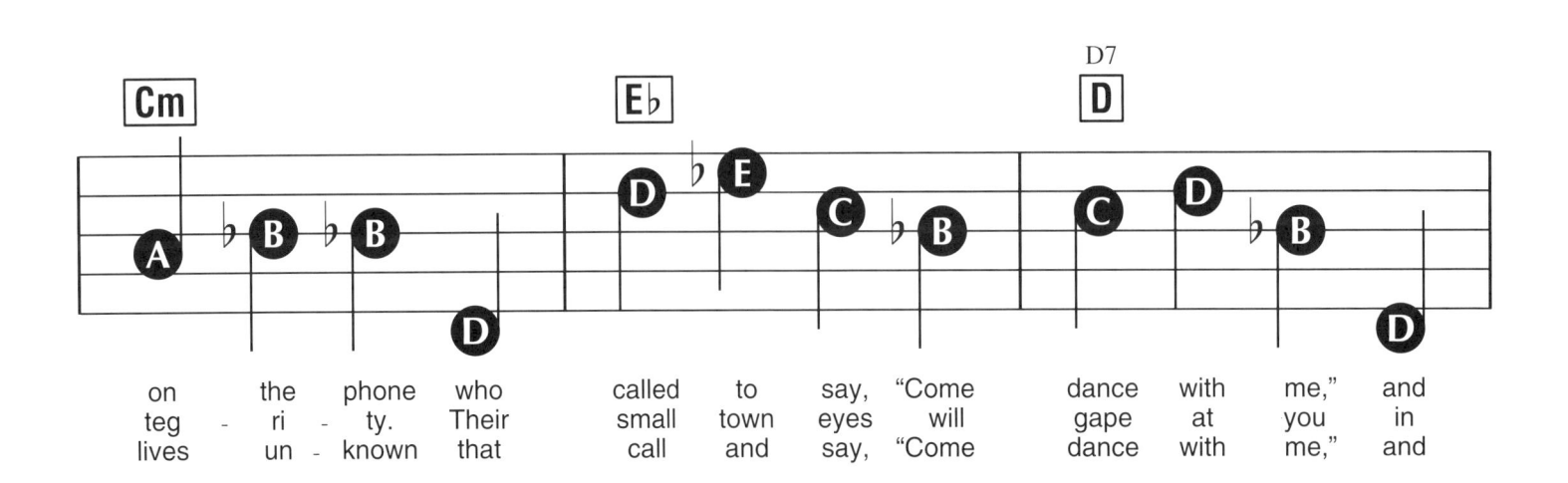

34

B♭: D D D B♭ | **E♭** D B♭ C

those of us with rav - aged fac - es,
mem - ber those who win the game ___
play the game and when we dare to

Am: C C C A | **D7 / D**: D C B♭ A

lose lack - ing in the so - cial grac - es,
the love they sought to gain in
cheat our - selves at Sol - i - taire in -

Gm: A B♭ B♭ A | **Cm**: A B♭ B♭ D | **Gm**: A B♭ B♭ B♭

des - p'rate - ly re - mained at home in - vent - ing lov - ers
de - ben - tures of qual - i - ty and du - bi - ous in -
vent - ing lov - ers on the phone, re - pent - ing oth - er

Cm: A B♭ B♭ D | **E♭**: D E♭ C B♭ | **D7 / D**: C D B♭ D

on the phone who called to say, "Come dance with me," and
teg - ri - ty. Their small town eyes will gape at you in
lives un - known that call and say, "Come dance with me," and

Gm | **Cm**

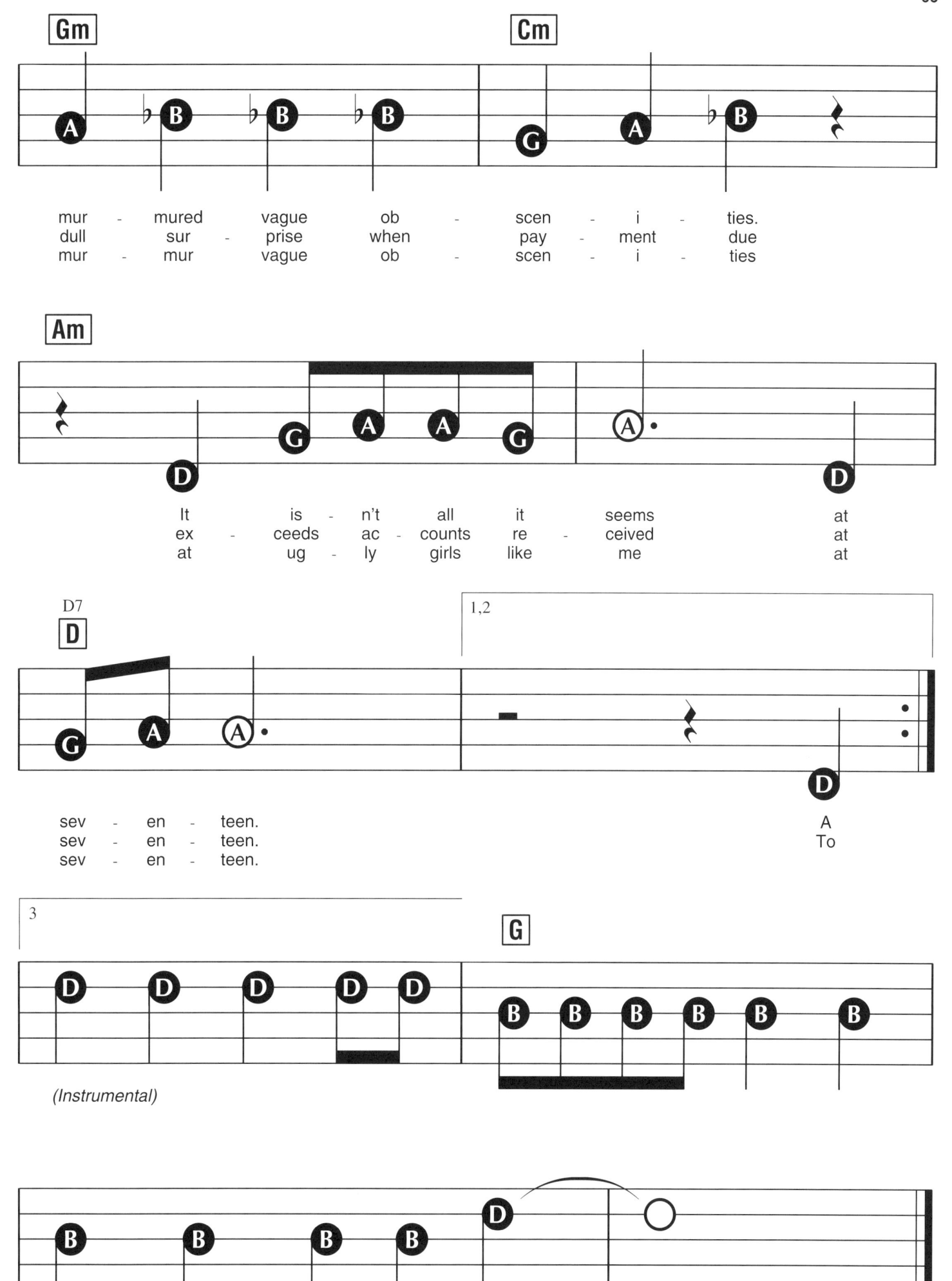

mur - mured vague ob - scen - i - ties.
dull sur - prise when pay - ment due
mur - mur vague ob - scen - i - ties

Am

It is - n't all it seems at
ex - ceeds ac - counts re - ceived at
at ug - ly girls like me at

D7
D

| 1,2

sev - en - teen.   A
sev - en - teen.   To
sev - en - teen.

3 | **G**

(Instrumental)

Best of My Love

Registration 8
Rhythm: Rock or Disco

Words and Music by John David Souther,
Don Henley and Glenn Frey

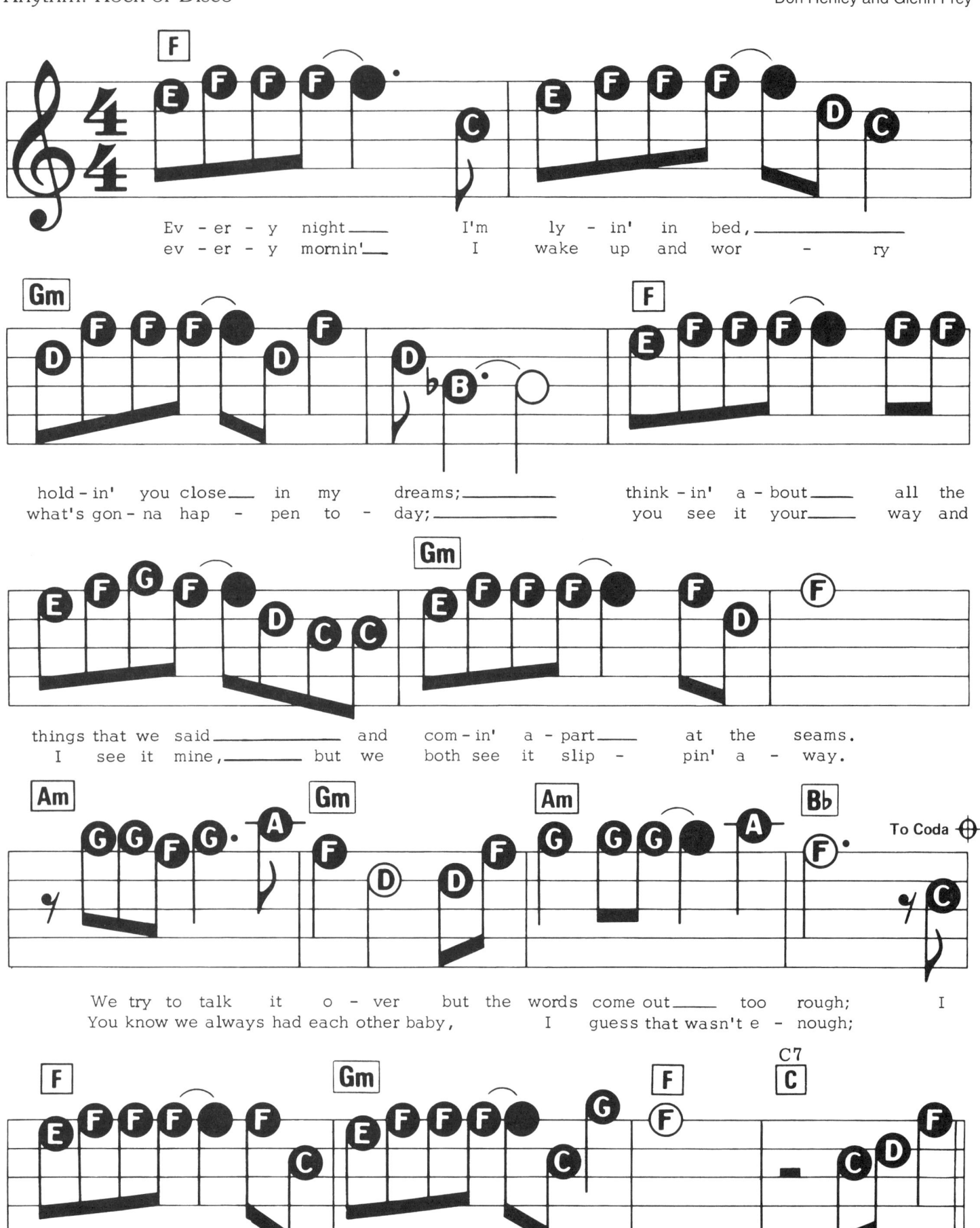

Ev - 'ry night___ I'm ly - in' in bed,___ hold - in' you close___ in my dreams;___ think - in' a - bout___ all the things that we said___ and com - in' a - part___ at the seams.

ev - 'ry mornin'___ I wake up and wor - ry what's gon - na hap - pen to - day;___ you see it your___ way and I see it mine,___ but we both see it slip - pin' a - way.

We try to talk it o - ver but the words come out___ too rough; I know you were try - in' to give me the best___ of your love. Oh,___

You know we al - ways had each oth - er ba - by, I guess that wasn't e - nough;

© 1974 (Renewed 2002) EMI BLACKWOOD MUSIC INC., CASS COUNTY MUSIC and RED CLOUD MUSIC
All Rights Reserved   International Copyright Secured   Used by Permission

sweet dar-lin', you get the best of my love, Oh,

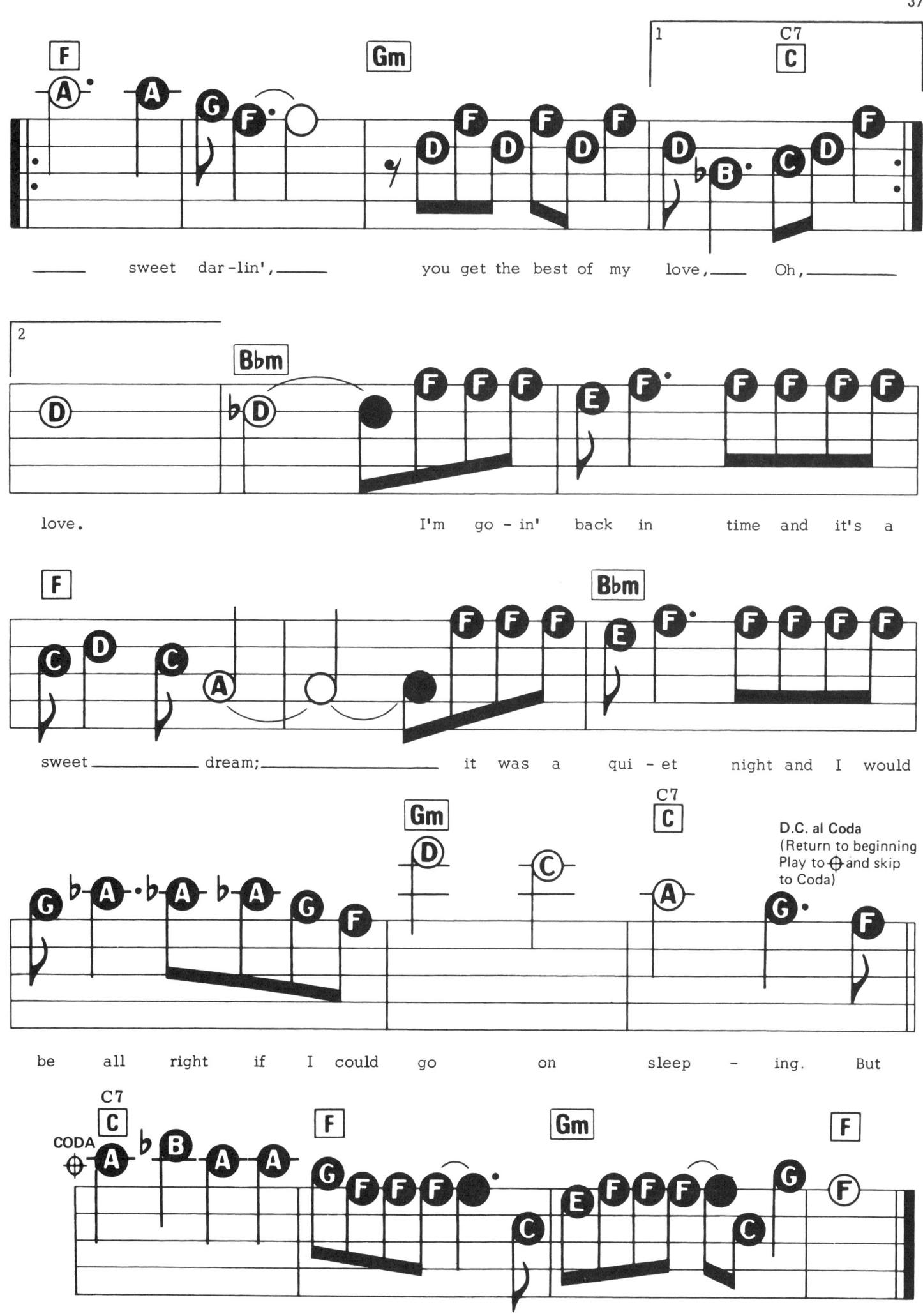

love. I'm go-in' back in time and it's a

sweet dream; it was a qui-et night and I would

be all right if I could go on sleep-ing. But

Oh, but here in my heart I give you the best of my love.

Blackbird

Registration 8
Rhythm: Rock

Words and Music by John Lennon
and Paul McCartney

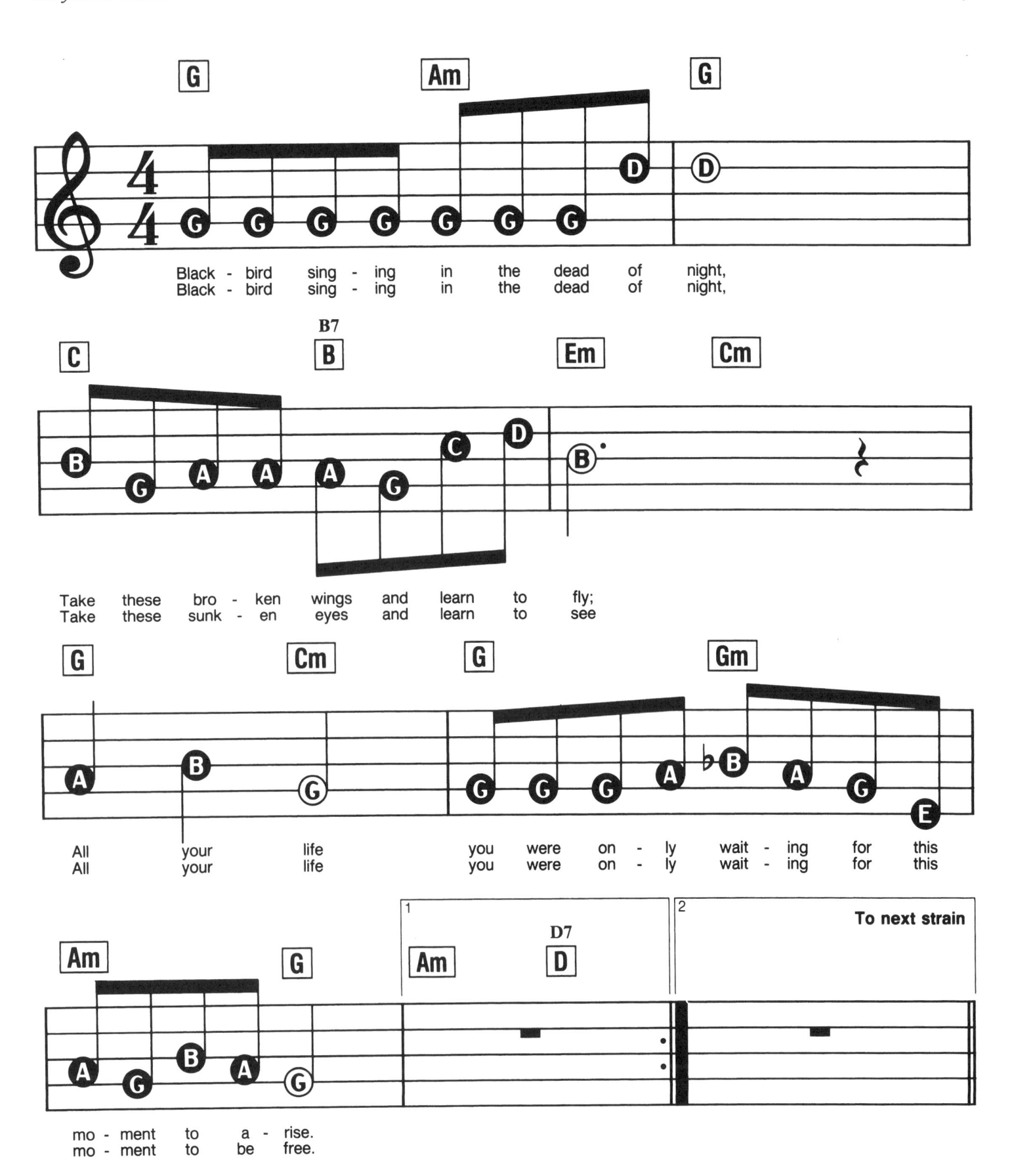

Black - bird sing - ing in the dead of night,
Black - bird sing - ing in the dead of night,

Take these bro - ken wings and learn to fly;
Take these sunk - en eyes and learn to see

All your life you were on - ly wait - ing for this
All your life you were on - ly wait - ing for this

mo - ment to a - rise.
mo - ment to be free.

To next strain

Copyright © 1968, 1969 Sony/ATV Music Publishing LLC
Copyright Renewed
All Rights Administered by Sony/ATV Music Publishing LLC, 8 Music Square West, Nashville, TN 37203
International Copyright Secured   All Rights Reserved

3 | Fine

| F | Dm | B♭ | C |

Black - bird, fly,

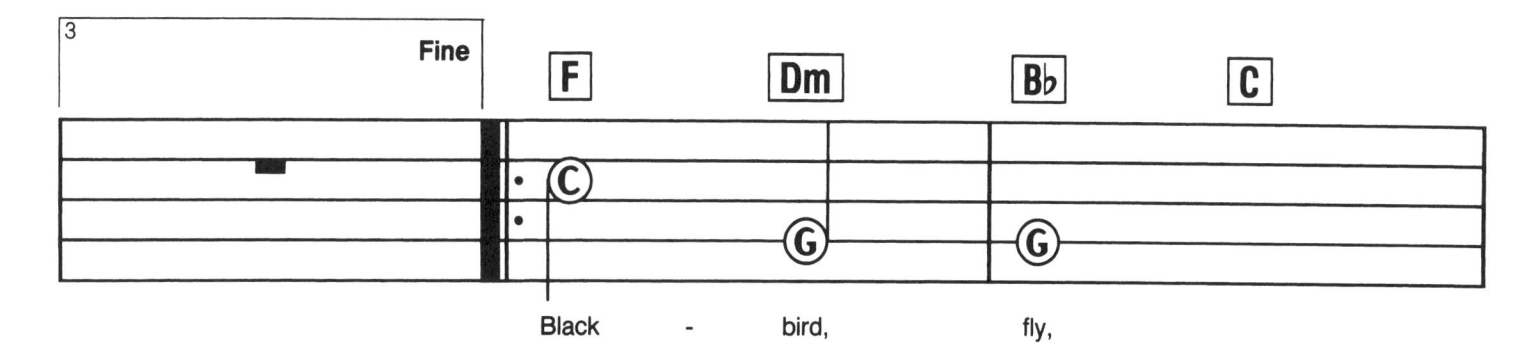

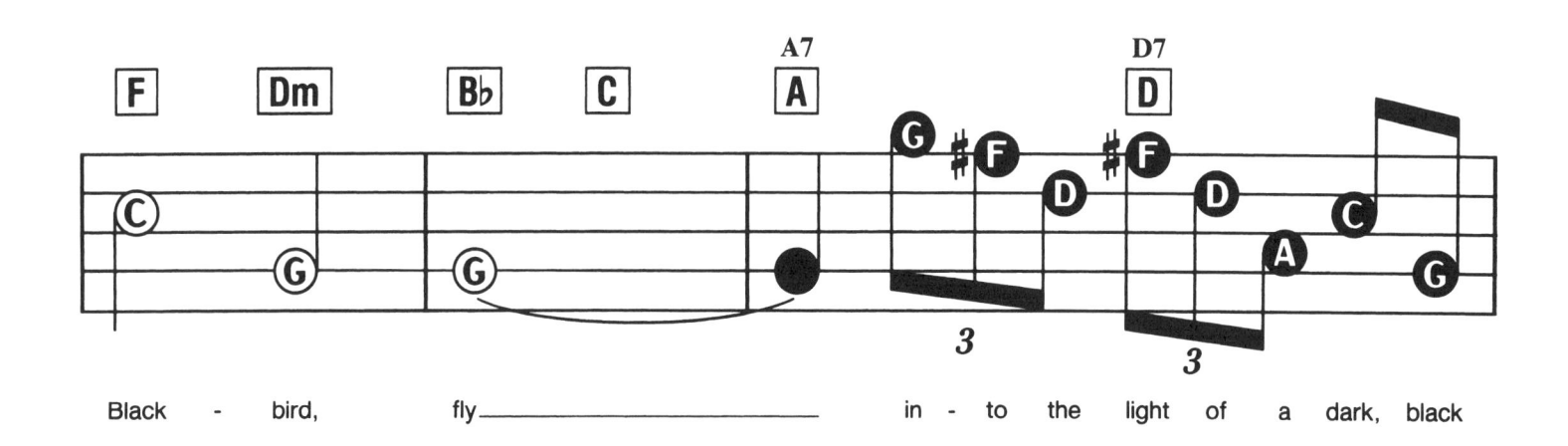

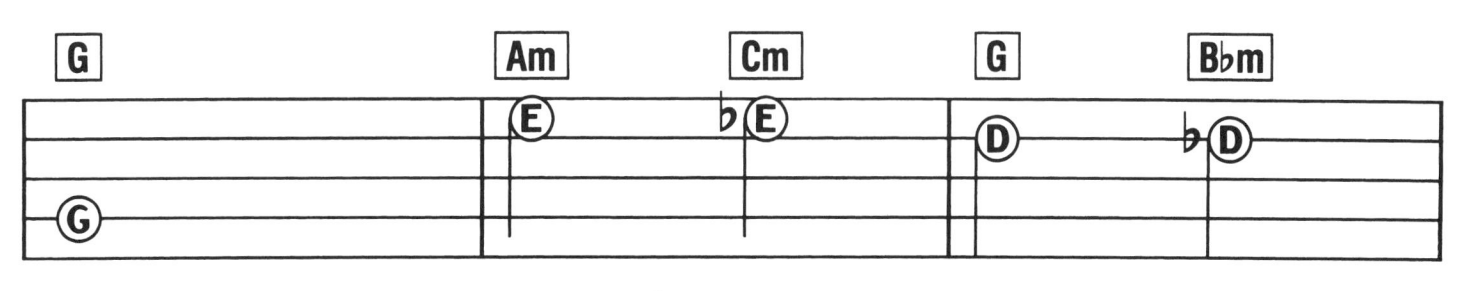

| F | Dm | B♭ | C | A7/A | D7/D |

Black - bird, fly _____ in - to the light of a dark, black

| G | Am | Cm | G | B♭m |

night.   *Instrumental*

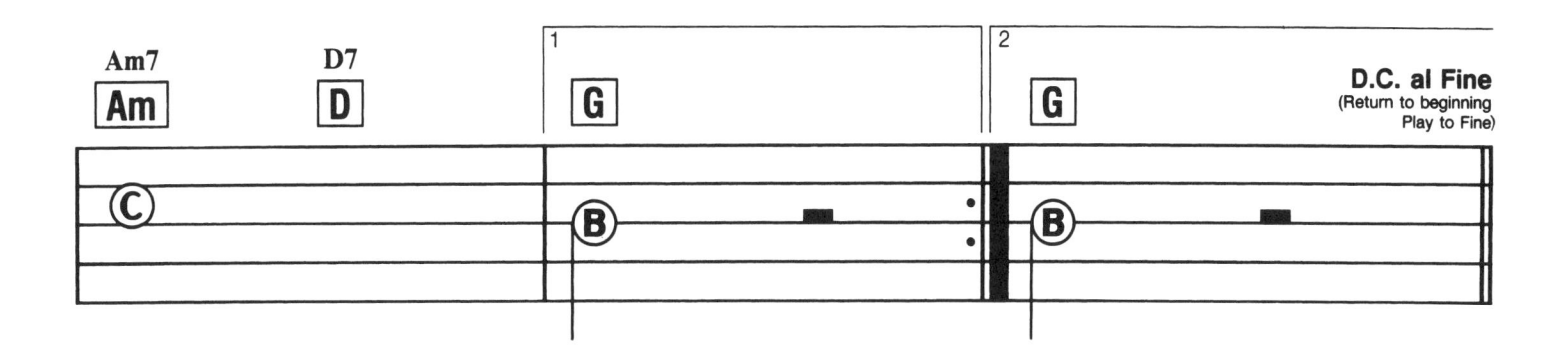

| Am7/Am | D7/D | **1** G | **2** G |

D.C. al Fine
(Return to beginning
Play to Fine)

Constant Craving

Registration 5
Rhythm: 8-Beat or Pop

Words and Music by K.D. Lang
and Ben Mink

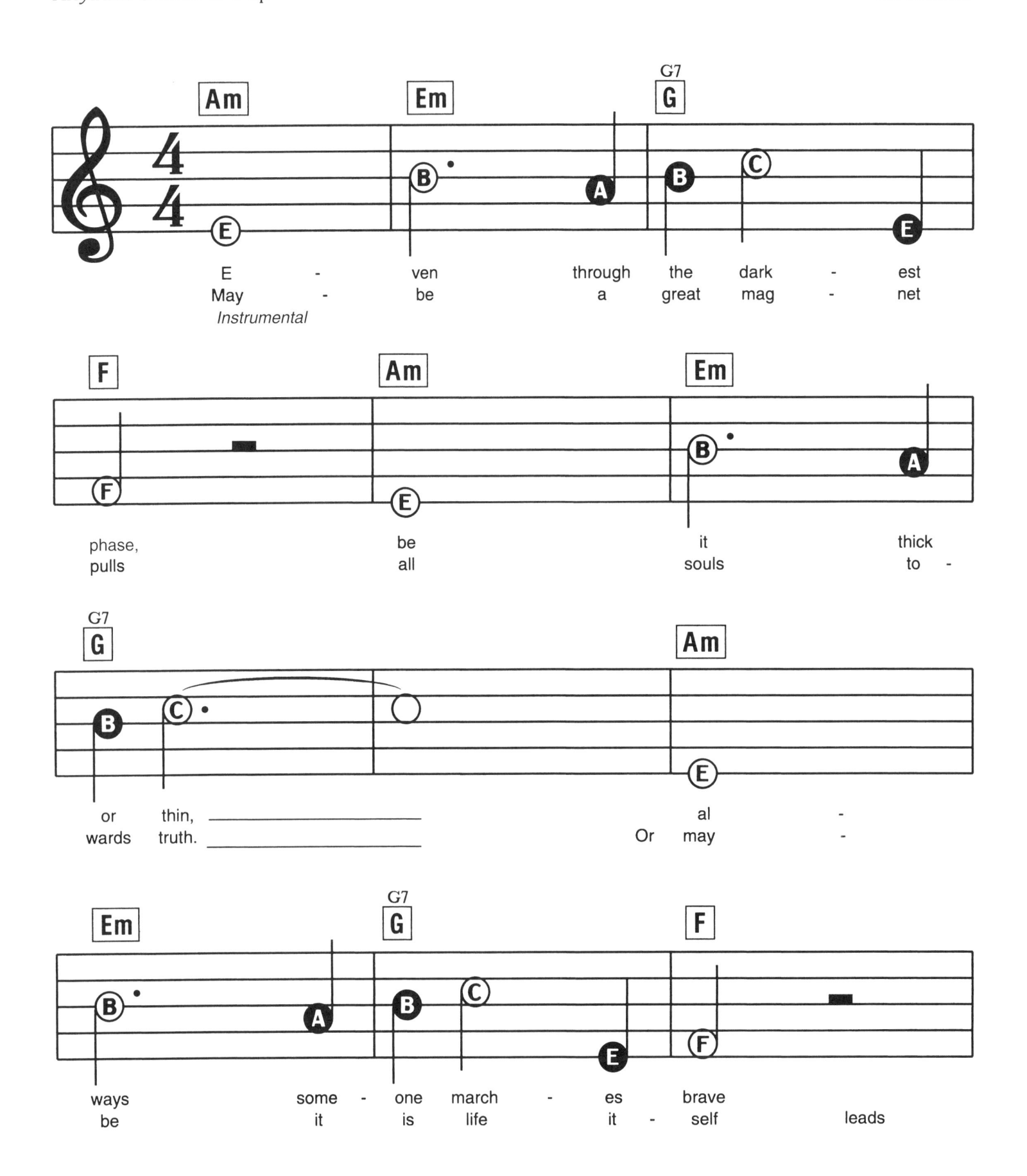

Am	Em	G7 / G

E - ven through the dark - est
May be

Instructional

F	Am	Em

phase, be it thick
pulls all souls to -

G7 / G	Am

or thin, _____ al -
wards truth. _____ Or may -

Em	G7 / G	F

ways some - one march - es brave
be it is life it - self leads

Copyright © 1992 UNIVERSAL - POLYGRAM INTERNATIONAL PUBLISHING, INC., Bumstead Productions U.S., Inc. and Zavion Enterprises, Inc.
All Rights for BUMSTEAD PRODUCTIONS U.S., INC. Controlled and Administered by UNIVERSAL - POLYGRAM INTERNATIONAL PUBLISHING, INC.
All Rights Reserved   Used by Permission

41

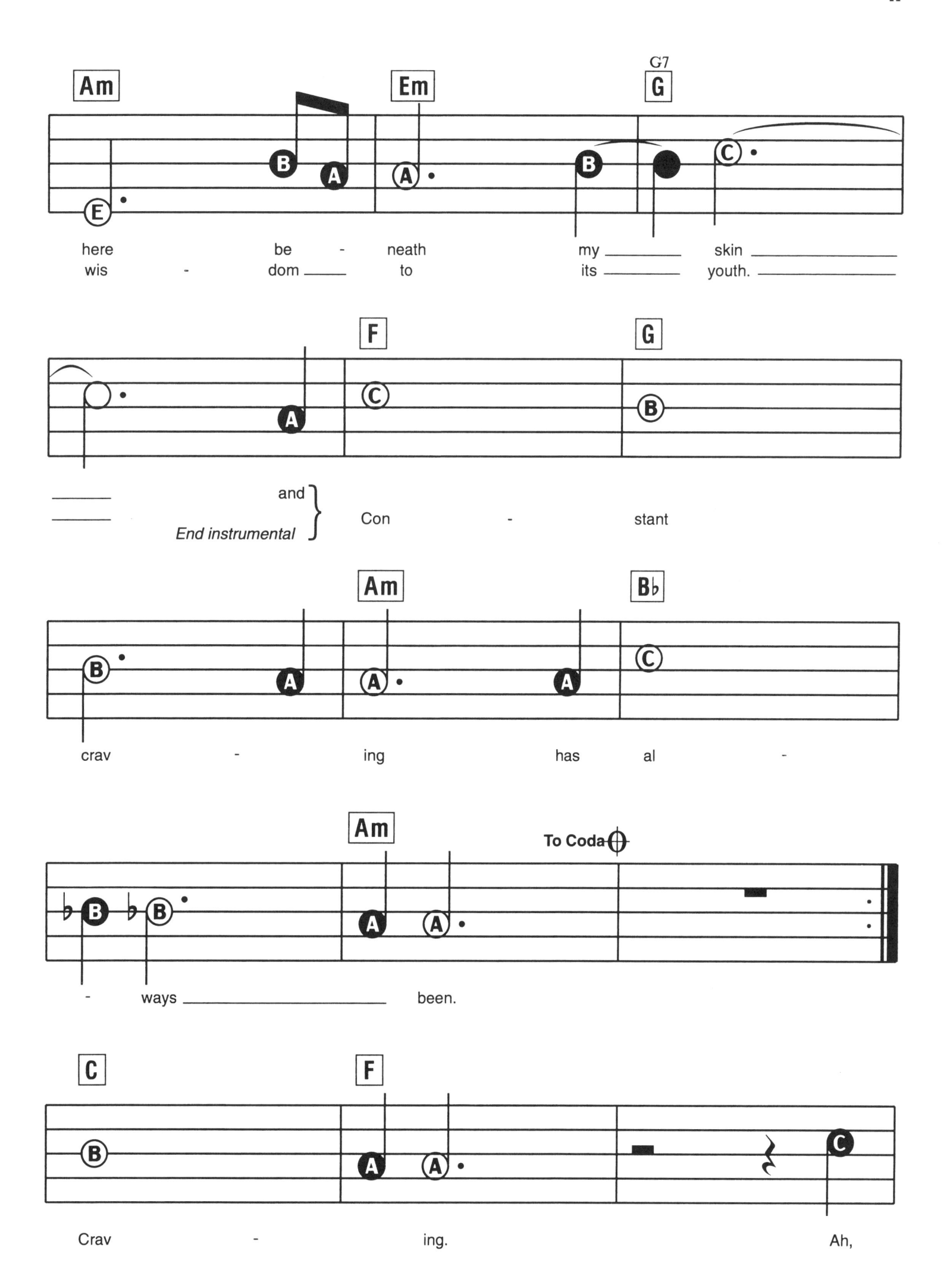

42

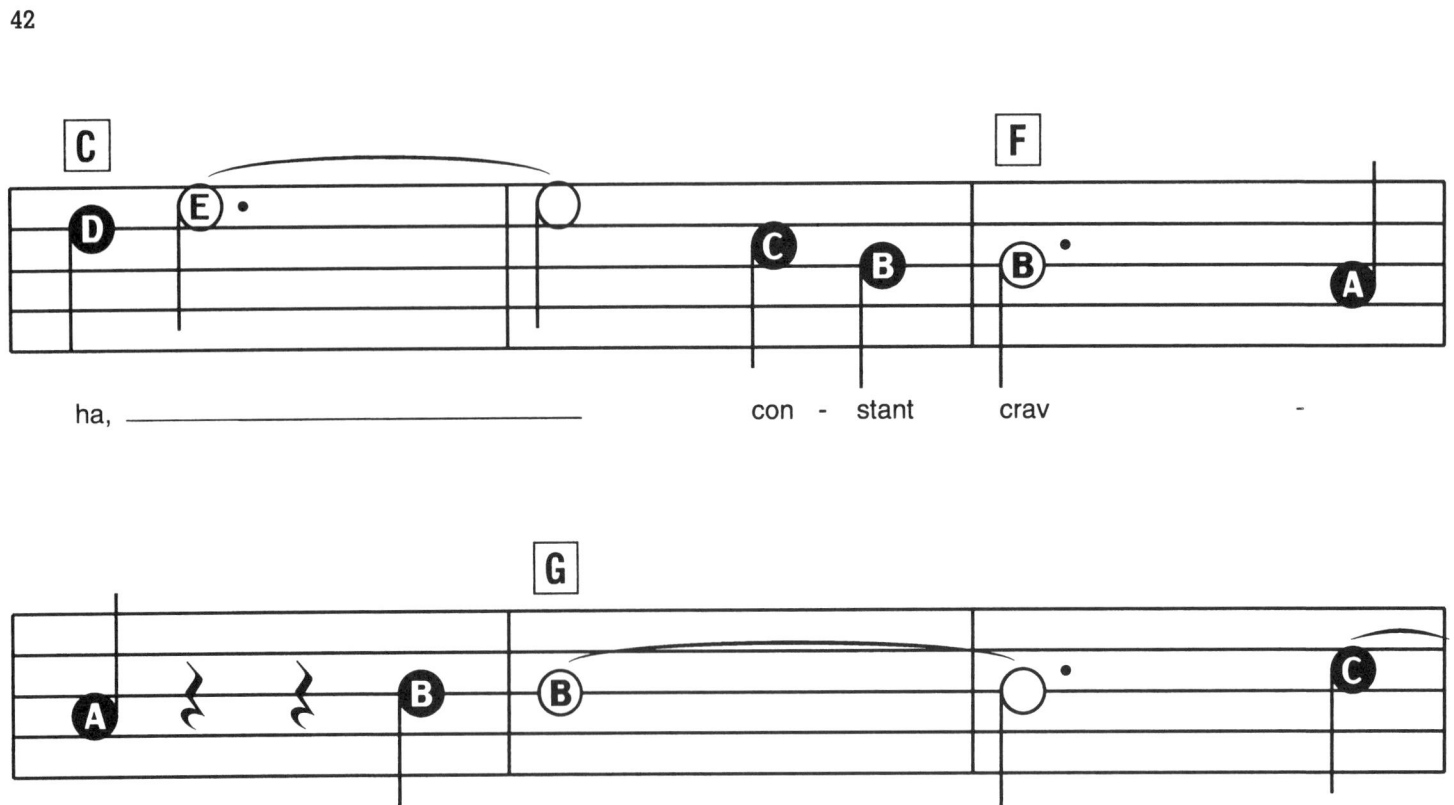

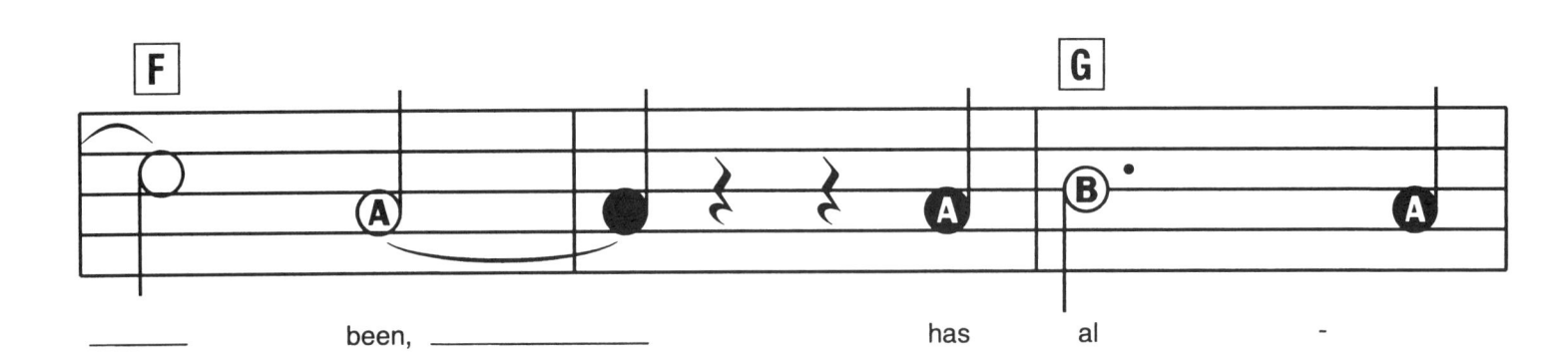

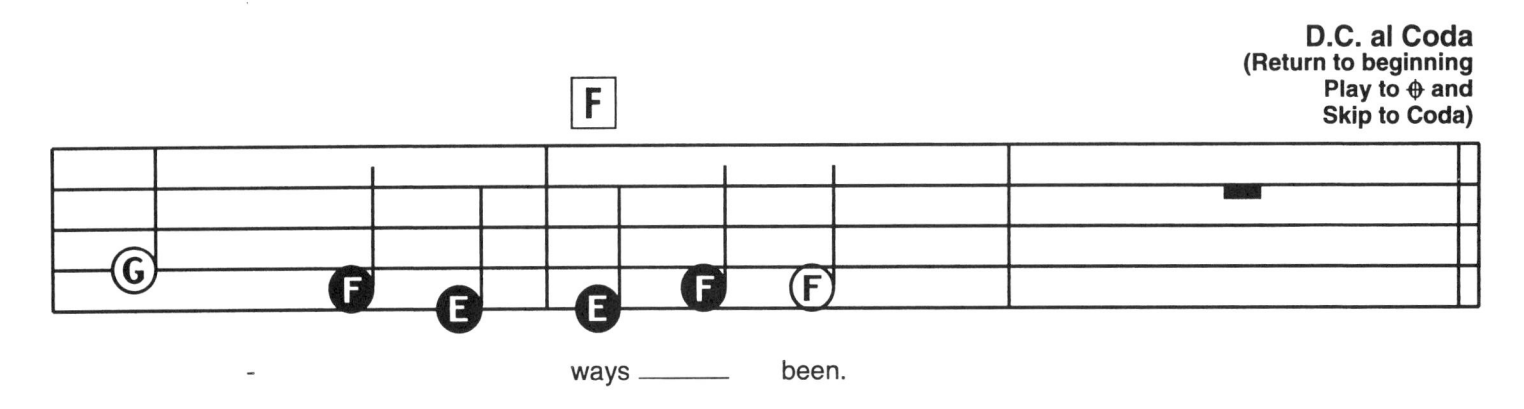

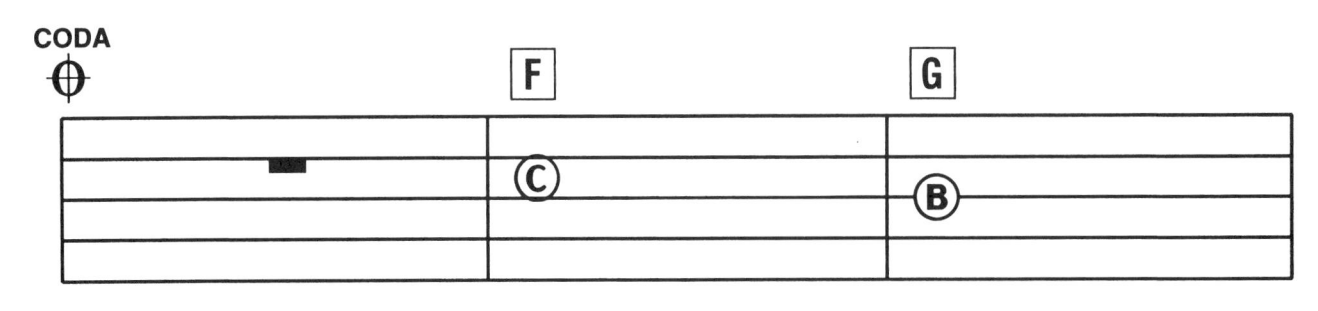

ha, con - stant crav - ing has al - ways

been, has al - ways been.

D.C. al Coda
(Return to beginning
Play to ⊕ and
Skip to Coda)

CODA

Con - stant

43

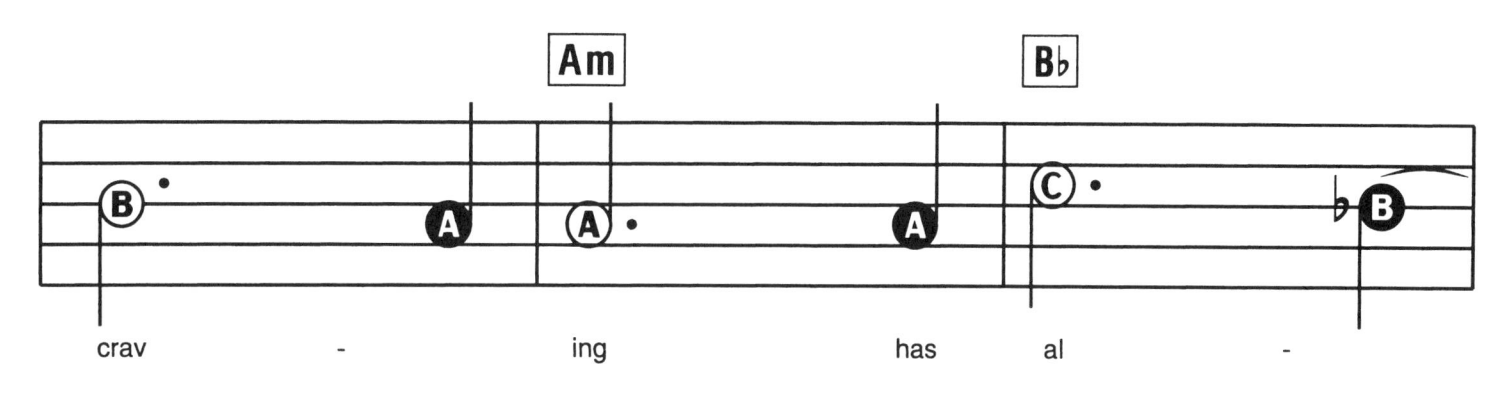

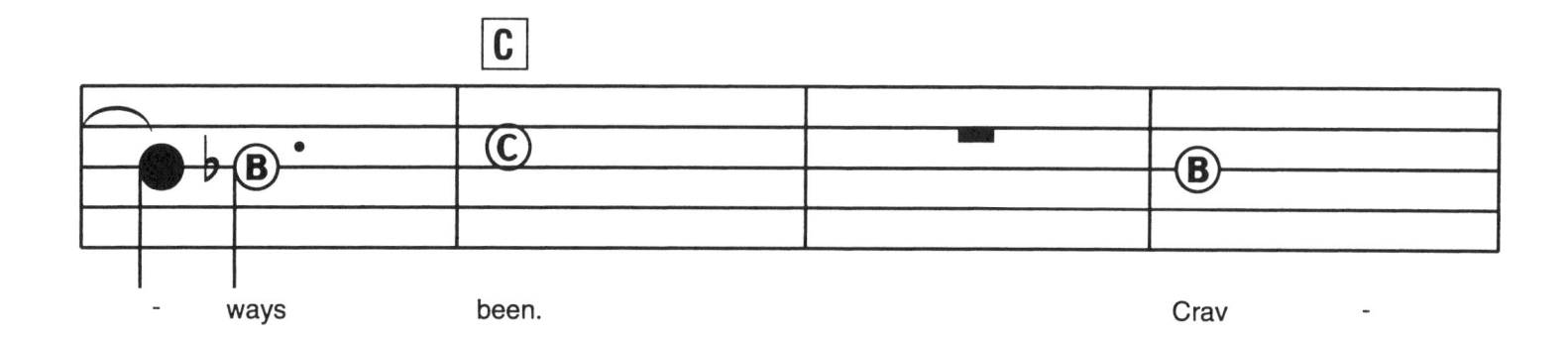

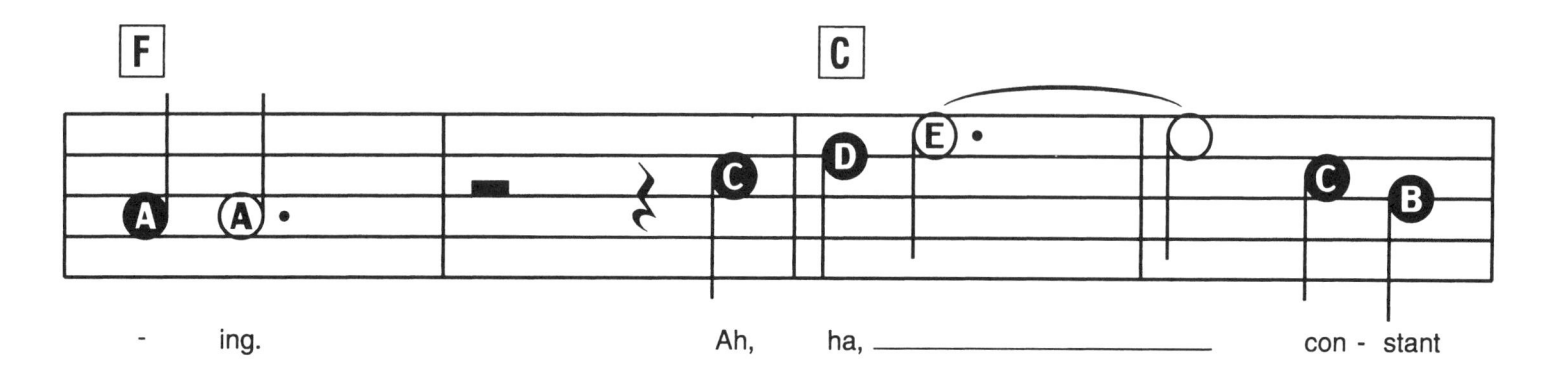

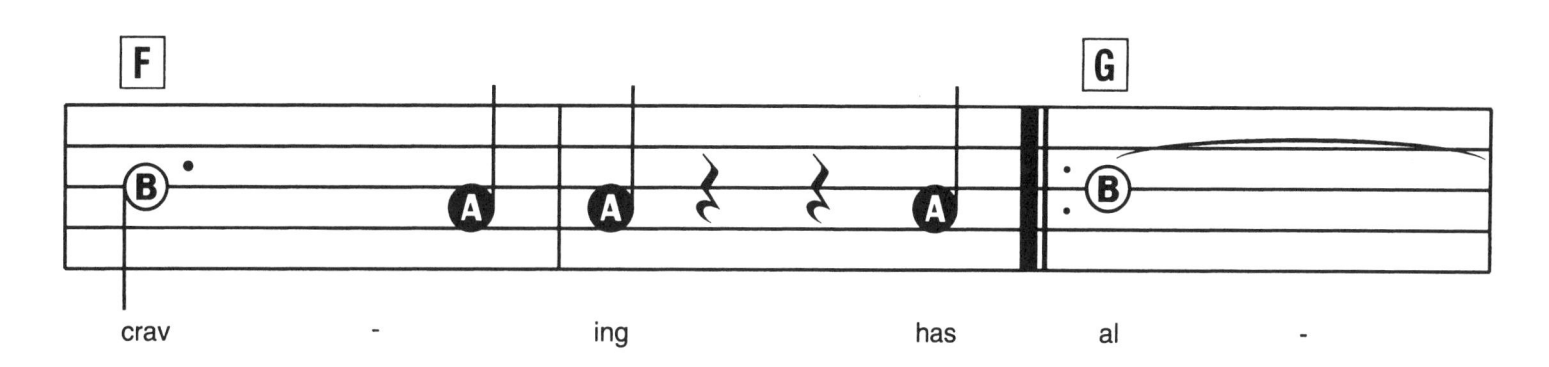

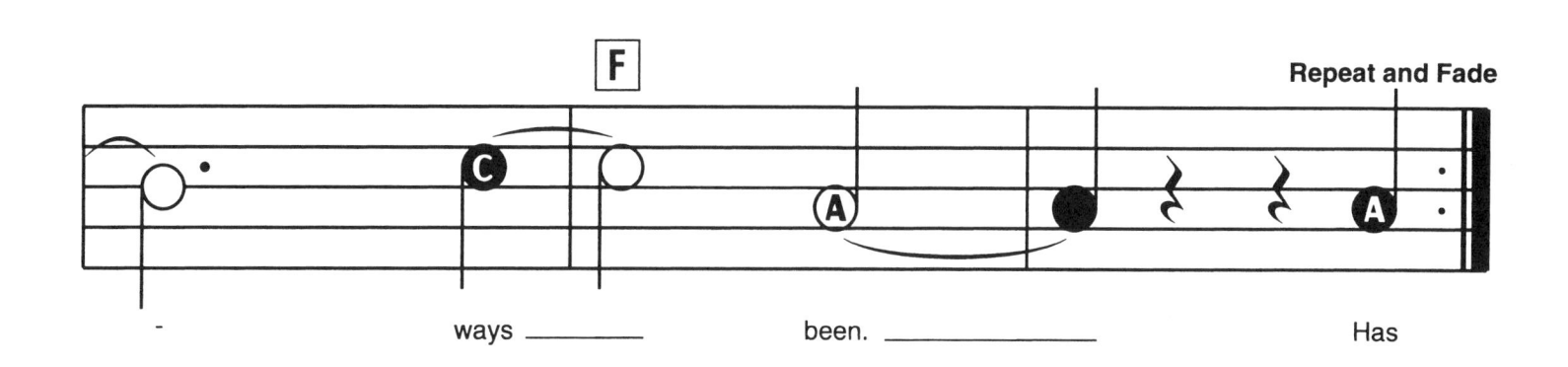

Cotton Fields
(The Cotton Song)

Registration 8
Rhythm: Country

Words and Music by
Huddie Ledbetter

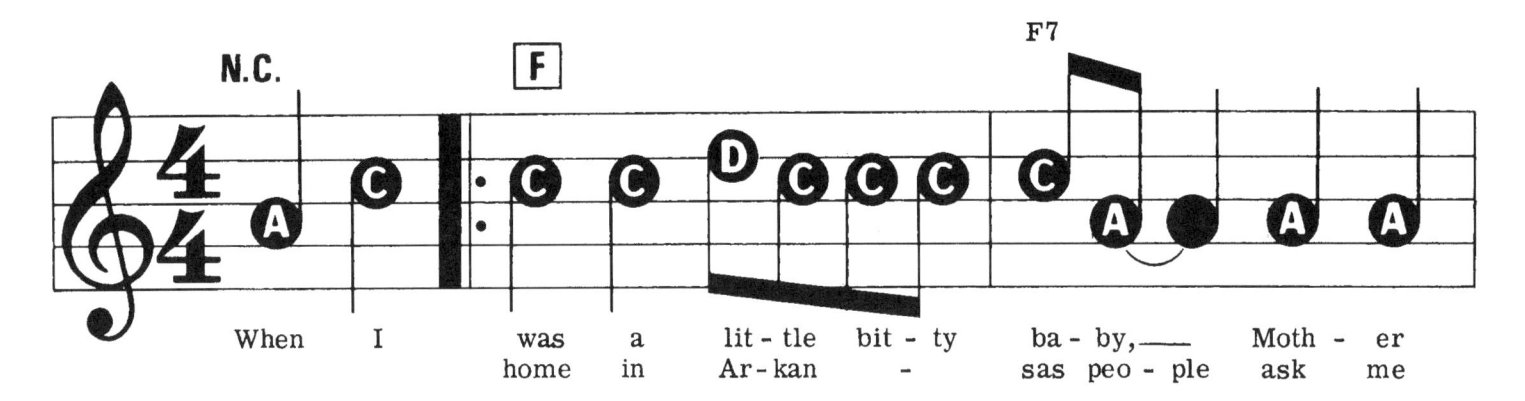

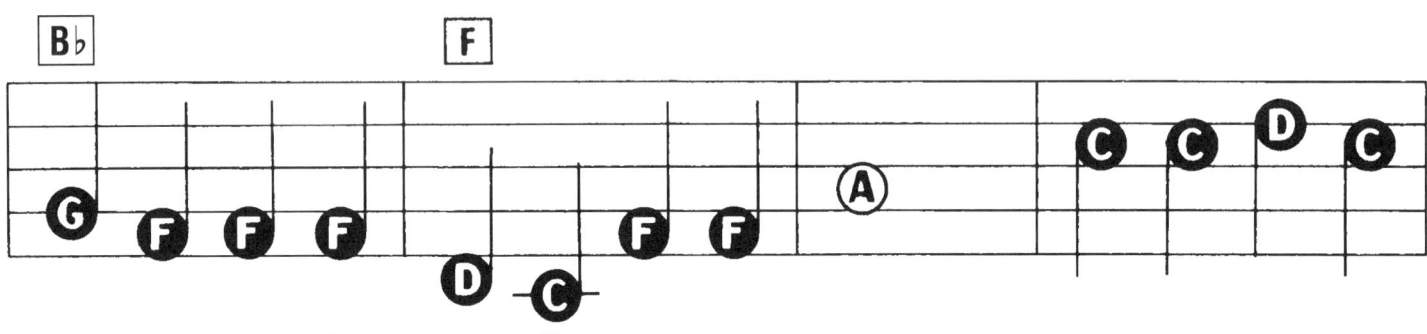

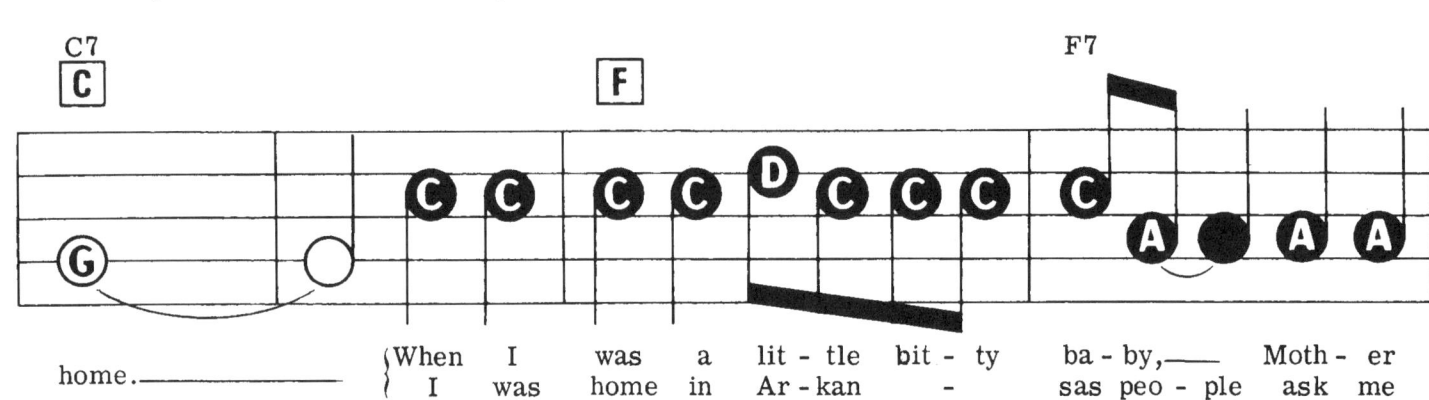

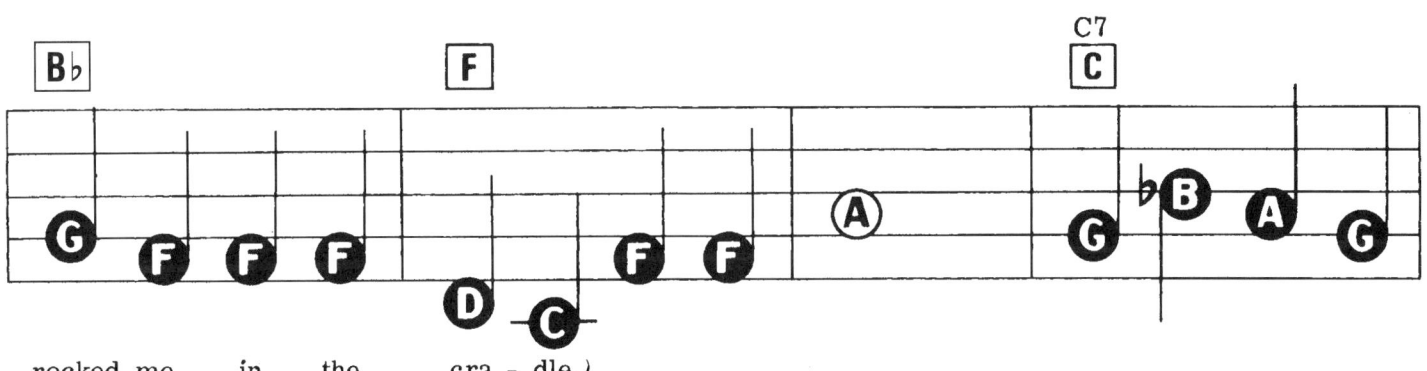

When I was a lit-tle bit-ty ba-by,— Moth-er rocked me in the cra-dle, In them old cot-ton fields at home.
I was home in Ar-kan-sas peo-ple ask me what you come here for,—

{When I was a lit-tle bit-ty ba-by,— Moth-er rocked me in the cra-dle,} In them old cot-ton fields at
{I was home in Ar-kan-sas peo-ple ask me what you come here for,—}

TRO - © Copyright 1962 (Renewed) Folkways Music Publishers, Inc., New York, NY
International Copyright Secured
All Rights Reserved Including Public Performance For Profit
Used by Permission

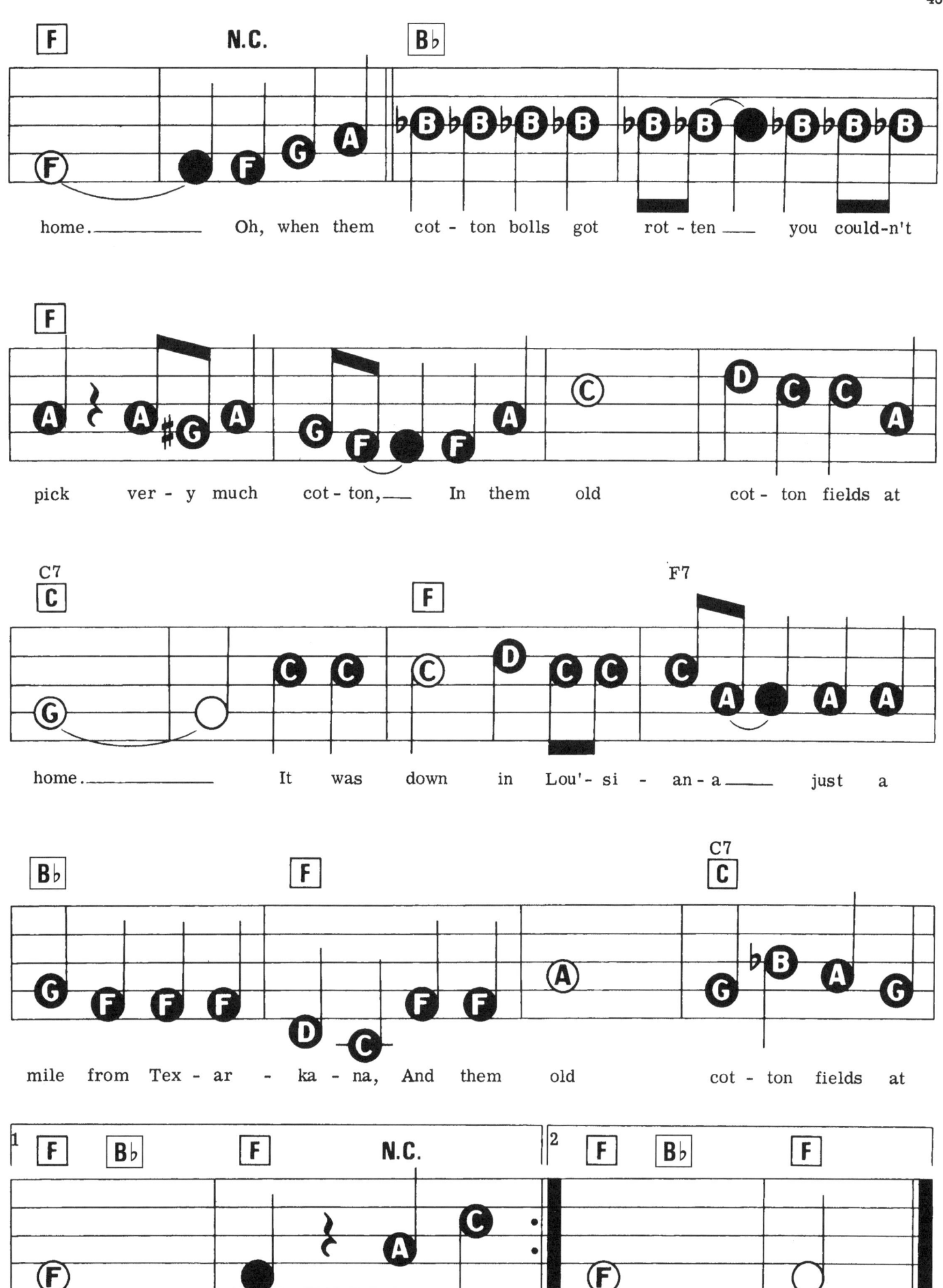

home. Oh, when them cot-ton bolls got rot-ten you could-n't pick ver-y much cot-ton, In them old cot-ton fields at home. It was down in Lou'-si-an-a just a mile from Tex-ar-ka-na, And them old cot-ton fields at home. I was home.

Don't Let the Rain Come Down
(Crooked Little Man)(Crooked Little House)

Registration 10
Rhythm: Rock or Pops

Words and Music by Ersel Hicky
and Ed E. Miller

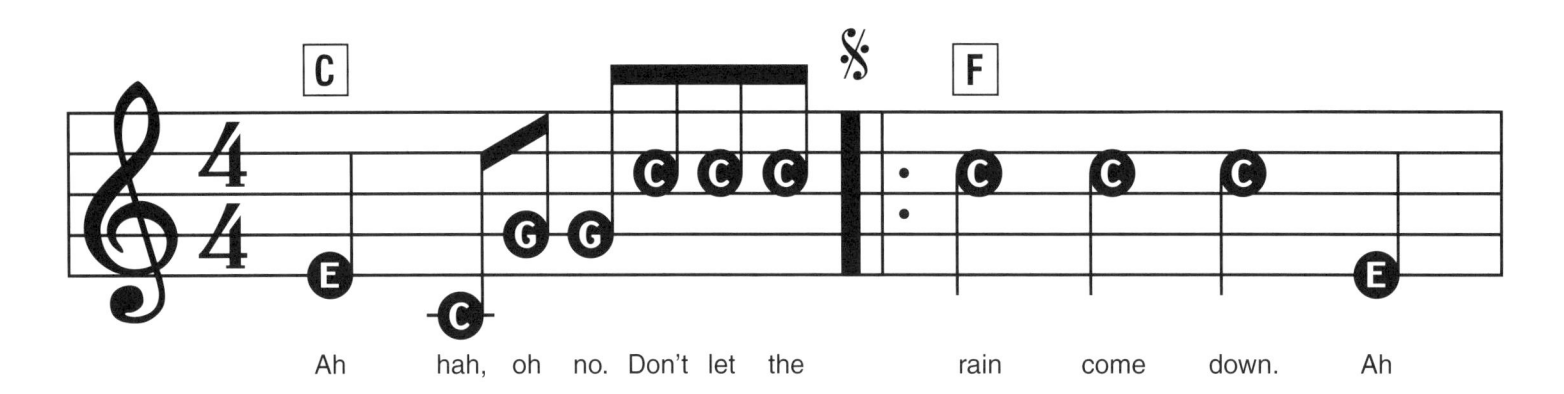

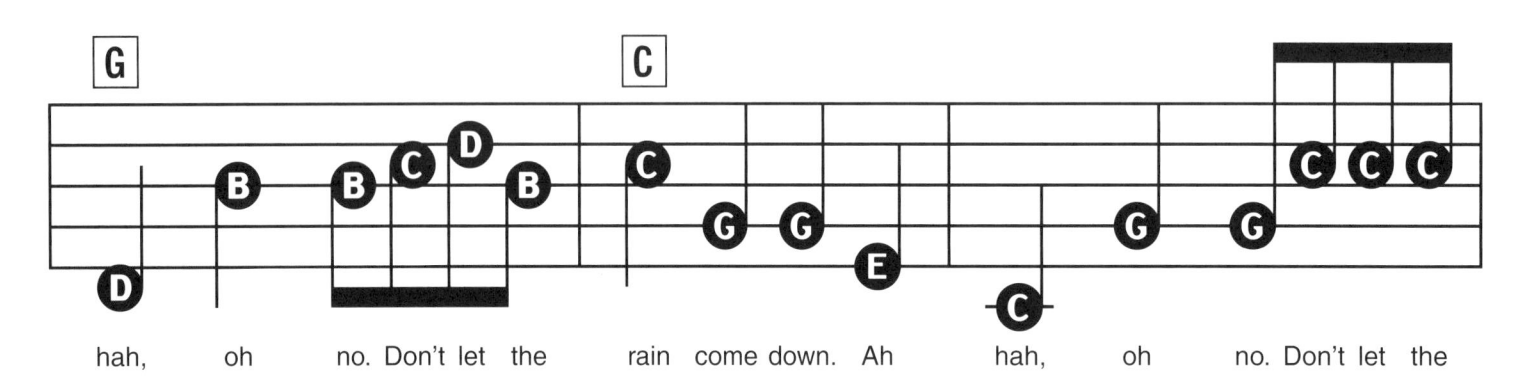

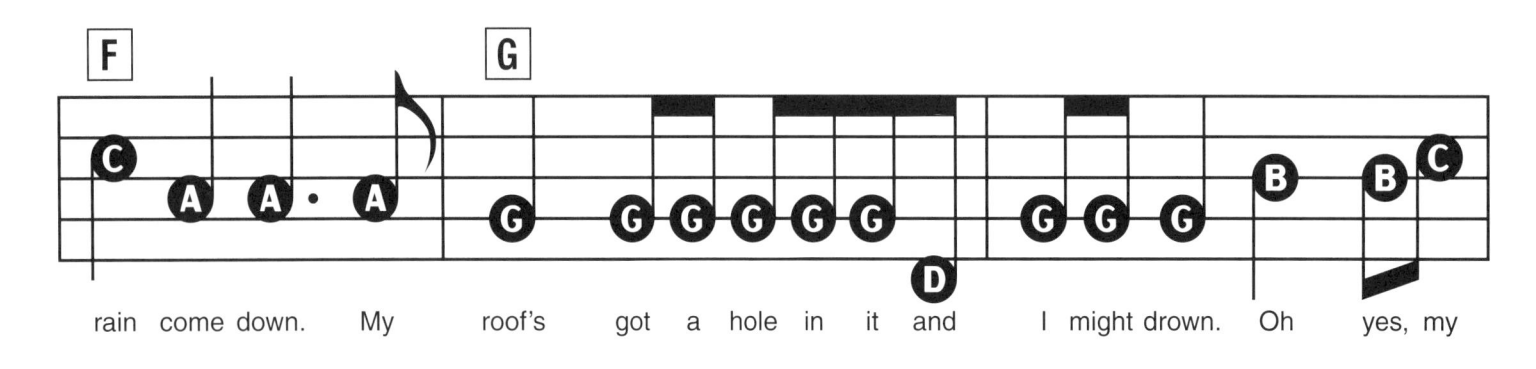

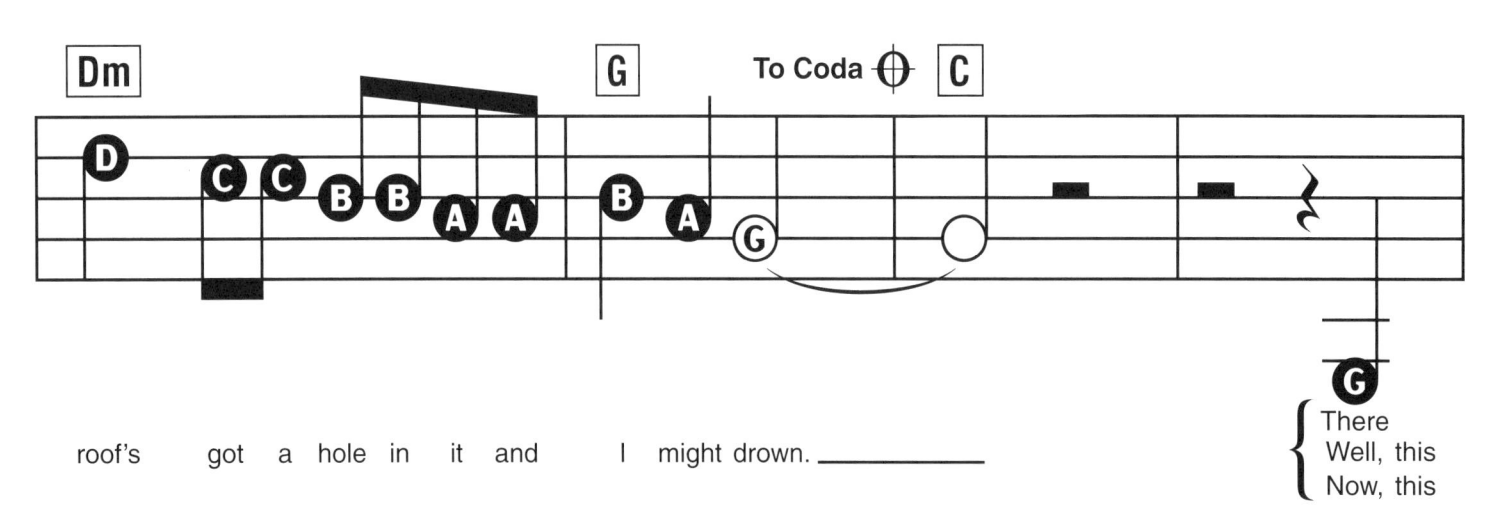

Ah hah, oh no. Don't let the rain come down. Ah hah, oh no. Don't let the rain come down. Ah hah, oh no. Don't let the rain come down. My roof's got a hole in it and I might drown. Oh yes, my roof's got a hole in it and I might drown. _____

{ There
  Well, this
  Now, this

© 1960 (Renewed 1988) SCREEN GEMS-EMI MUSIC INC. and SERENDIPITY PUBLISHING CORP.
All Rights Controlled and Administered by SCREEN GEMS-EMI MUSIC INC.
All Rights Reserved   International Copyright Secured   Used by Permission

was a crook-ed man and he had a crook-ed smile,
crook-ed lit-tle man and his crook-ed lit-tle smile,
crook-ed lit-tle man and his crook-ed cat and mouse, they

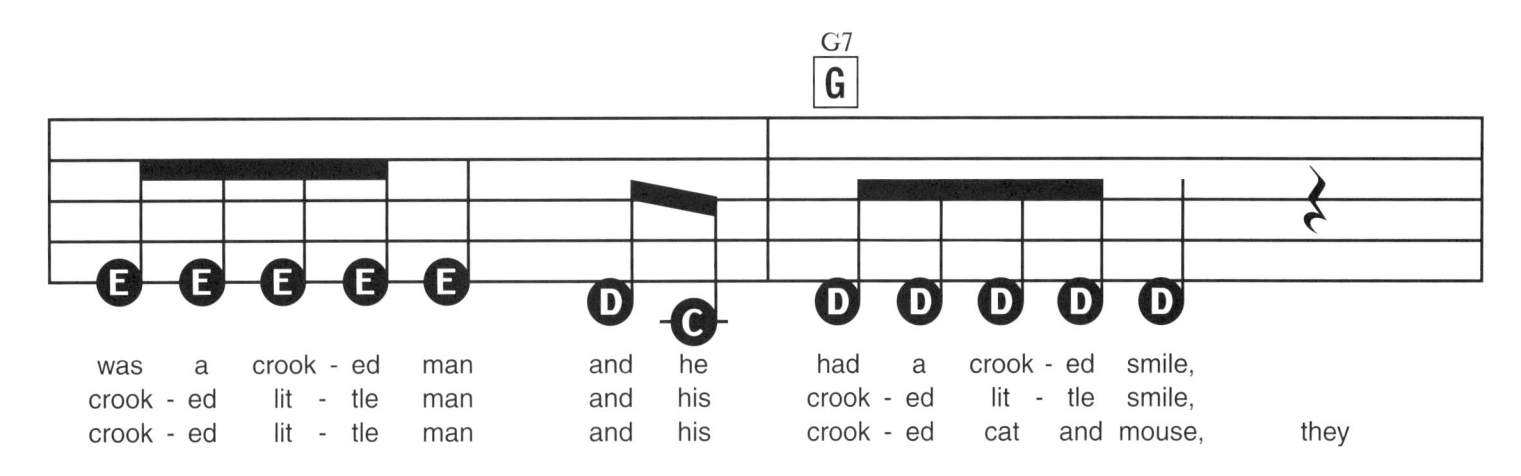

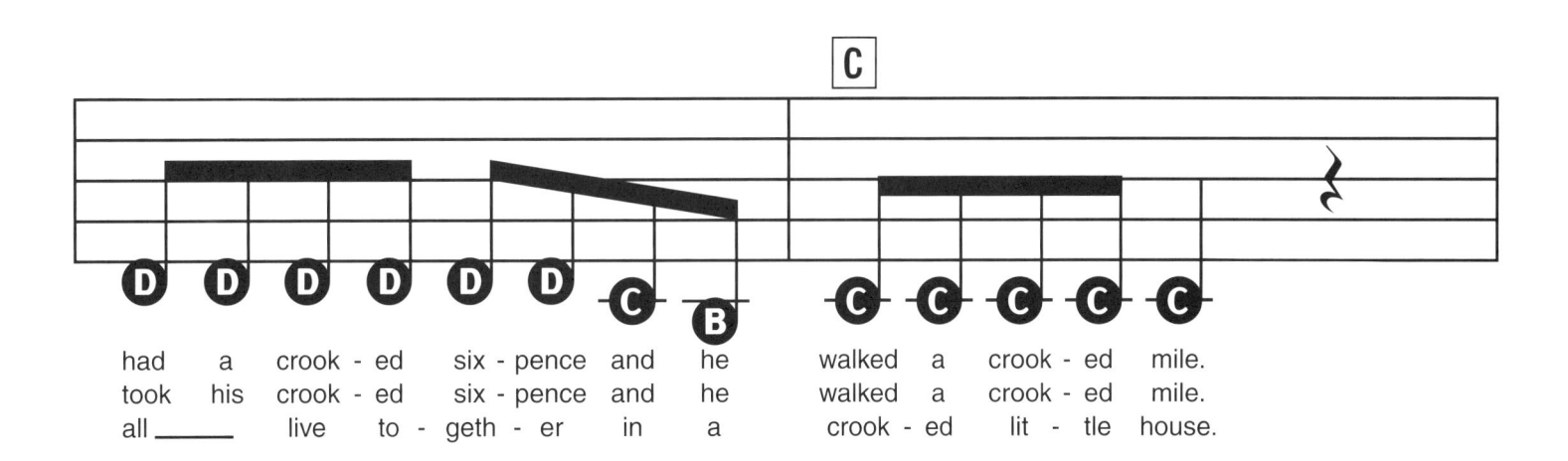

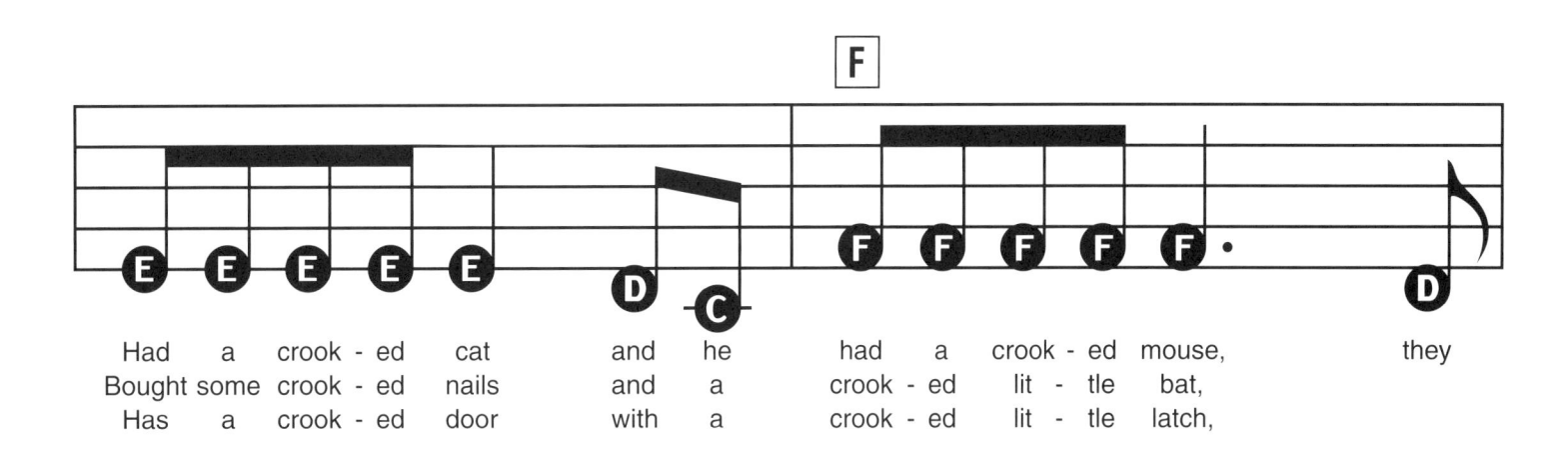

had a crook-ed six-pence and he walked a crook-ed mile.
took his crook-ed six-pence and he walked a crook-ed mile.
all ___ live to-geth-er in a crook-ed lit-tle house.

Had a crook-ed cat and he had a crook-ed mouse, they
Bought some crook-ed nails and a crook-ed lit-tle bat,
Has a crook-ed door with a crook-ed lit-tle latch,

all lived to-geth-er in a crook-ed lit-tle house.
tried to fix his roof with a rat-tat-tat-tat-tat. Ah
has a crook-ed roof with a crook-ed lit-tle patch.

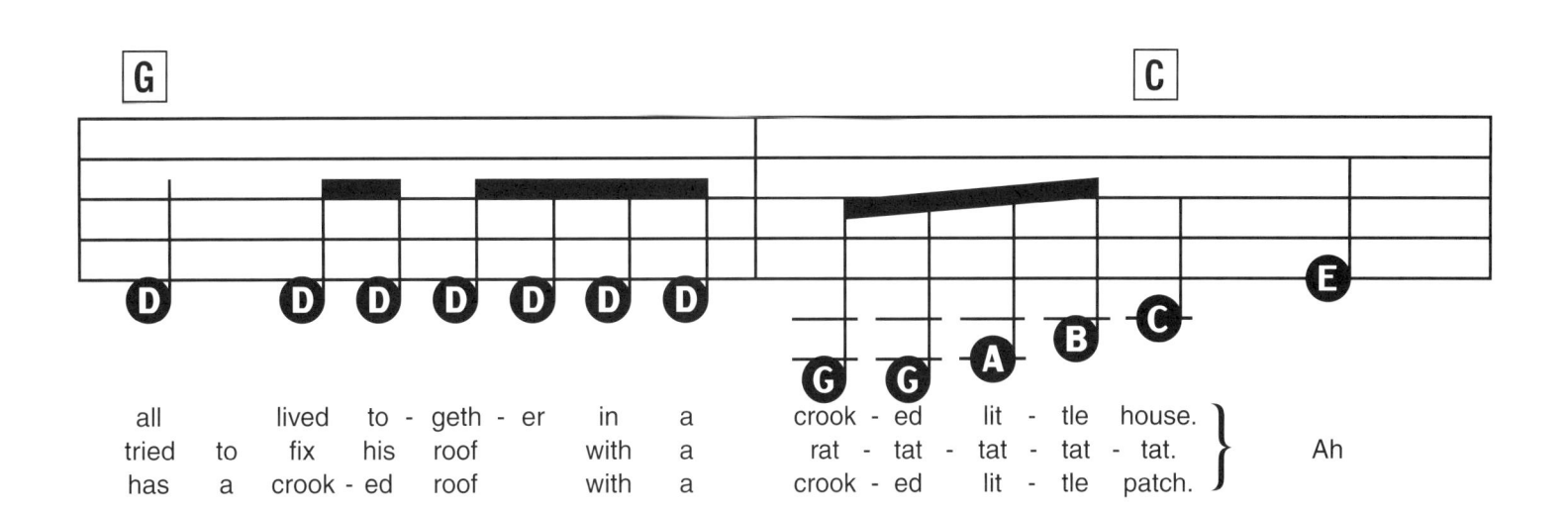

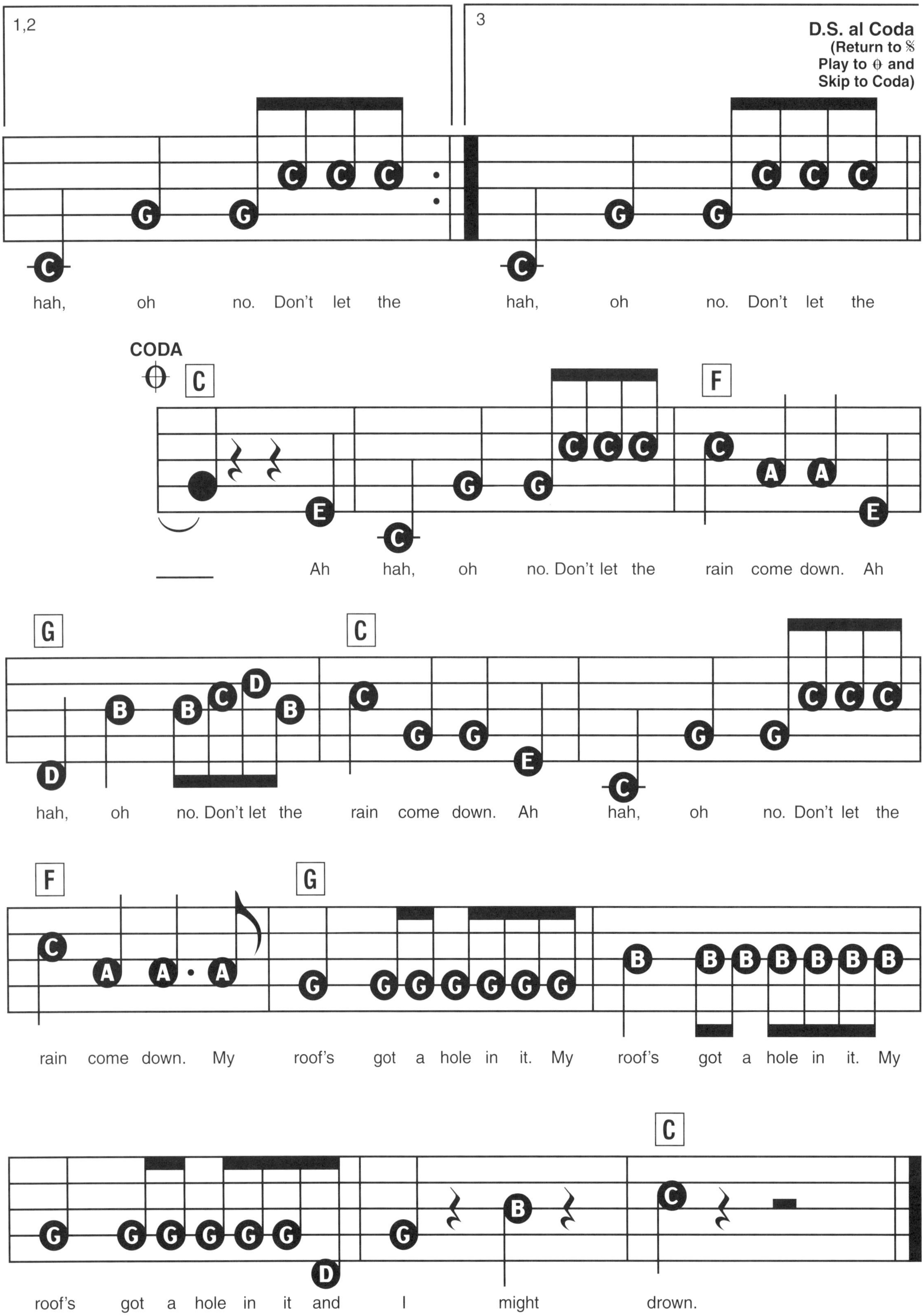
1,2
3
D.S. al Coda
(Return to 𝄋
Play to ⊕ and
Skip to Coda)
hah, oh no. Don't let the
hah, oh no. Don't let the
CODA
C
F
Ah hah, oh no. Don't let the rain come down. Ah
G
C
hah, oh no. Don't let the rain come down. Ah hah, oh no. Don't let the
F
G
rain come down. My roof's got a hole in it. My roof's got a hole in it. My
C
roof's got a hole in it and I might drown.

Everything I Own

Registration 4
Rhythm: Reggae or 8-Beat

Words and Music by
David Gates

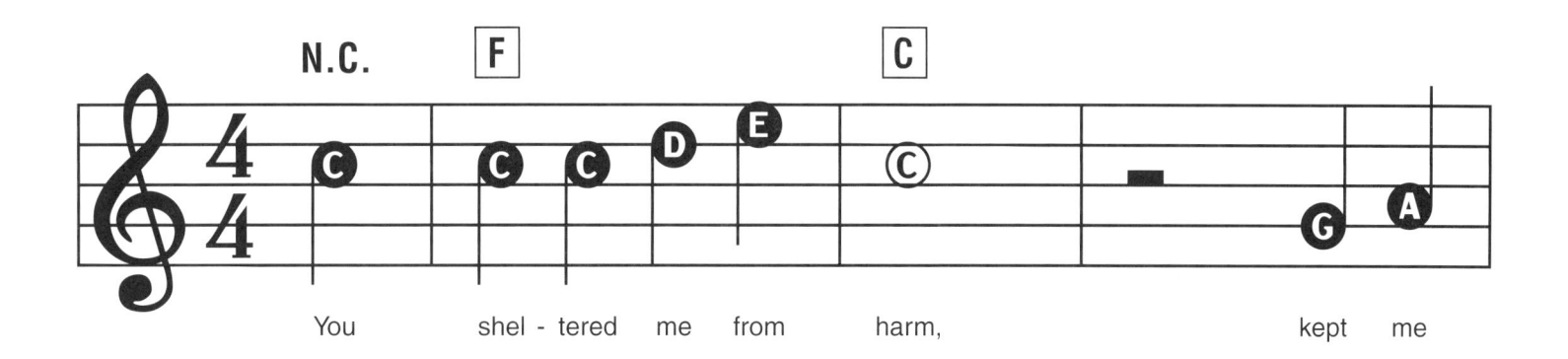

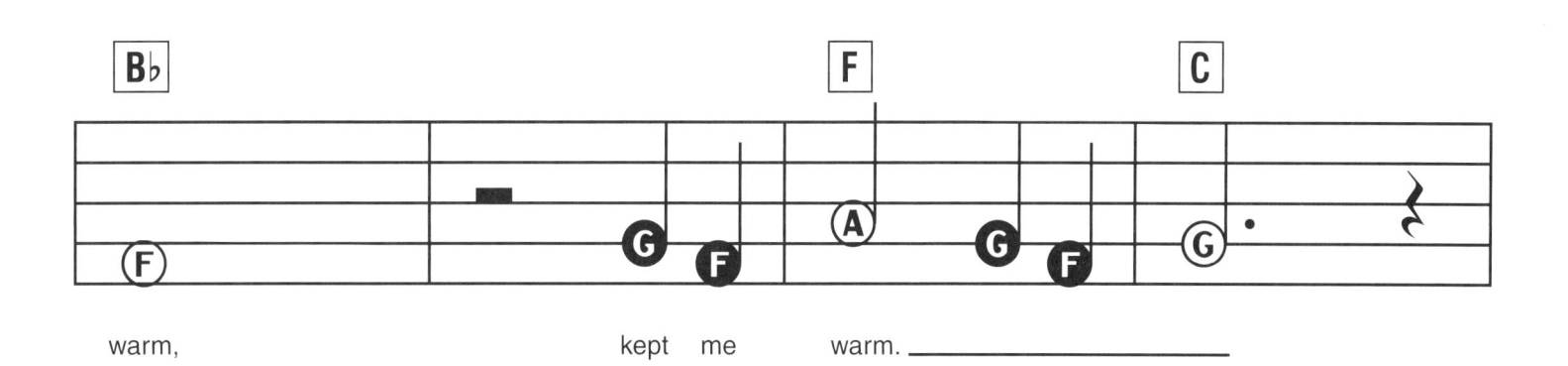

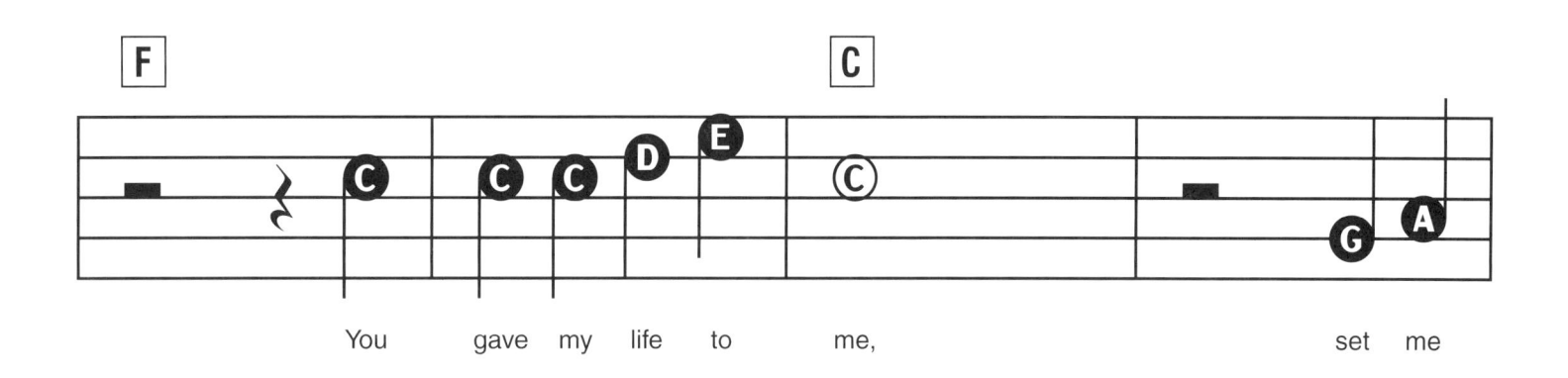

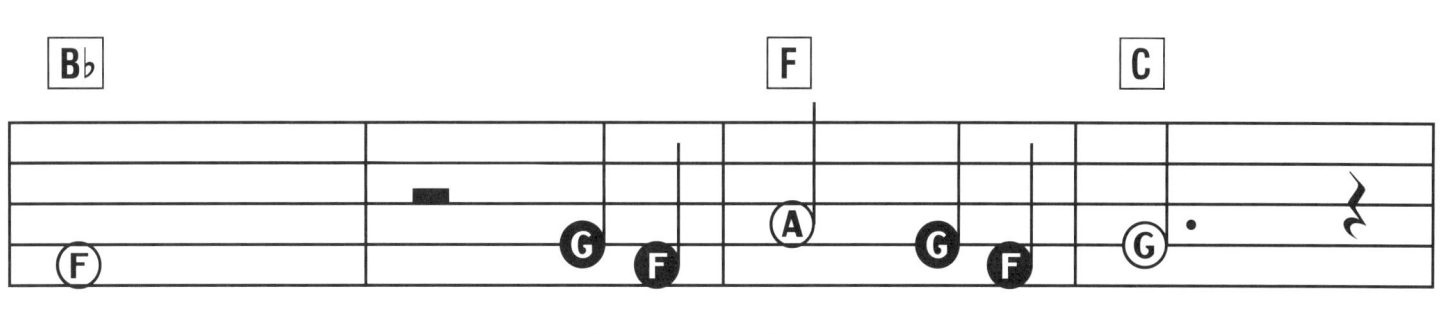

You shel-tered me from harm, kept me warm, kept me warm.

You gave my life to me, set me free, set me free.

Copyright © 1972 Sony/ATV Music Publishing LLC
Copyright Renewed
All Rights Administered by Sony/ATV Music Publishing LLC, 8 Music Square West, Nashville, TN 37203
International Copyright Secured All Rights Reserved

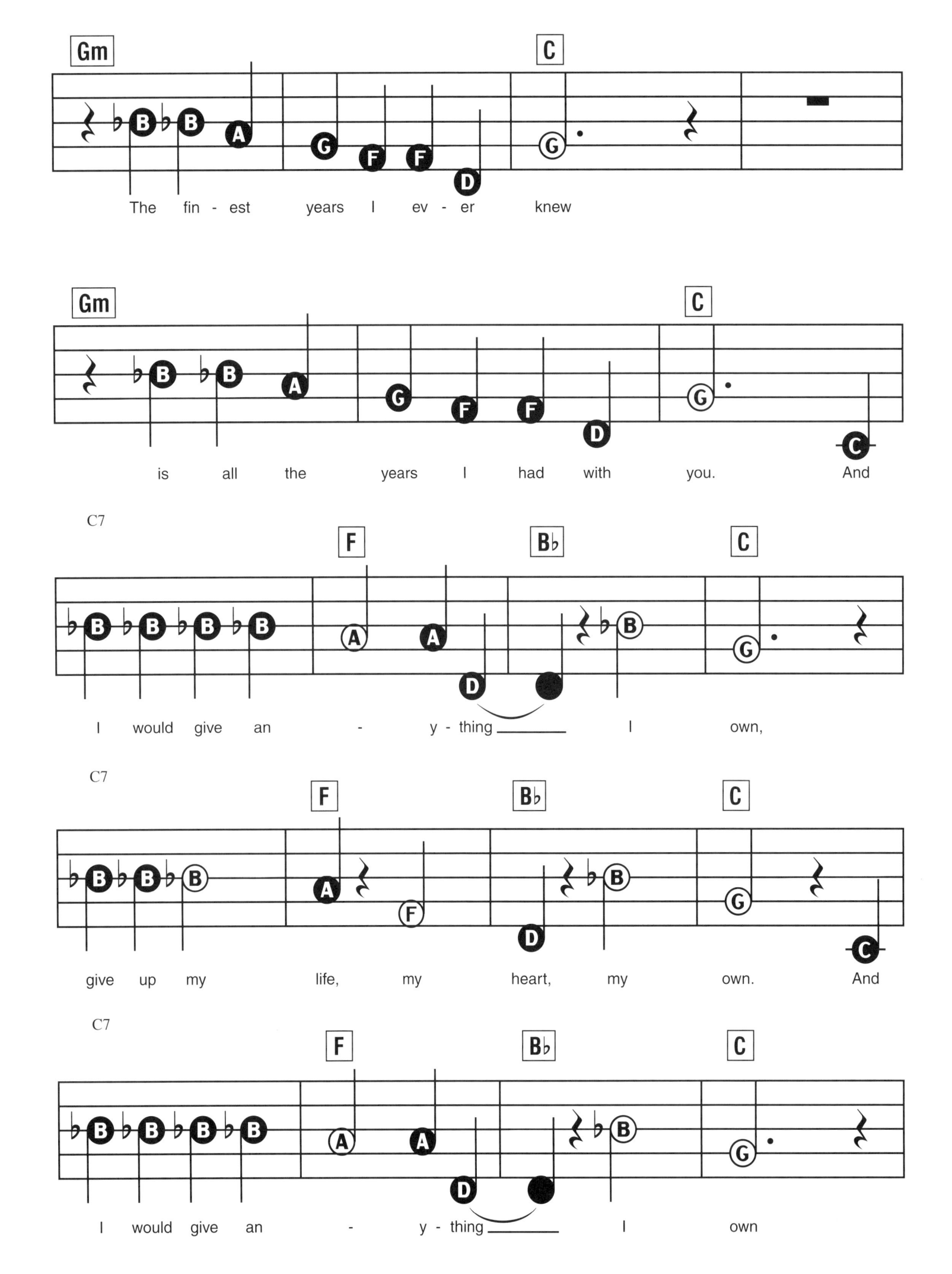

The fin-est years I ev-er knew is all the years I had with you. And I would give an-y-thing I own, give up my life, my heart, my own. And I would give an-y-thing I own

51

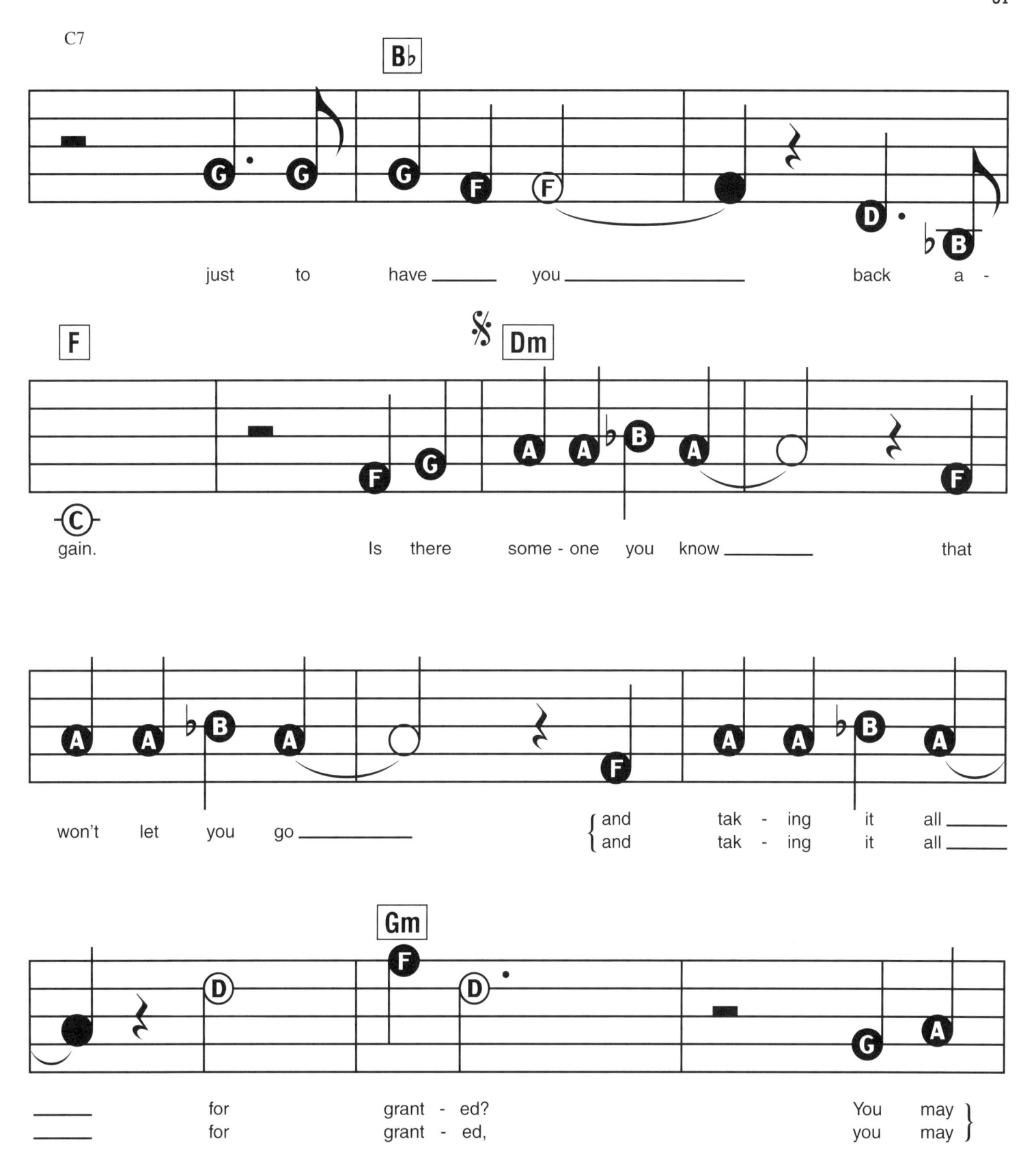

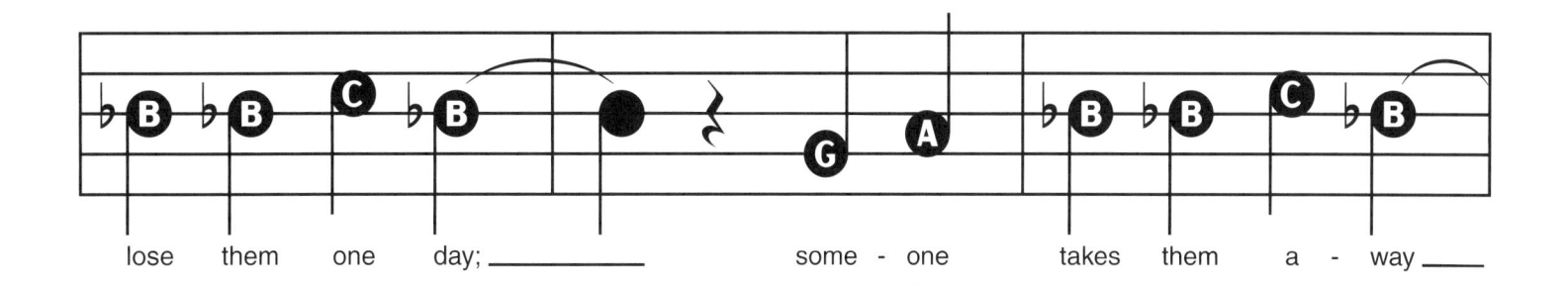

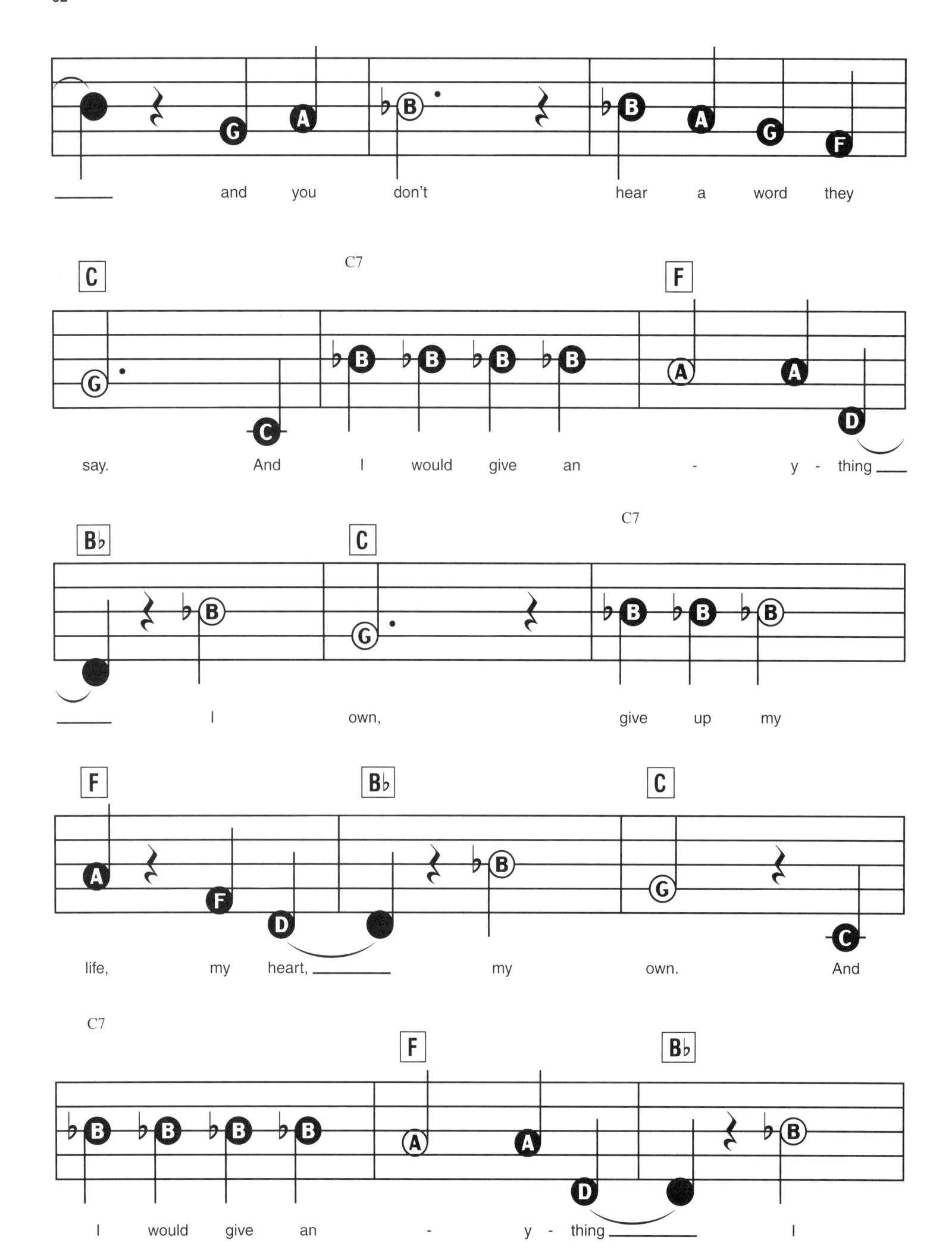

and you don't hear a word they say. And I would give anything I own, give up my life, my heart, my own. And I would give anything I own ... just to have ____ you ____ back a - gain, just to talk to you once a - gain. If there's

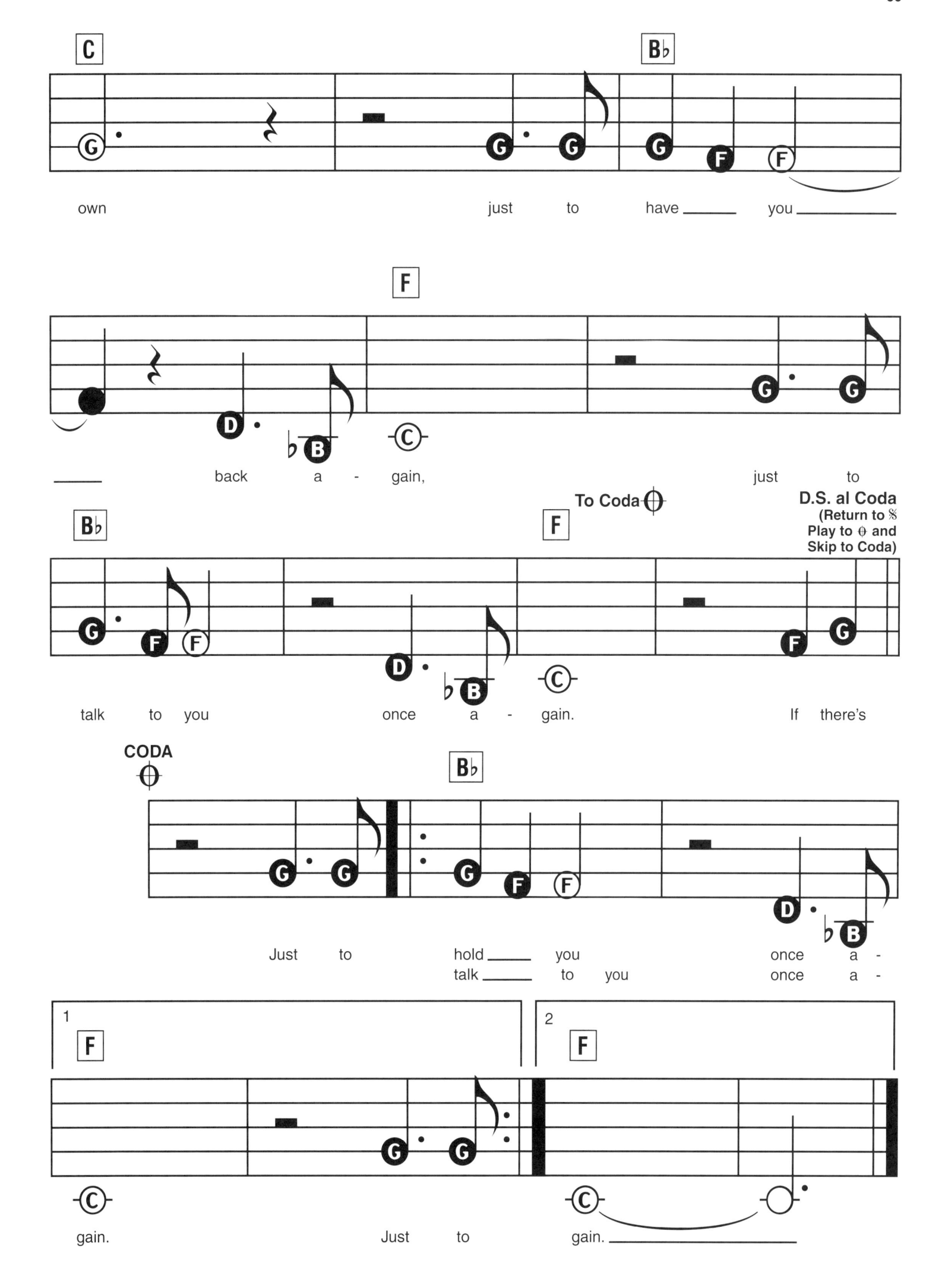

CODA

Just to hold ____ you once a -
talk ____ to you once a -

1. gain. Just to
2. gain. ____

Dust in the Wind

Registration 10
Rhythm: Rock

Words and Music by
Kerry Livgren

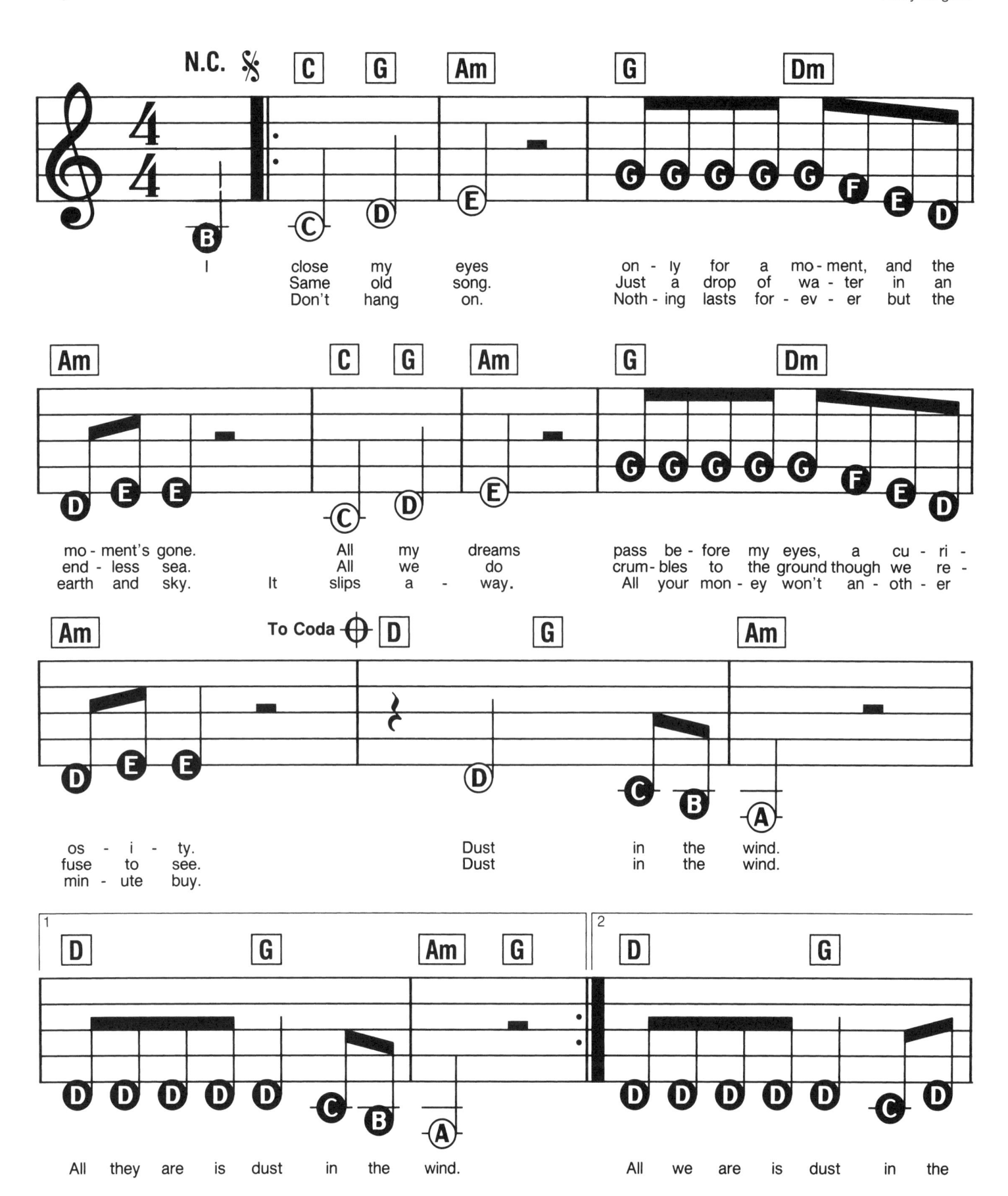

I close my eyes only for a moment, and the
Same old song.   Just a drop of water in an
Don't hang on.   Nothing lasts forever but the

moment's gone.   All my dreams pass before my eyes, a cu-ri-
endless sea.   All we do crumbles to the ground though we re-
earth and sky.   It slips away.   All your money won't an-oth-er

os-i-ty.   Dust in the wind.
fuse to see.   Dust in the wind.
min-ute buy.

1. All they are is dust in the wind.

2. All we are is dust in the

© 1977 (Renewed 2005), 1978 EMI BLACKWOOD MUSIC INC. and DON KIRSHNER MUSIC
All Rights Controlled and Administered by EMI BLACKWOOD MUSIC INC.
All Rights Reserved   International Copyright Secured   Used by Permission

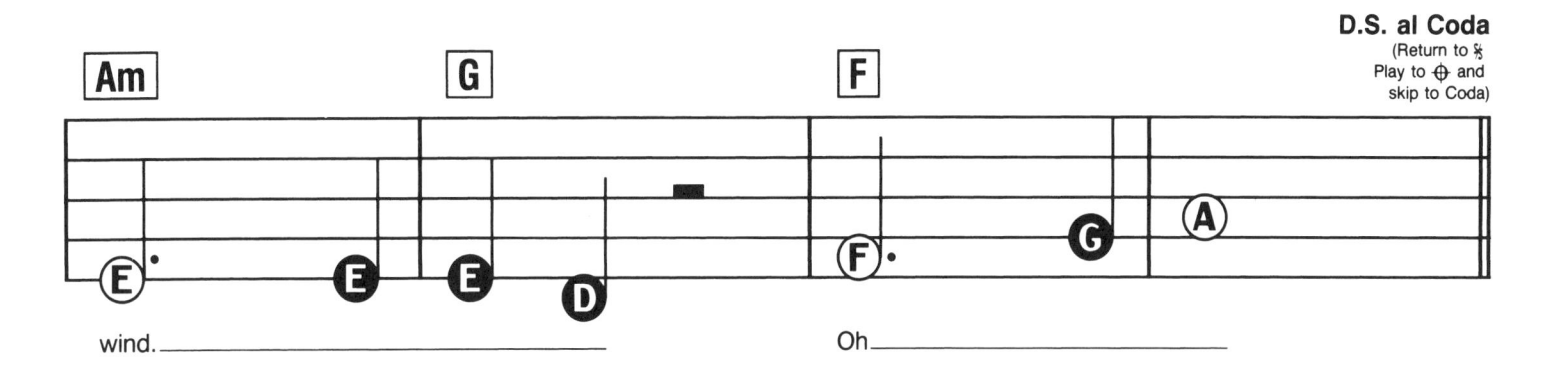

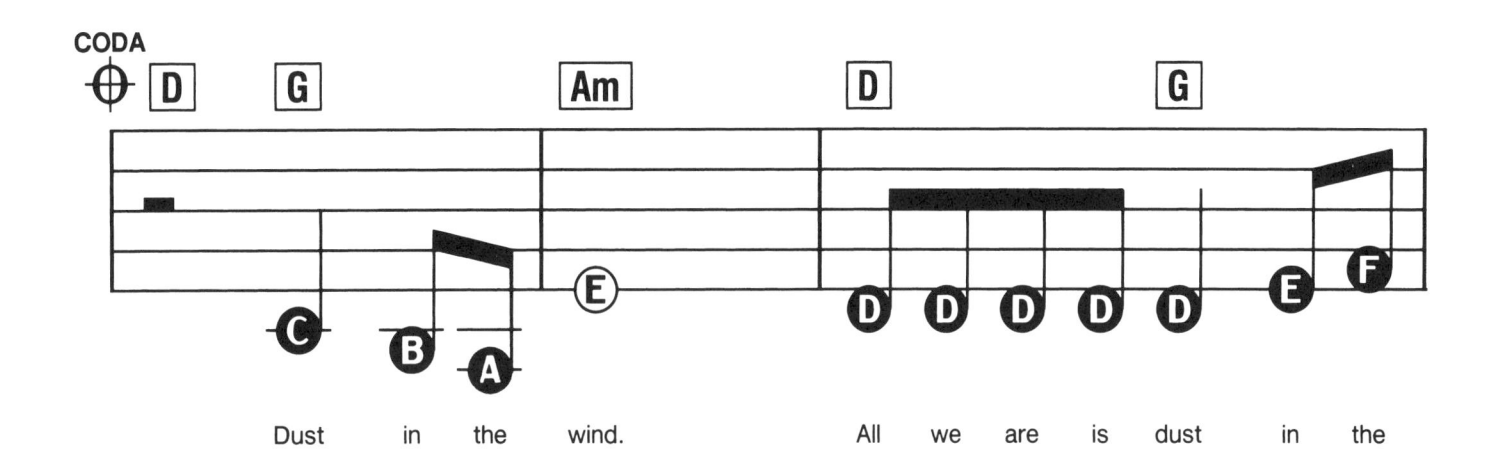

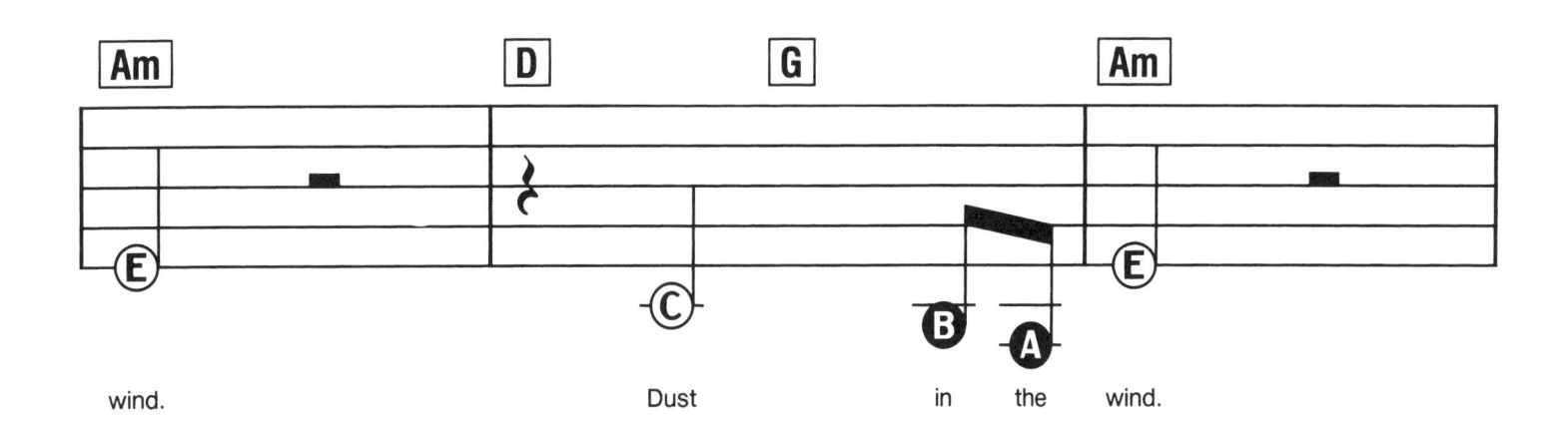

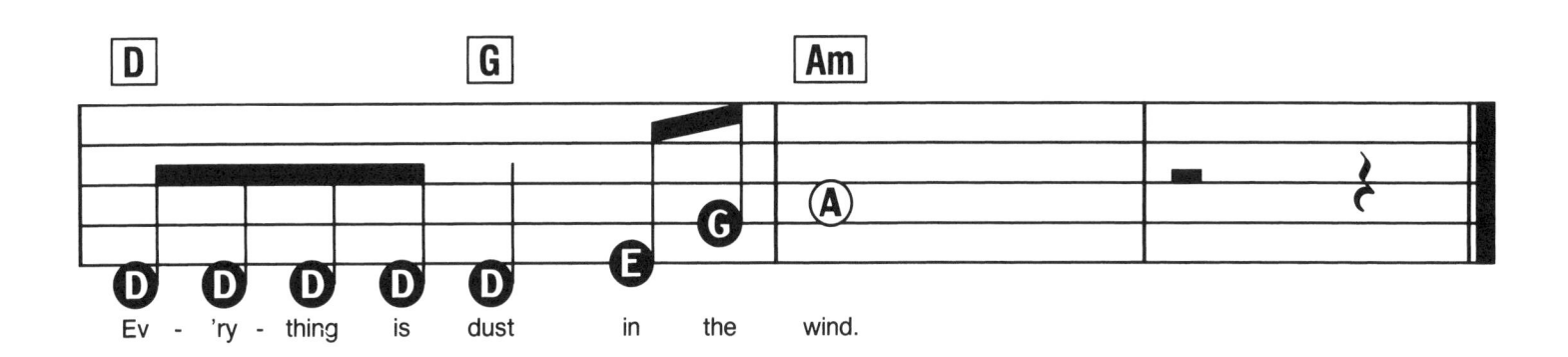

55

D.S. al Coda
(Return to 𝄋
Play to ⊕ and
skip to Coda)

Am	G	F	

E. E E D F. G A

wind._____ Oh_____

CODA
⊕ D G   Am   D   G

C B A   E   D D D D D   E F

Dust in the wind.   All we are is dust in the

| Am | D G | Am |

E   C   B A   E

wind.   Dust   in the wind.

| D   G | Am |

D D D D D E G   A

Ev - 'ry - thing is dust in the wind.

Everybody's Talkin'

(Echoes)

from MIDNIGHT COWBOY

Registration 6
Rhythm: Rock

Words and Music by
Fred Neil

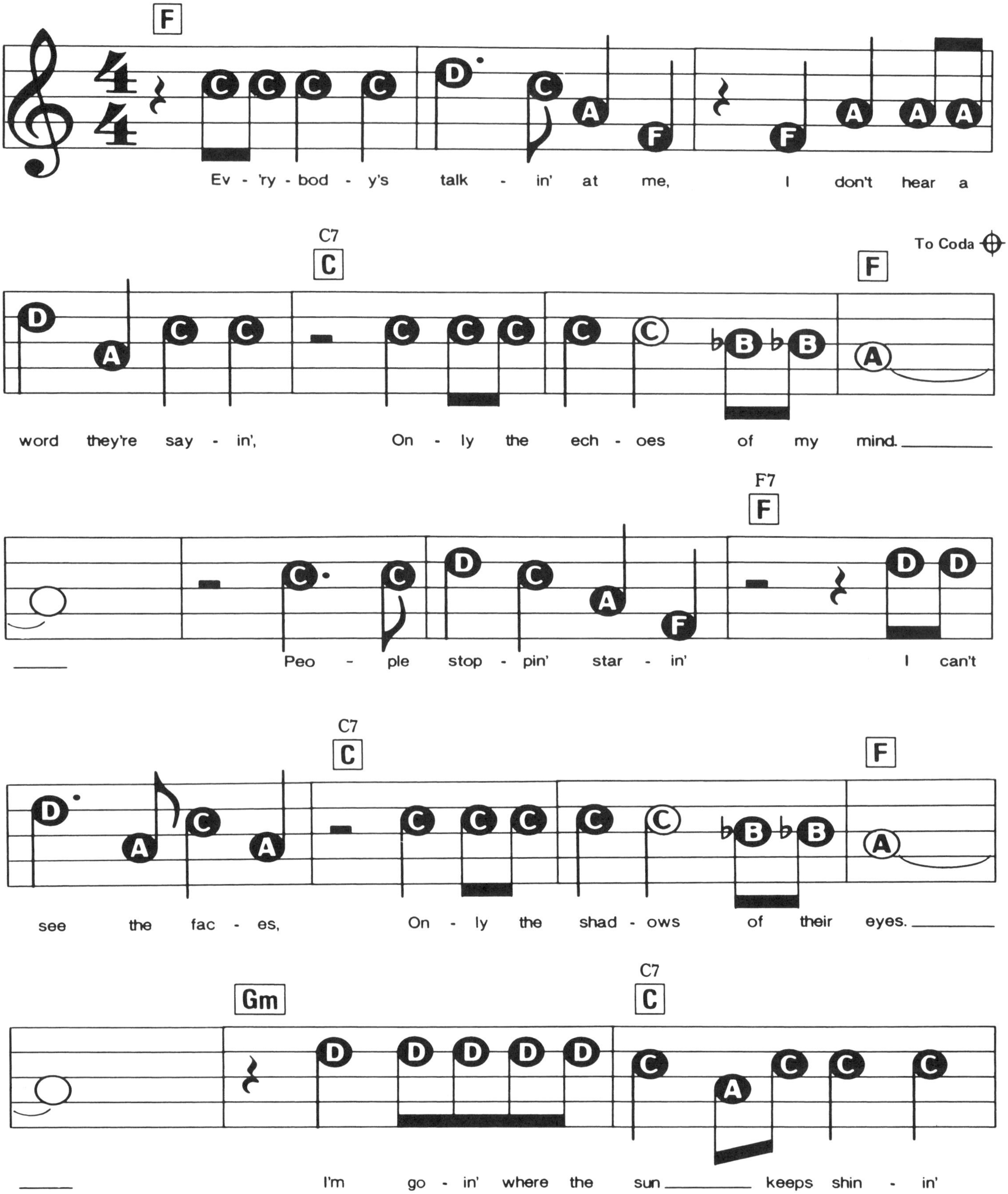

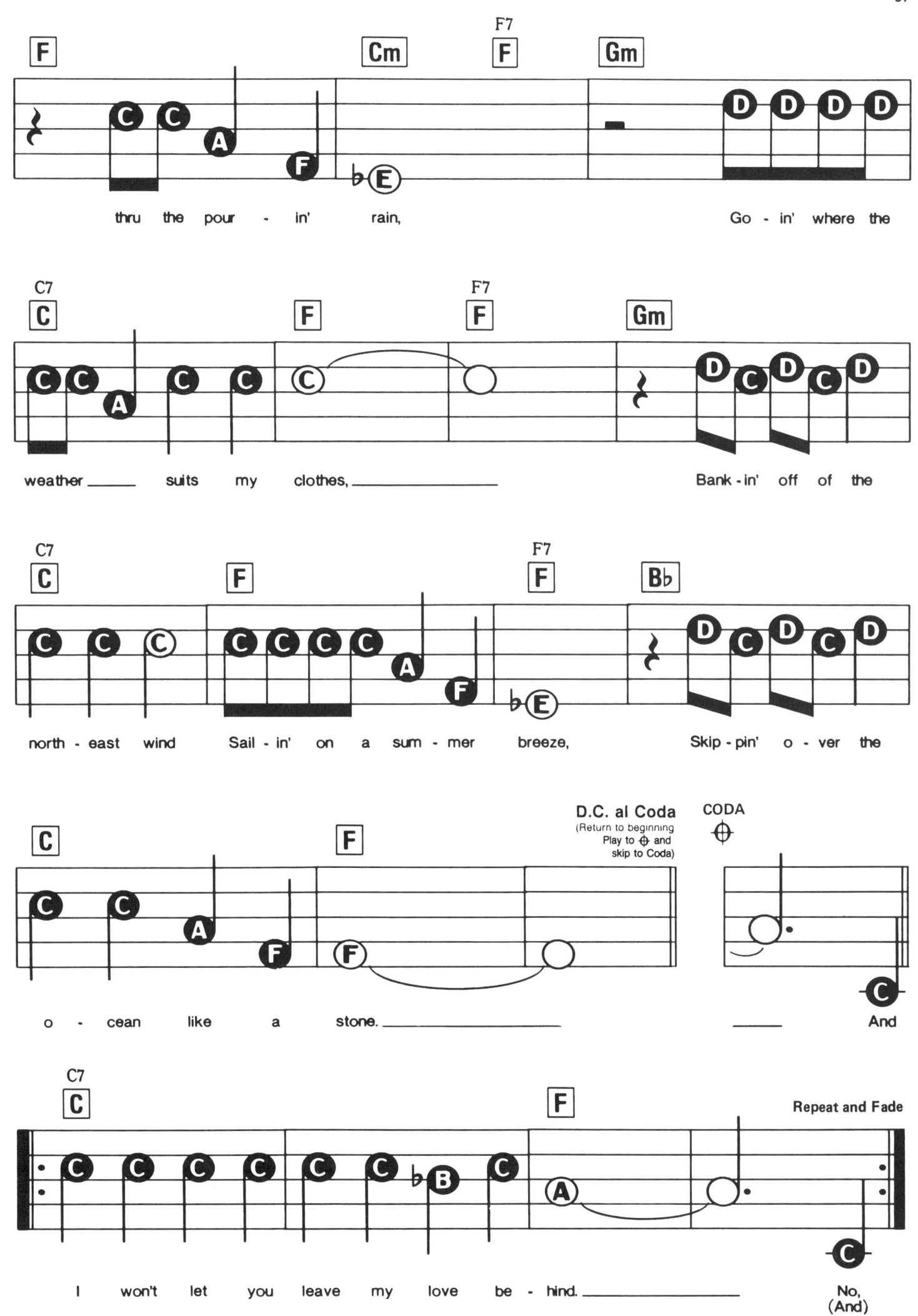

thru the pour - in' rain, Go - in' where the weather suits my clothes, Bank - in' off of the north - east wind Sail - in' on a sum - mer breeze, Skip - pin' over the o - cean like a stone. And I won't let you leave my love be - hind. No, (And)

Fast Car

Registration 9
Rhythm: Rock

Words and Music by
Tracy Chapman

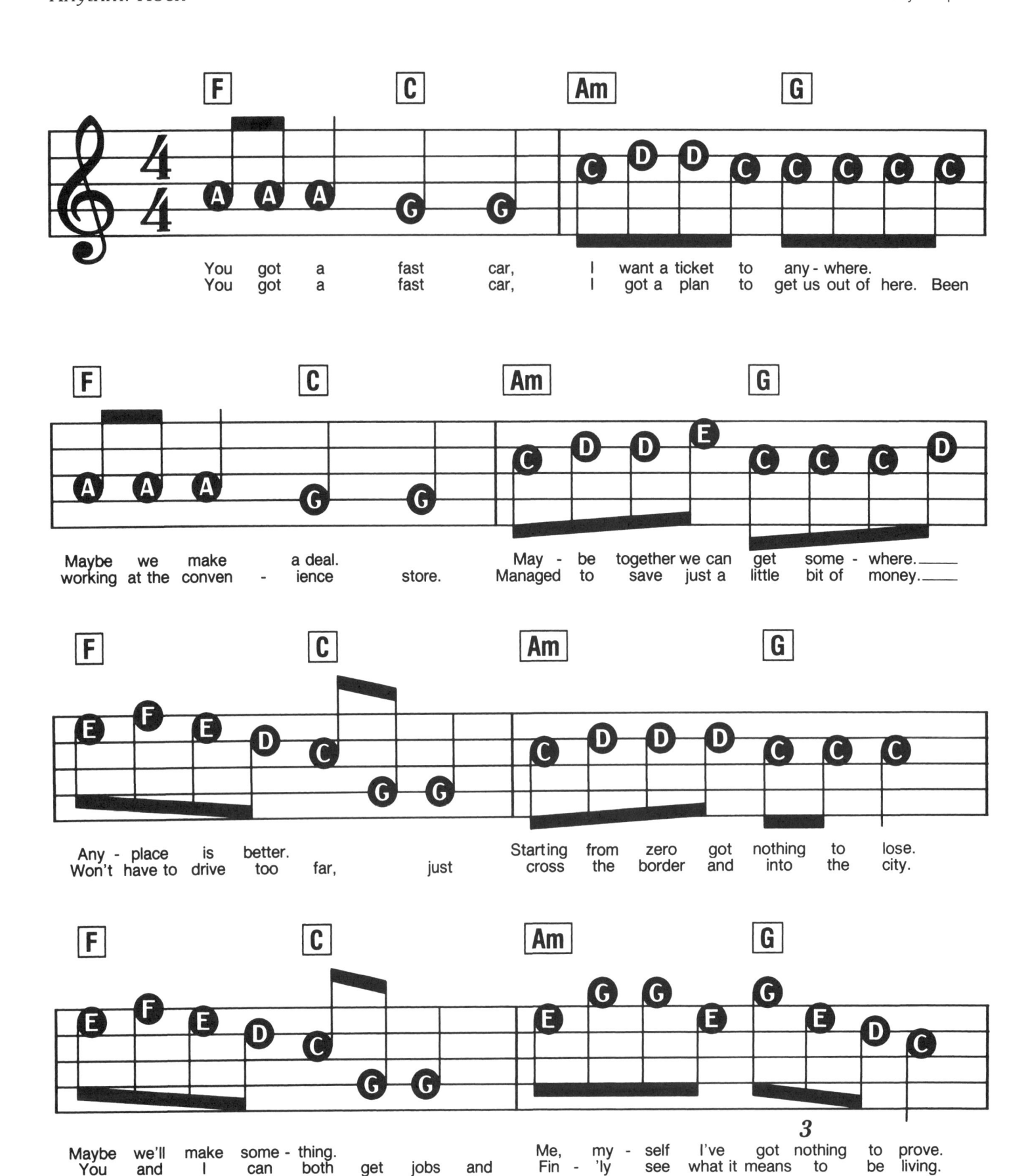

You got a fast car, I want a ticket to any-where.
You got a fast car, I got a plan to get us out of here. Been

Maybe we make a deal. May-be together we can get some-where.
working at the conven-ience store. Managed to save just a little bit of money.

Any-place is better. Starting from zero got nothing to lose.
Won't have to drive too far, just cross the border into the city.

Maybe we'll make some-thing. Me, my-self I've got nothing to prove.
You and I can both get jobs and Fin-'ly see what it means to be living.

© 1987 EMI APRIL MUSIC INC. and PURPLE RABBIT MUSIC
All Rights Reserved   International Copyright Secured   Used by Permission

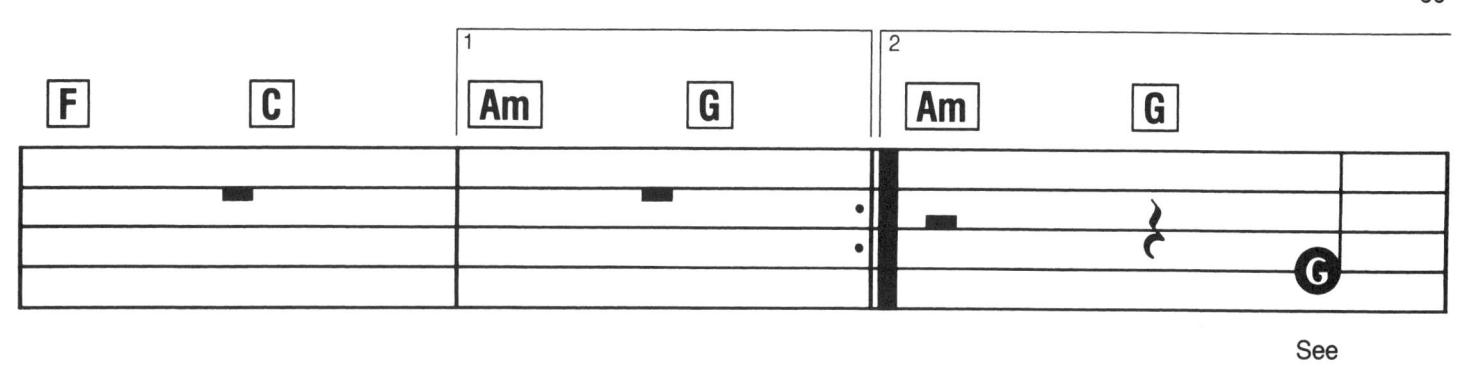

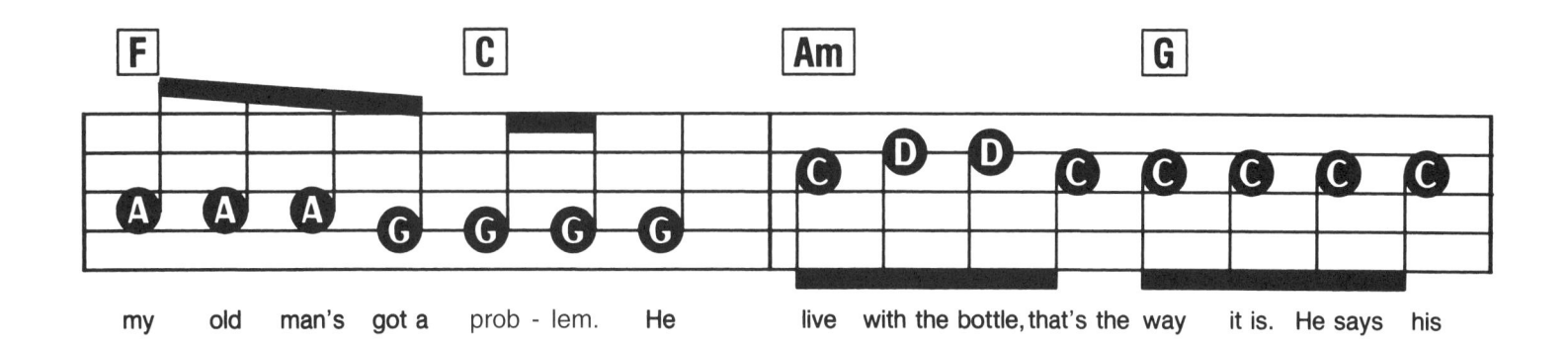

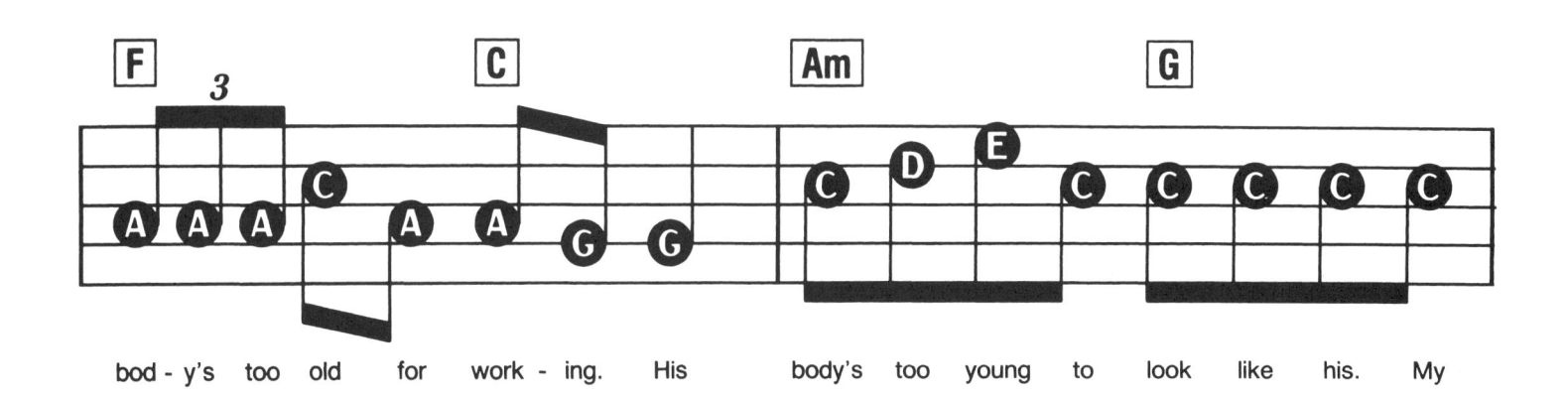

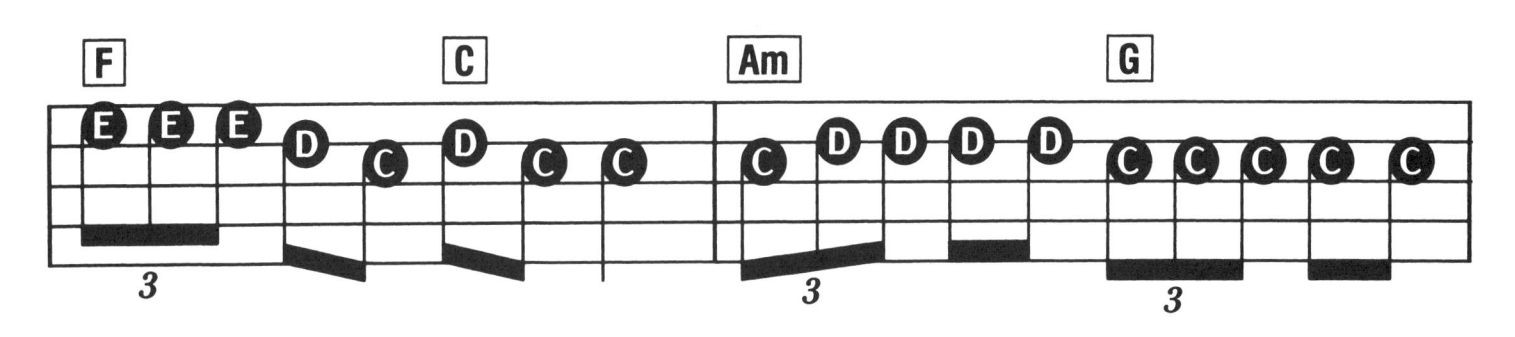

See my old man's got a problem. He live with the bottle, that's the way it is. He says his body's too old for working. His body's too young to look like his. My mama went off and left him. She wanted more from life than he could give. I said somebody's got to take care of him. So I quit school and that's what I did.

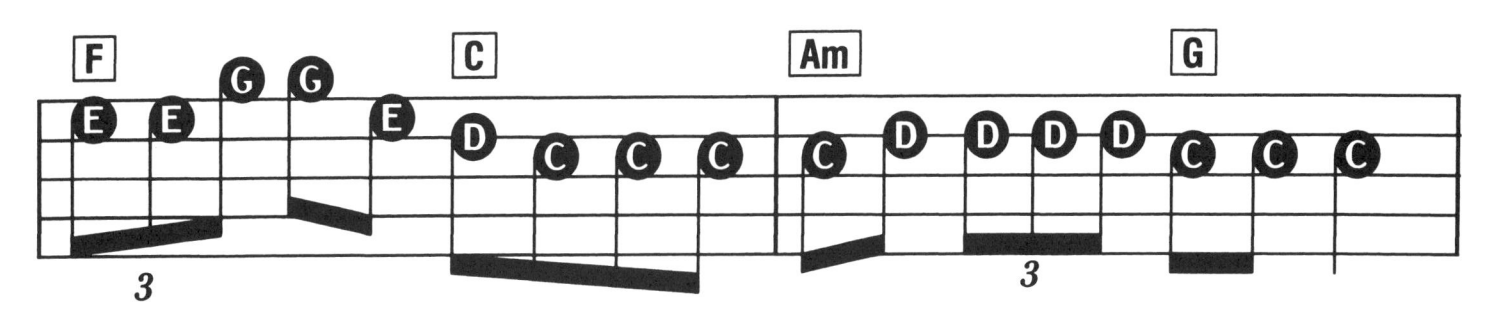

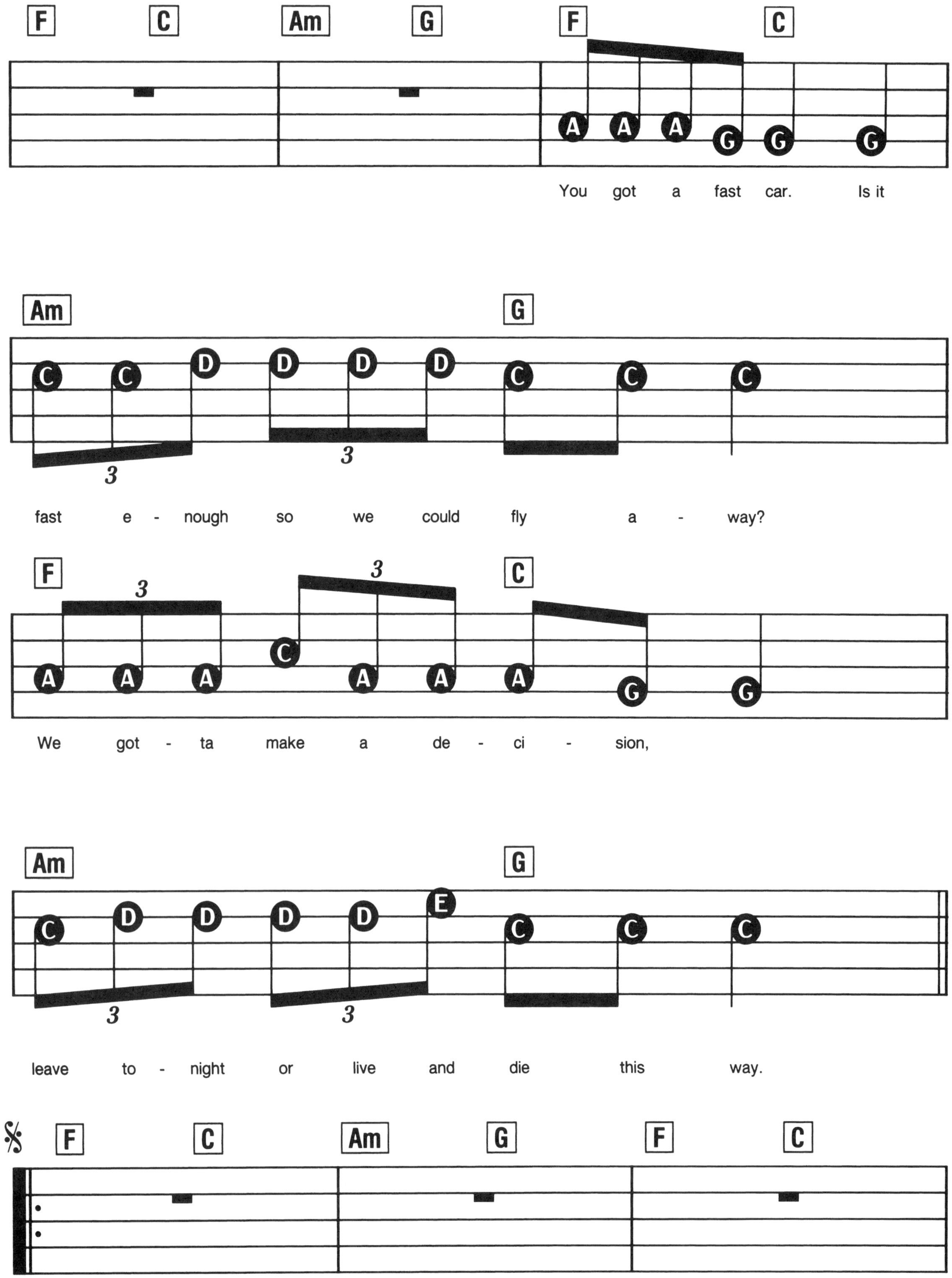
F C Am G F C
A A A G G G
You got a fast car. Is it
Am G
C C D D D D C C C
fast e - nough so we could fly a - way?
F C
3 3
A A A C A A A G G
We got - ta make a de - ci - sion,
Am G
C D D D D E C C C
3 3
leave to - night or live and die this way.
F C Am G F C

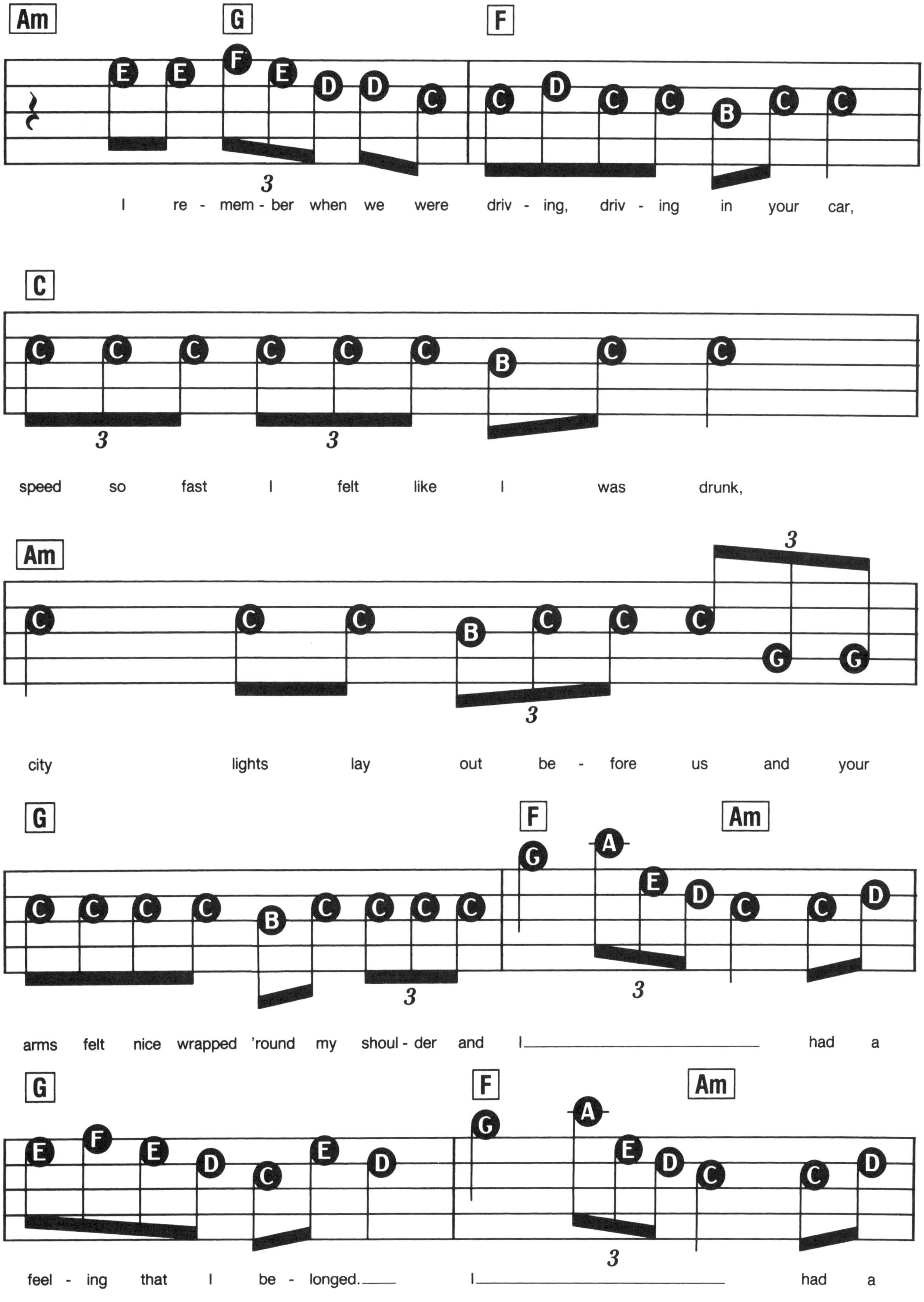
Am G F
I re - mem - ber when we were driv - ing, driv - ing in your car,
C
speed so fast I felt like I was drunk,
Am
city lights lay out be - fore us and your
G F Am
arms felt nice wrapped 'round my shoul - der and I had a
G F Am
feel - ing that I be - longed. I had a

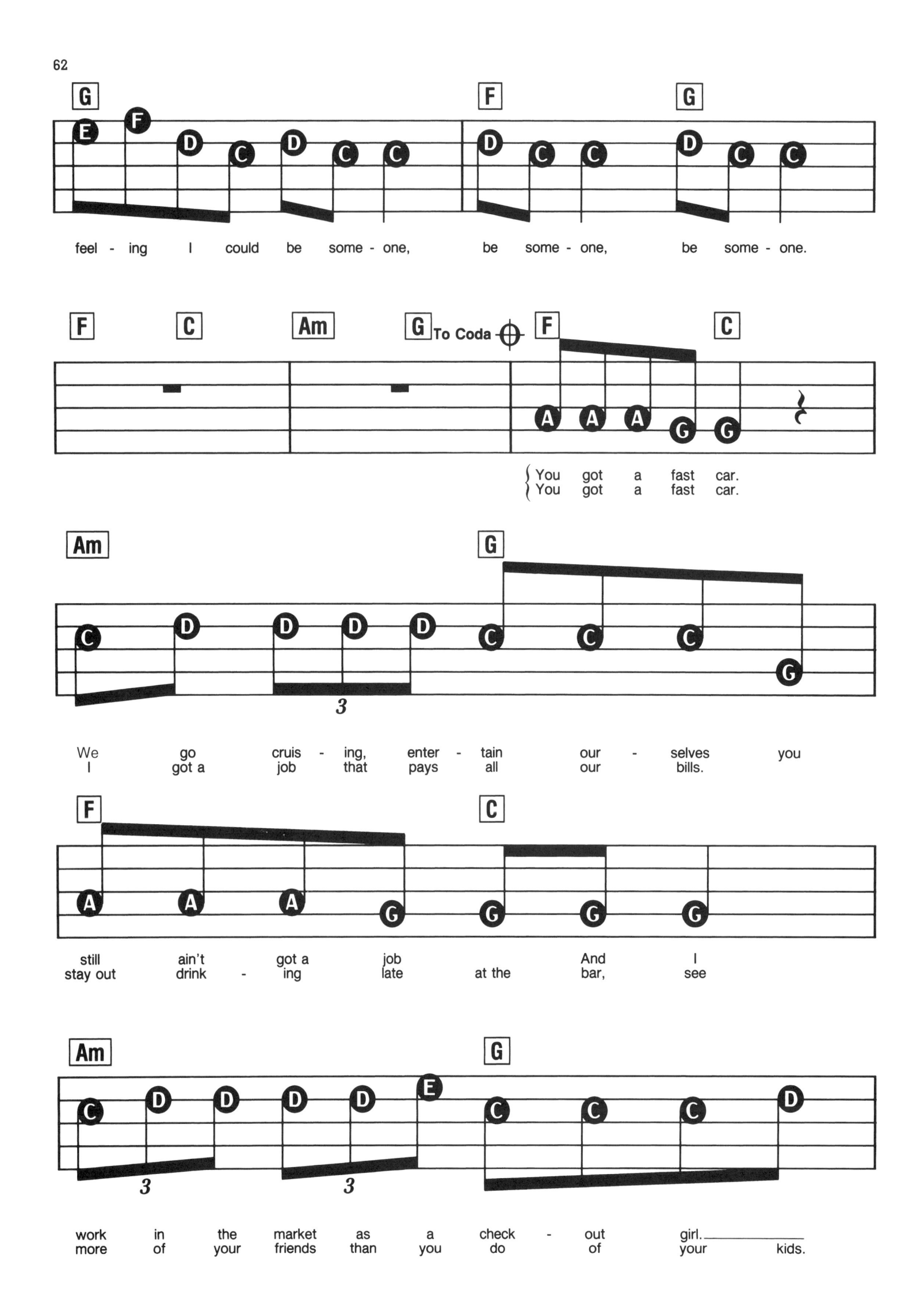

feel - ing I could be some - one, be some - one, be some - one.

You got a fast car.
You got a fast car.

We go cruis - ing, enter - tain our - selves you
I got a job that pays all our bills.

still ain't got a job And I
stay out drink - ing late at the bar, see

work in the market as a check - out girl.
more of your friends than you do of your kids.

I know things will get bet - ter.
I'd always hoped for bet - ter, thought

You'll find work and I'll get pro - mot - ed.
may - be to - gether you and me'd find it. I

We'll move out of the shel - ter,
got no plans, I ain't going, no - where, so

1.
buy a big house and live in the sub - urbs.

2.
D.S. al Coda
(Return to 𝄋
Play to ⊕ and
skip to Coda)

take your fast car and keep driv - ing.

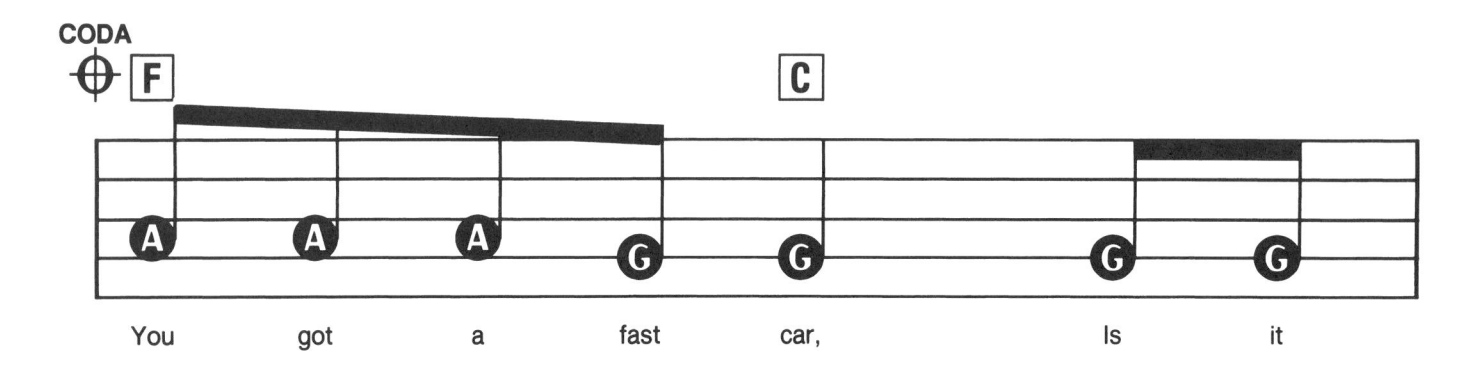

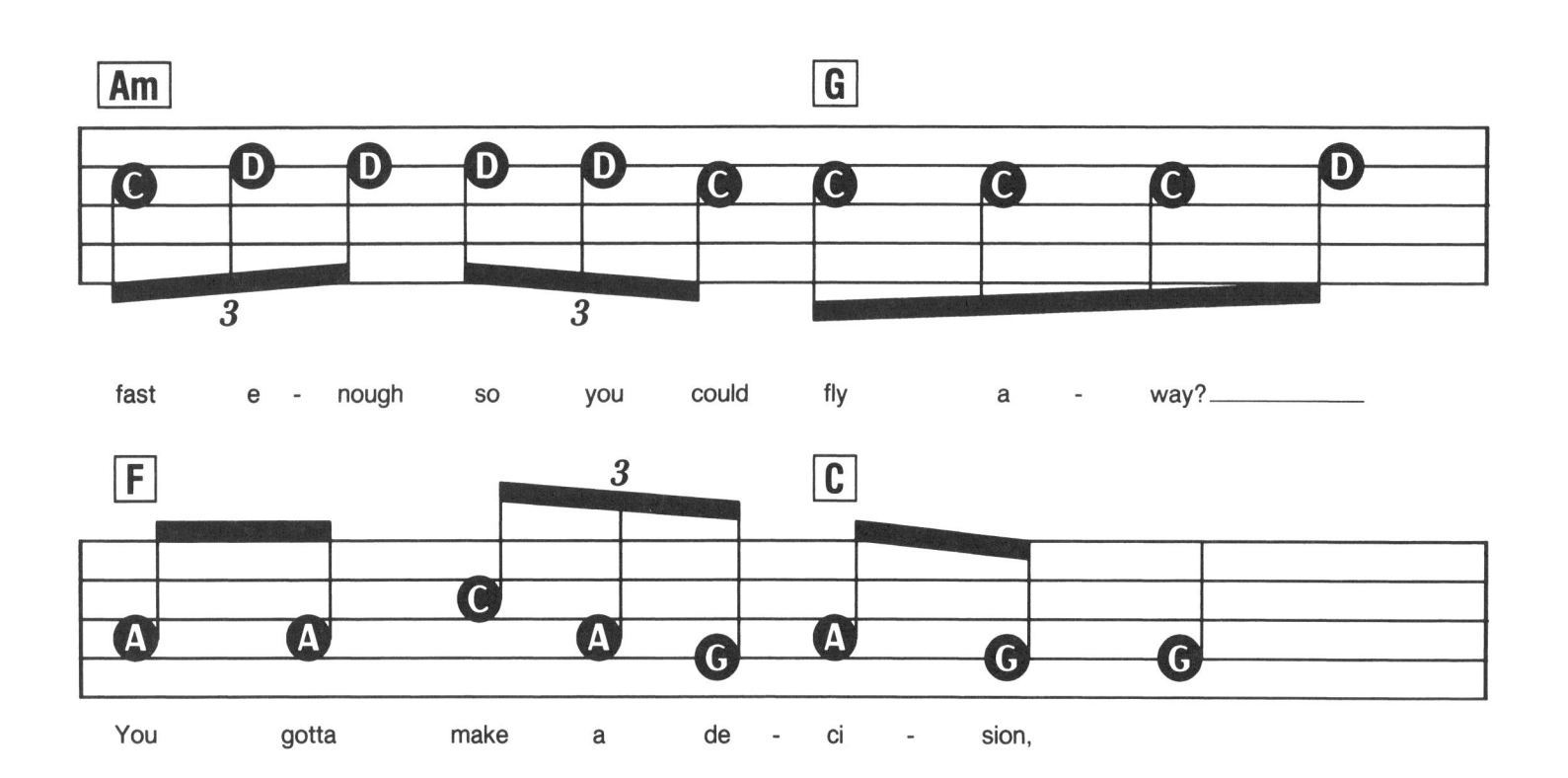

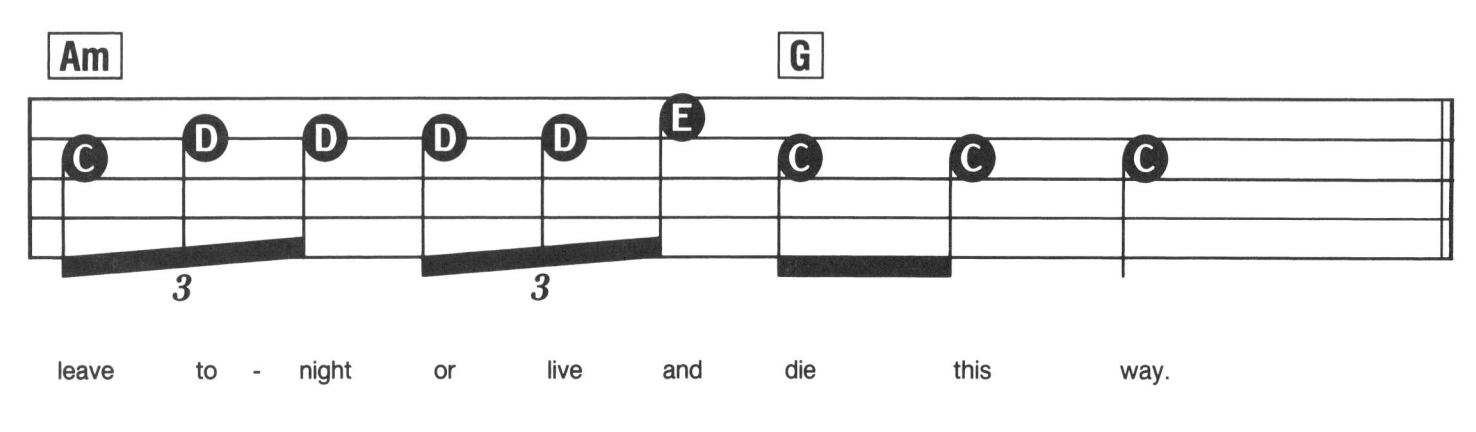

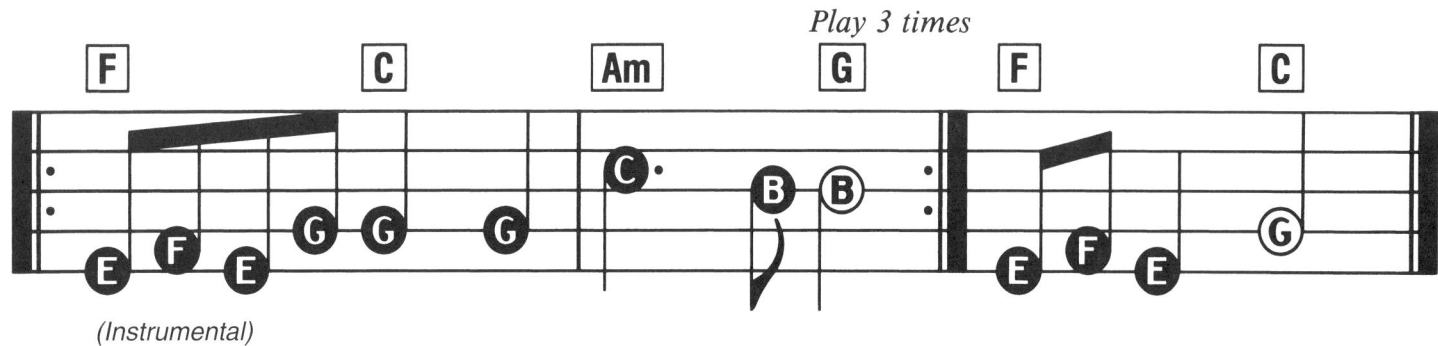

64

CODA

F | | **C** |
A A A G G | G G

You got a fast car, Is it

Am | | **G** |
C D D D D C C C C D
(3) (3)

fast e-nough so you could fly a - way?

F | | **C** |
A A C A G A G G
(3)

You gotta make a de-ci-sion,

Am | | **G** |
C D D D D E C C C
(3) (3)

leave to-night or live and die this way.

Play 3 times

F | **C** | **Am** | **G** | **F** | **C** |
E F E G G G C. B B E F E G

(Instrumental)

Get Closer

Registration 4
Rhythm: Country Rock or Rock

Words and Music by James Seals
and Dash Crofts

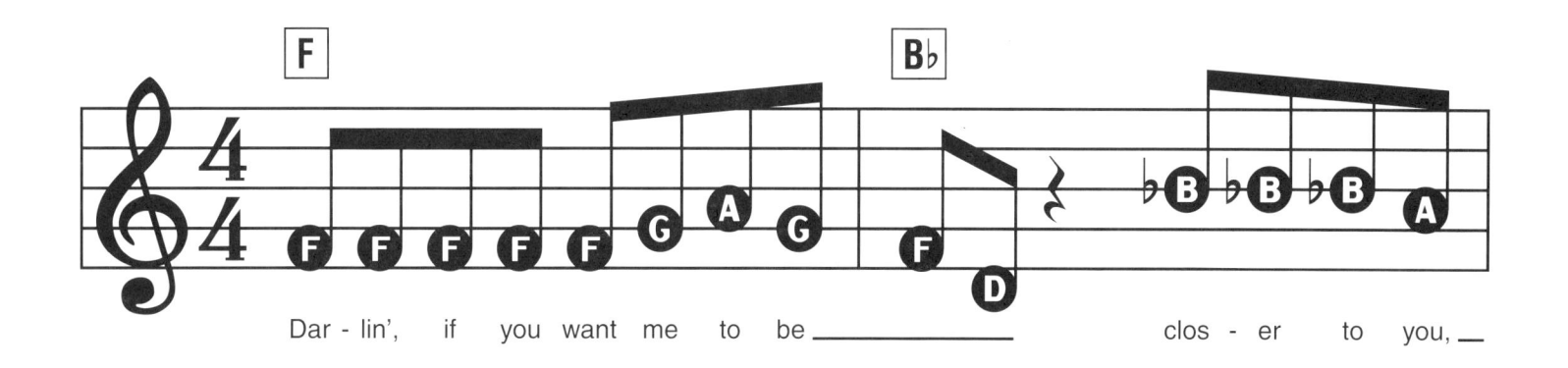

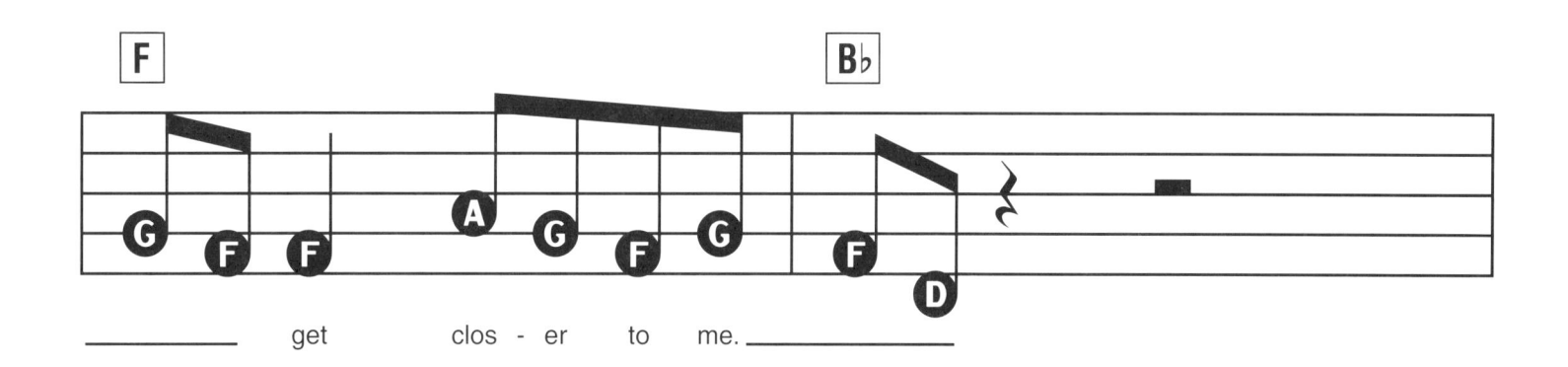

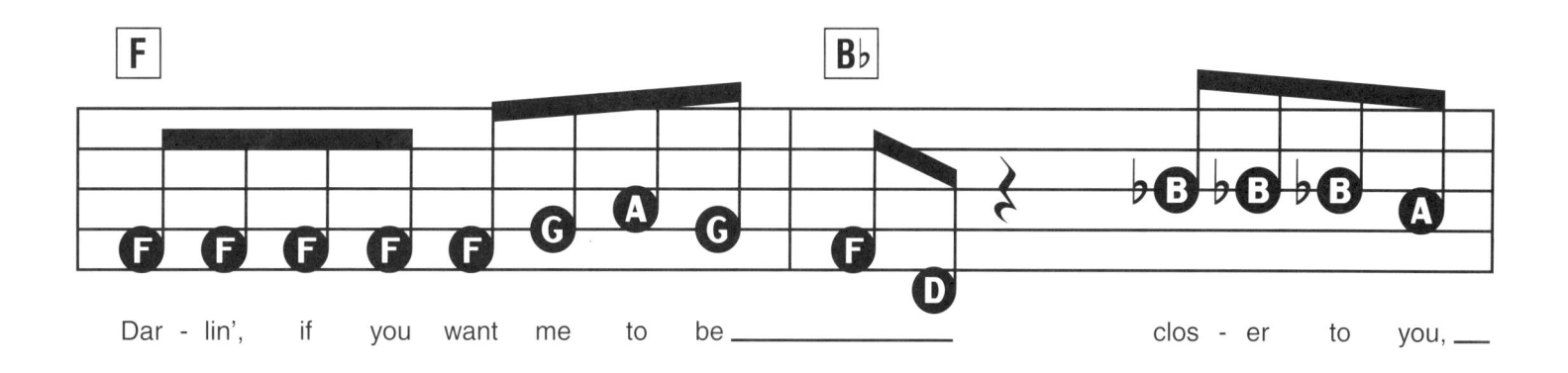

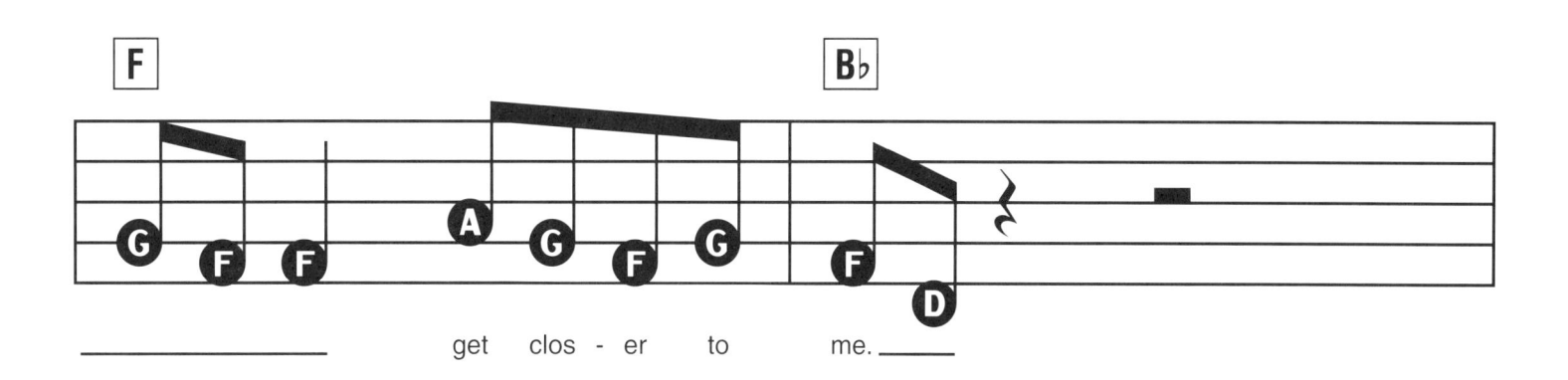

F · F F F F F F G A G | B♭ · F D (rest) ♭B ♭B ♭B A
Dar - lin', if you want me to be _____ clos - er to you, _____

F · G F F A G F G | B♭ · F D (rest)
_____ get clos - er to me. _____

F · F F F F F G A G | B♭ · F D (rest) ♭B ♭B ♭B A
Dar - lin', if you want me to be _____ clos - er to you, _____

F · G F F A G F G | B♭ · F D (rest)
_____ get clos - er to me. _____

© 1976 Sutjujo Music and Faizilu Publishing/BMI (admin. by ICG)
All Rights Reserved   Used by Permission

66

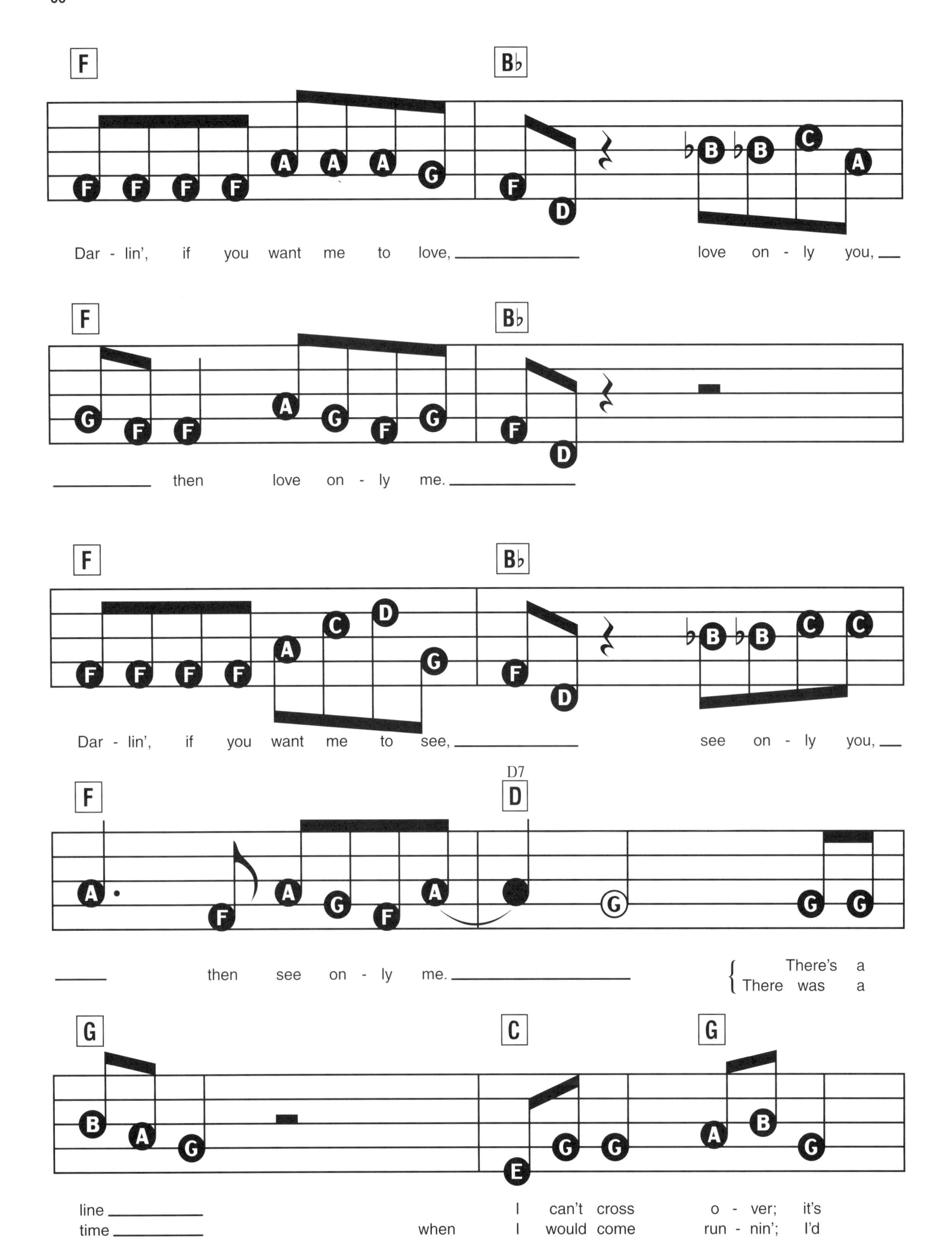

F								Bb							

Dar-lin', if you want me to love, ____ love on-ly you, ____

| F | | | | | | | | Bb | | | | | | | |

____ then love on-ly me. ____

| F | | | | | | | | Bb | | | | | | | |

Dar-lin', if you want me to see, ____ see on-ly you, ____

| F | | | | | | | | D (D7) | | | | | | | |

____ then see on-ly me. ____ { There's a / There was a

| G | | | | | | | | C | | | | | | G | |

line ____ I can't cross o-ver; it's
time ____ when I would come run-nin'; I'd

67

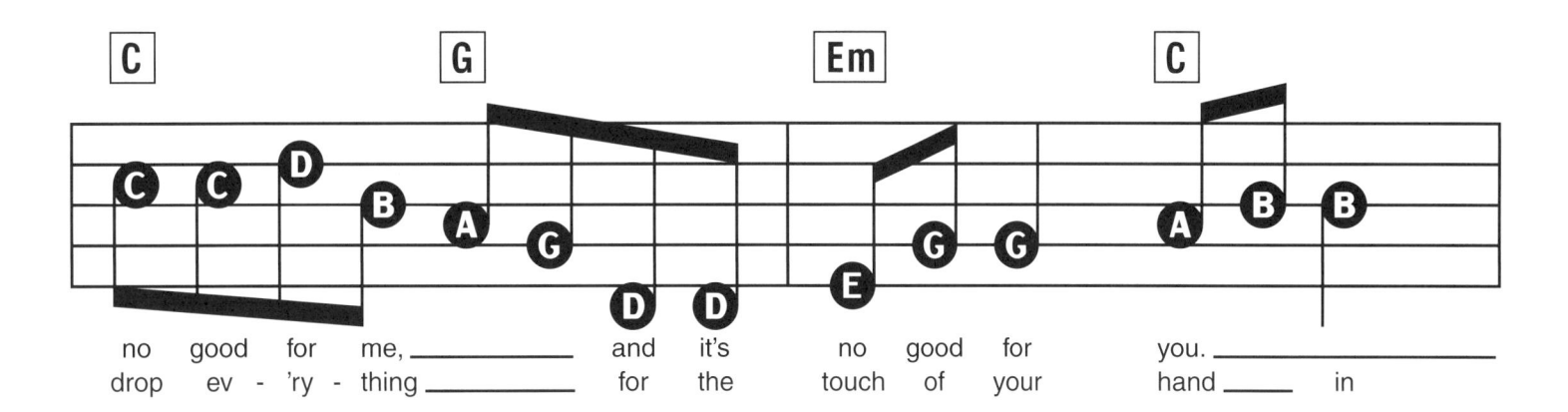

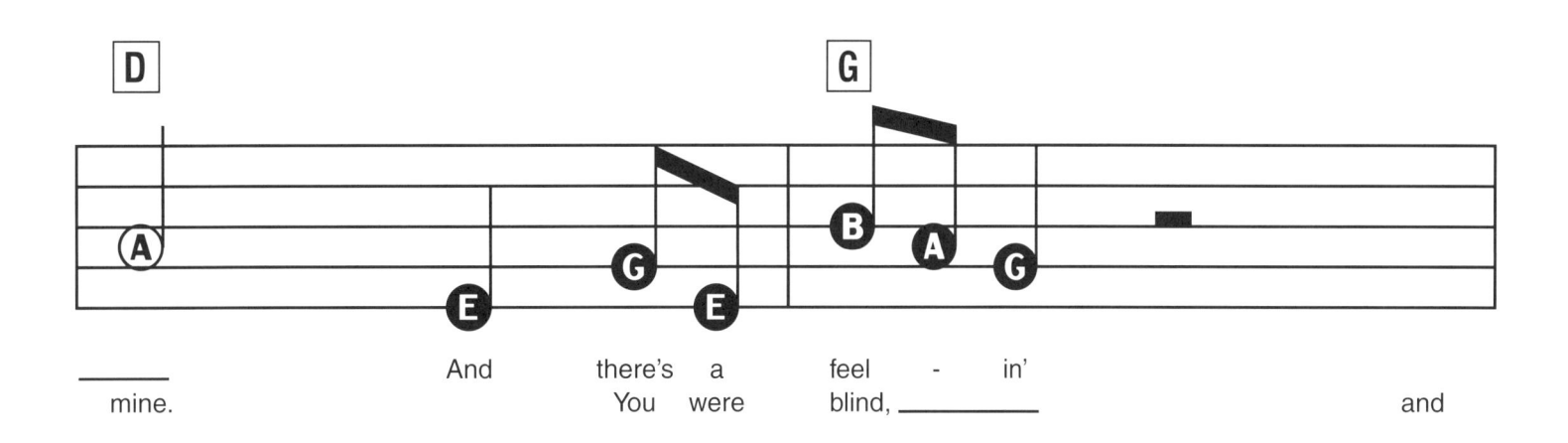

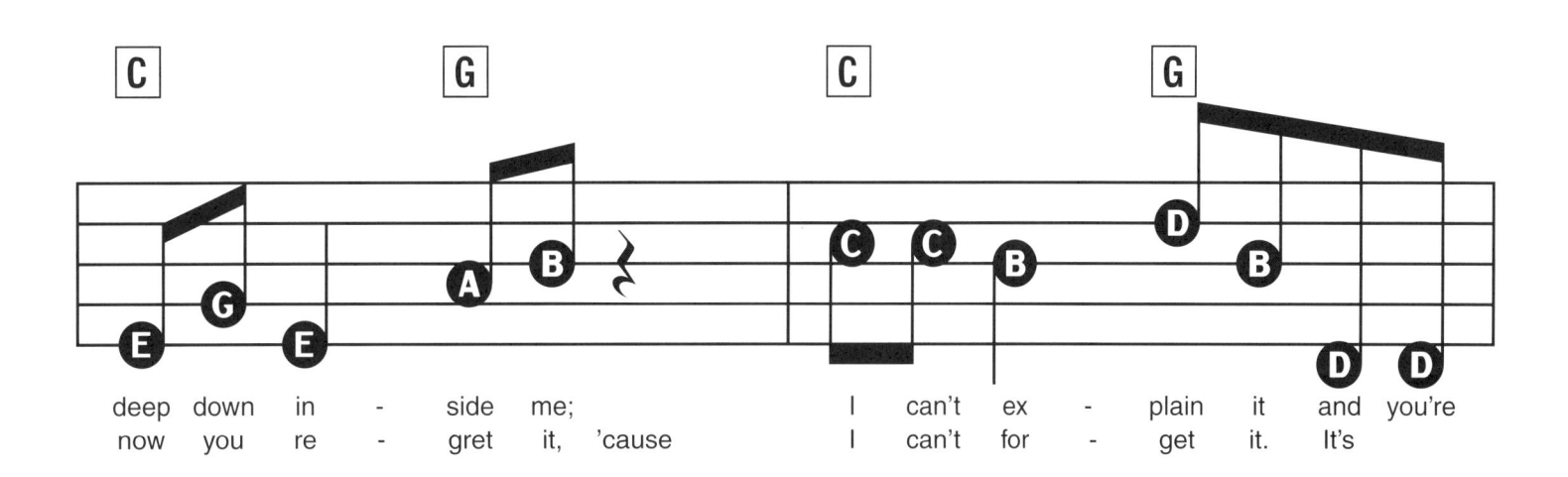

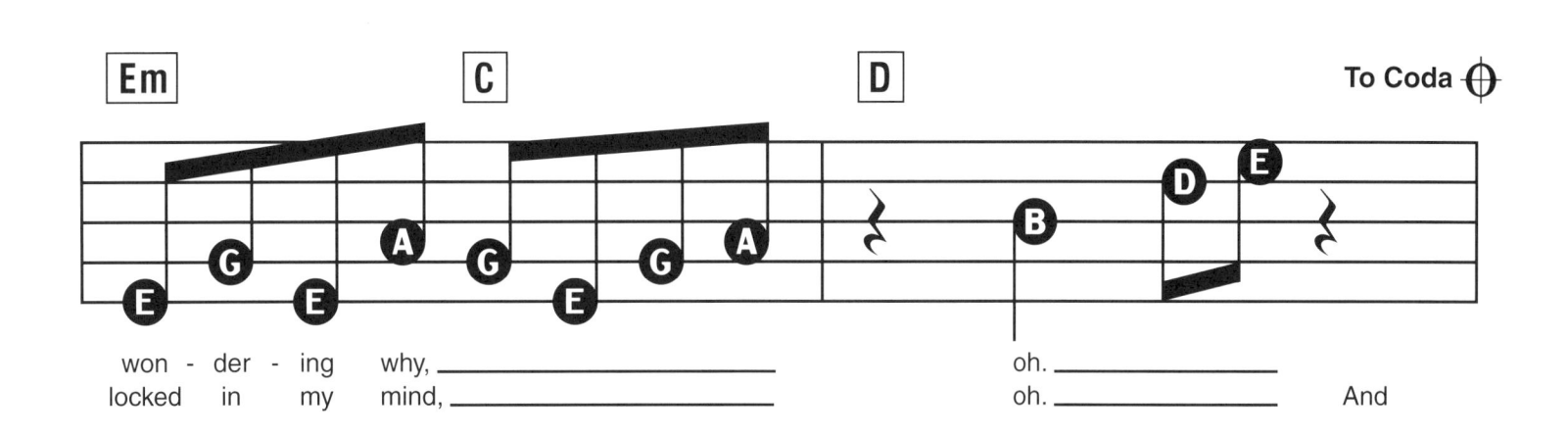

68

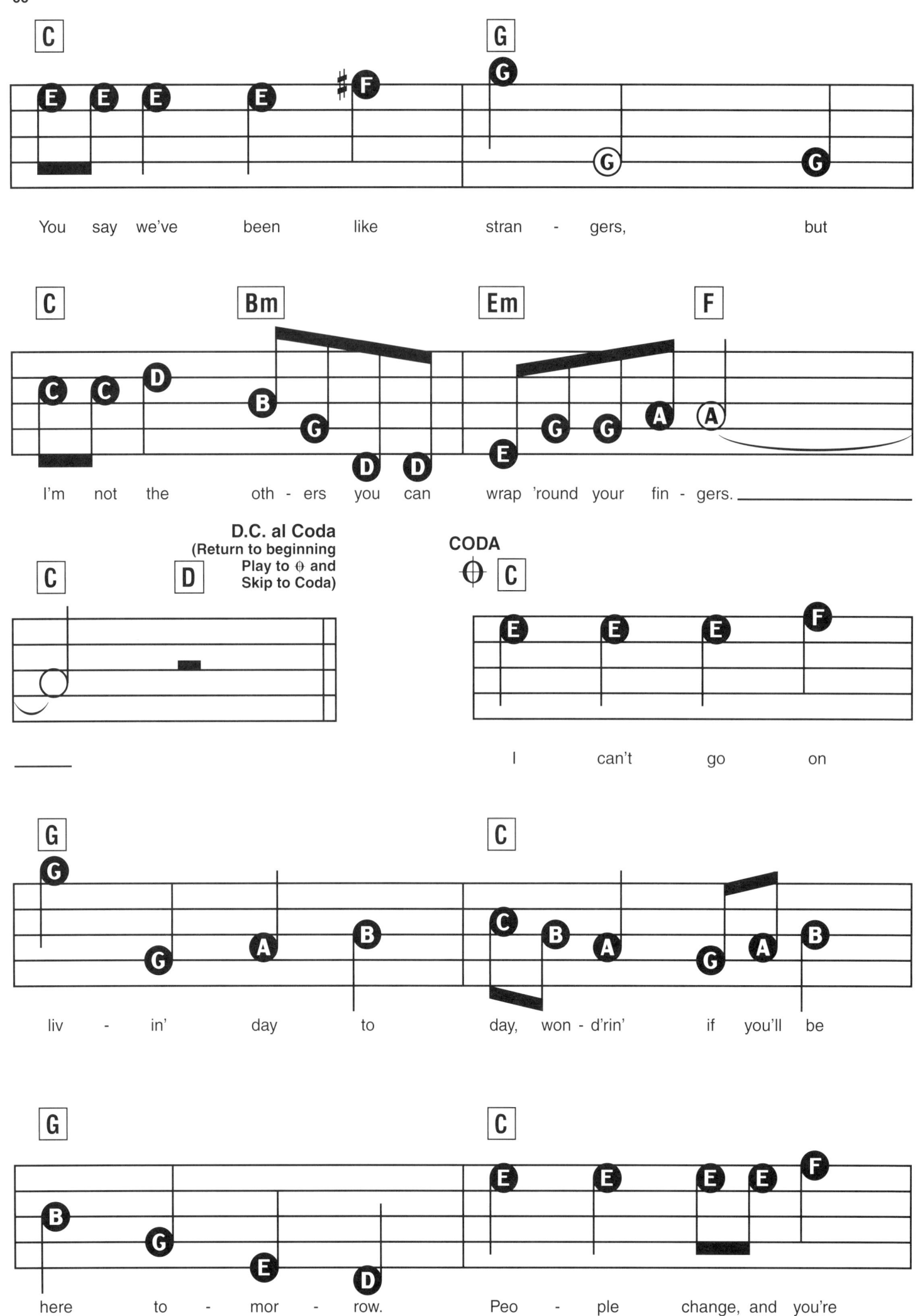

You say we've been like stran - gers, but I'm not the oth - ers you can wrap 'round your fin - gers.

D.C. al Coda
(Return to beginning
Play to ⊕ and
Skip to Coda)

CODA

I can't go on liv - in' day to day, won - d'rin' if you'll be here to - mor - row. Peo - ple change, and you're chang - in', and I've giv - en you ___ my all; ___ there's

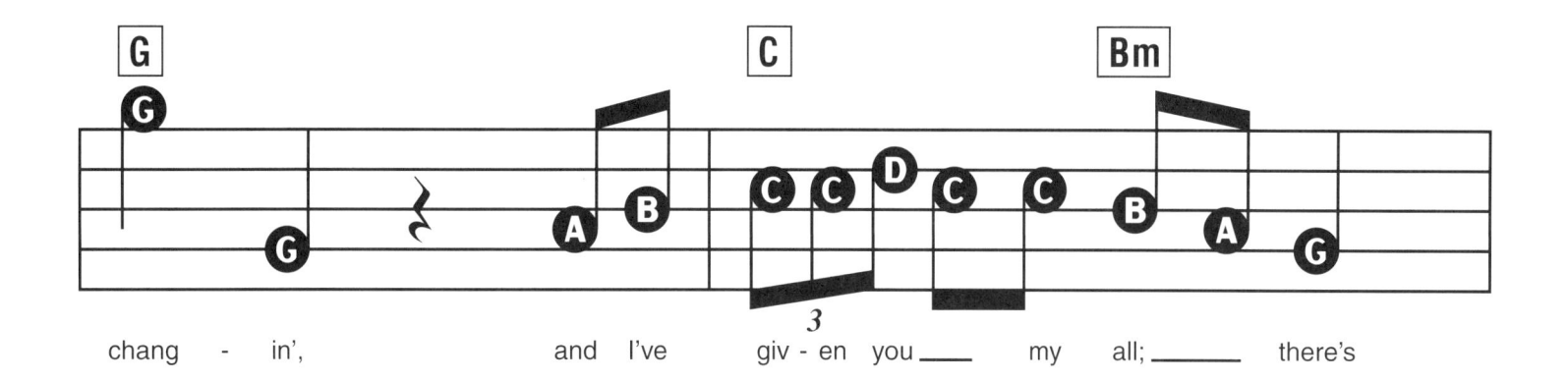

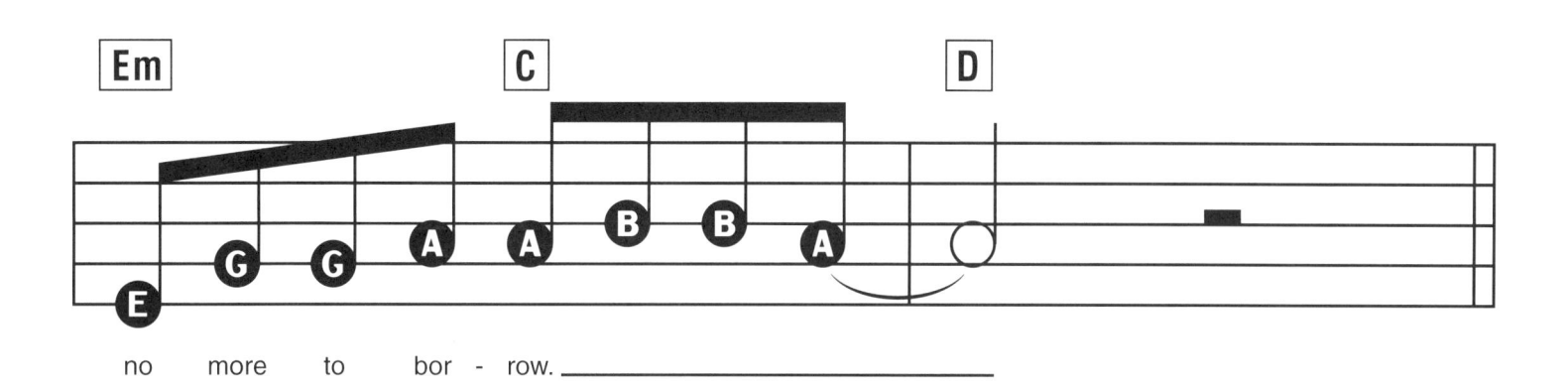

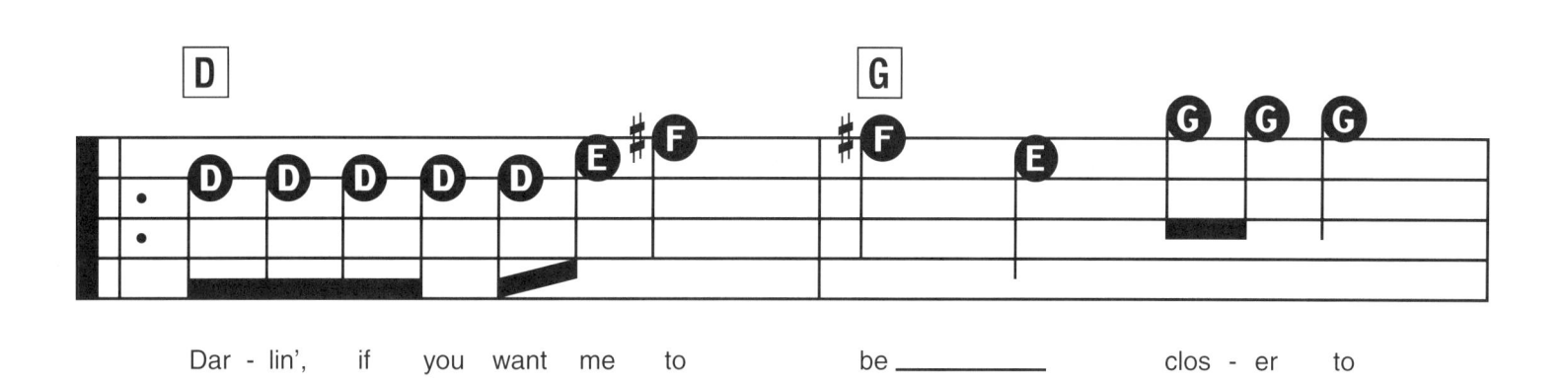

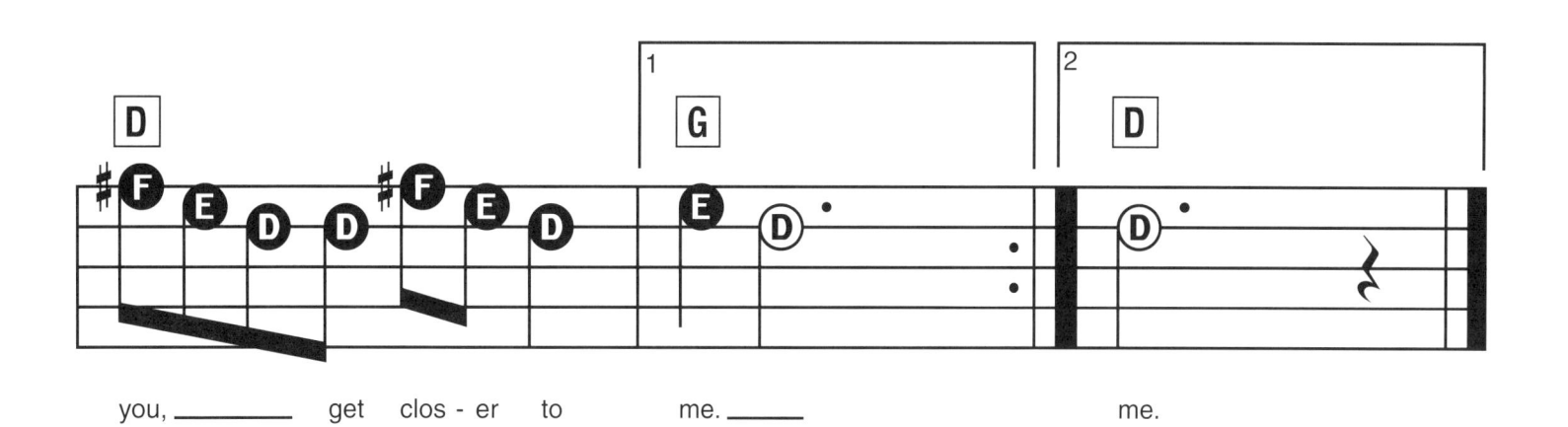

no more to bor - row. ___

Dar - lin', if you want me to be ___ clos - er to

you, ___ get clos - er to me. ___ me.

Happy Together

Registration 4
Rhythm: Rock

Words and Music by Garry Bonner
and Alan Gordon

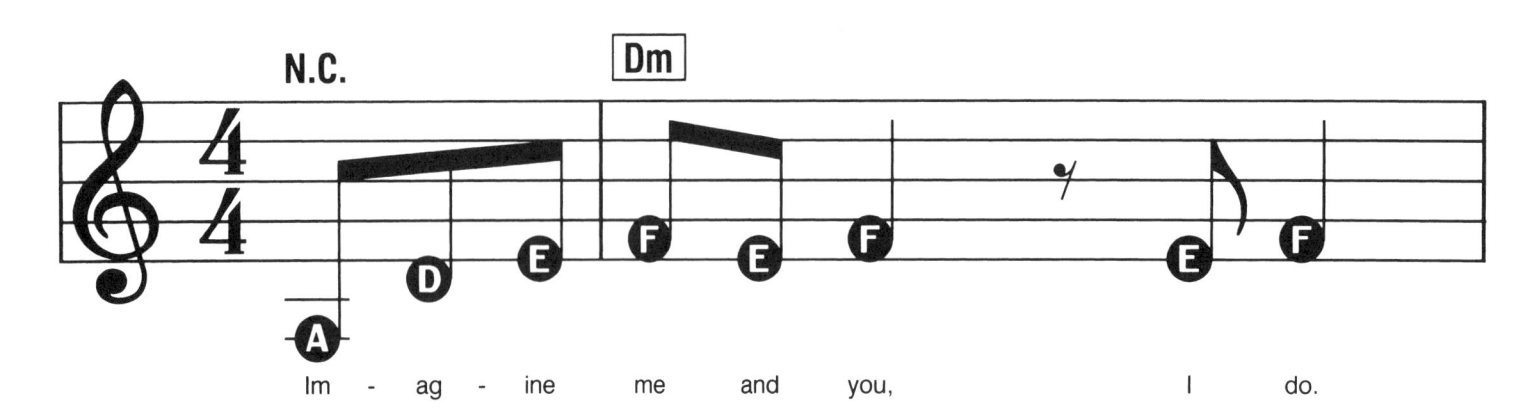

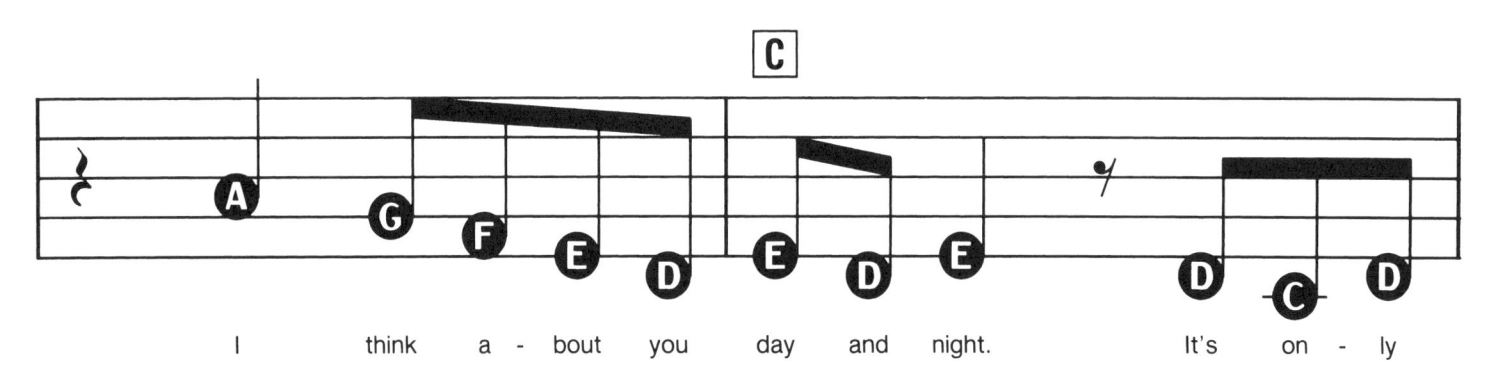

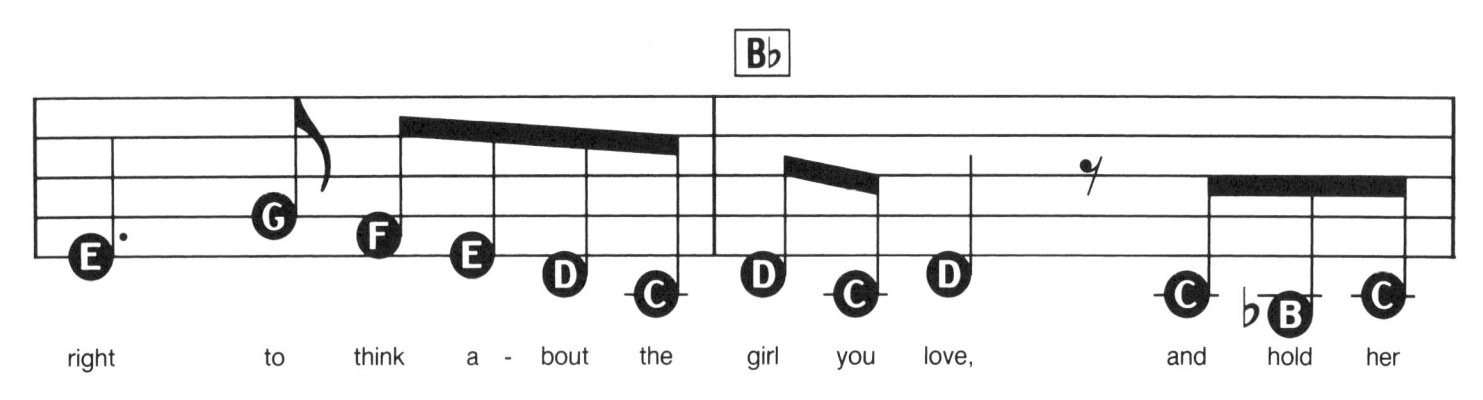

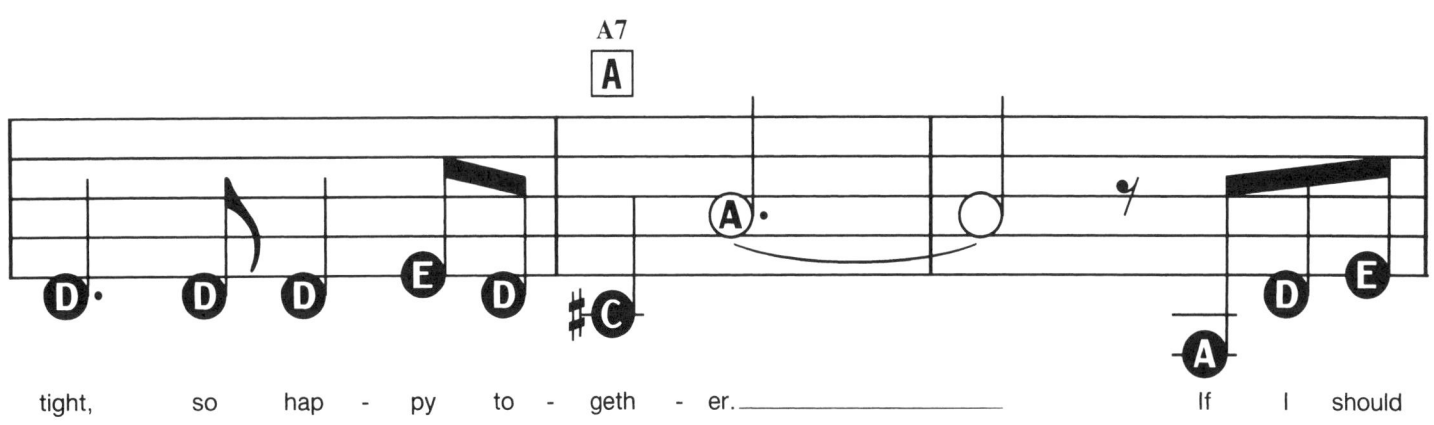

N.C. A D E | **Dm** F E F — E F
Im-ag-ine me and you, I do.

A G F E E D E D E — D C D
I think a-bout you day and night. It's on-ly

E. G F E D C | **B♭** D C D — C ♭B C
right to think a-bout the girl you love, and hold her

D. D D E D #C | **A** / **A7** A.— / A D E
tight, so hap-py to-geth-er.___ If I should

Copyright © 1966, 1967 by Alley Music Corp. and Bug Music-Trio Music Company
Copyright Renewed
International Copyright Secured   All Rights Reserved
Used by Permission

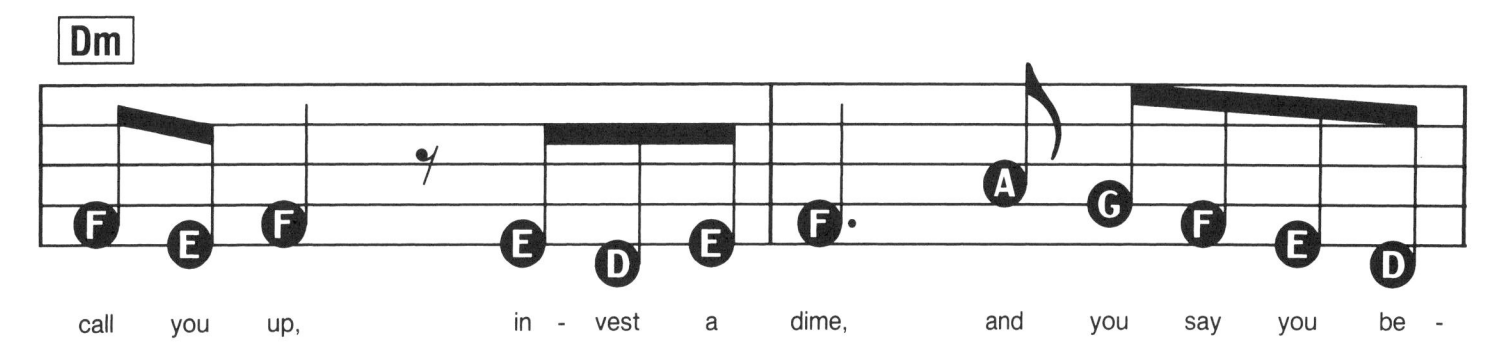

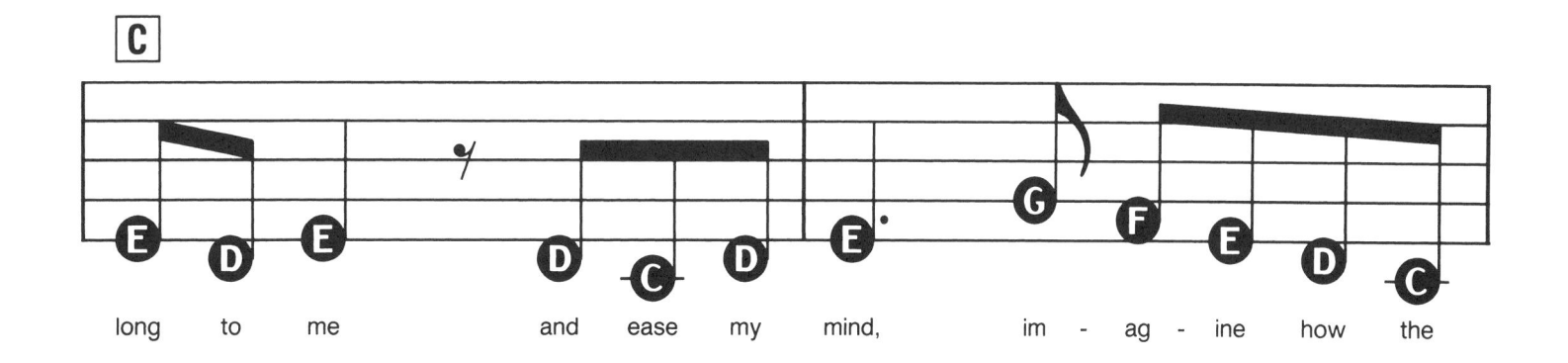

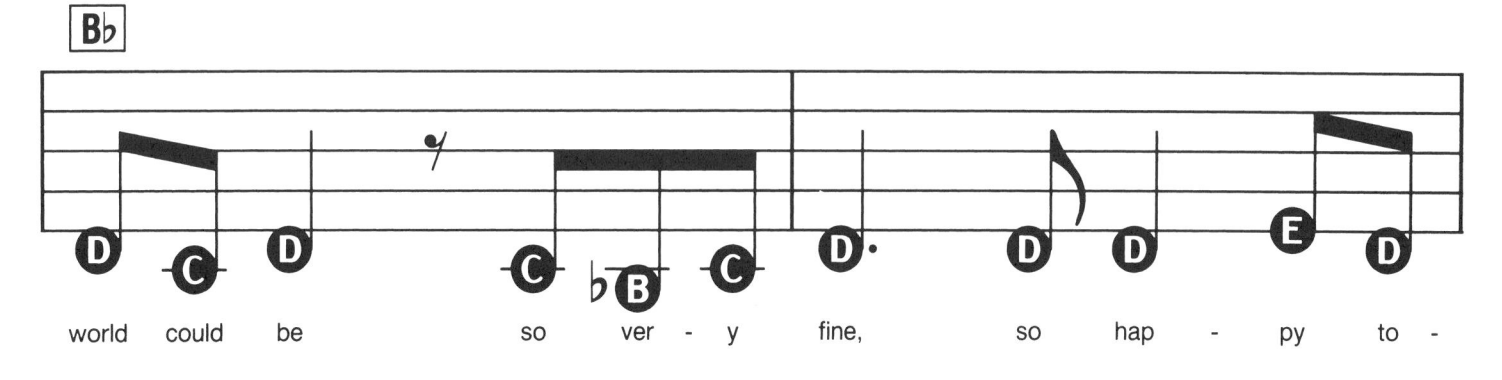

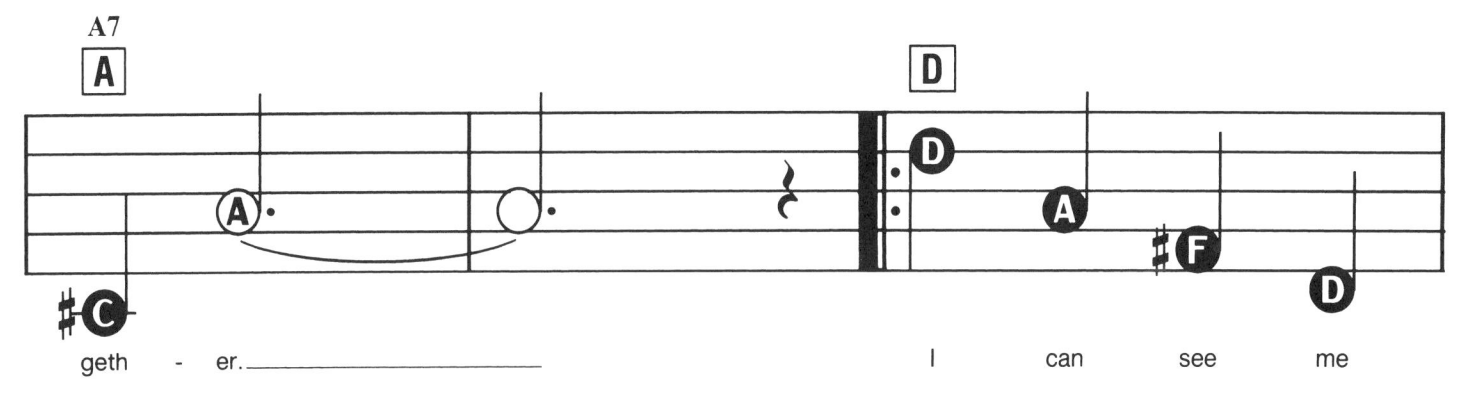

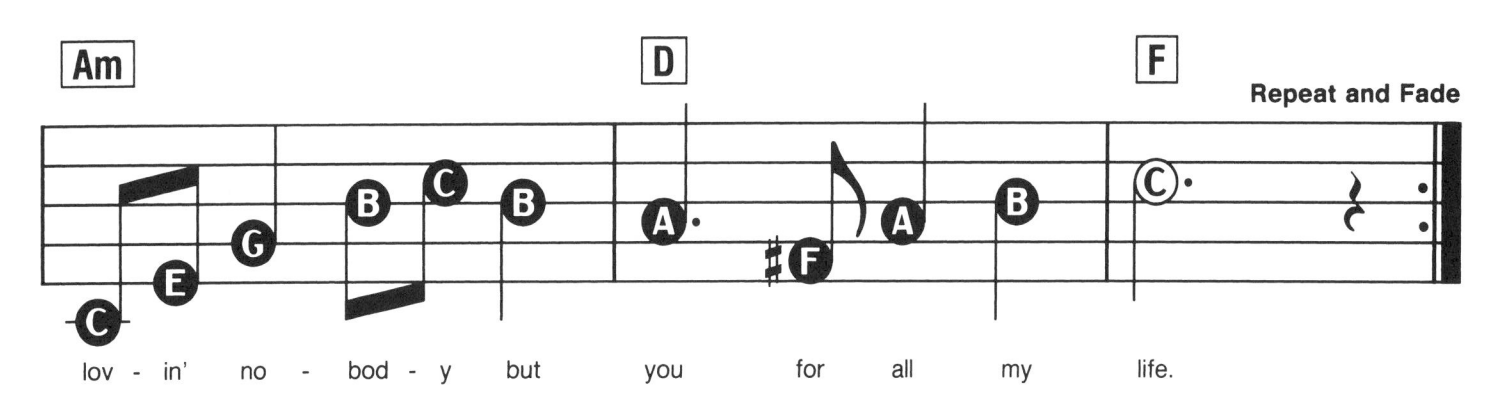

71

Dm

call you up, in-vest a dime, and you say you be-

C

long to me and ease my mind, im-ag-ine how the

B♭

world could be so ver-y fine, so hap-py to-

A (A7)   **D**

geth - er. _____ I can see me

Am   **D**   **F**

Repeat and Fade

lov - in' no - bod - y but you for all my life.

Hello, It's Me

Registration 1
Rhythm: Ballad

Words and Music by
Todd Rundgren

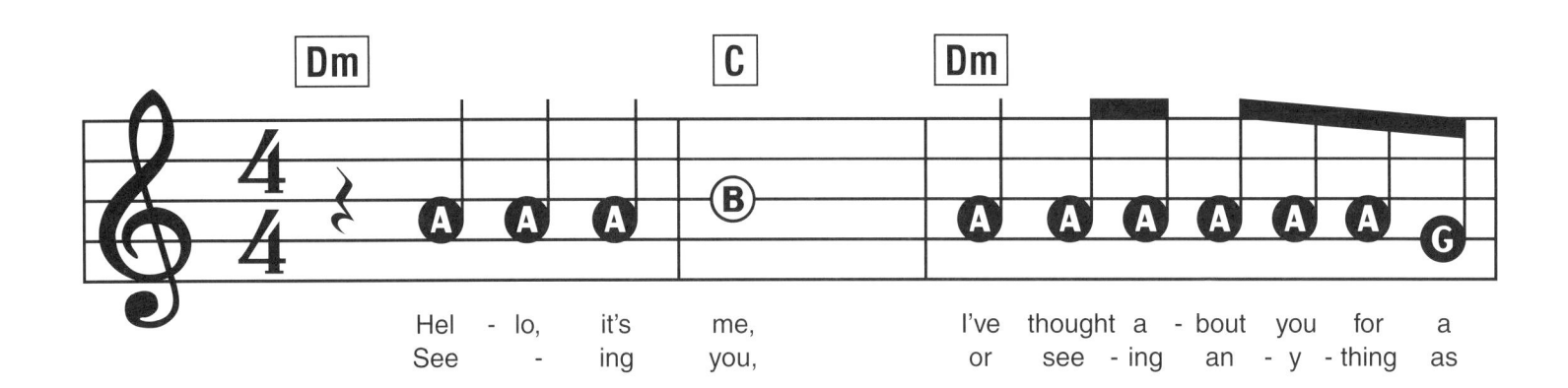

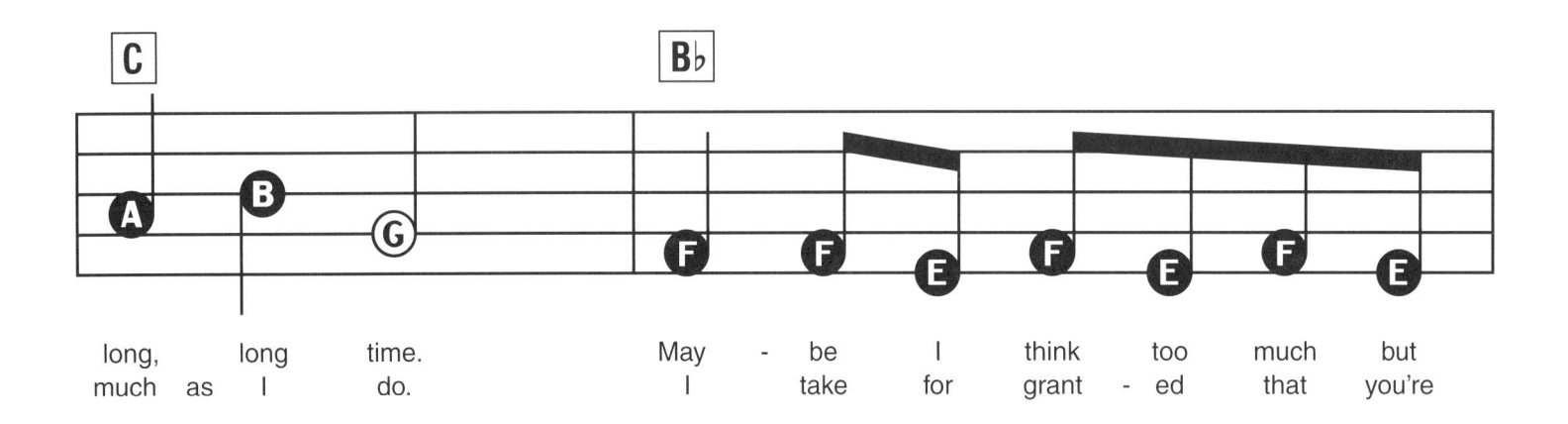

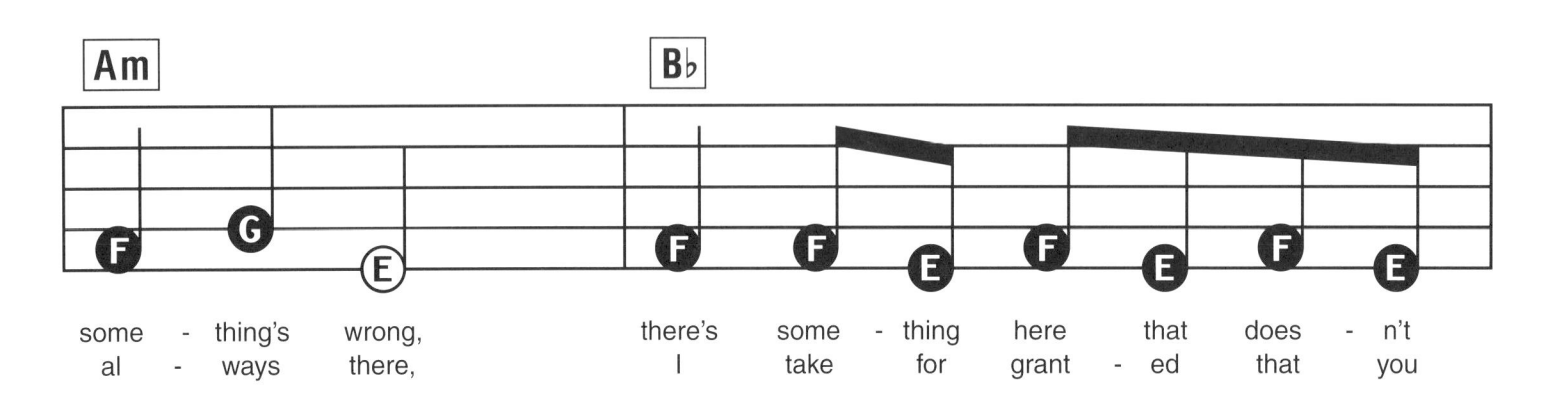

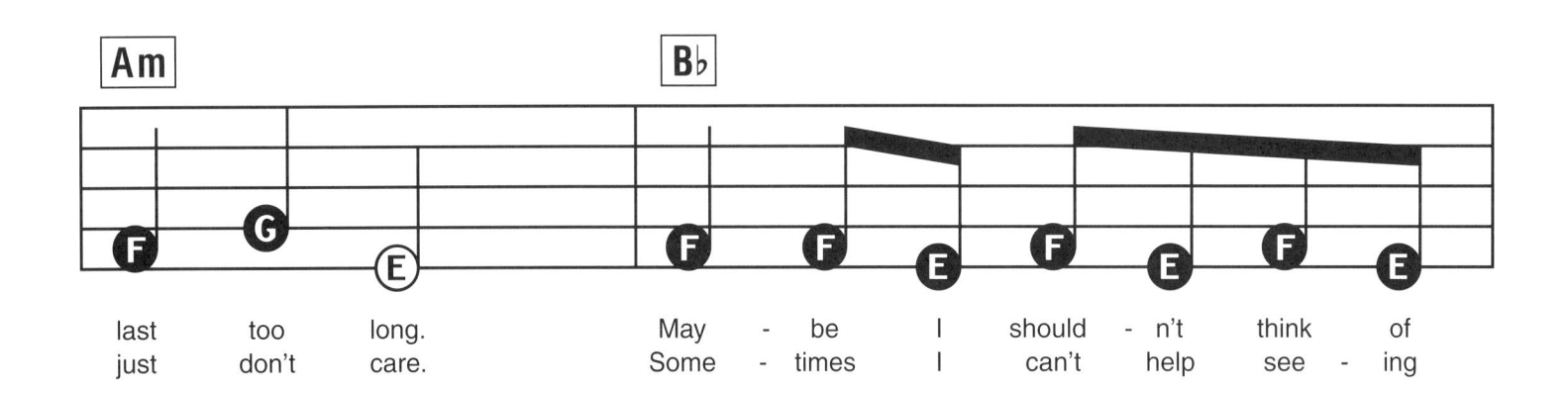

Hel - lo, it's me, I've thought a - bout you for a
See - ing you, or see - ing an - y - thing as

long, long time. May - be I think too much but
much as I do. I take for grant - ed that you're

some - thing's wrong, there's some - thing here that does - n't
al - ways there, I take for grant - ed that you

last too long. May - be I should - n't think of
just don't care. Some - times I can't help see - ing

© 1968 (Renewed 1996) SCREEN GEMS-EMI MUSIC INC.
All Rights Reserved   International Copyright Secured   Used by Permission

you as mine.
all the way through.

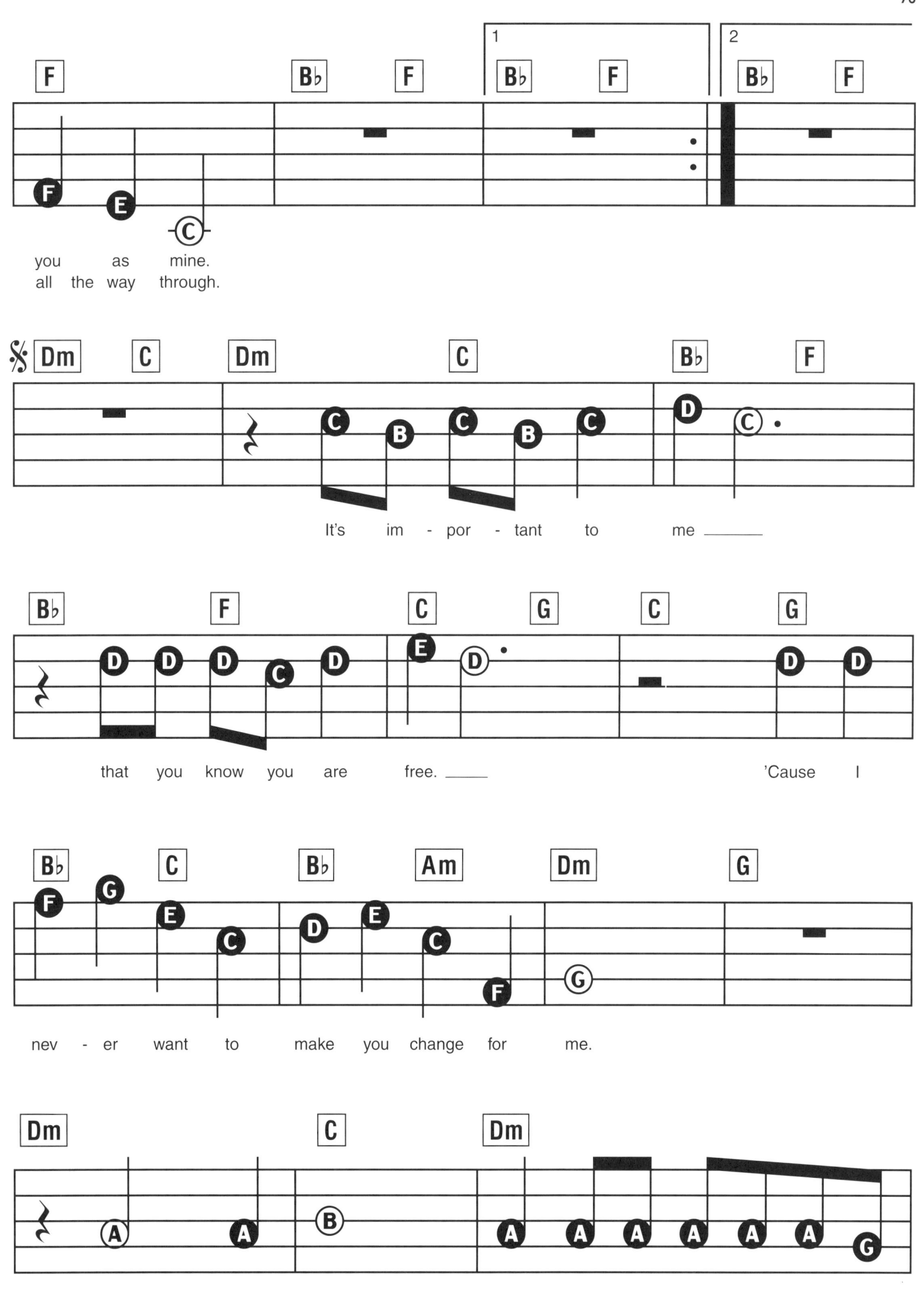

It's im - por - tant to me

that you know you are free. 'Cause I

nev - er want to make you change for me.

Think of me, you know that I'd be with you

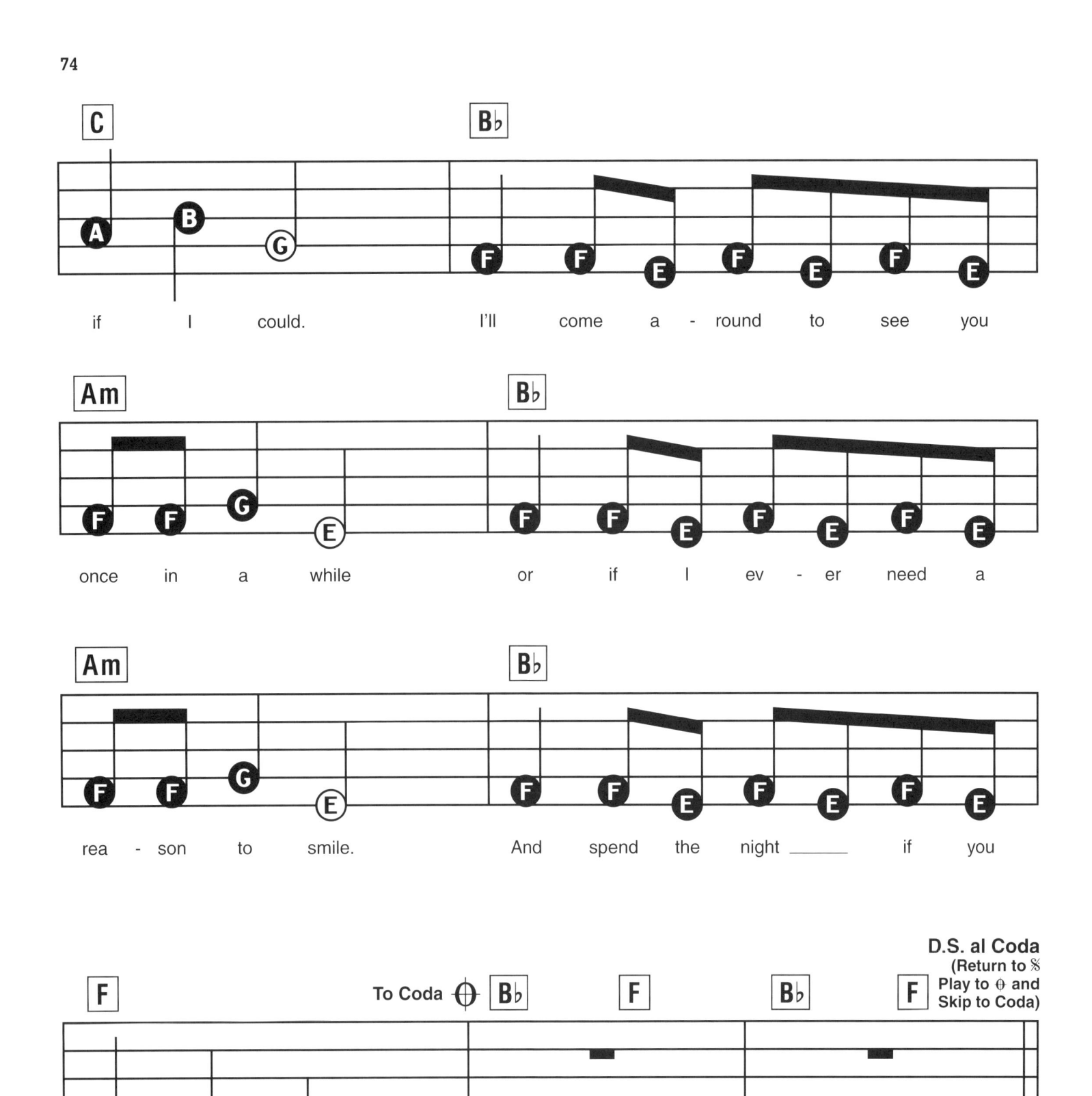

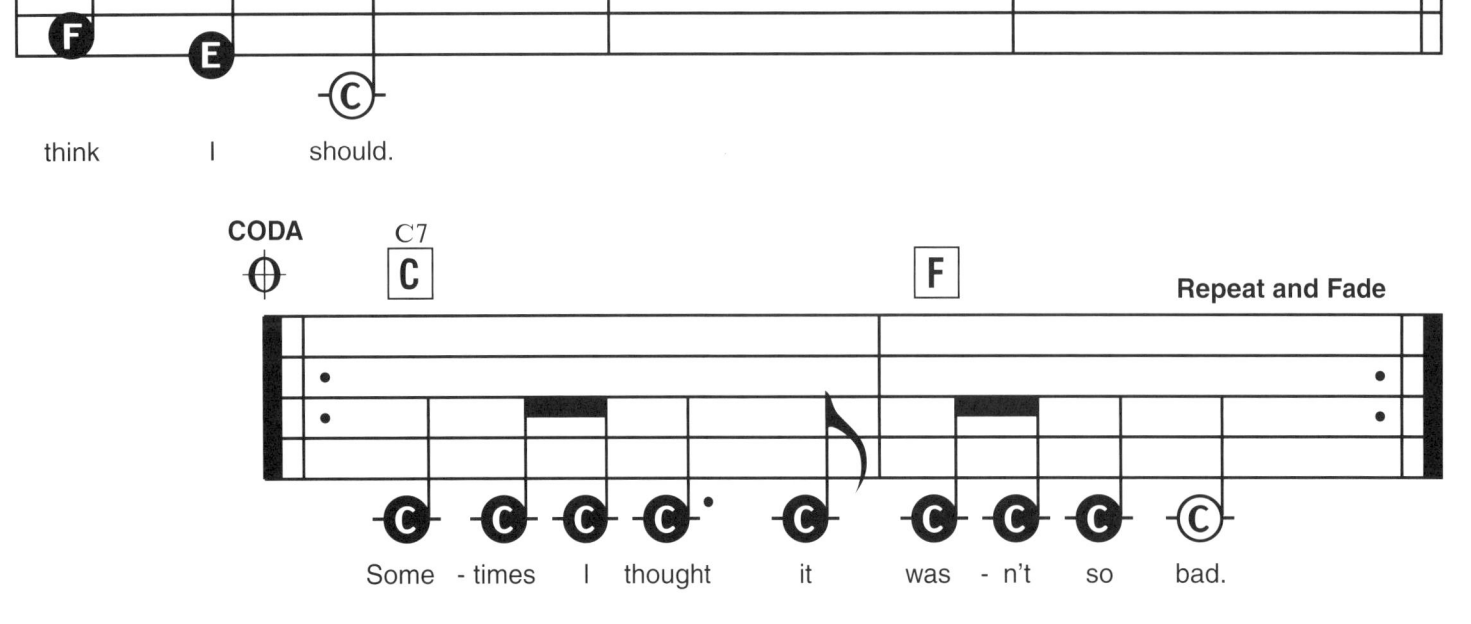

C			Bb						
A	B	G	F	F	E	F	E	F	E
if	I	could.	I'll	come	a-	round	to	see	you

Am				Bb						
F	F	G	E	F	F	E	F	E	F	E
once	in	a	while	or	if	I	ev-	er	need	a

Am				Bb						
F	F	G	E	F	F	E	F	E	F	E
rea-	son	to	smile.	And	spend	the	night ___		if	you

D.S. al Coda
(Return to 𝄋
Play to ϕ and
Skip to Coda)

To Coda ϕ

F			Bb	F	Bb	F
F	E	C				
think	I	should.				

CODA ϕ

C (C7)					F				**Repeat and Fade**
C	C	C	C.	C	C	C	C	C	
Some-	times	I	thought	it	was-	n't	so	bad.	

Her Town Too

Registration 2
Rhythm: Rock

Words and Music by John David Souther,
James Taylor and Robert Wachtel

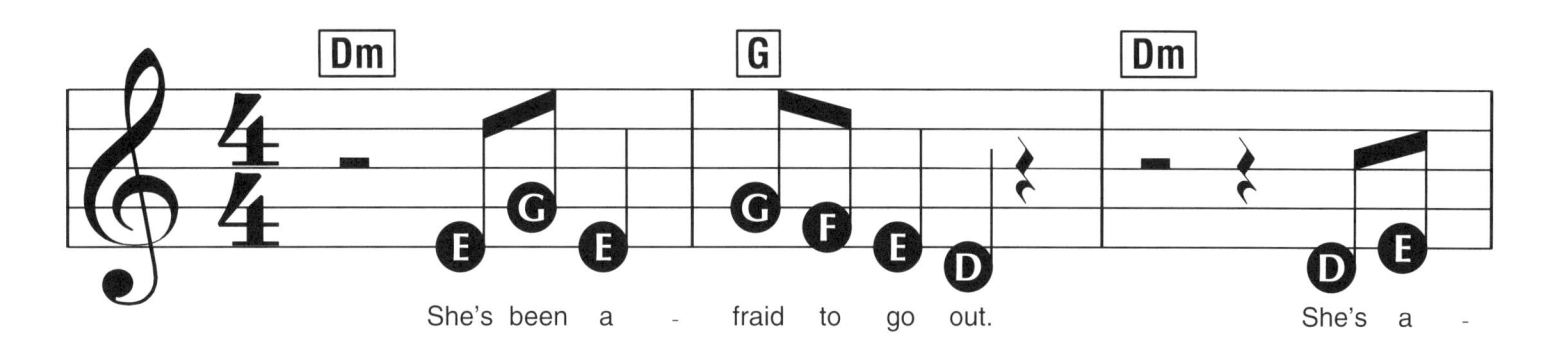

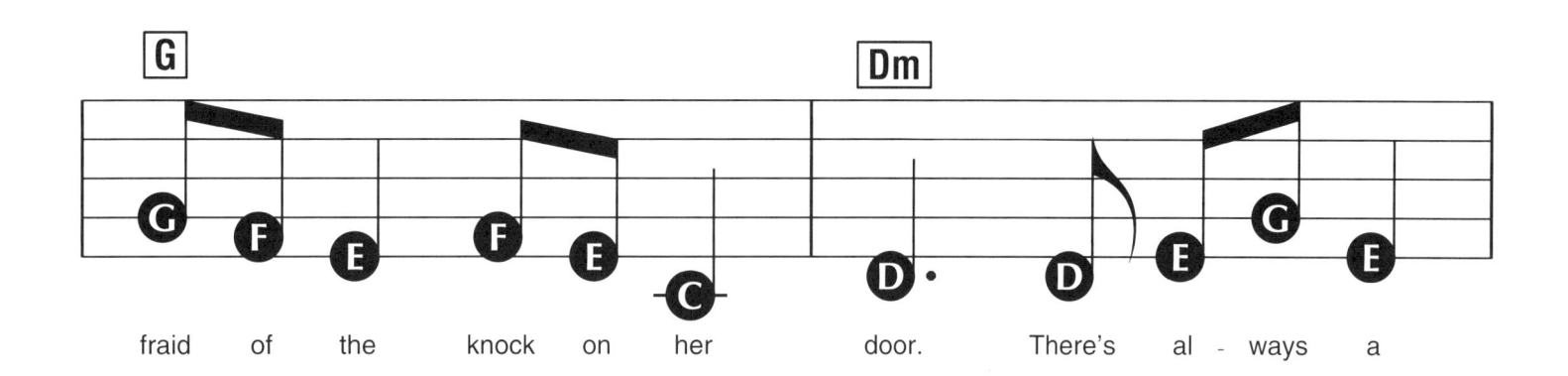

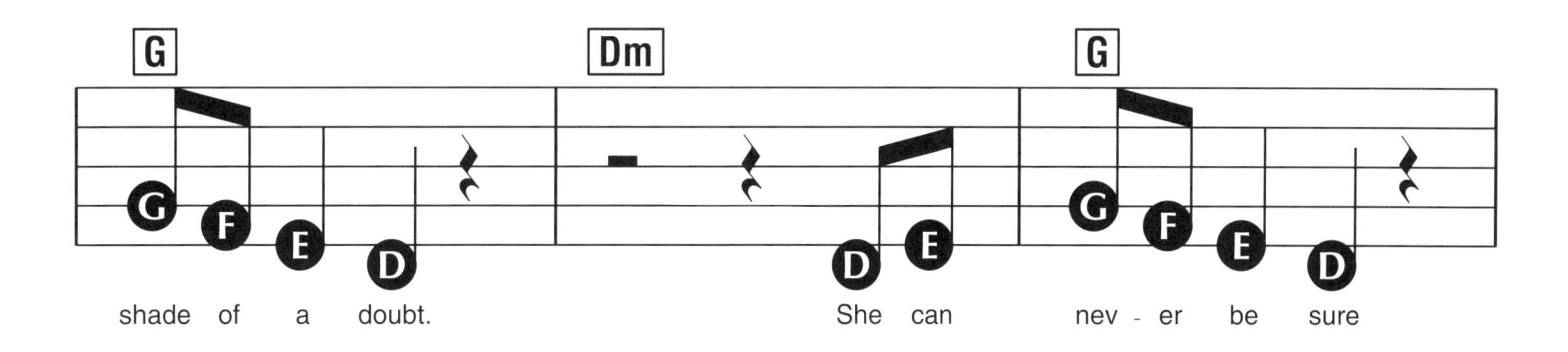

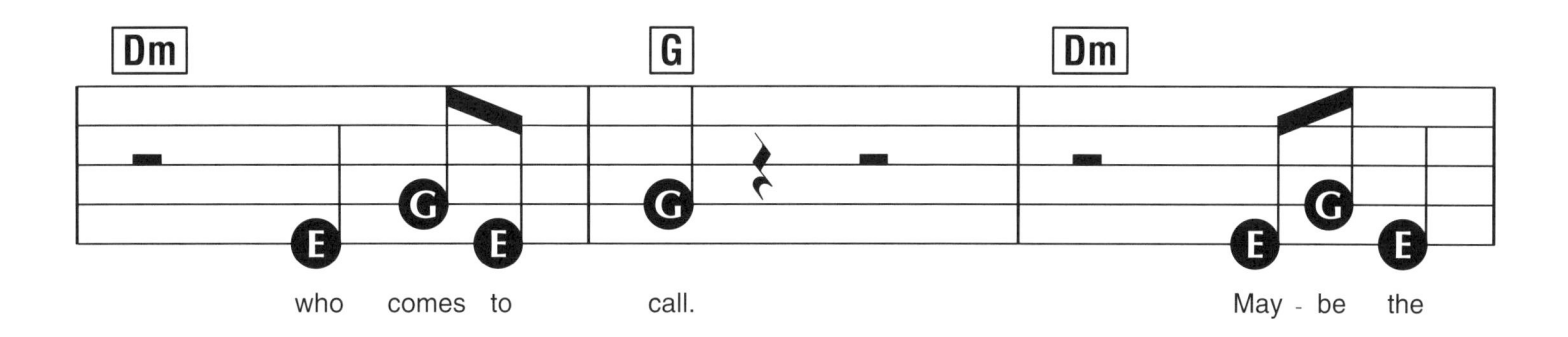

She's been a-fraid to go out. She's a-fraid of the knock on her door. There's al-ways a shade of a doubt. She can nev-er be sure who comes to call. May-be the

© 1981 EMI APRIL MUSIC INC., COUNTRY ROAD MUSIC and LEADSHEETLAND MUSIC
All Rights Reserved   International Copyright Secured   Used by Permission

friend of a friend of a friend; an-y-one at

all, _____ an-y-thing but noth-ing a - gain. It

used to be her town. _____ It

used to be her town, too. It

used to be her town. _____ It

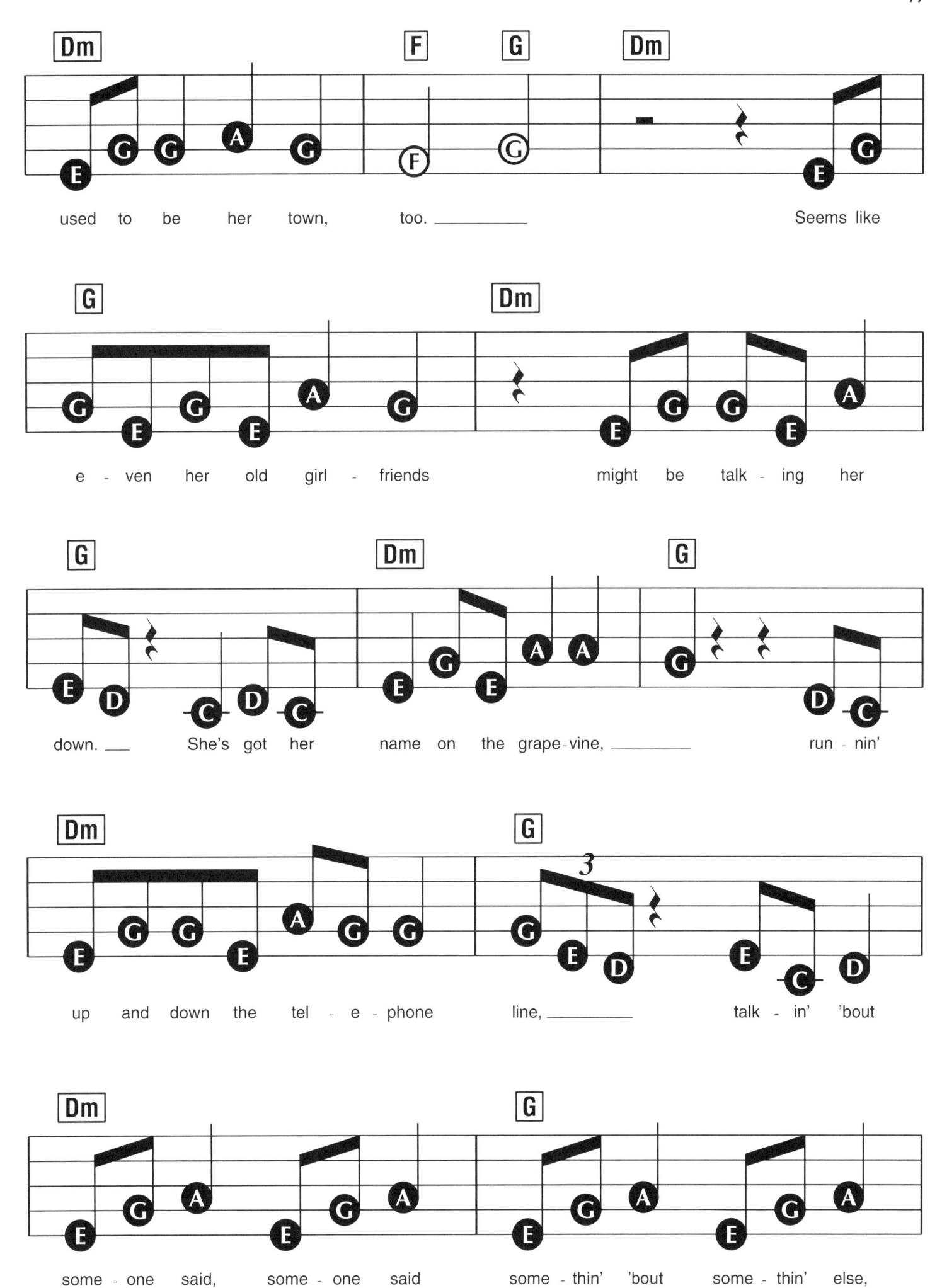

used to be her town, too. _____ Seems like e - ven her old girl - friends might be talk - ing her down. ___ She's got her name on the grape - vine, _____ run - nin' up and down the tel - e - phone line, _____ talk - in' 'bout some - one said, some - one said some - thin' 'bout some - thin' else,

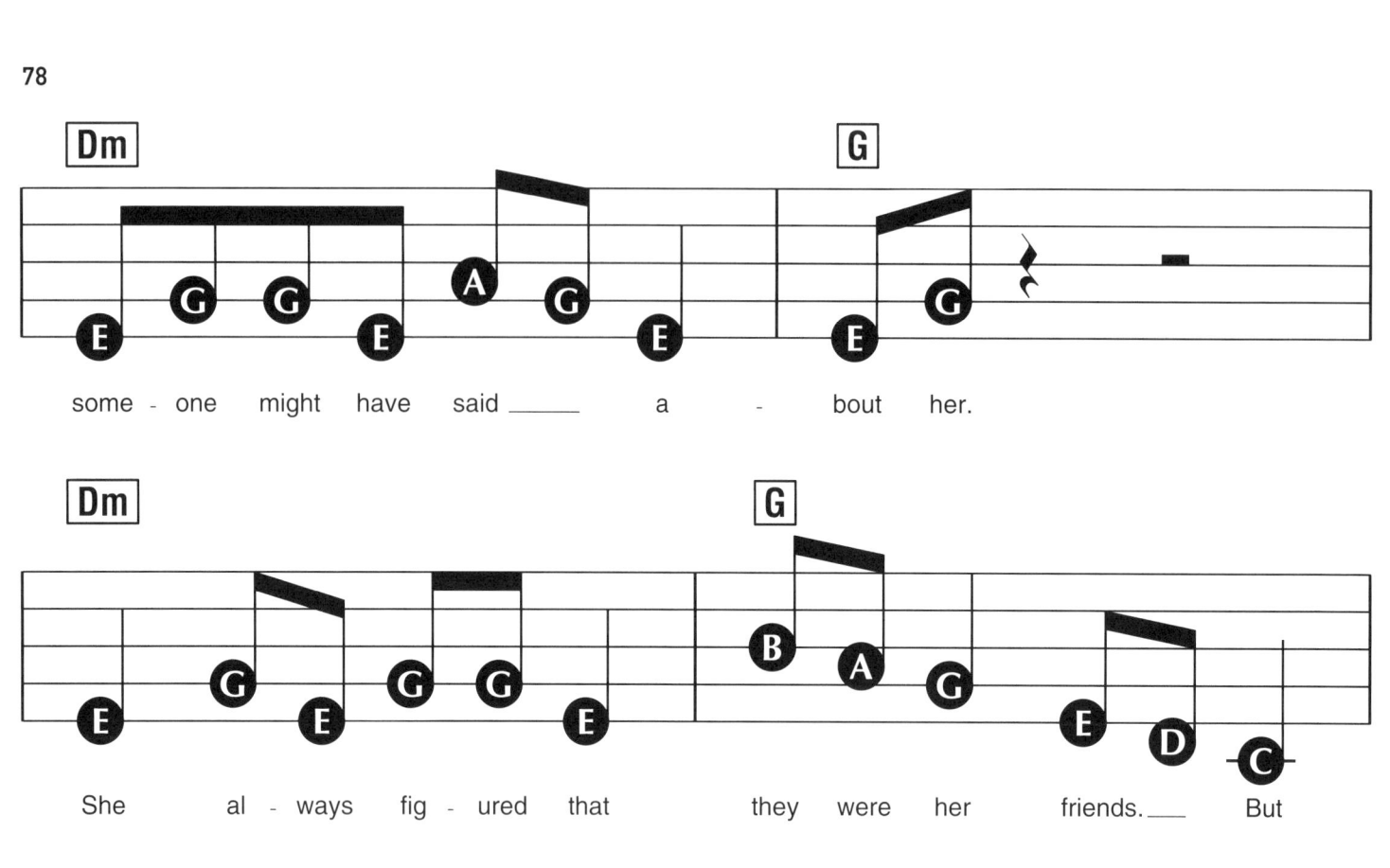

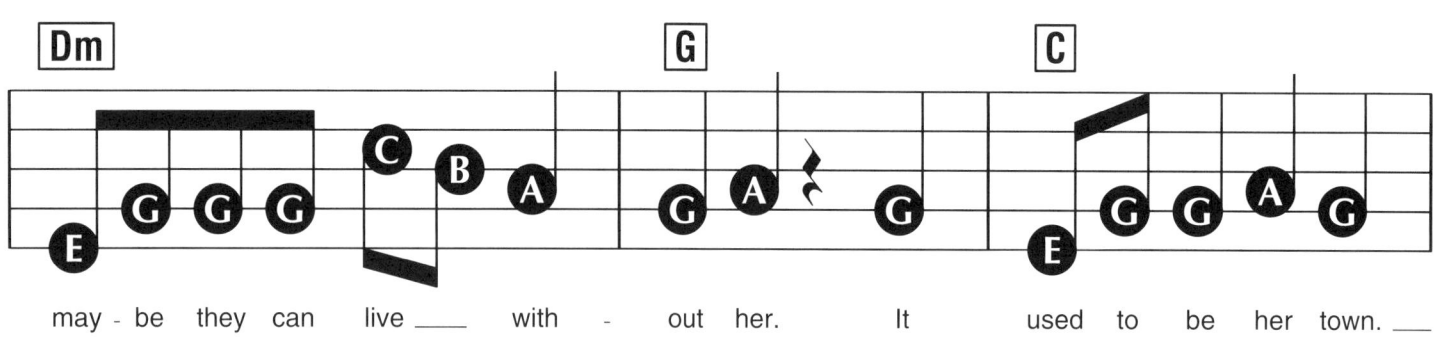

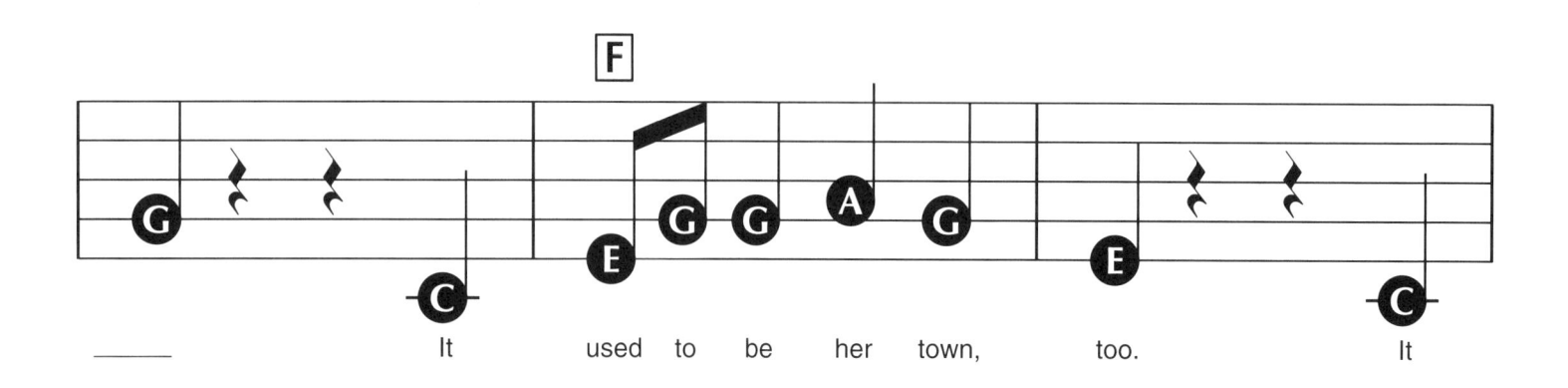

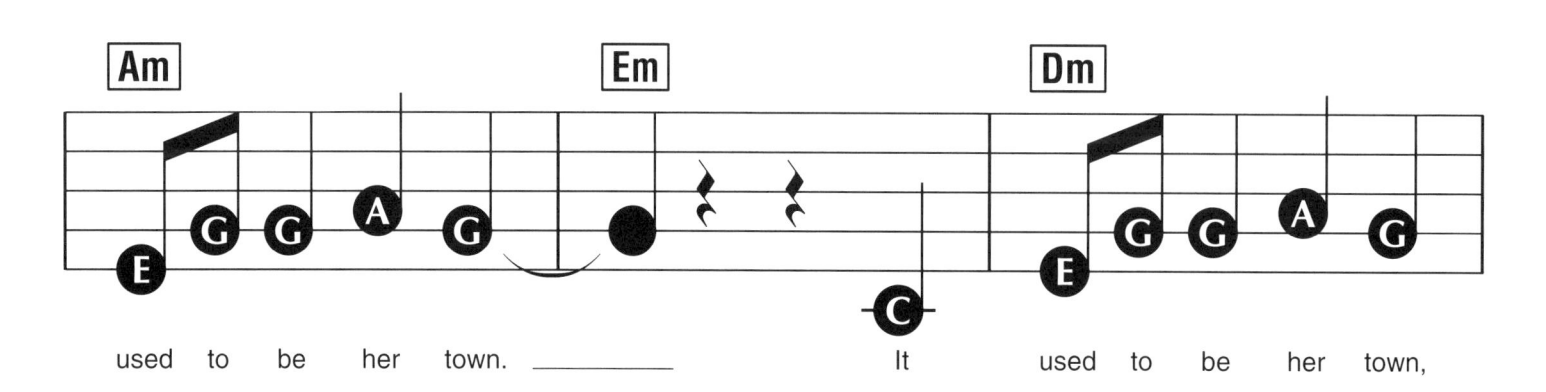

78

Dm | **G**
some-one might have said ___ a - bout her.

Dm | **G**
She al-ways fig-ured that they were her friends. ___ But

Dm | **G** | **C**
may-be they can live ___ with - out her. It used to be her town. ___

F
___ It used to be her town, too. It

Am | **Em** | **Dm**
used to be her town. ___ It used to be her town,

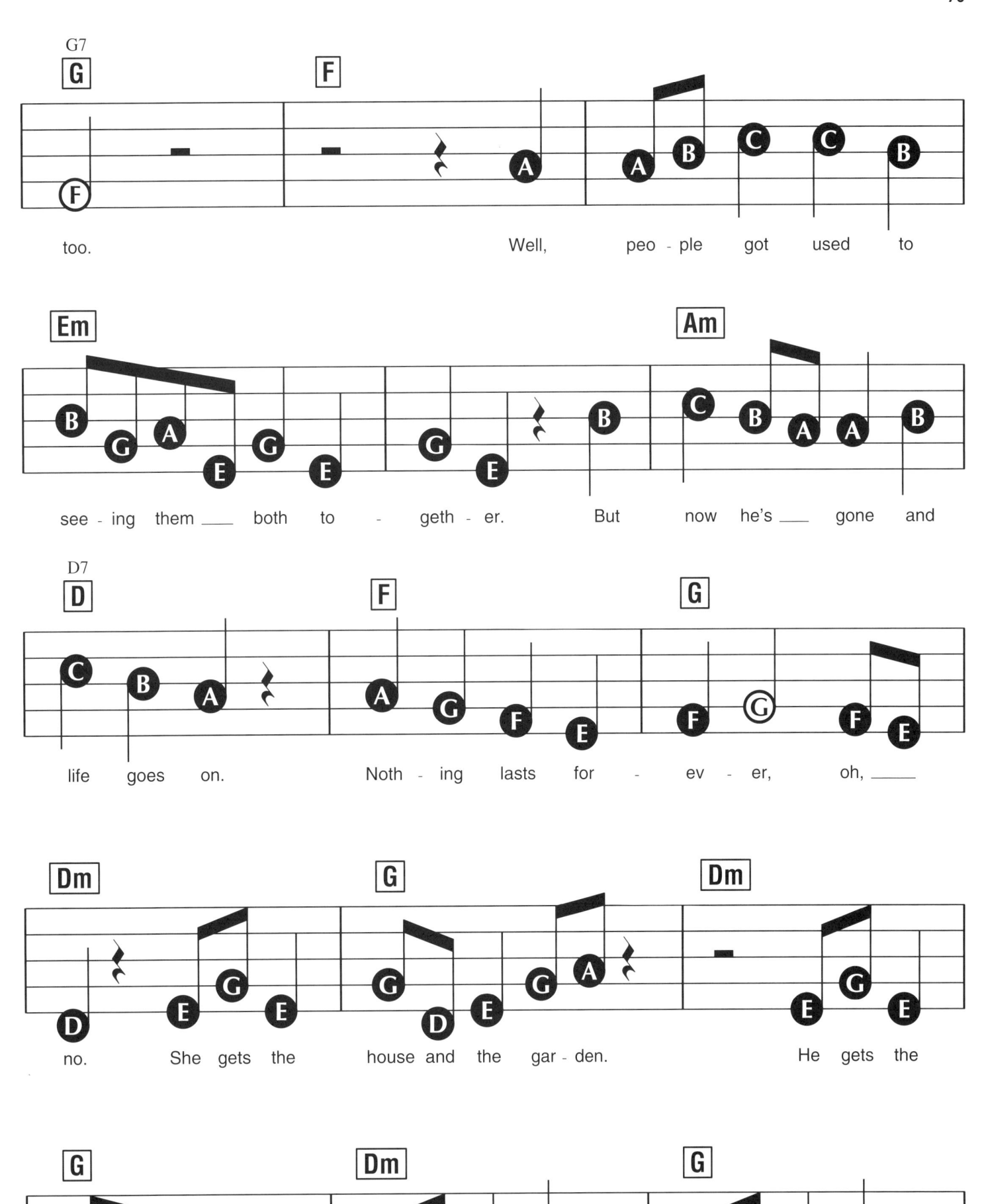

too. Well, peo - ple got used to see - ing them both to - geth - er. But now he's gone and life goes on. Noth - ing lasts for - ev - er, oh, no. She gets the house and the gar - den. He gets the boys in the band, some of them his friends, some of them her friends.

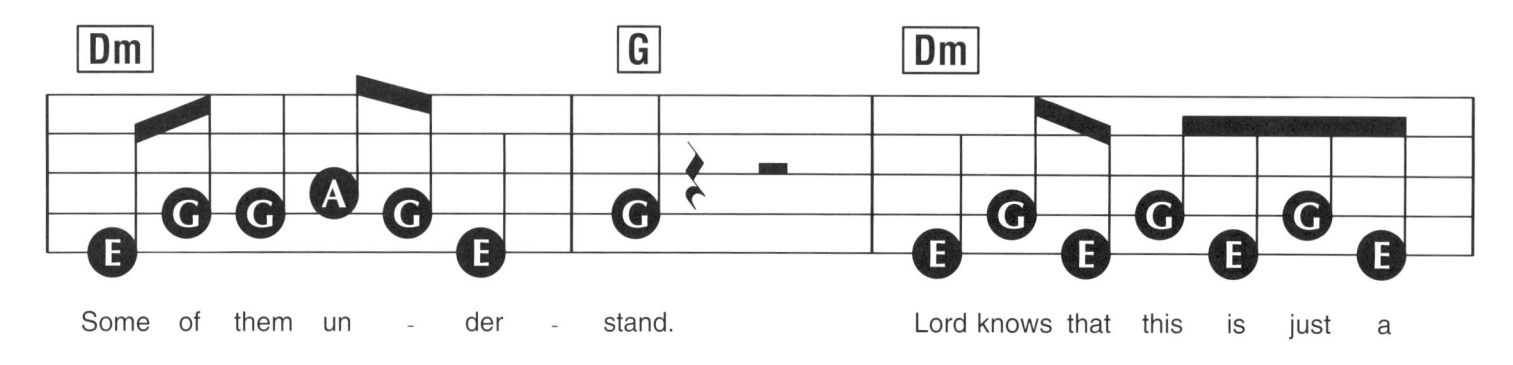

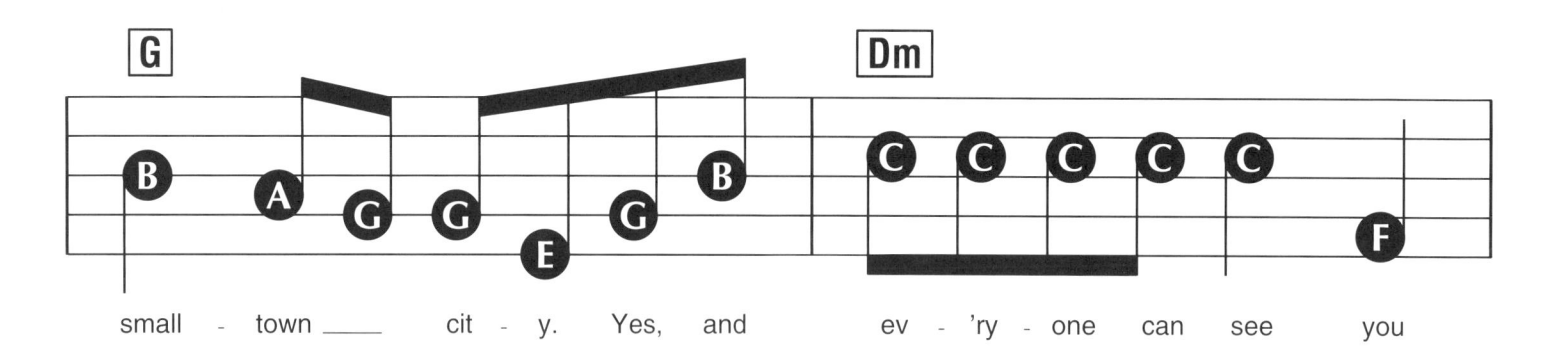

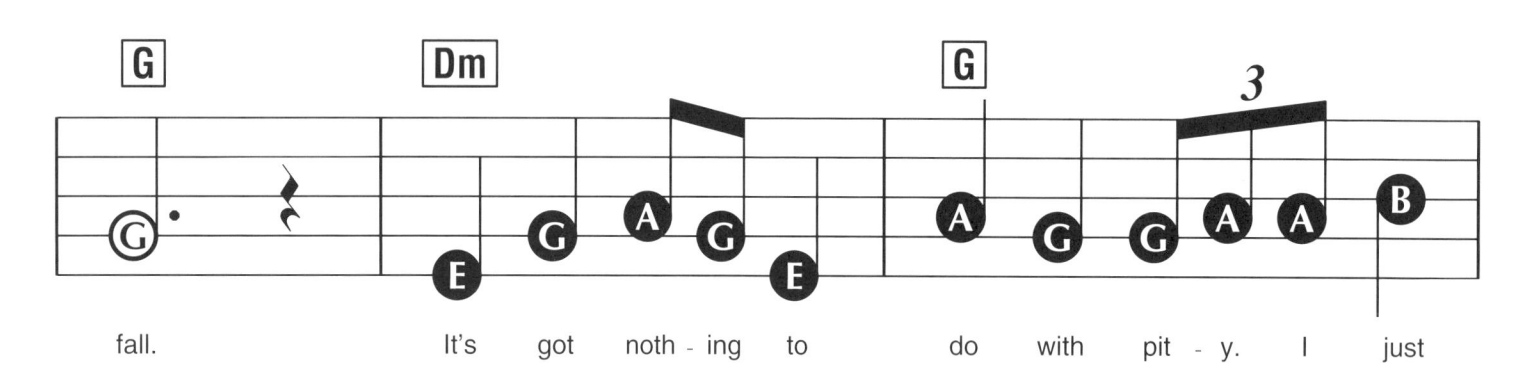

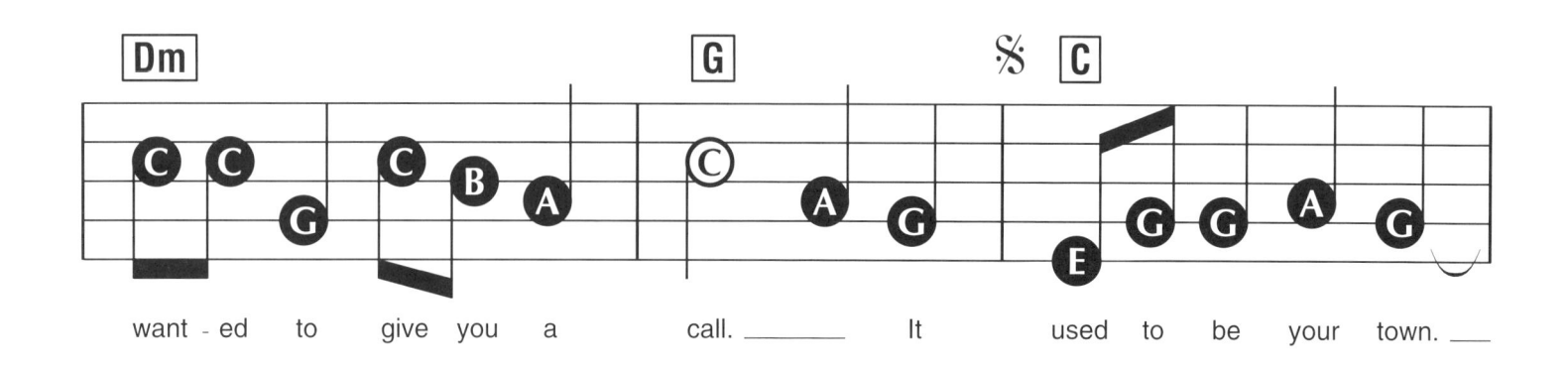

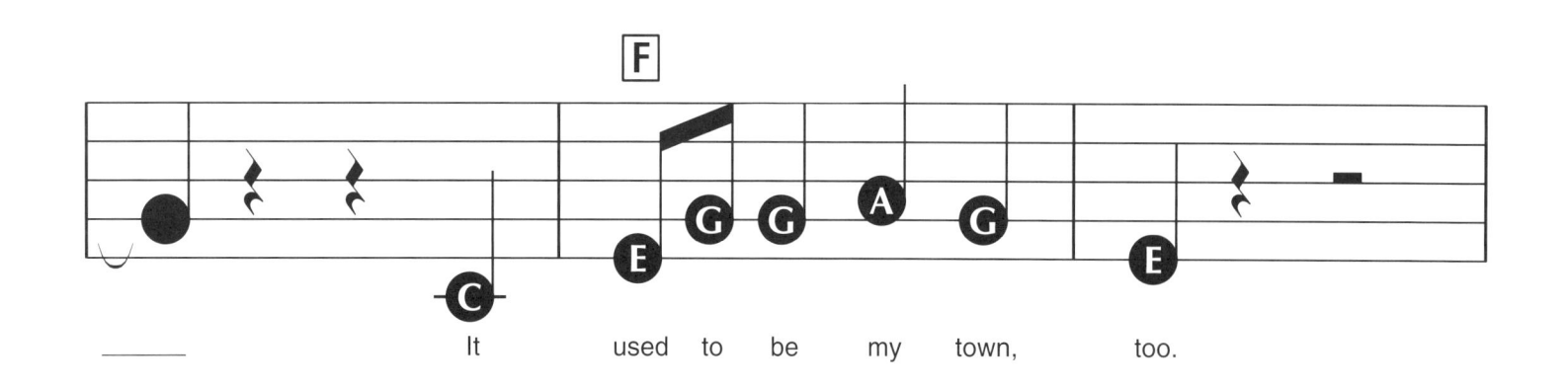

Some of them un-der-stand. Lord knows that this is just a small-town city. Yes, and ev-'ry-one can see you fall. It's got noth-ing to do with pit-y. I just want-ed to give you a call. It used to be your town. It used to be my town, too.

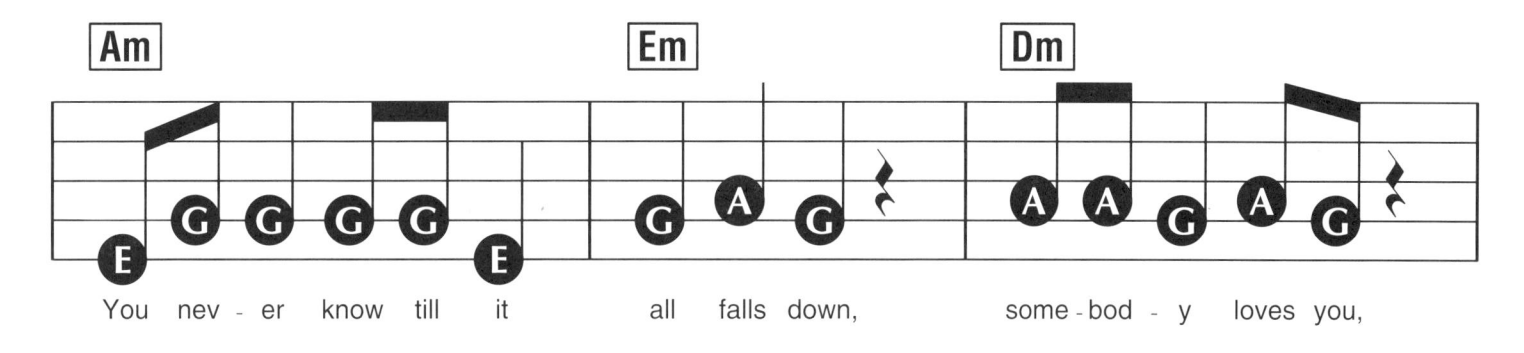

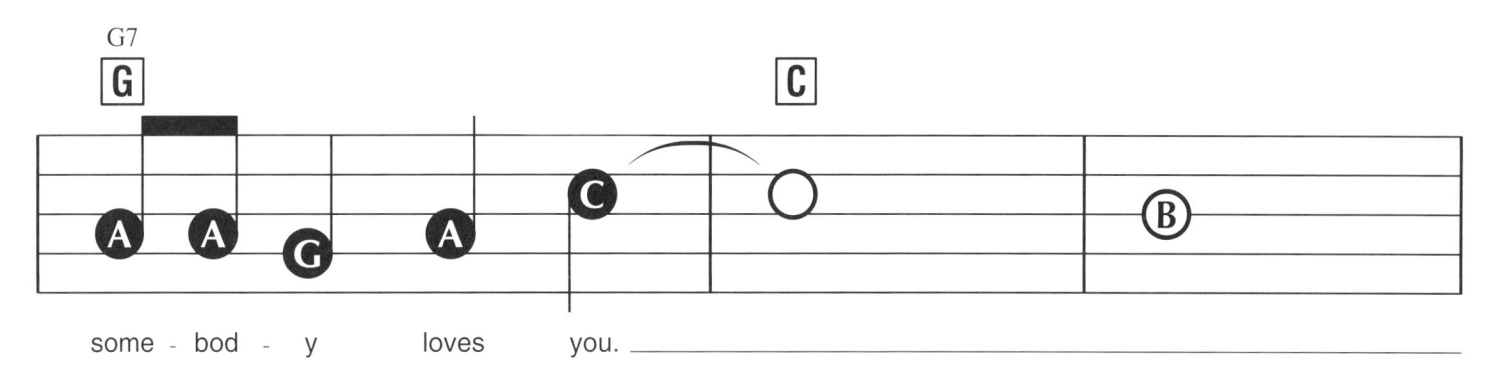

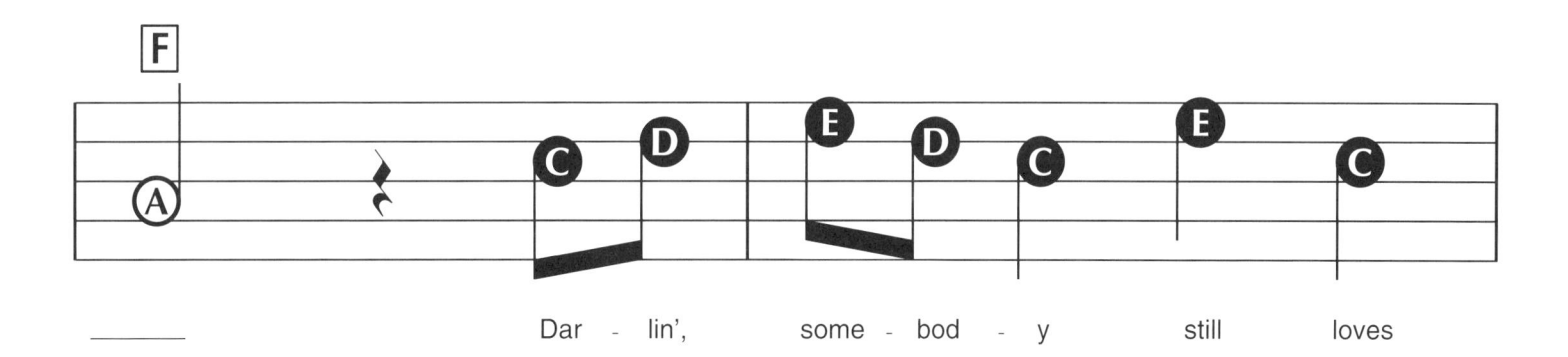

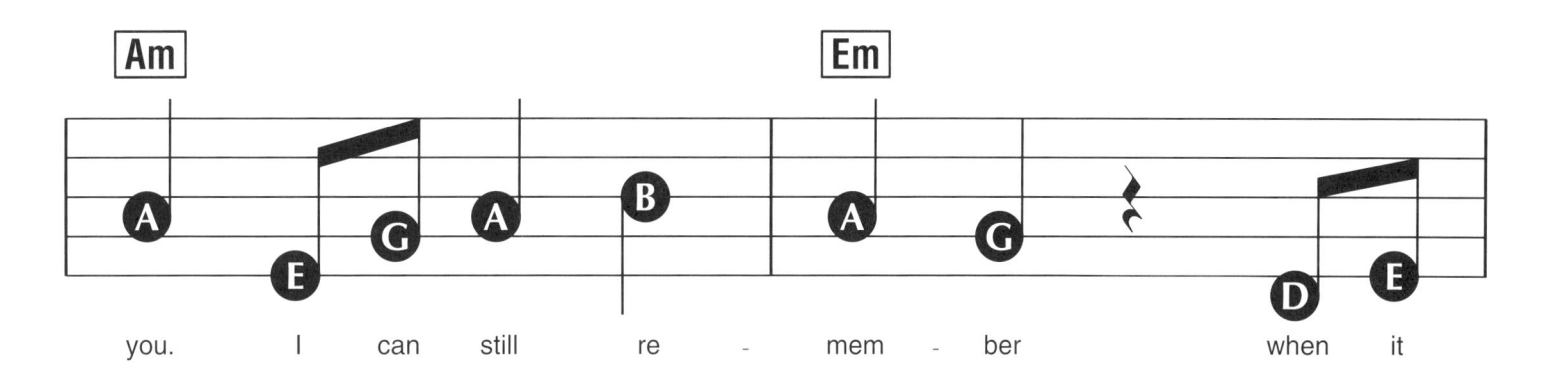

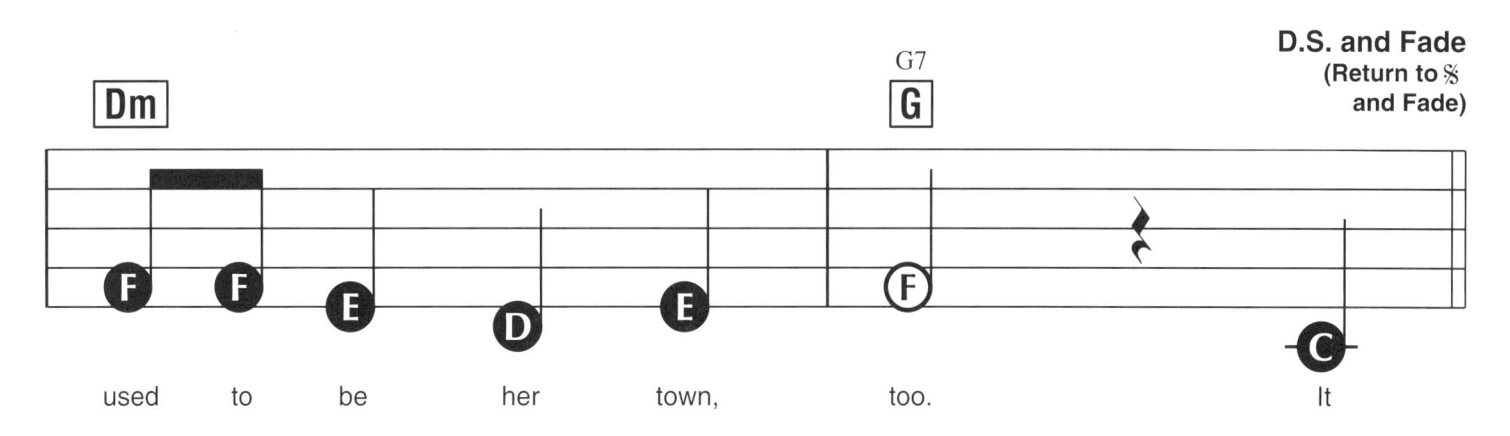

| Am | Em | Dm |

You nev-er know till it all falls down, some-bod-y loves you,

| G (G7) | C |

some-bod-y loves you.

| F |

Dar-lin', some-bod-y still loves

| Am | Em |

you. I can still re-mem-ber when it

D.S. and Fade
(Return to 𝄋 and Fade)

| Dm | G (G7) |

used to be her town, too. It

Help Me Make It Through the Night

Registration 2
Rhythm: Rock or 8 Beat

Words and Music by
Kris Kristofferson

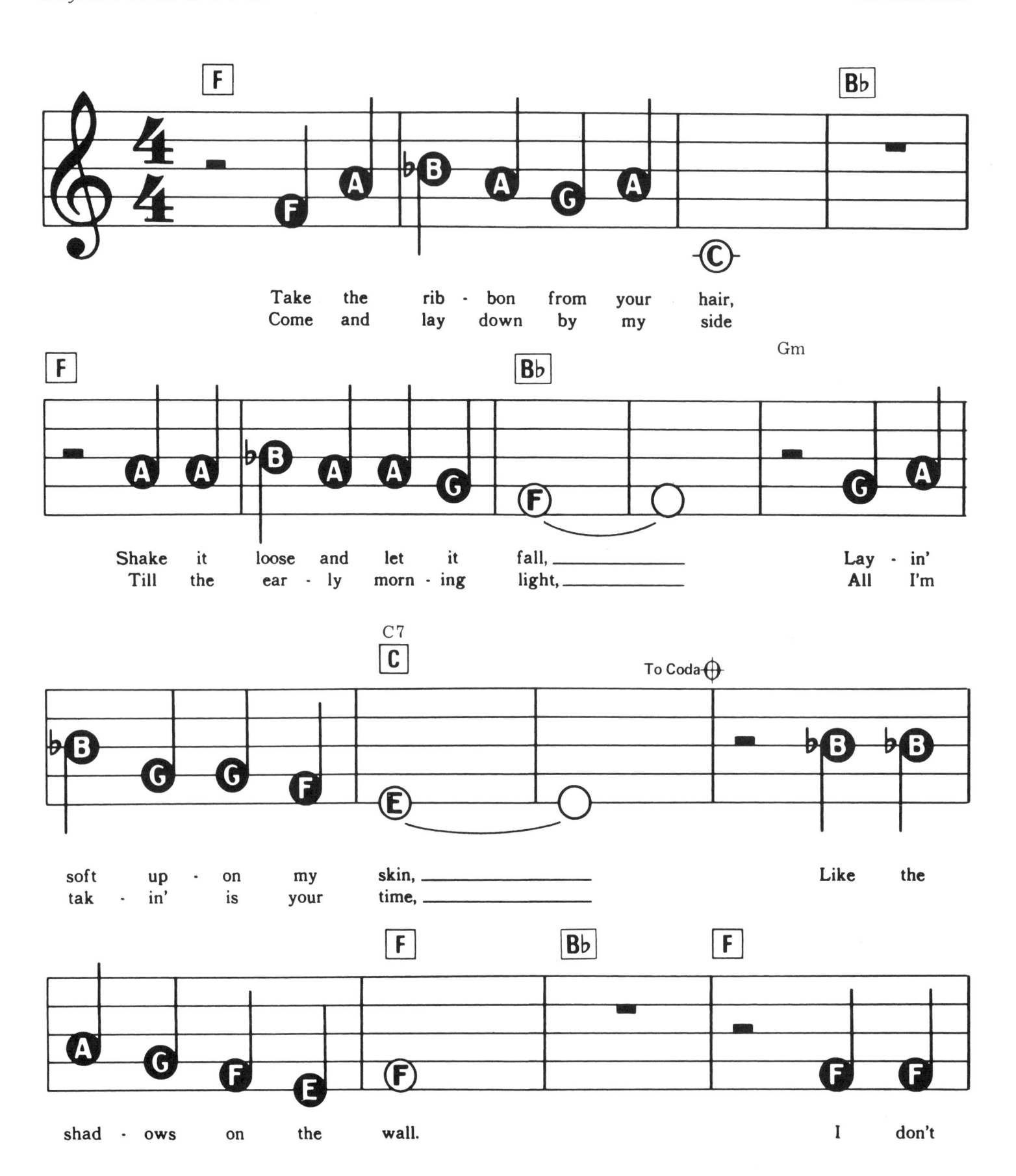

Take the rib-bon from your hair,
Come and lay down by your my side

Shake it loose and let it fall, Lay - in'
Till the ear - ly morn - ing light, All I'm

soft up - on my skin, Like the
tak - in' is your time,

shad - ows on the wall. I don't

© 1970 (Renewed 1998) TEMI COMBINE INC.
All Rights Controlled by COMBINE MUSIC CORP. and Administered by EMI BLACKWOOD MUSIC INC.
All Rights Reserved   International Copyright Secured   Used by Permission

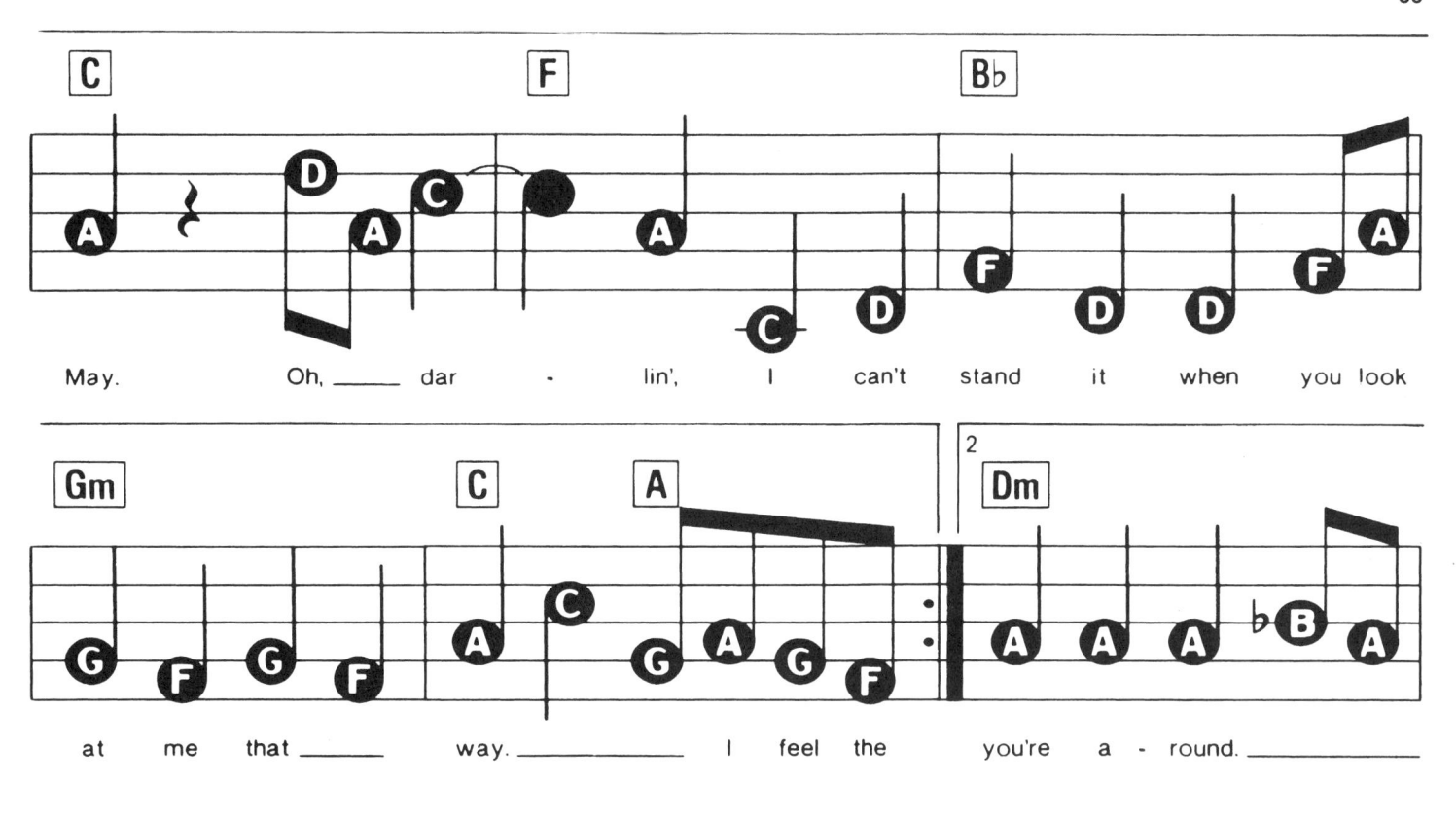

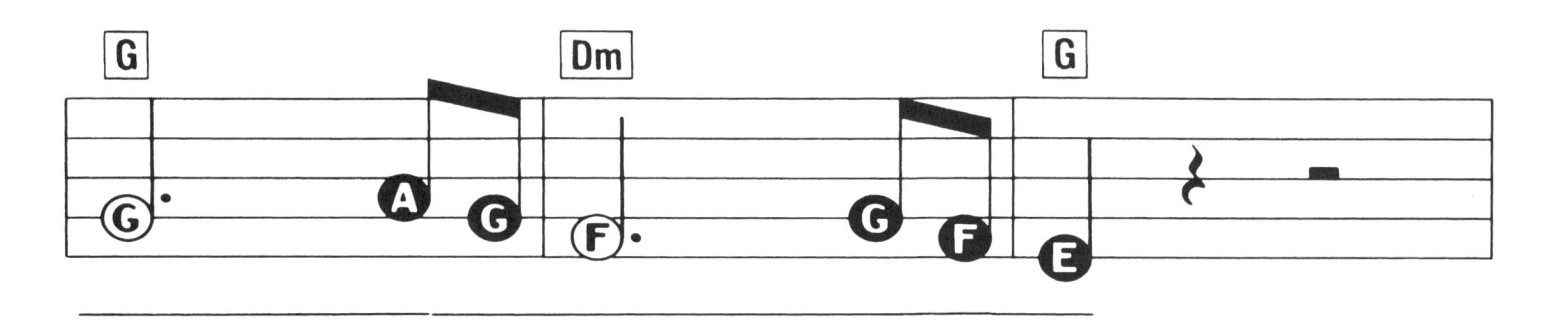

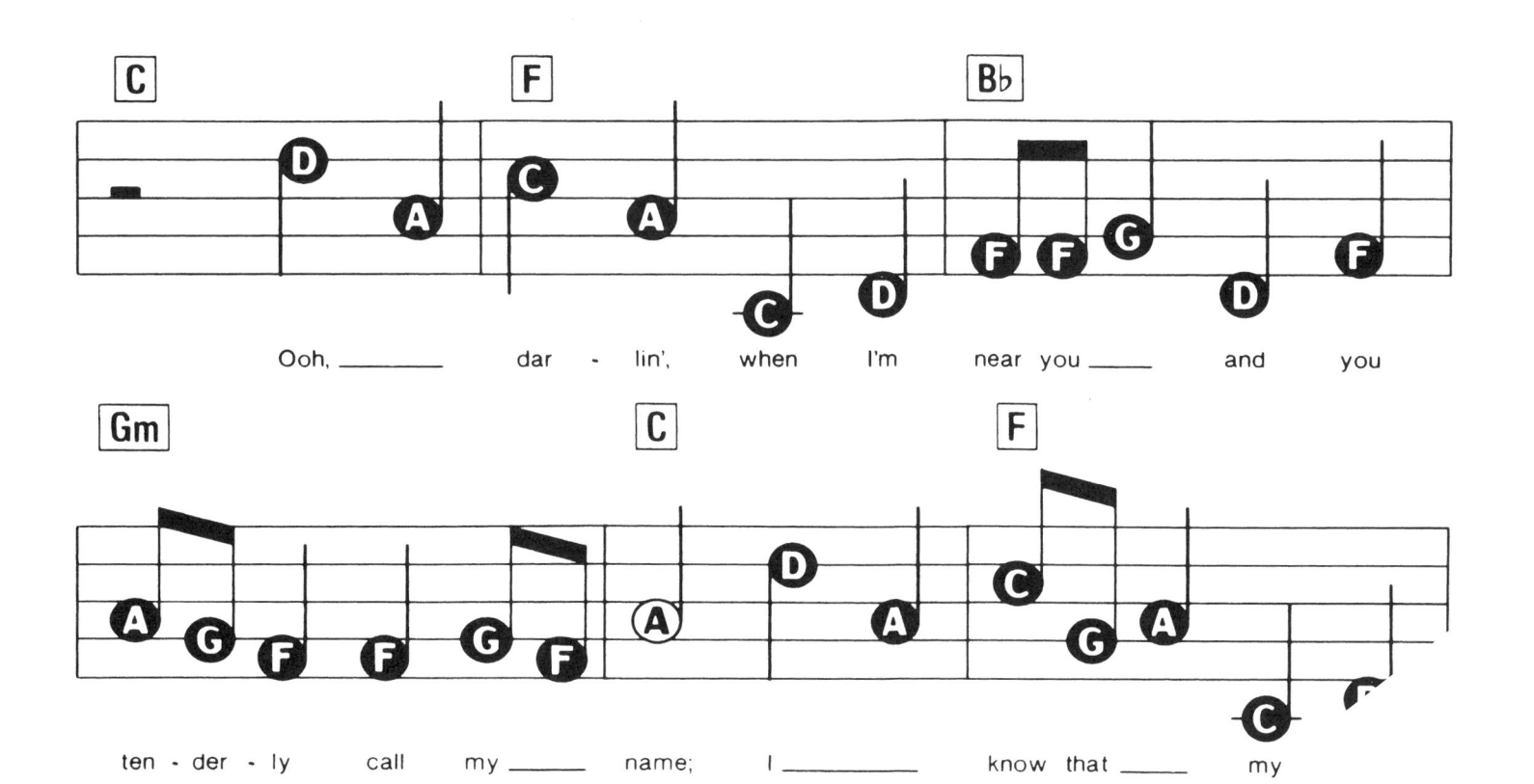

May. Oh, ____ dar - lin', I can't stand it when you look

at me that ____ way. ____ I feel the you're a - round. ____

Ooh, ____ dar - lin', when I'm near you ____ and you

ten - der - ly call my ____ name; I ____ know that ____ my

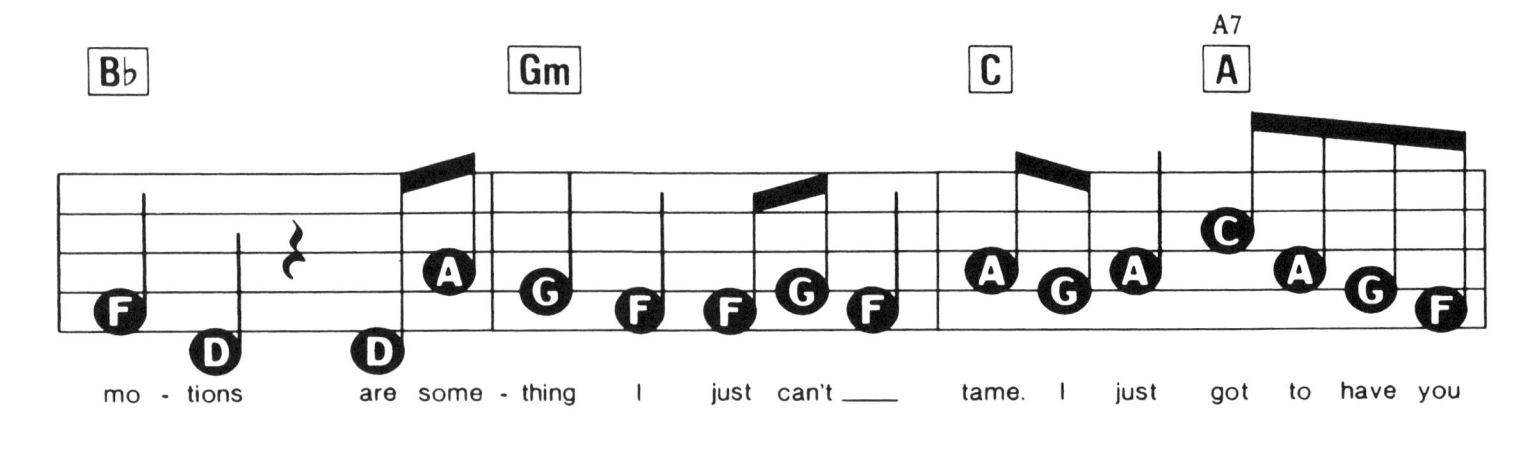

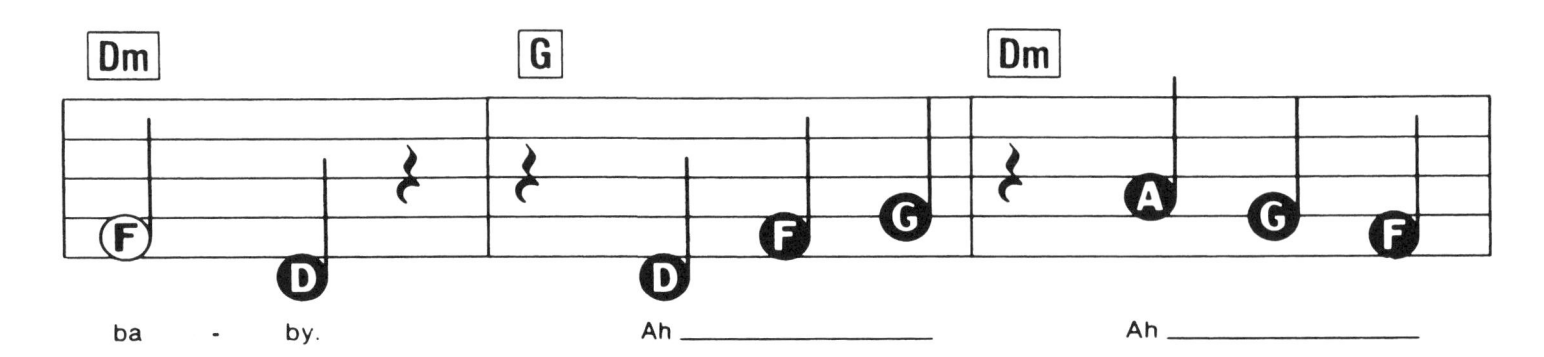

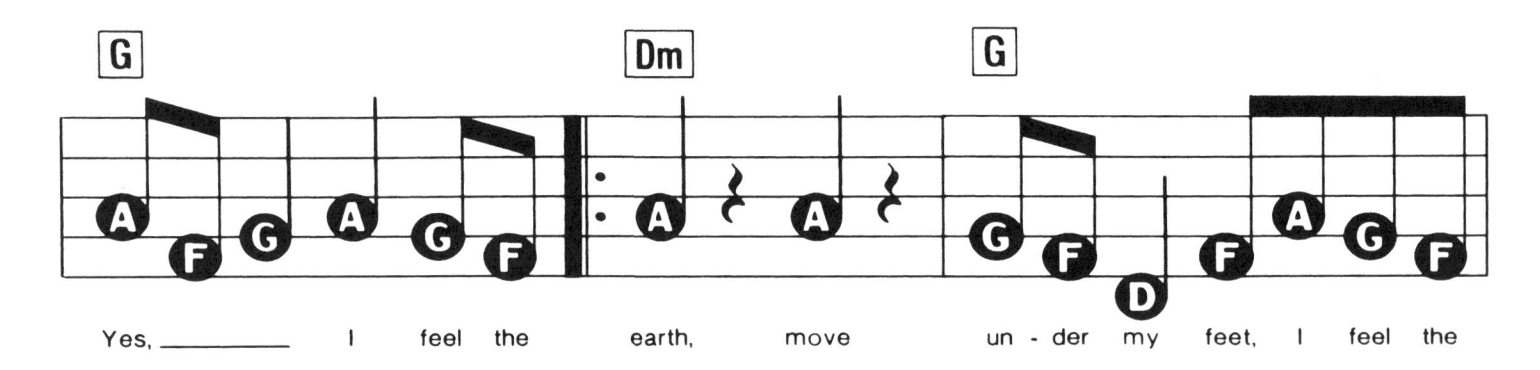

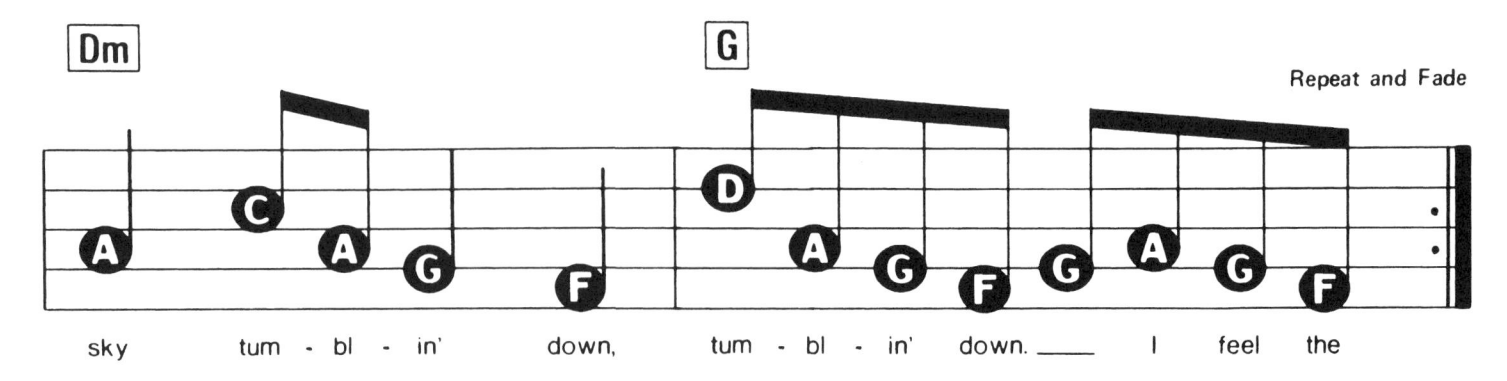

Additional Lyrics

I just lose control down to my very soul,
I get hot and cold all over, all over, all over.

Last Goodbye

Registration 4
Rhythm: Country Pop or 8-Beat

Words and Music by
Jeff Buckley

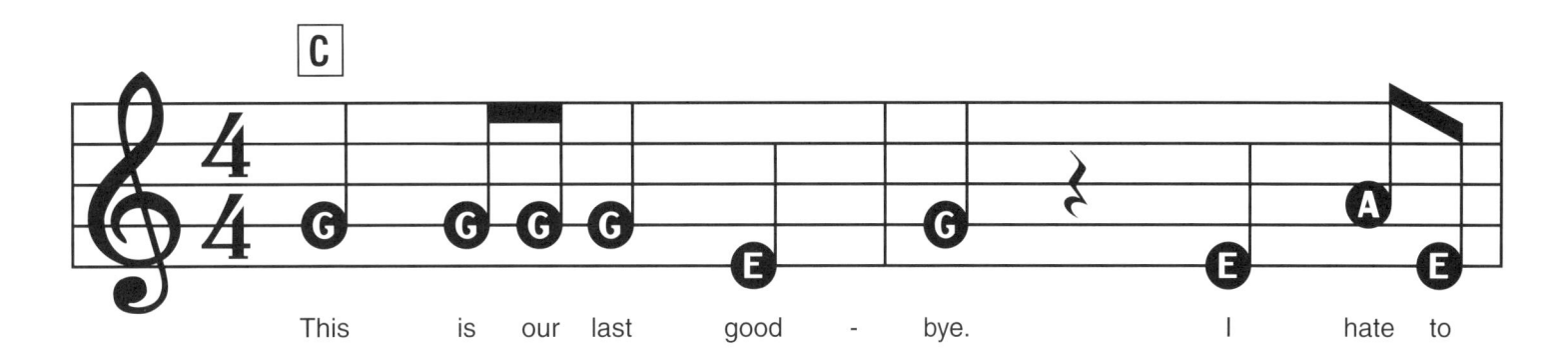

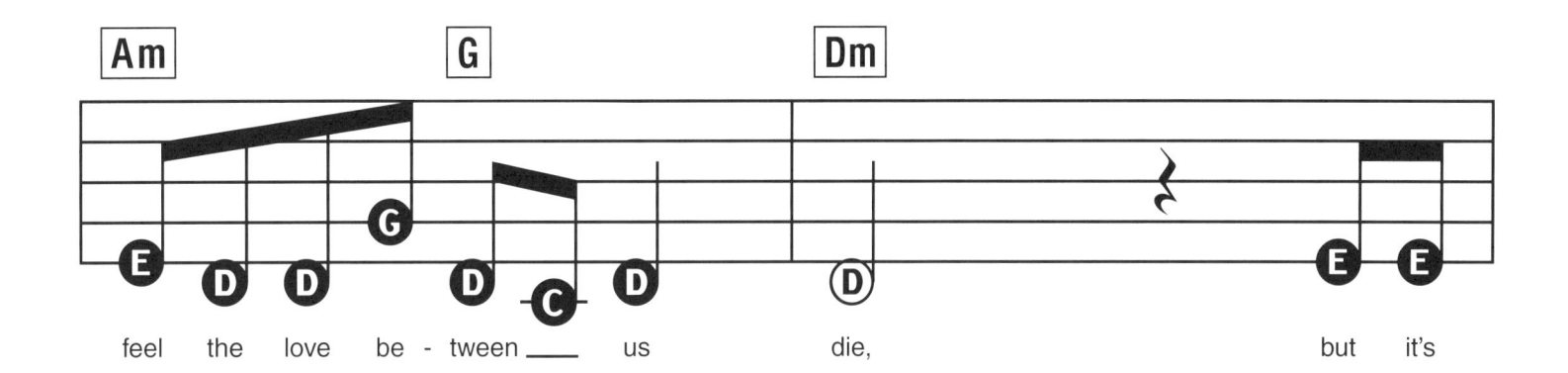

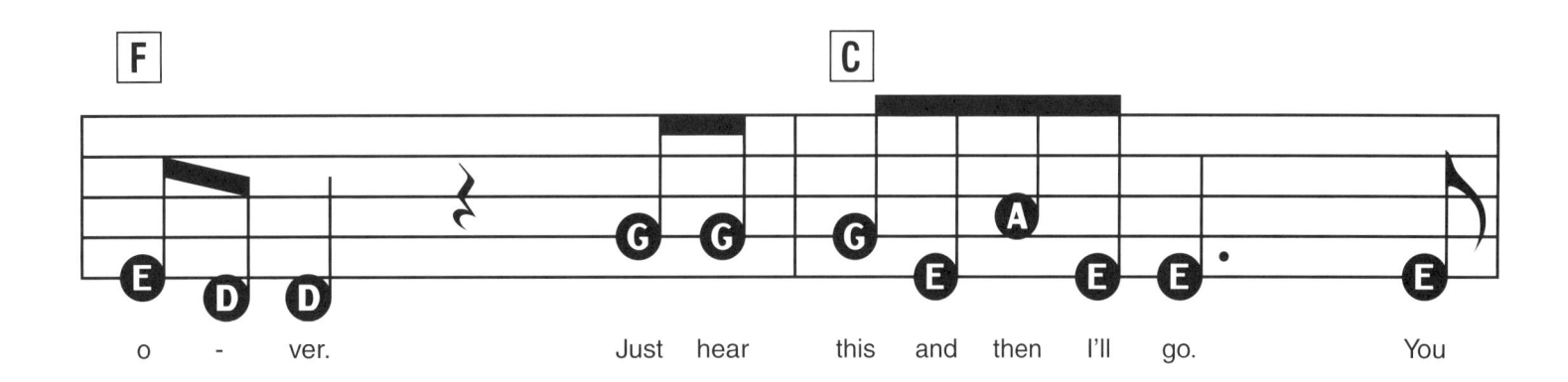

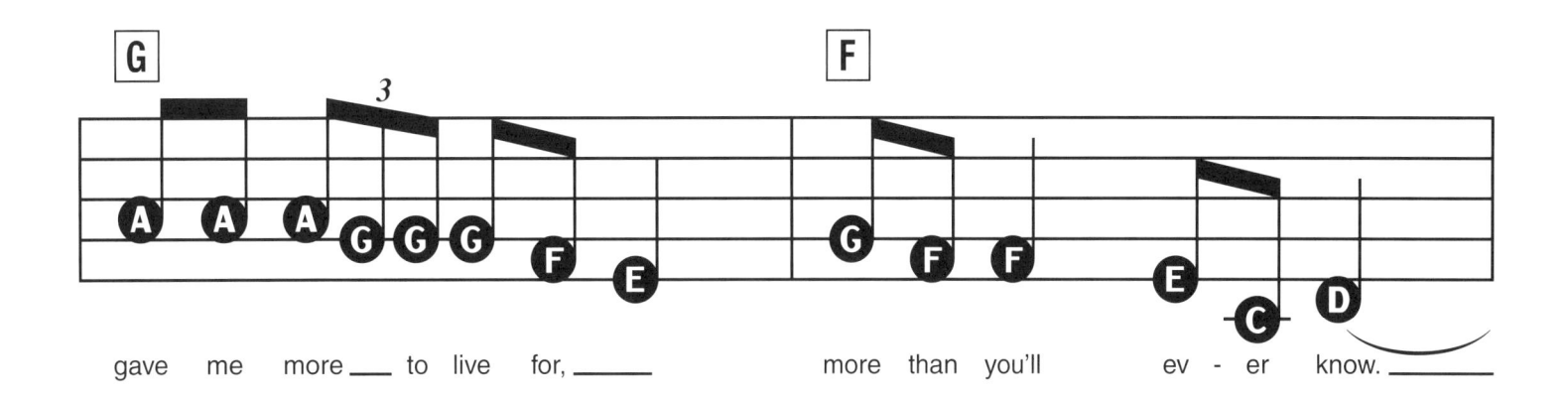

C

G G G G E G E A E

This is our last good-bye. I hate to

Am **G** **Dm**

E D D G D C D D E E

feel the love be-tween us die, but it's

F **C**

E D D G G G A E E E E

o-ver. Just hear this and then I'll go. You

G **F**

A A A G G G F E G F F E C D

gave me more to live for, more than you'll ev-er know.

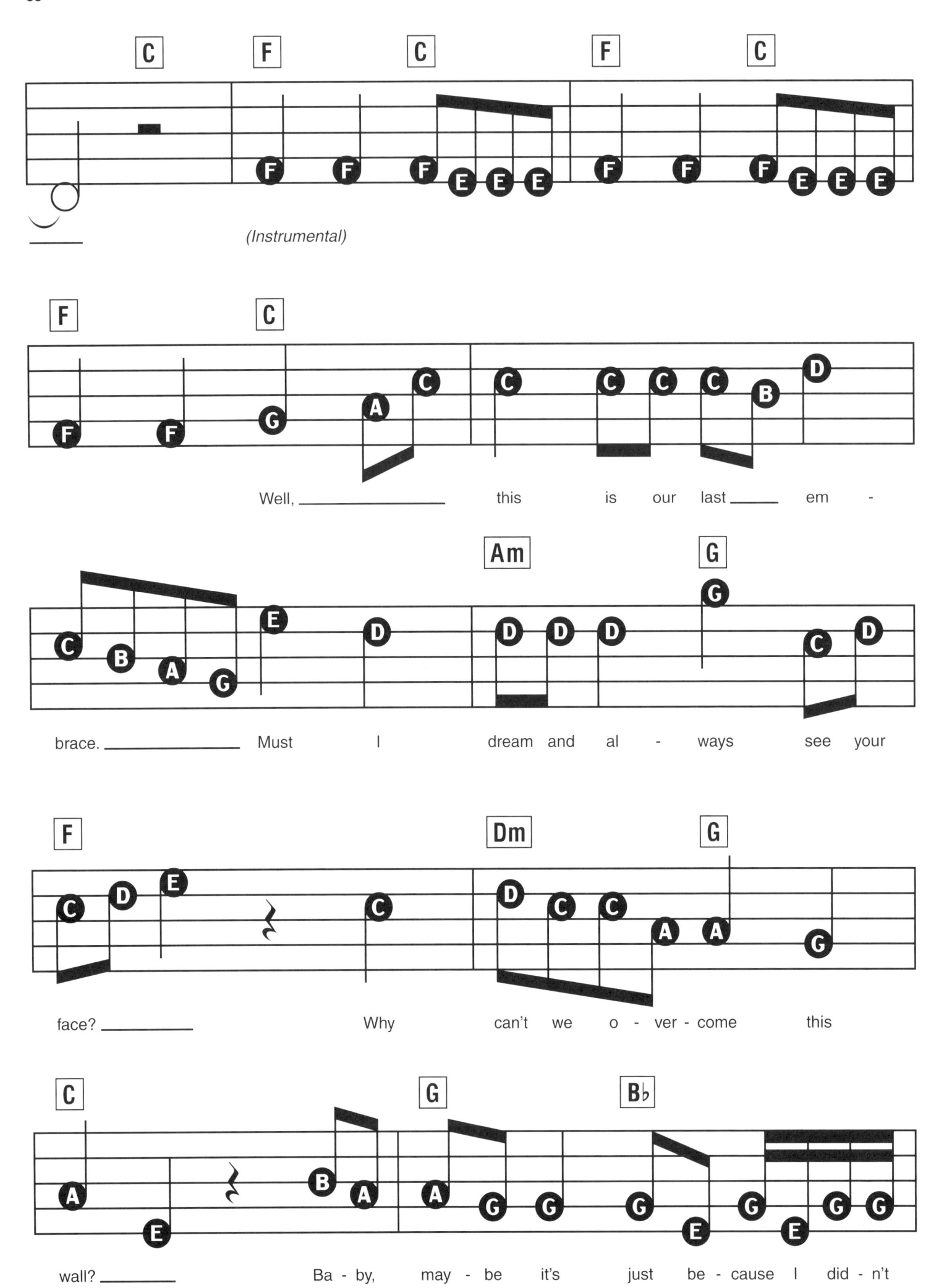

(Instrumental)

Well, this is our last em-brace. Must I dream and al-ways see your face? Why can't we o-ver-come this wall? Ba-by, may-be it's just be-cause I did-n't know you at all. _____ Kiss me, please kiss _____ me. _____ Kiss me out of de-sire, ba-by, no con-so-la-tion. Oh, you know it makes me so an-gry, 'cause I know that in time, I'll on-ly make you cry. _____ This is our last good-bye. Oh, did you say,

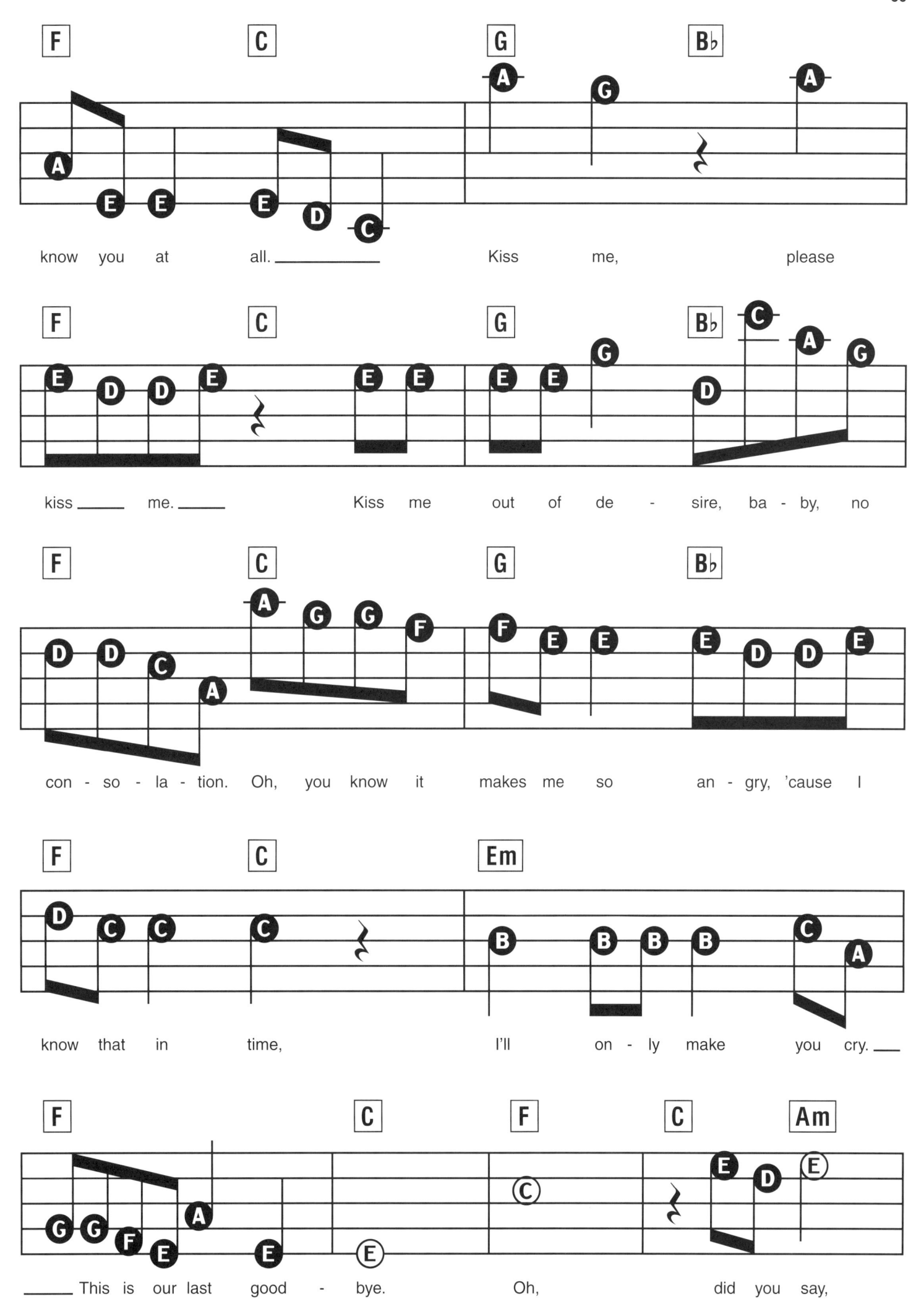

90

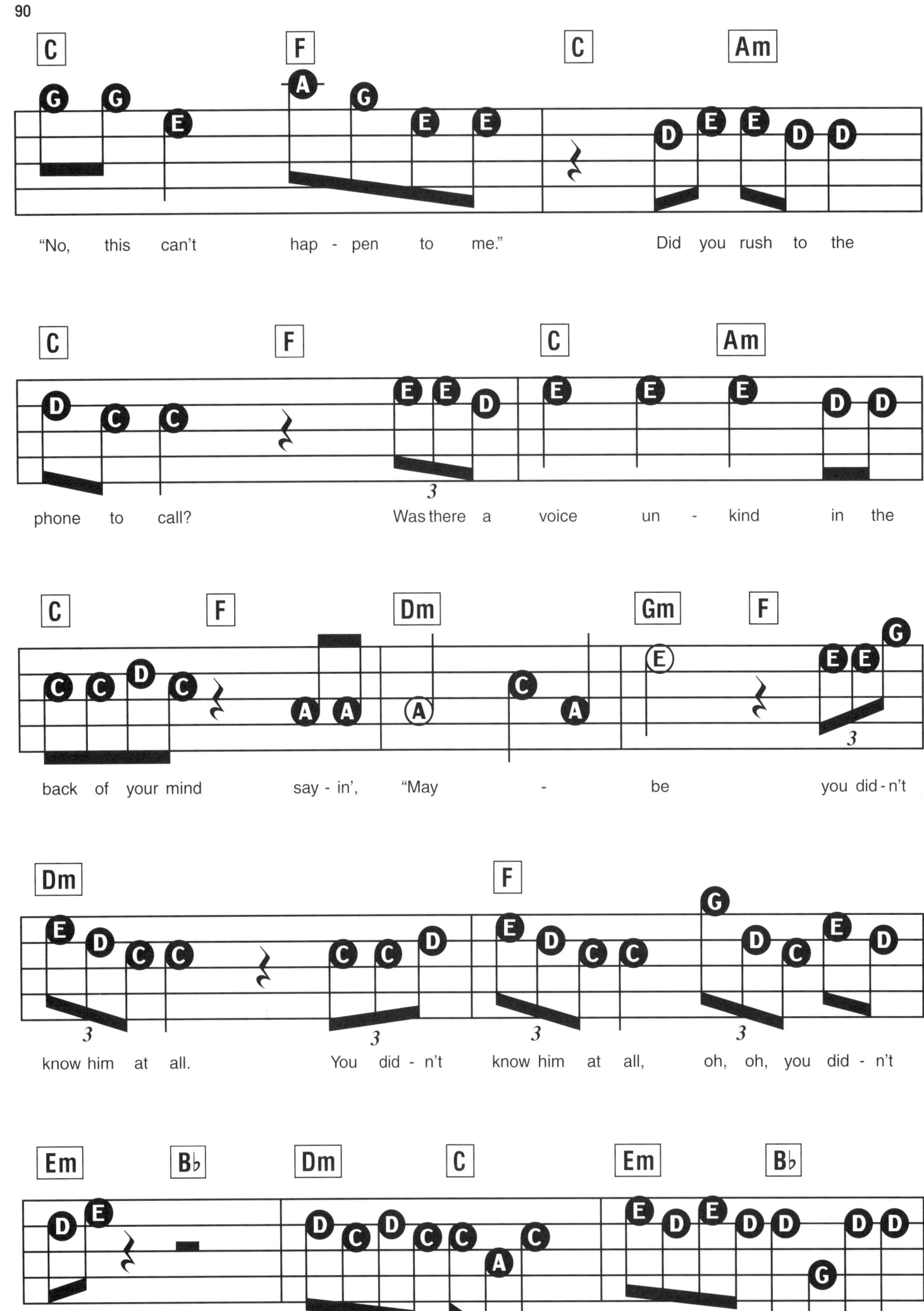

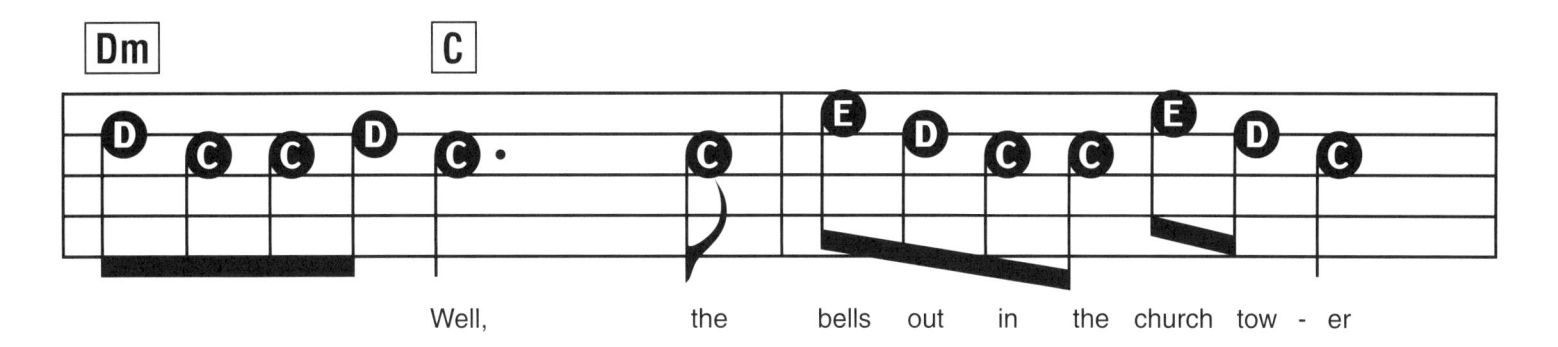

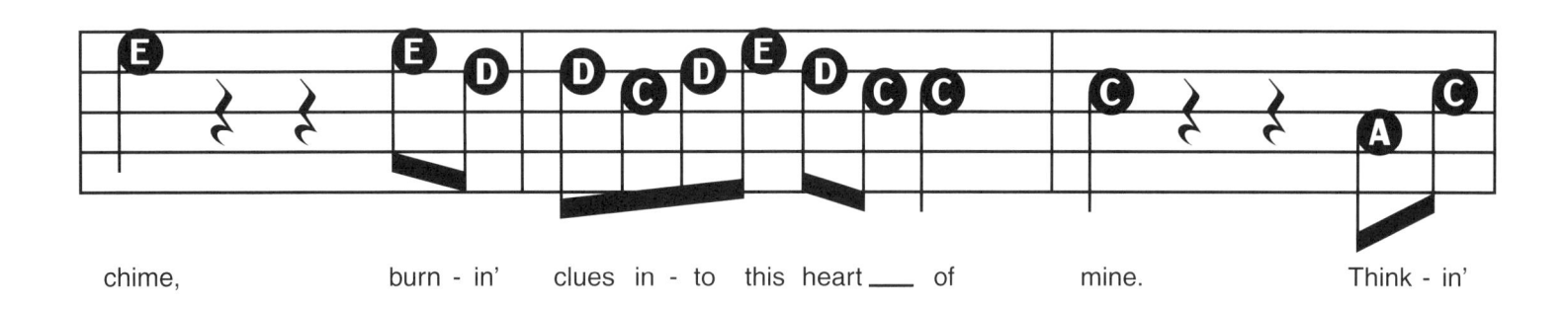

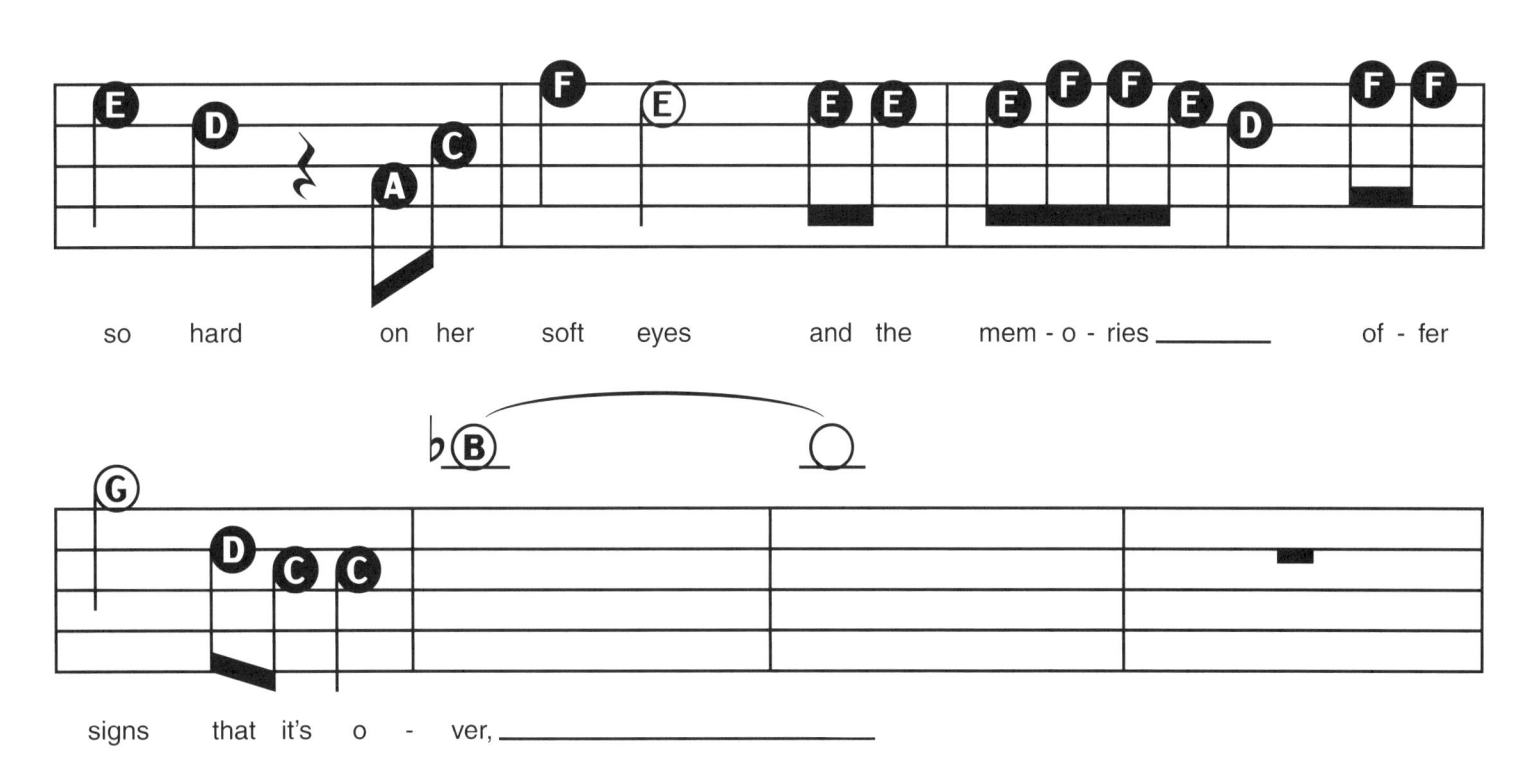

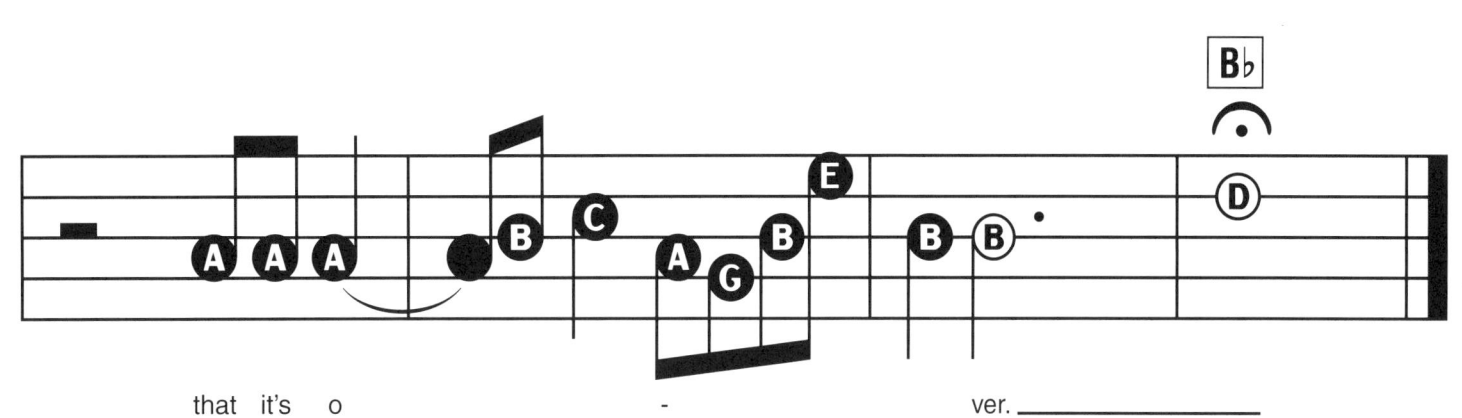

Well, the bells out in the church tow-er chime, burn-in' clues in-to this heart of mine. Think-in' so hard on her soft eyes and the mem-o-ries of-fer signs that it's o-ver, that it's o - ver.

I'll Have to Say I Love You in a Song

Registration 2
Rhythm: Slow Rock or Ballad

Words and Music by
Jim Croce

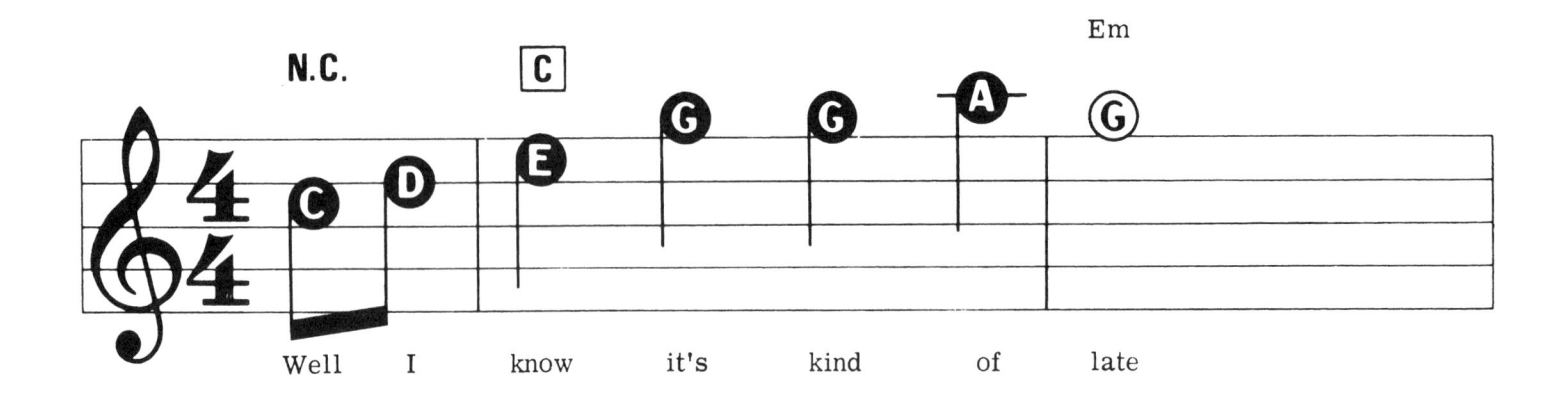

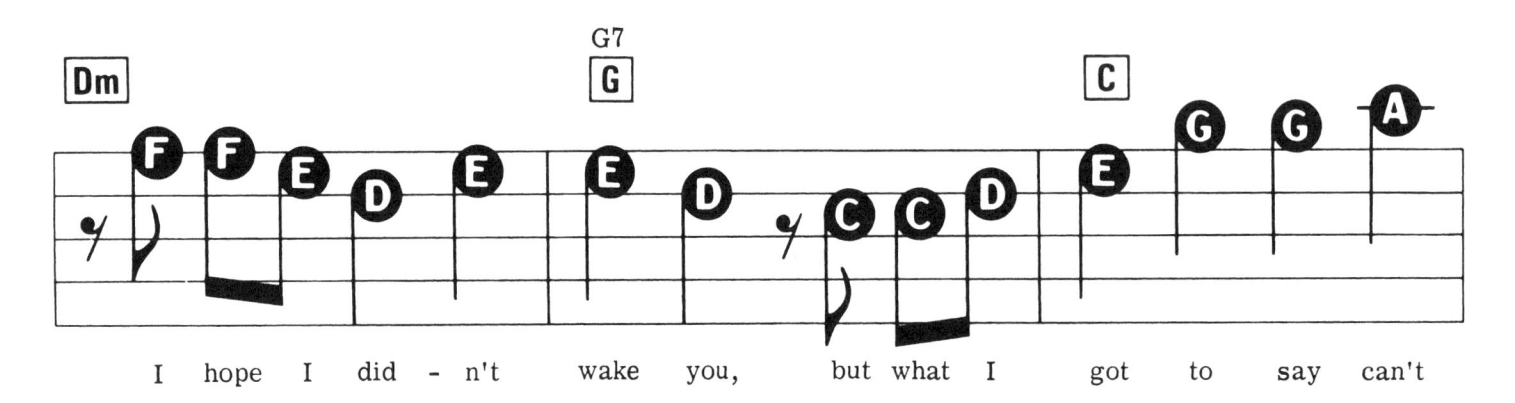

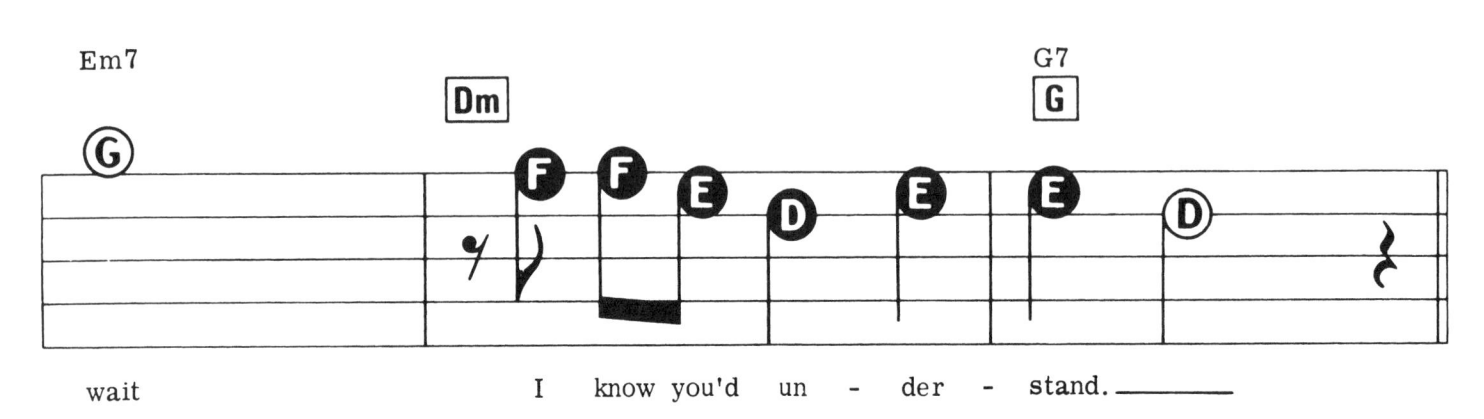

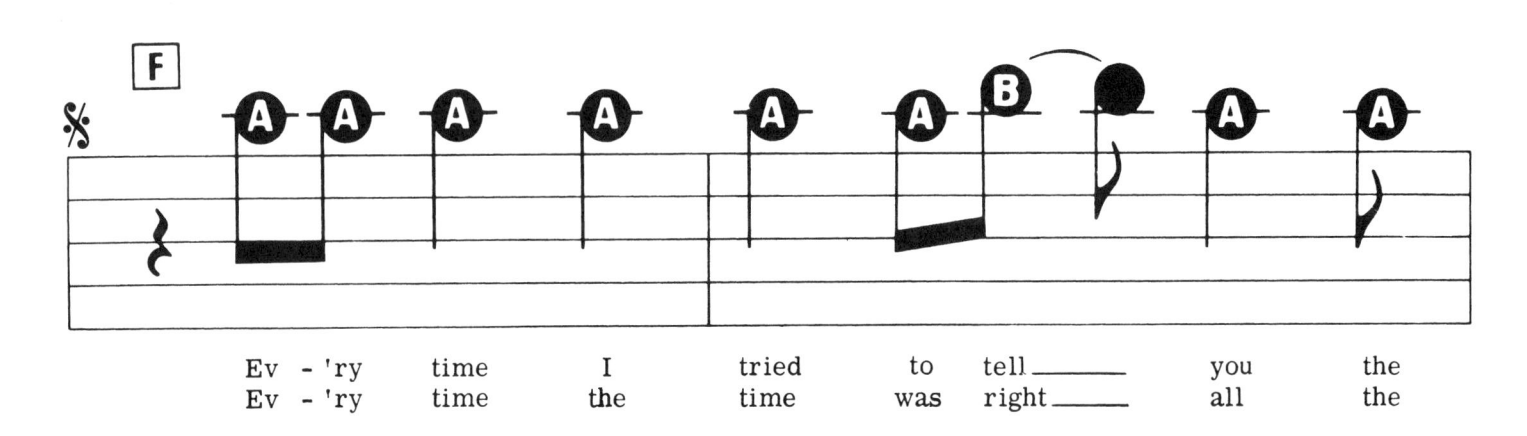

N.C. | **C** | **Em**

C D E G G A G

Well I know it's kind of late

Dm | **G7 / G** | **C**

F F E D E D C C D E G G A

I hope I did-n't wake you, but what I got to say can't

Em7 | **Dm** | **G7 / G**

G F F E D E E D

wait I know you'd un-der-stand.___

𝄋 F

A A A A A A B ● A A

Ev - 'ry time I tried to tell___ you the
Ev - 'ry time the time was right___ all the

© 1973 (Renewed 2001) TIME IN A BOTTLE PUBLISHING and CROCE PUBLISHING
All Rights Controlled and Administered by EMI APRIL MUSIC INC.
All Rights Reserved   International Copyright Secured   Used by Permission

words just came out wrong,
words just came out wrong⎱ So I'll have to say I love you in a song. ____ Yeah, I know it's kind of late I hope I didn't wake you, But there's some-thin' that I just got to say I know you'd un-der-stand. ____ song. ____

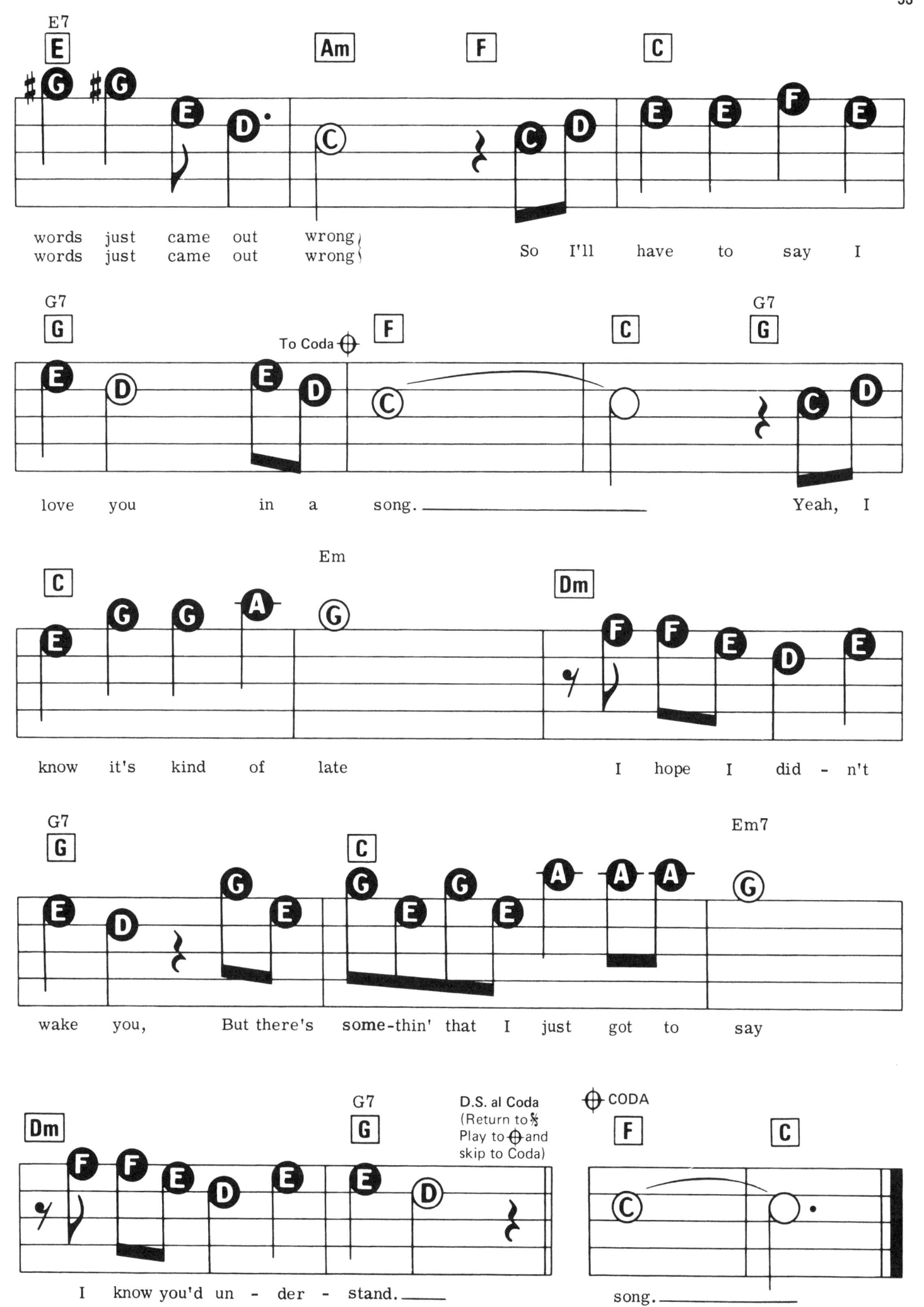

If I Were a Carpenter

Registration 3
Rhythm: Country

Words and Music by
Tim Hardin

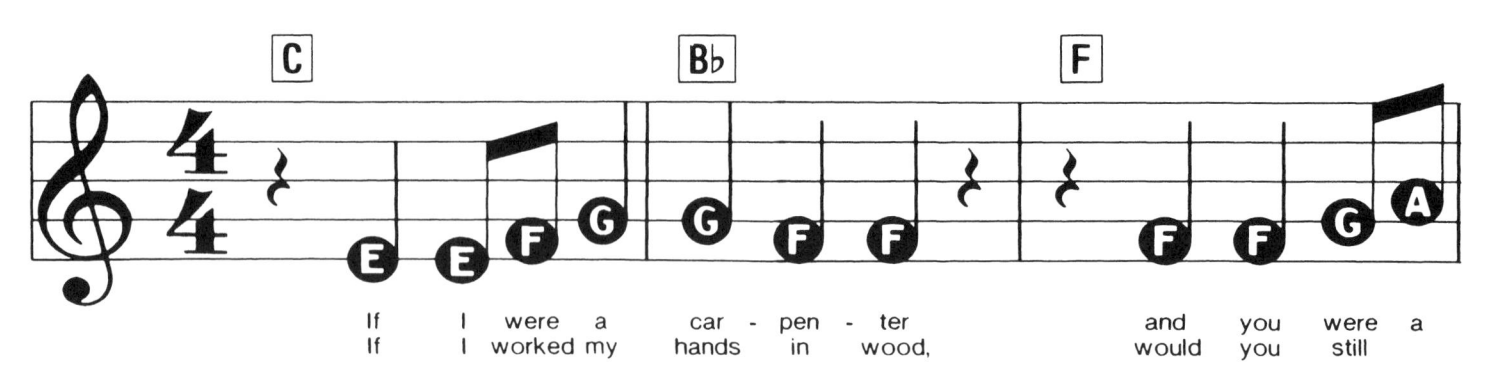

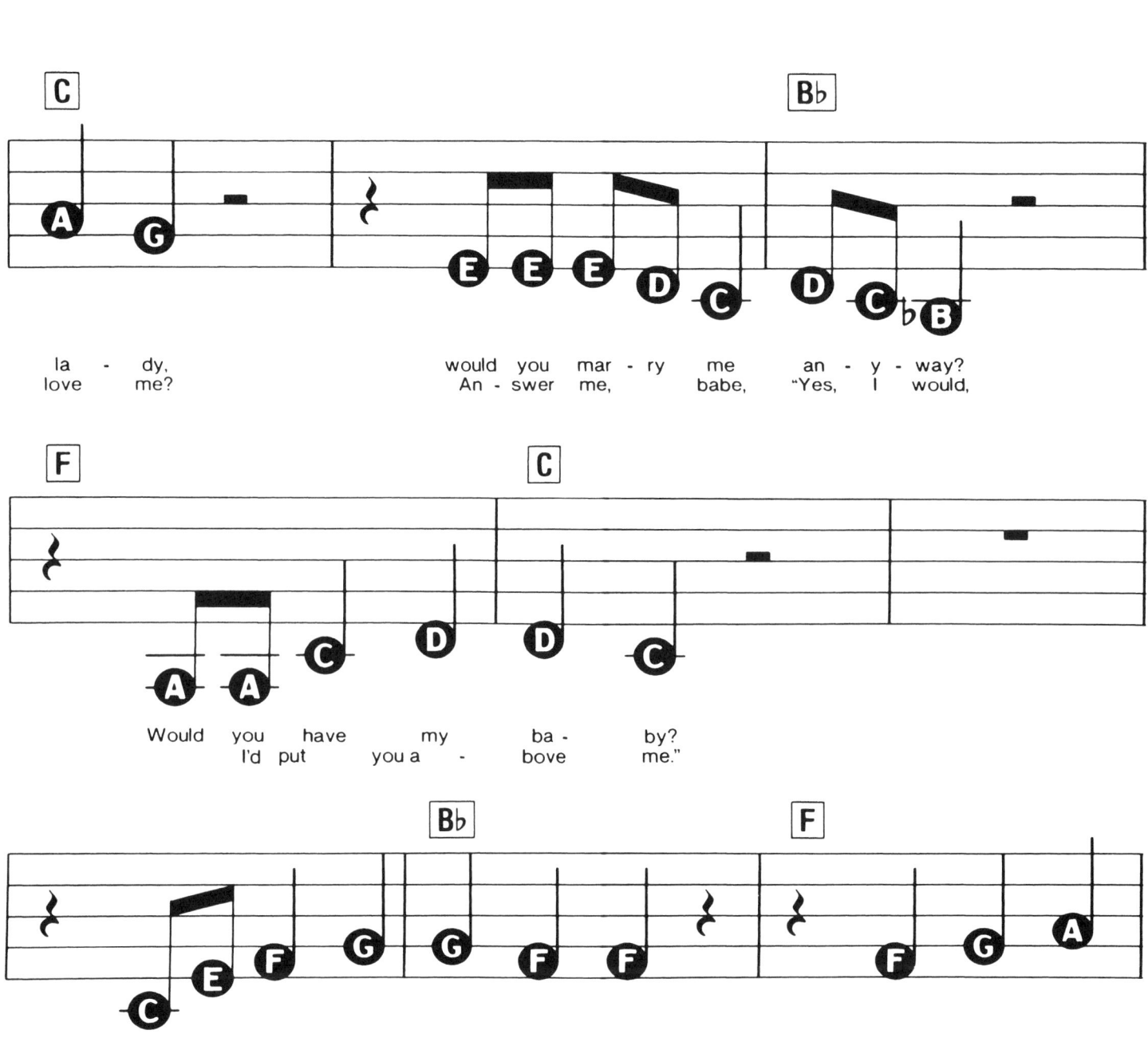

If I were a car-pen-ter, and you were a la-dy, would you mar-ry me an-y-way? Would you have my ba-by?

If I worked my hands in wood, would you still love me? An-swer me, babe, "Yes, I would, I'd put you a-bove me."

If a tin-ker were my trade, would you still
If I were a mil-ler, at a mill wheel

Copyright © 1966 (Renewed) Allen Stanton Productions
International Copyright Secured   All Rights Reserved
Used by Permission

95

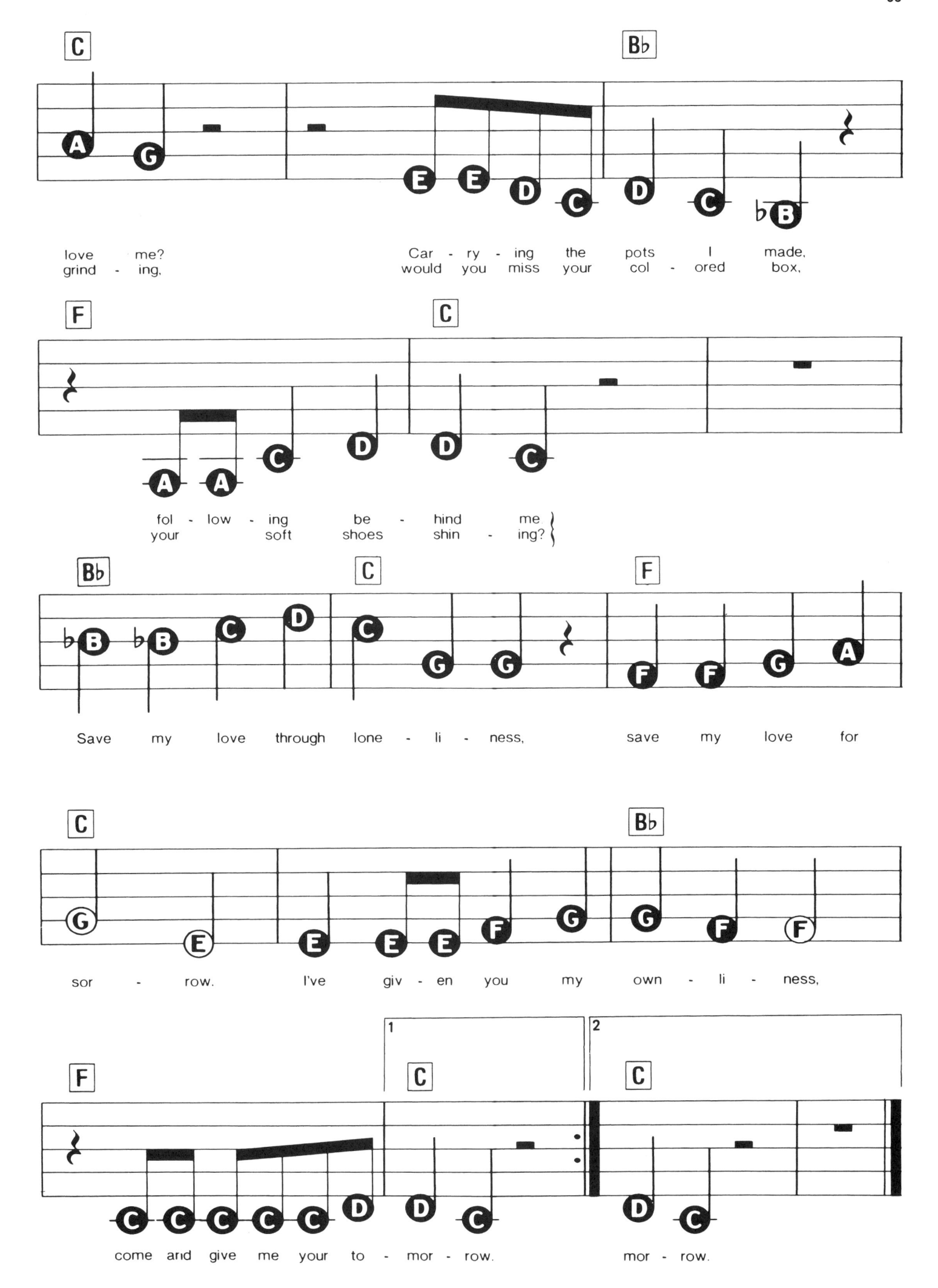

love me? / grind - ing,
Car - ry - ing the pots I made, / would you miss your col - ored box,

fol - low - ing be - hind me / your soft shoes shin - ing?

Save my love through lone - li - ness, save my love for

sor - row. I've giv - en you my own - li - ness,

come and give me your to - mor - row.

mor - row.

Leaving on a Jet Plane

Registration 1
Rhythm: Rock or Slow Rock

Words and Music by
John Denver

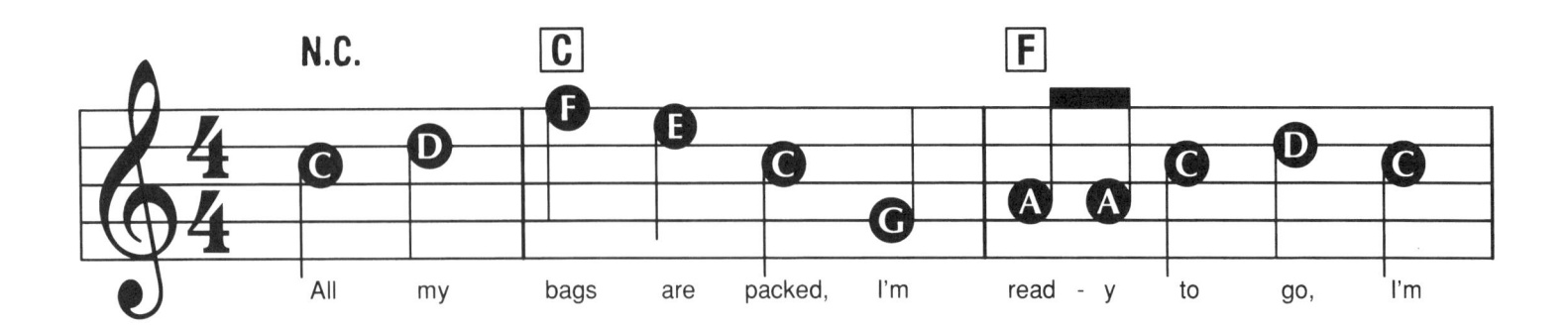

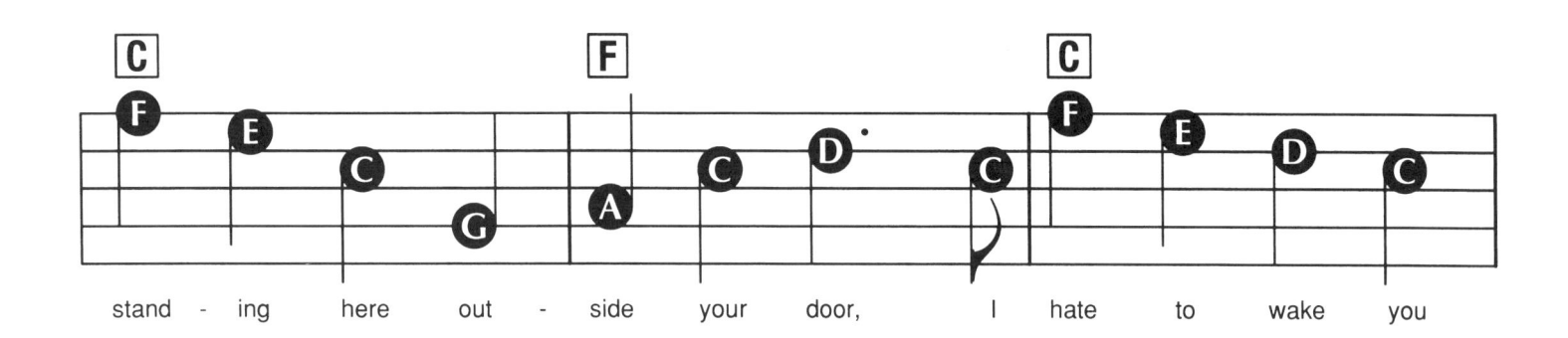

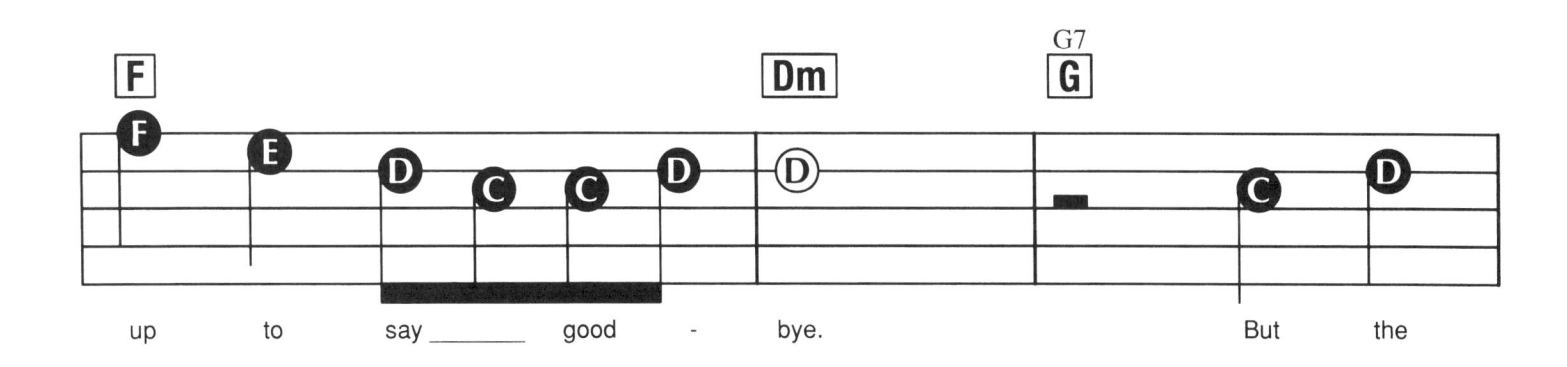

All my bags are packed, I'm ready to go, I'm standing here outside your door, I hate to wake you up to say _____ good - bye. But the

Copyright © 1967; Henewed 1995 Cherry Lane Music Publishing Company, Inc. (ASCAP), FSMGI (IMRO) and State One Songs America (ASCAP)
All Rights Controlled and Administered jointly by Cherry Lane Music Publishing Company, Inc. and State One Songs America (ASCAP)
International Copyright Secured   All Rights Reserved

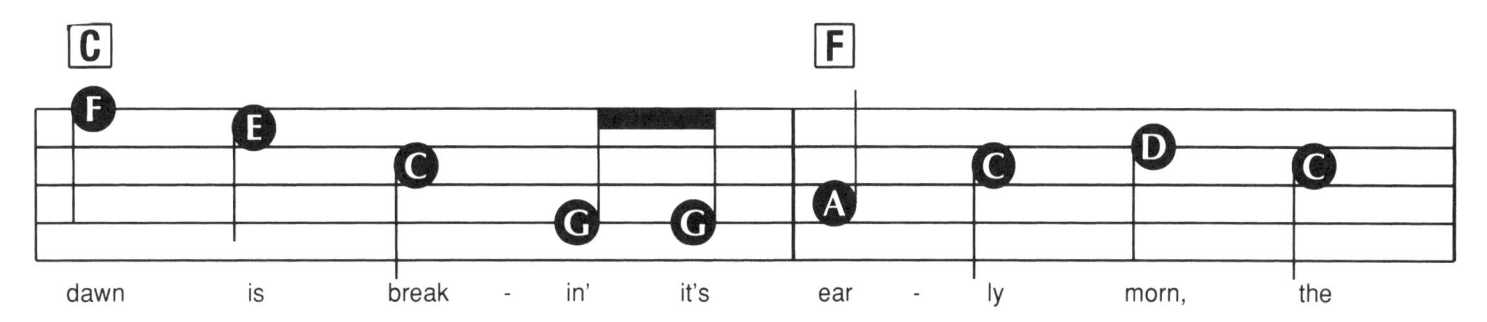

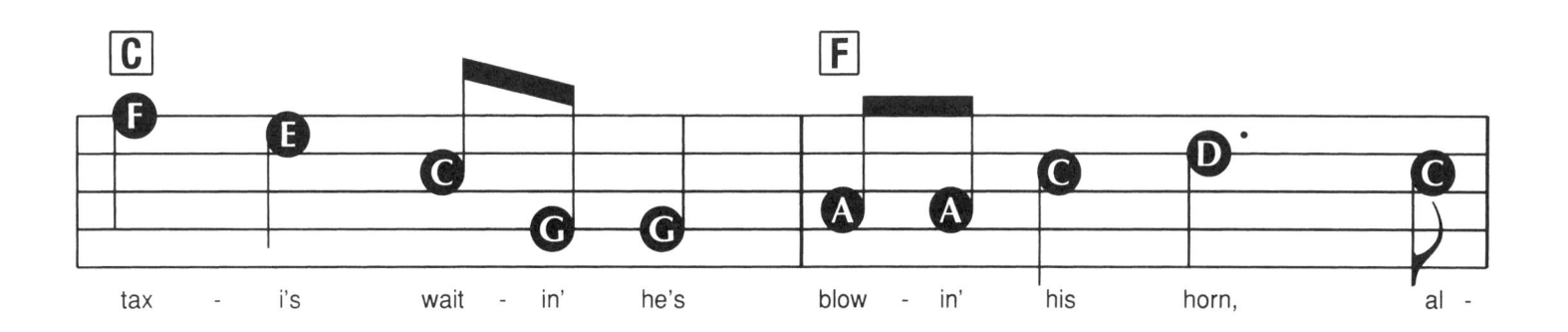

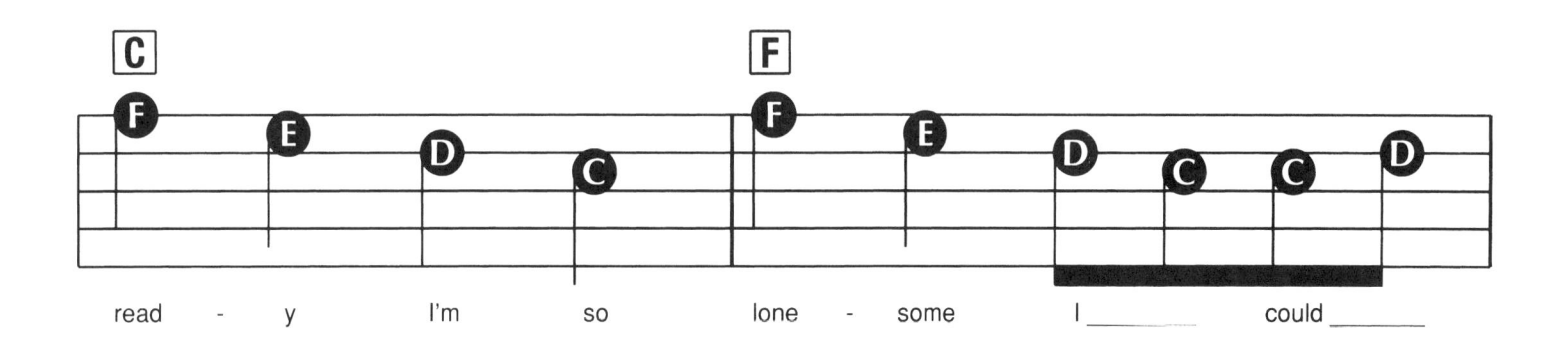

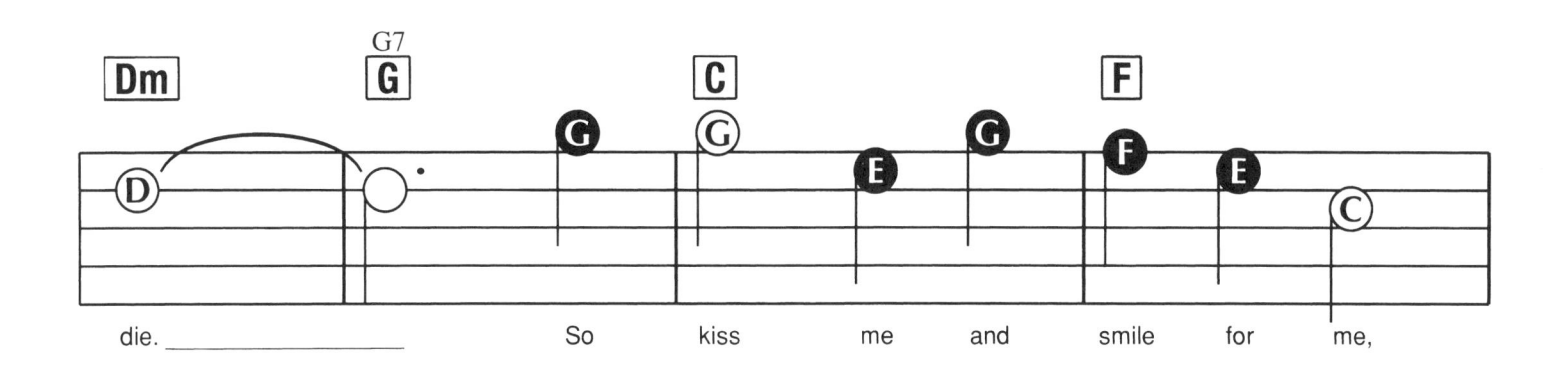

dawn is break - in' it's ear - ly morn, the tax - i's wait - in' he's blow - in' his horn, al - read - y I'm so lone - some I could die. So kiss me and smile for me,

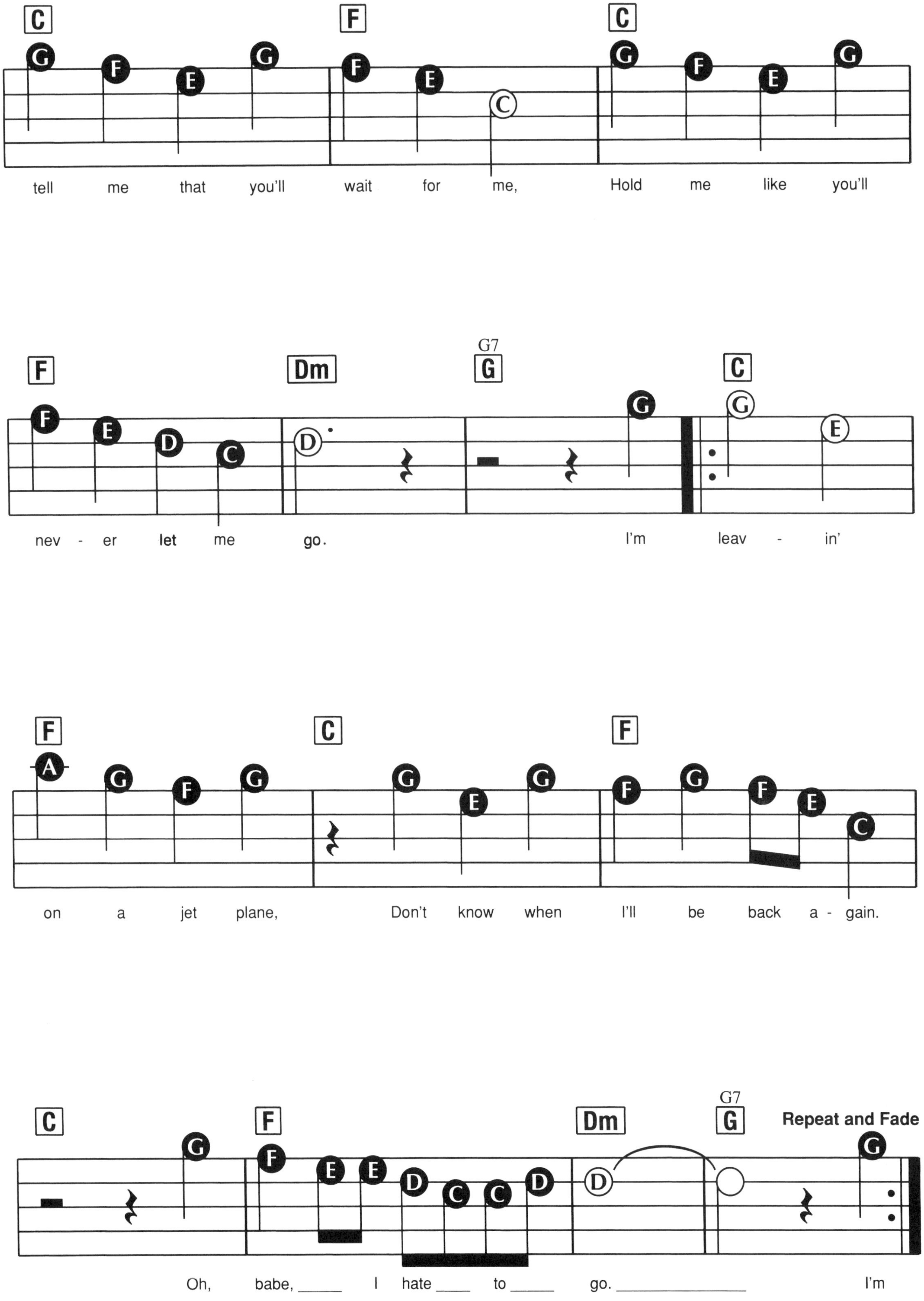
C F C
tell me that you'll wait for me, Hold me like you'll
F Dm G7 G C
nev - er let me go. I'm leav - in'
F C F
on a jet plane, Don't know when I'll be back a - gain.
C F Dm G7 G
Repeat and Fade
Oh, babe, I hate to go. I'm

Lemon Tree

Registration 5
Rhythm: Calypso or Fox Trot

Words and Music by
Will Holt

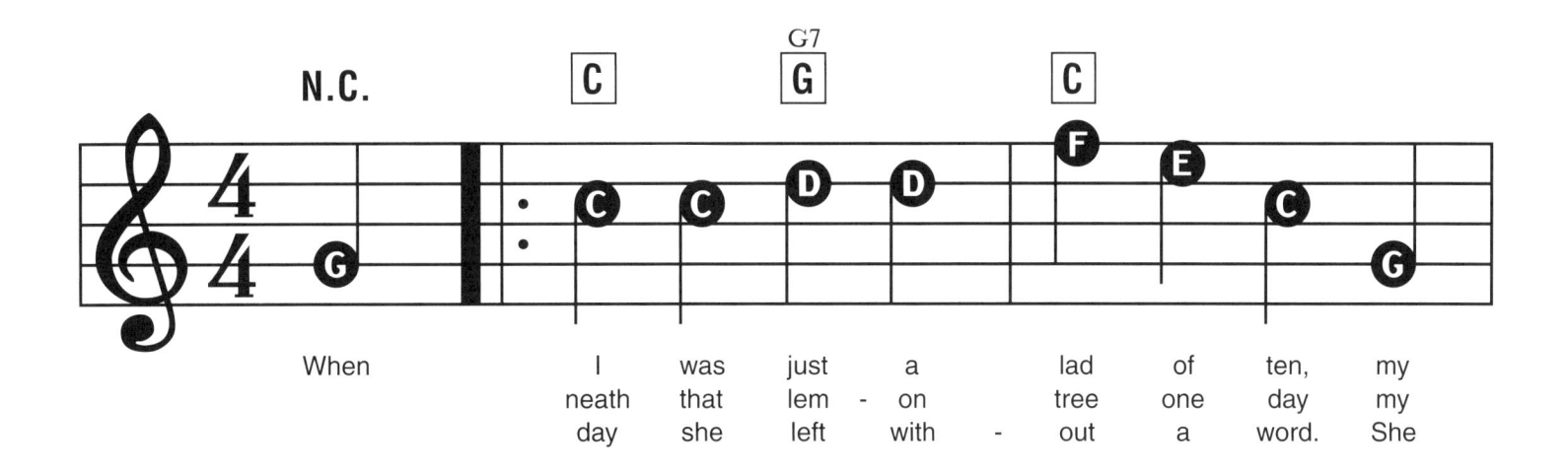

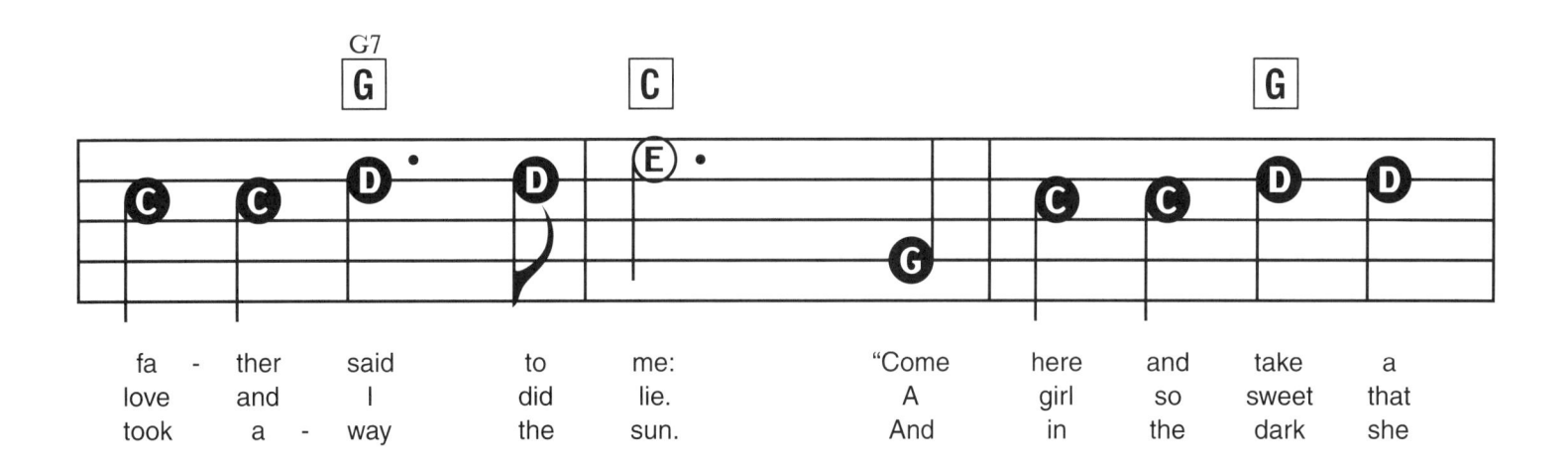

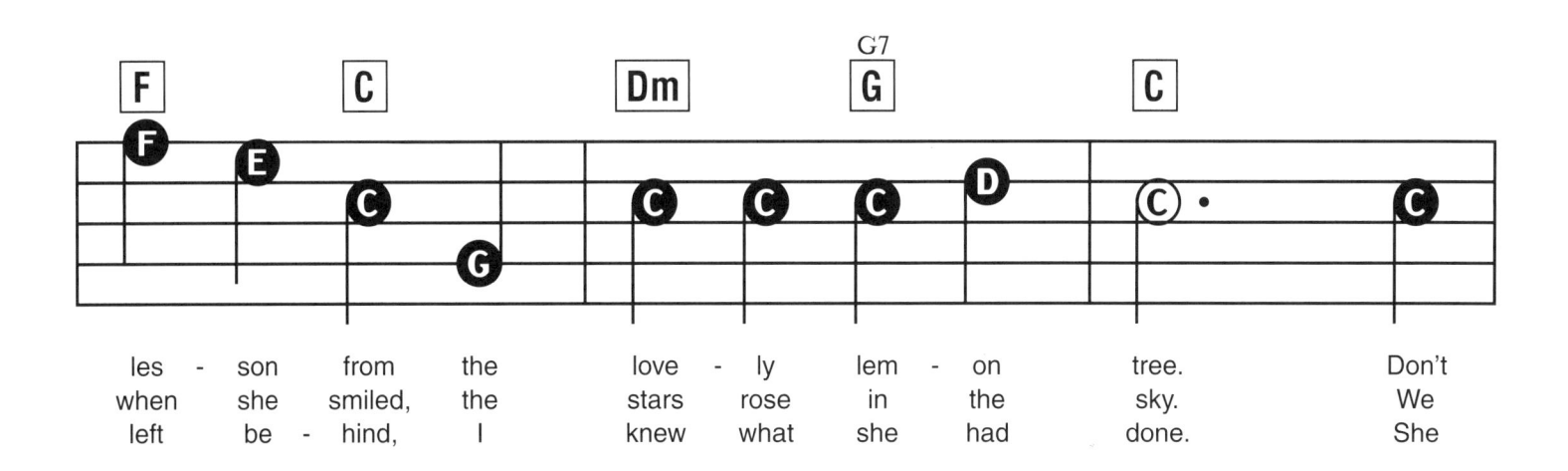

When I was just a lad of ten, my
neath that lem - on tree one day my
day she left with - out a word. She

fa - ther said to me: "Come here and take a
love and I did lie. A girl so sweet that
took a - way the sun. And in the dark she

les - son from the love - ly lem - on tree. Don't
when she smiled, the stars rose in the sky. We
left be - hind, I knew what she had done. She

Copyright © 1960 (Renewed) by Wise Brothers Music, LLC (ASCAP)
International Copyright Secured All Rights Reserved
Reprinted by Permission

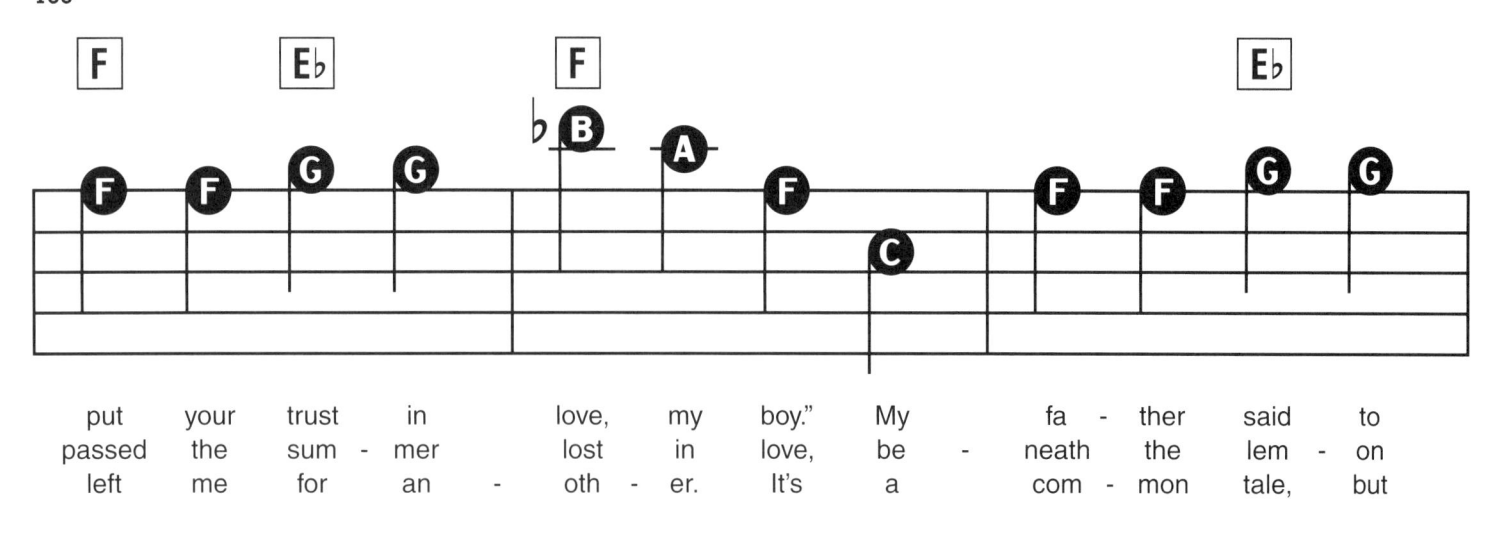

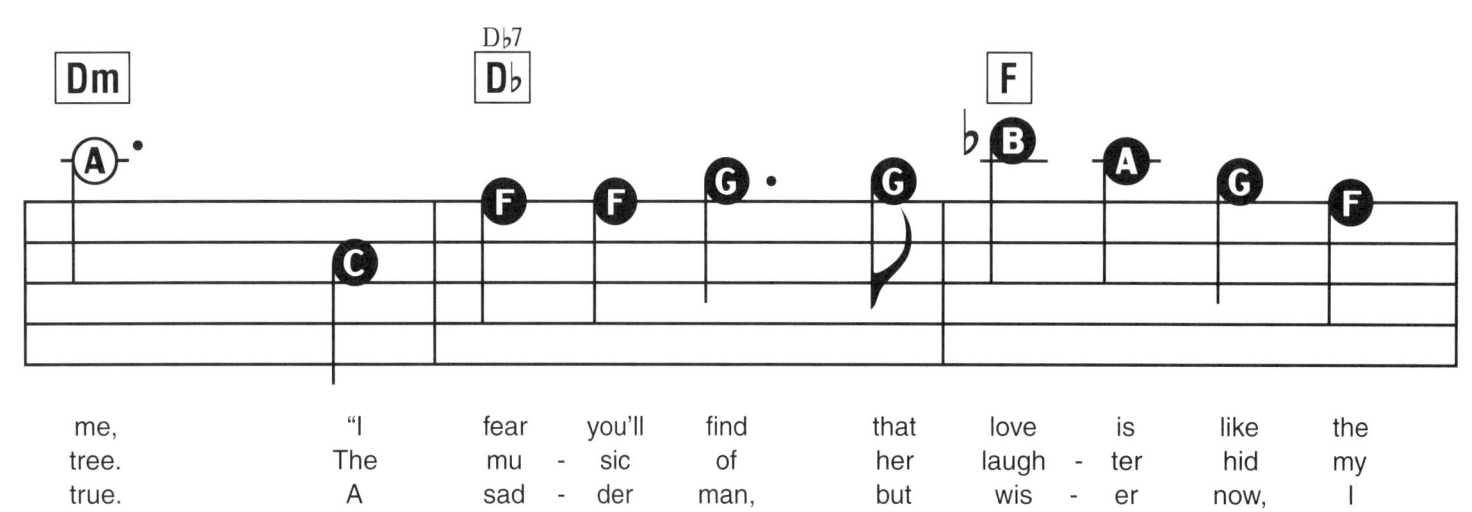

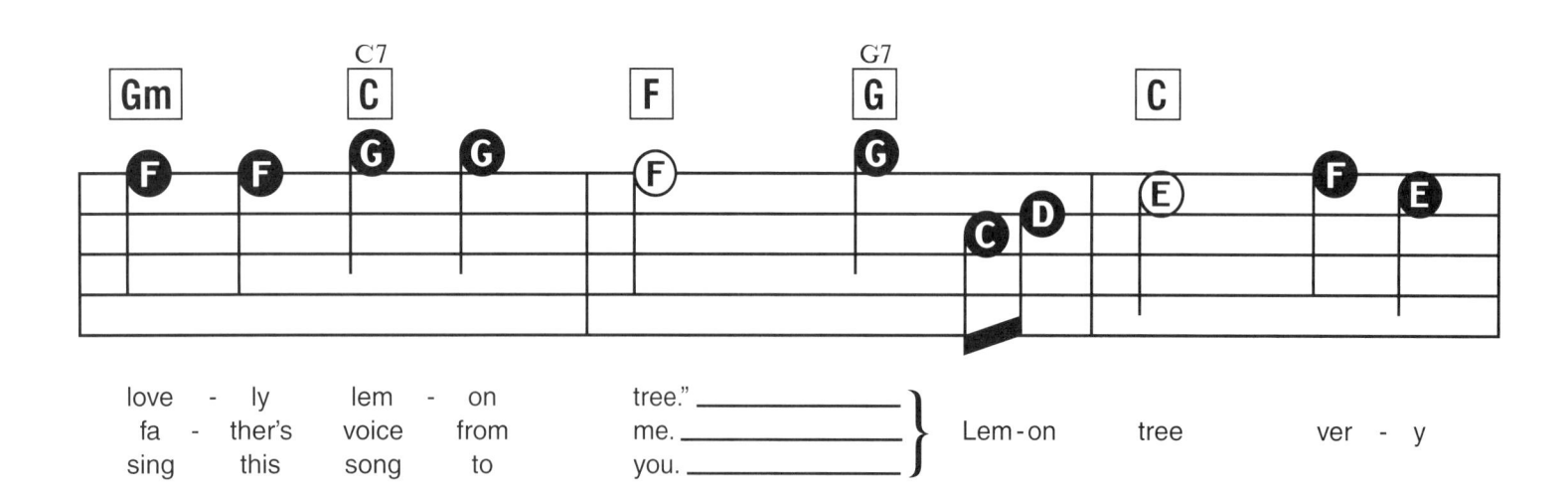

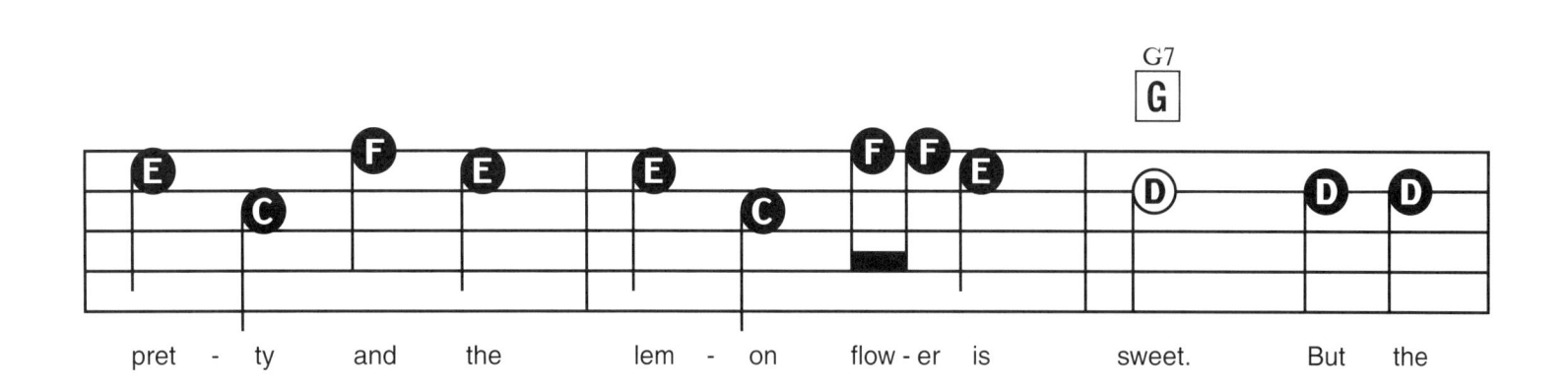

put your trust in love, my boy." My fa - ther said to
passed the sum - mer lost in love, be - neath the lem - on
left me for an - oth - er. It's a com - mon tale, but

me, "I fear you'll find that love is like the
tree. The mu - sic of her laugh - ter hid my
true. A sad - der man, but wis - er now, I

love - ly lem - on tree."
fa - ther's voice from me.   Lem - on tree ver - y
sing this song to you.

pret - ty and the lem - on flow - er is sweet. But the

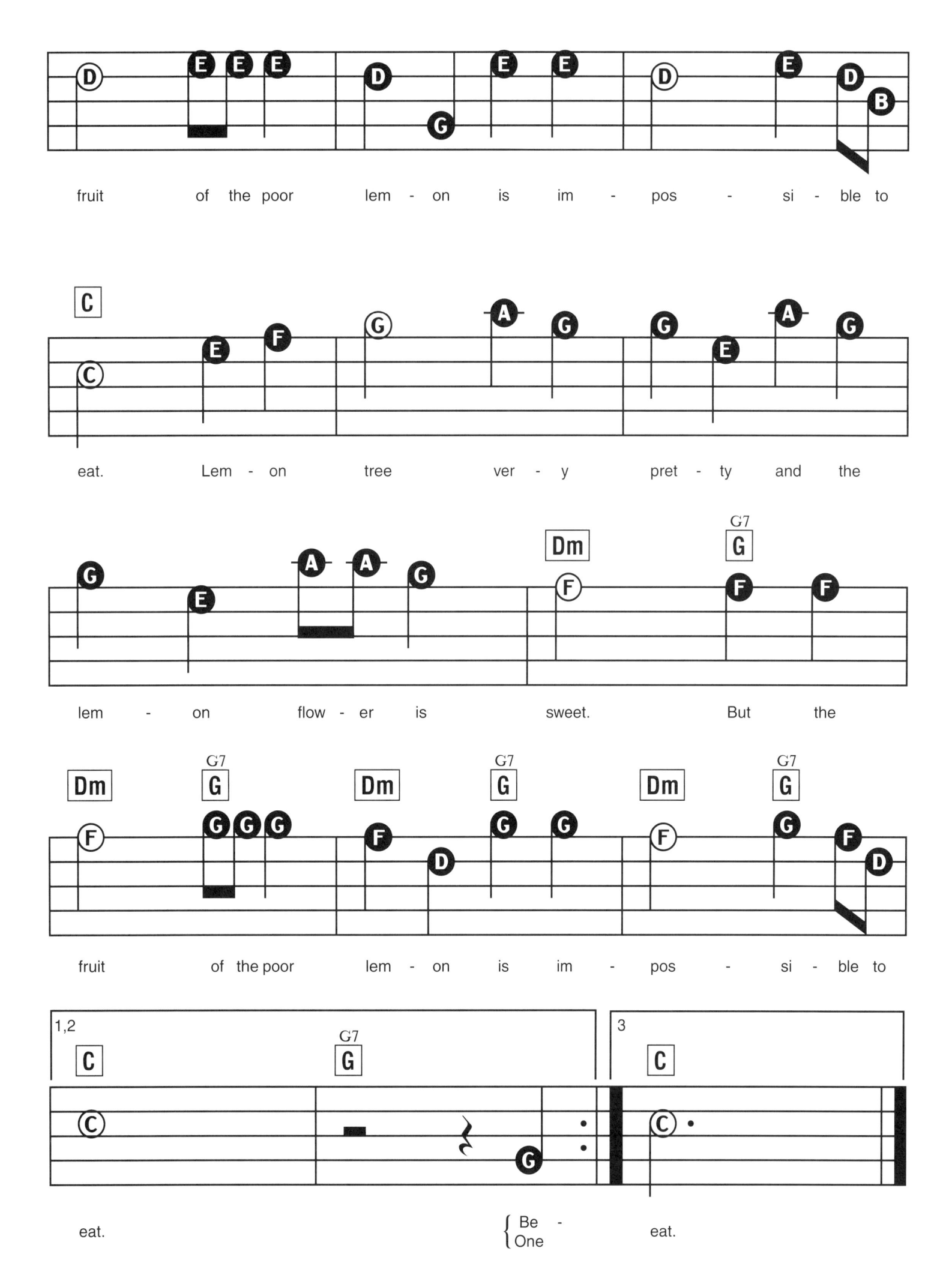

fruit of the poor lem-on is im-pos-si-ble to eat. Lem-on tree ver-y pret-ty and the lem-on flow-er is sweet. But the fruit of the poor lem-on is im-pos-si-ble to eat.

{ Be-
{ One   eat.

Longer

Registration 4
Rhythm: Rock or 8 Beat

Words and Music by
Dan Fogelberg

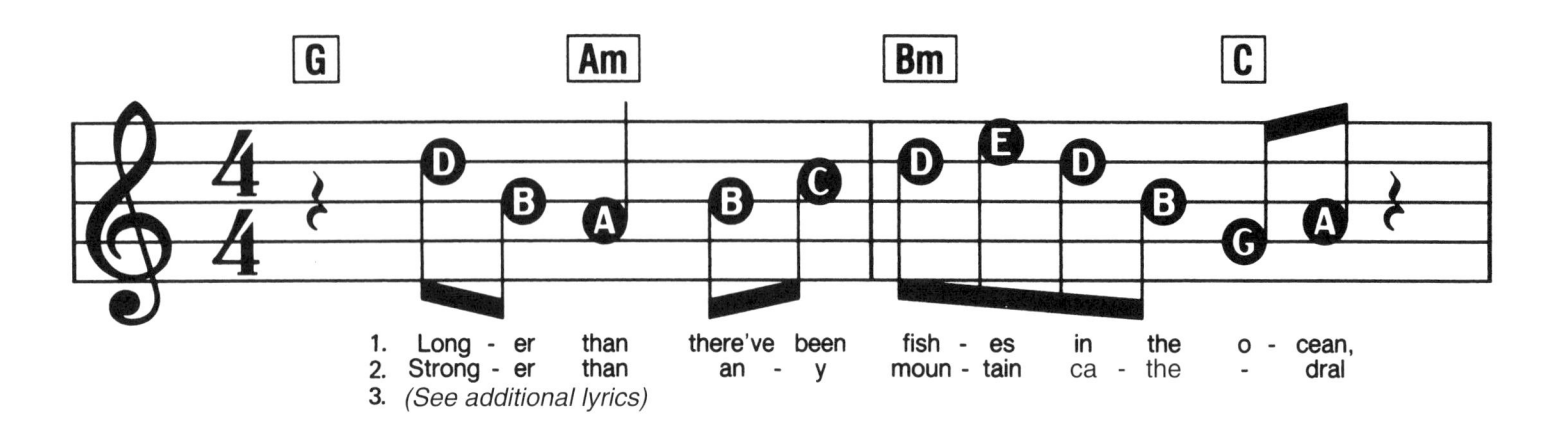

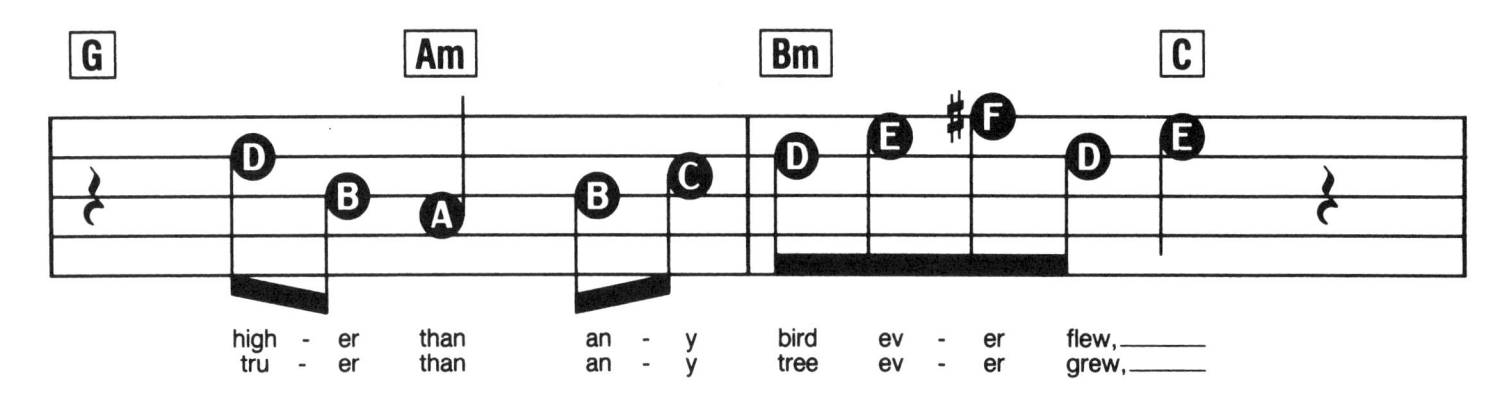

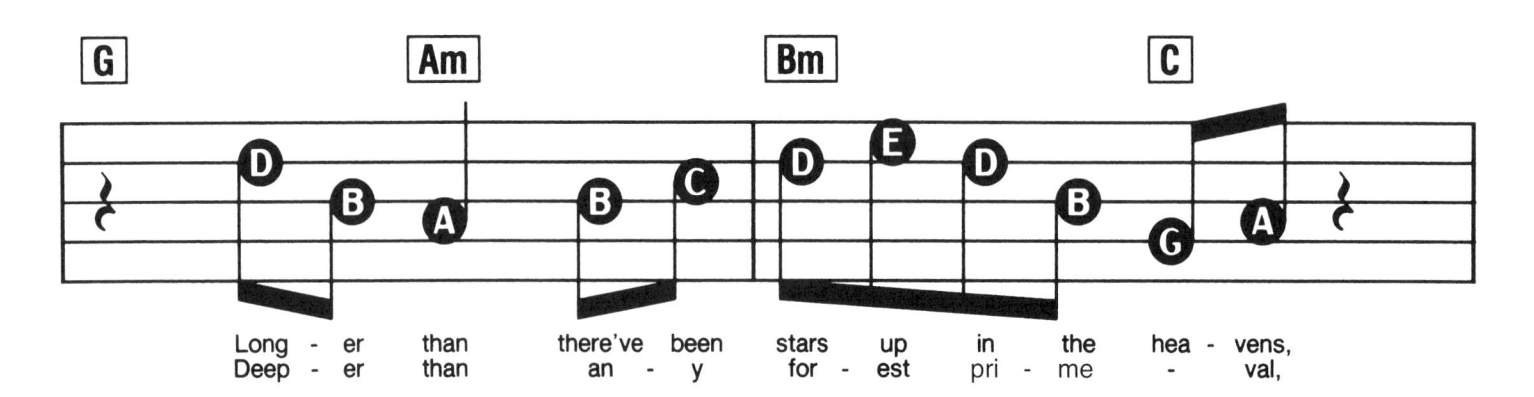

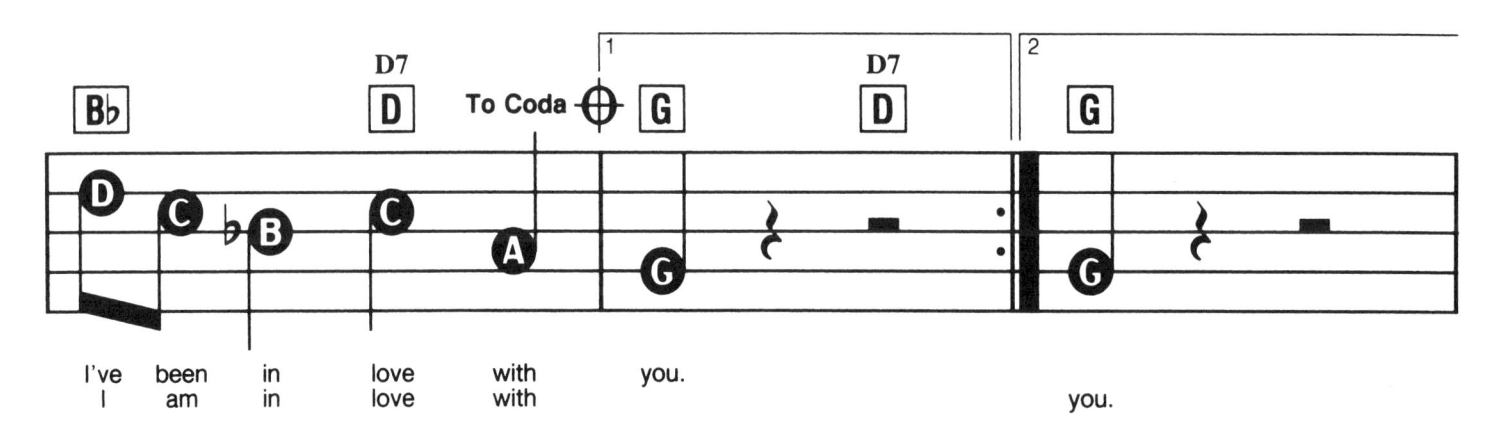

1. Long-er than there've been fish-es in the o-cean,
2. Strong-er than an-y moun-tain ca-the-dral
3. *(See additional lyrics)*

high-er than an-y bird ev-er flew,
tru-er than an-y tree ev-er grew,

Long-er than there've been stars up in the heav-ens,
Deep-er than an-y for-est pri-me-val,

I've been in love with you.
I am in love with you.

© 1979 EMI APRIL MUSIC INC. and HICKORY GROVE MUSIC
All Rights Controlled and Administered by EMI APRIL MUSIC INC.
All Rights Reserved   International Copyright Secured   Used by Permission

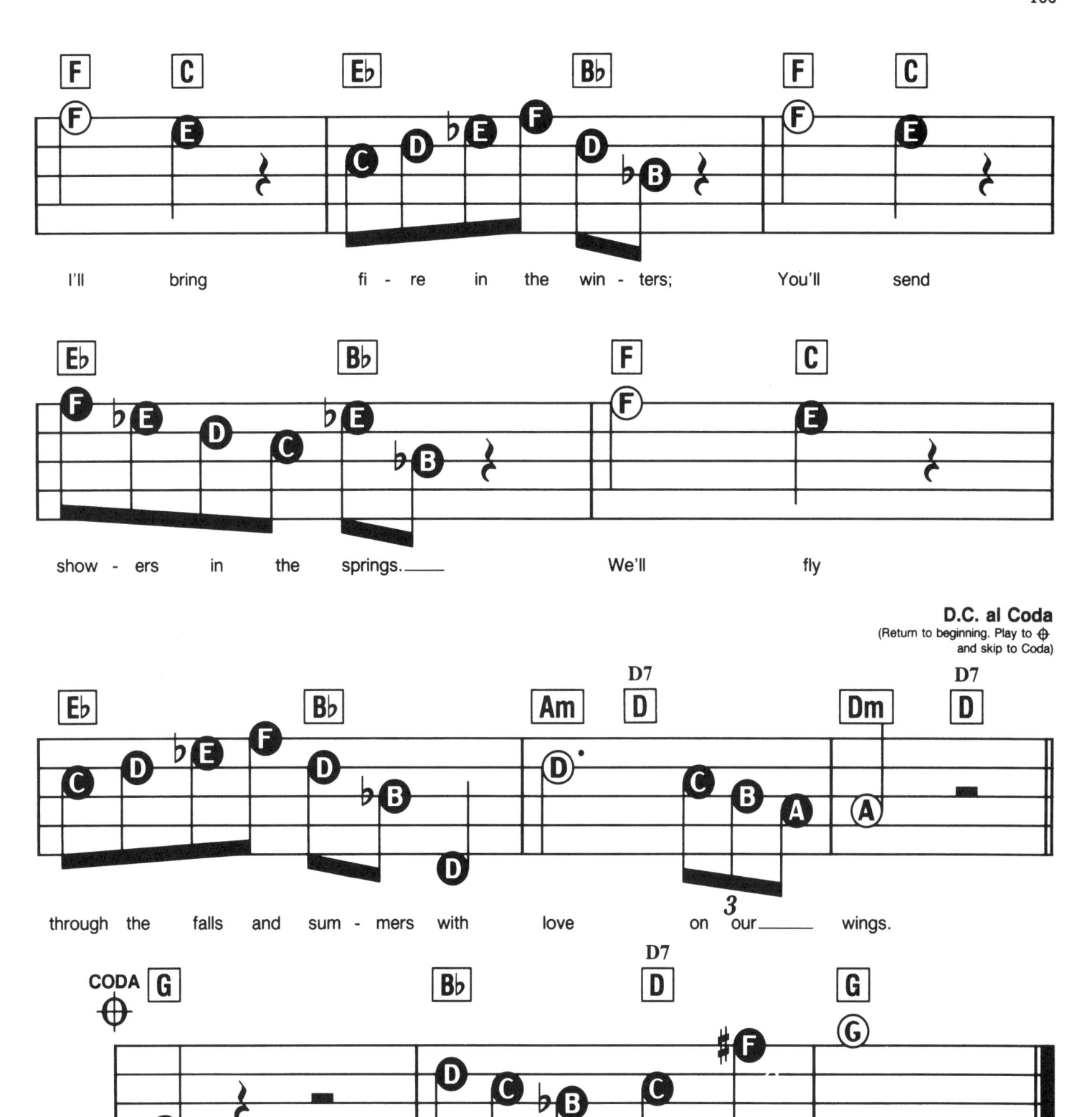

Additional Lyrics

3. Through the years as the fire starts to mellow,
   Burning lines in the book of our lives.
   Though the binding cracks and the pages start to yellow,
   I'll be in love with you.

Love the One You're With

Registration 8
Rhythm: Rock or Folk

Words and Music by
Stephen Stills

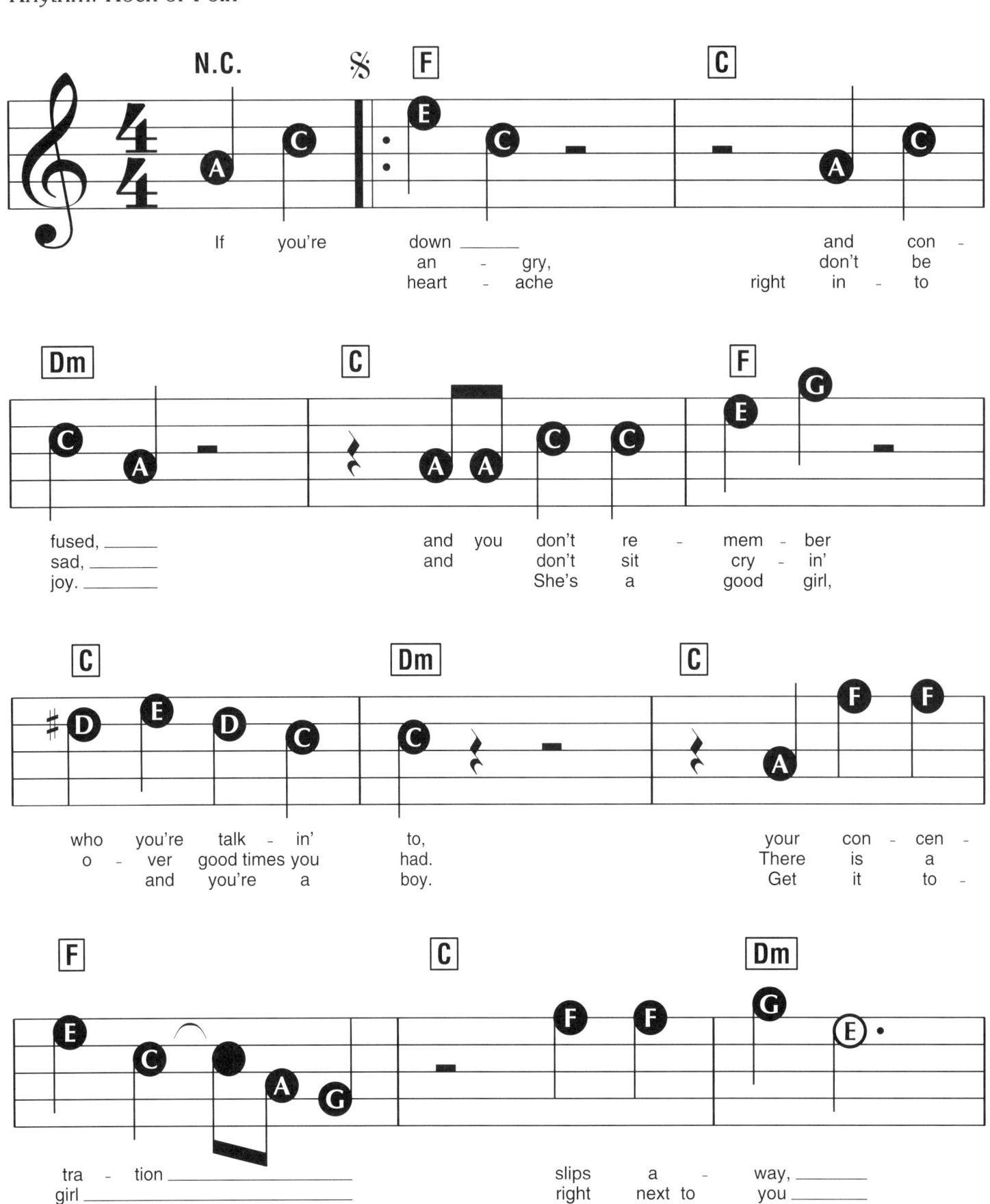

If you're down and con-
an - gry, don't be
heart - ache right in - to

fused, and you don't re - mem - ber
sad, and don't sit cry - in'
joy. She's a good girl,

who you're talk - in' to, your con - cen -
o - ver good times you had. There is a
and you're a boy. Get it to -

tra - tion slips a - way,
girl right next to you
geth - er and make it to - night,

Copyright © 1970 Gold Hill Music, Inc.
Copyright Renewed
International Copyright Secured   All Rights Reserved

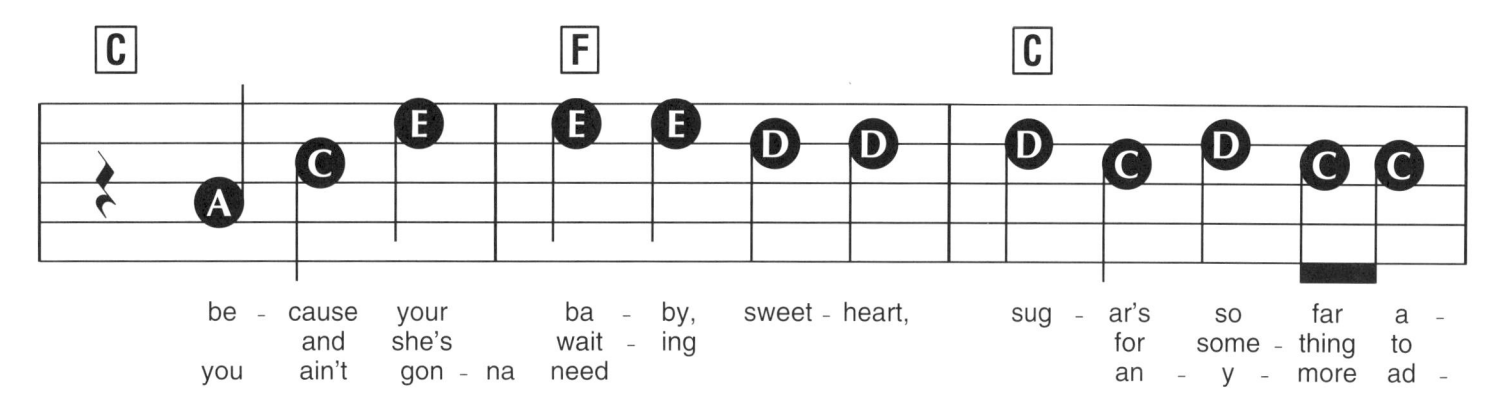

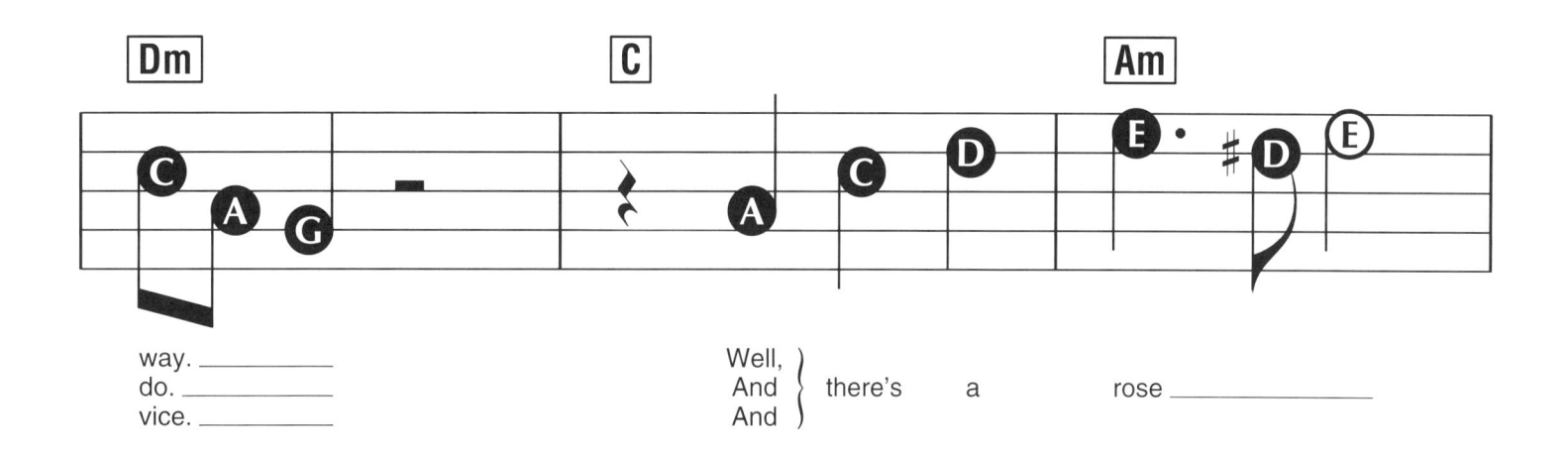

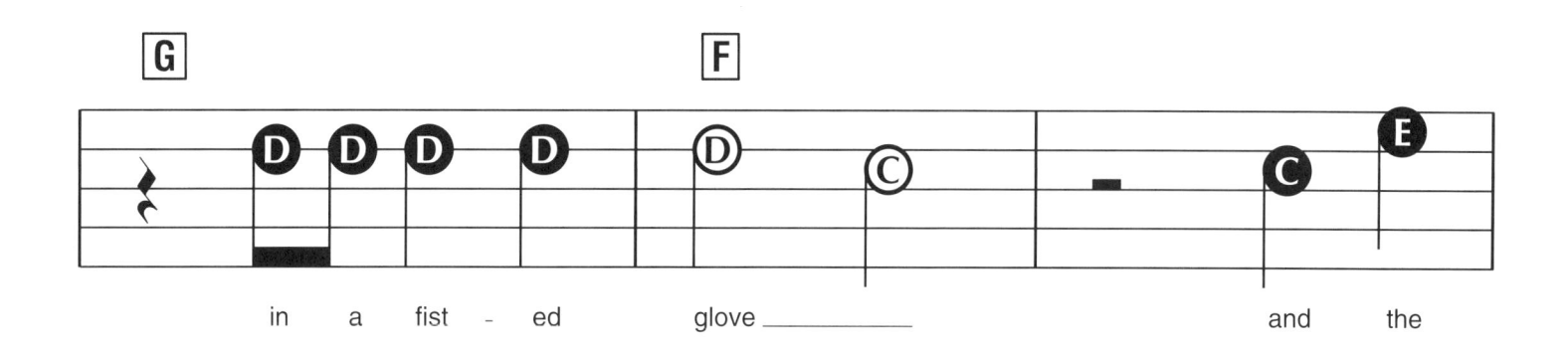

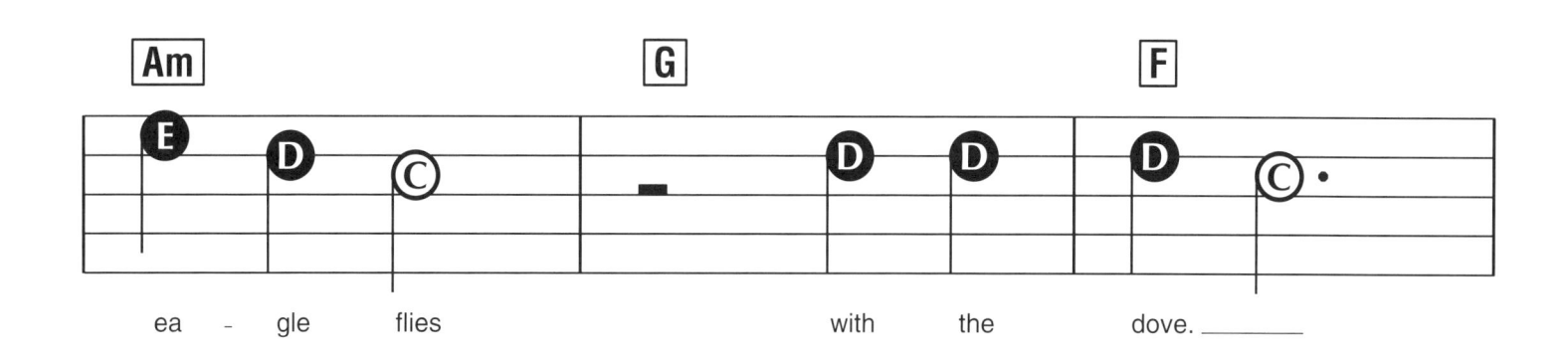

C		F		C	

be - cause your ba - by, sweet - heart, sug - ar's so far a -
and she's wait - ing for some - thing to
you ain't gon - na need an - y - more ad -

| Dm | | C | | Am | |

way.
do.
vice.

Well,
And } there's a rose
And

| G | | F | | | |

in a fist - ed glove and the

| Am | | G | | F | |

ea - gle flies with the dove.

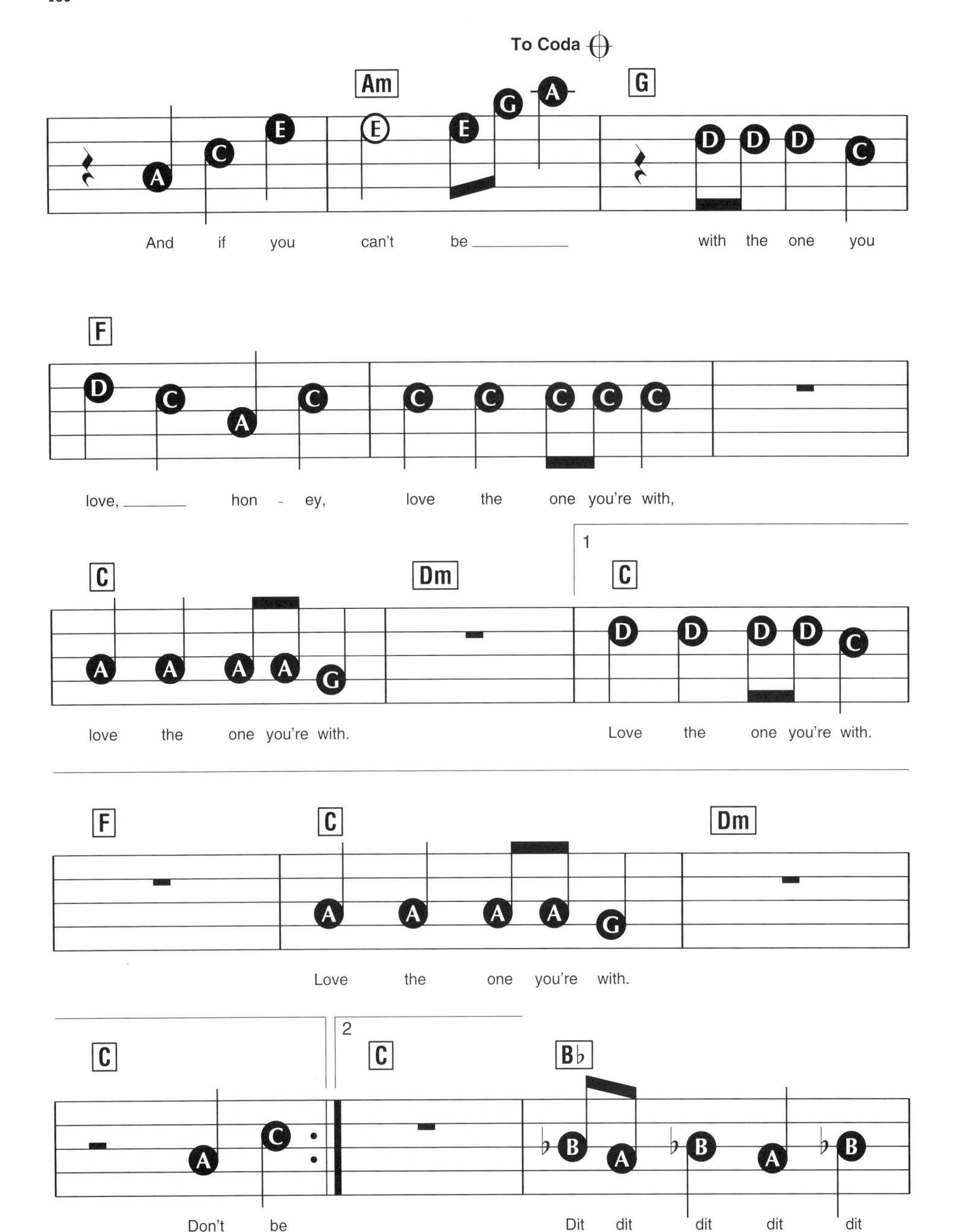

And if you can't be _____ with the one you love, _____ hon-ey, love the one you're with, love the one you're with. Love the one you're with.

Love the one you're with.

Don't be   Dit dit dit dit dit

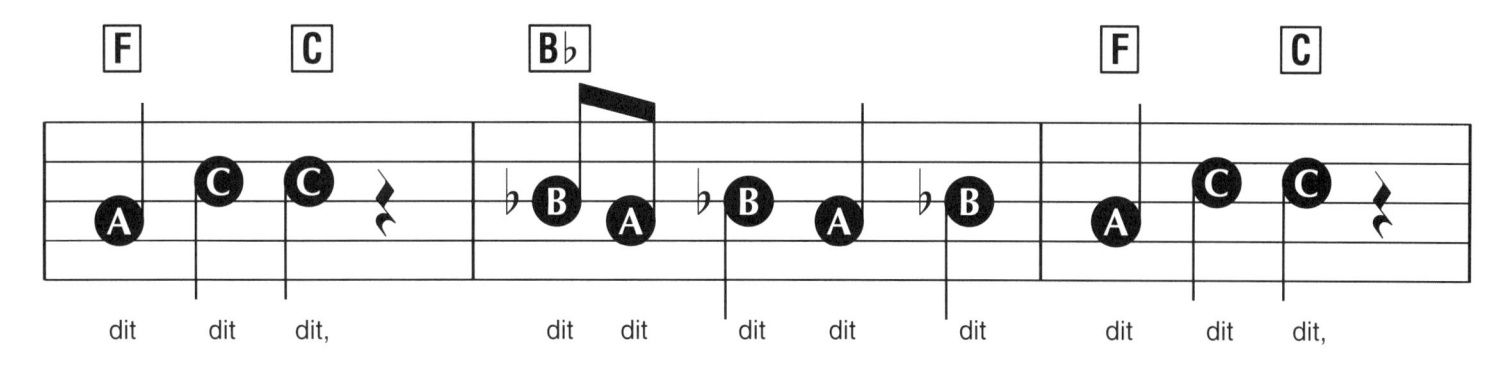

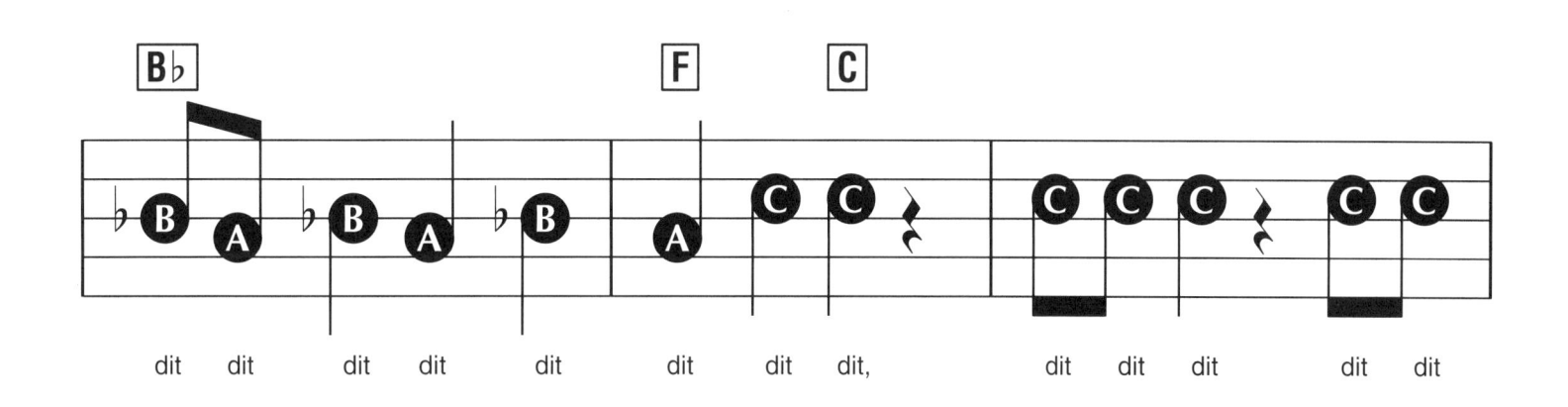

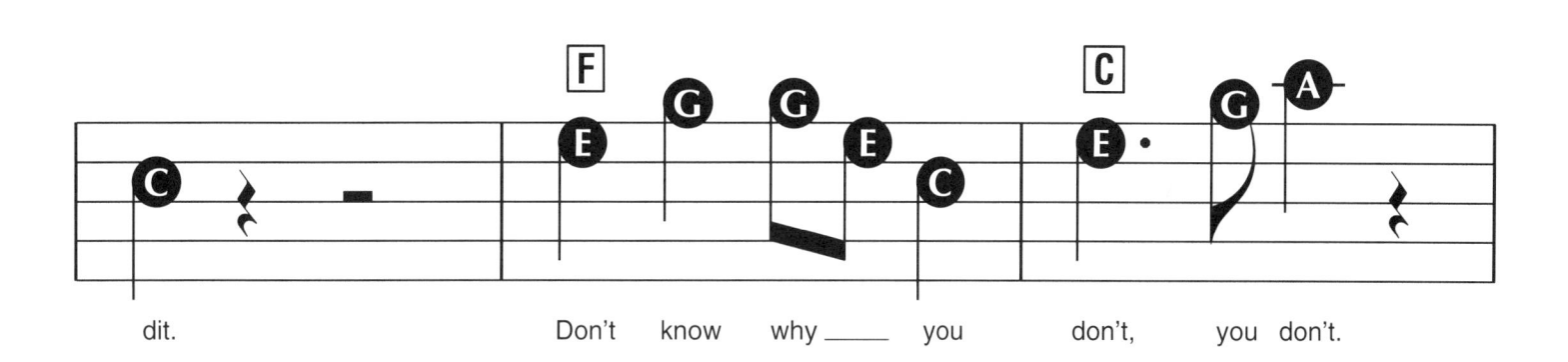

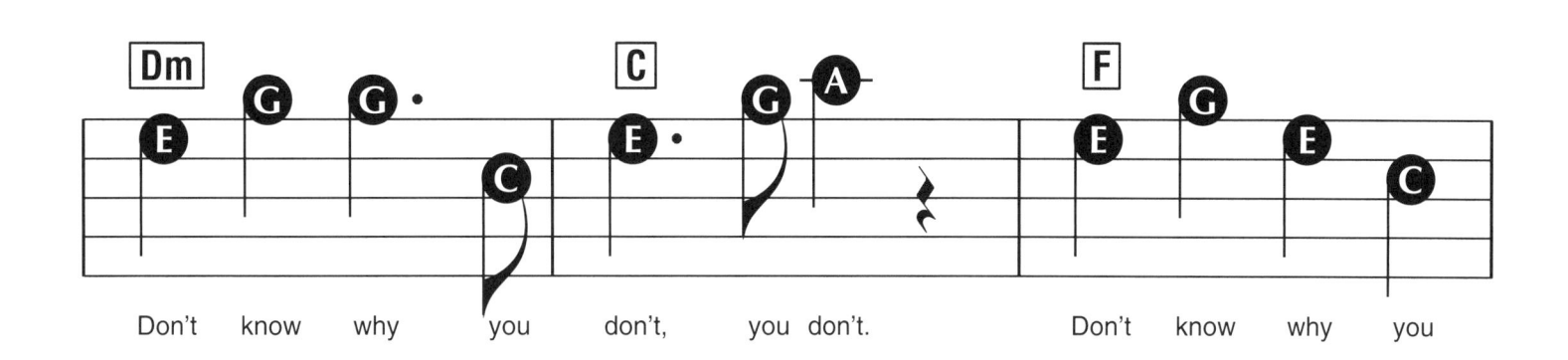

107

dit dit dit, dit dit dit dit dit dit dit dit,

dit dit dit dit dit dit dit dit, dit dit dit dit dit

dit. Don't know why ____ you don't, you don't.

Don't know why you don't, you don't. Don't know why you

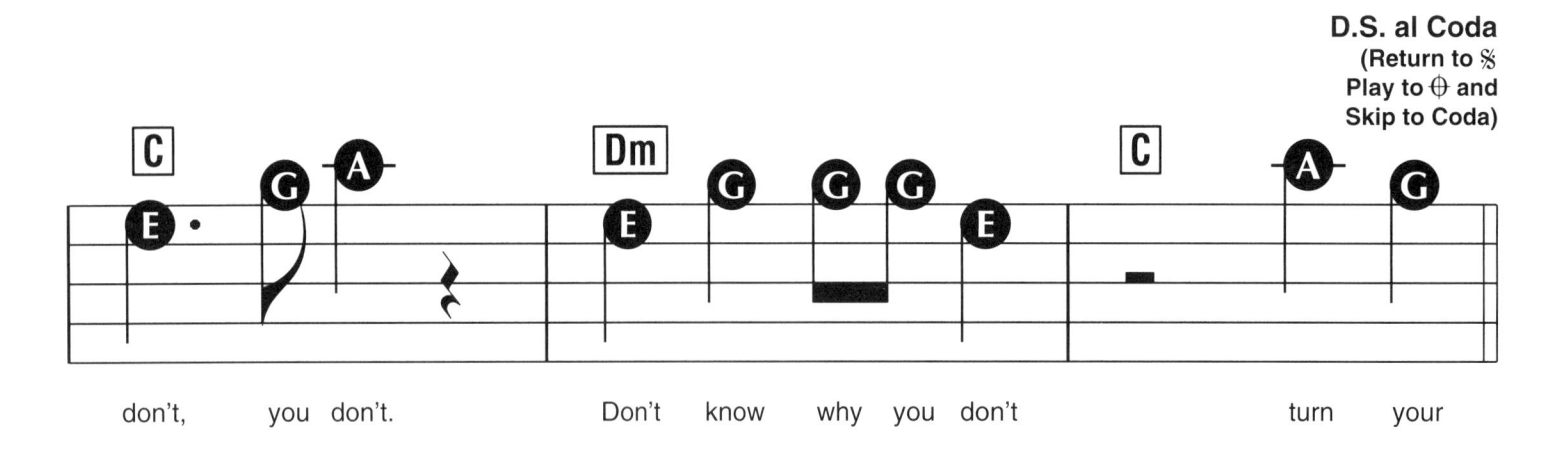

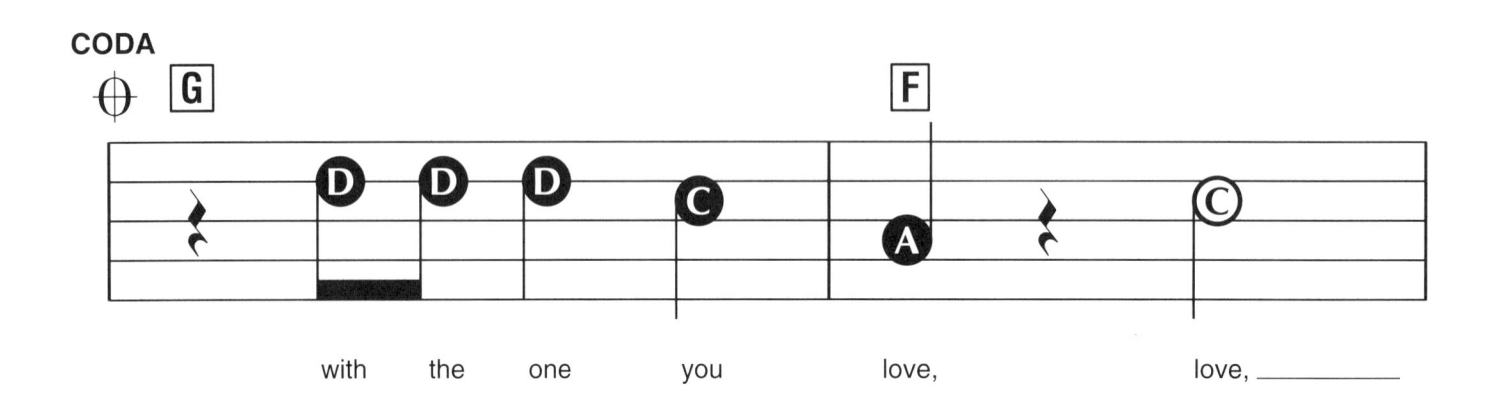

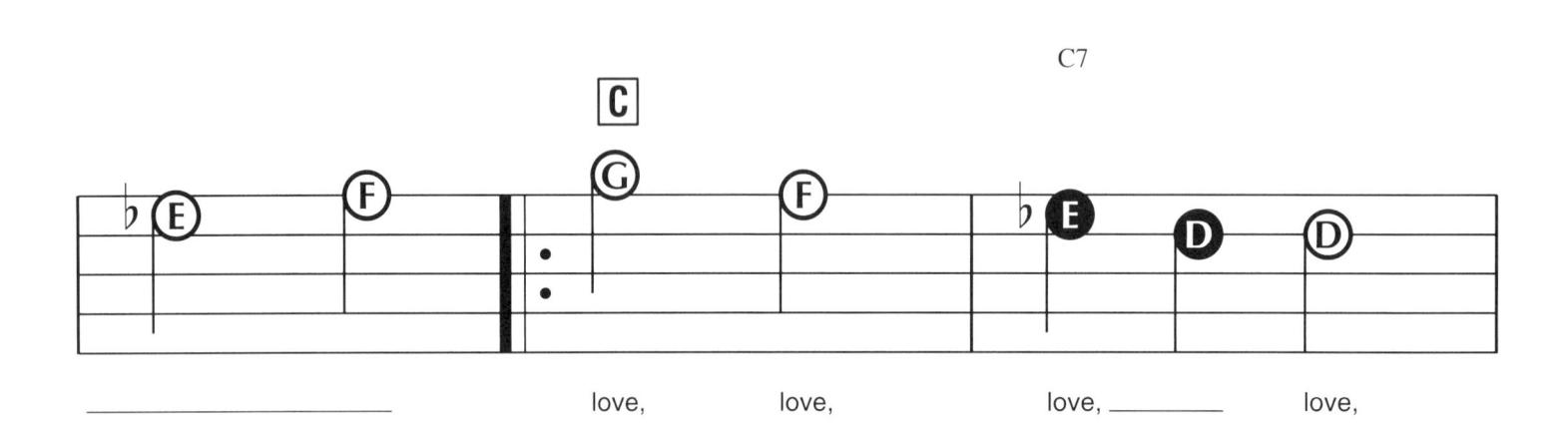

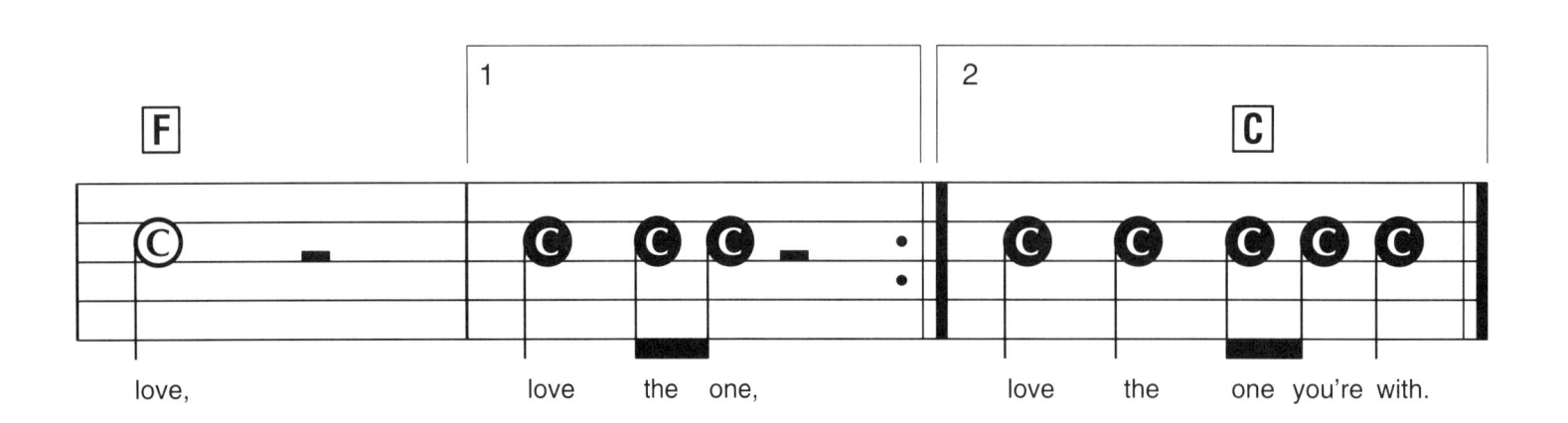

D.S. al Coda
(Return to 𝄋
Play to ⊕ and
Skip to Coda)

don't, you don't. Don't know why you don't turn your

CODA
with the one you love, love, _____

_____ love, love, love, _____ love,

love, love the one, love the one you're with.

Mrs. Robinson
from THE GRADUATE

Registration 5
Rhythm: Swing

Words and Music by
Paul Simon

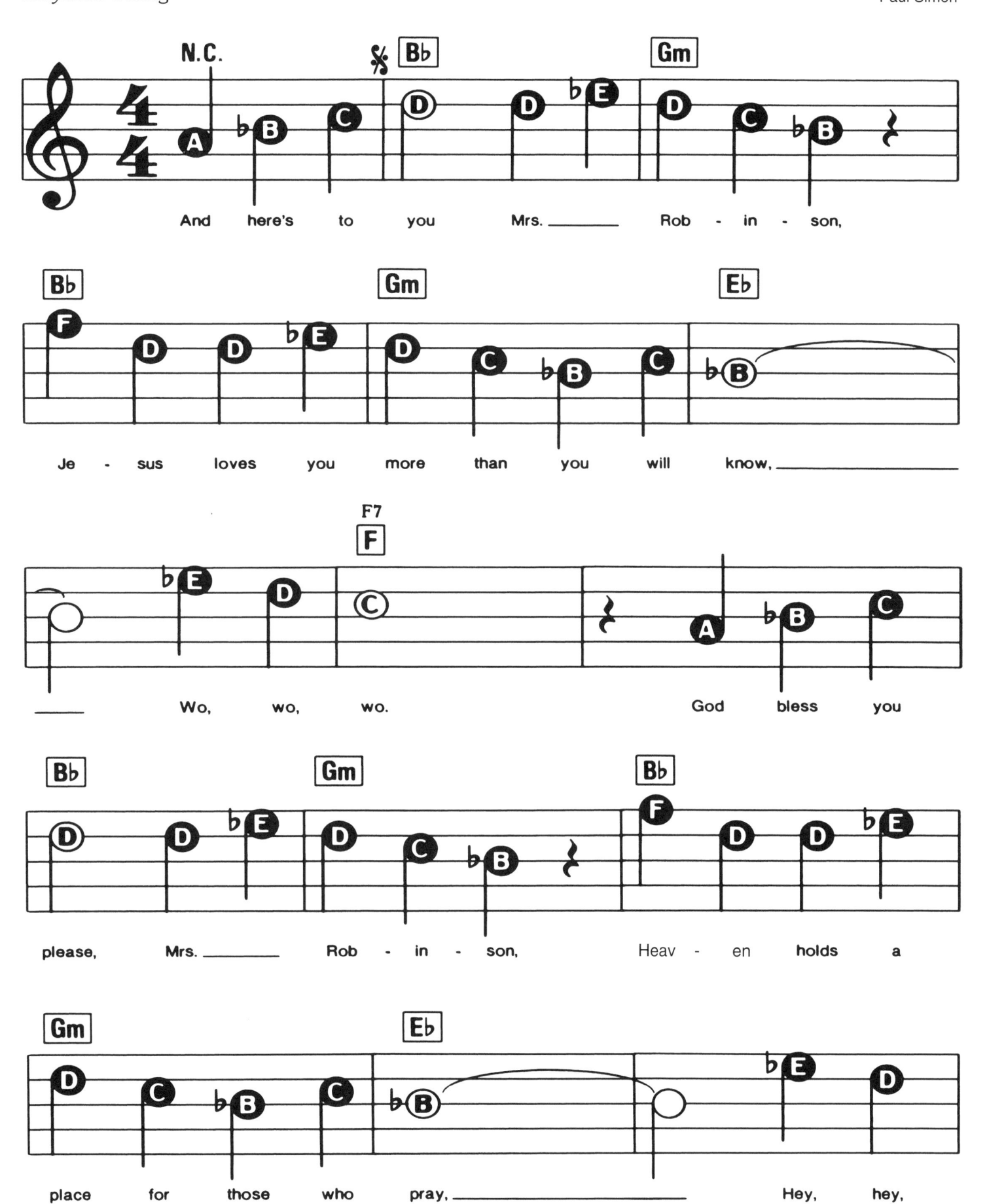

And here's to you Mrs. ____ Rob - in - son,

Je - sus loves you more than you will know, ____

Wo, wo, wo. God bless you

please, Mrs. ____ Rob - in - son, Heav - en holds a

place for those who pray, ____ Hey, hey,

Copyright © 1968 (Renewed), 1970 (Renewed) Paul Simon (BMI)
International Copyright Secured   All Rights Reserved
Reprinted by Permission of Music Sales Corporation

hey, _____ Hey, hey, hey. _____

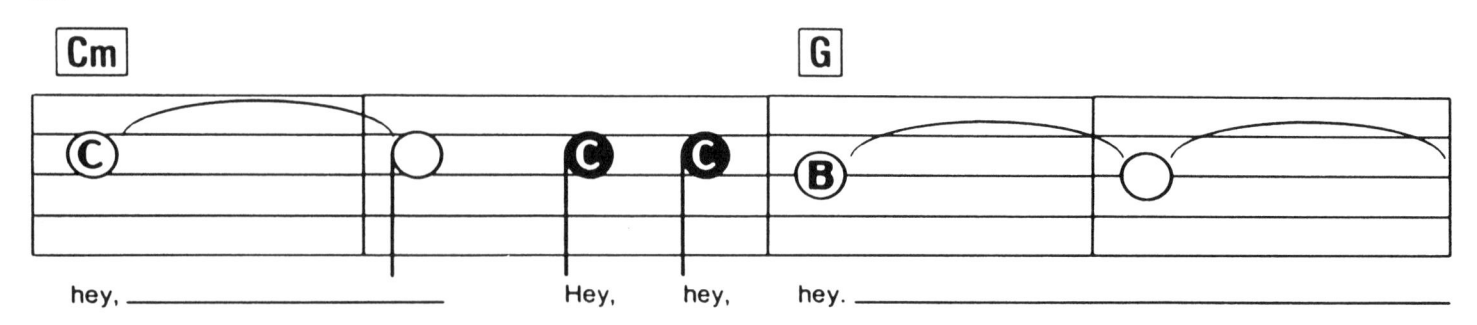

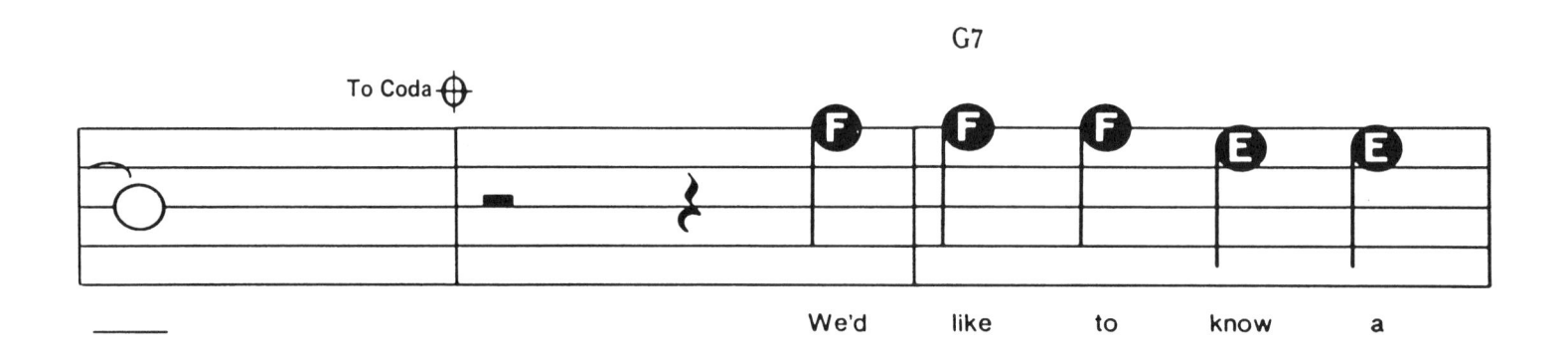

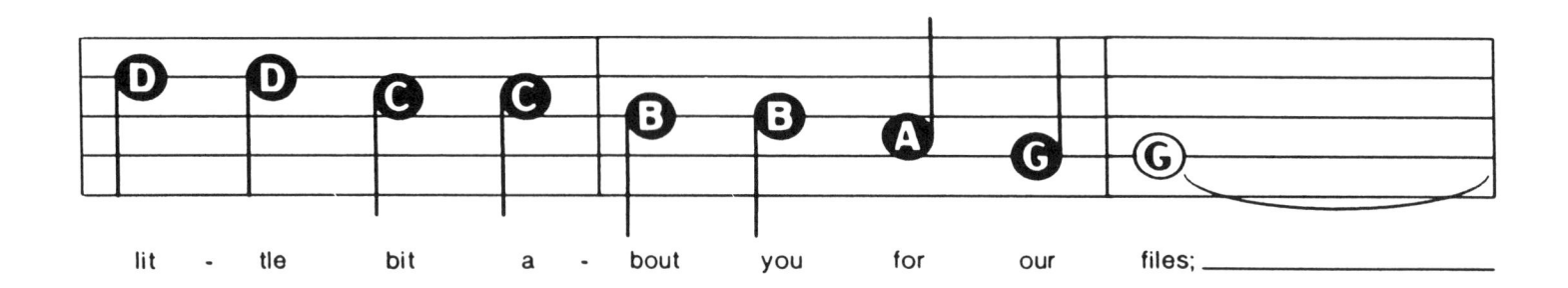

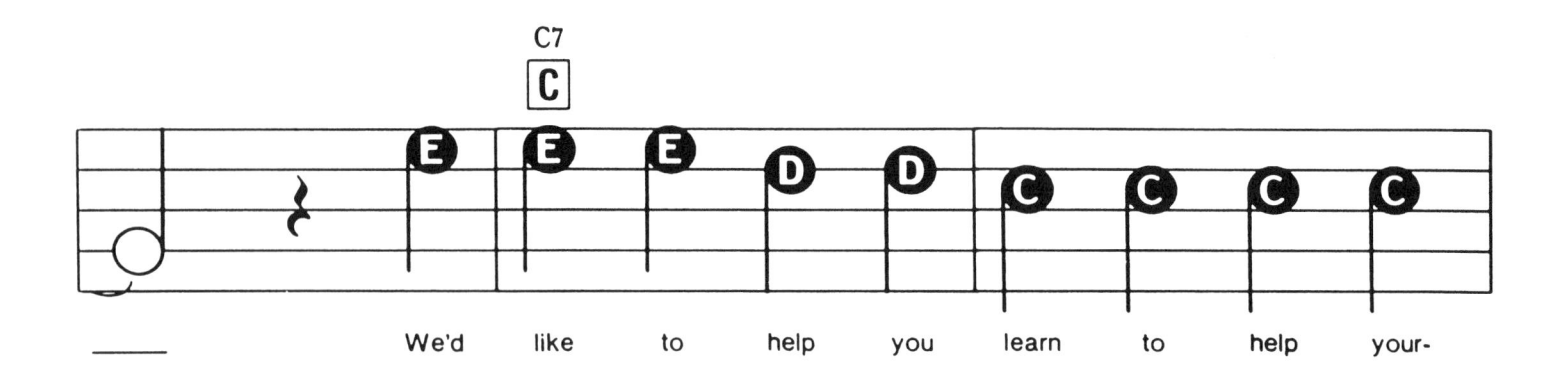

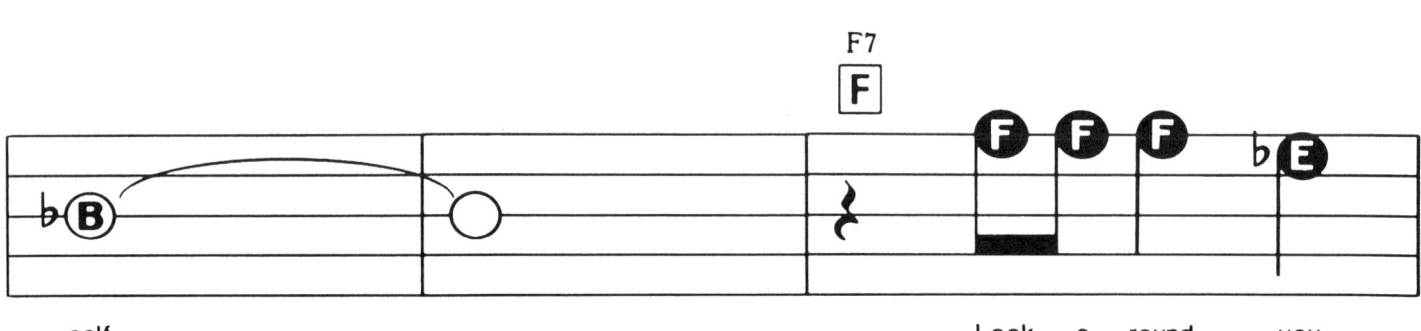

We'd like to know a little bit about you for our files; _____ We'd like to help you learn to help your-self. _____ Look a-round you,

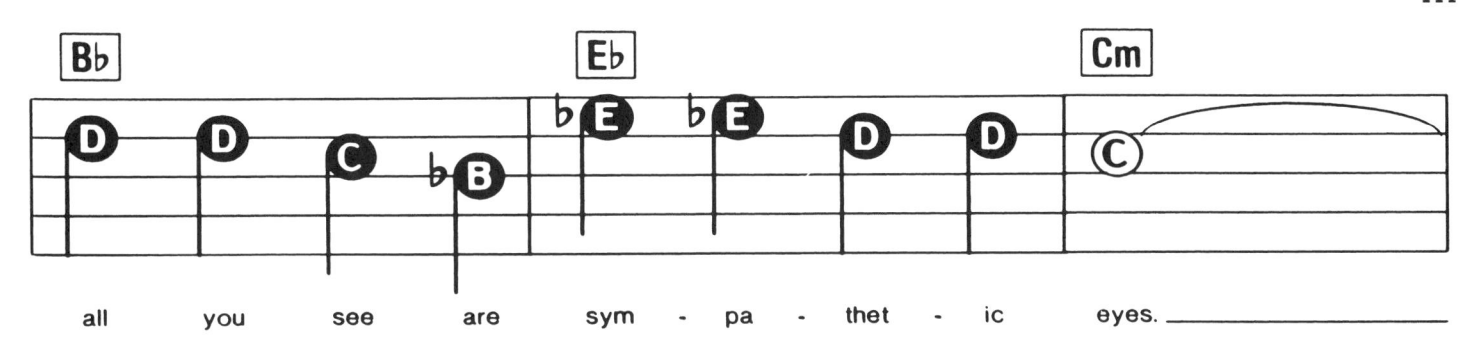

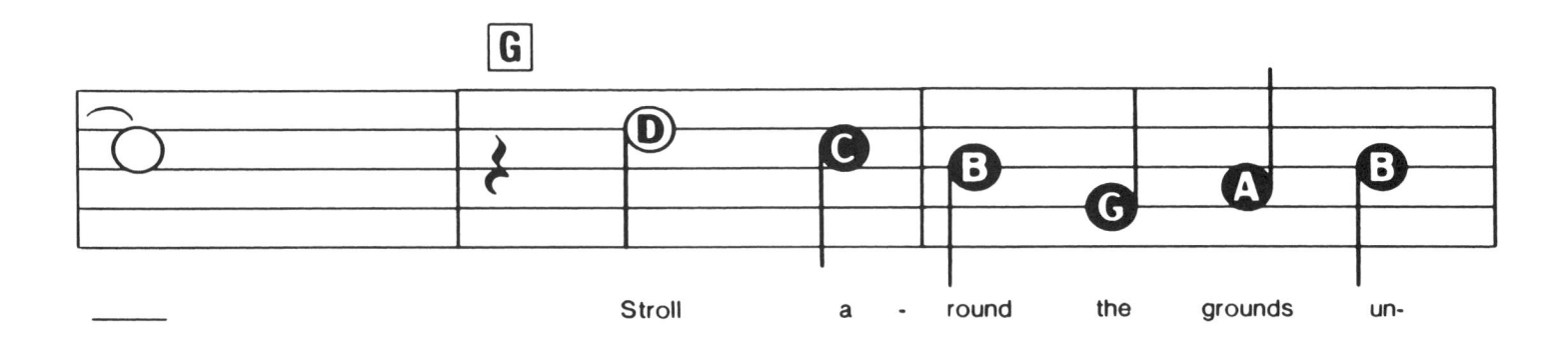

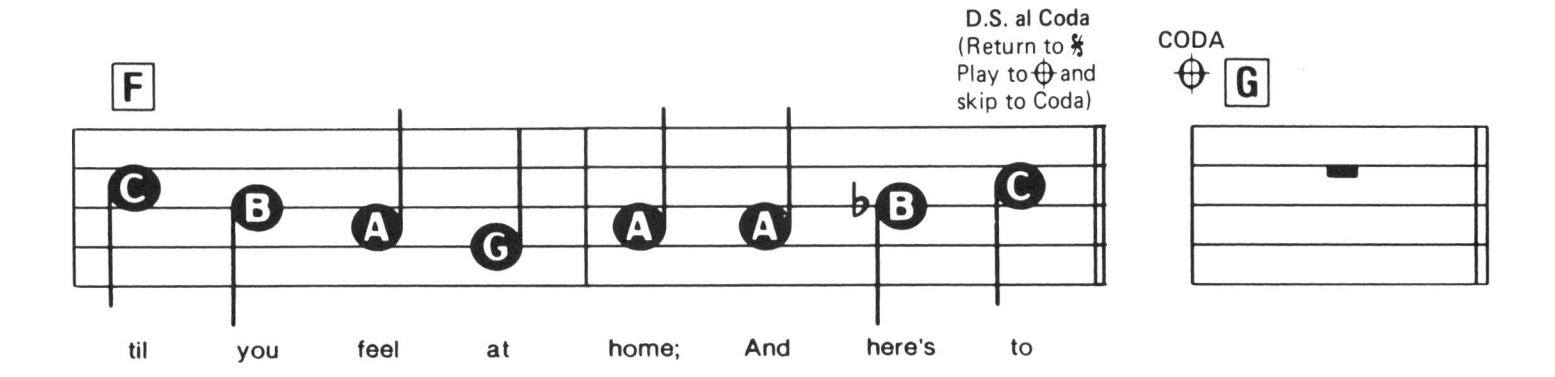

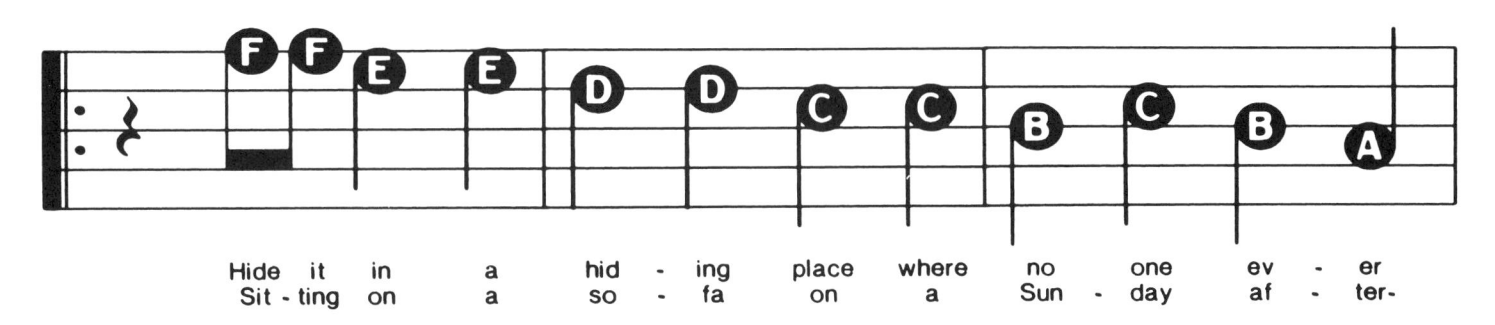

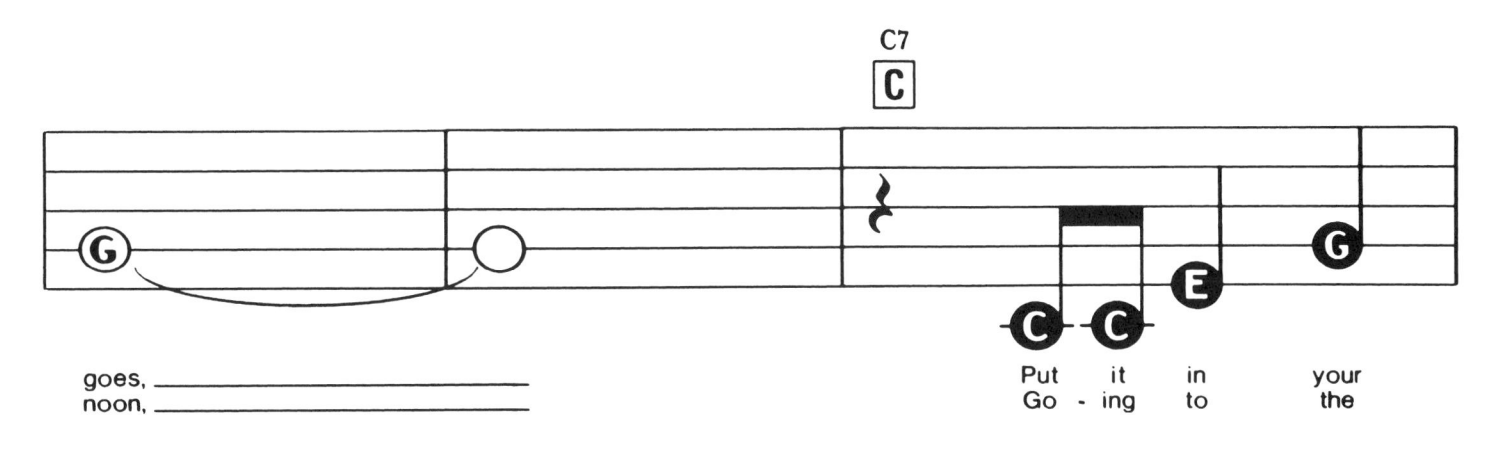

111

all you see are sym-pa-thet-ic eyes._____

_____ Stroll a-round the grounds un-

til you feel at home; And here's to

D.S. al Coda (Return to 𝄋 Play to ⊕ and skip to Coda)

CODA

G7

Hide it in a hid-ing place where no one ev-er
Sit-ting on a so-fa place on a Sun-day af-ter-

C7

goes,_____
noon,_____ Put it in your
Go-ing to the

pan - try with your cup - cakes, ___
can - di - dates de - bate,

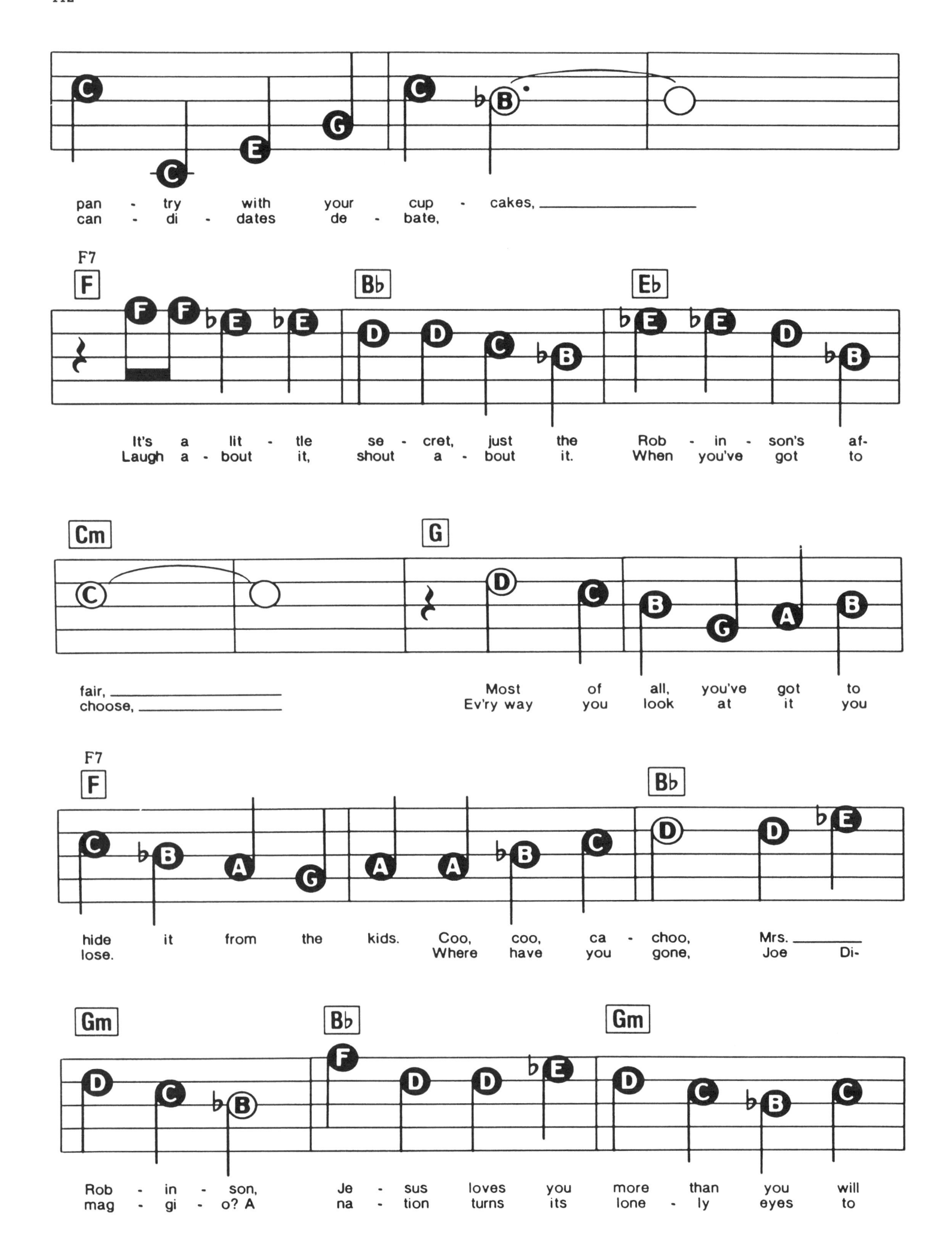

It's a lit - tle se - cret, just the Rob - in - son's af-
Laugh a - bout it, shout a - bout it. When you've got to

fair, ___ Most of all, you've got to
choose, ___ Ev'ry way you look at it you

hide it from the kids. Coo, coo, ca - choo, Mrs. ___
lose. Where have you gone, Mrs. Joe Di-

Rob - in - son, Je - sus loves you more than you will
mag - gi - o? A na - tion turns its lone - ly eyes to

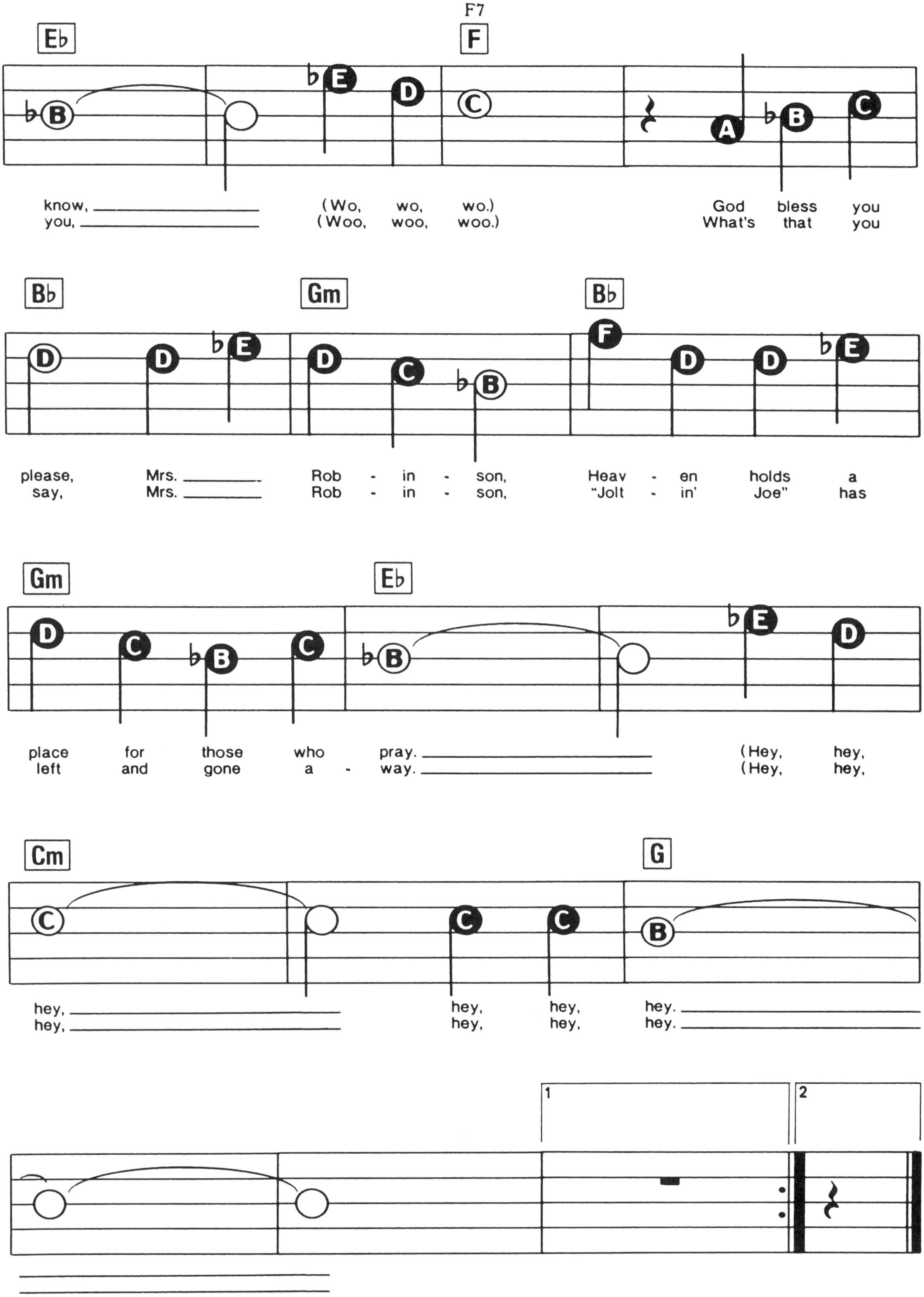
Eb
F7
F
know, (Wo, wo, wo.) God bless you
you, (Woo, woo, woo.) What's that you
Bb
Gm
Bb
please, Mrs. Rob - in - son, Heav - en holds a
say, Mrs. Rob - in - son, "Jolt - in' Joe" has
Gm
Eb
place for those who pray. (Hey, hey,
left and those gone a - way. (Hey, hey,
Cm
G
hey, hey, hey, hey.
hey, hey, hey, hey.
1
2

Make It with You

Registration 1
Rhythm: Ballad

Words and Music by
David Gates

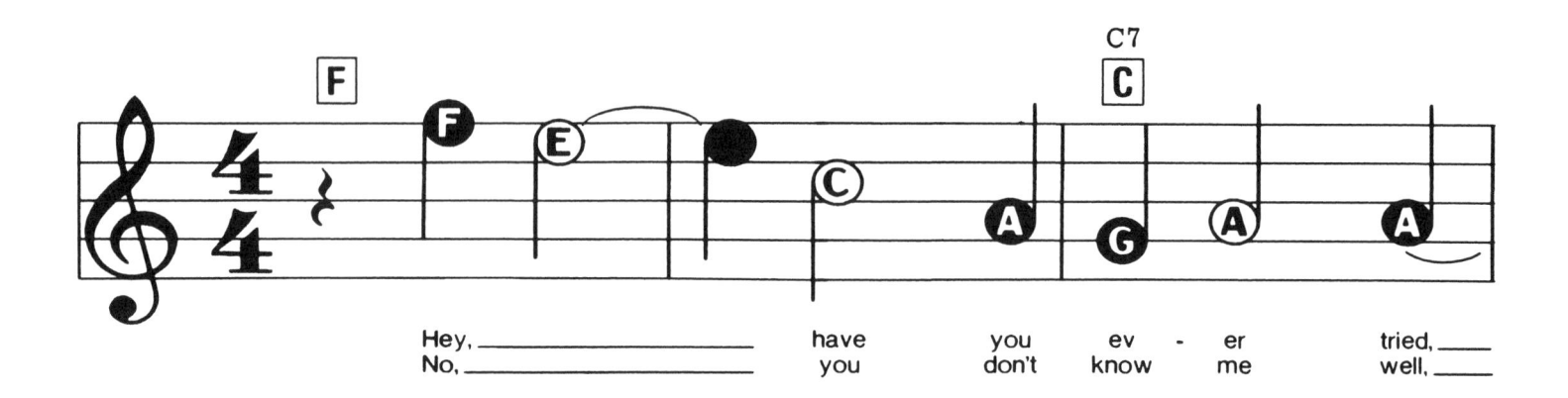

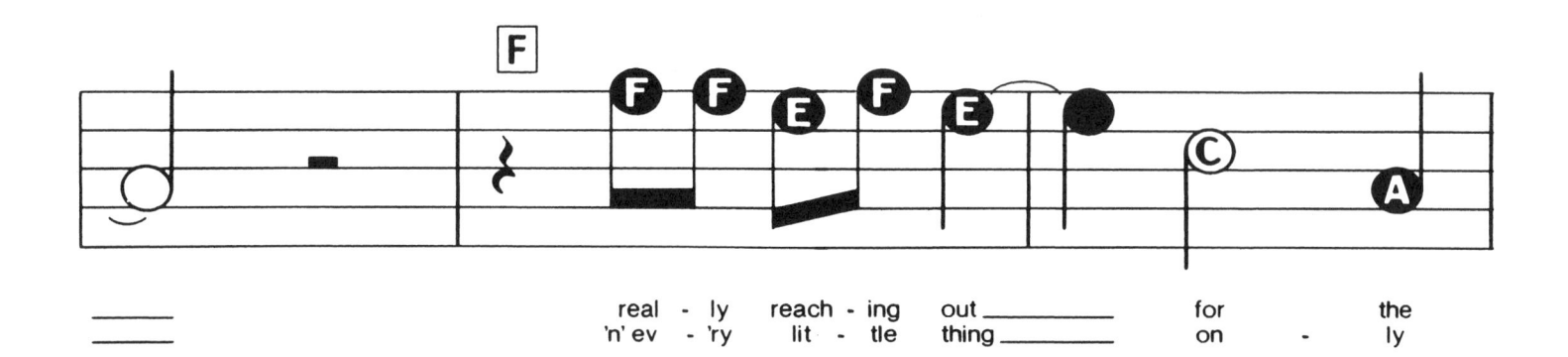

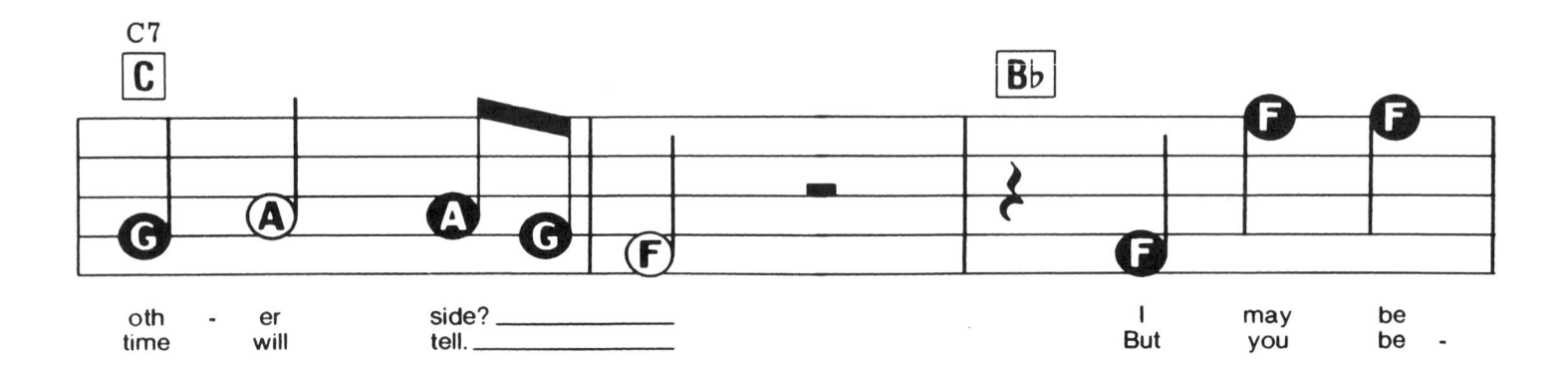

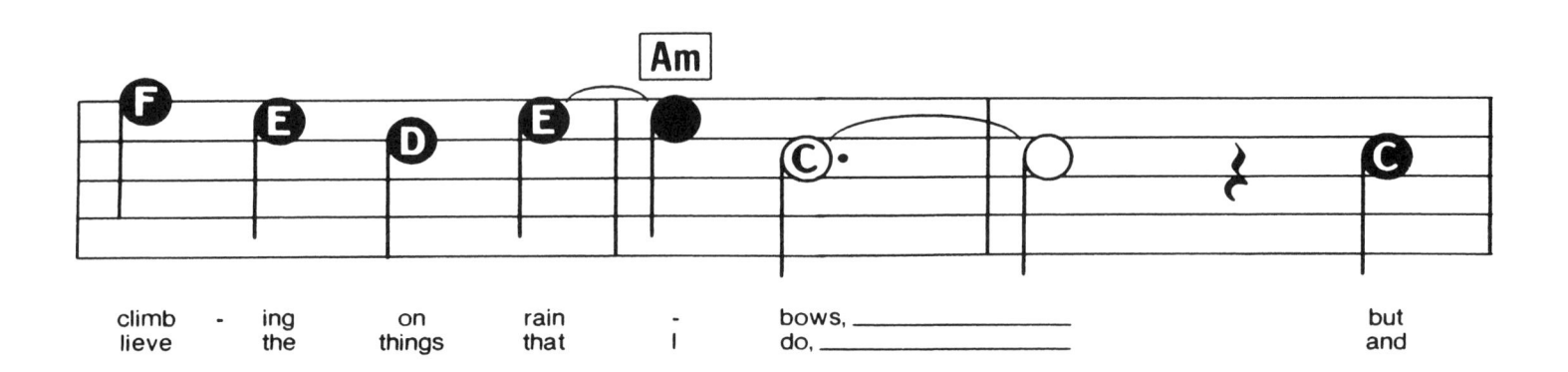

Hey, _____ have you ev - er tried, _____ real - ly reach - ing out _____ for the oth - er side? _____ I may be climb - ing on rain - bows, _____ but

No, _____ you don't know me well, _____ 'n' ev - 'ry lit - tle thing _____ on - ly time will tell. _____ But you be - lieve - ing the things that I do, _____ and

Copyright © 1970 Sony/ATV Music Publishing LLC
Copyright Renewed
All Rights Administered by Sony/ATV Music Publishing LLC, 8 Music Square West, Nashville, TN 37203
International Copyright Secured All Rights Reserved

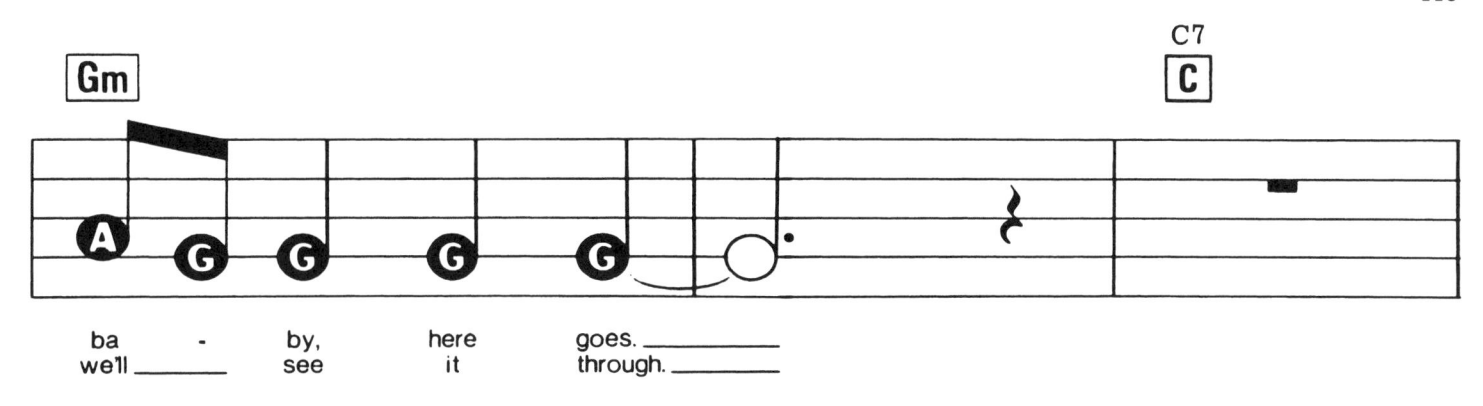

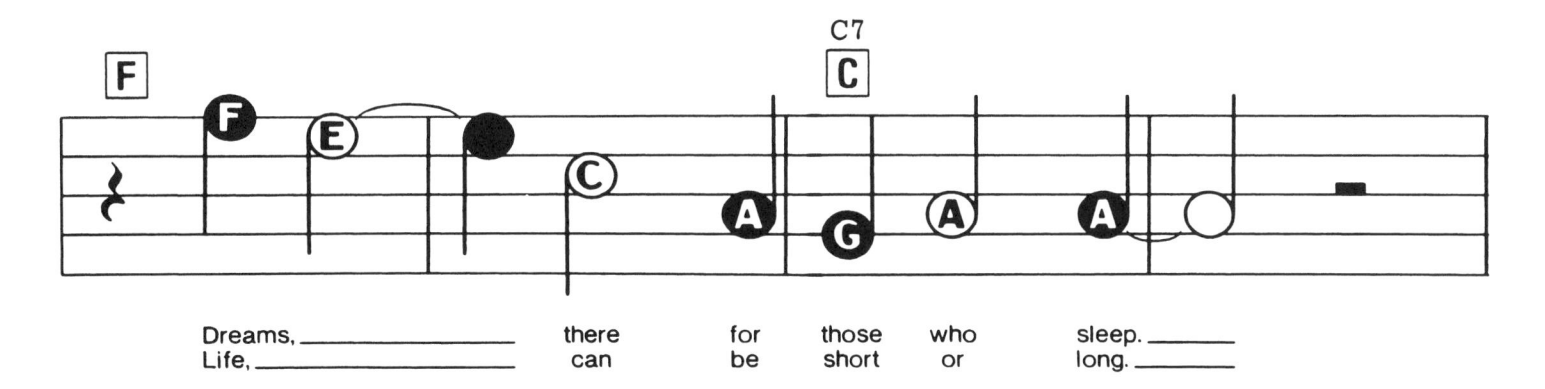

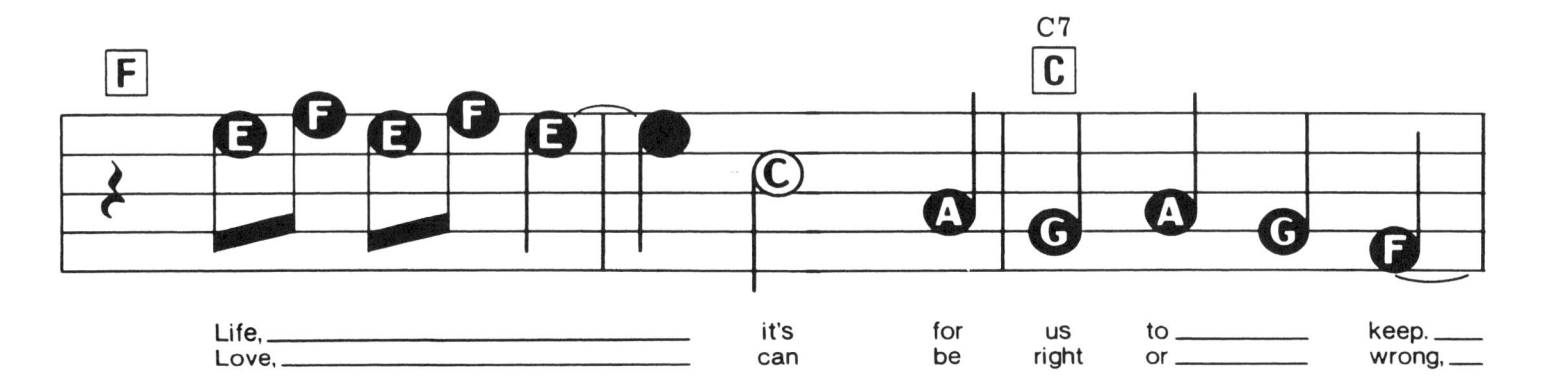

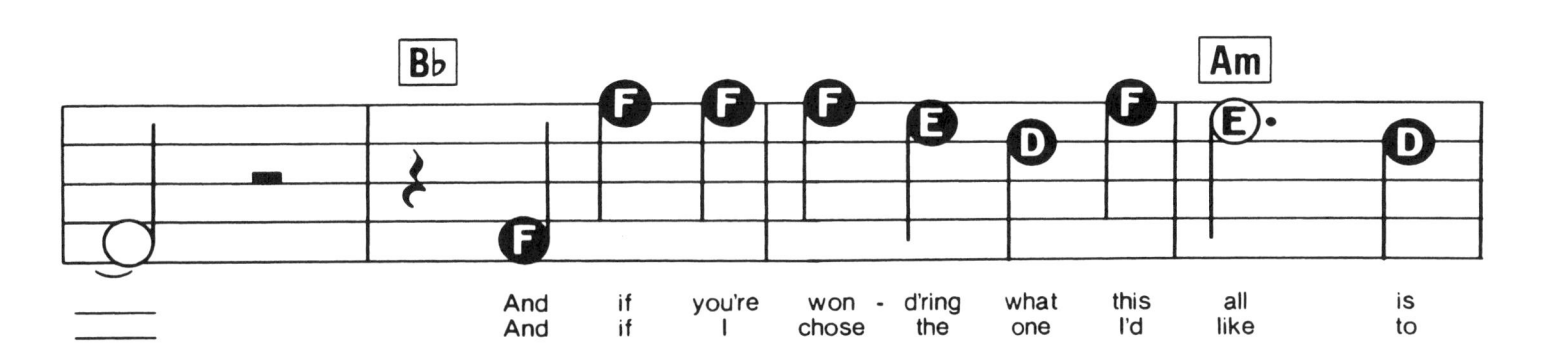

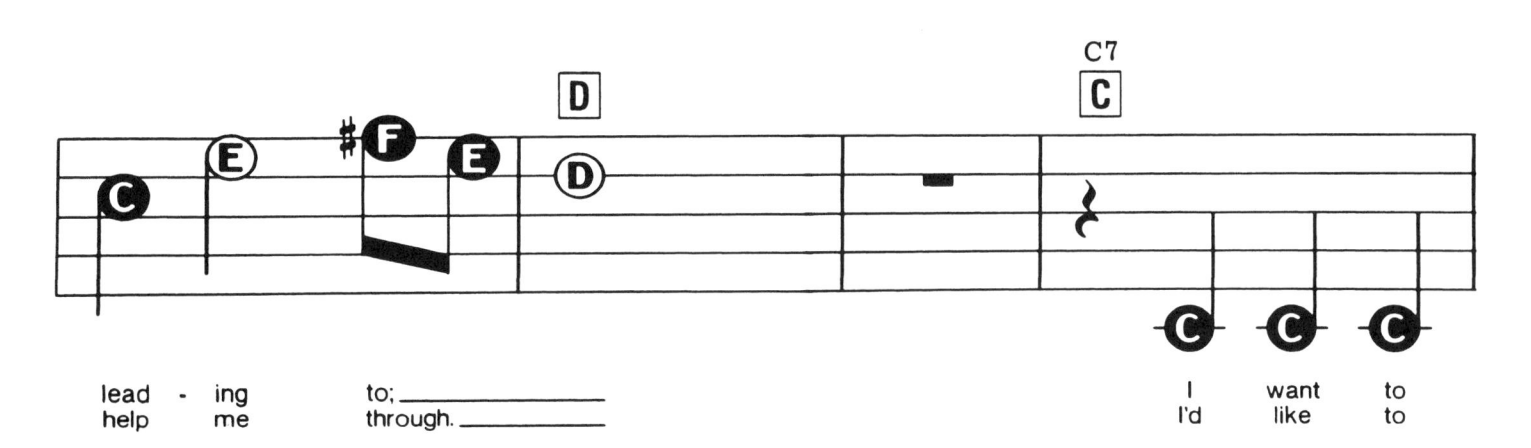

ba - by, here goes.
we'll see it through.

Dreams, there for those who sleep.
Life, can be short or long.

Life, it's for us to keep.
Love, can be right or wrong,

And if you're won-d'ring what this all is
And if I chose the one I'd like to

lead - ing to; I want to
help me through. I'd like to

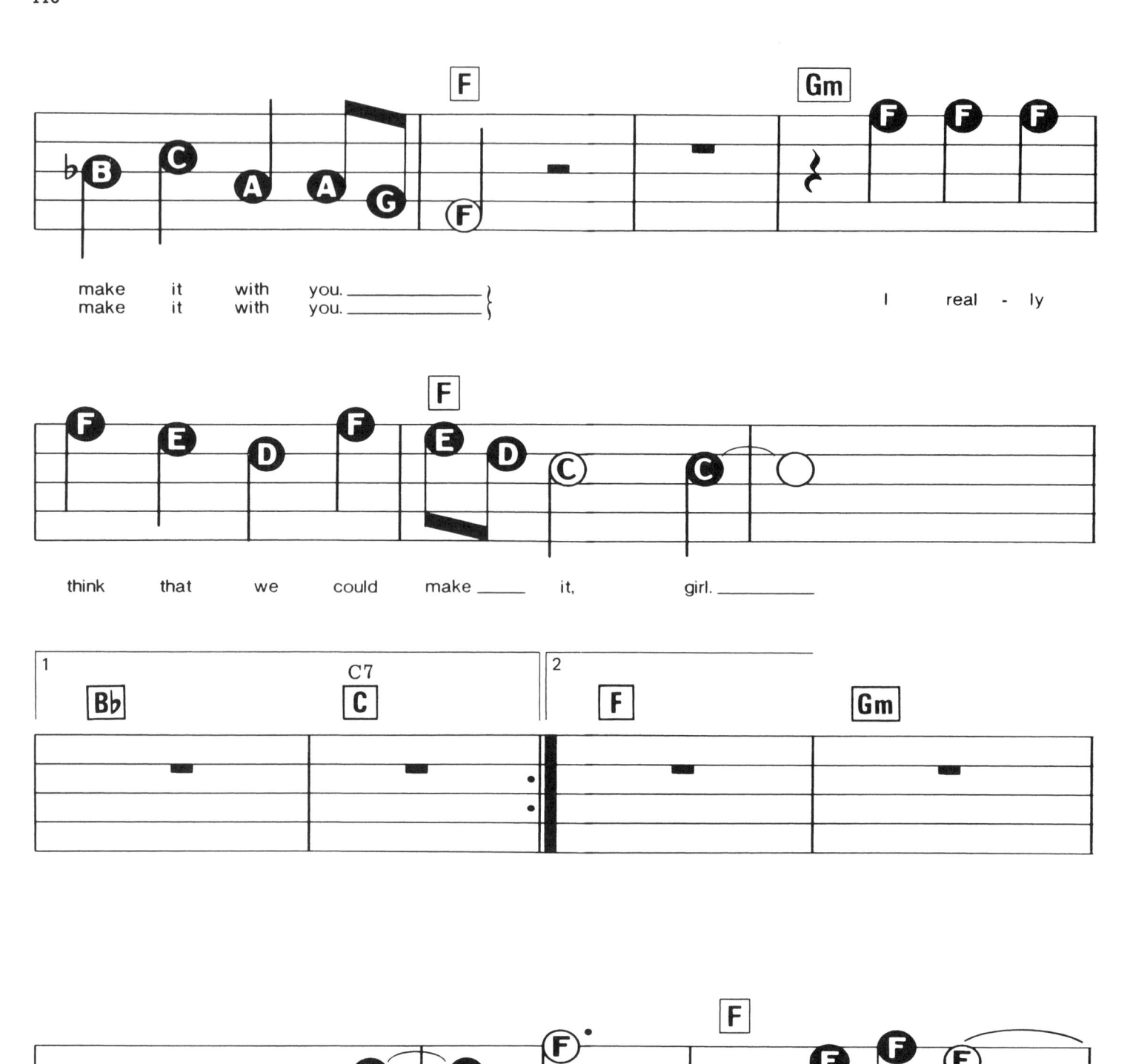

make it with you. _____
make it with you. _____ I real - ly

think that we could make ___ it, girl. _____

Ba - by, you know ___ that dreams, _____

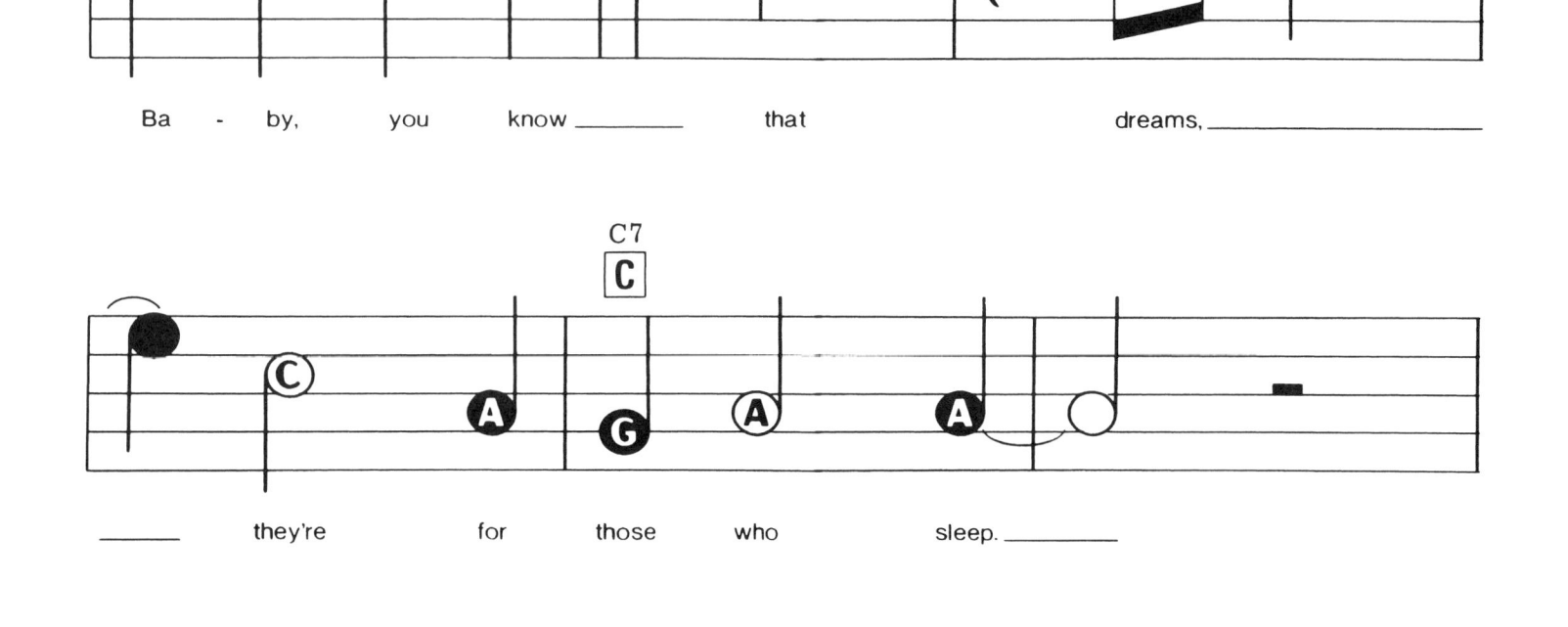

_____ they're for those who sleep. _____

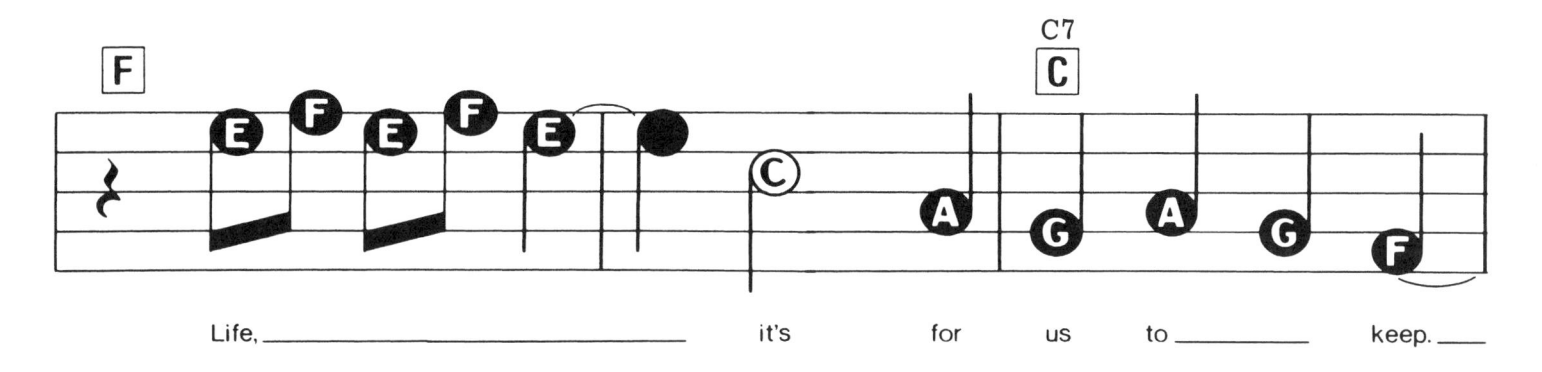

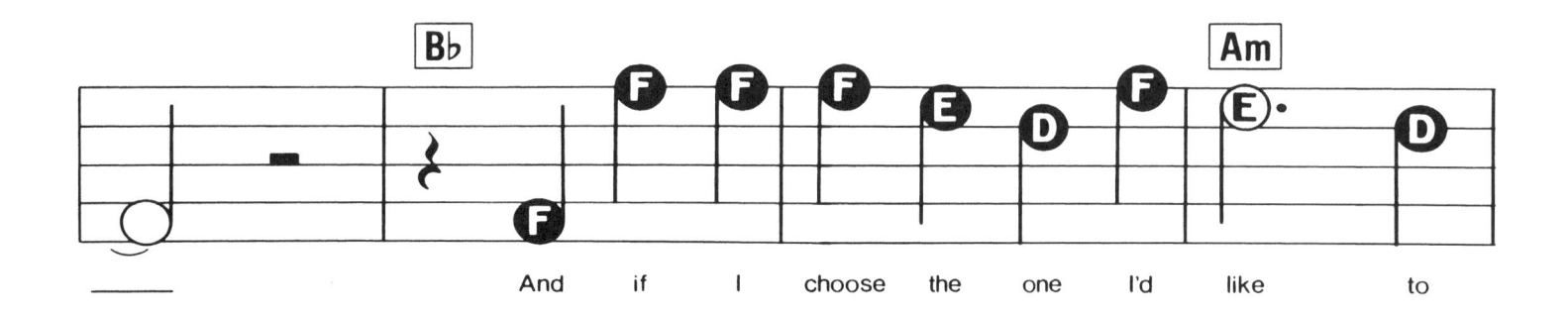

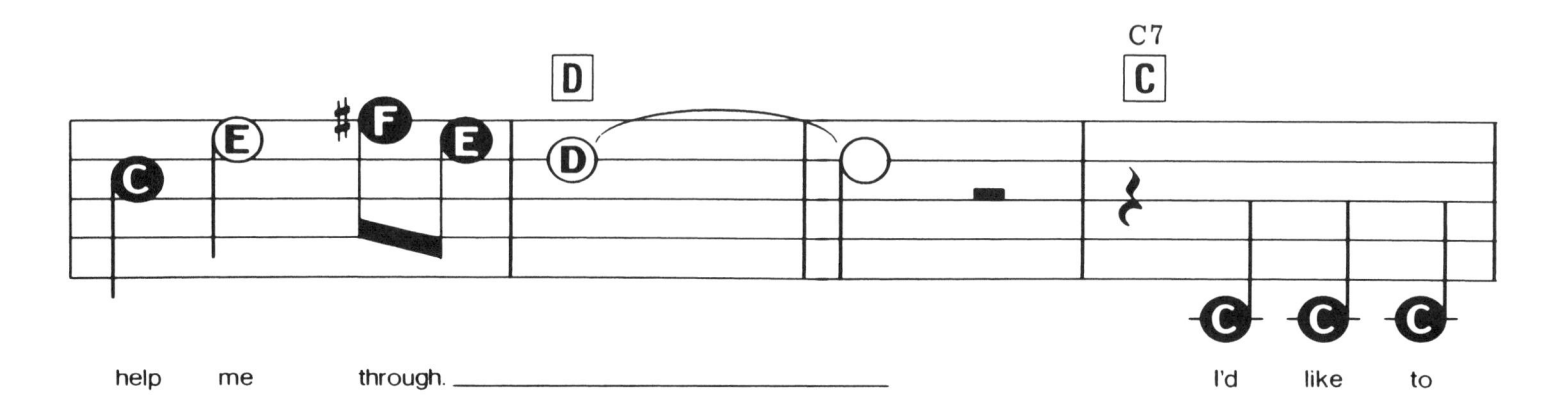

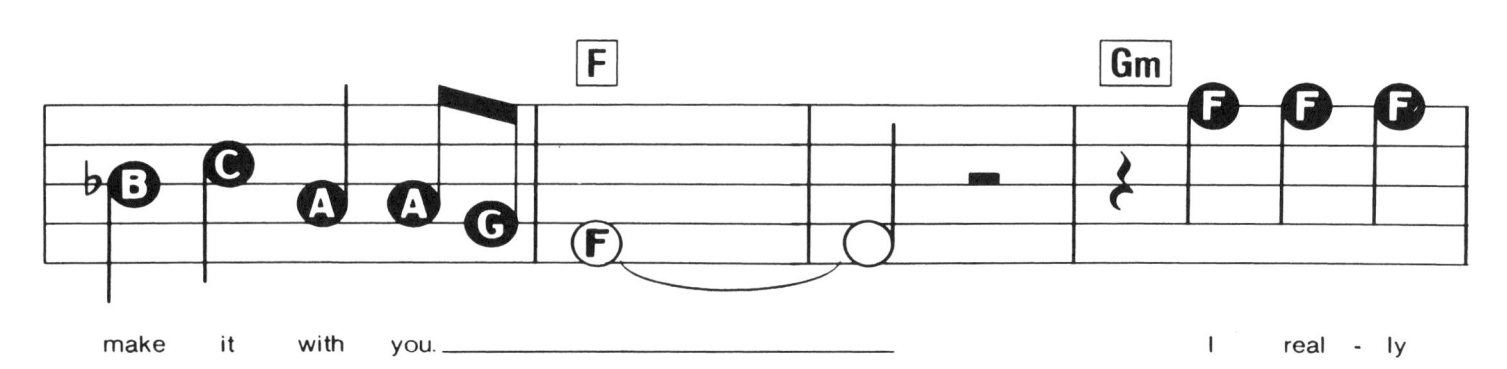

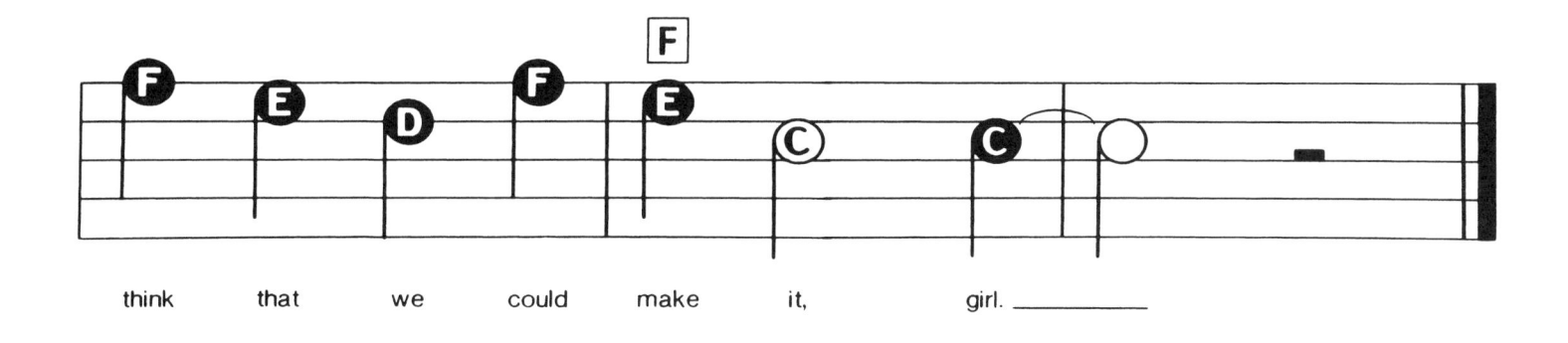

Life, _____ it's for us to _____ keep. _____ And if I choose the one I'd like to help me through. _____ I'd like to make it with you. _____ I real-ly think that we could make it, girl. _____

Me and Bobby McGee

Registration 4
Rhythm: Country Rock

Words and Music by Kris Kristofferson and Fred Foster

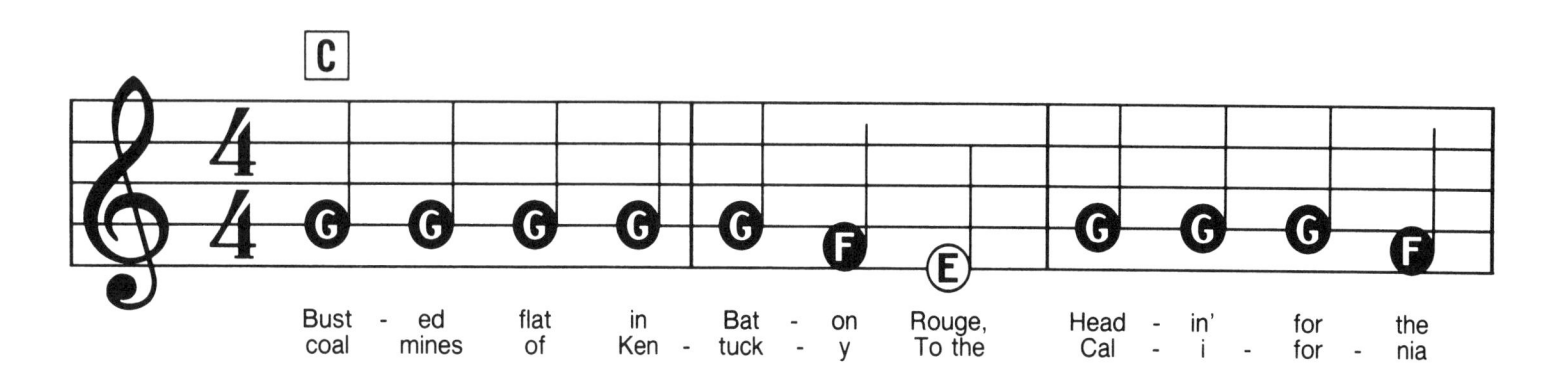

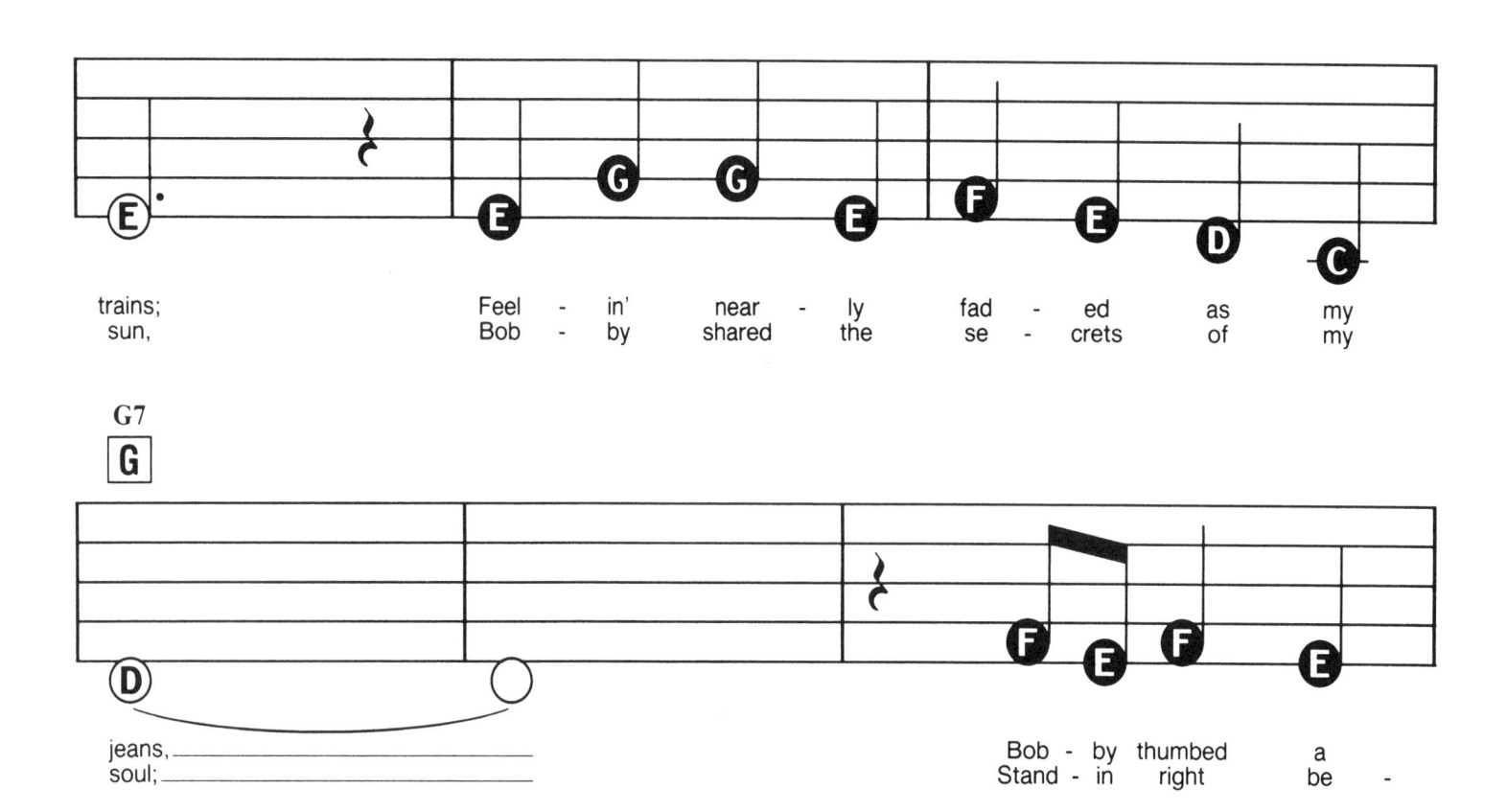

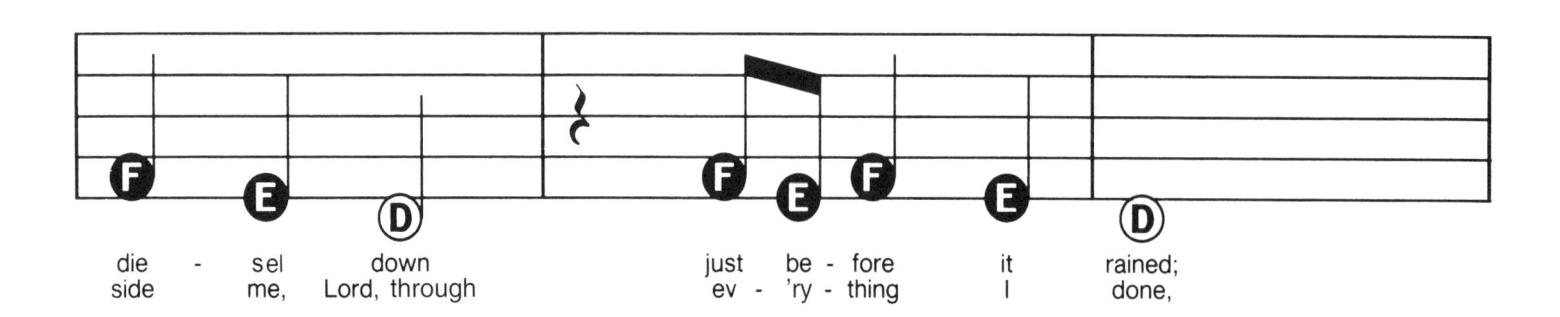

C

Bust - ed flat in Bat - on Rouge, Head - in' for the
coal mines of Ken - tuck - y To the Cal - i - for - nia

trains; Feel - in' near - ly fad - ed as my
sun, Bob - by shared the se - crets of my

G7

jeans, Bob - by thumbed a
soul; Stand - in right be -

die - sel down just be - fore it rained;
side me, Lord, through ev - 'ry - thing I done,

© 1969 (Renewed 1997) TEMI COMBINE INC.
All Rights Controlled by COMBINE MUSIC CORP. and Administered by EMI BLACKWOOD MUSIC INC.
All Rights Reserved   International Copyright Secured   Used by Permission

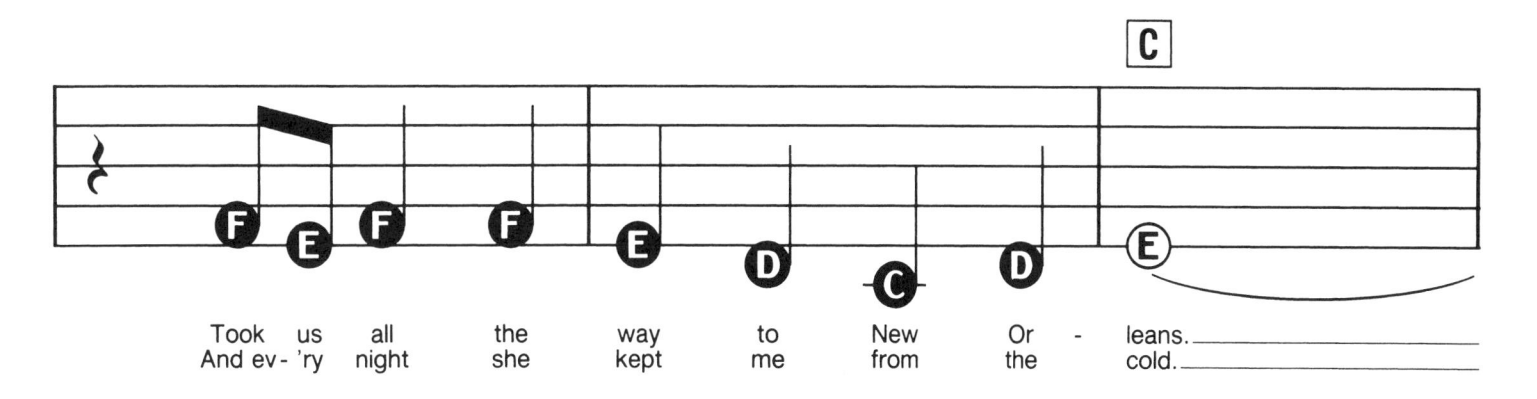

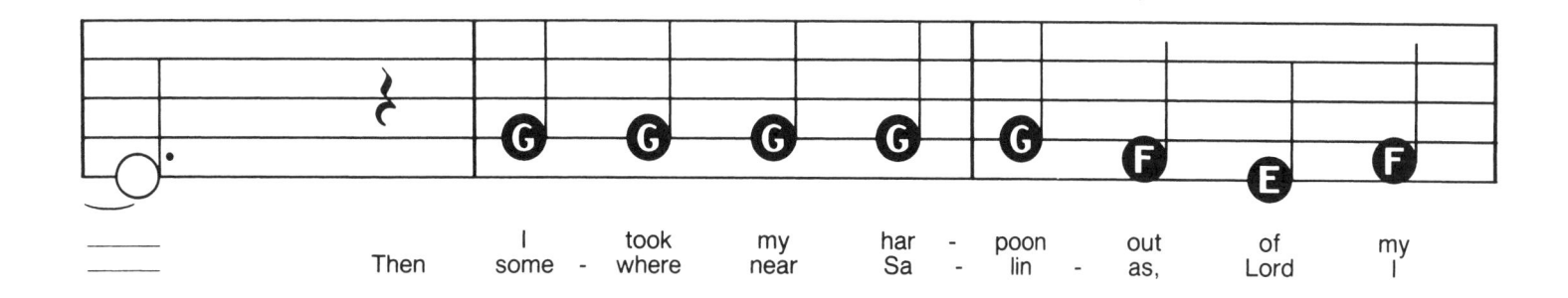

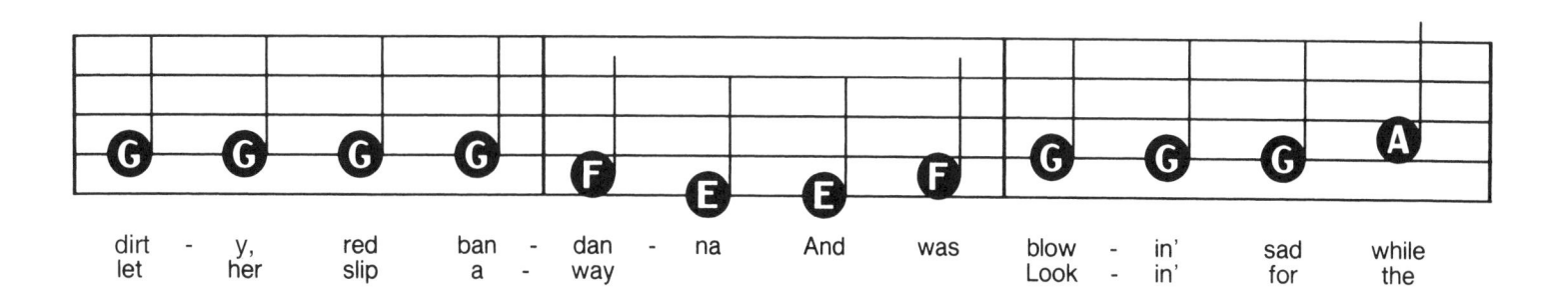

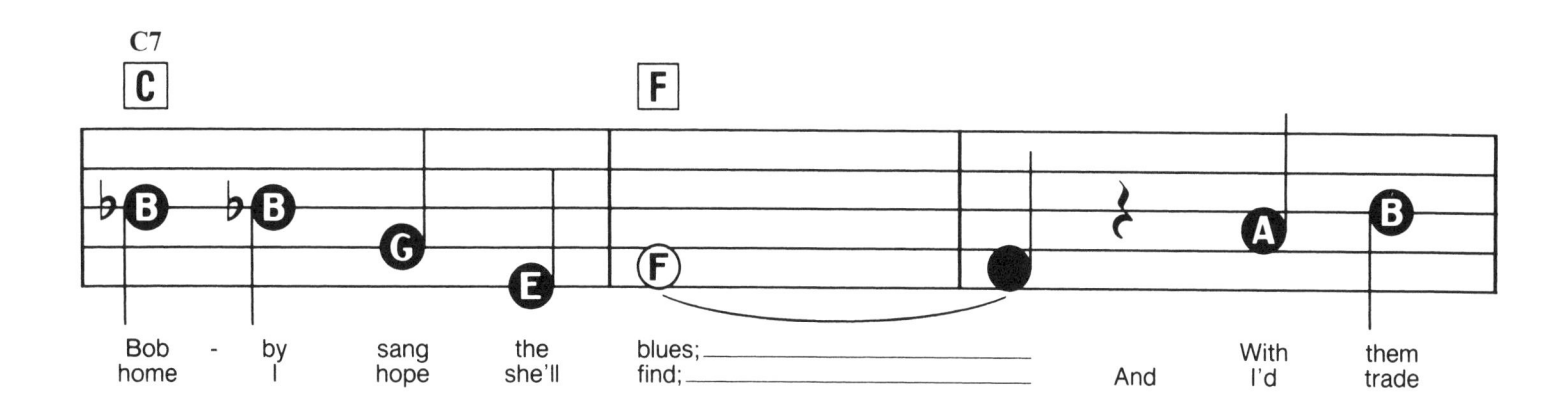

119

Took us all the way to New Or - leans.
And ev-'ry night she kept me from the cold.

Then I took my har - poon out of my
somewhere near Sa - lin - as, Lord I

dirt - y, red ban - dan - na And was blow - in' sad while
let her slip a - way Look - in' sad for the

C7

Bob - by sang the blues; And With
home I hope she'll find; I'd them trade

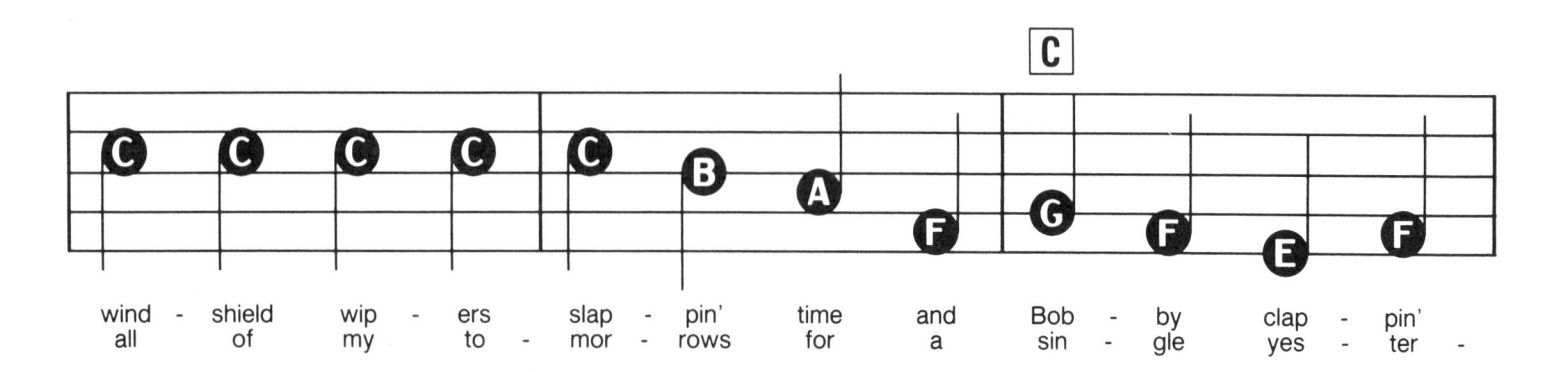

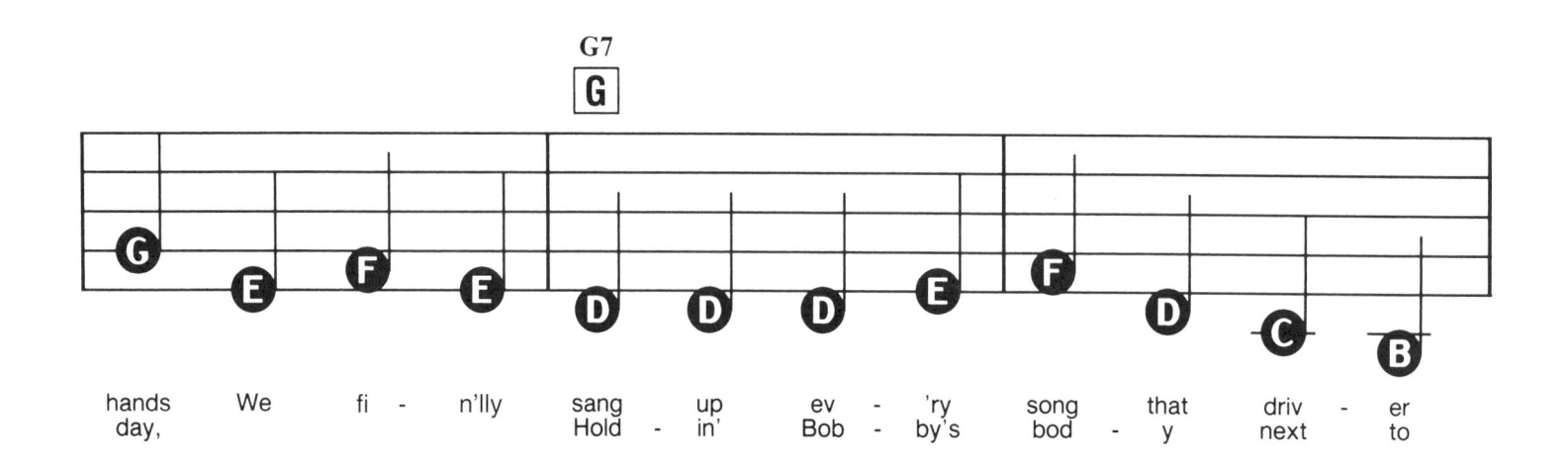

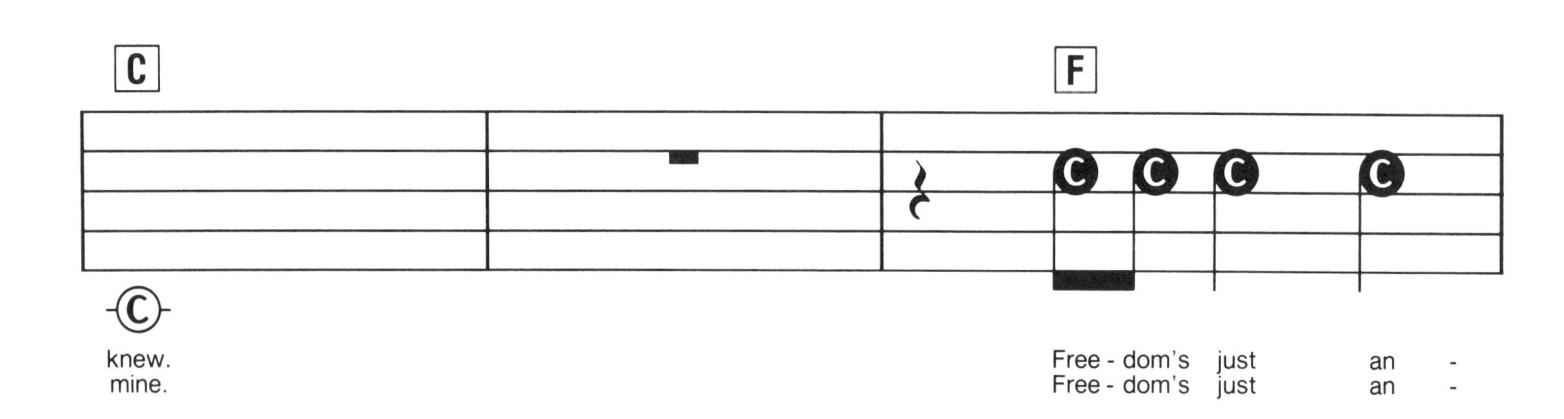

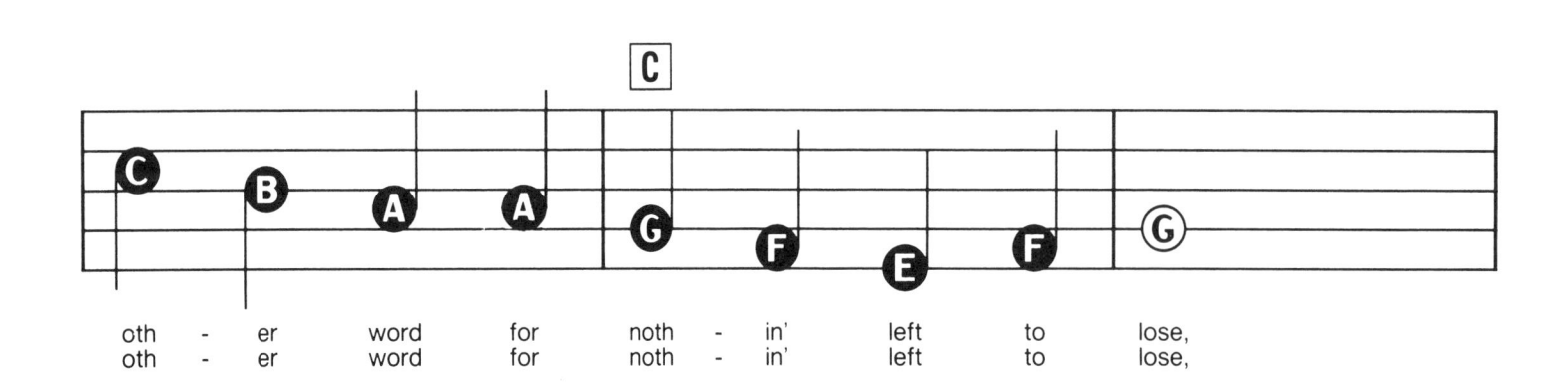

120

wind - shield wip - ers slap - pin' time and a Bob - by clap - pin'
all of my to - mor - rows time for a sin - gle yes - ter -

hands We fi - n'lly sang up ev - 'ry song that driv - er
day, Hold - in' Bob - by's bod - y next to

knew.
mine.
Free - dom's just an -
Free - dom's just an -

oth - er word for noth - in' left to lose,
oth - er word for noth - in' left to lose,

Nothin' ain't worth nothin', but it's free;
Nothin' left is all she but left it's for me;

Feelin' good was easy, Lord, When Bobby sang the

blues; And feelin' good was good enough for me,
And, buddy, that was good enough for me,

Good enough for me and Bobby Mc-

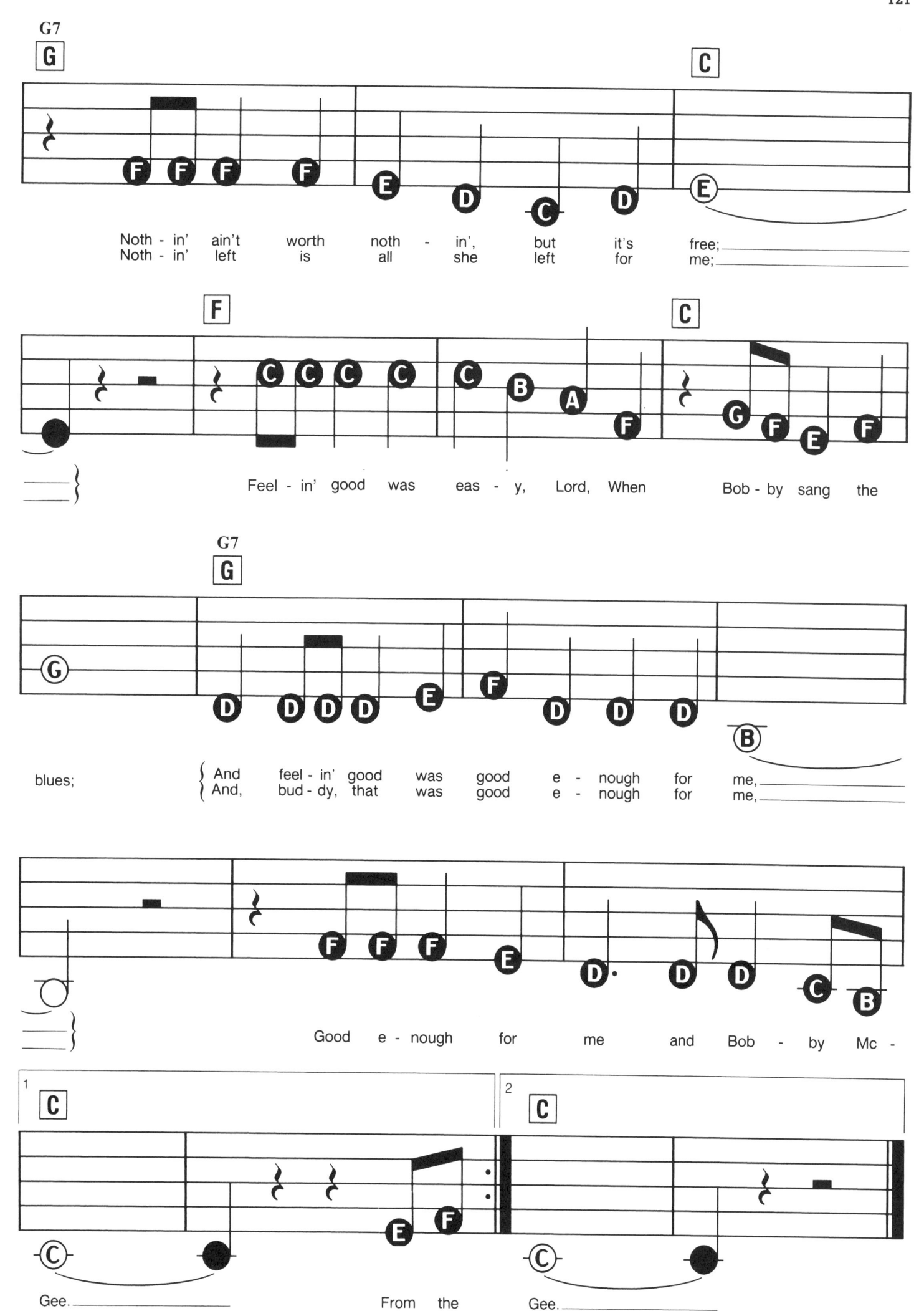

Gee.   From the Gee.

Monday, Monday

Registration 4
Rhythm: Rock

Words and Music by
John Phillips

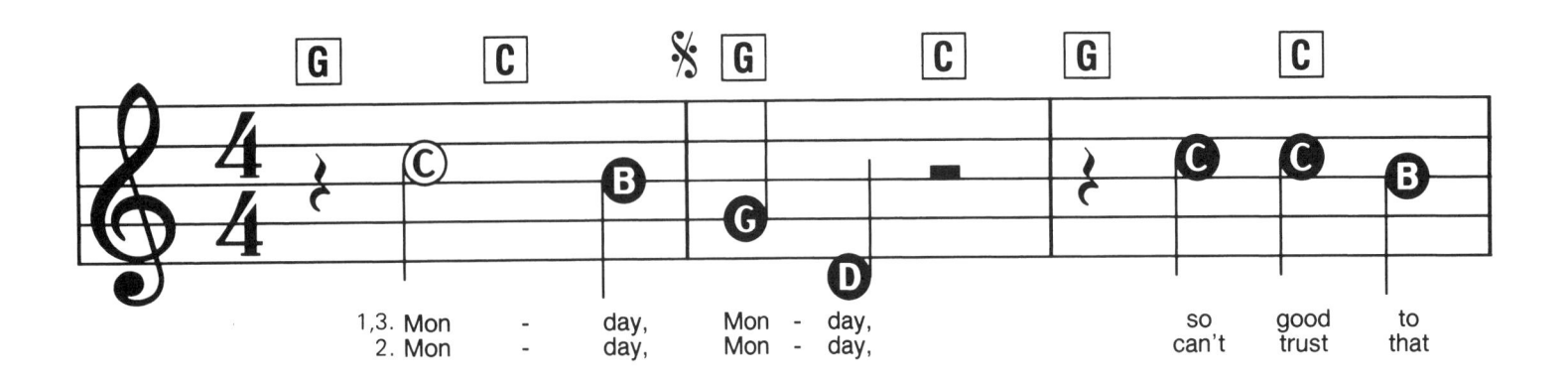

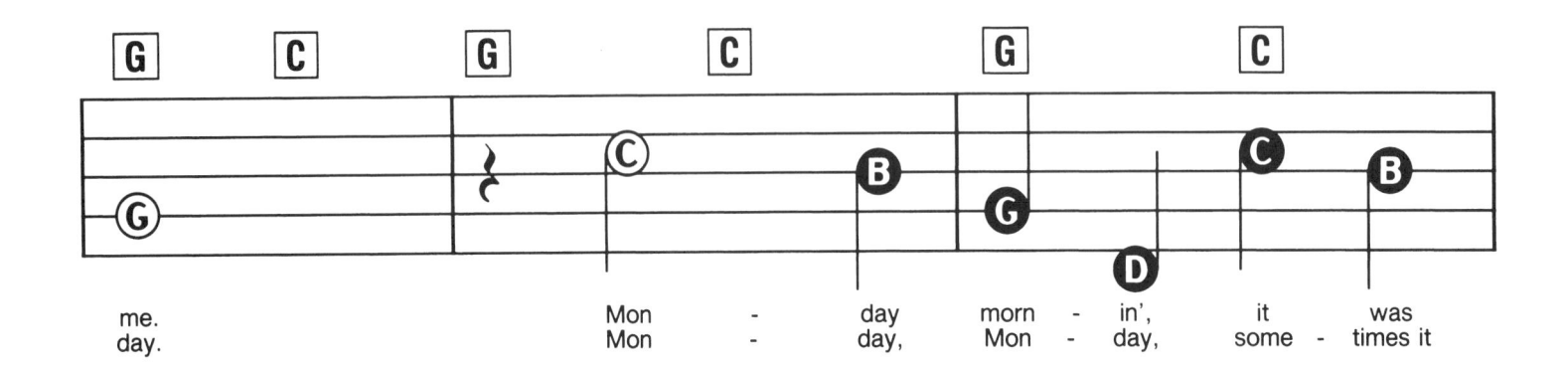

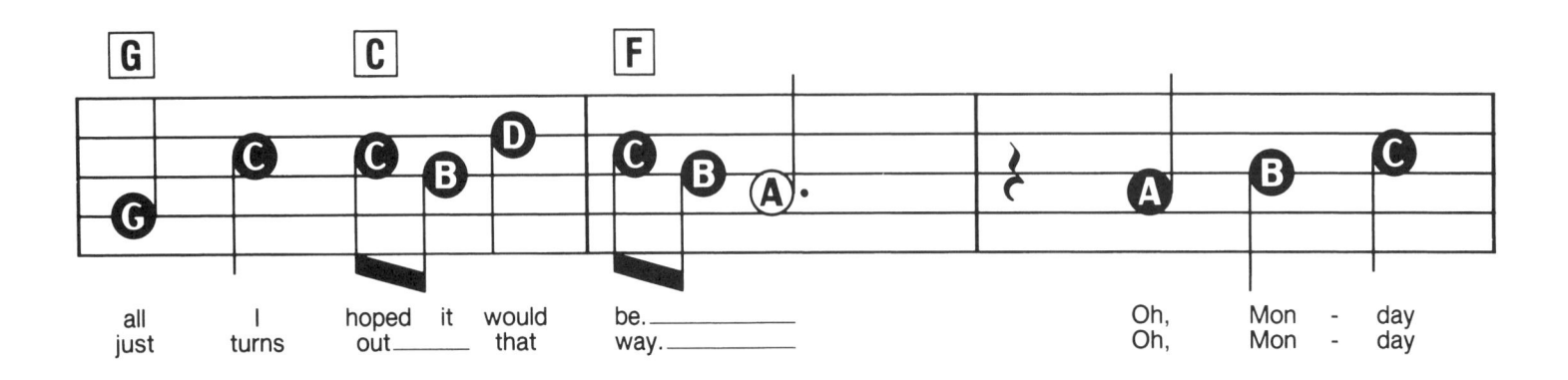

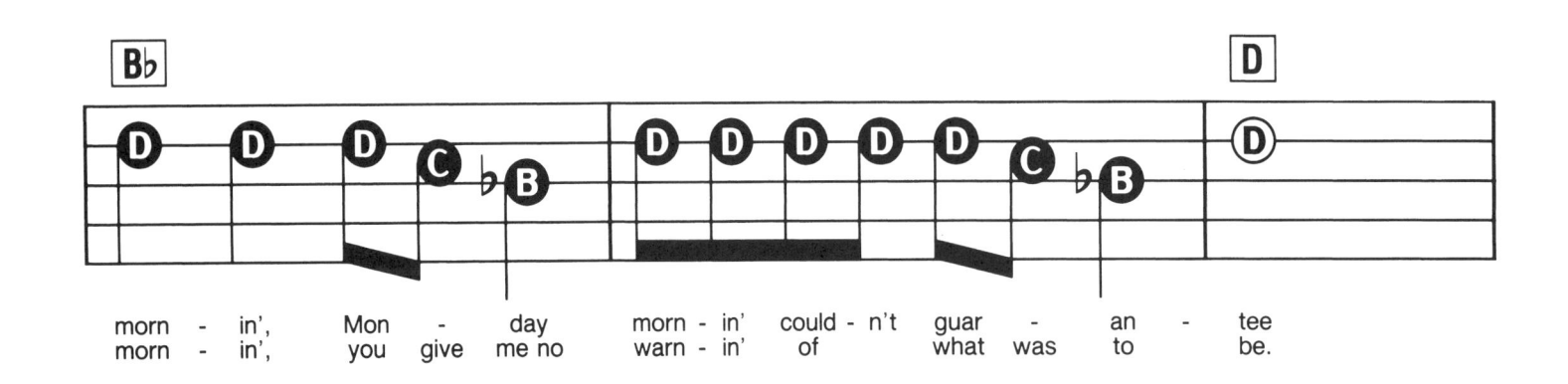

1,3. Mon - day, Mon - day, so good to
2. Mon - day, Mon - day, can't trust that

me. Mon - day morn - in', it was
day. Mon - day, Mon - day, some - times it

all I hoped it would be._____ Oh, Mon - day
just turns out____ that way._____ Oh, Mon - day

morn - in', Mon - day morn - in' could - n't guar - an - tee
morn - in', you give me no warn - in' of what was to be.

Copyright © 1966 UNIVERSAL MUSIC CORP.
Copyright Renewed
All Rights Reserved   Used by Permission

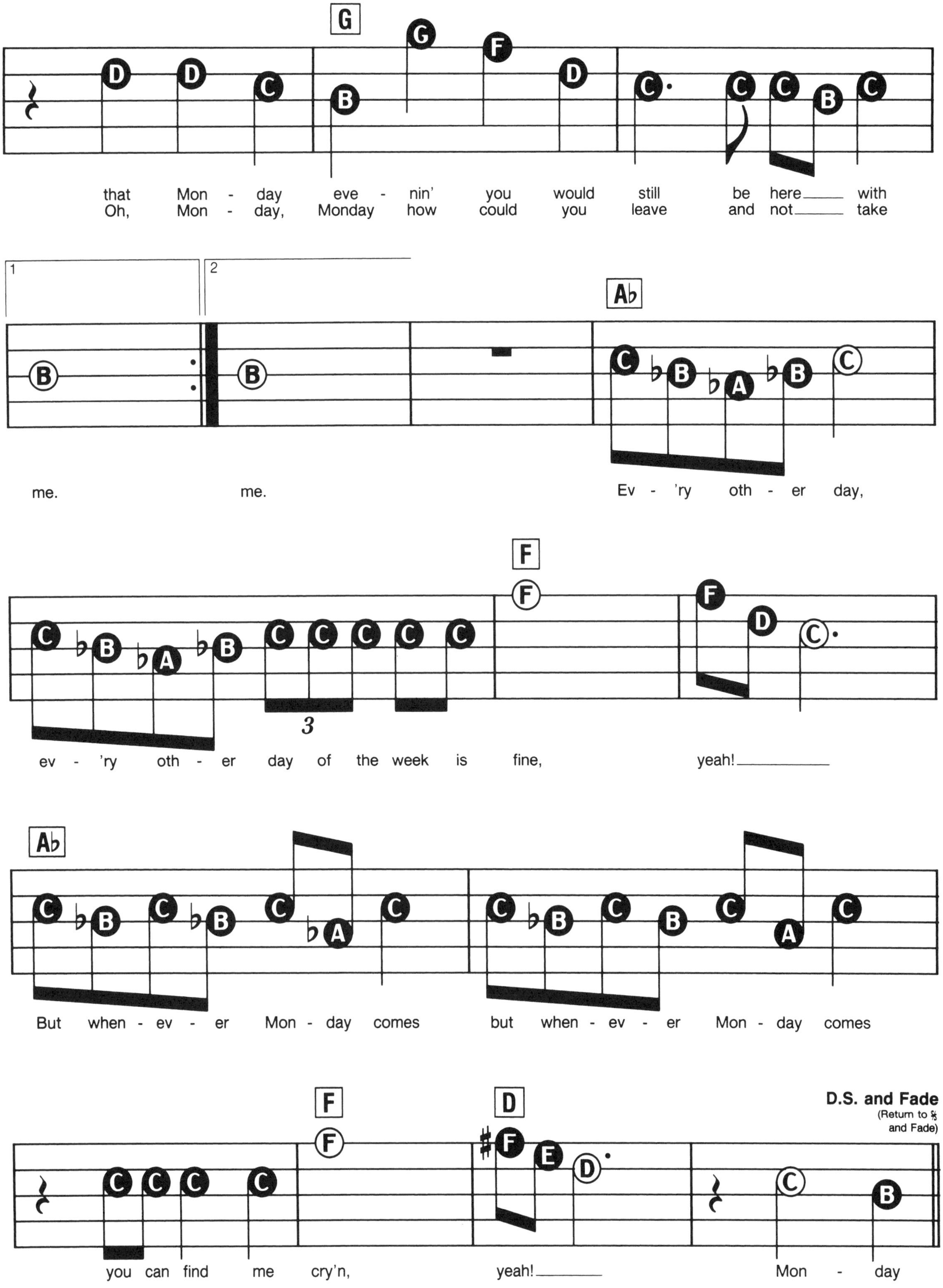
G
that Mon - day eve - nin' you would still be here with
Oh, Mon - day, Monday how could you leave and not take
1
2
me. me.
Ab
Ev - 'ry oth - er day,
F
ev - 'ry oth - er day of the week is fine,
3
yeah!
Ab
But when - ev - er Mon - day comes but when - ev - er Mon - day comes
F
D
D.S. and Fade
(Return to 𝄋 and Fade)
you can find me cry'n, yeah!
Mon - day

Nights in White Satin

Registration 6
Rhythm: Waltz

Words and Music by
Justin Hayward

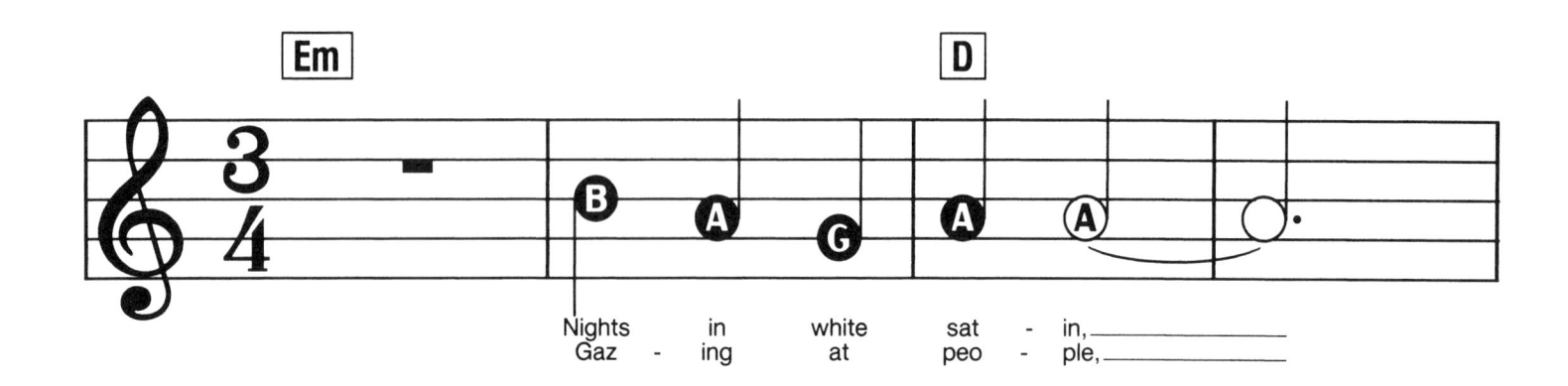

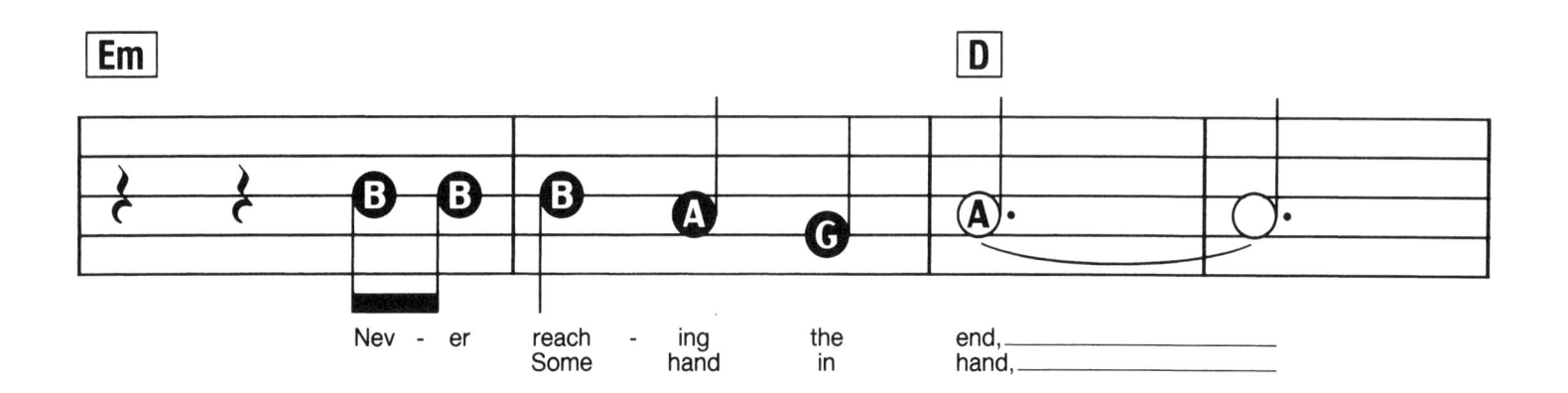

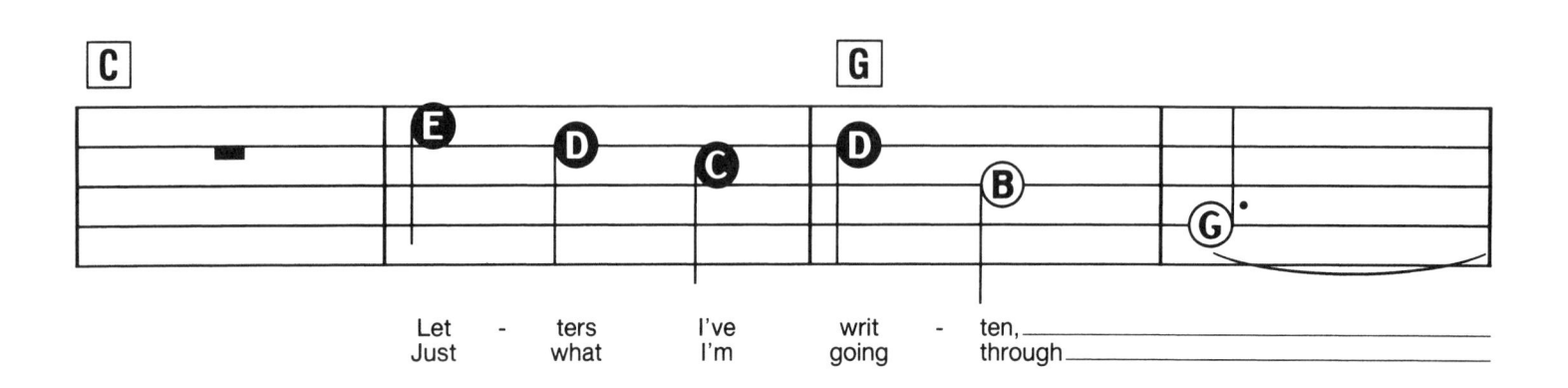

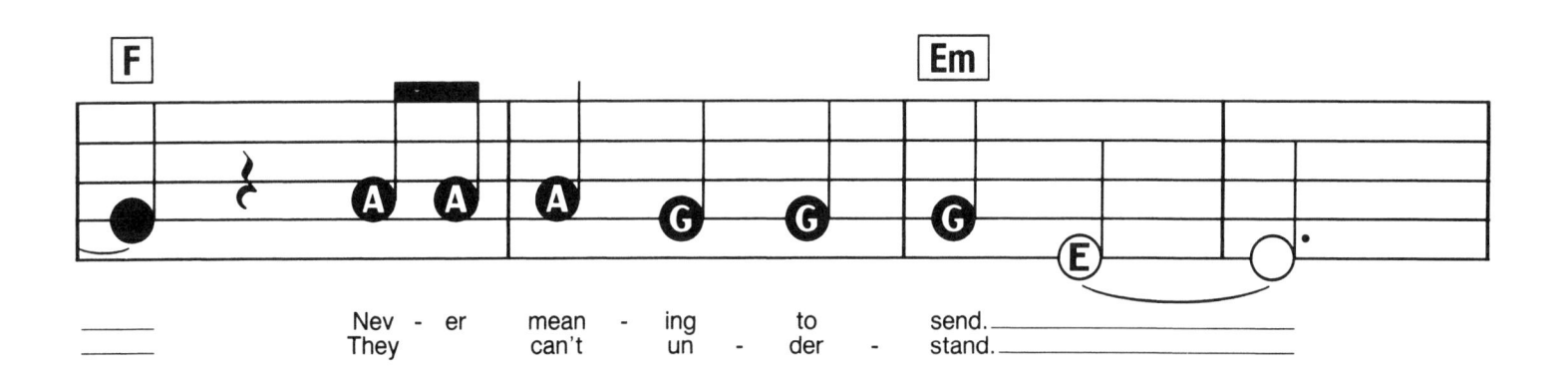

Nights in white sat - in,_____
Gaz - ing at peo - ple,_____

Nev - er reach - ing the end,_____
Some hand in hand,_____

Let - ters I've writ - ten,_____
Just what I'm going through_____

Nev - er mean - ing to send._____
They can't un - der - stand._____

© Copyright 1967 (Renewed), 1968 (Renewed) and 1970 (Renewed) Tyler Music Ltd., London, England
TRO - Essex Music, Inc., New York, controls all publication rights for the U.S.A. and Canada
International Copyright Secured
All Rights Reserved Including Public Performance For Profit
Used by Permission

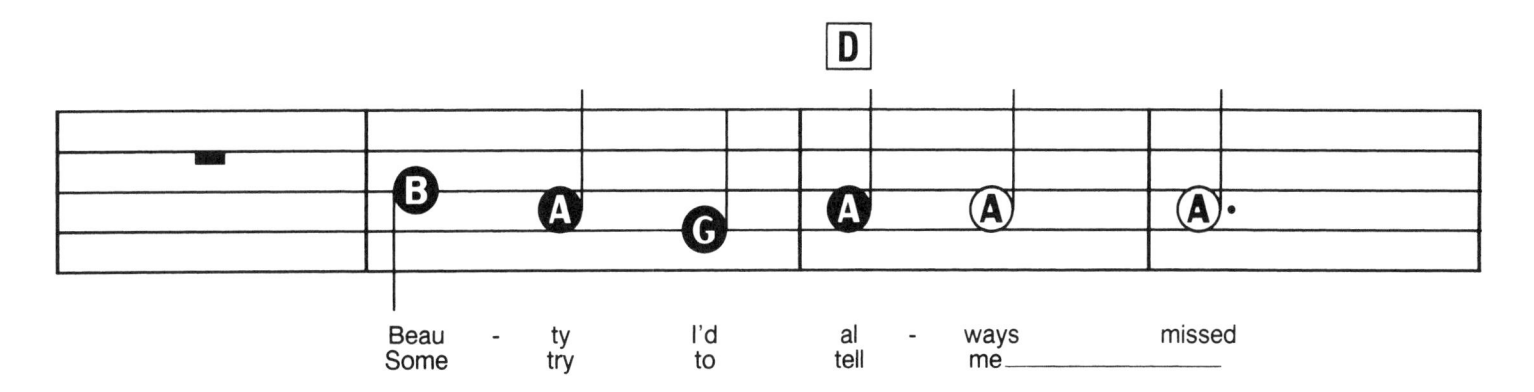

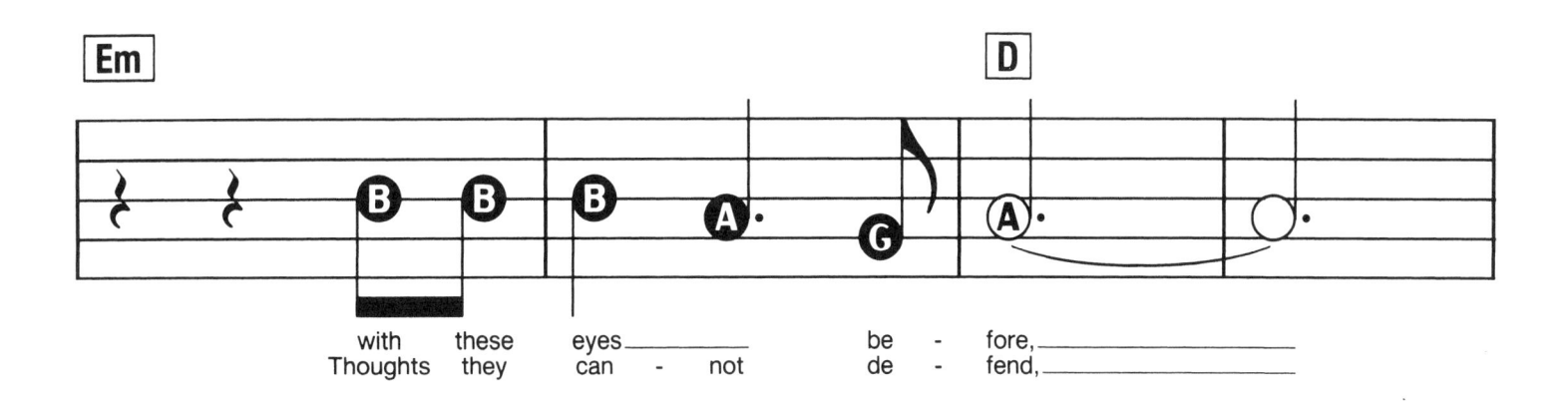

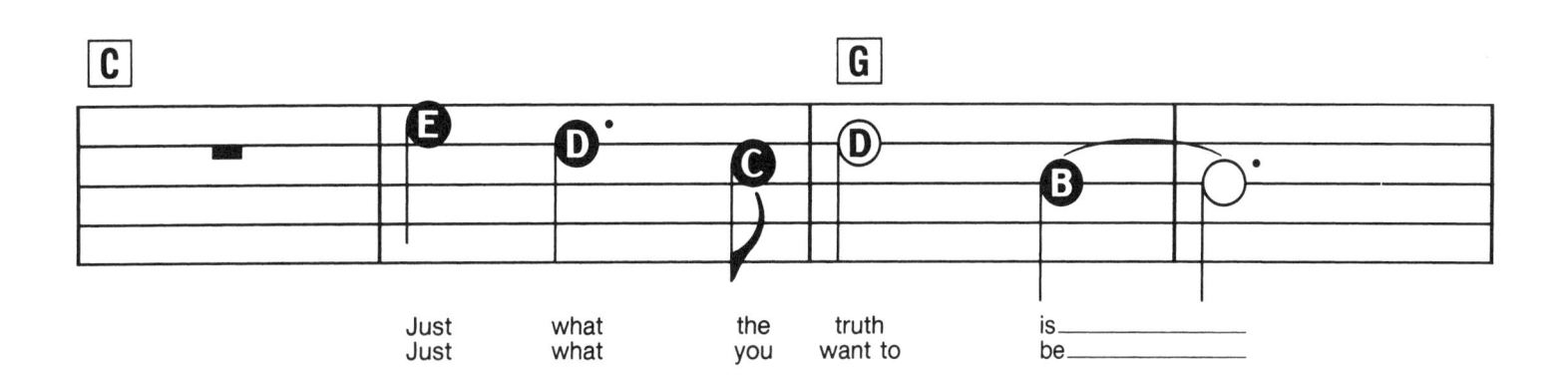

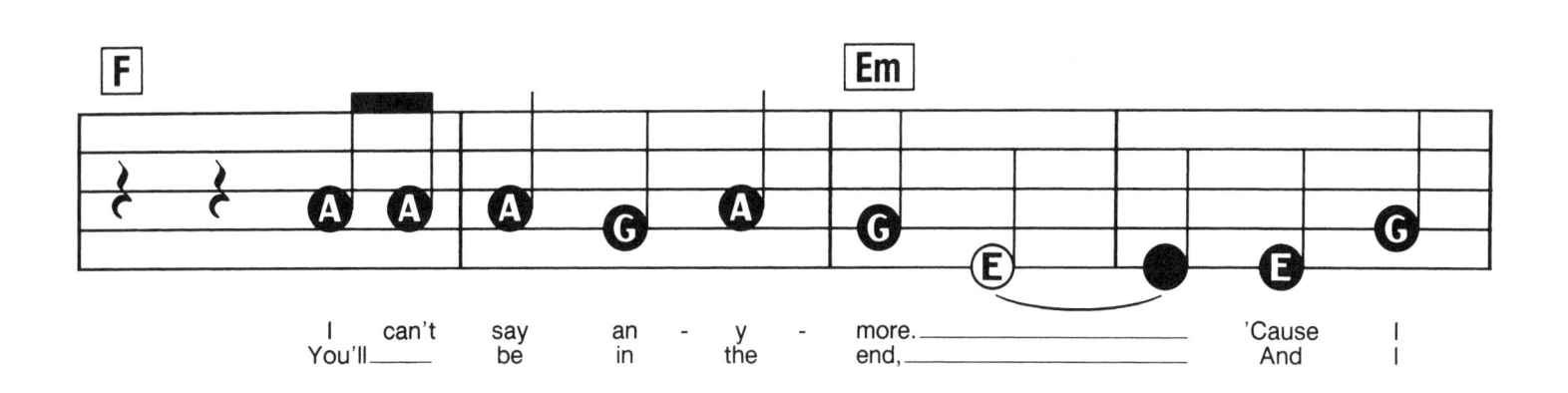

Beau - ty I'd al - ways missed with these eyes be - fore,
Some try to tell me Thoughts they can - not de - fend,

Just what the truth is
Just what what you want to be

I can't say an - y - more. 'Cause I
You'll be in the end, And I

126

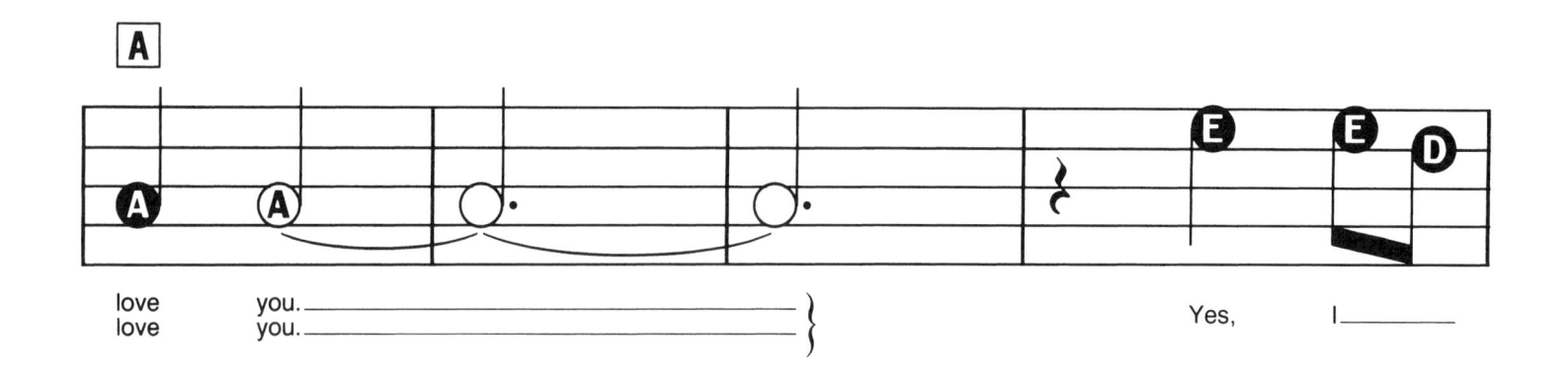

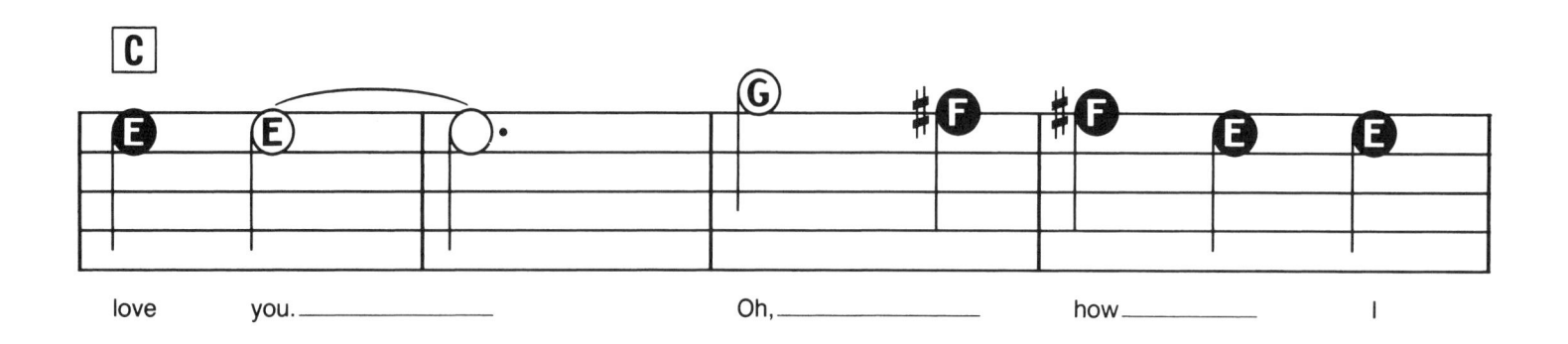

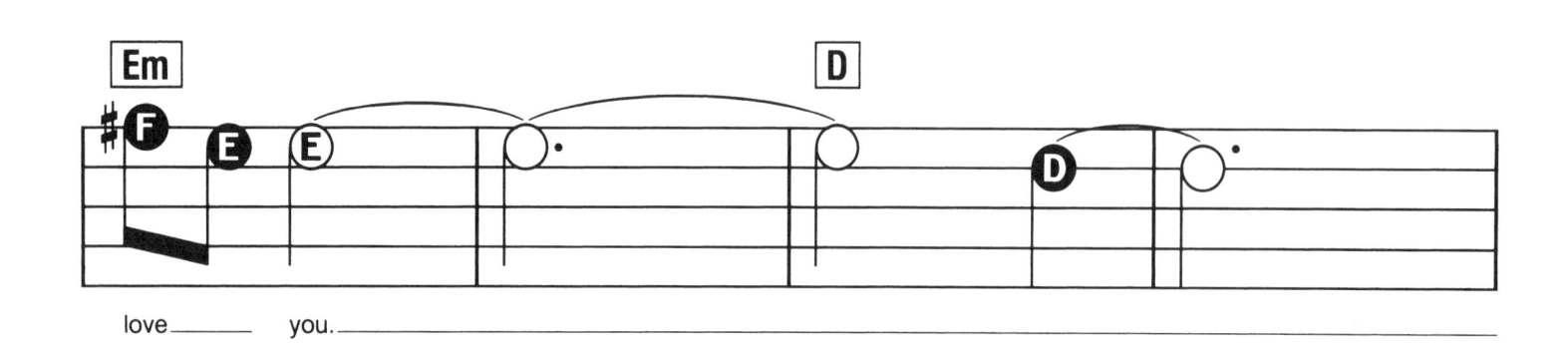

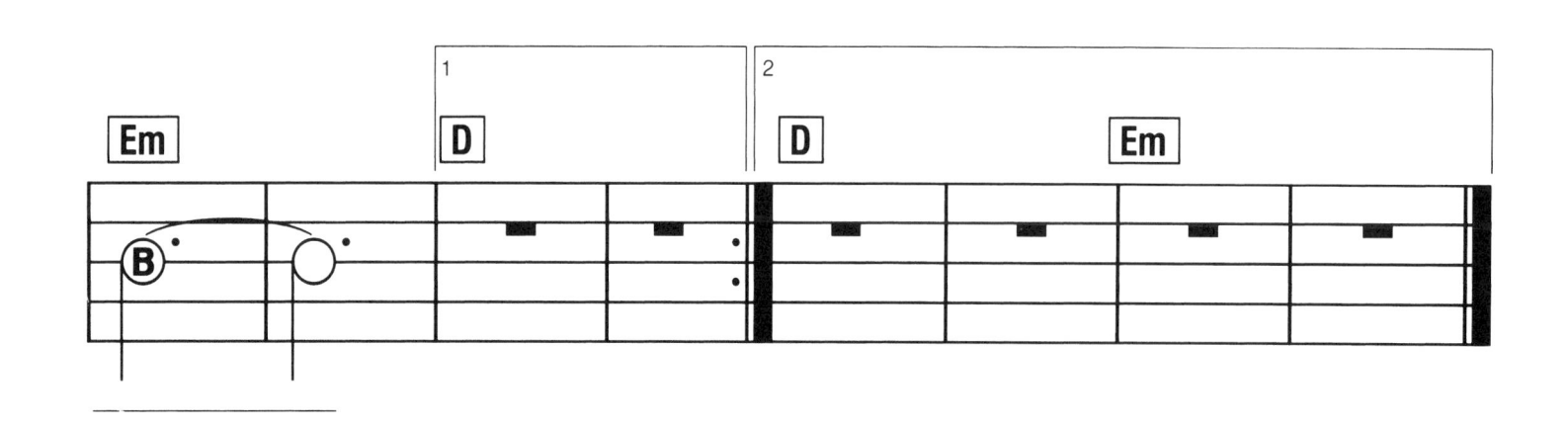

Norwegian Wood
(This Bird Has Flown)

Registration 8
Rhythm: Waltz

Words and Music by John Lennon
and Paul McCartney

| G | F | G | F |

3/4

D · E D C B · A C B

I once had a girl, or should I

| G | F | G | F |

G · C F E D · —

say she once had me;

| G | F | G | F |

D · E D C B · A C B

She showed me her room, is-n't it

| G | F | G |

G · C F E D · ♪ ♪ G

good Nor-we-gian wood? She

Copyright © 1965 Sony/ATV Music Publishing LLC
Copyright Renewed
All Rights Administered by Sony/ATV Music Publishing LLC, 8 Music Square West, Nashville, TN 37203
International Copyright Secured All Rights Reserved

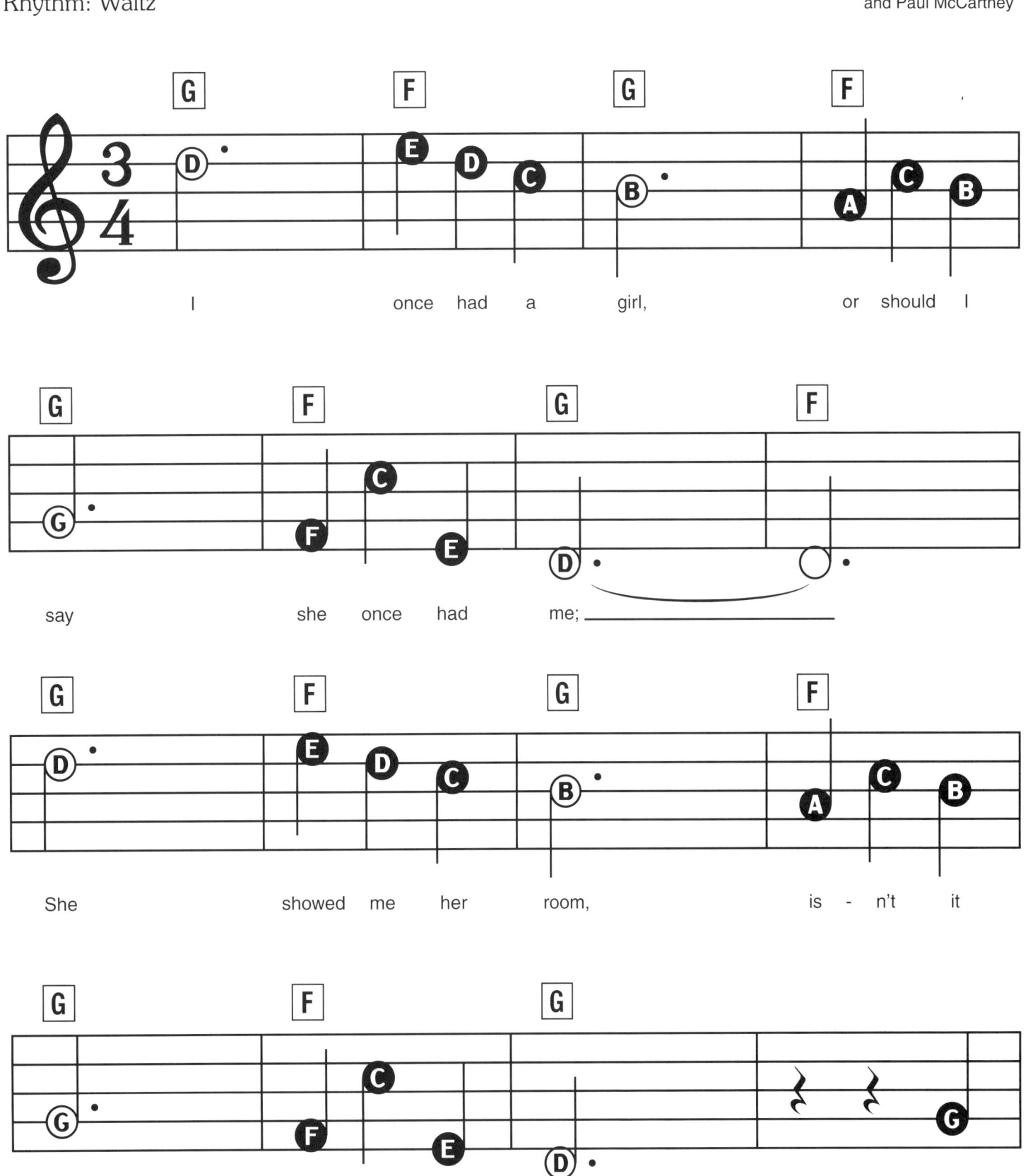

Gm

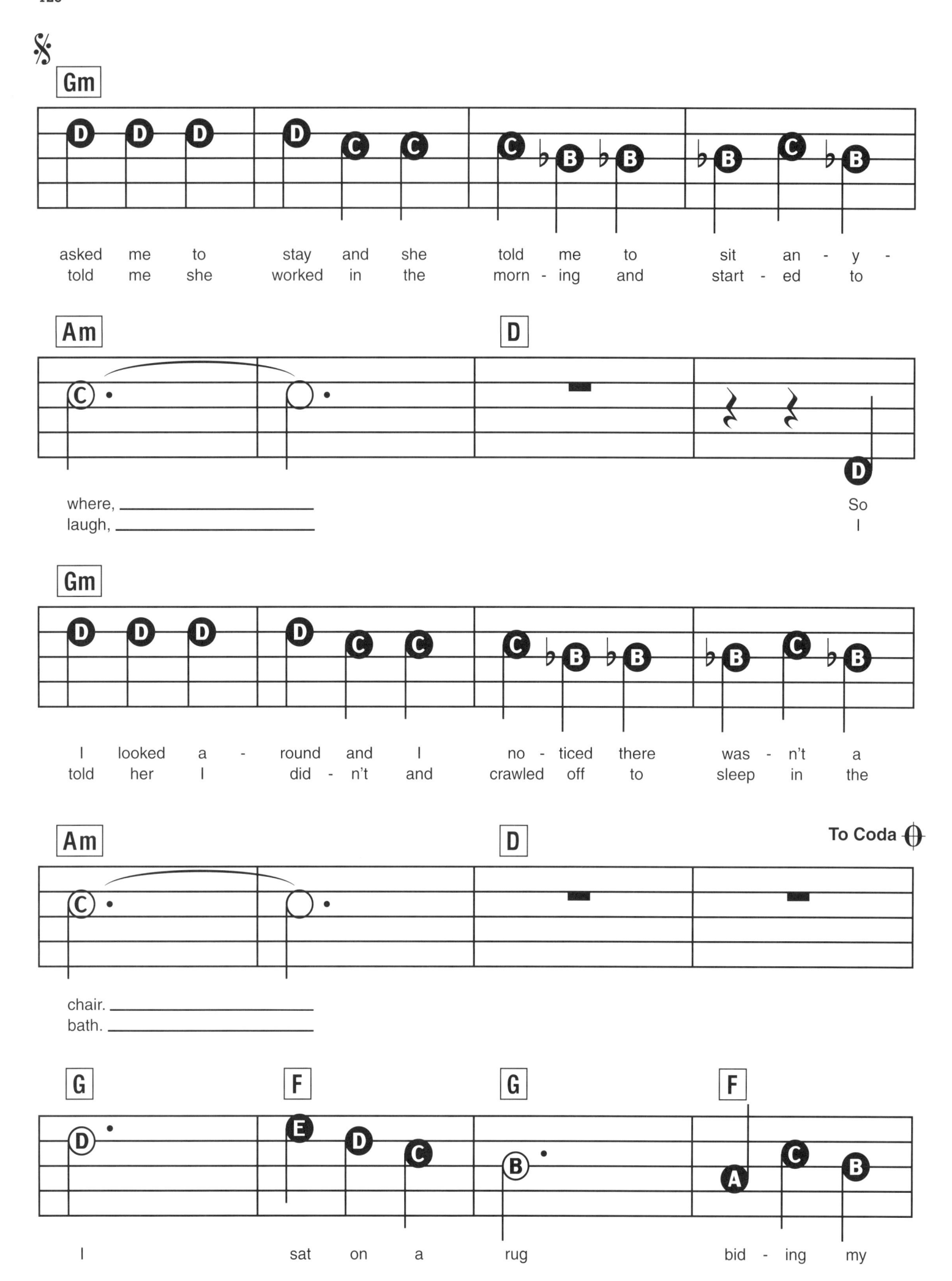

asked me to / told me she — stay and she / worked in the — told me to / morn-ing and — sit an-y- / start-ed to

Am — **D**

where, / laugh, — So / I

Gm

I looked a- / told her I — round and I / did-n't and — no-ticed there / crawled off to — was-n't a / sleep in the

Am — **D** — To Coda

chair. / bath.

G — **F** — **G** — **F**

I — sat on a rug — bid-ing my

time, drink-ing her wine. _____

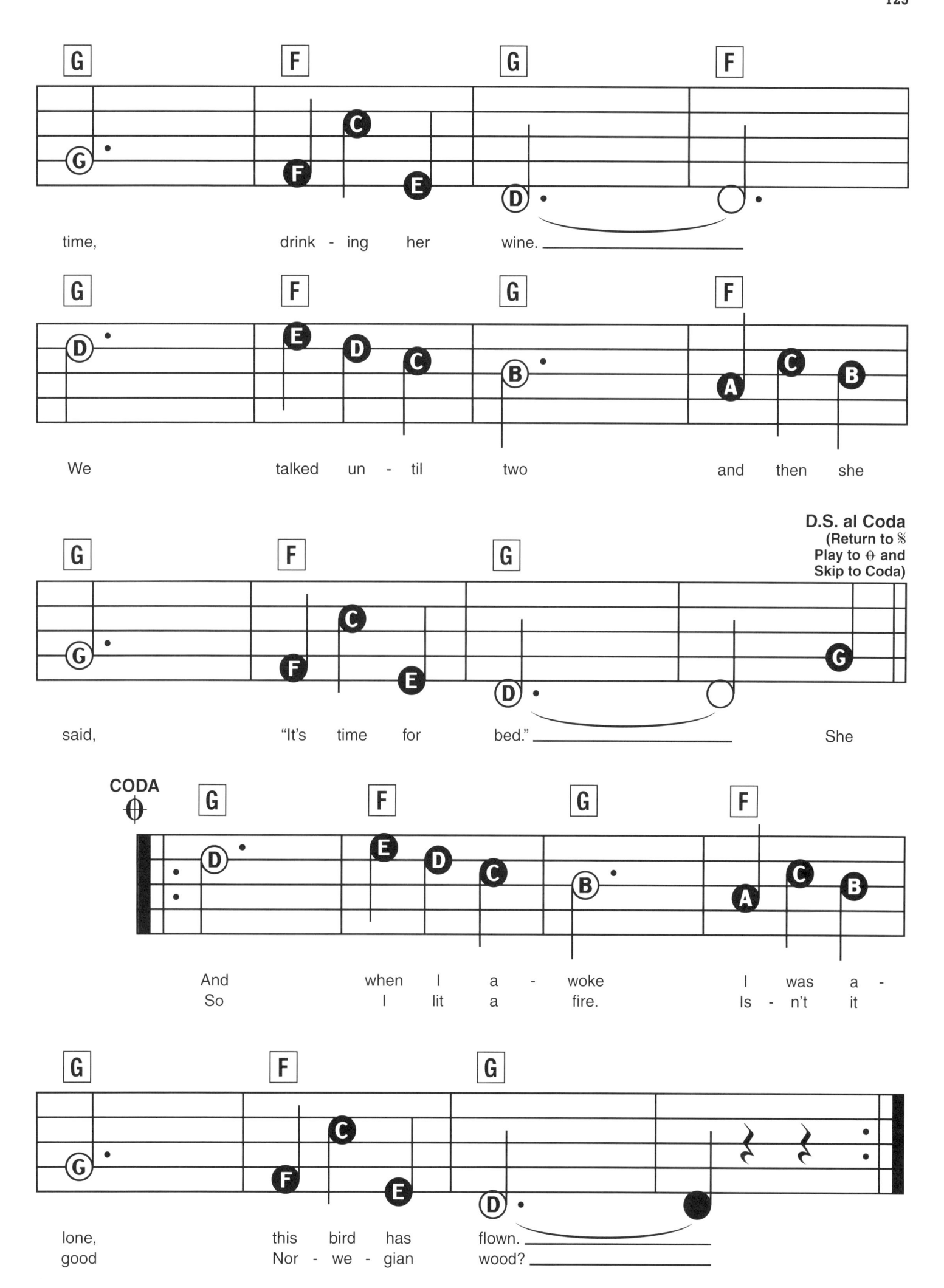

We talked un-til two and then she

D.S. al Coda
(Return to 𝄋
Play to ✛ and
Skip to Coda)

said, "It's time for bed." _____ She

CODA

And when I a-woke I was a-
So I lit a fire. Isn't it

lone, this bird has flown. _____
good Nor-we-gian wood? _____

Operator
(That's Not the Way It Feels)

Registration 1
Rhythm: 8 Beat or Rock

Words and Music by
Jim Croce

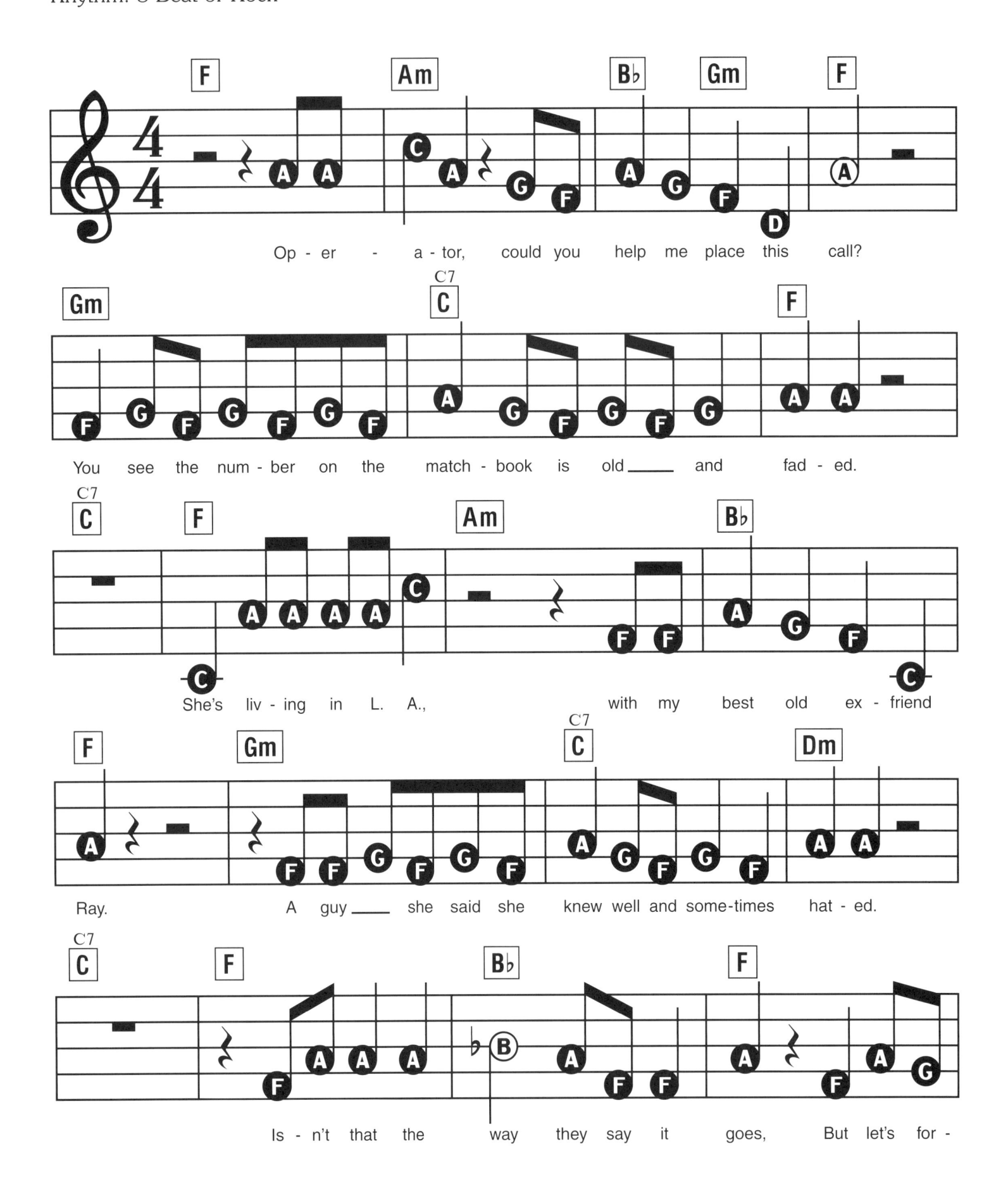

Op - er - a - tor, could you help me place this call?

You see the num - ber on the match - book is old ___ and fad - ed.

She's liv - ing in L. A., with my best old ex - friend

Ray. A guy ___ she said she knew well and some - times hat - ed.

Is - n't that the way they say it goes, But let's for -

© 1971 (Renewed 1999) TIME IN A BOTTLE PUBLISHING and CROCE PUBLISHING
All Rights Controlled and Administered by EMI APRIL MUSIC INC.
All Rights Reserved   International Copyright Secured   Used by Permission

get all that, And give me the num-ber, if you can find it, So I can ___ call just to tell them I'm fine and to show ___ I've o-ver-come the blow, I've learned to take it well, I on-ly wish my words could just con-vince my-self That it just was-n't real, ___ But that's not the way it feels. ___

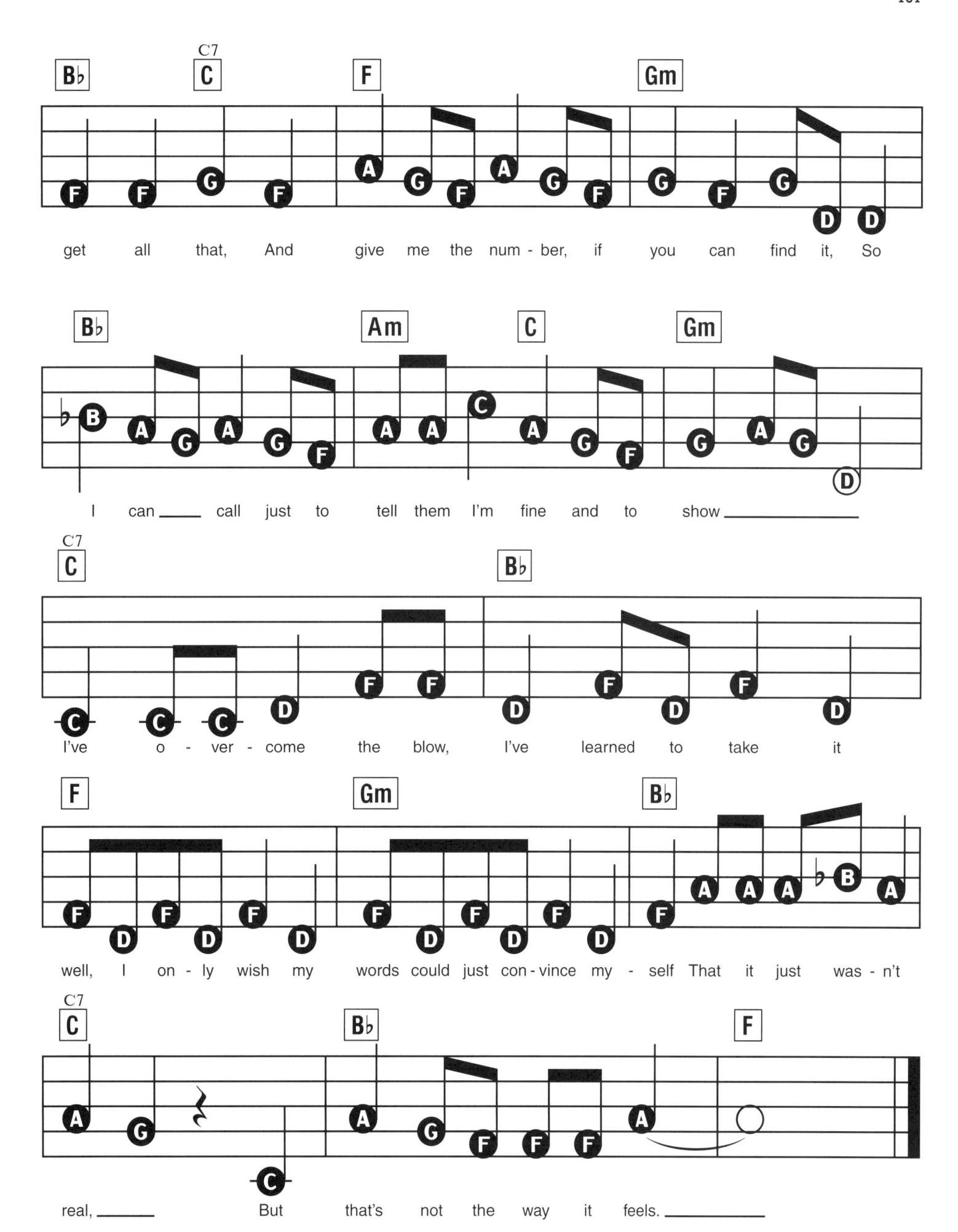

Puff the Magic Dragon

Registration 2
Rhythm: Swing

Words and Music by Lenny Lipton
and Peter Yarrow

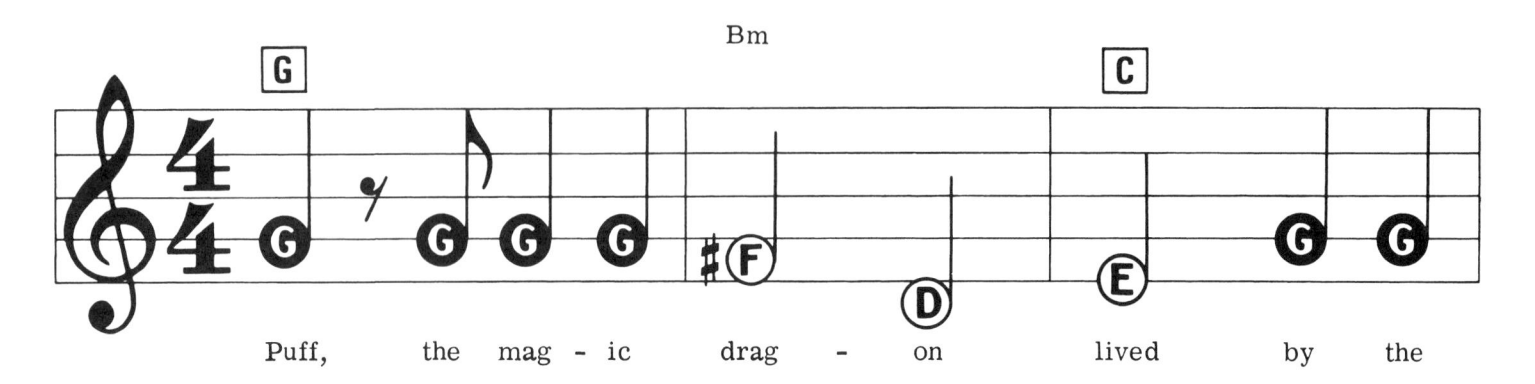

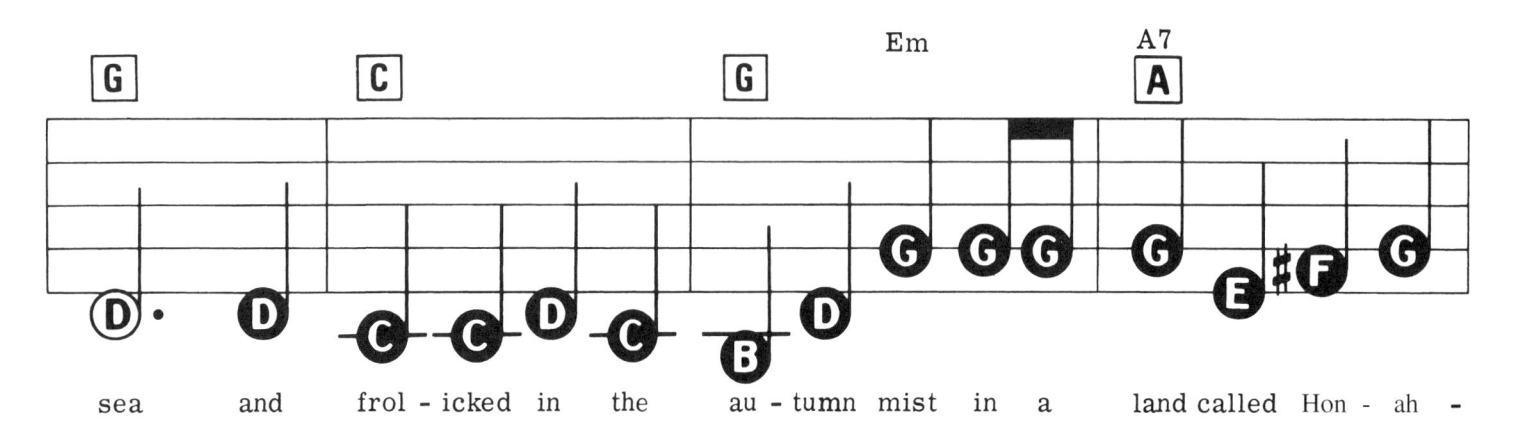

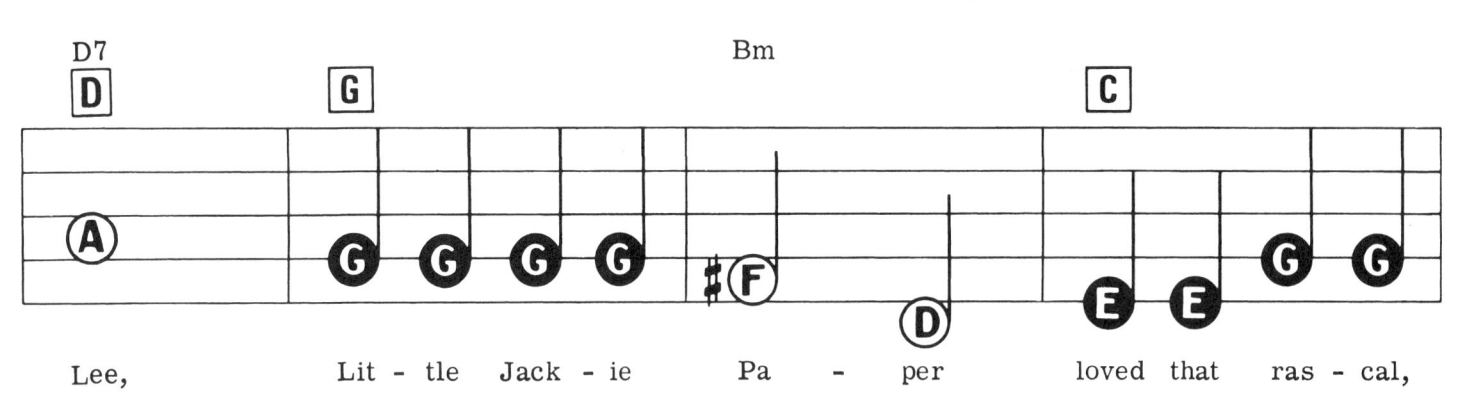

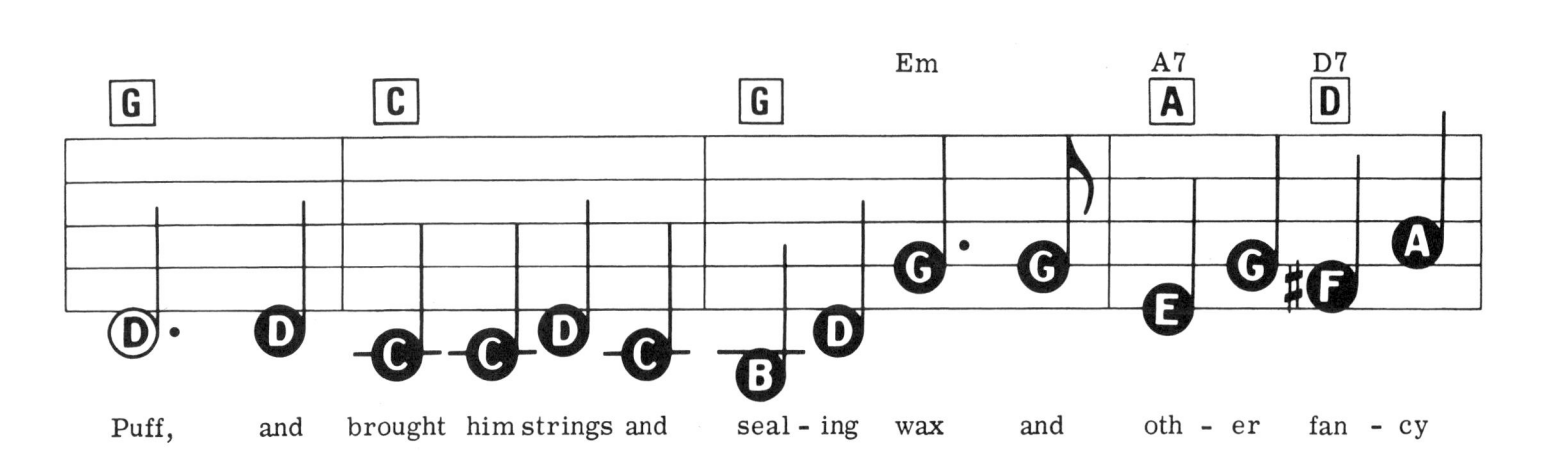

Puff, the mag-ic drag-on lived by the sea and frol-icked in the au-tumn mist in a land called Hon-ah- Lee, Lit-tle Jack-ie Pa-per loved that ras-cal, Puff, and brought him strings and seal-ing wax and oth-er fan-cy

Copyright © 1963; Renewed 1991 Honalee Melodies (ASCAP) and Silver Dawn Music (ASCAP)
Worldwide Rights for Honalee Melodies Administered by Cherry Lane Music Publishing Company, Inc.
Worldwide Rights for Silver Dawn Music Administered by WB Music Corp.
International Copyright Secured   All Rights Reserved

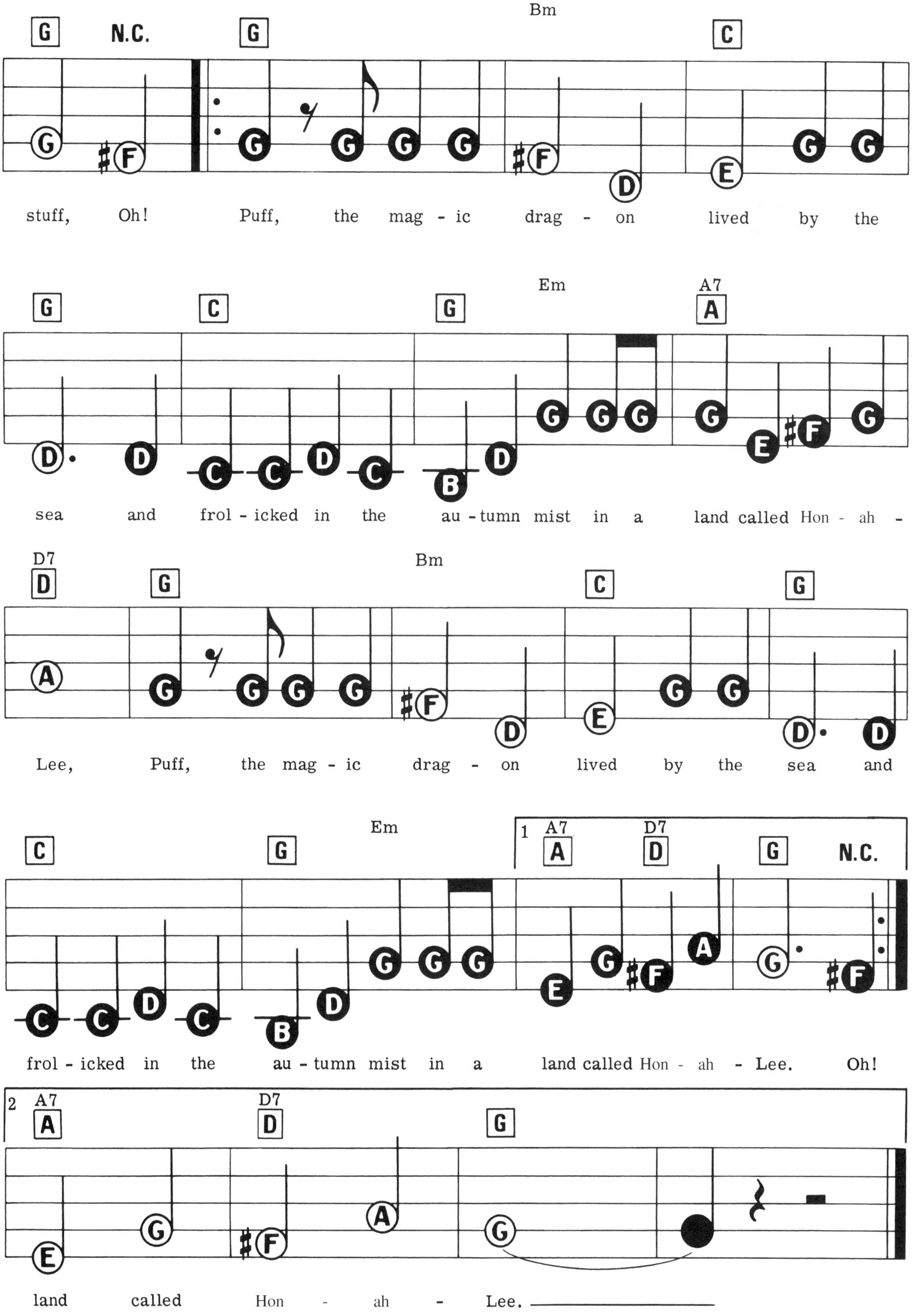
G N.C. G Bm C
stuff, Oh! Puff, the mag - ic drag - on lived by the
G C G Em A7 A
sea and frol - icked in the au - tumn mist in a land called Hon - ah -
D7 D G Bm C G
Lee, Puff, the mag - ic drag - on lived by the sea and
C G Em 1 A7 A D7 D G N.C.
frol - icked in the au - tumn mist in a land called Hon - ah - Lee. Oh!
2 A7 A D7 D G
land called Hon - ah - Lee.

Same Old Lang Syne

Registration 7
Rhythm: Fox Trot or Ballad

Words and Music by
Dan Fogelberg

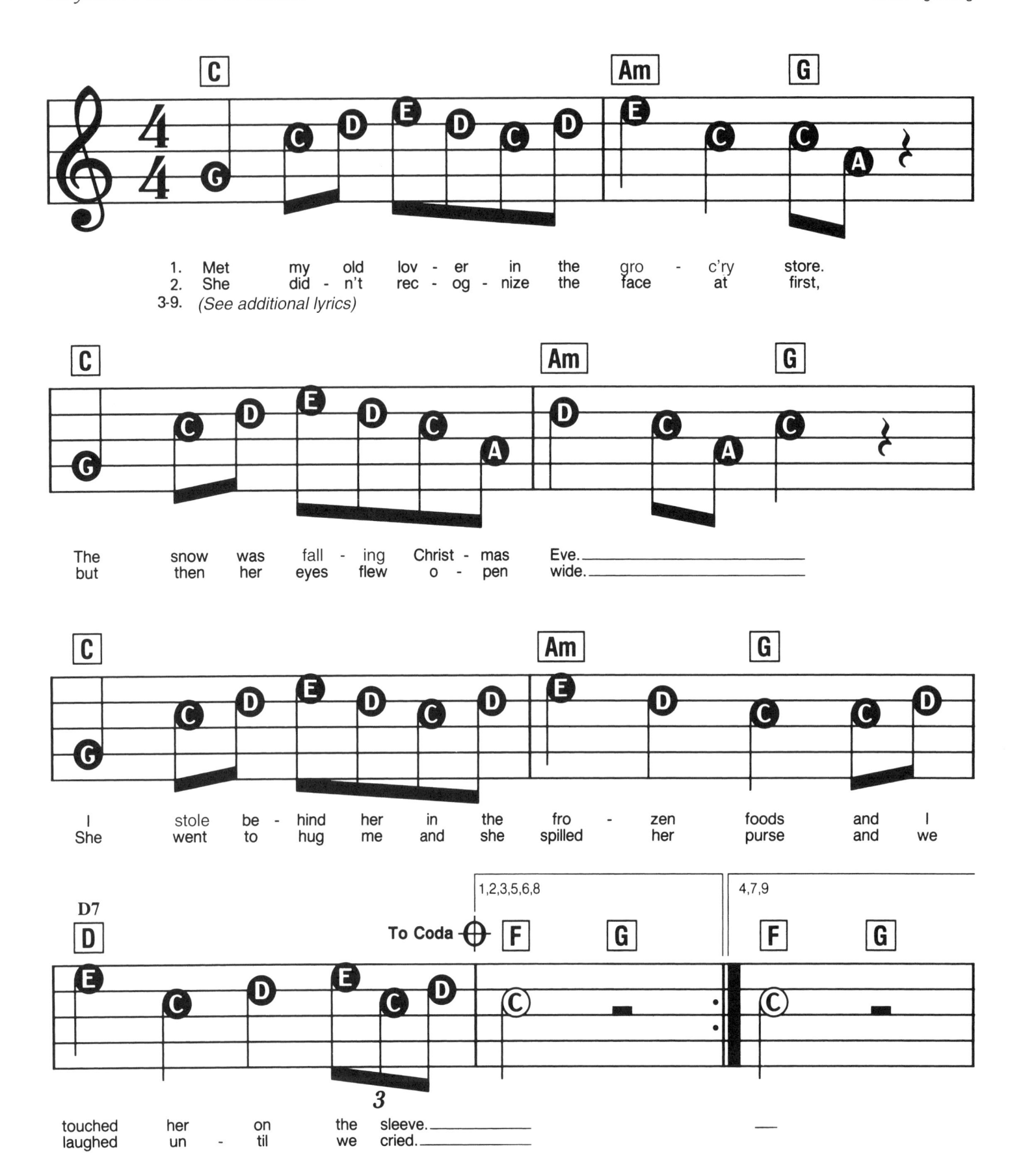

1. Met my old lov-er in the gro-c'ry store.
2. She did-n't rec-og-nize the face at first,
3-9. *(See additional lyrics)*

The snow was fall-ing Christ-mas Eve.
but then her eyes flew o-pen wide.

I stole be-hind her in the fro-zen foods and I
She went to hug me and she spilled her purse and we

touched her on the sleeve.
laughed un-til we cried.

© 1979, 1981 EMI APRIL MUSIC INC. and HICKORY GROVE MUSIC
All Rights Controlled and Administered by EMI APRIL MUSIC INC.
All Rights Reserved   International Copyright Secured   Used by Permission

135

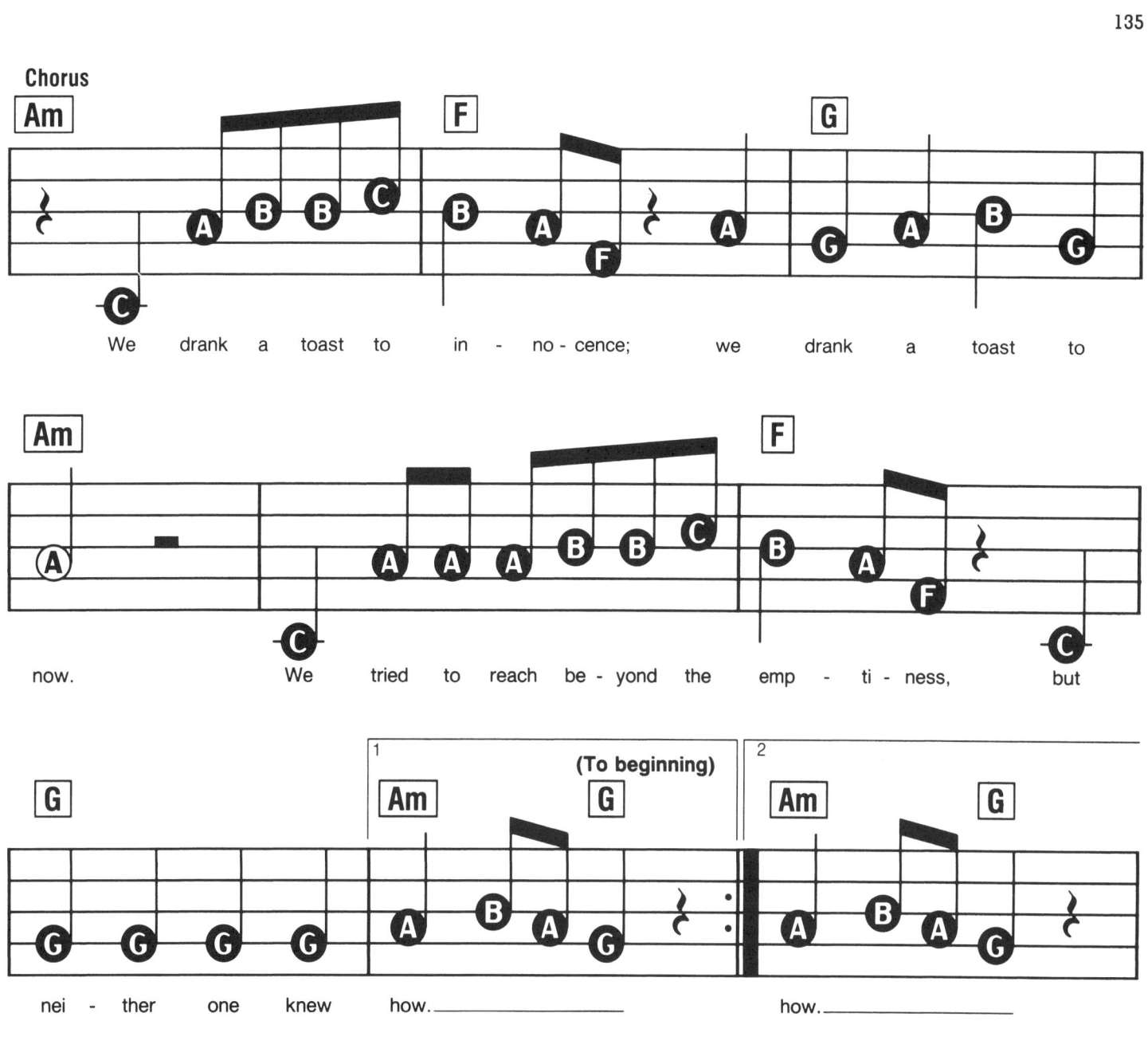

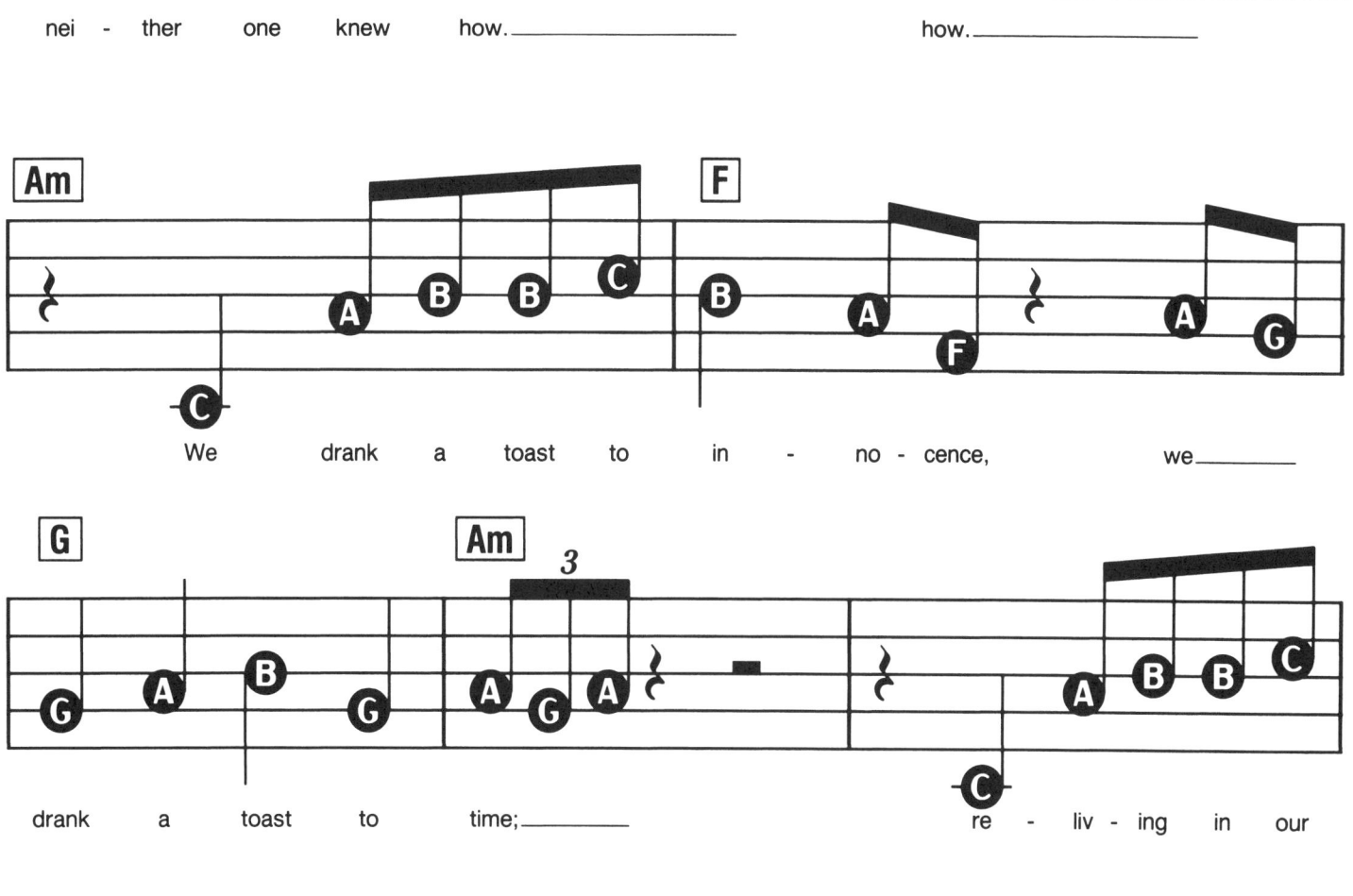

el-o-quence, an-oth-er "Auld Lang Syne."

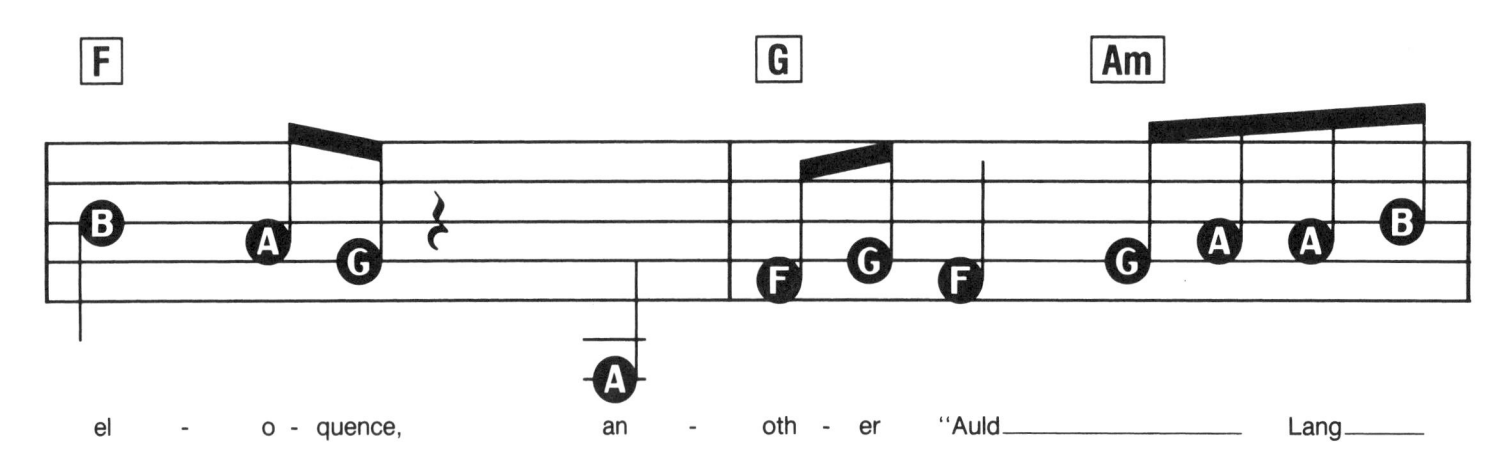

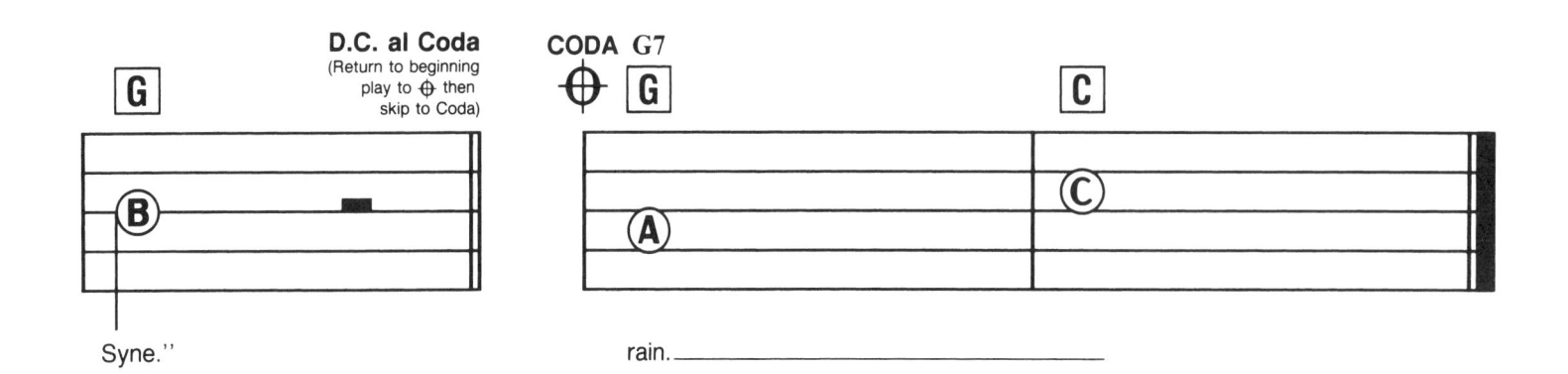

rain.

Additional Lyrics

3. We took her groc'ries to the check out stand;
   The food was totalled up and bagged.
   We stood there, lost in our embarrassment,
   As the conversation lagged.

4. We went to have ourselves a drink or two,
   But couldn't find an open bar.
   We bought a six-pack at the liquor store
   And we drank it in her car.

5. She said she's married her an architect,
   Who kept her warm and safe and dry.
   She would have liked to say she loved the man,
   But she didn't like to lie.

6. I said the years had been a friend to her
   And that her eyes were still as blue.
   But in those eyes I wasn't sure if I
   Saw doubt or gratitude.

7. She said she saw me in the record stores,
   And that I must be doing well.
   I said the audience was heavenly,
   But the traveling was hell.

8. The beer was empty and our tongues were tired,
   And running out of things to say.
   She gave a kiss to me as I got out,
   And I watched her drive away.

9. Just for a moment I was back at school
   And felt that old familiar pain.
   And as I turned to make my way back home,
   The snow turned into rain.

Sara Smile

Registration 3
Rhythm: Rock

Words and Music by Daryl Hall
and John Oates

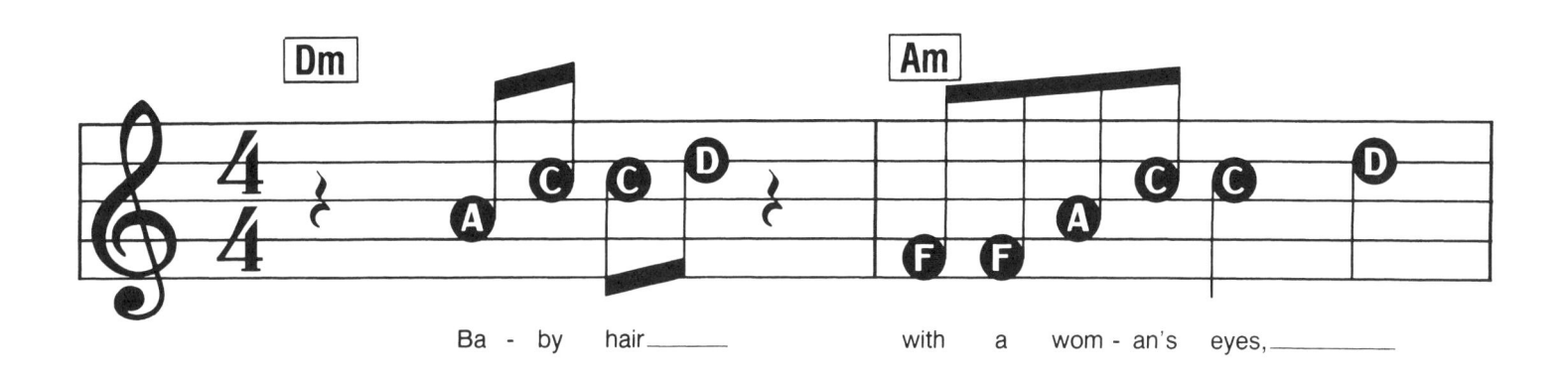

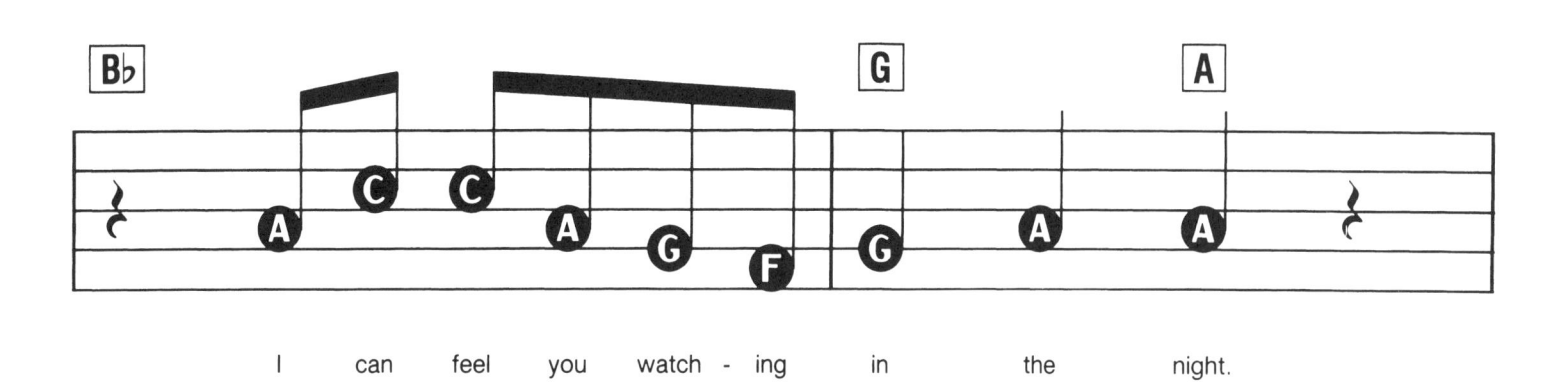

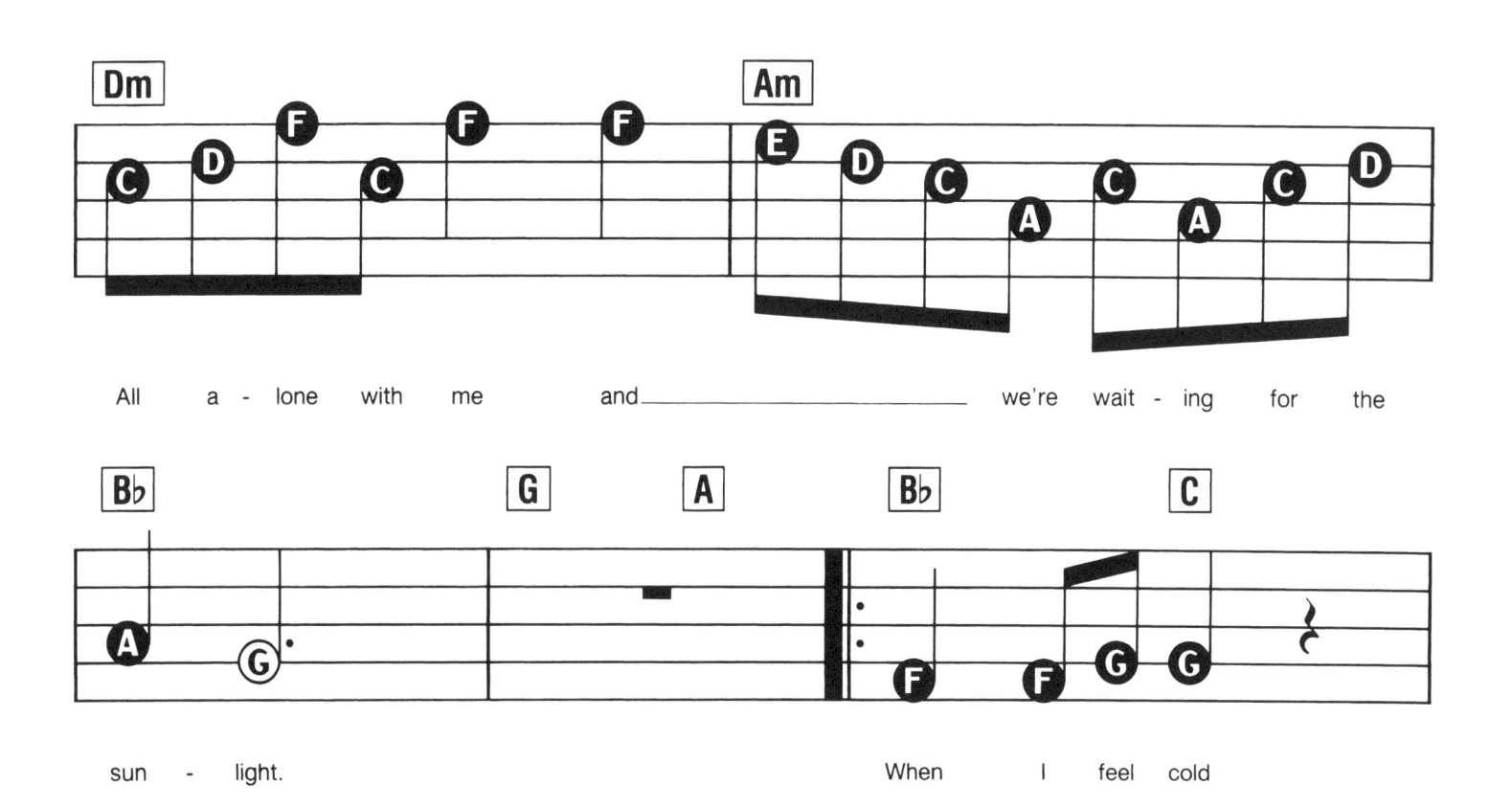

Ba - by hair_____ with a wom - an's eyes,_____

I can feel you watch - ing in the night.

All a - lone with me and_____ we're wait - ing for the

sun - light. When I feel cold

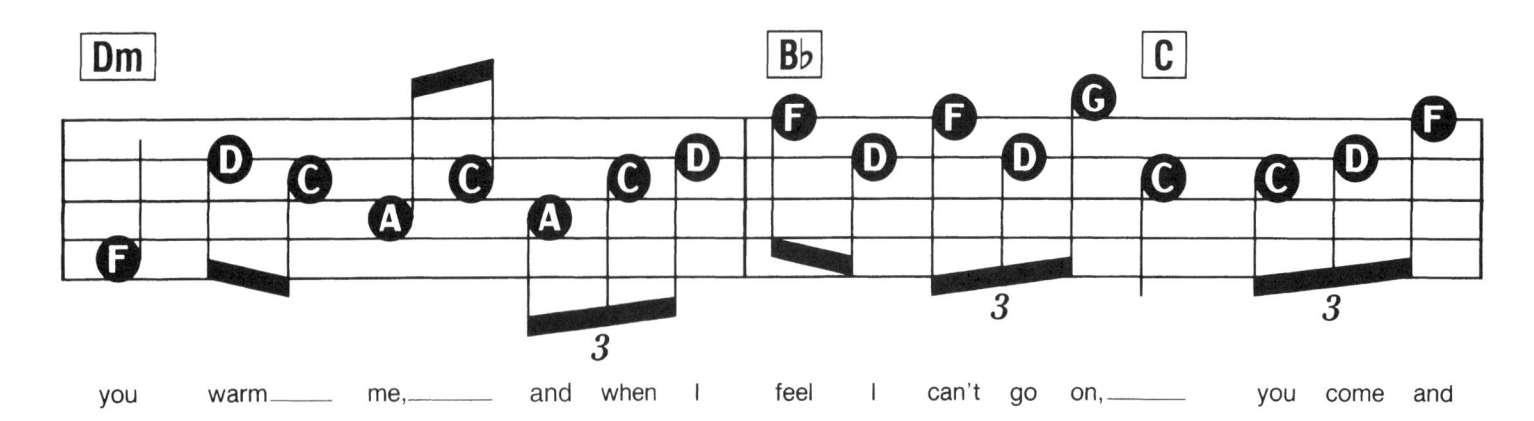

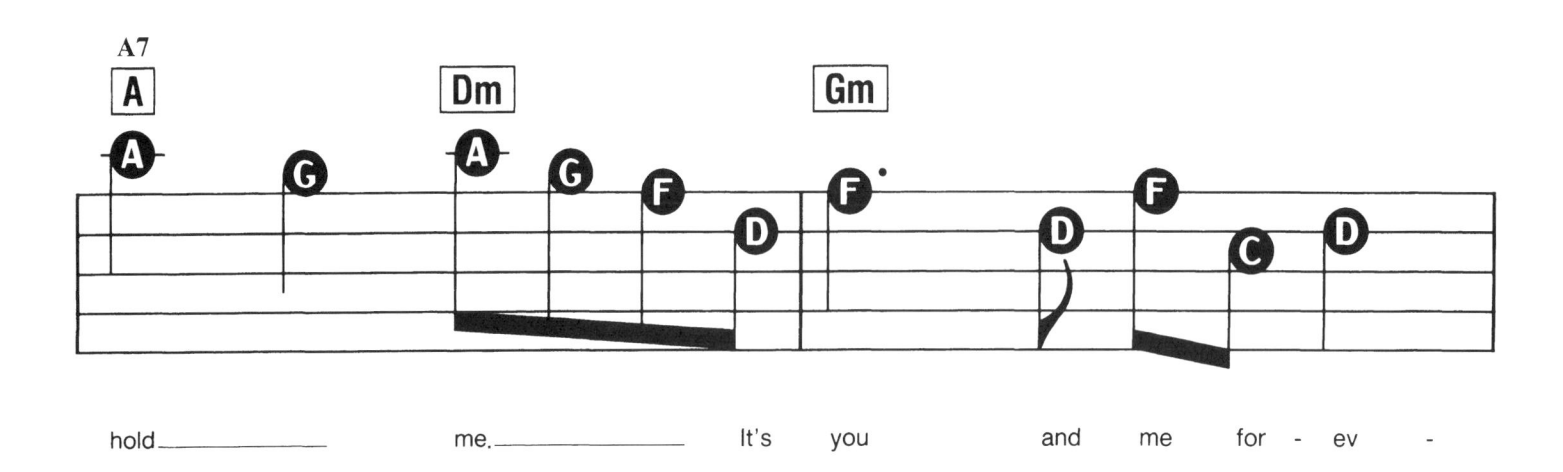

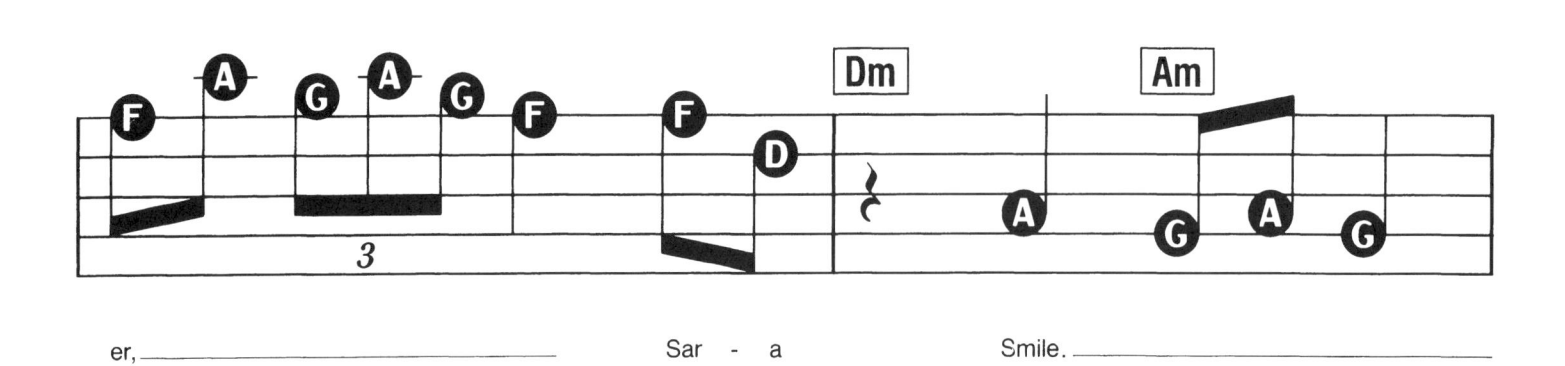

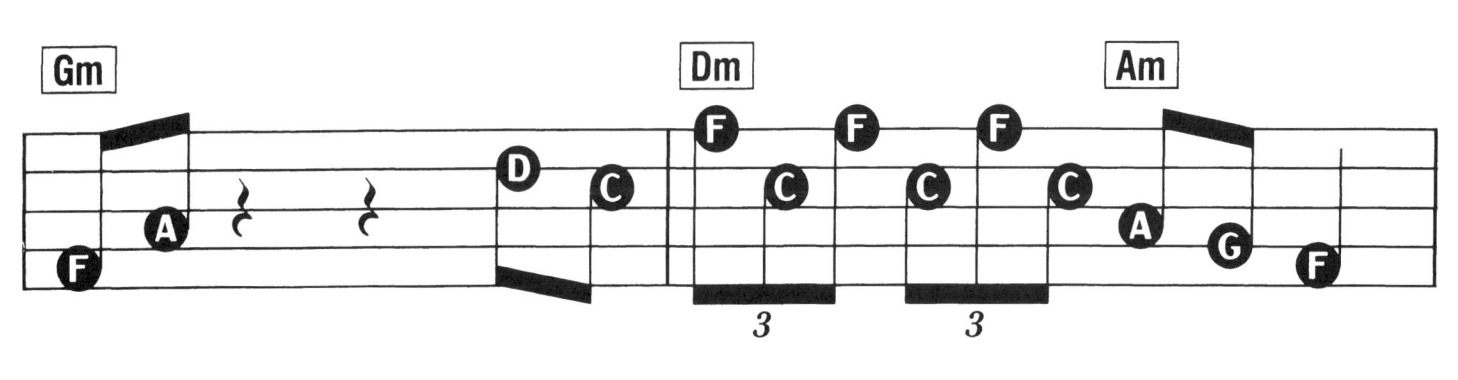

you warm me, and when I feel I can't go on, you come and hold me. It's you and me for-ev-er, Sar-a Smile. Won't you smile a while for me, Sar-a?

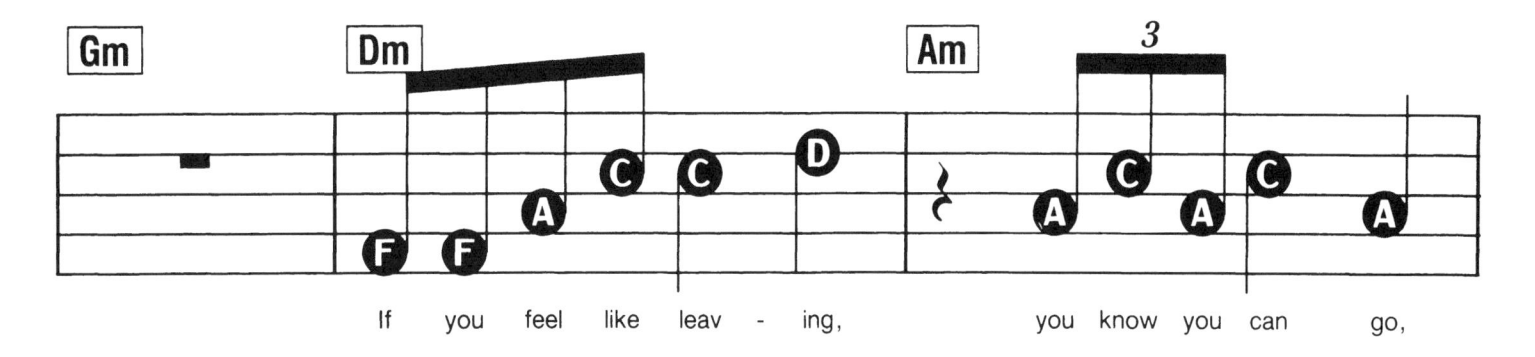

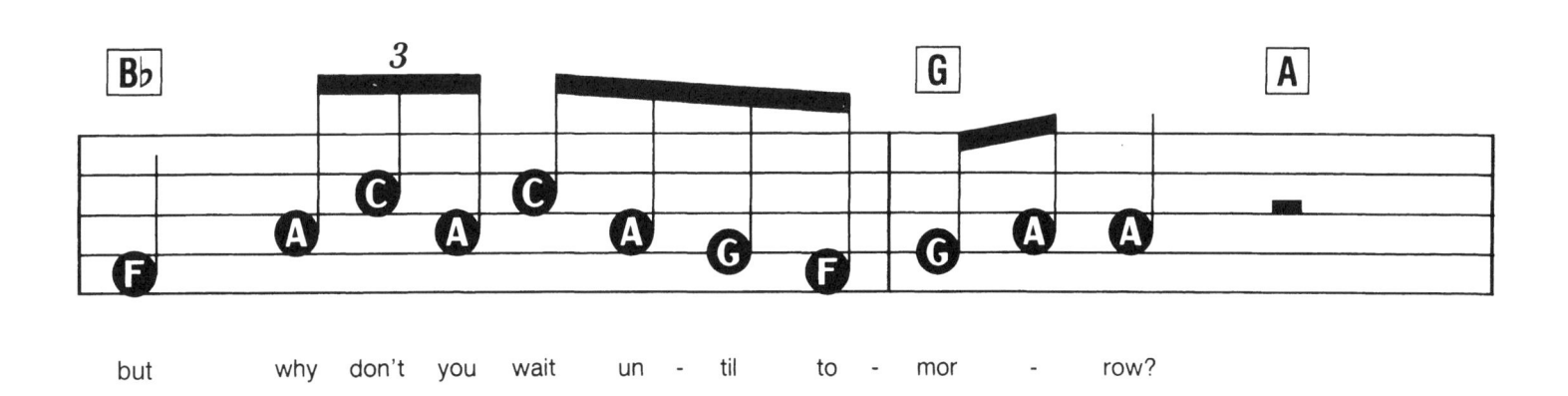

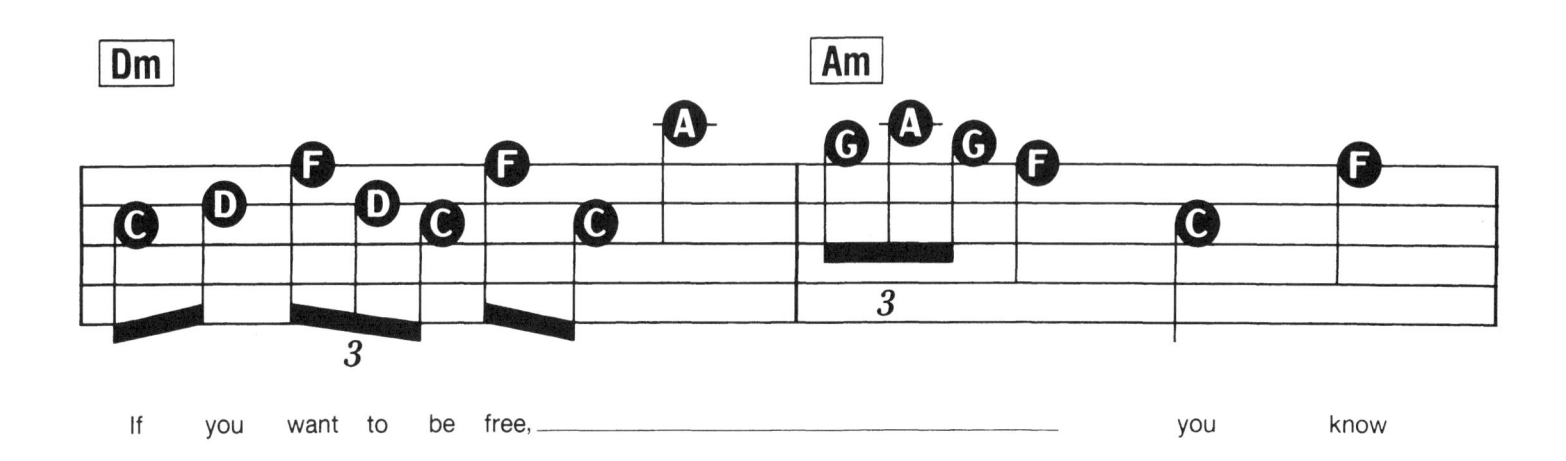

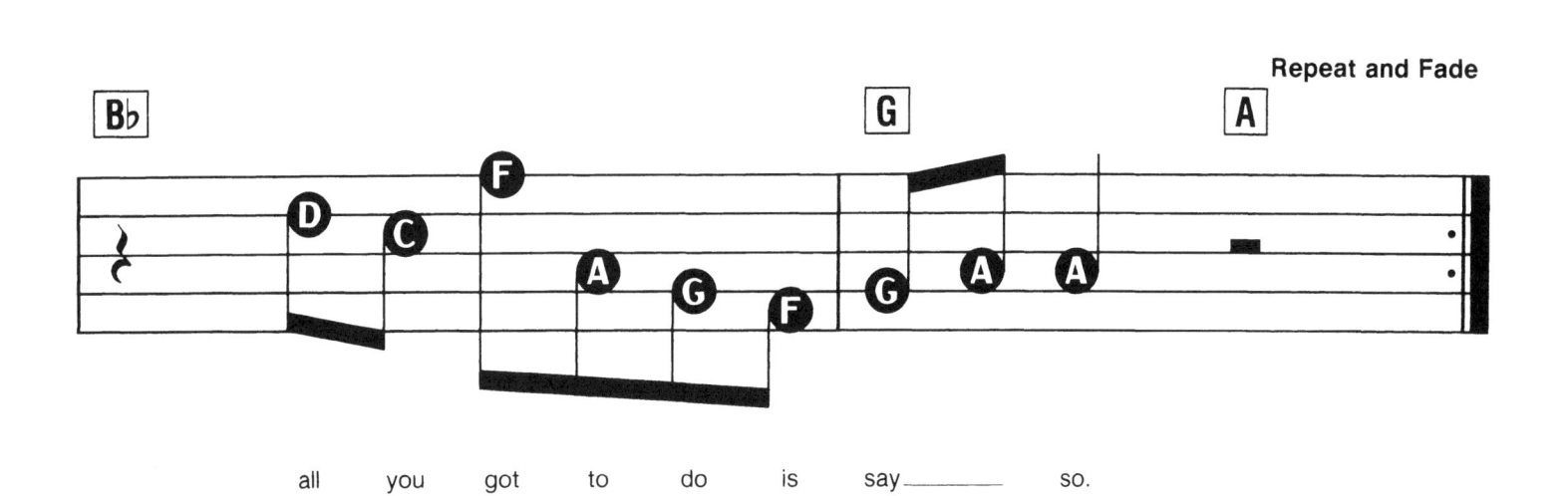

If you feel like leav-ing, you know you can go, but why don't you wait un-til to-mor-row? If you want to be free, you know all you got to do is say so.

San Francisco
(Be Sure to Wear Some Flowers in Your Hair)

Registration 2
Rhythm: Rock

Words and Music by
John Phillips

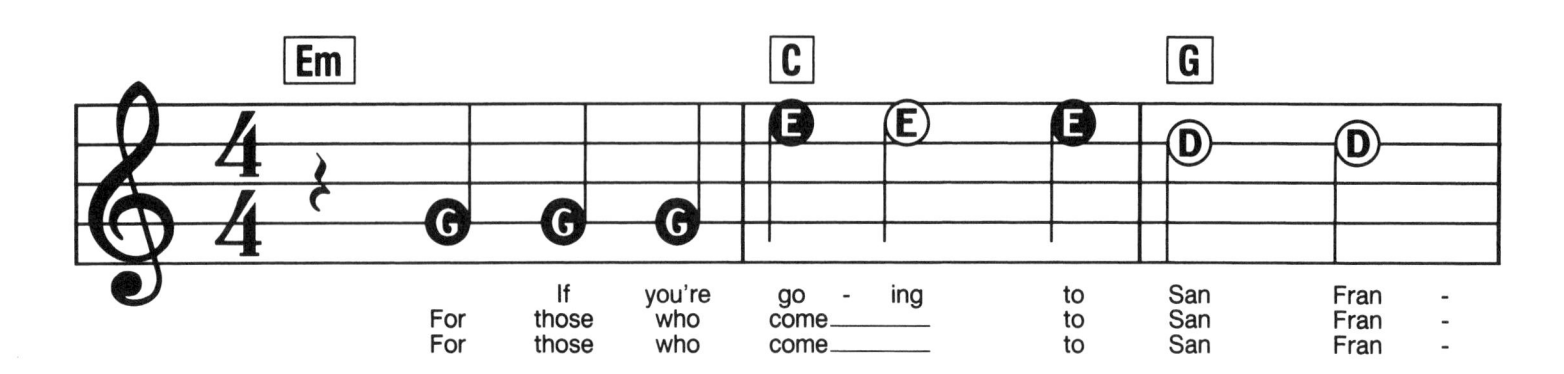

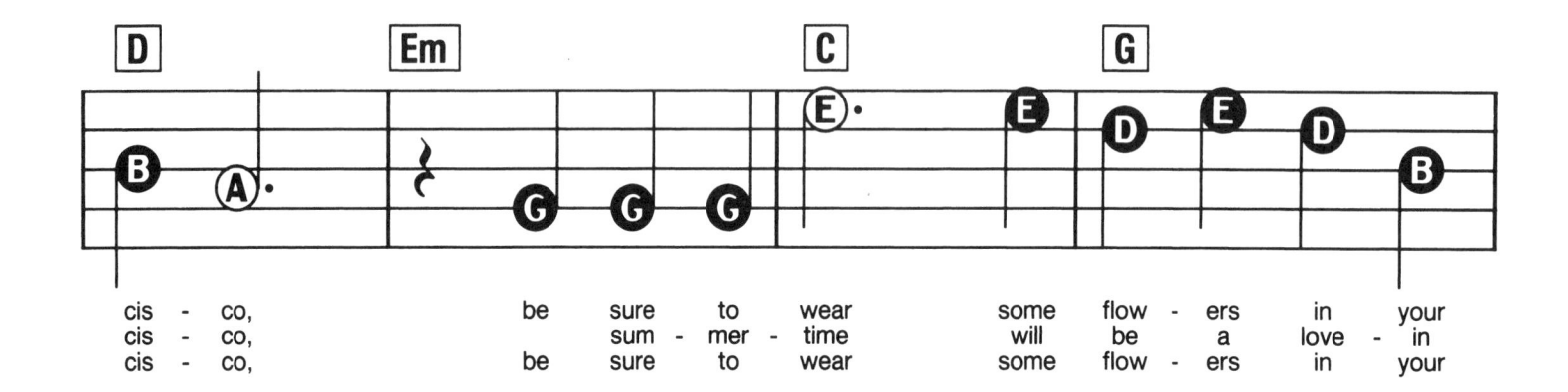

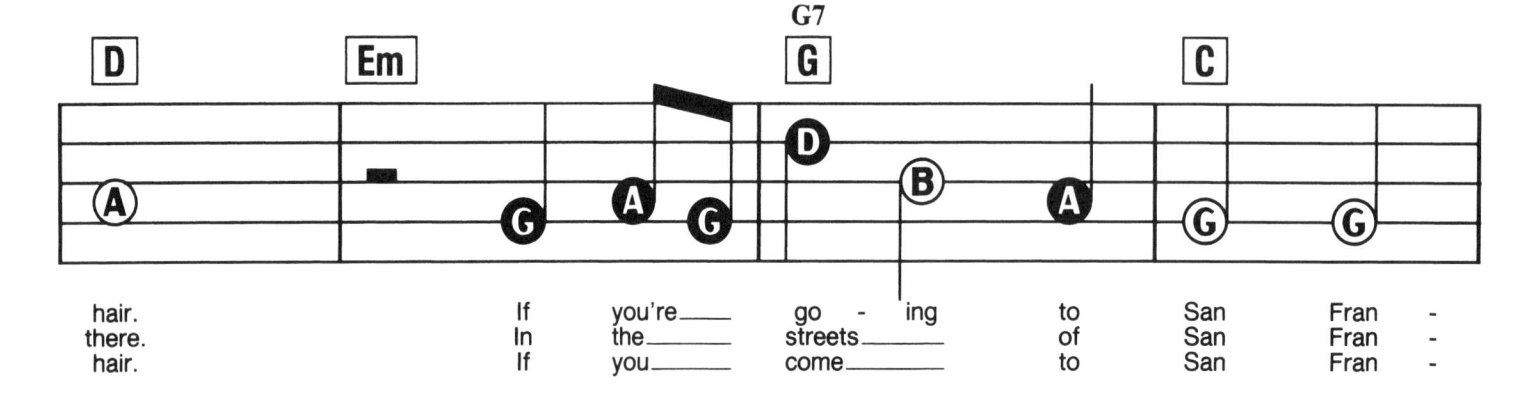

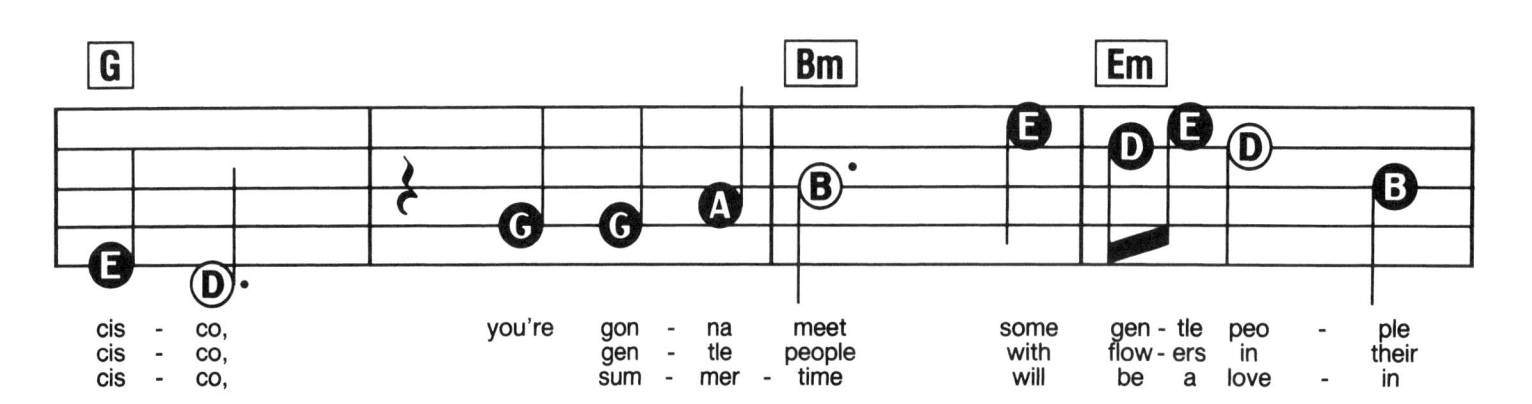

For / If you're / going to San Fran-
For those who come to San Fran-
For those who come to San Fran-

cis-co, / be sure to wear / some flow-ers in your
cis-co, / sum-mer-time / will be a love-in
cis-co, / be sure to wear / some flow-ers in your

hair. / If you're going to San Fran-
there. / In the streets of San Fran-
hair. / If you come to San Fran-

cis-co, / you're gon-na meet / some gen-tle peo-ple
cis-co, / gen-tle people / with flow-ers in their
cis-co, / sum-mer-time / will be a love-in

Copyright © 1967 UNIVERSAL MUSIC CORP.
Copyright Renewed
All Rights Reserved Used by Permission

141

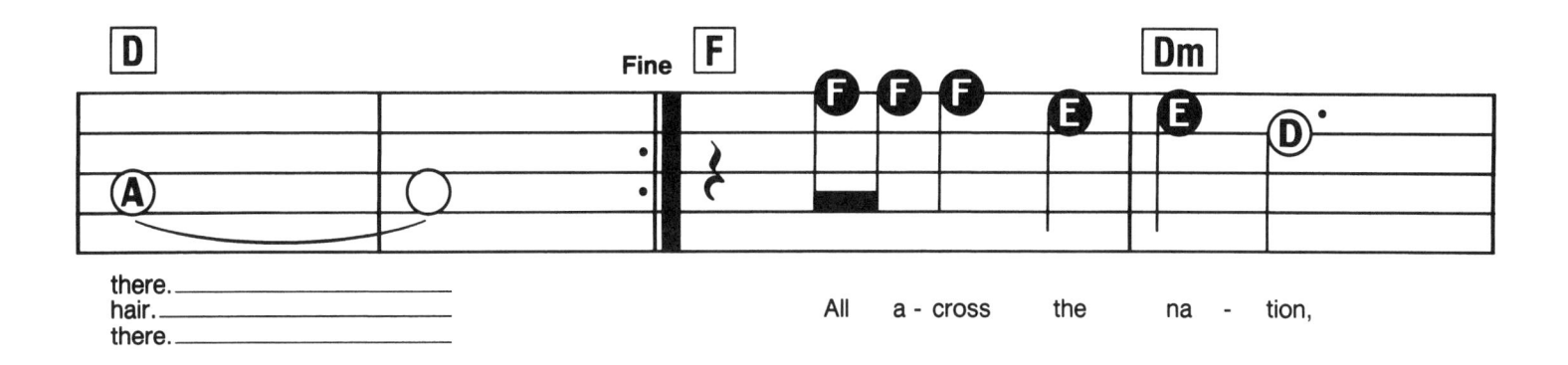

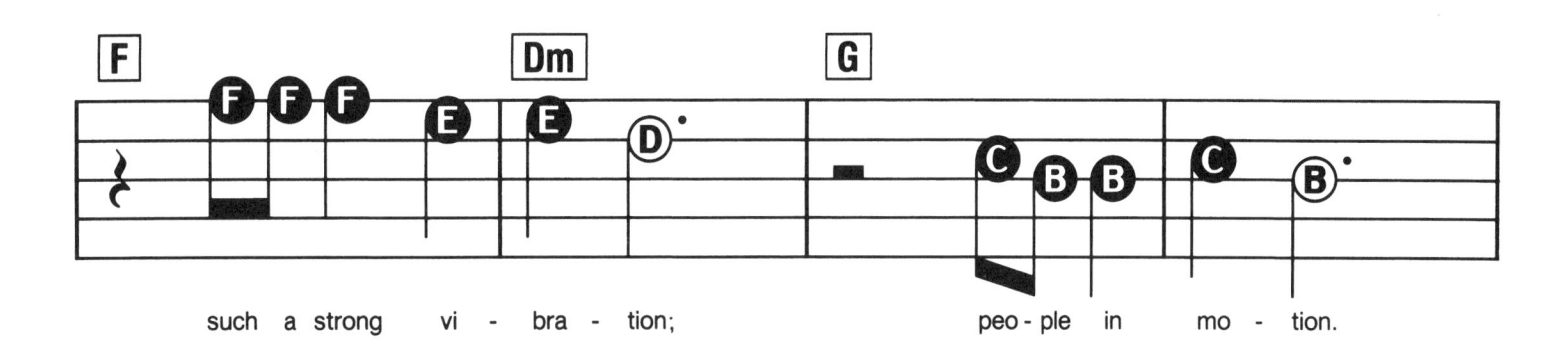

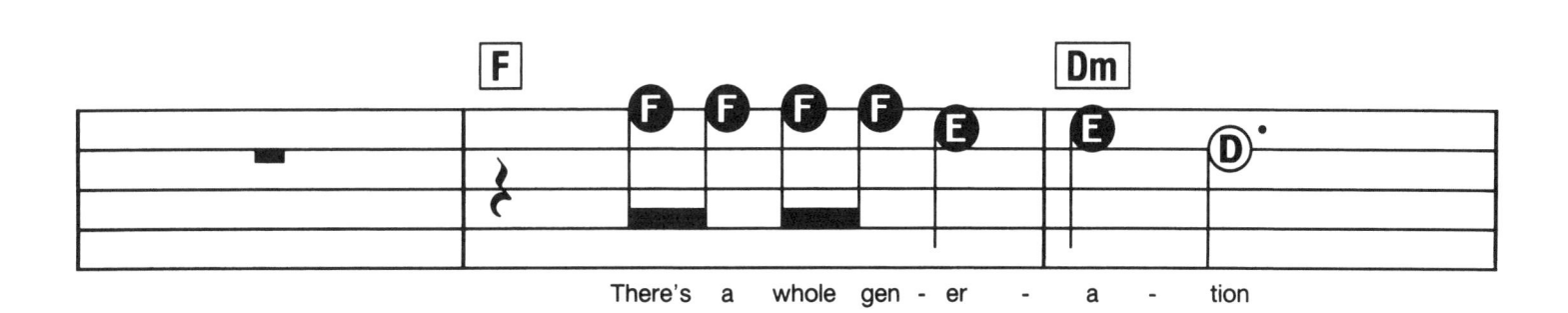

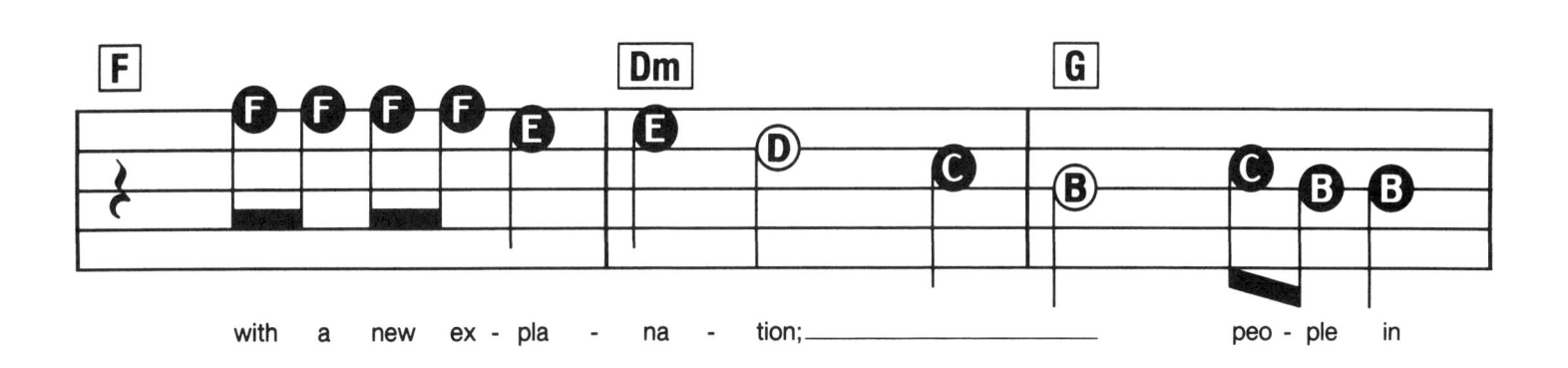

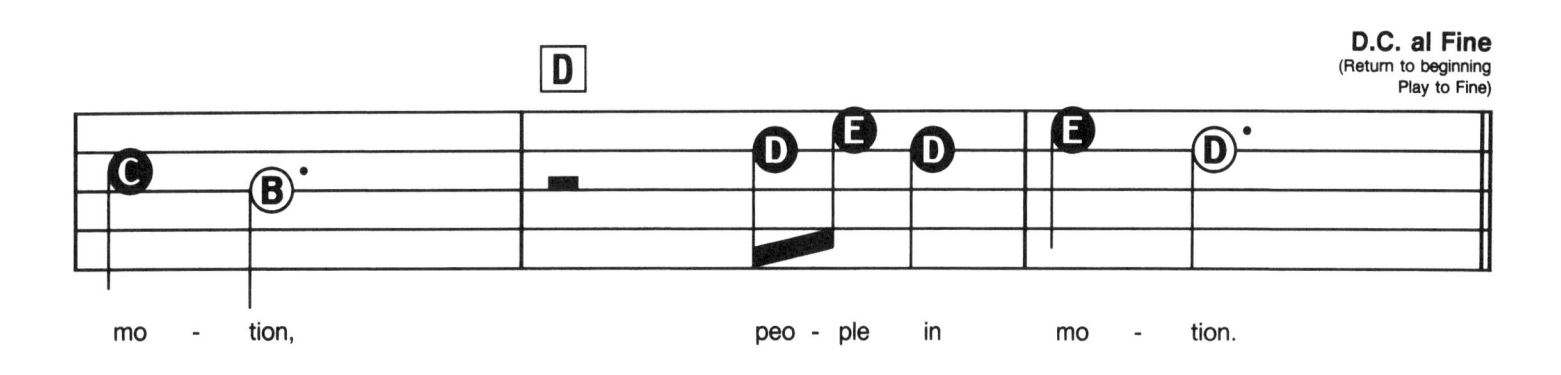

Scotch and Soda

Registration 8
Rhythm: Swing or Jazz

Words and Music by
Dave Guard

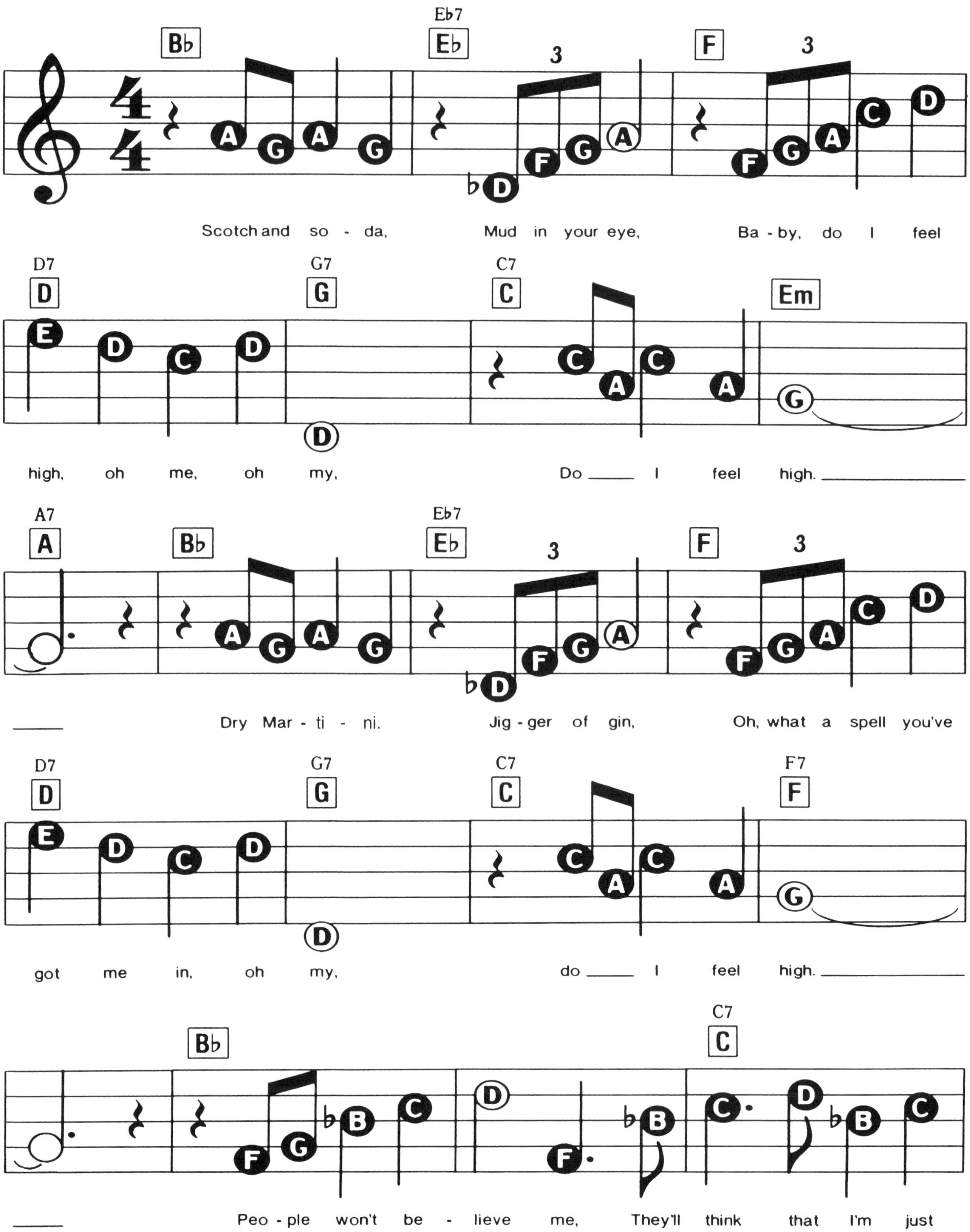

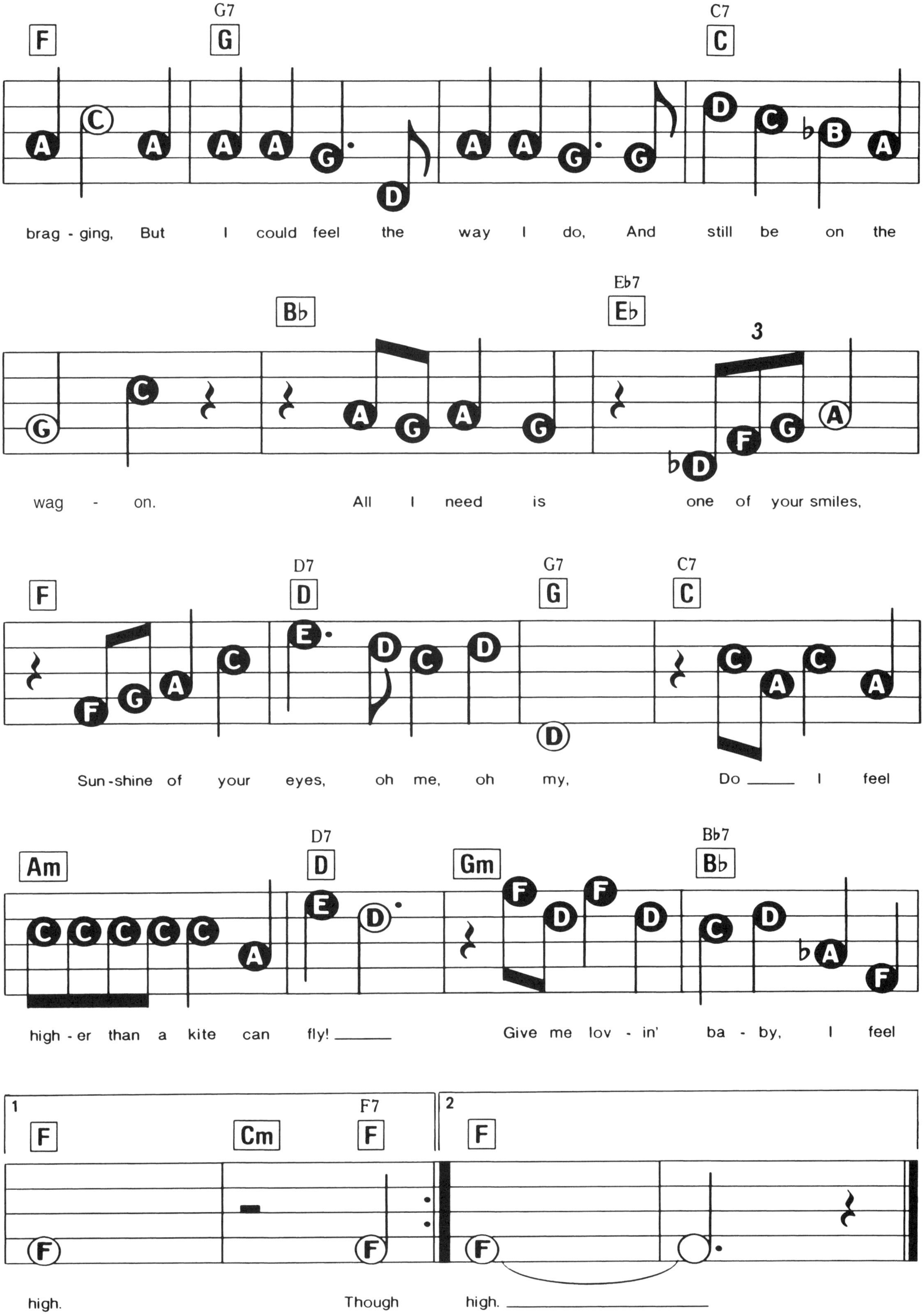
F G7 G C7 C
brag - ging, But I could feel the way I do, And still be on the
Bb Eb7 Eb
3
wag - on. All I need is one of your smiles,
F D7 D G7 G C7 C
Sun-shine of your eyes, oh me, oh my, Do I feel
Am D7 D Gm Bb7 Bb
high - er than a kite can fly! Give me lov - in' ba - by, I feel
1 F Cm F7 F
high. Though
2 F
high.

Sentimental Lady

Registration 2
Rhythm: Country

Words and Music by
Robert Welch

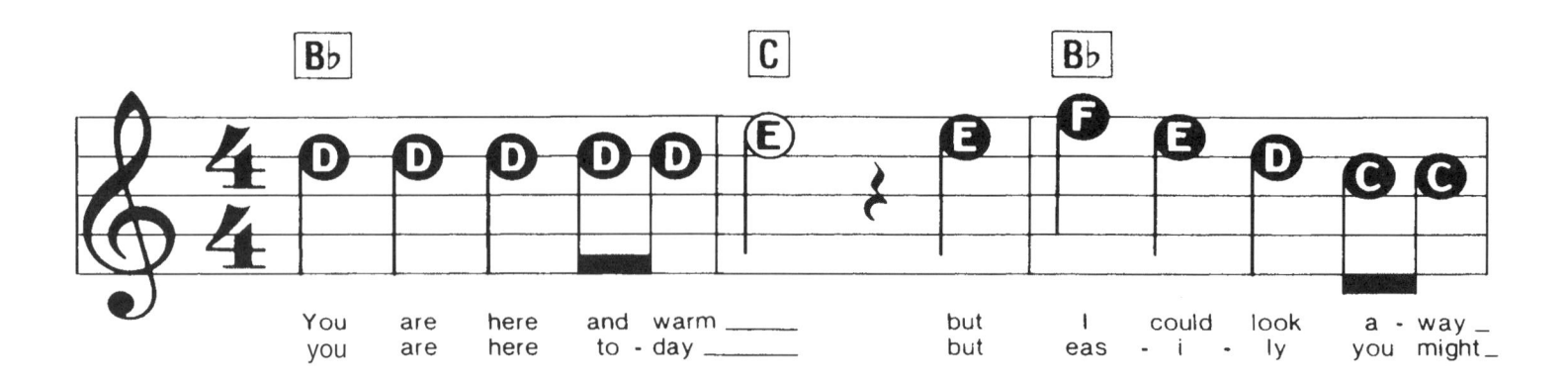

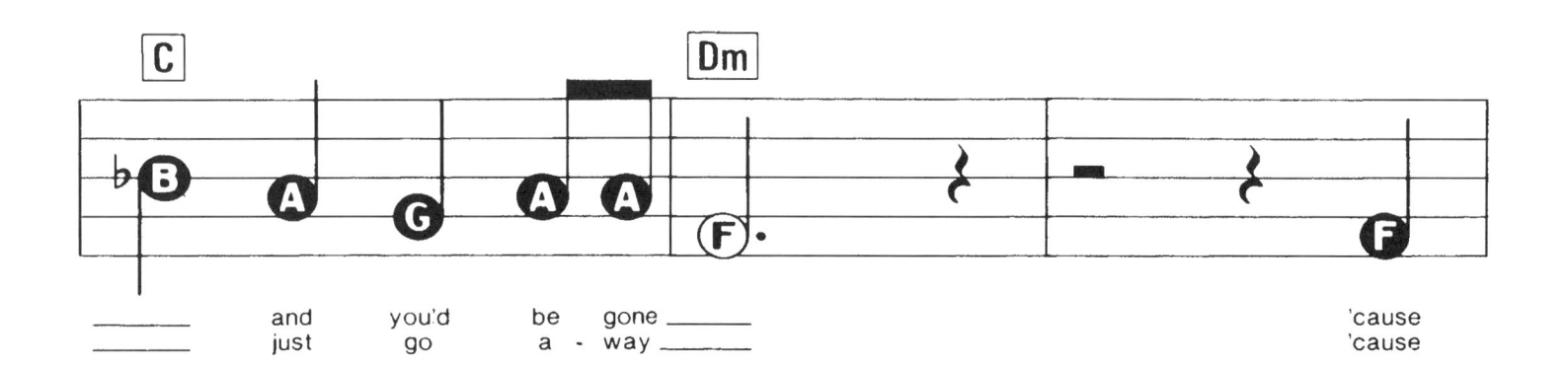

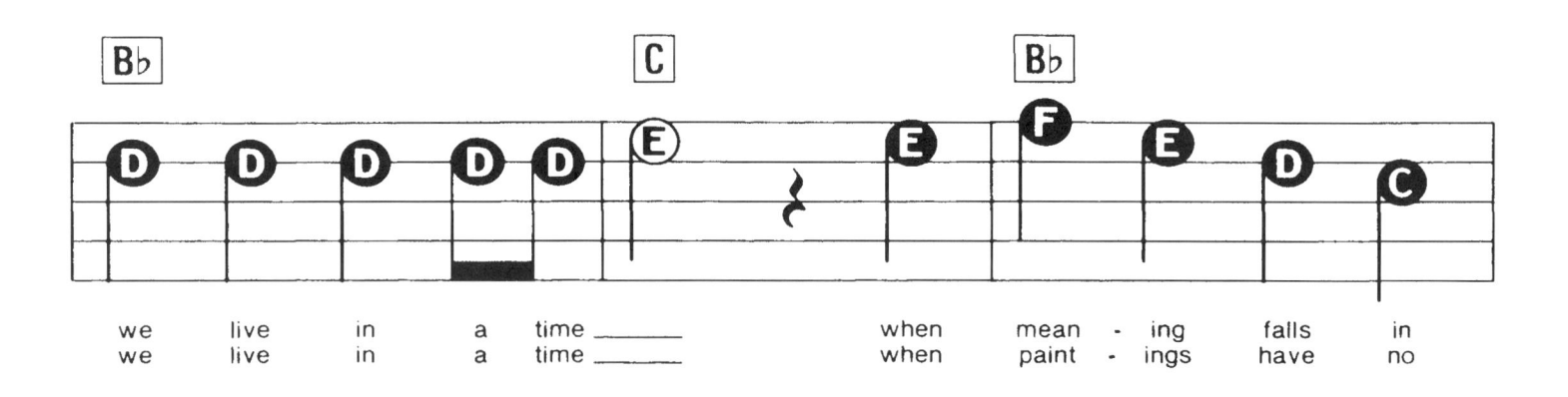

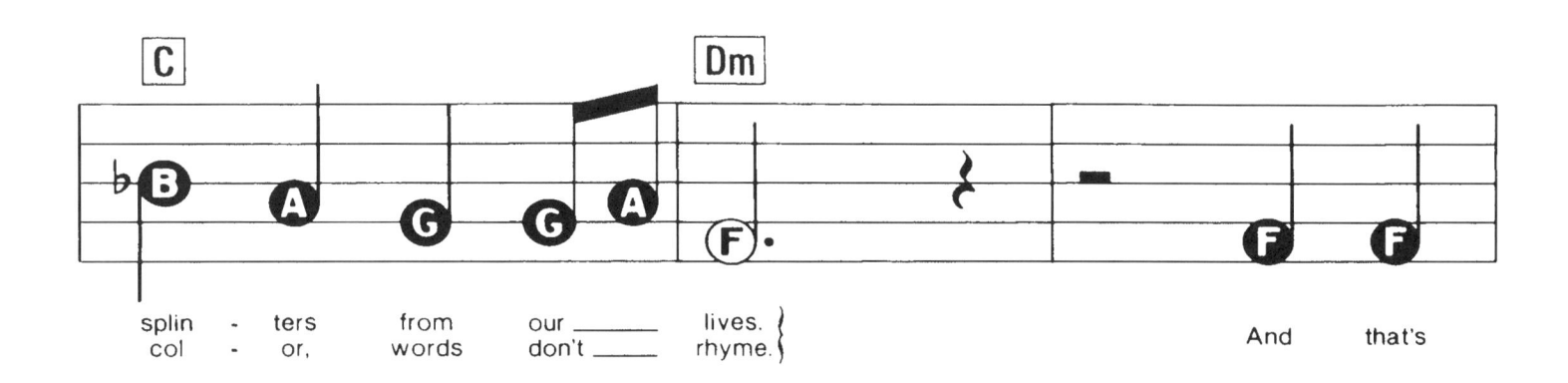

You are here and warm — but I could look a-way
you are here to-day — but eas-i-ly you might

— and you'd be gone — 'cause
— just go a-way — 'cause

we live in a time — when mean-ing falls in
we live in a time — when paint-ings have no

splin-ters from our — lives.
col - or, words don't — rhyme.

And that's

Copyright © 1972 (Renewed) Palan Music Publishing Ltd.
All Rights Controlled and Administered by Palan Songs America
International Copyright Secured   All Rights Reserved

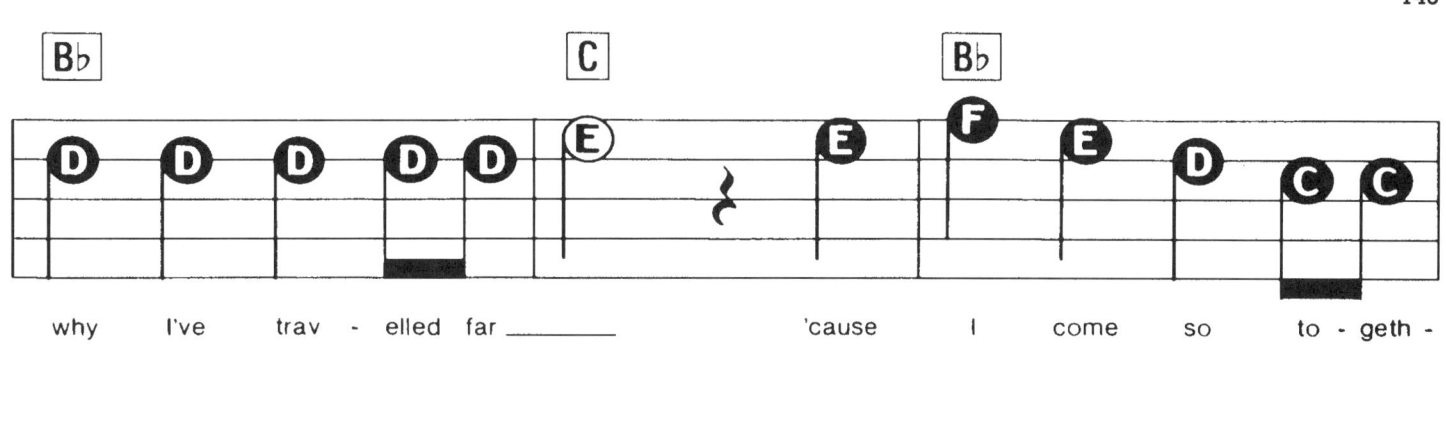

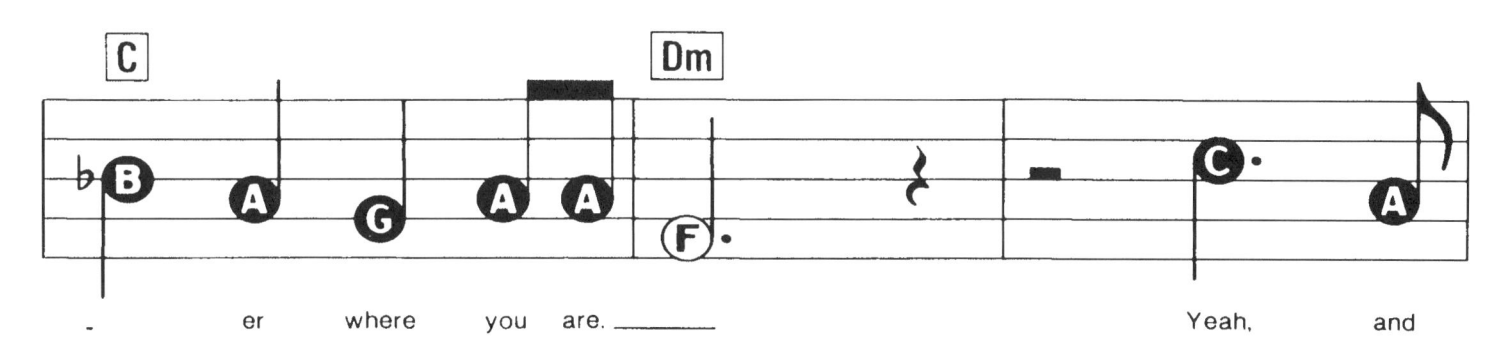

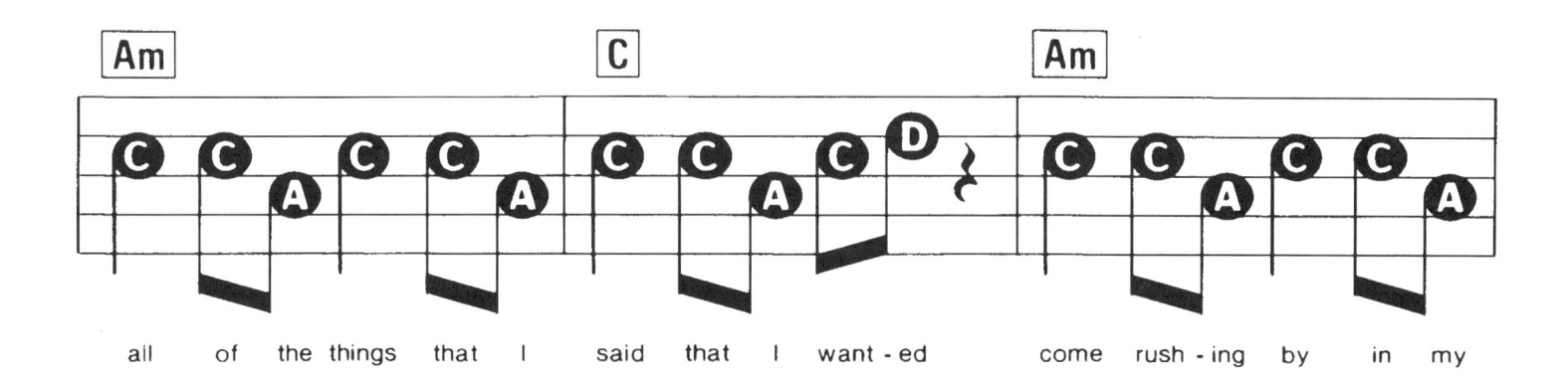

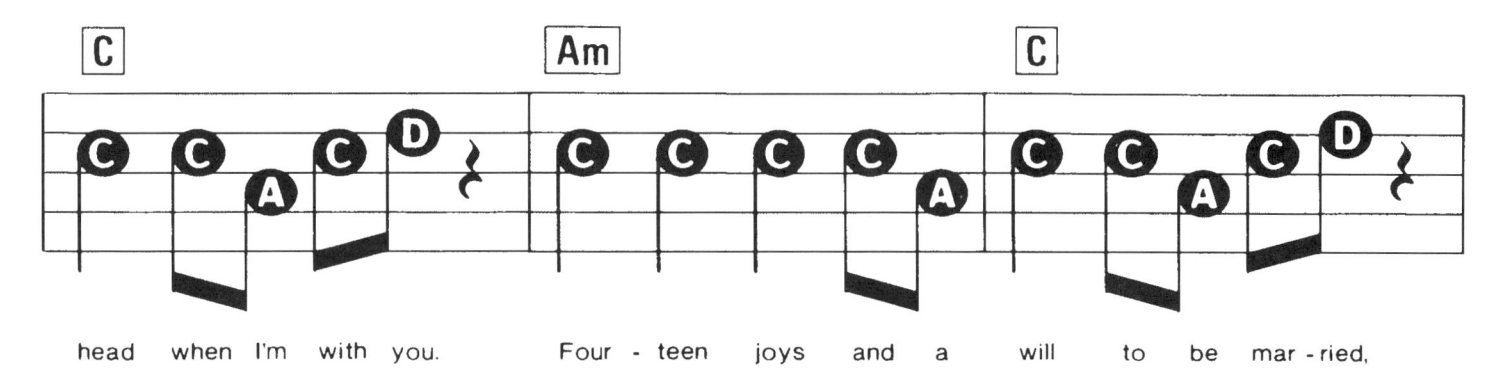

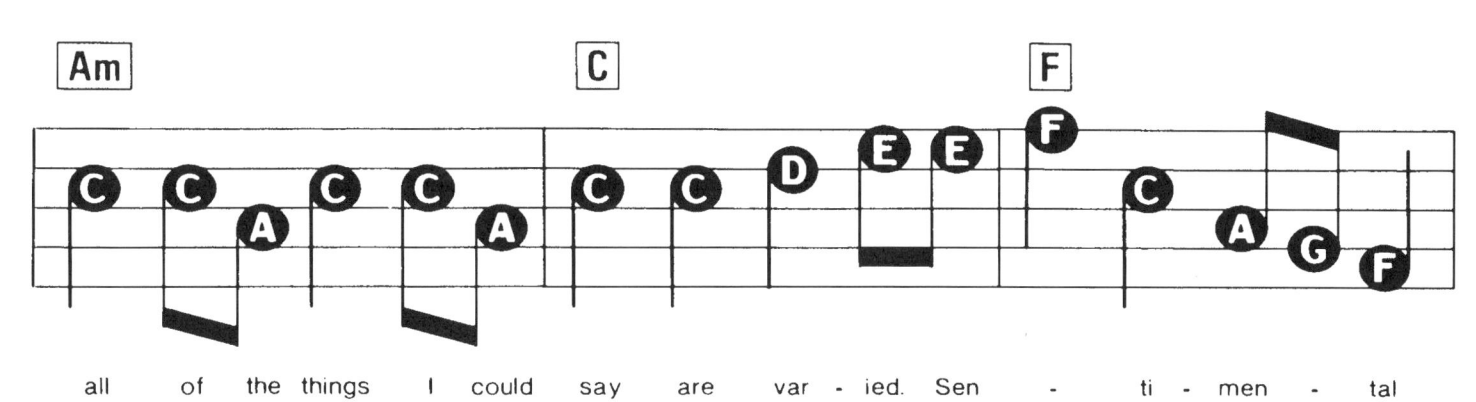

why I've trav-elled far _____ 'cause I come so to-geth- er where you are. _____ Yeah, and all of the things that I said that I want-ed come rush-ing by in my head when I'm with you. Four-teen joys and a will to be mar-ried, all of the things I could say are var-ied. Sen - ti - men - tal

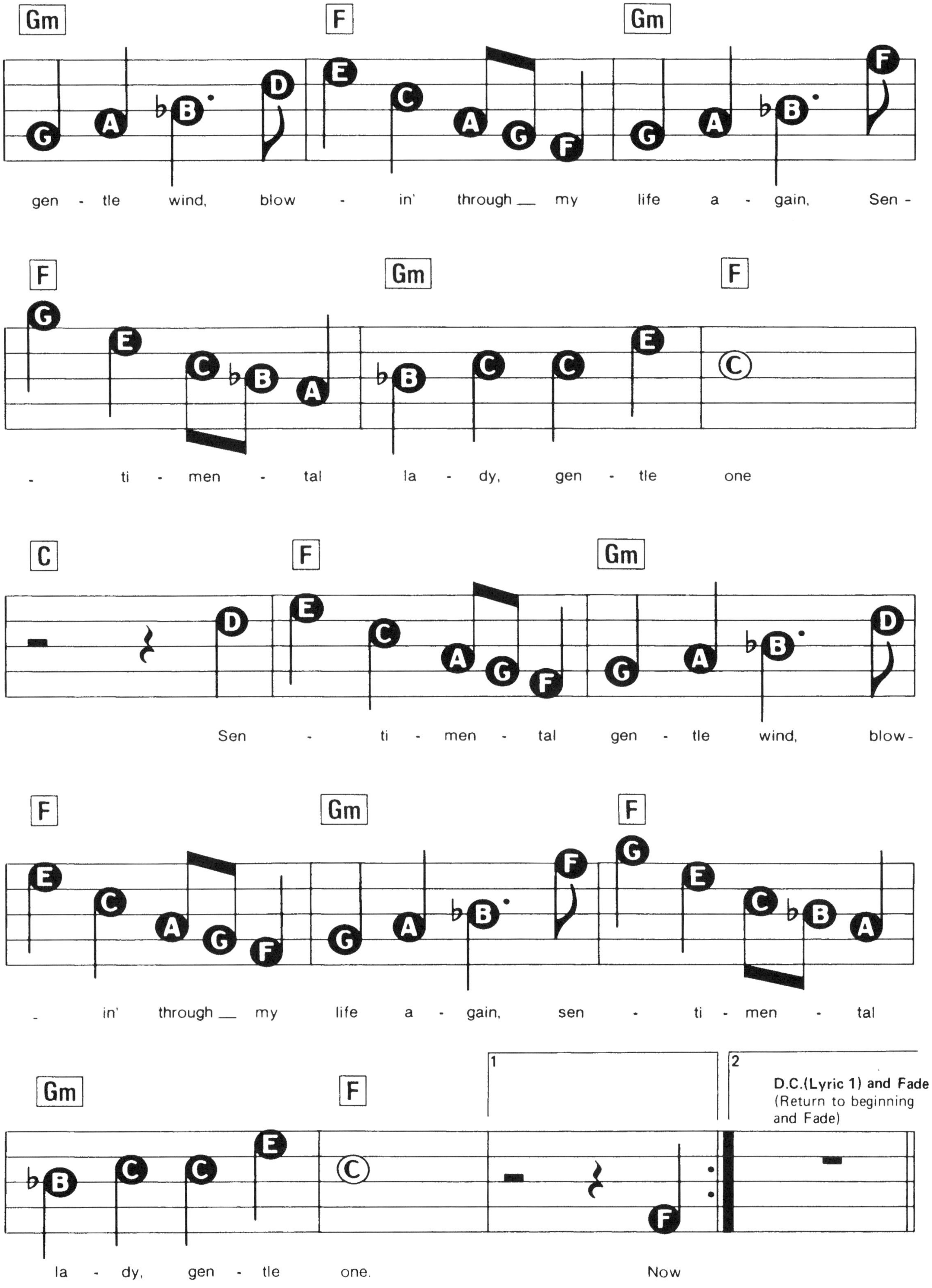
Gm F Gm
gen - tle wind, blow - in' through ___ my life a - gain, Sen -
F Gm F
- ti - men - tal la - dy, gen - tle one
C F Gm
Sen - ti - men - tal gen - tle wind, blow-
F Gm F
- in' through ___ my life a - gain, sen - ti - men - tal
Gm F
la - dy, gen - tle one.
1
Now
2
D.C.(Lyric 1) and Fade
(Return to beginning and Fade)

Somebody to Love

Registration 8
Rhythm: Rock or Pop

Words and Music by
Darby Slick

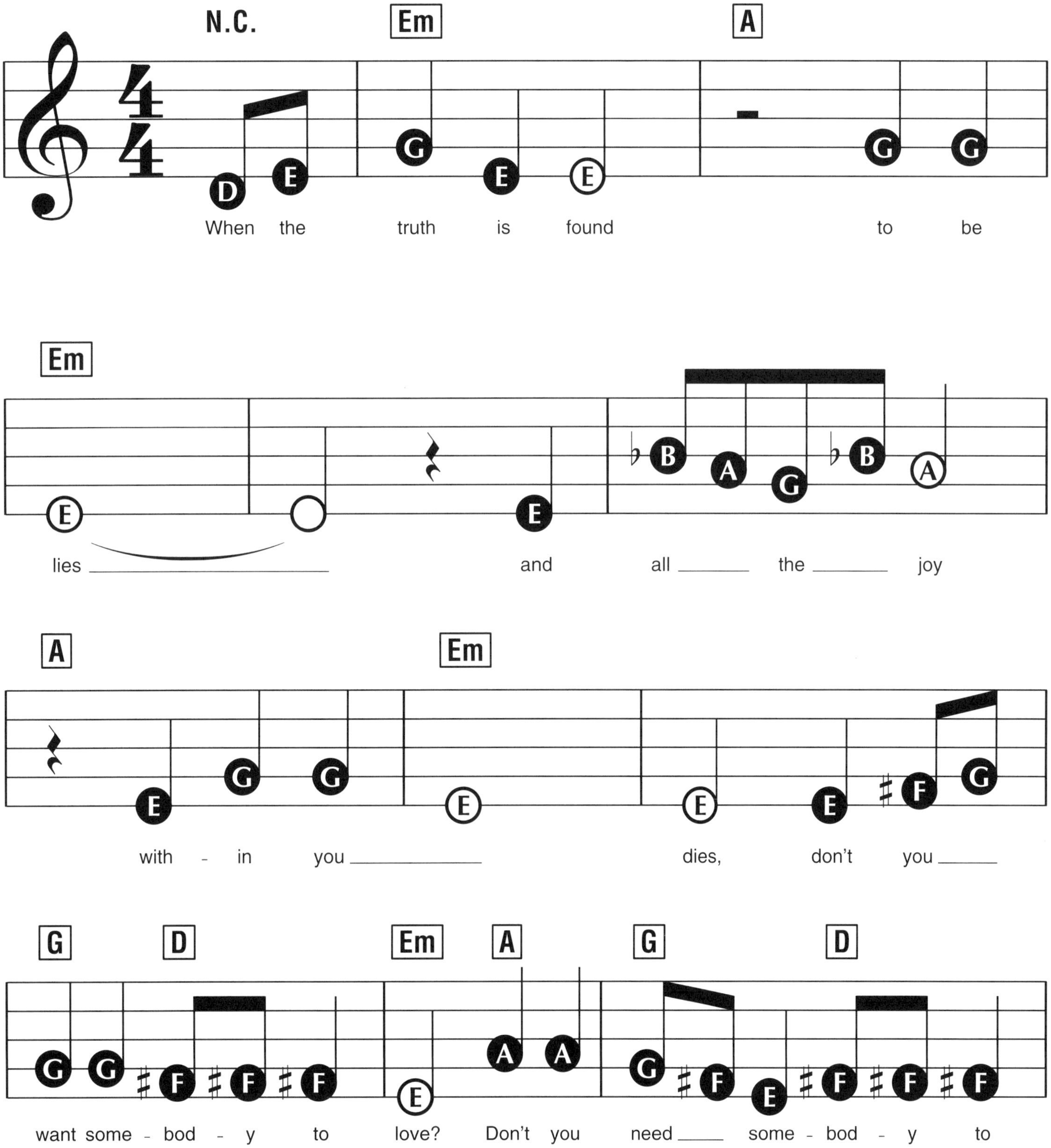

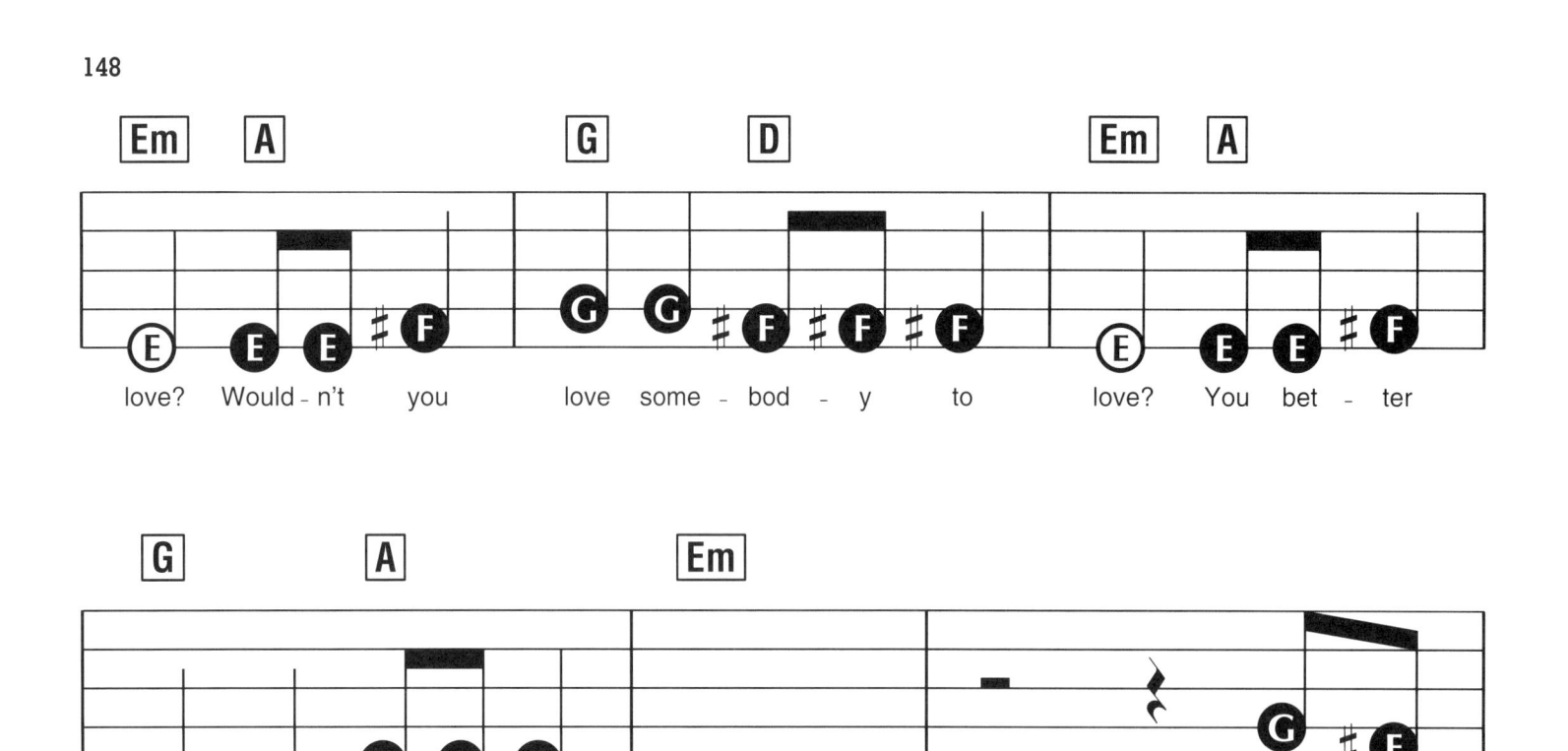

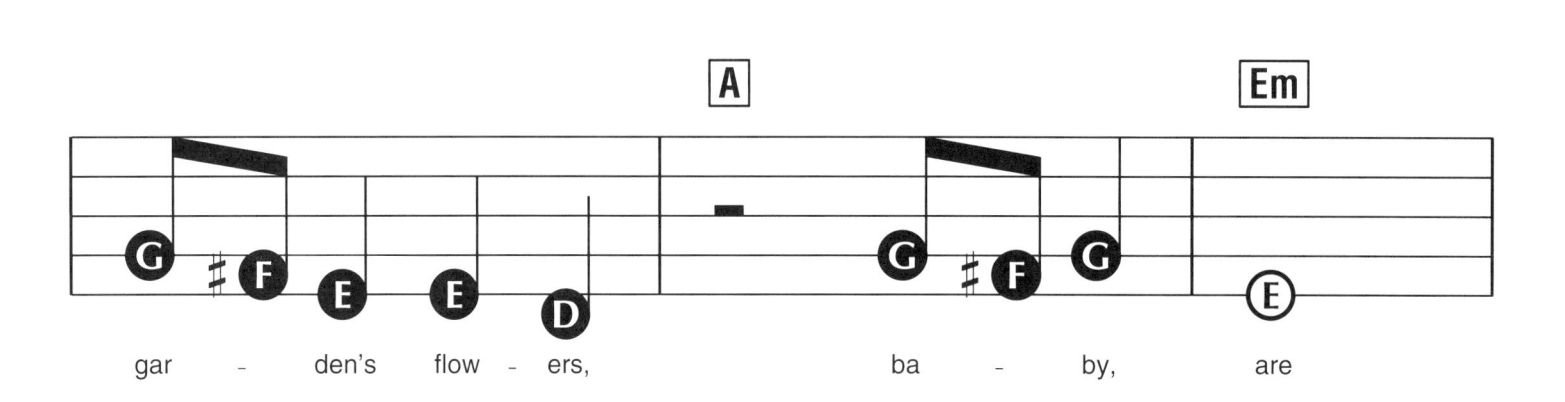

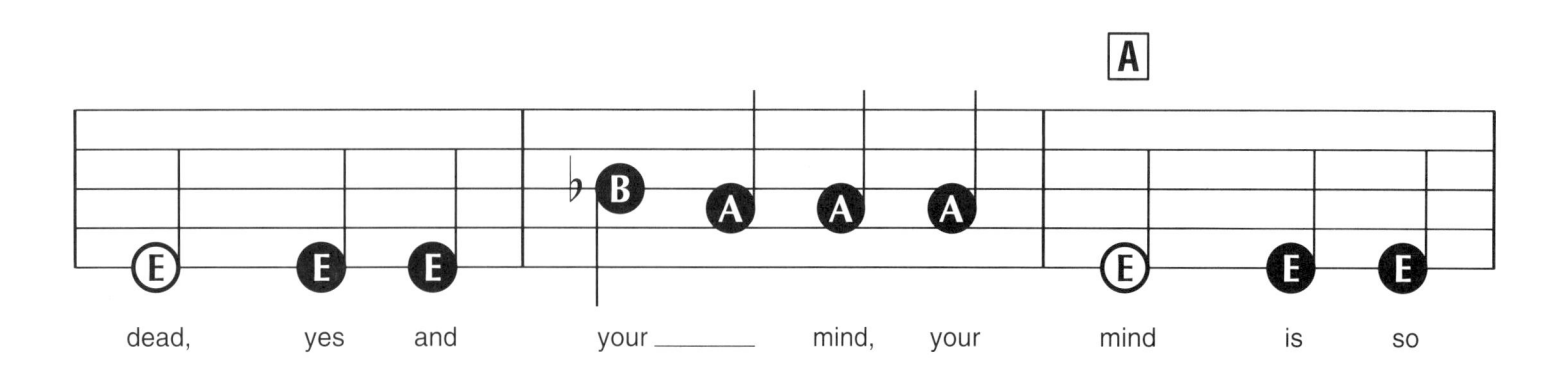

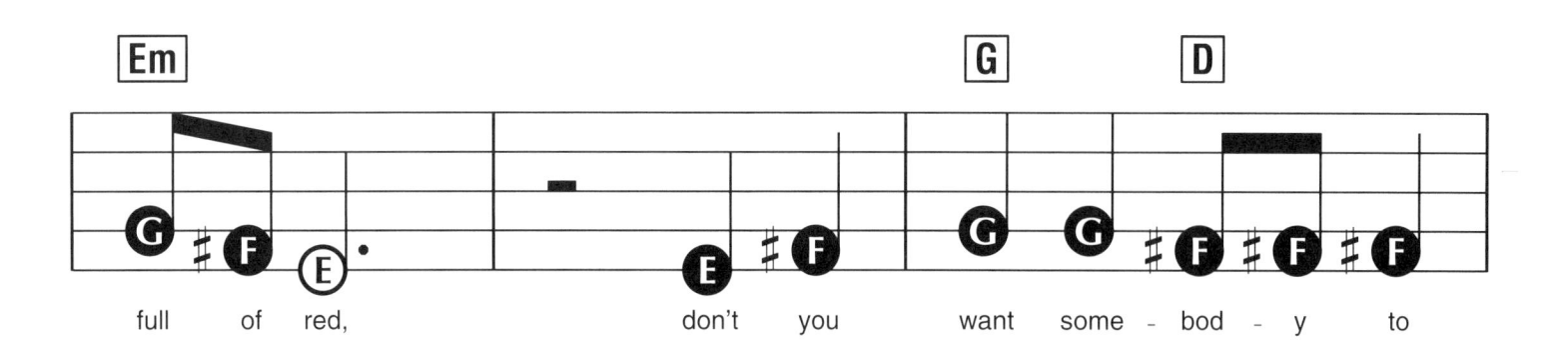

love? Would-n't you love some-bod-y to love? You bet-ter

find some-bod-y to love. When the

gar-den's flow-ers, ba-by, are

dead, yes and your mind, your mind is so

full of red, don't you want some-bod-y to

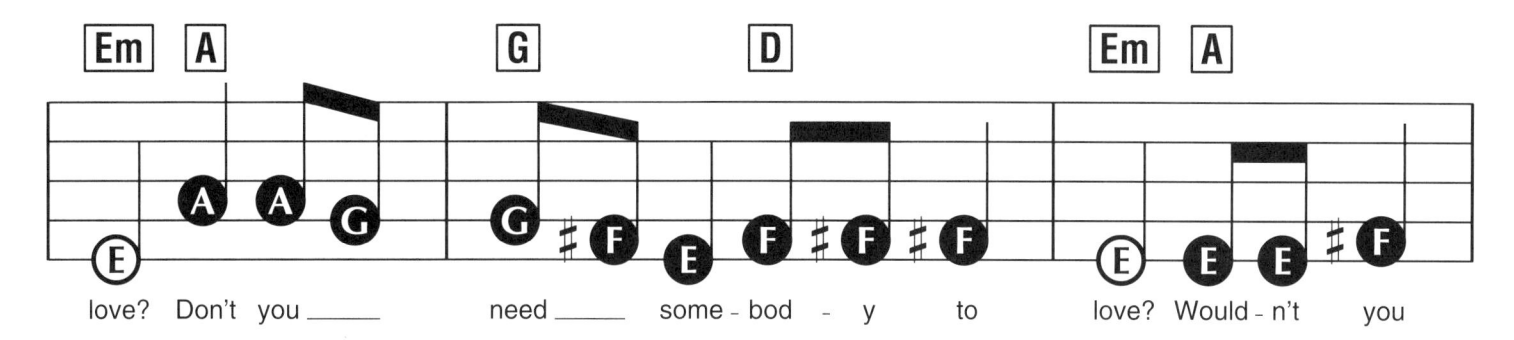

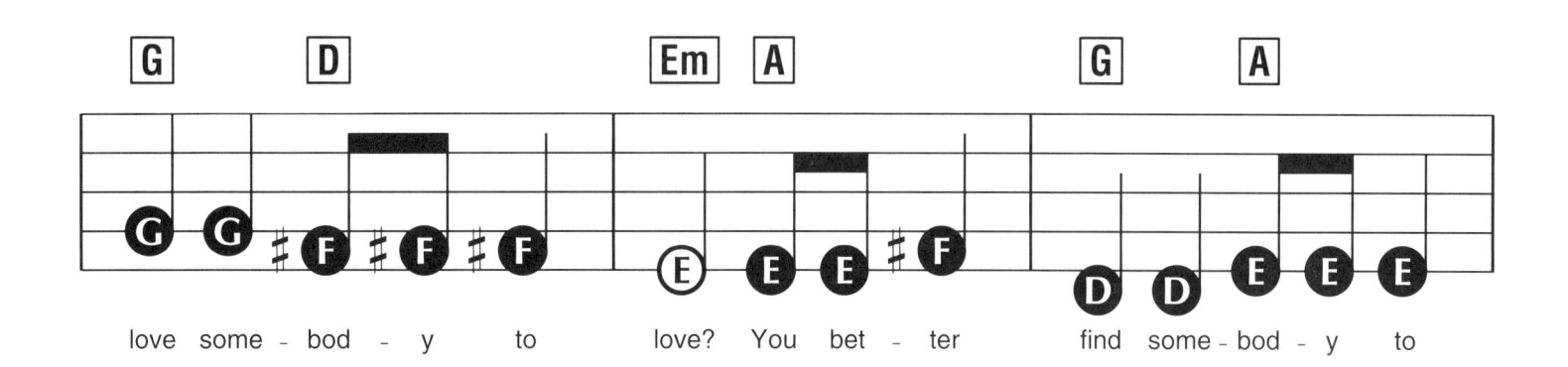

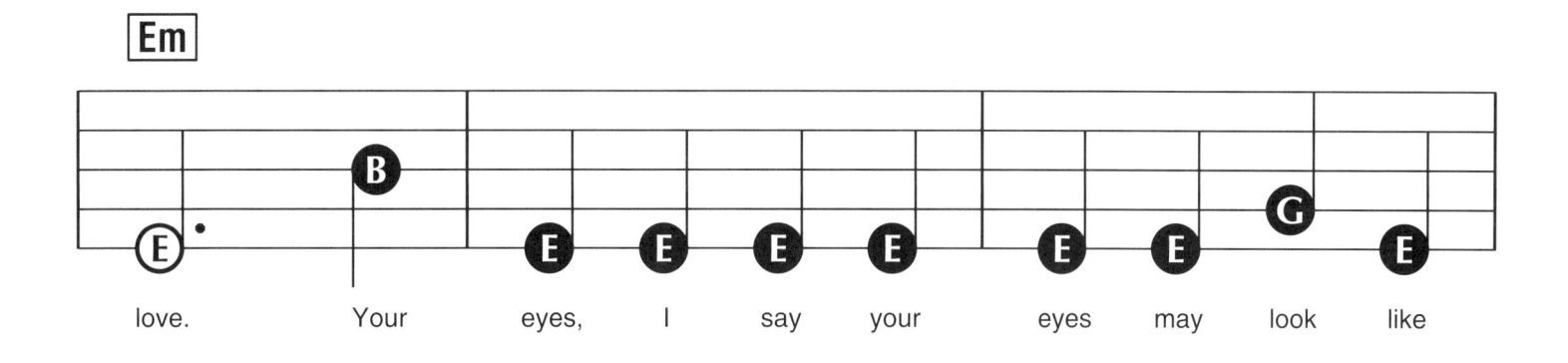

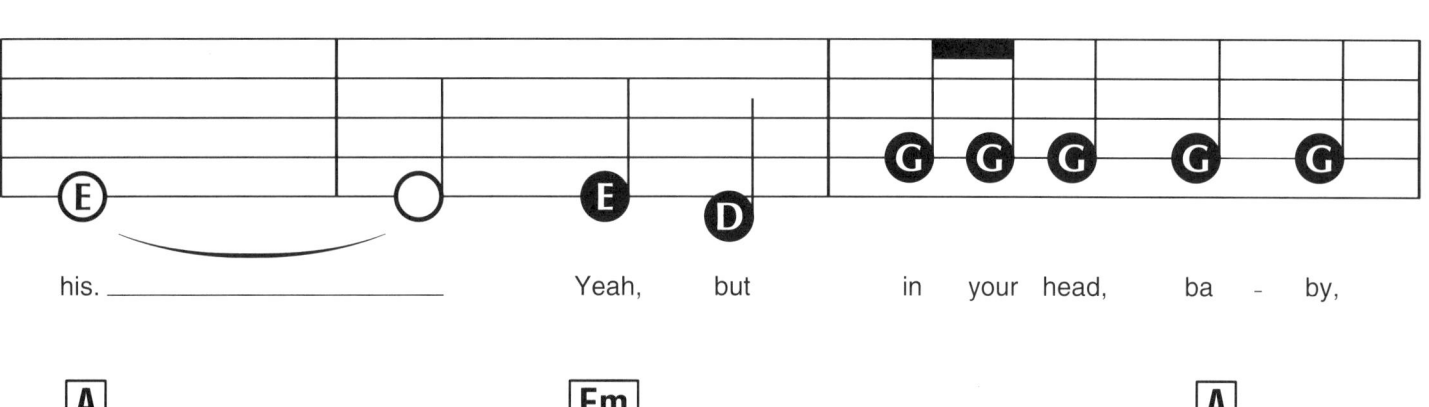

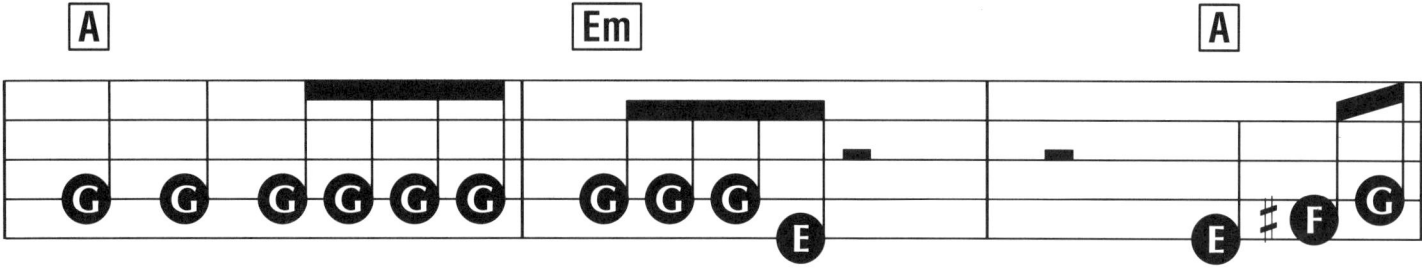

love? Don't you need some-bod-y to love? Would-n't you love some-bod-y to love? You bet-ter find some-bod-y to love. Your eyes, I say your eyes may look like his. Yeah, but in your head, ba-by, I'm a-fraid you don't know where it is. Don't you

150

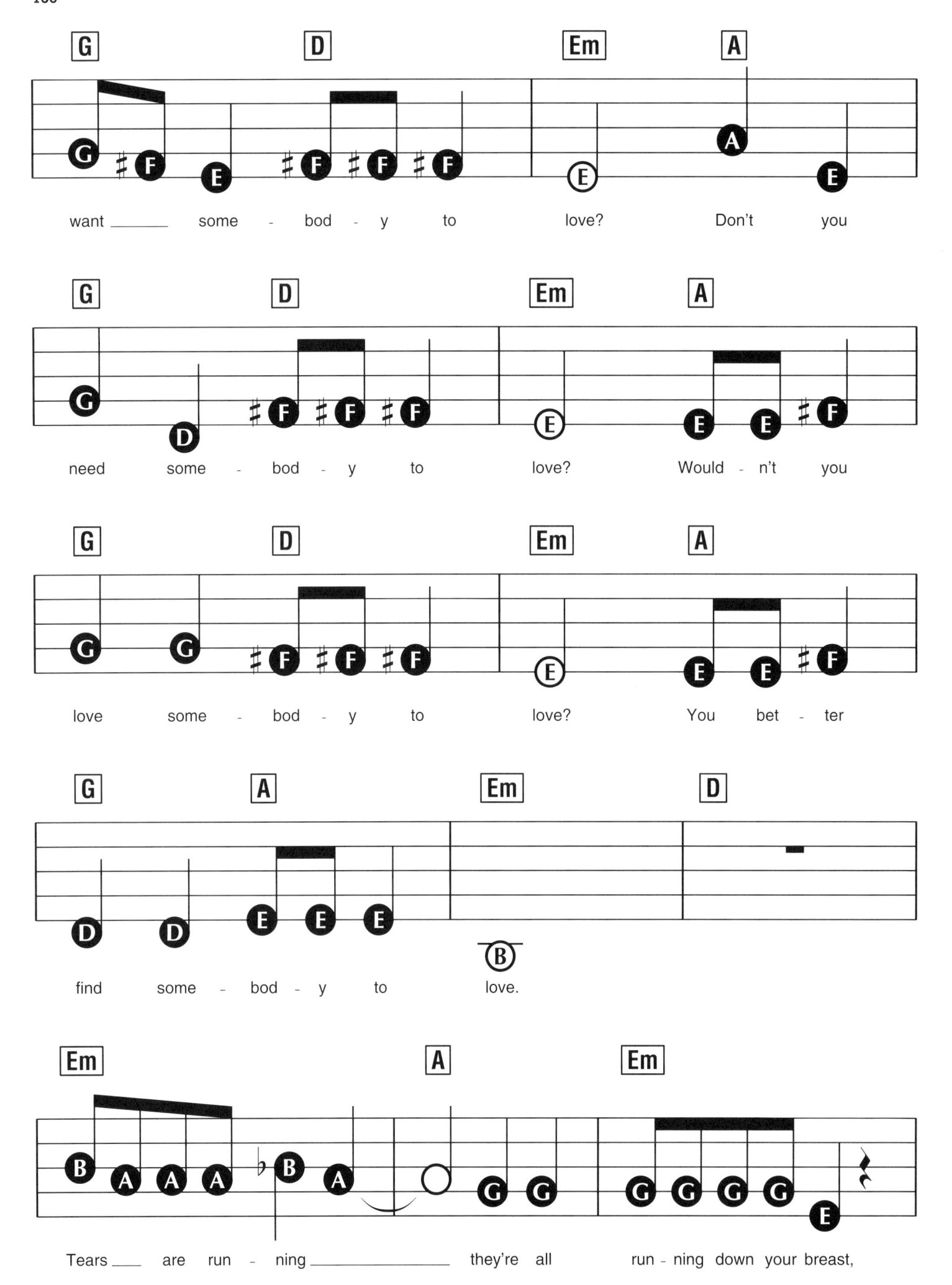

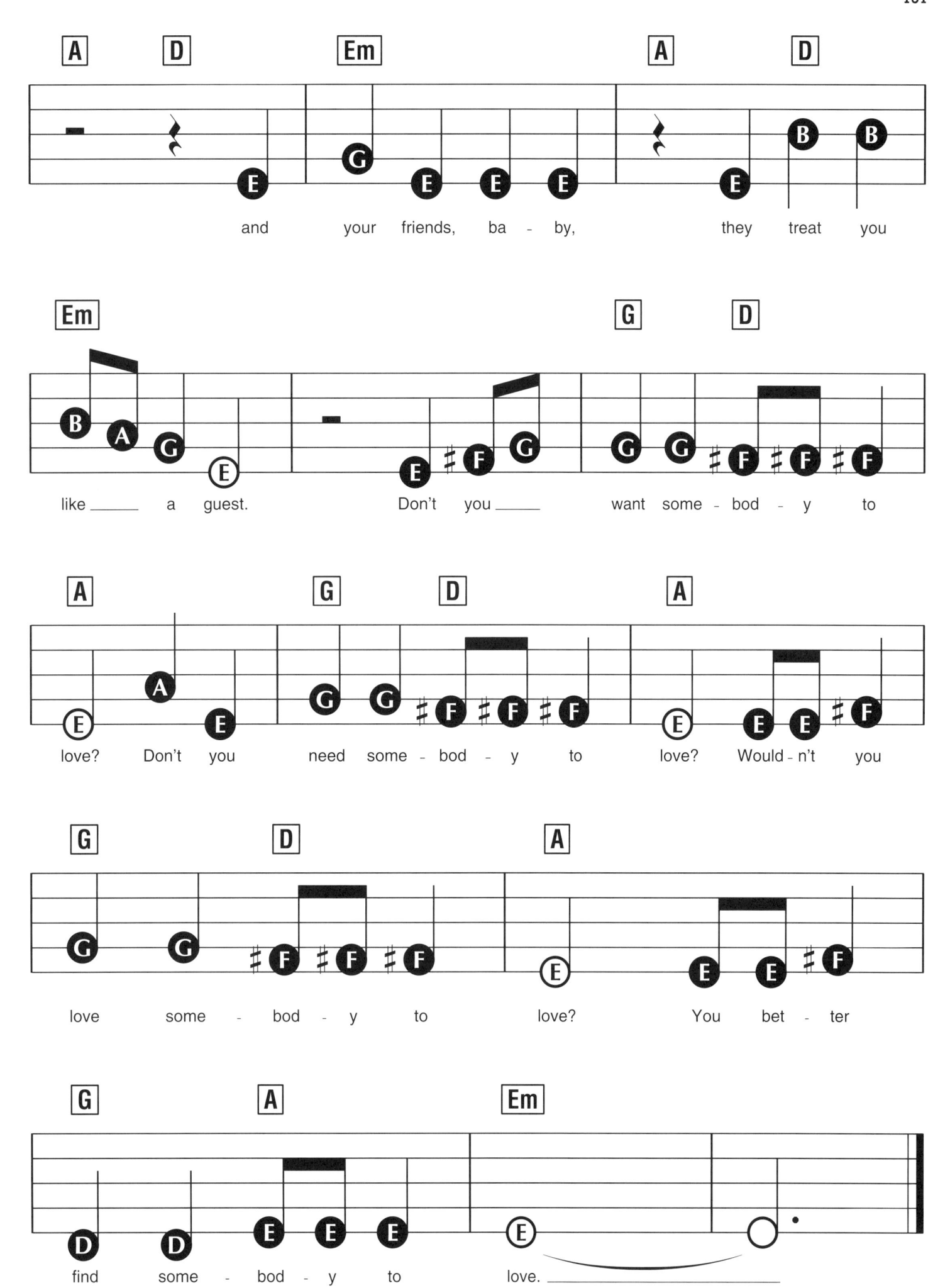

and your friends, ba-by, they treat you like a guest. Don't you want some-bod-y to love? Don't you need some-bod-y to love? Would-n't you love some-bod-y to love? You bet-ter find some-bod-y to love.

Sunshine
(Go Away Today)

Registration 4
Rhythm: Folk or Country Rock

Written by
Jonathan Edwards

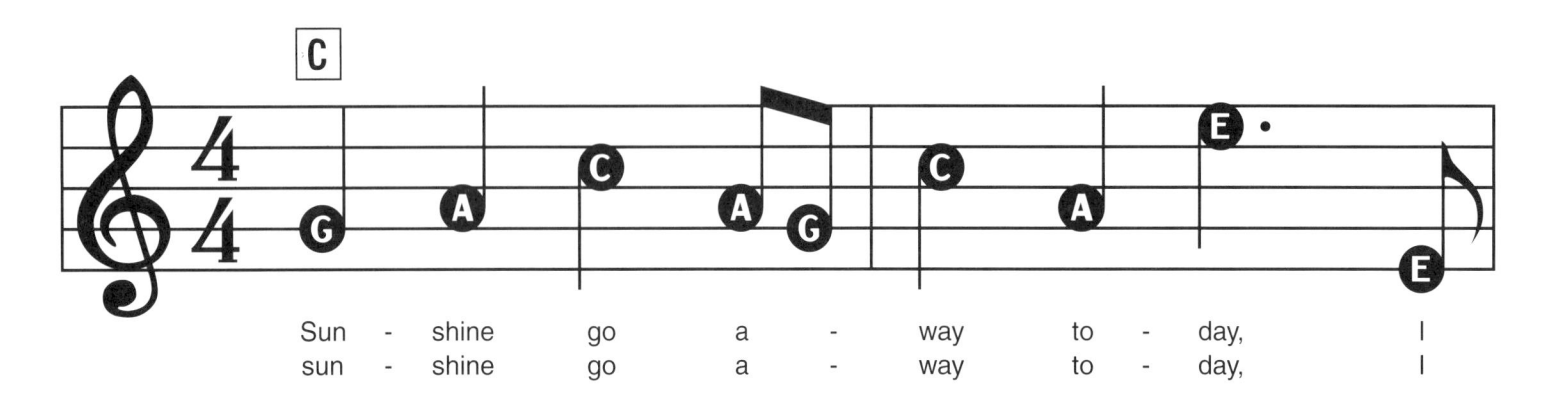

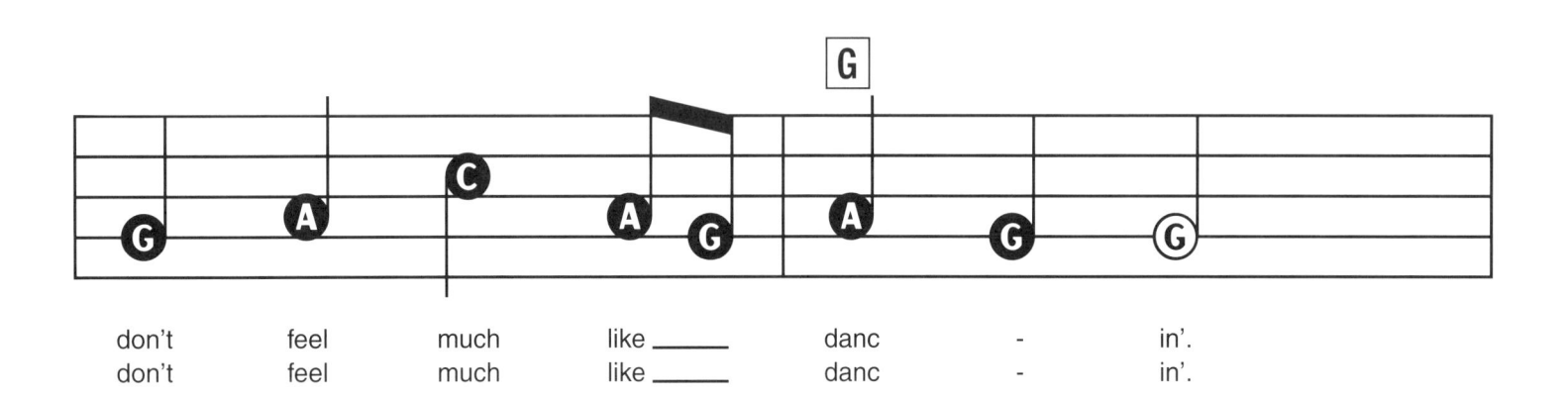

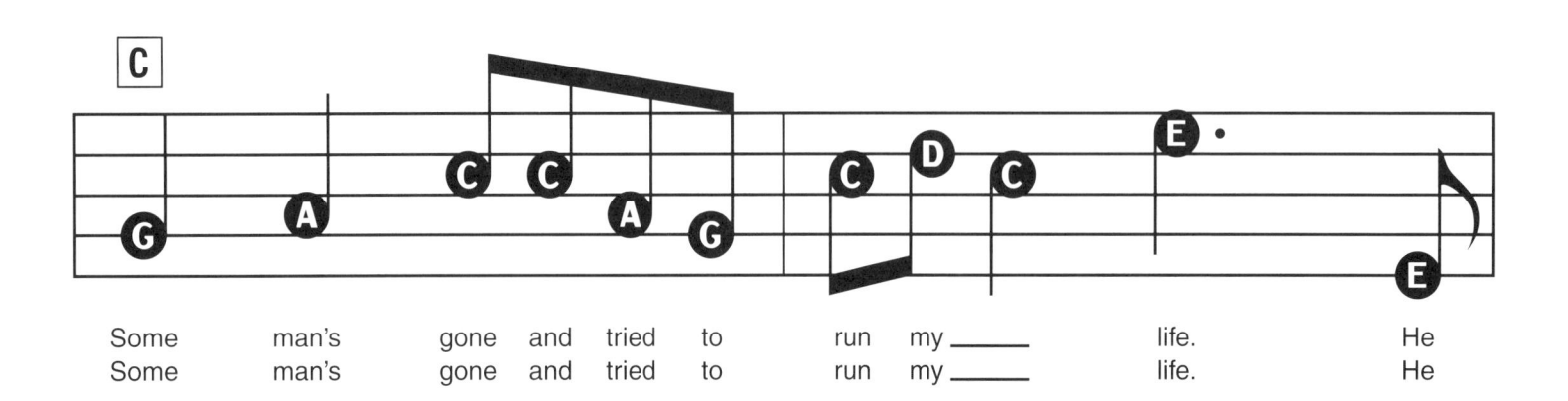

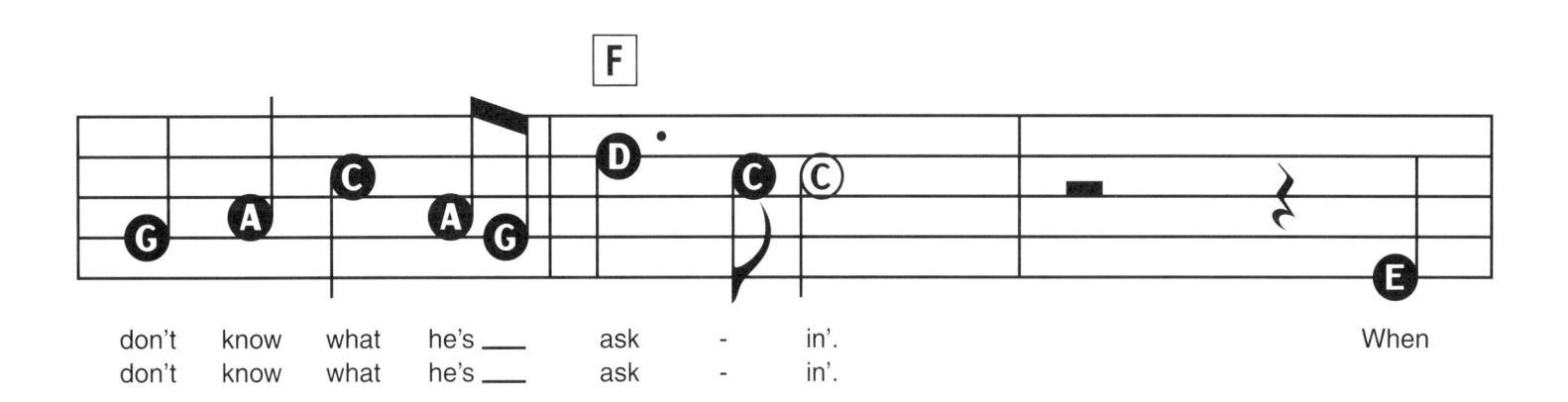

Sun - shine go a - way to - day, I
sun - shine go a - way to - day, I

don't feel much like danc - in'.
don't feel much like danc - in'.

Some man's gone and tried to run my life. He
Some man's gone and tried to run my life. He

don't know what he's ask - in'. When
don't know what he's ask - in'.

© 1971 (Renewed 1999) CASTLE HILL PUBLISHING LTD. (ASCAP)/Administered by BUG MUSIC
All Rights Reserved Used by Permission

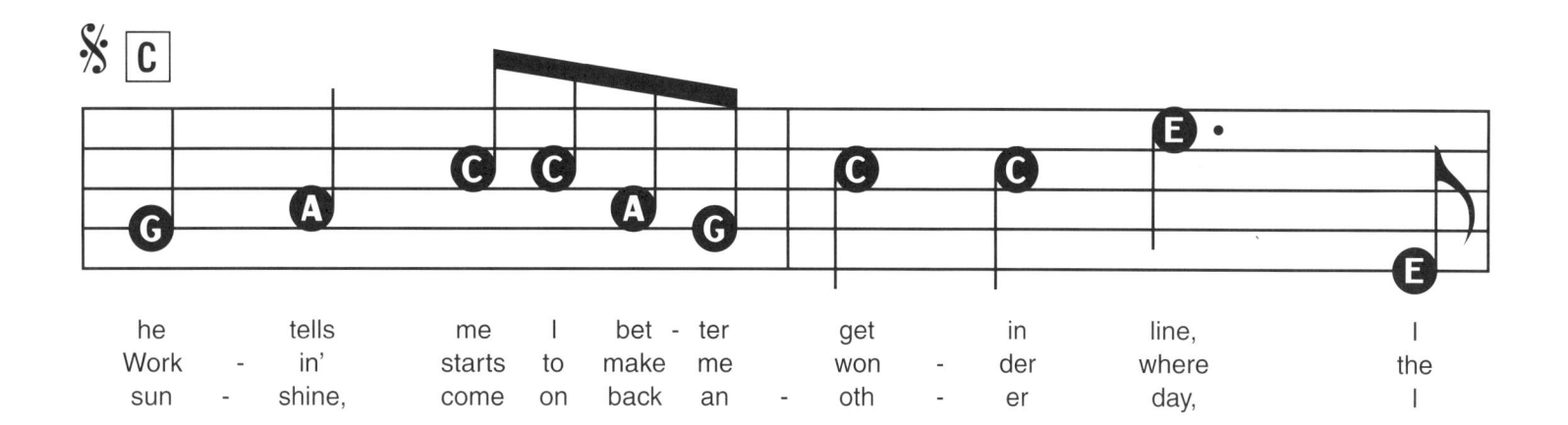

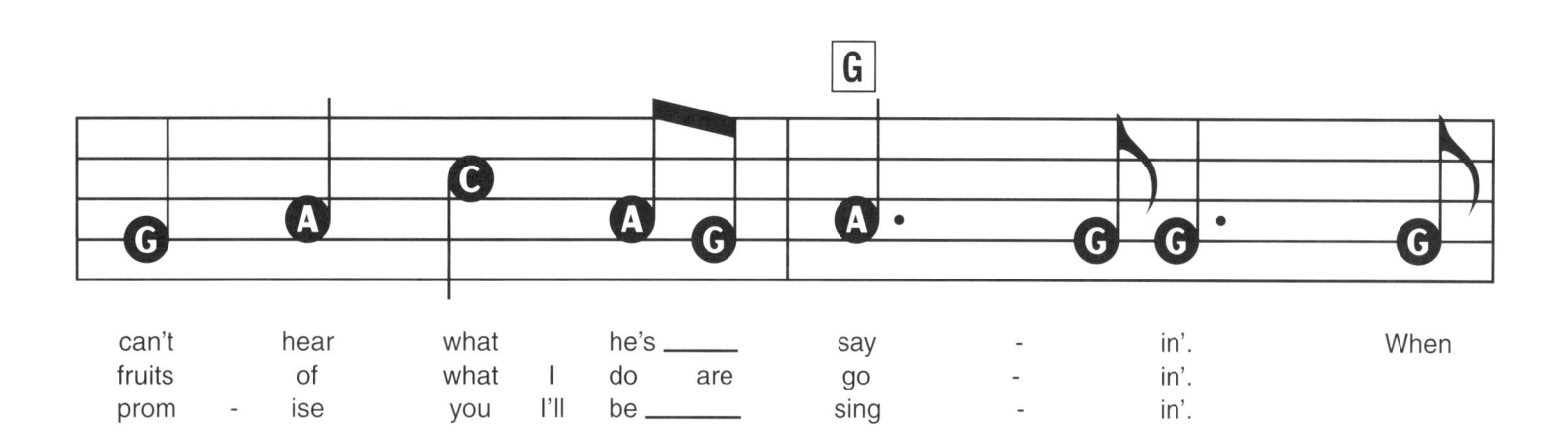

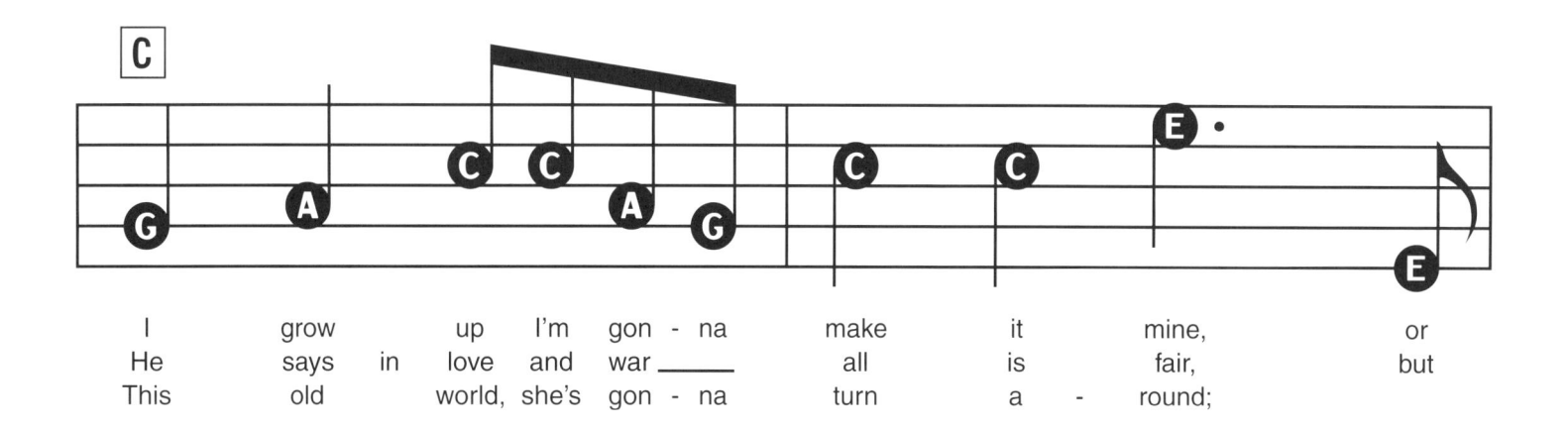

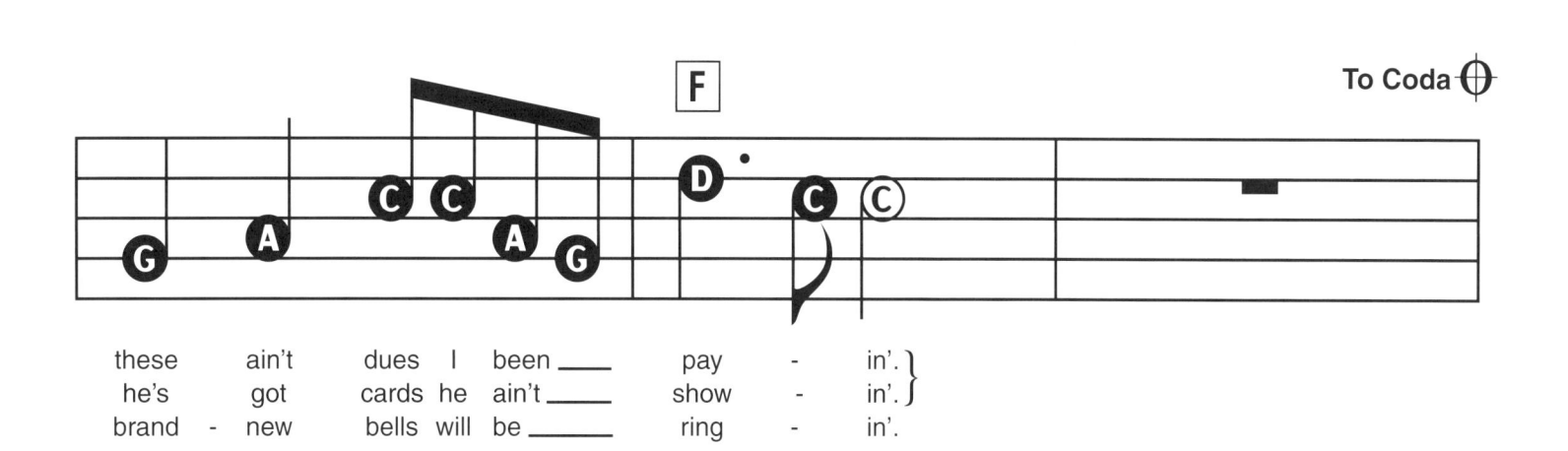

| C |

he tells me I better get in line, I
Work - in' starts to make me won - der where the
sun - shine, come on back an - oth - er day, I

| G |

can't hear what he's _____ say - in'. When
fruits of what I do are go - in'.
prom - ise you I'll be _____ sing - in'.

| C |

I grow up I'm gon - na make it mine, or
He says in love and war _____ all is fair, but
This old world, she's gon - na turn a - round;

To Coda ⊕

| F |

these ain't dues I been _____ pay - in'.
he's got cards he ain't _____ show - in'.
brand - new bells will be _____ ring - in'.

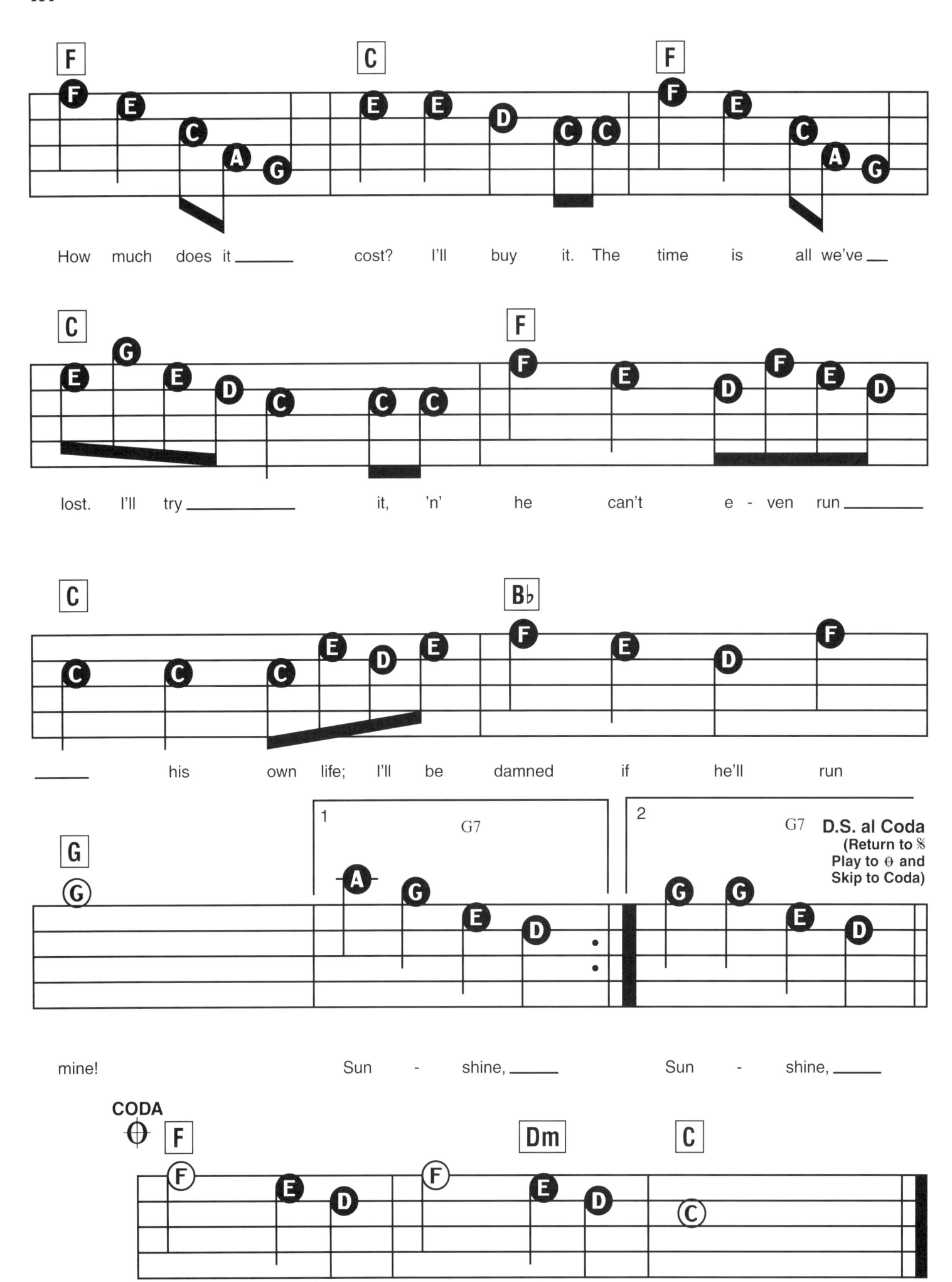

How much does it ____ cost? I'll buy it. The time is all we've ____ lost. I'll try ____ it, 'n' he can't e - ven run ____ his own life; I'll be damned if he'll run mine! Sun - shine, ____ Sun - shine, ____

(Instrumental)

Sunshine Superman

Registration 4
Rhythm: Country Rock or Rock

Words and Music by
Donovan Leitch

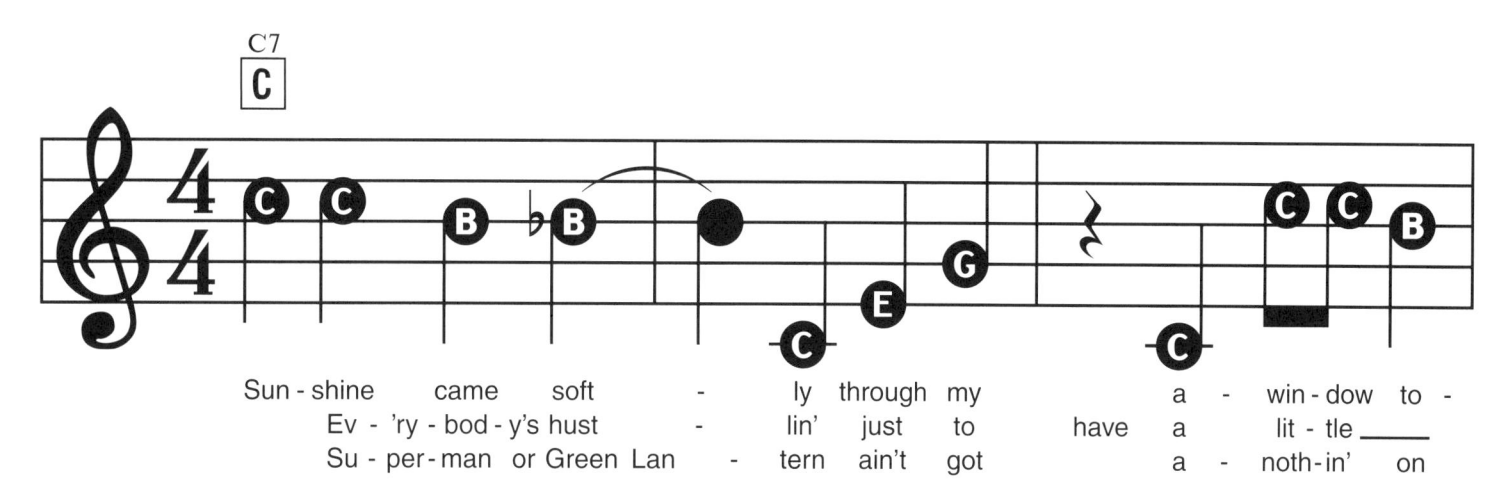

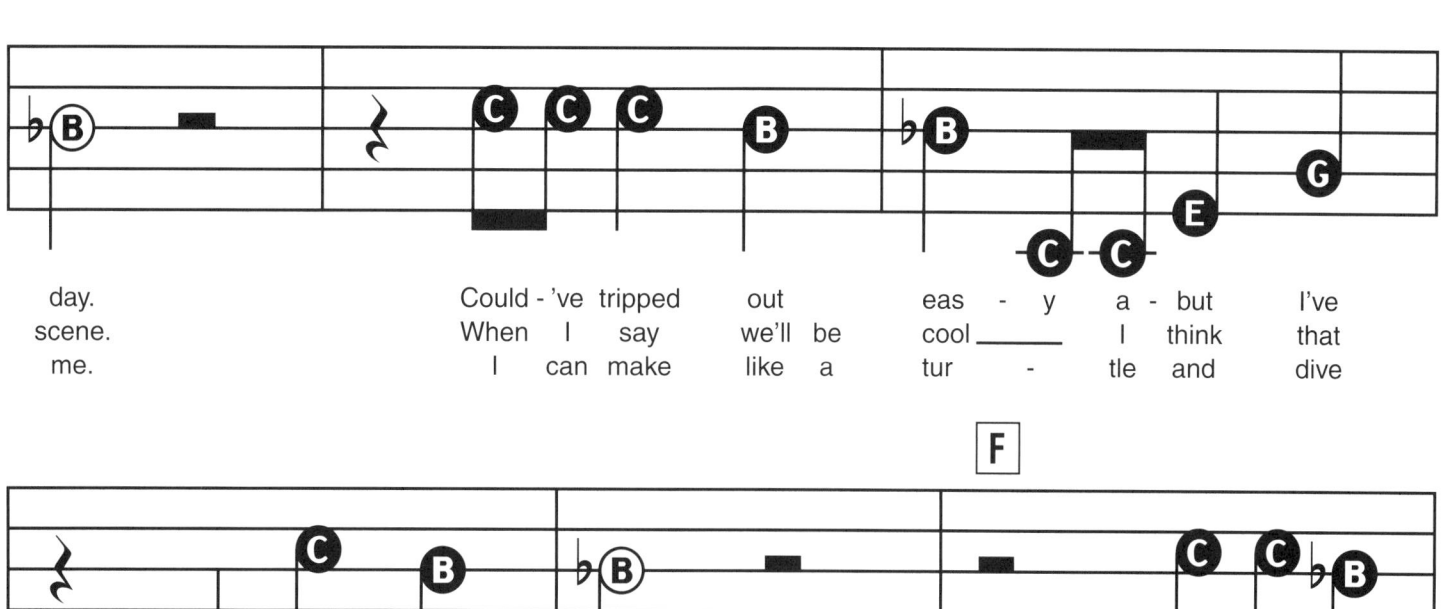

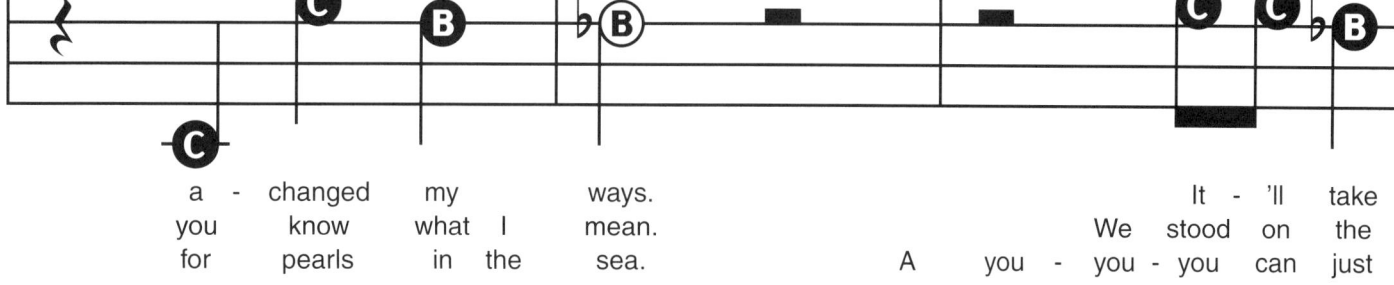

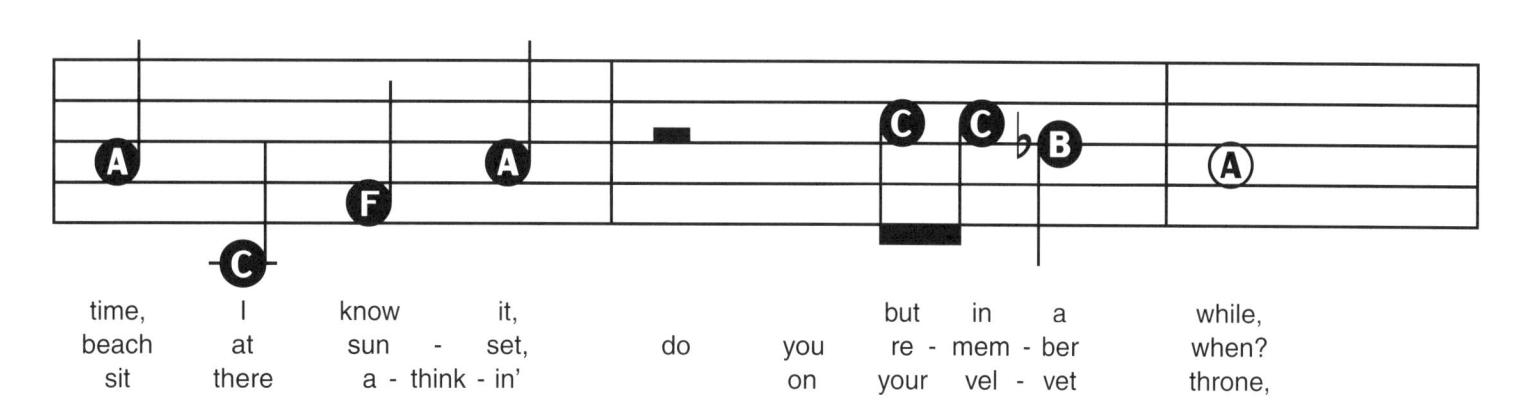

Sun - shine came soft - ly through my a - win - dow to - day.
Ev - 'ry - bod - y's hust - lin' just to have a lit - tle scene.
Su - per - man or Green Lan - tern ain't got a - noth - in' on me.

Could - 've tripped out eas - y a - but I've a - changed my ways.
When I say we'll be cool I think that you know what I mean.
I can make like a tur - tle and dive for pearls in the sea.

It - 'll take time, I know it, but in a while,
We stood on the beach at sun - set, do you re - mem - ber when?
A you - you - you can just sit there a - think - in' on your vel - vet throne,

Copyright © 1966 by Donovan (Music) Ltd.
Copyright Renewed
All Rights Administered by Peer International Corporation
International Copyright Secured All Rights Reserved

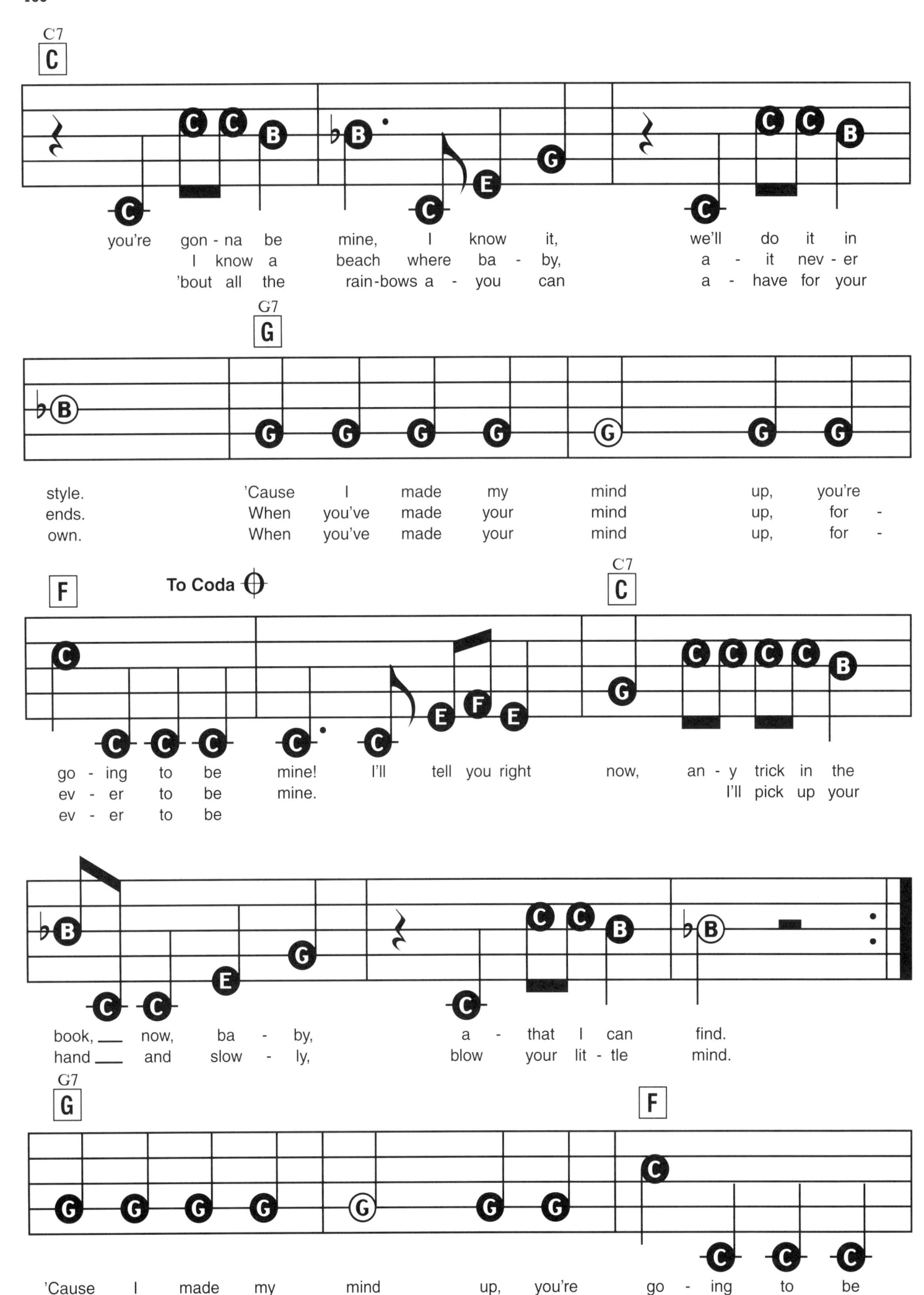

you're gon-na be mine, I know it, we'll do it in
I know a beach where ba - by, a - it nev - er
'bout all the rain-bows a - you can a - have for your

style. 'Cause I made my mind up, you're
ends. When you've made your mind up, for -
own. When you've made your mind up, for -

To Coda

go - ing to be mine! I'll tell you right now, an - y trick in the
ev - er to be mine. I'll pick up your
ev - er to be

book, now, ba - by, a - that I can find.
hand and slow - ly, blow your lit - tle mind.

'Cause I made my mind up, you're go - ing to be

mine. I'll tell you right now, an-y trick in the

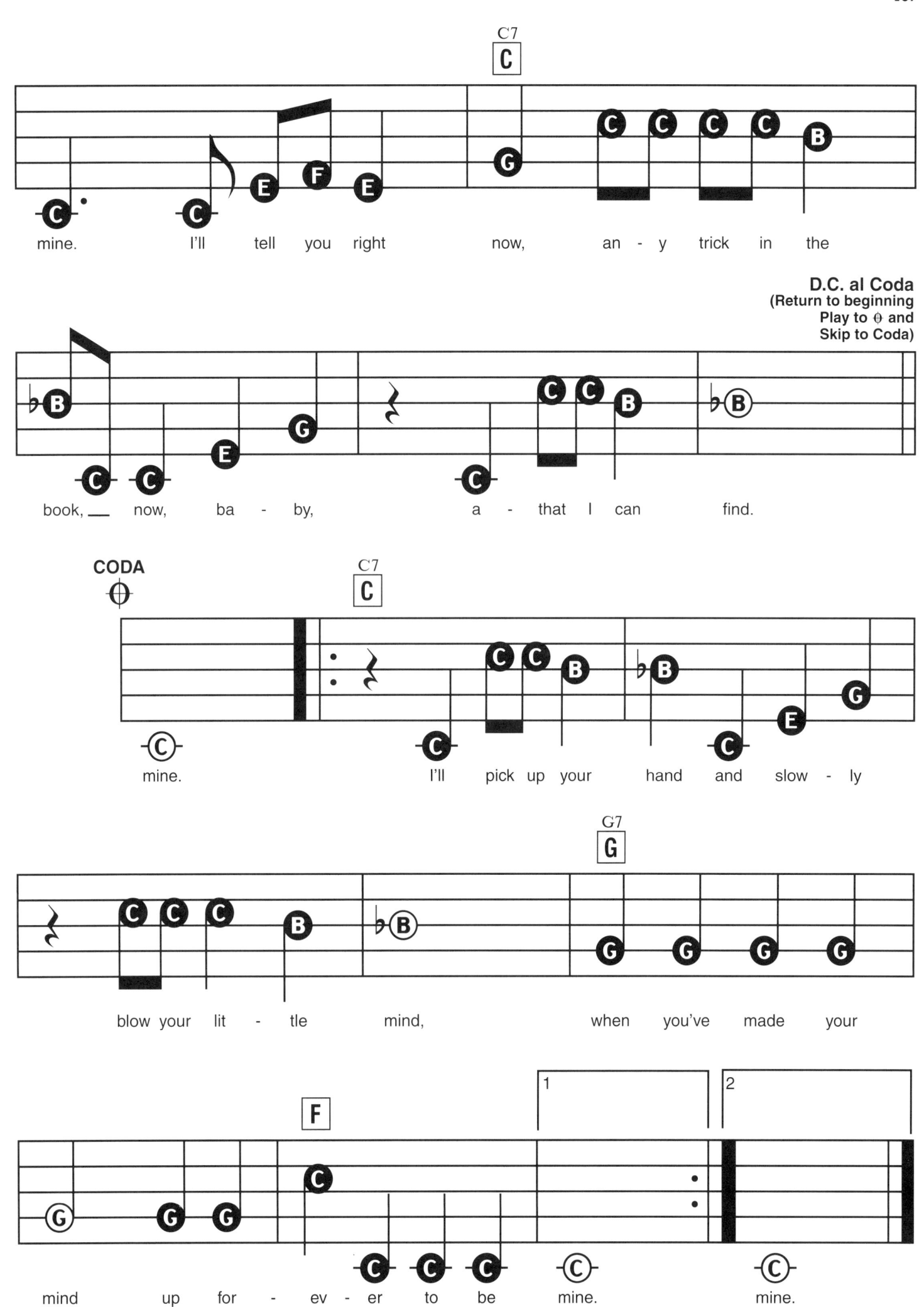

D.C. al Coda
(Return to beginning
Play to ϴ and
Skip to Coda)

book,__ now, ba-by, a - that I can find.

CODA

mine. I'll pick up your hand and slow-ly

blow your lit-tle mind, when you've made your

mind up for-ev-er to be mine. mine.

This Land Is Your Land

Registration 9
Rhythm: Country or Swing

Words and Music by
Woody Guthrie

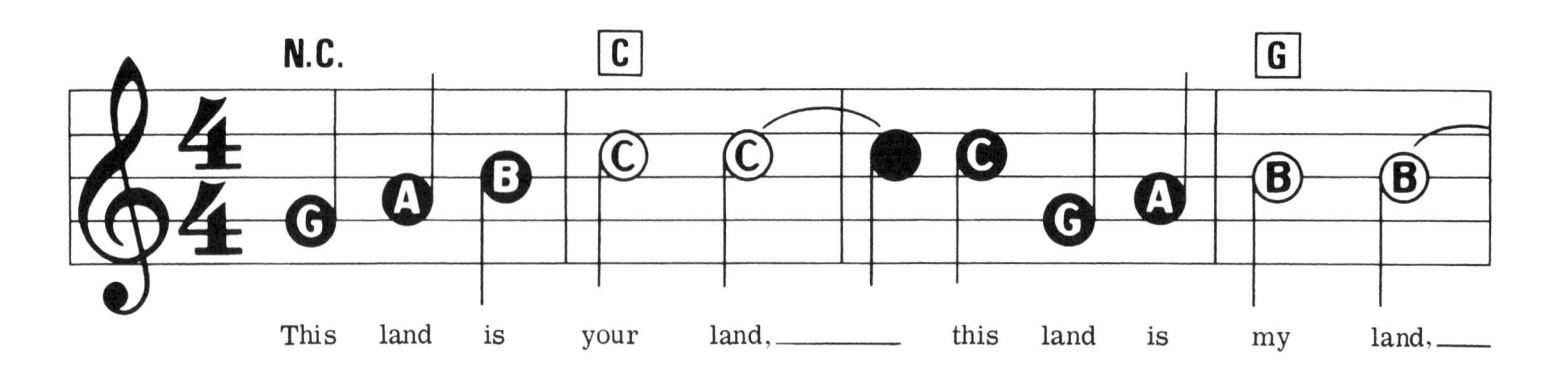

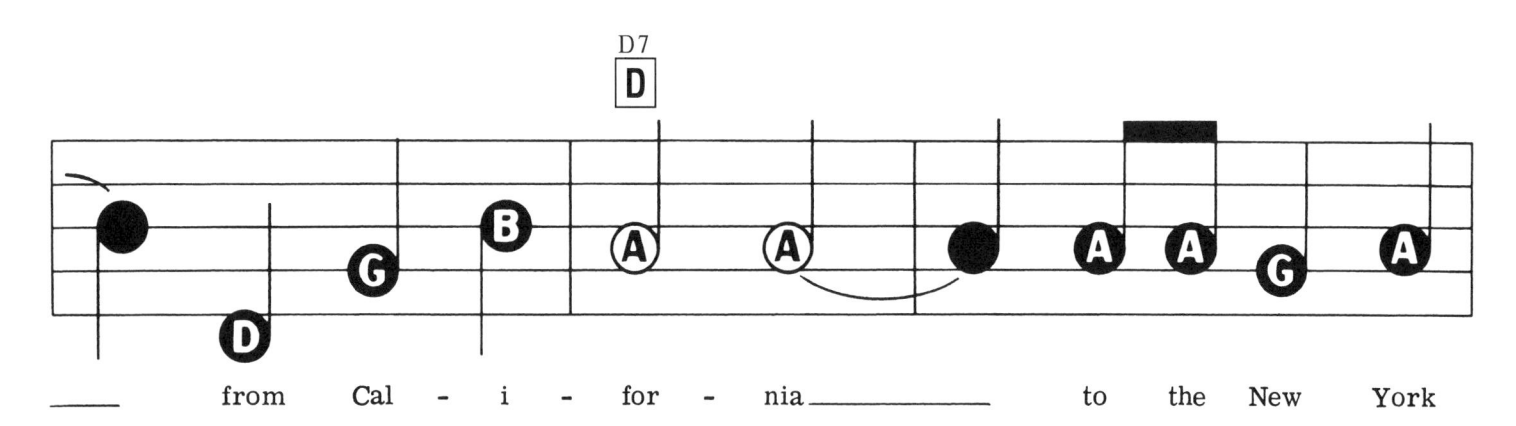

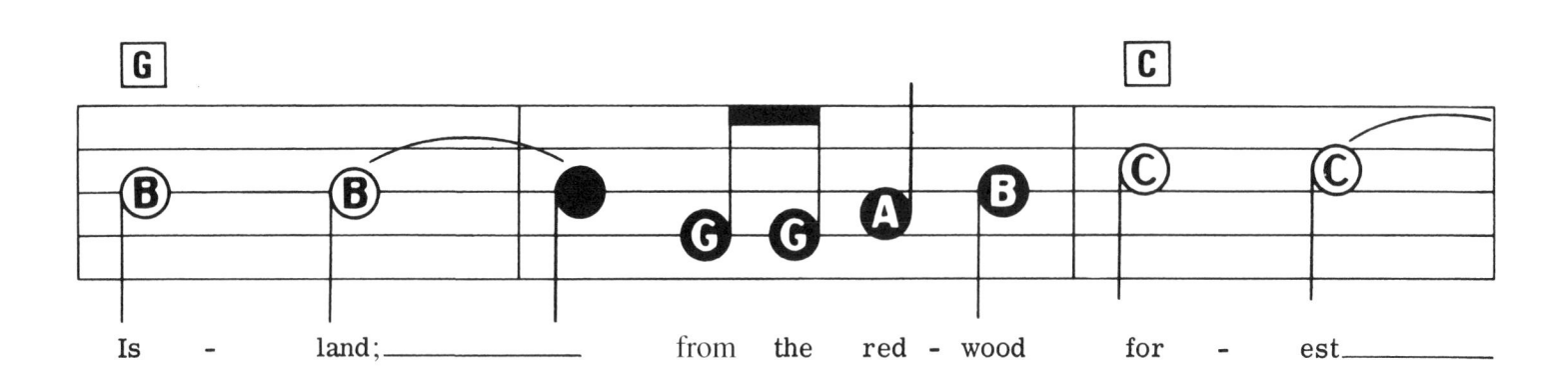

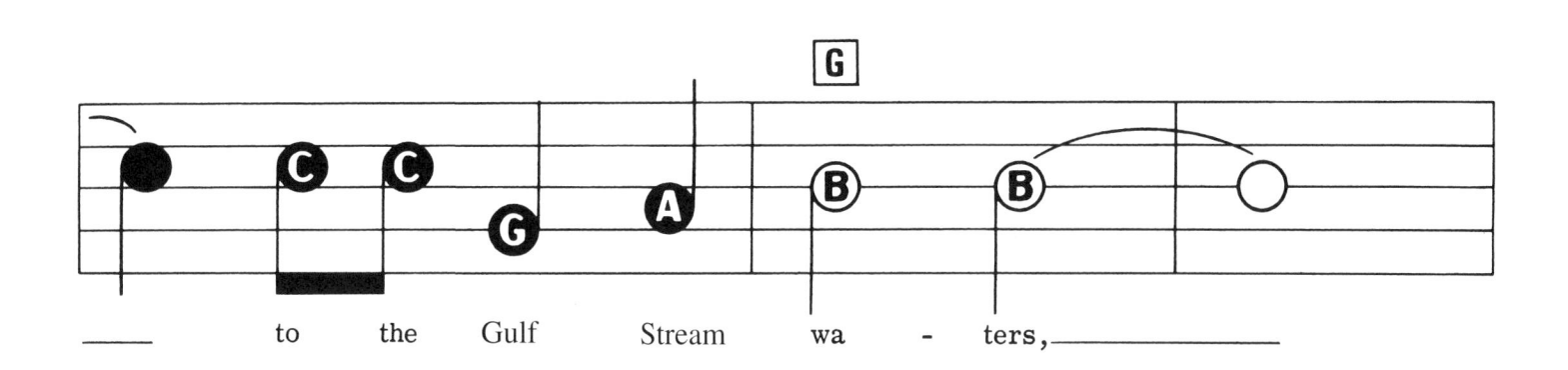

This land is your land, _____ this land is my land, _____ from Cal-i-for-nia _____ to the New York Is-land; _____ from the red-wood for-est _____ to the Gulf Stream wa-ters, _____

TRO - © 1956 (Renewed), 1958 (Renewed), 1970 (Renewed) and 1972 (Renewed) Ludlow Music, Inc., New York, NY
International Copyright Secured
All Rights Reserved Including Public Performance For Profit
Used by Permission

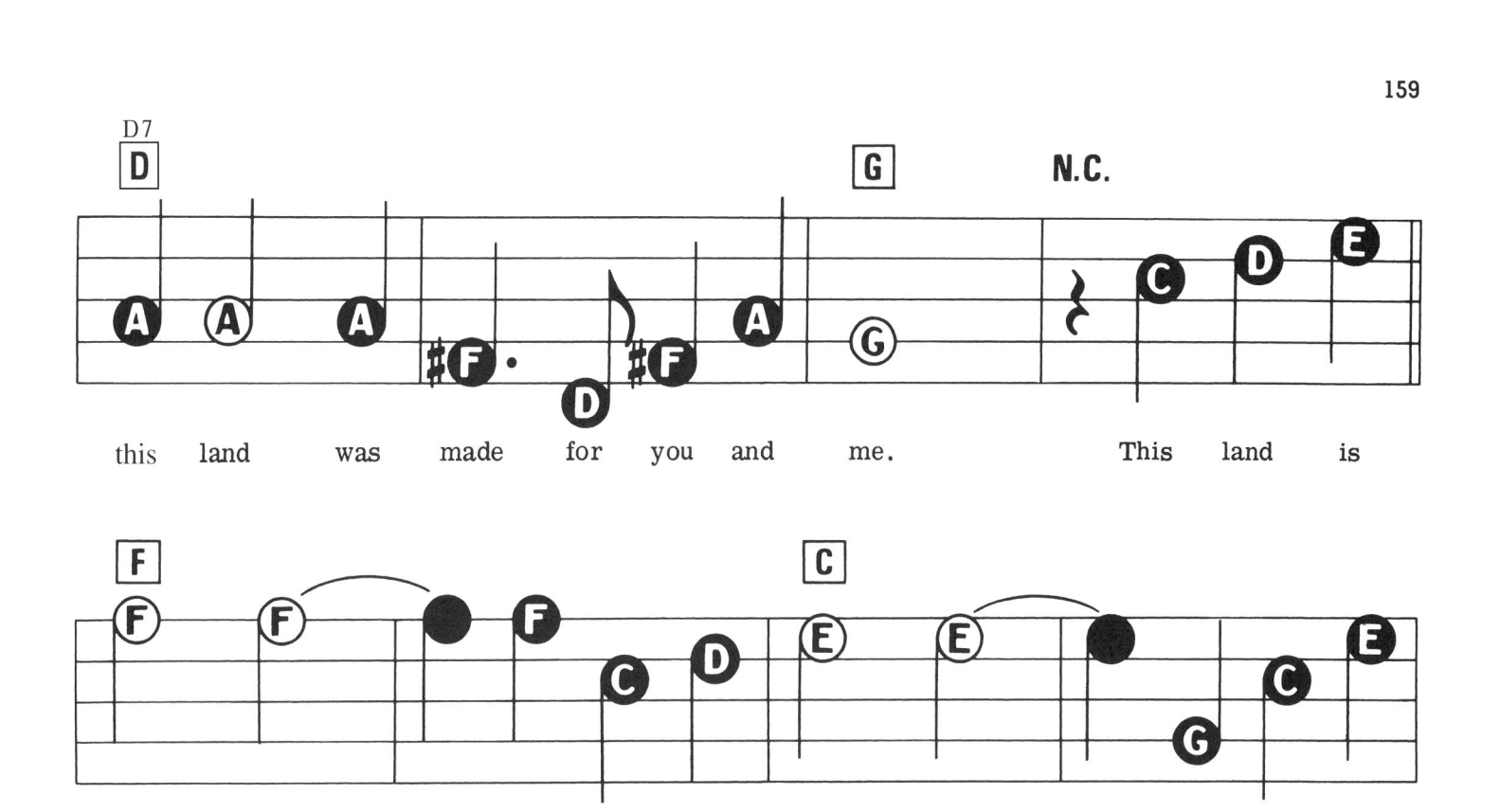

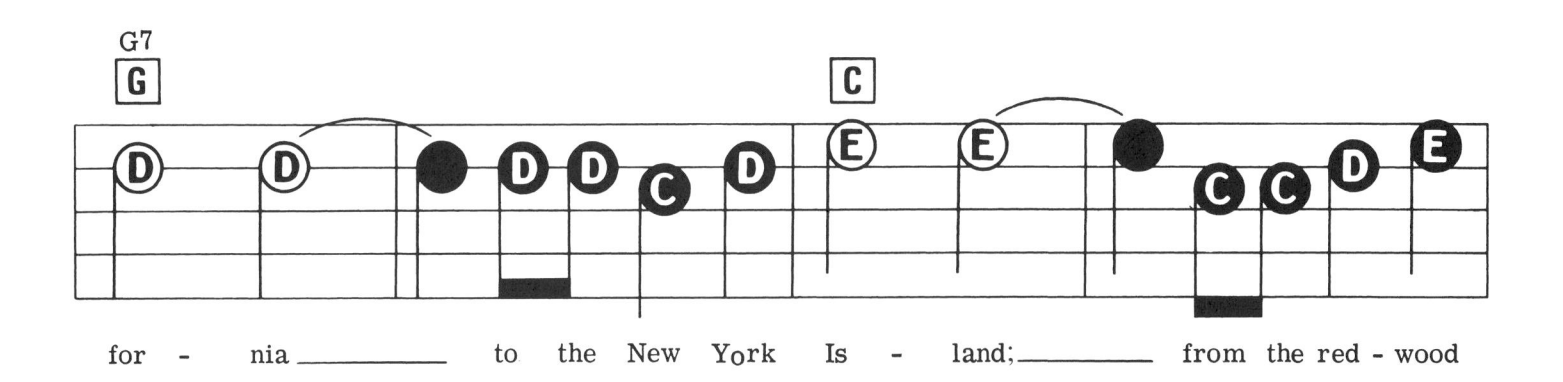

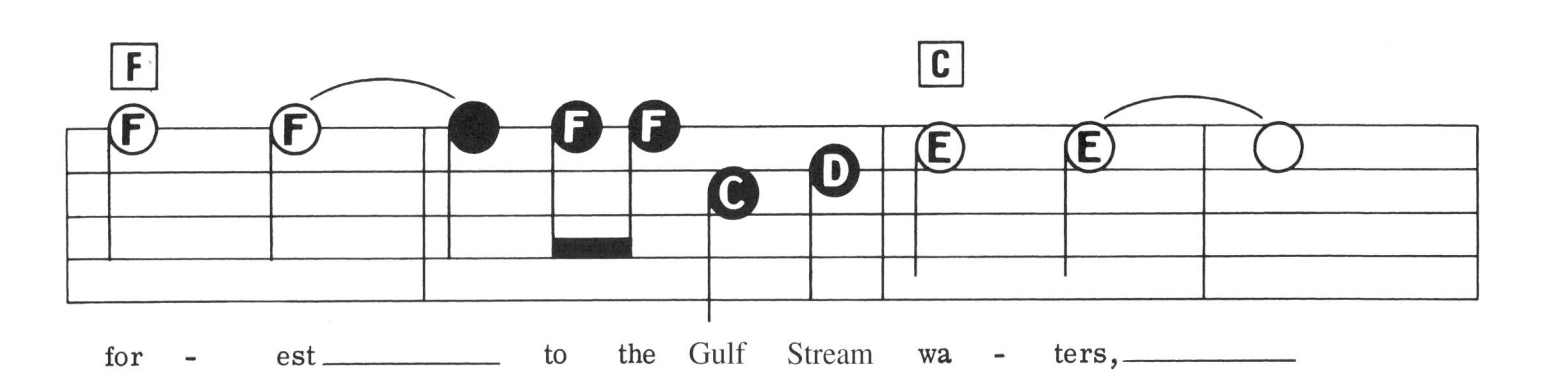

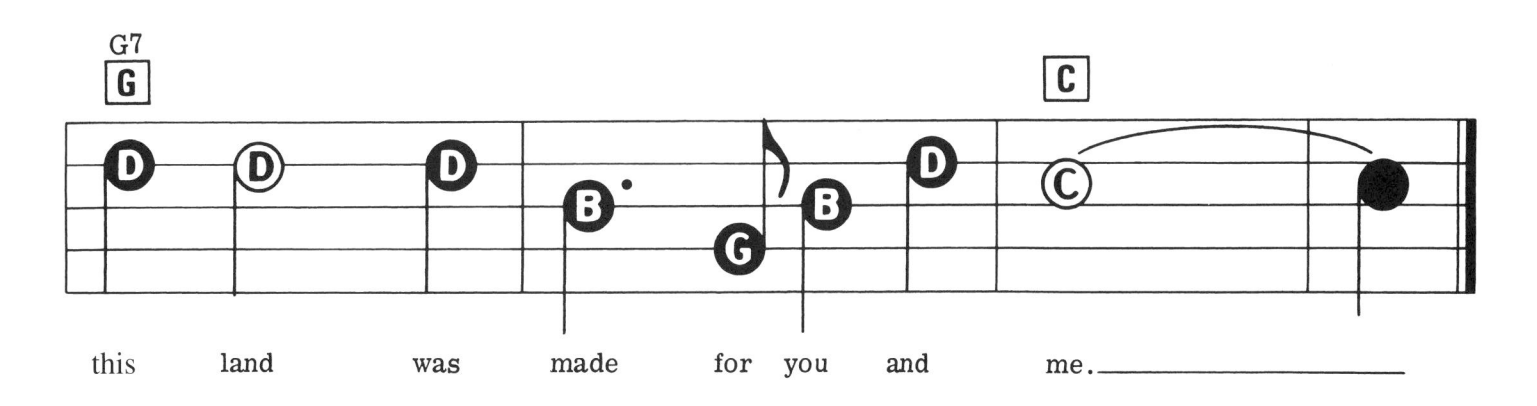

this land was made for you and me. This land is your land, this land is my land, from California to the New York Island; from the redwood forest to the Gulf Stream waters, this land was made for you and me.

Those Were the Days

Registration 3
Rhythm: Fox Trot or March

Words and Music by
Gene Raskin

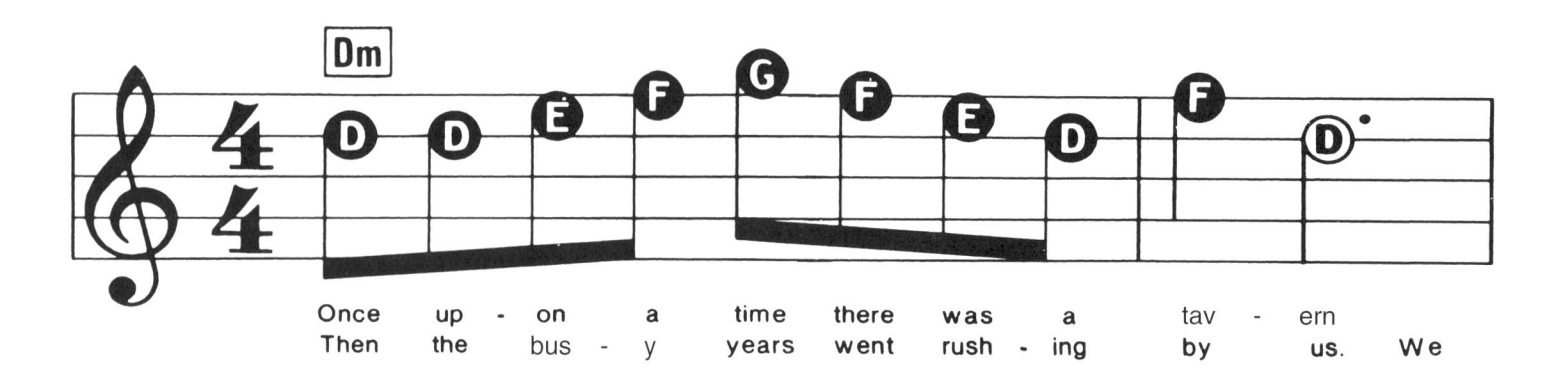

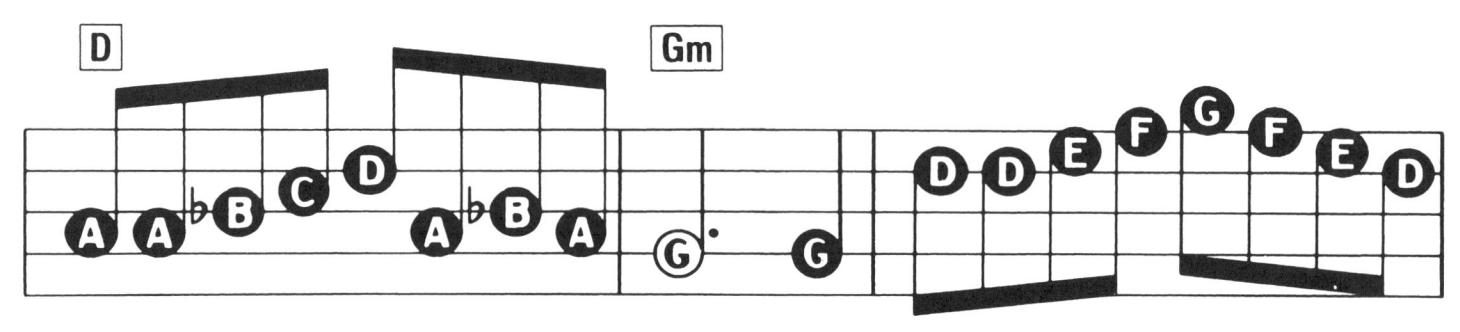

Once up-on a time there was a tav-ern
Then the bus-y years went rush-ing by us. We

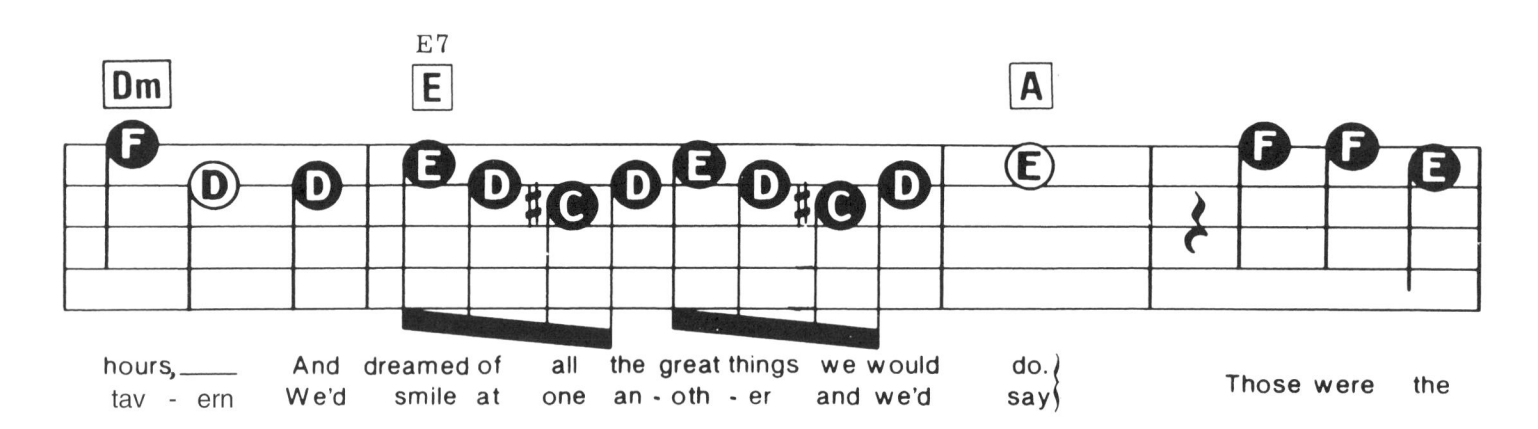

Where we used to raise a glass or two. Re- mem-ber how we laughed a-way the
lost our star-ry no-tions on the way. If by chance I'd see you in the

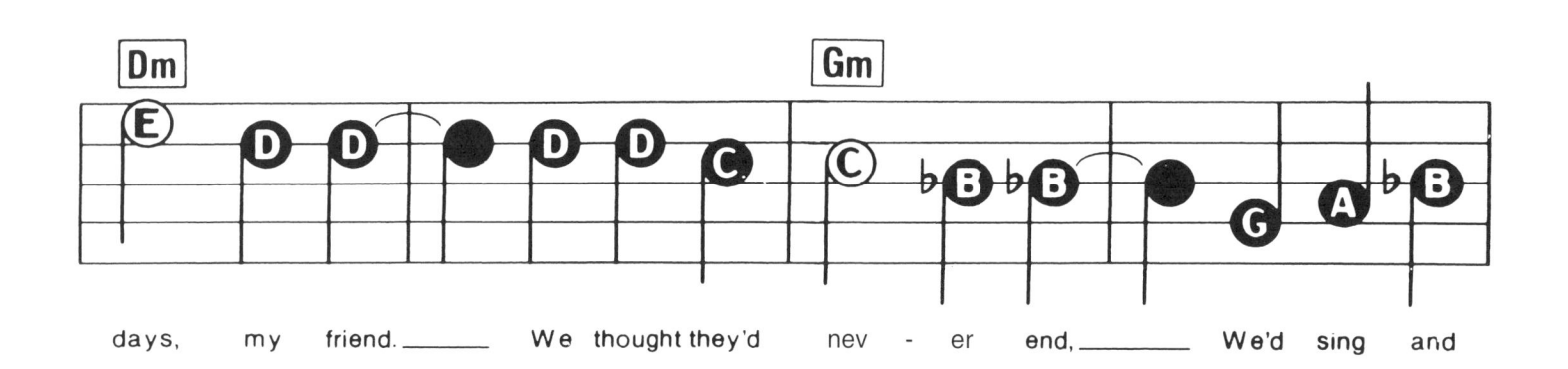

hours,___ And dreamed of all the great things we would do.
tav-ern We'd smile at one an-oth-er and we'd say

Those were the

days, my friend.___ We thought they'd nev-er end,___ We'd sing and

TRO - © Copyright 1962 (Renewed) and 1968 (Renewed) Essex Music, Inc., New York, NY
International Copyright Secured
All Rights Reserved Including Public Performance For Profit
Used by Permission

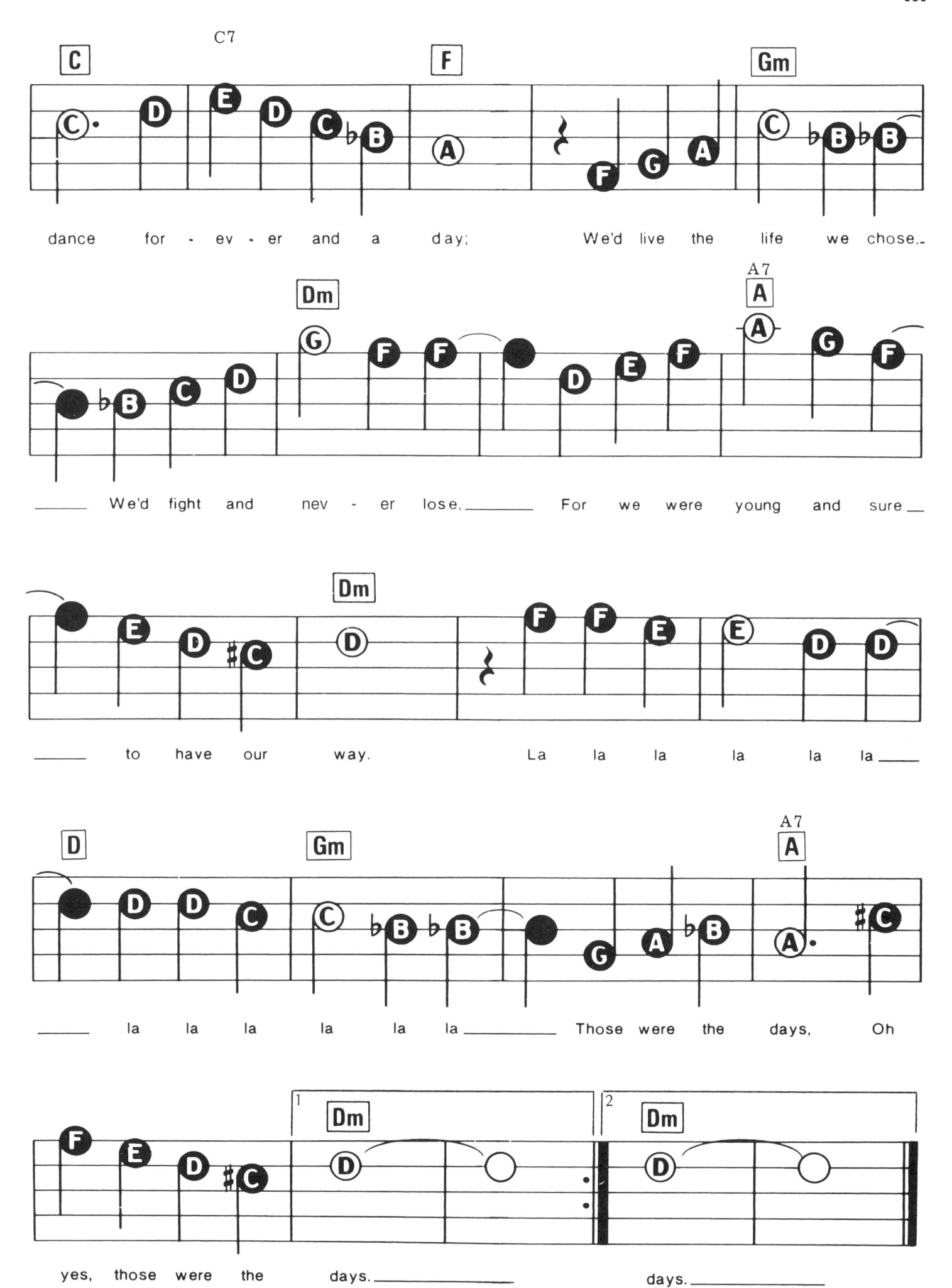

dance for-ev-er and a day; We'd live the life we chose,

We'd fight and nev-er lose, For we were young and sure

to have our way. La la la la la la

la la la la la la Those were the days, Oh

yes, those were the days. days.

Time in a Bottle

Registration 8
Rhythm: Waltz

Words and Music by
Jim Croce

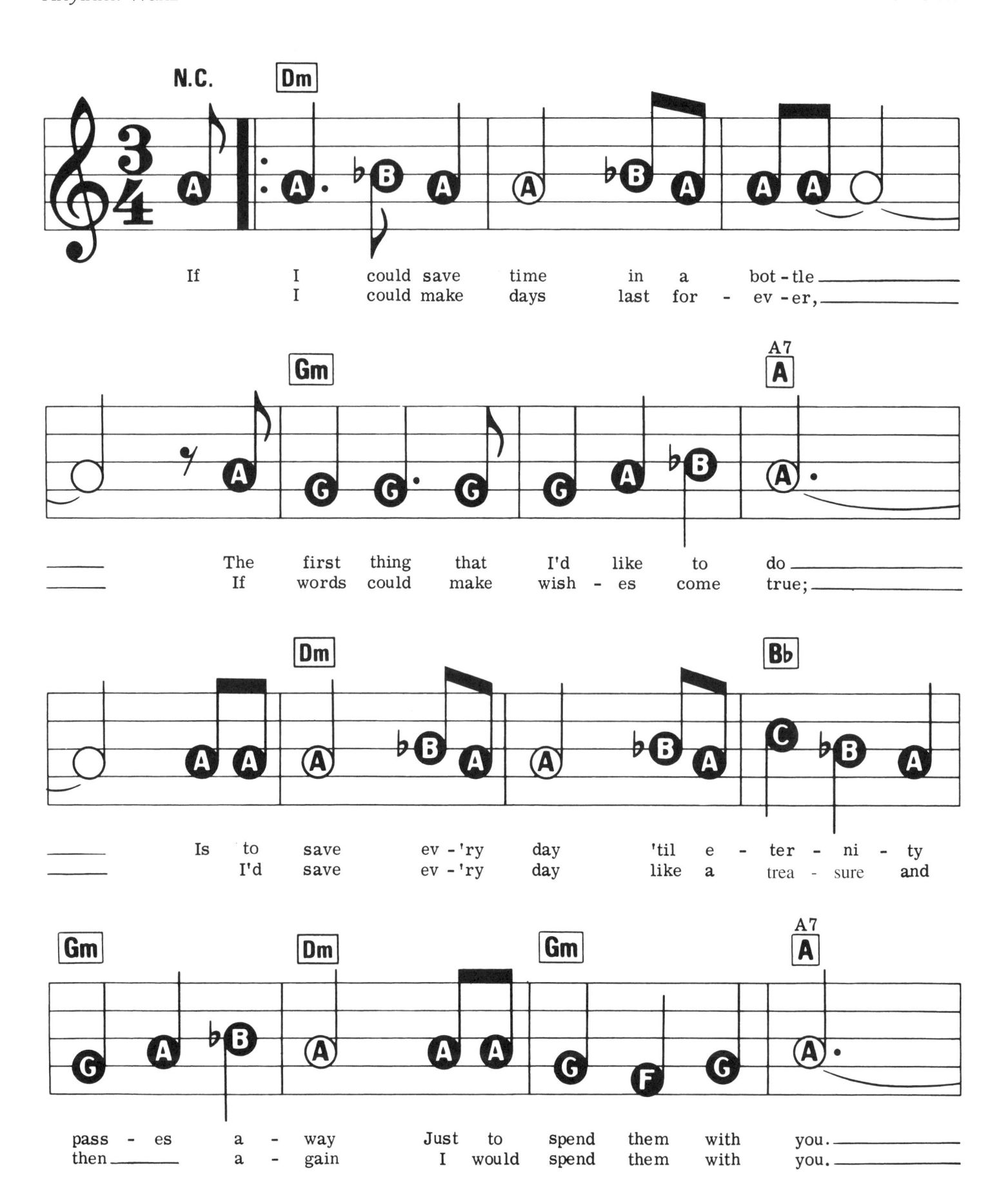

If I could save time in a bottle
I could make days last for-ev-er,

The first thing that I'd like to do
If words could make wish-es come true;

Is to save ev-'ry day 'til e-ter-ni-ty
I'd save ev-'ry day like a trea-sure and

pass-es a-way Just to spend them with you.
then a-gain I would spend them with you.

© 1971 (Renewed 1999) TIME IN A BOTTLE PUBLISHING and CROCE PUBLISHING
All Rights Controlled and Administered by EMI APRIL MUSIC INC.
All Rights Reserved   International Copyright Secured   Used by Permission

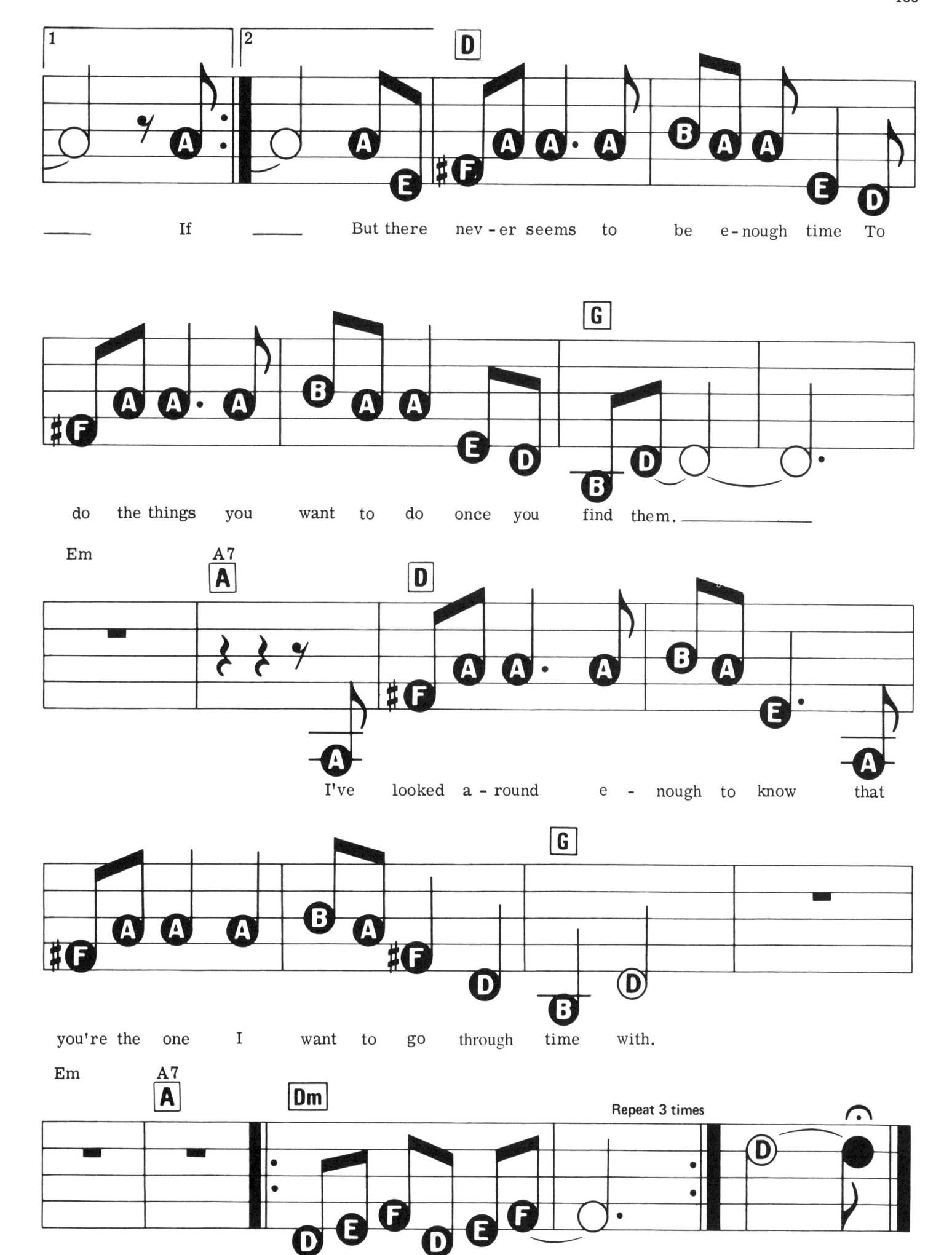

If ____ But there nev-er seems to be e-nough time To do the things you want to do once you find them. ____

I've looked a-round e-nough to know that you're the one I want to go through time with.

(Instrumental)

Repeat 3 times

Vincent
(Starry Starry Night)

Registration 7
Rhythm: 8 Beat or Pops

Words and Music by
Don McLean

Star - ry, star - ry night, paint your pal - ette
night, flam - ing flow'rs that
night, por - traits hung in

blue and grey; look out on a sum - mer's day, with
bright - ly blaze; swirl - ing clouds in vio - let haze with re -
emp - ty halls; frame - less heads on name - less walls, with

eyes that know the dark - ness in my soul. Shad - ows on the
flect in Vin - cent's eyes of Chi - na blue. Col - ors chang - ing
eyes that watch the world and can't for - get. Like the stran - gers that you've

hills, sketch the trees and the daf - fo - dils,
hue, morn - ing fields of am - ber grain,
met, the rag - ged men in rag - ged clothes,

Copyright © 1971, 1972 BENNY BIRD CO., INC.
Copyrights Renewed
All Rights Controlled and Administered by SONGS OF UNIVERSAL, INC.
All Rights Reserved   Used by Permission

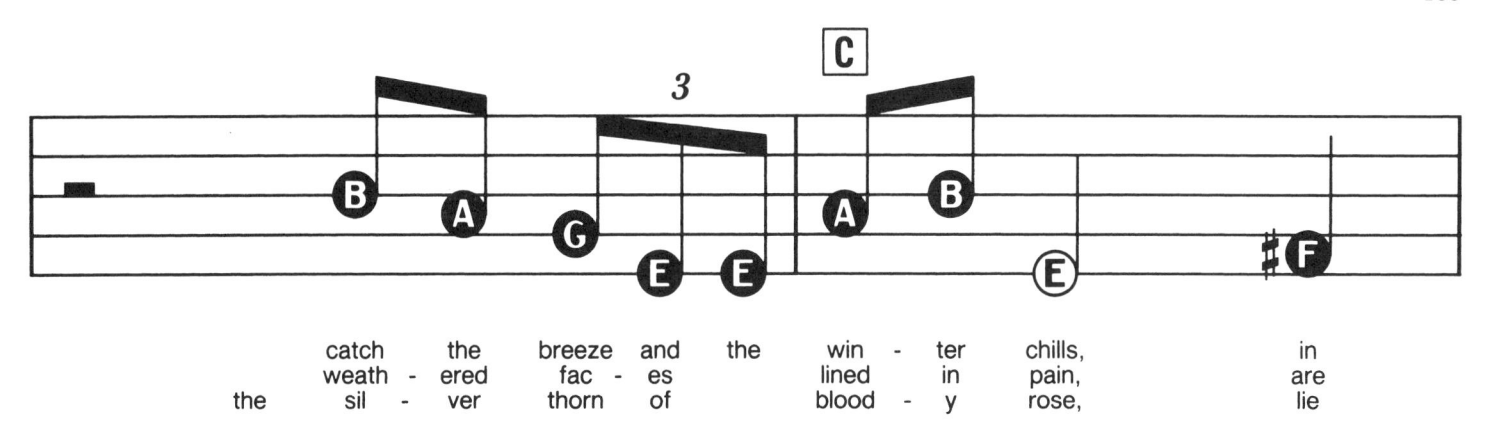

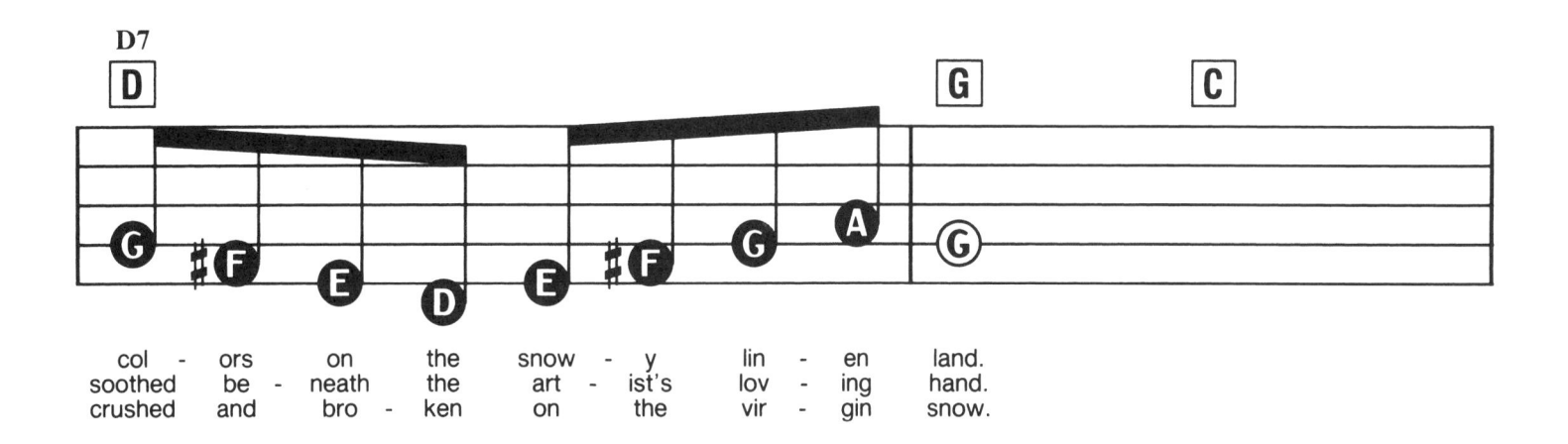

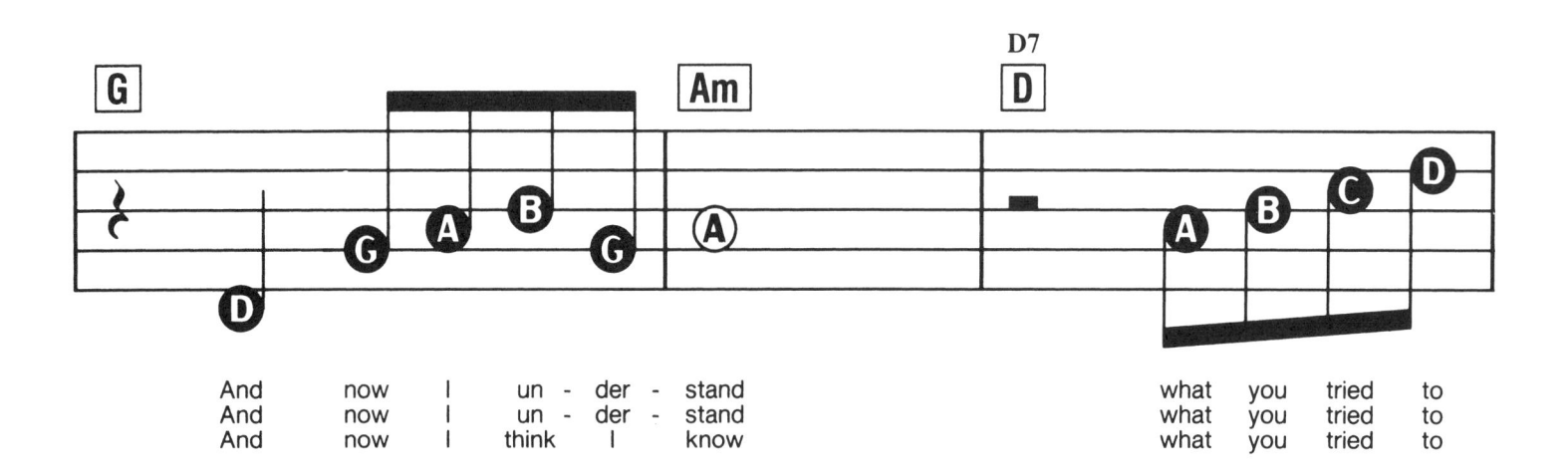

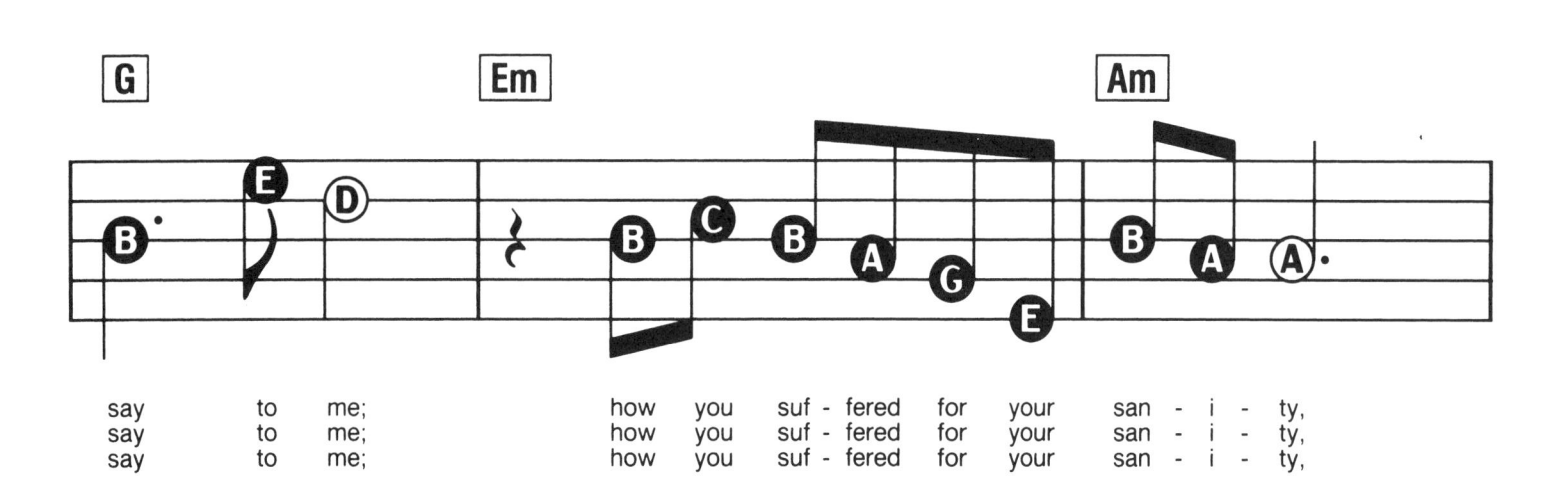

catch the breeze and the win - ter chills, in
weath - ered fac - es lined in pain, are
the sil - ver thorn of blood - y rose, lie

col - ors on the snow - y lin - en land.
soothed be - neath the art - ist's lov - ing hand.
crushed and bro - ken on the vir - gin snow.

And now I un - der - stand what you tried to
And now I un - der - stand what you tried to
And now I think I know what you tried to

say to me; how you suf - fered for your san - i - ty,
say to me; how you suf - fered for your san - i - ty,
say to me; how you suf - fered for your san - i - ty,

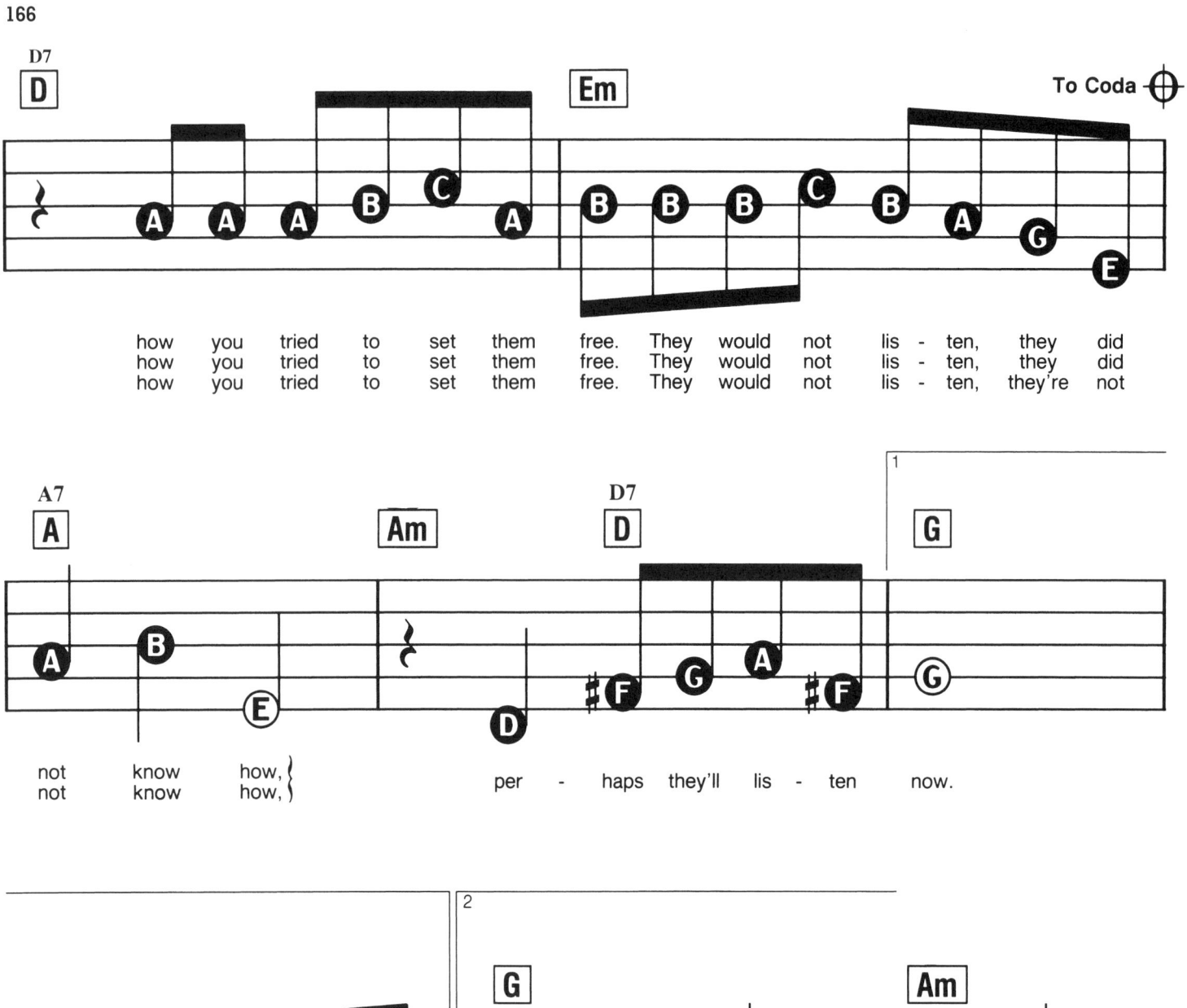

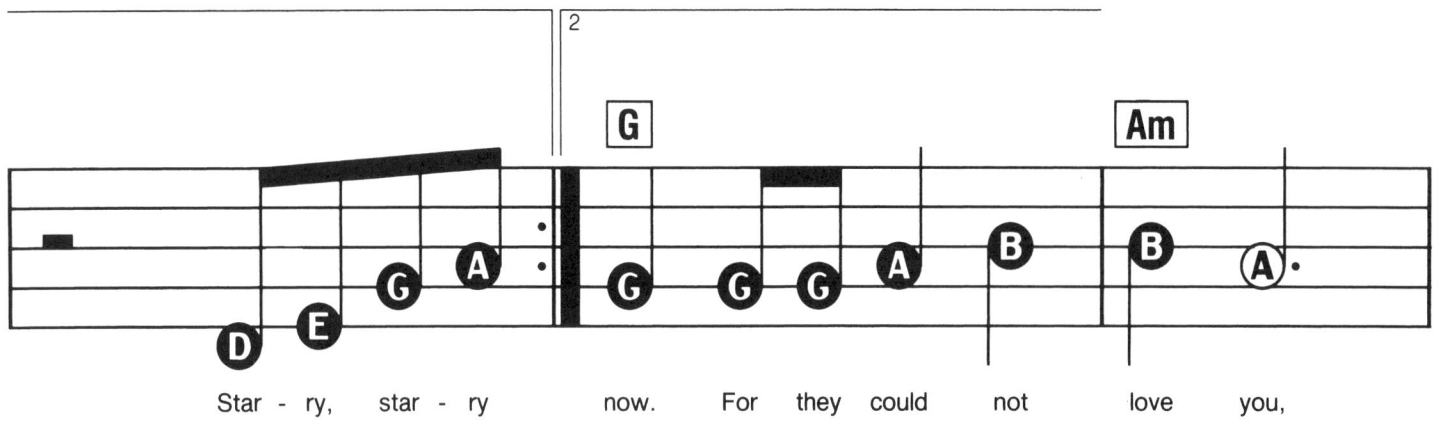

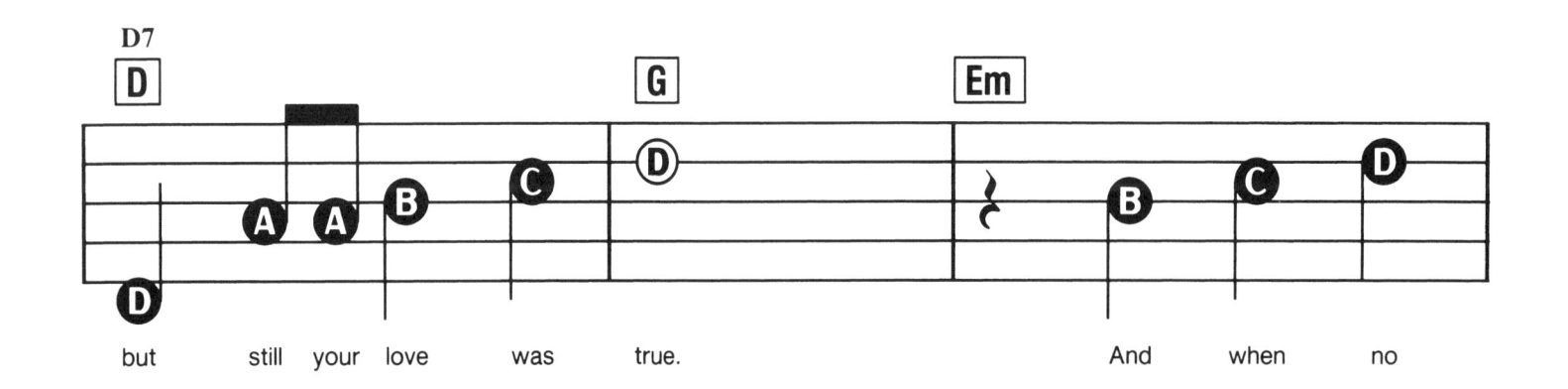

how you tried to set them free. They would not lis - ten, they did
how you tried to set them free. They would not lis - ten, they did
how you tried to set them free. They would not lis - ten, they're not

not know how, / per - haps they'll lis - ten now.
not know how, \

Star - ry, star - ry now. For they could not love you,

but still your love was true. And when no

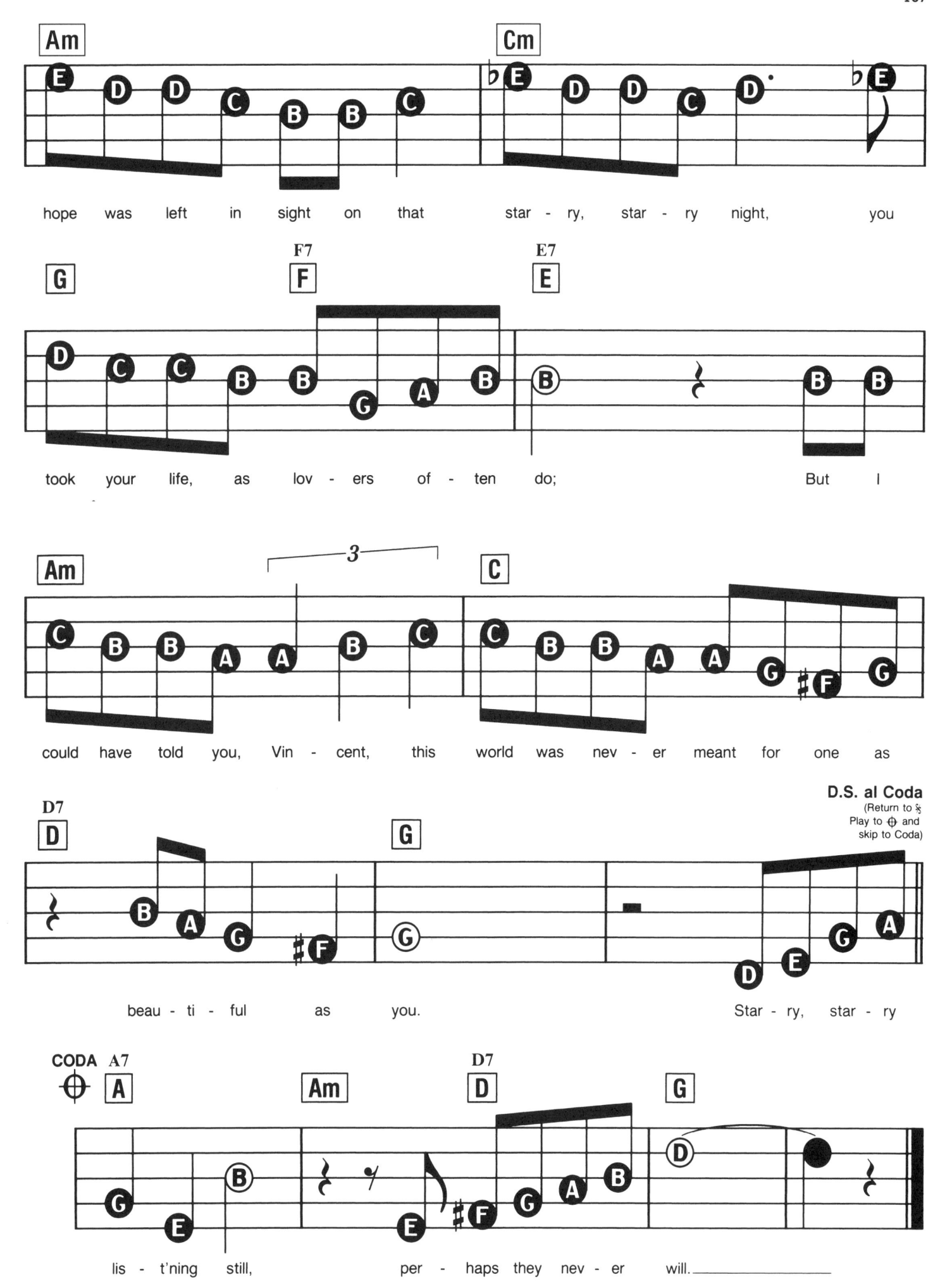

hope was left in sight on that star-ry, star-ry night, you took your life, as lov-ers of-ten do; But I could have told you, Vin-cent, this world was nev-er meant for one as beau-ti-ful as you. Star-ry, star-ry lis-t'ning still, per-haps they nev-er will.

We Just Disagree

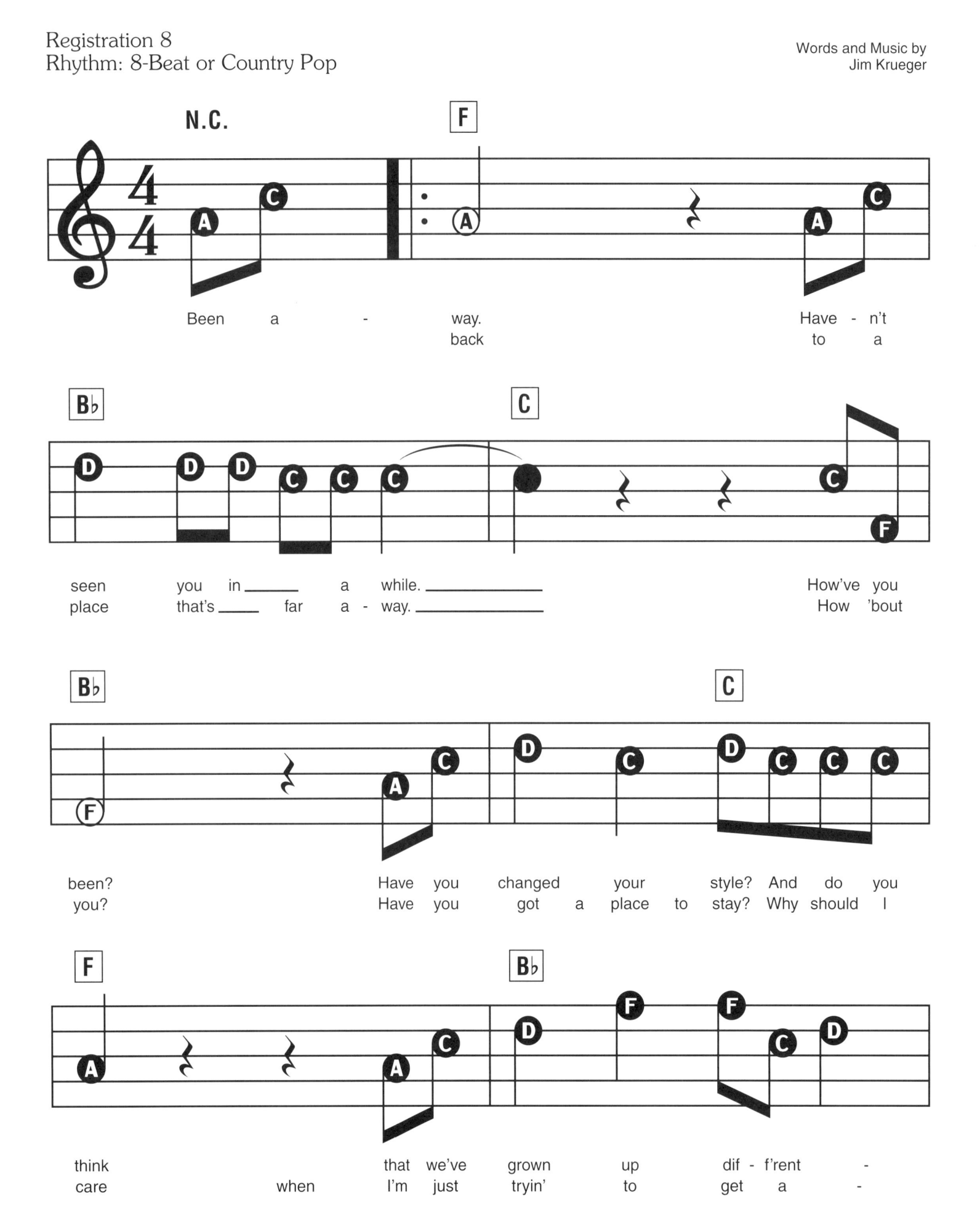

Registration 8
Rhythm: 8-Beat or Country Pop

Words and Music by
Jim Krueger

Been a - way. Have - n't
back to a

seen you in a while. How've you
place that's far a - way. How 'bout

been? Have you changed your style? And do you
you? Have you got a place to stay? Why should I

think that we've grown up dif - f'rent -
care when I'm just tryin' to get a -

© 1976, 1977 (Renewed 2004, 2005) EMI BLACKWOOD MUSIC INC. and BRUISER MUSIC
All Rights Controlled and Administered by EMI BLACKWOOD MUSIC INC.
All Rights Reserved   International Copyright Secured   Used by Permission

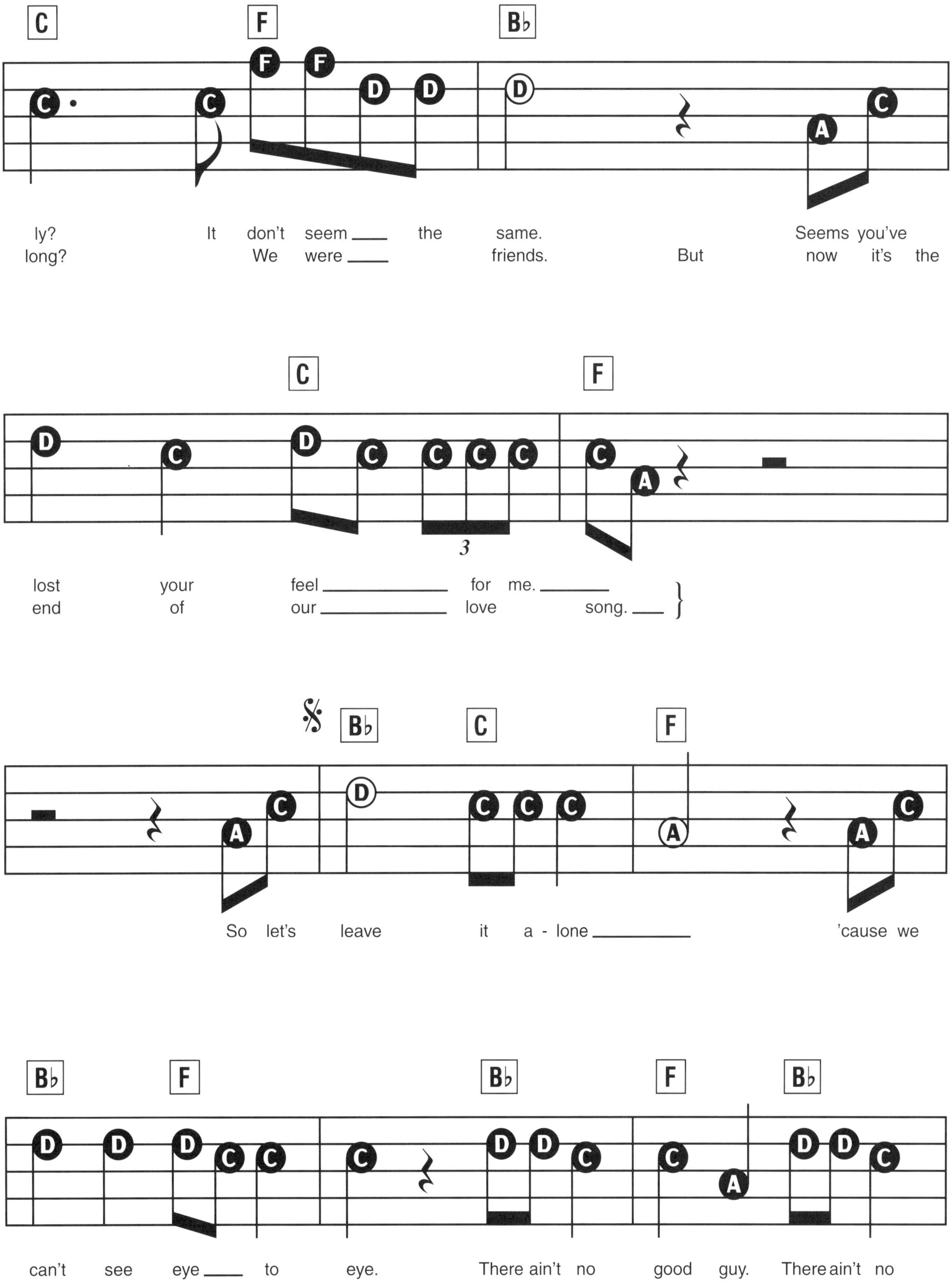
C F B♭
C C F F D D D A C
ly? It don't seem the same. Seems you've
long? We were friends. But now it's the
C F
D C D C C C C C A
3
lost your feel for me.
end of our love song.
𝄋 B♭ C F
A C D C C C A A C
So let's leave it a - lone 'cause we
B♭ F B♭ F B♭
D D D C C C D D C C A D D C
can't see eye to eye. There ain't no good guy. There ain't no

bad guy. There's on-ly you and me, and we just dis-a-

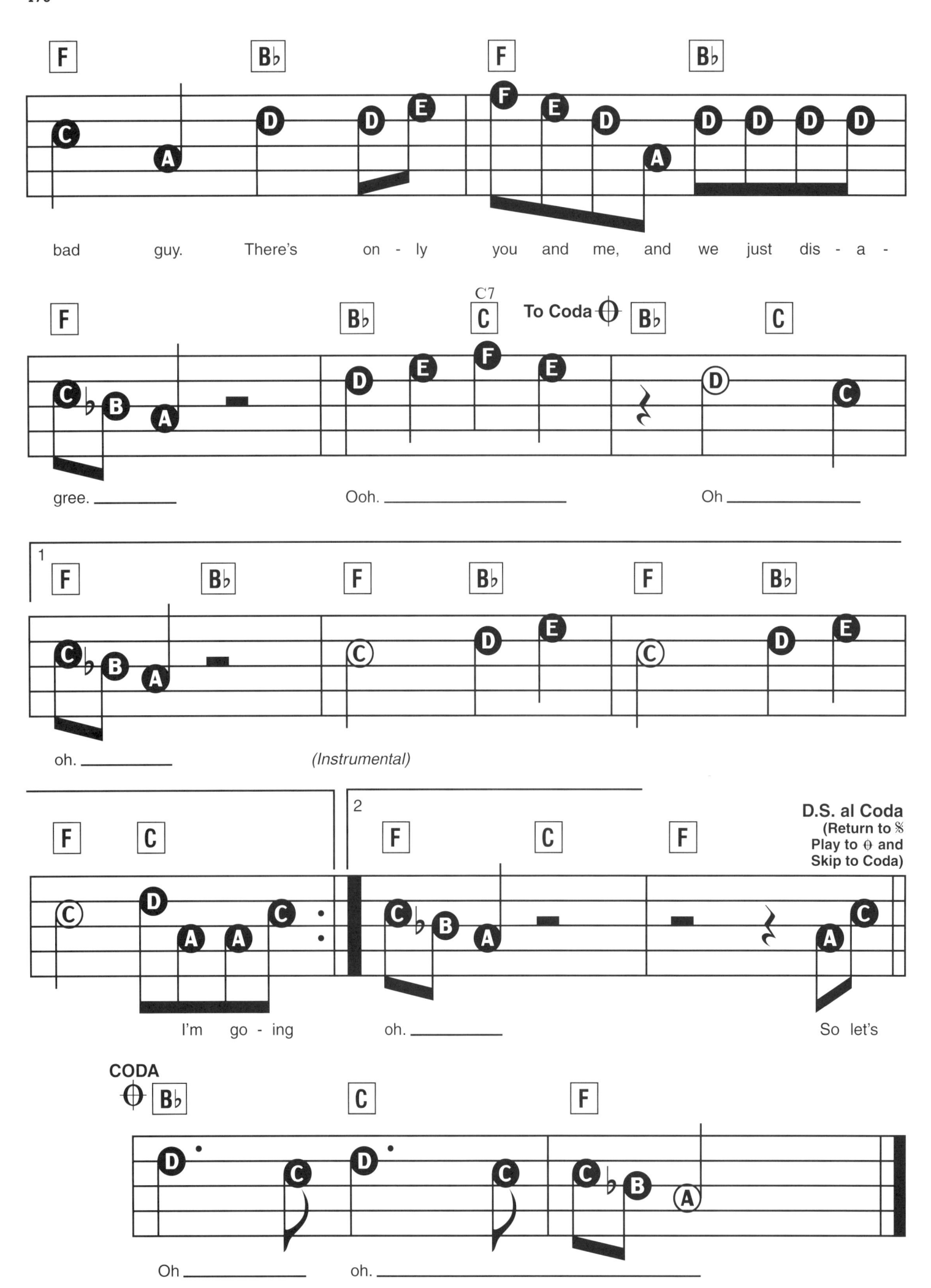

gree. _____ Ooh. _____ Oh _____

oh. _____ (Instrumental)

I'm go-ing oh. _____ So let's

Oh _____ oh. _____

You're Only Lonely

Registration 4
Rhythm: Country Rock or 8-Beat

Words and Music by
John David Souther

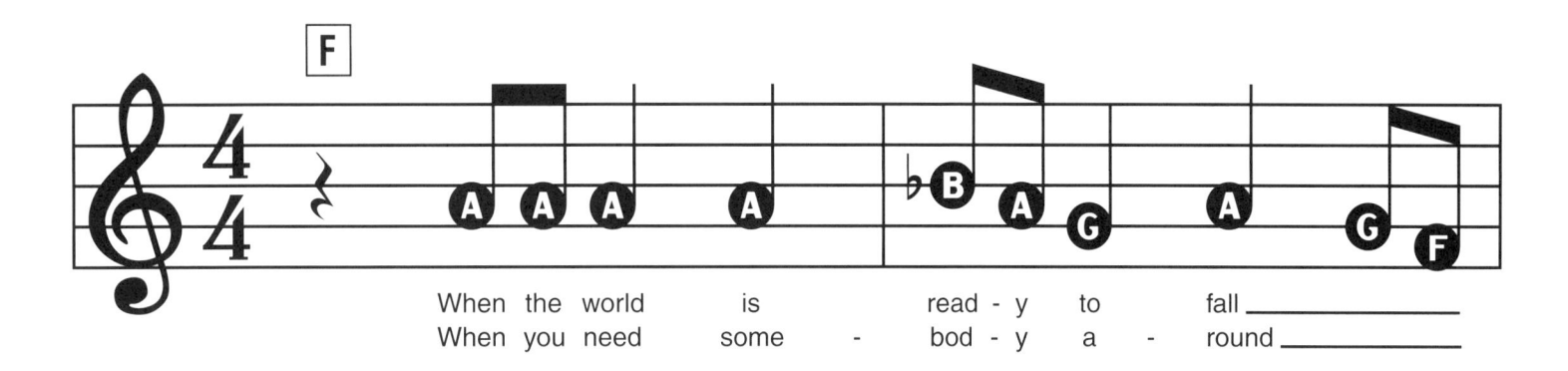

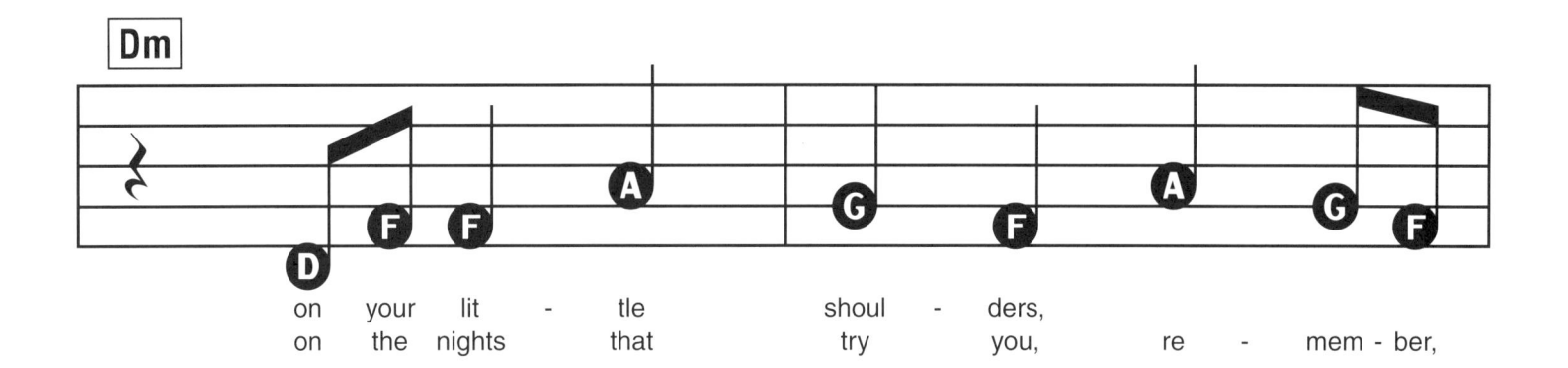

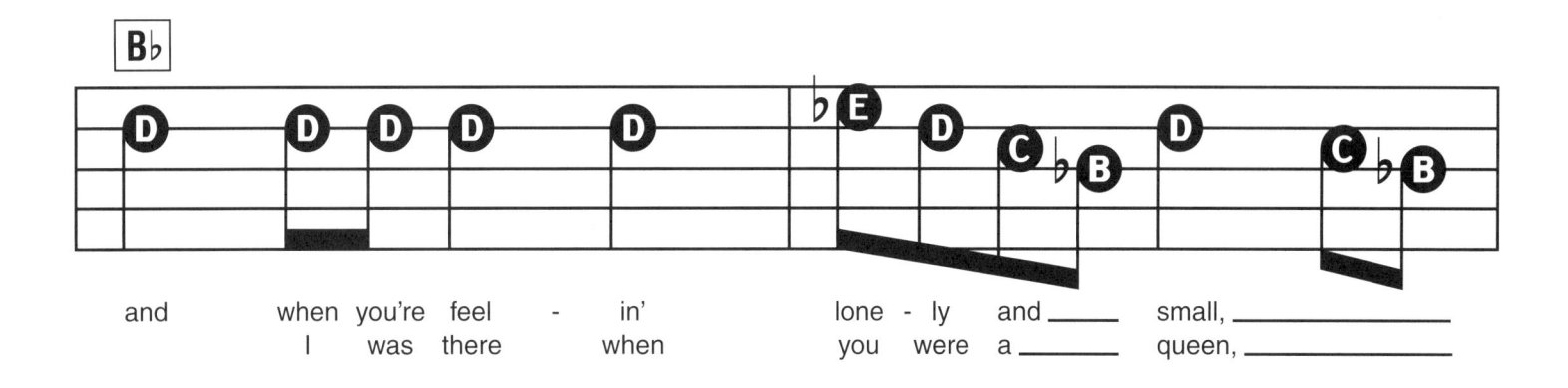

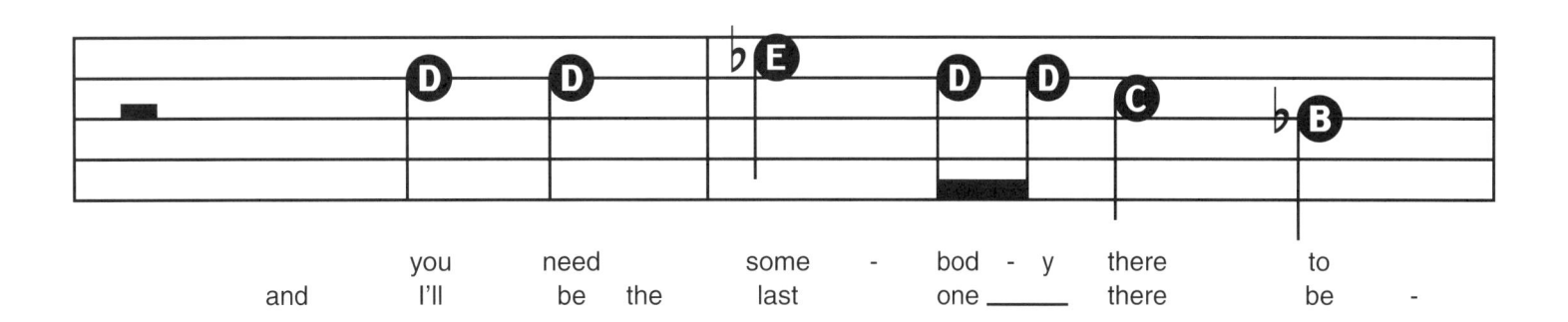

[F]

When the world is read-y to fall
When you need some-bod-y a-round

[Dm]

on your lit-tle shoul-ders,
on the nights that try you, re-mem-ber,

[B♭]

and when you're feel-in' lone-ly and small,
I was there when you were a queen,

you need some-bod-y there to
and I'll be the last one there be-

© 1979 EMI BLACKWOOD MUSIC INC.
All Rights Reserved   International Copyright Secured   Used by Permission

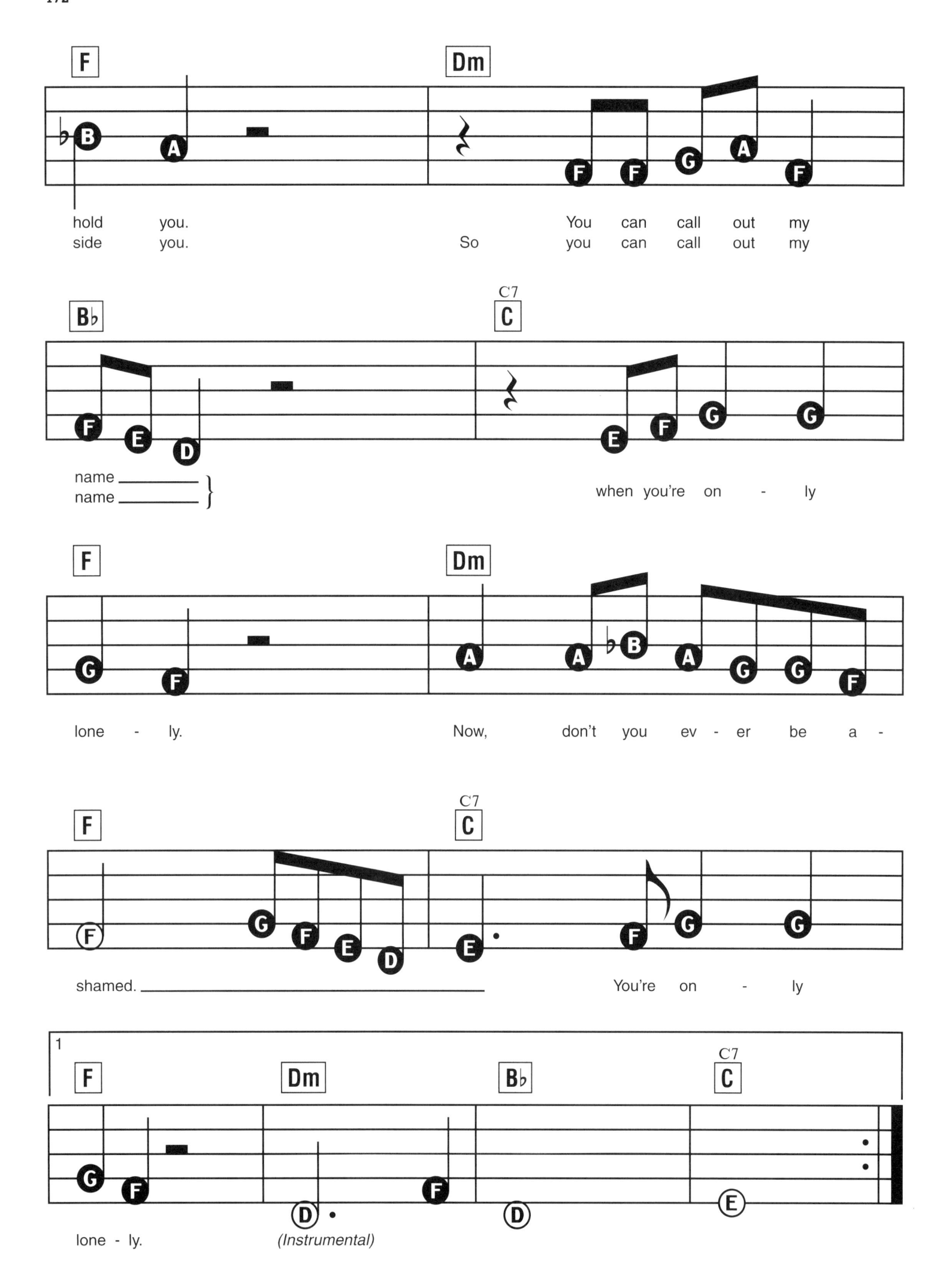

hold you.
side you. So you can call out my
name
name when you're on - ly
lone - ly. Now, don't you ev - er be a-
shamed. You're on - ly
lone - ly. *(Instrumental)*

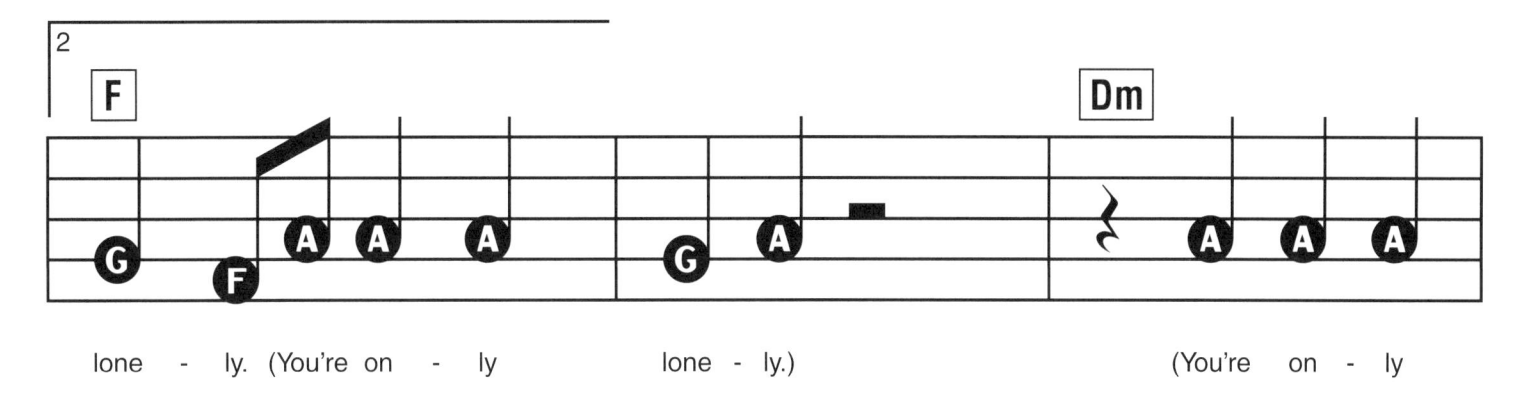

lone - ly. (You're on - ly lone - ly.) (You're on - ly lone - ly.) (You're on - ly lone - ly.)

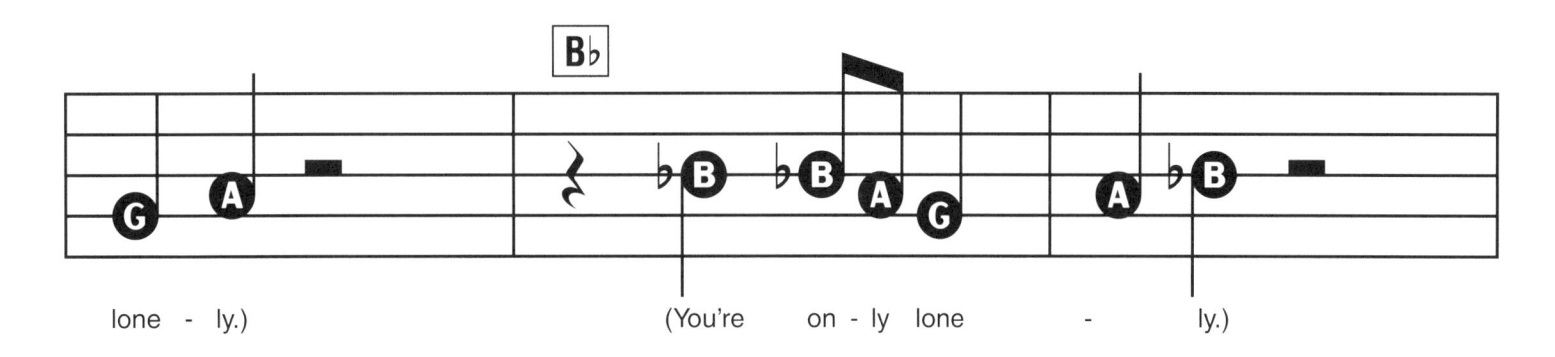

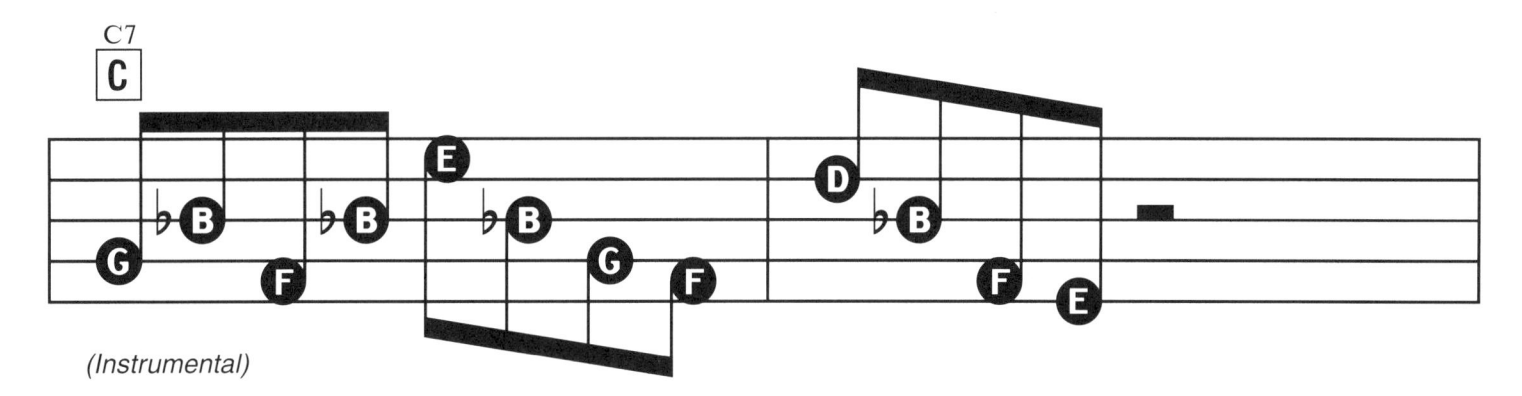

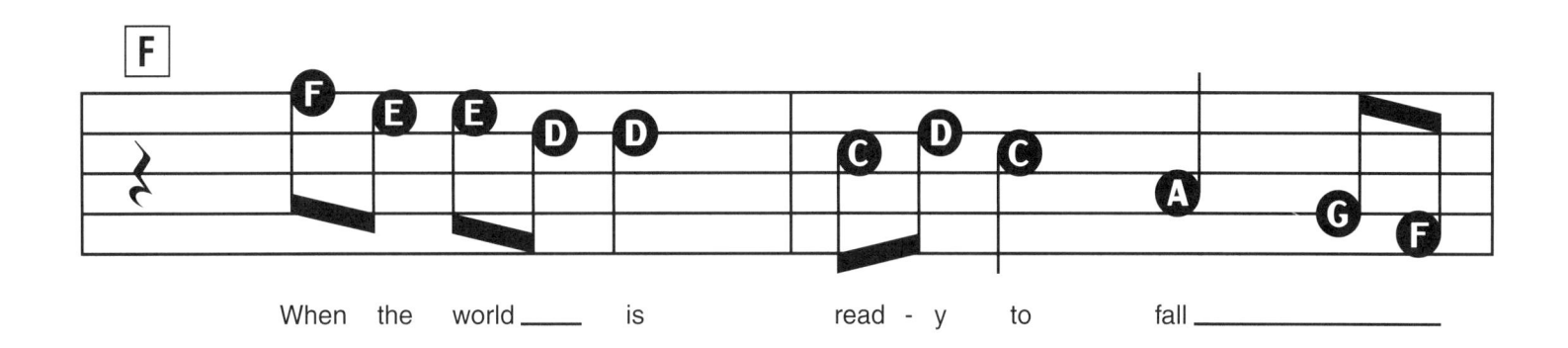

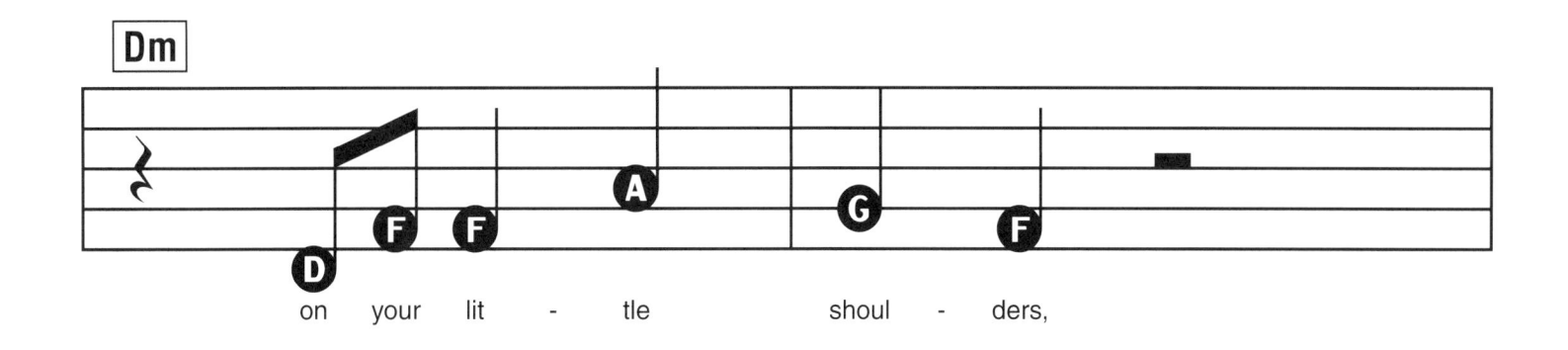

(Instrumental)

When the world ___ is read - y to fall ___

on your lit - tle shoul - ders,

and when you're feel - in' lone - ly and ____ small, ____

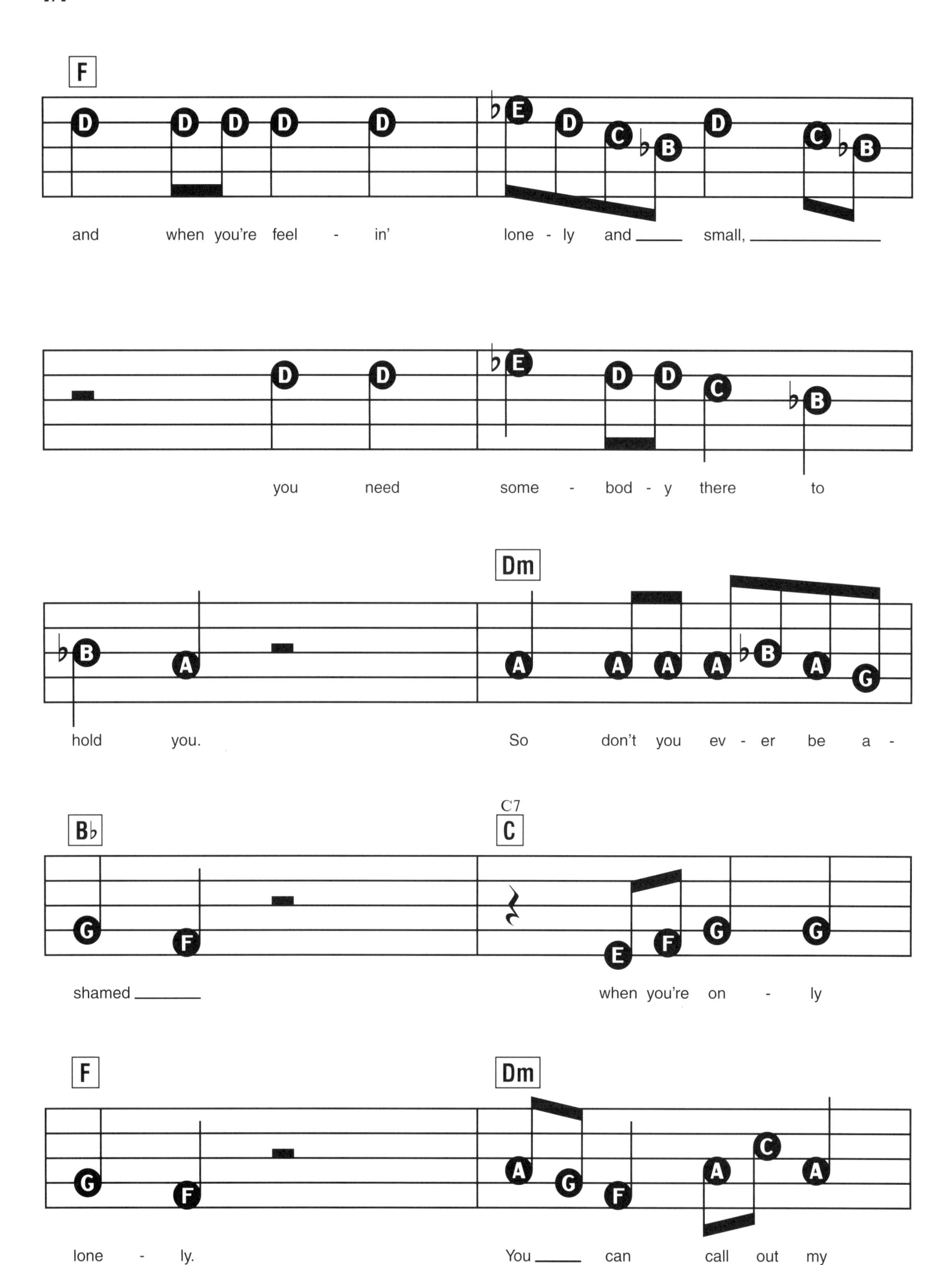

you need some - bod - y there to

hold you. So don't you ev - er be a-

shamed ____ when you're on - ly

lone - ly. You ____ can call out my

name _____ when you're on - ly

lone - ly. (You're on - ly lone - ly.)

(You're on - ly lone - ly.)

(You're on - ly lone - ly.)

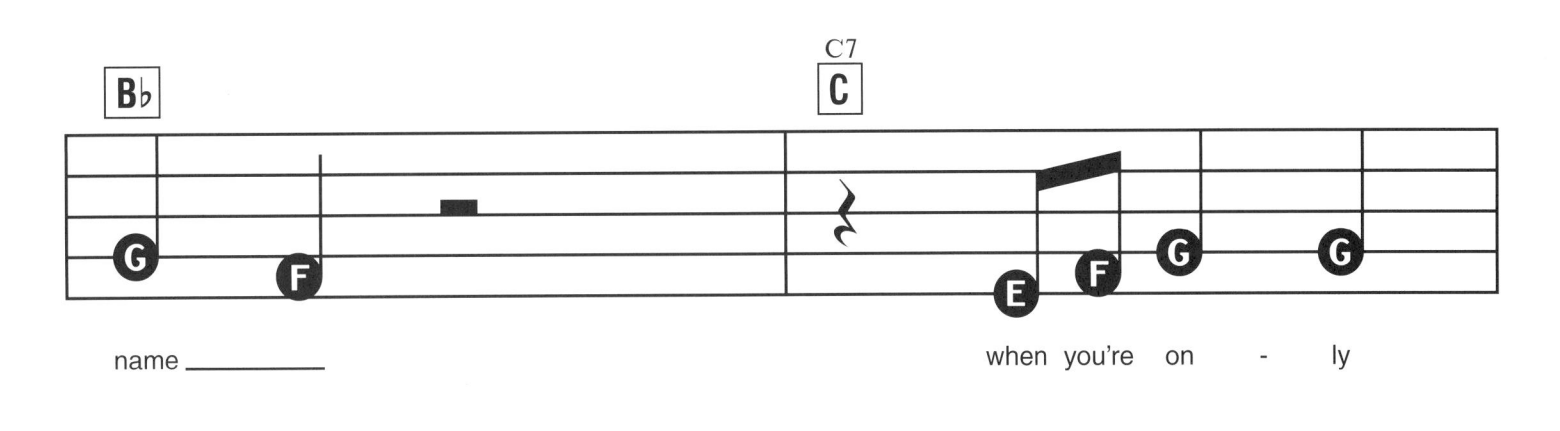

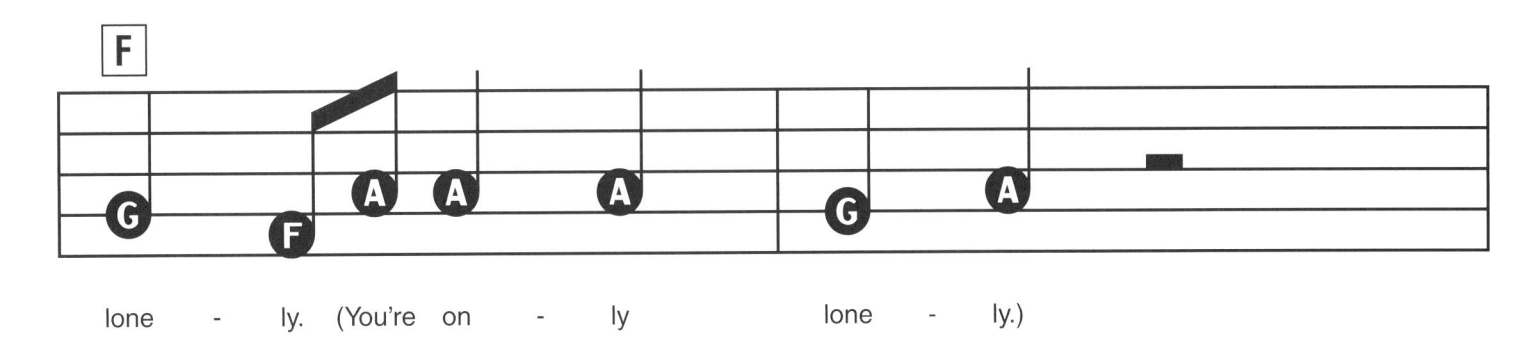

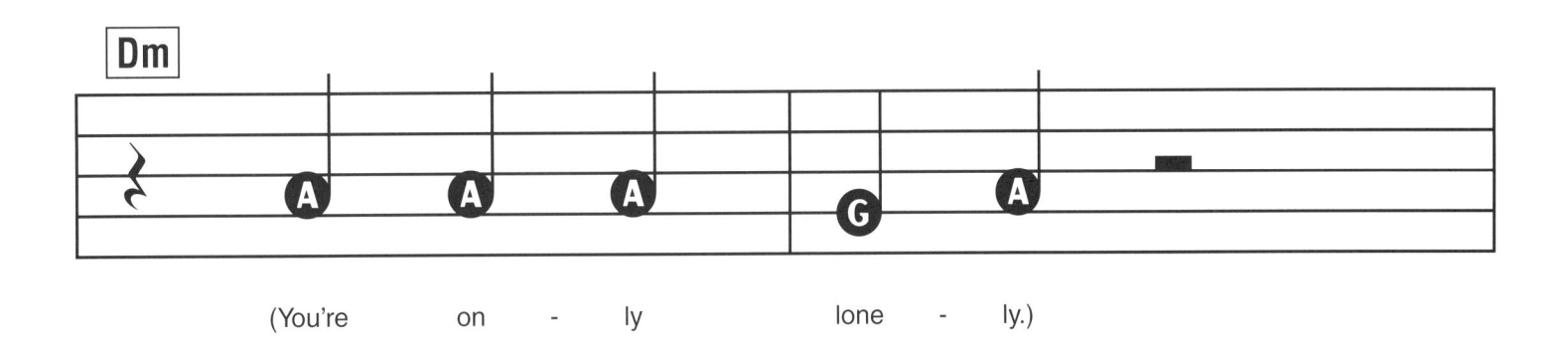

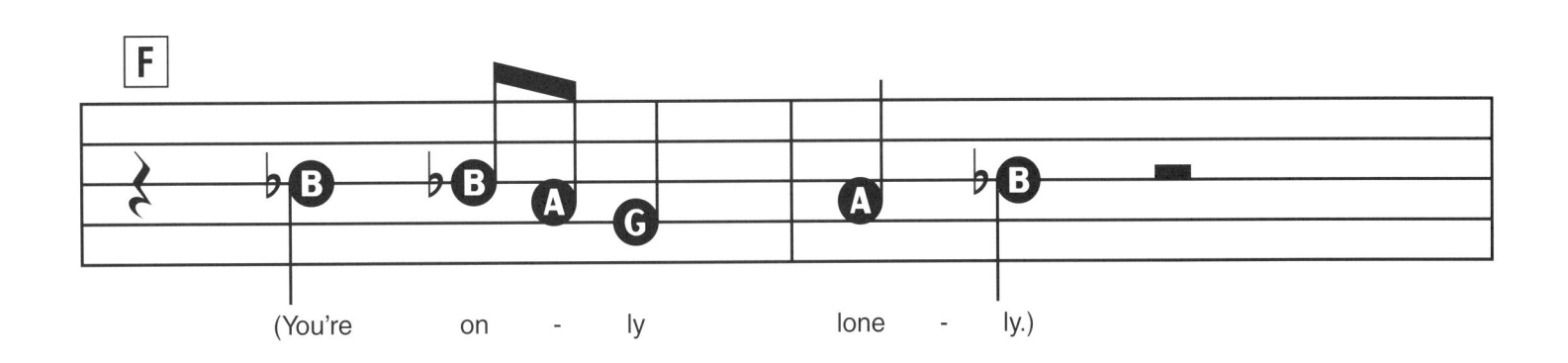

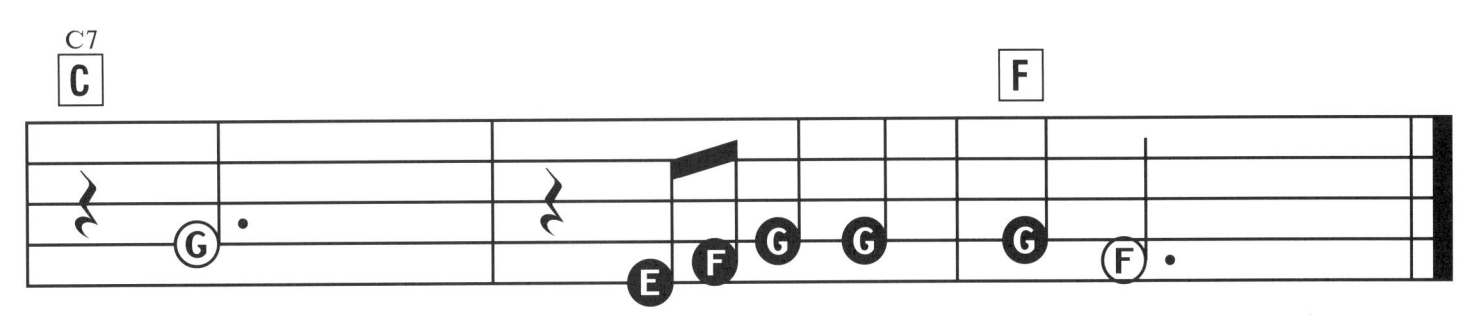

(Instrumental)

Where Have All the Flowers Gone?

Registration 10
Rhythm: Ballad

Words and Music by
Pete Seeger

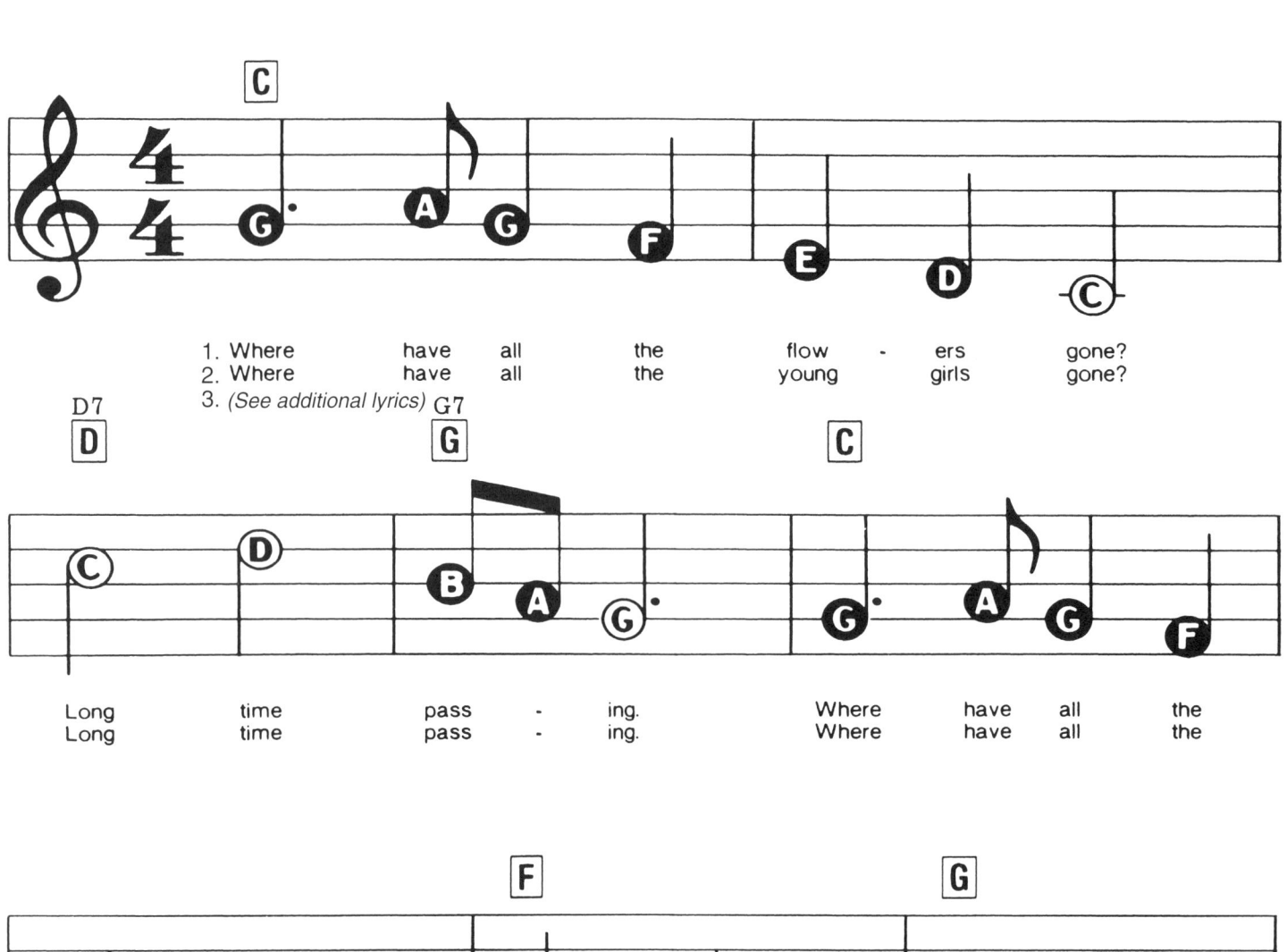

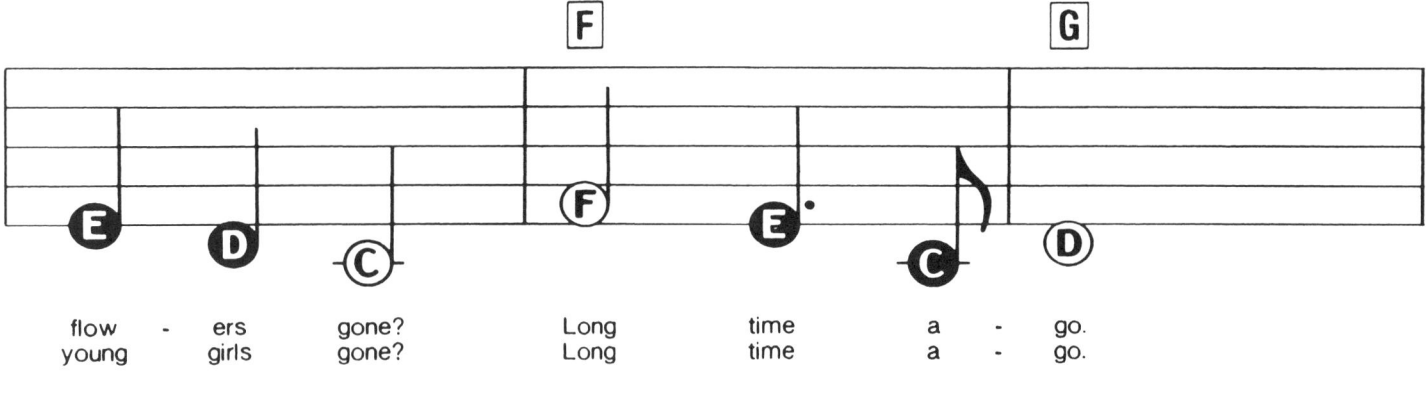

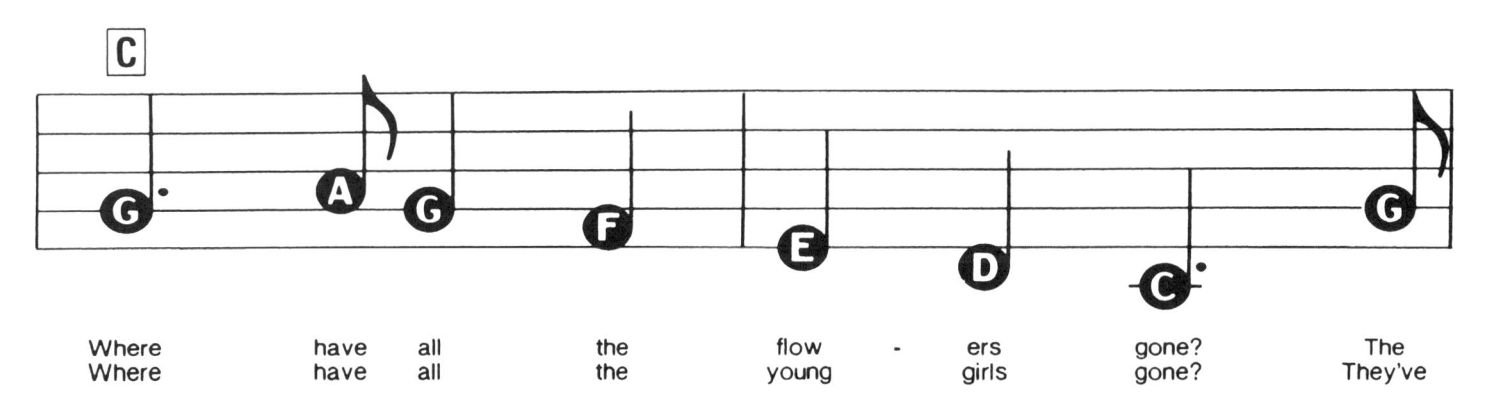

1. Where have all the flow - ers gone? Long time pass - ing. Where have all the flow - ers gone? Long time a - go. Where have all the flow - ers gone? The
2. Where have all the young girls gone? Long time pass - ing. Where have all the young girls gone? Long time a - go. Where have all the young girls gone? They've

3. *(See additional lyrics)*

Copyright © 1961 (Renewed) by Sanga Music, Inc.
All Rights Reserved   Used by Permission

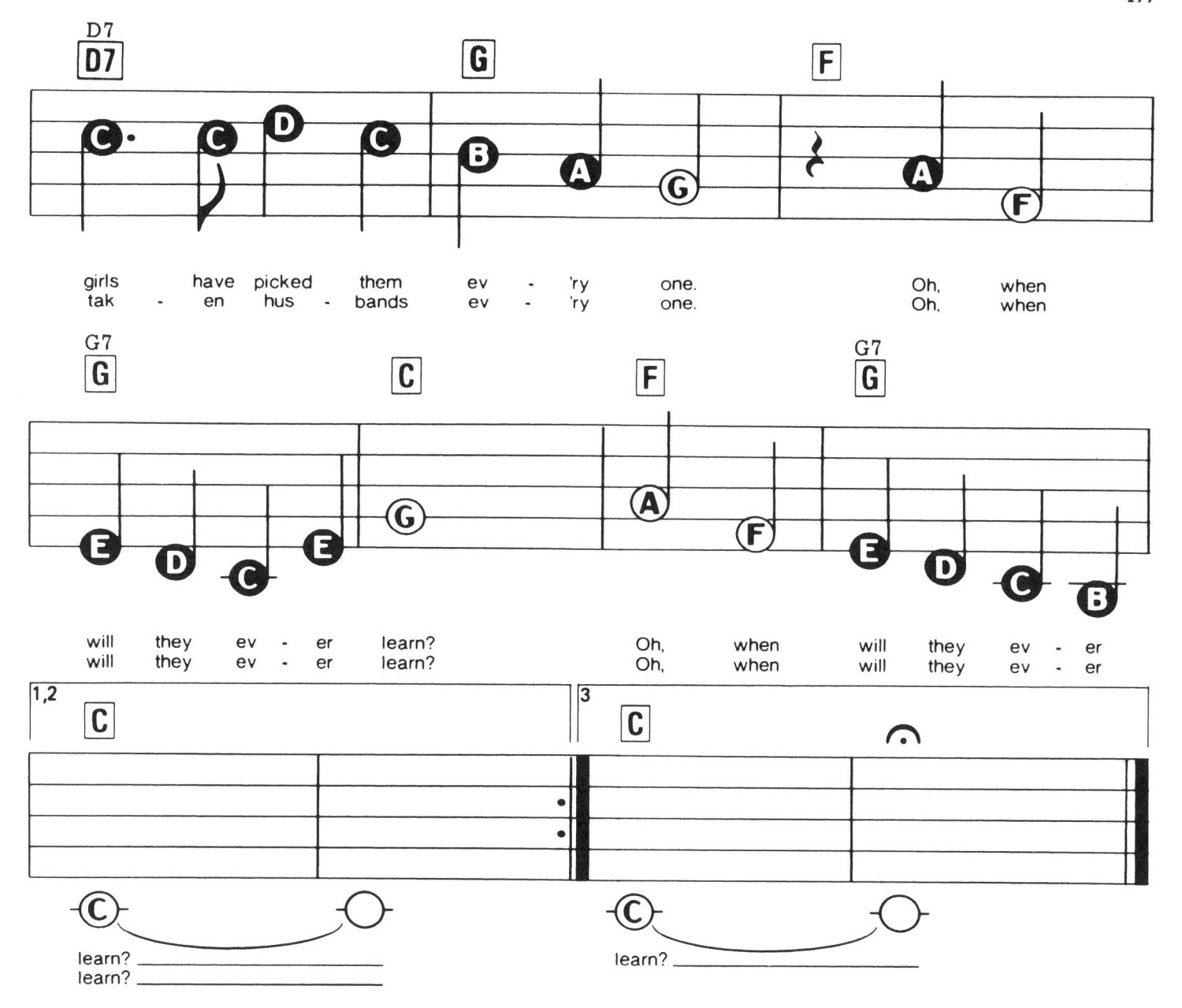

girls have picked them ev - 'ry one. Oh, when
tak - en hus - bands ev - 'ry one. Oh, when

will they ev - er learn? Oh, when will they ev - er
will they ev - er learn? Oh, when will they ev - er

learn?
learn?

learn?

Additional Lyrics

3. Where have all the young men gone?
   Long time passing.
   Where have all the young men gone?
   Long time ago.
   Where have all the young men gone?
   They're all in uniform.
   Oh, when will they ever learn?
   Oh, when will they ever learn?

You've Got a Friend

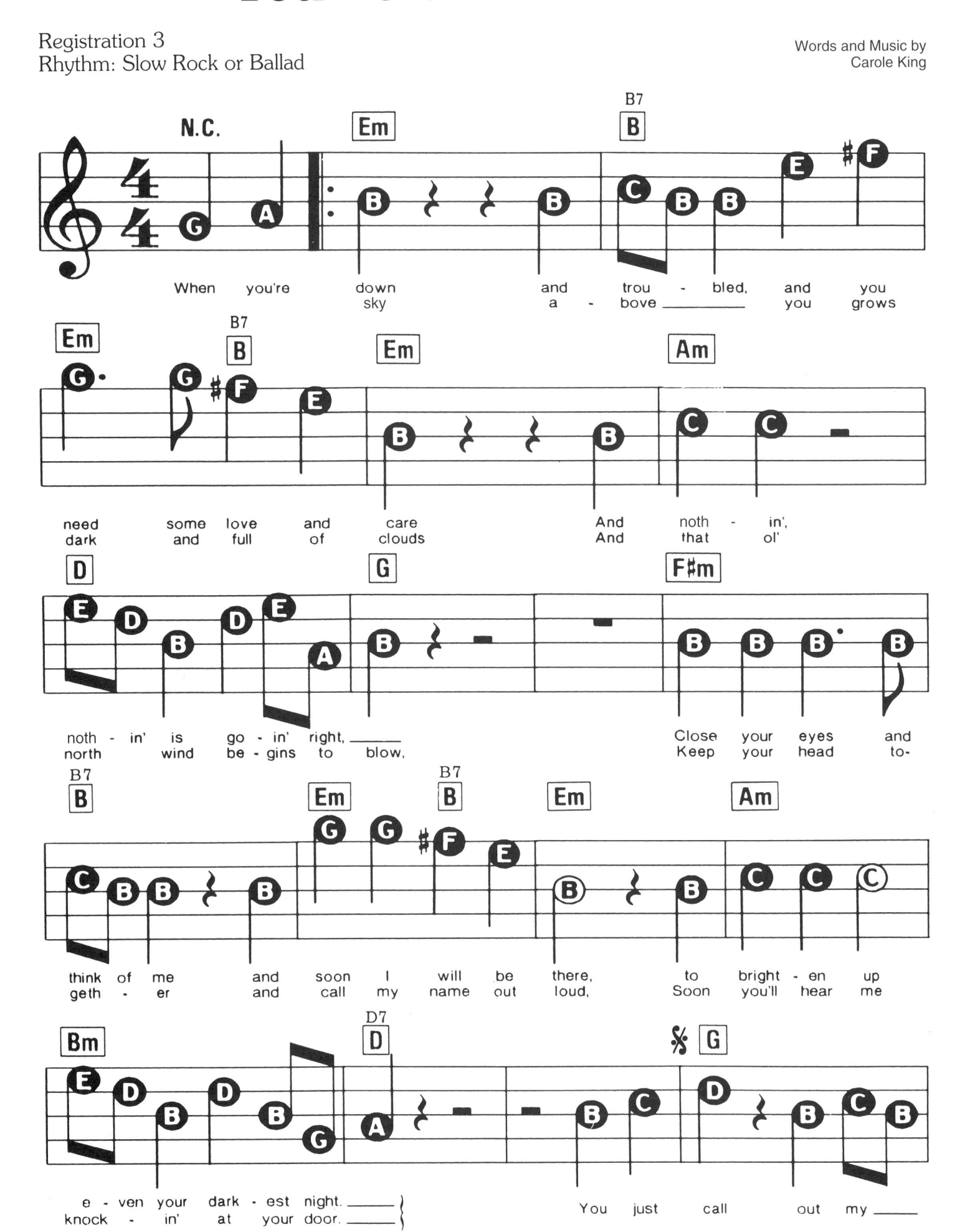

Registration 3
Rhythm: Slow Rock or Ballad

Words and Music by
Carole King

When you're down and troubled, and you
sky a-bove _____ you grows

need some love and care And nothin',
dark and full of clouds And that ol'

nothin' is go-in' right, _____ Close your eyes and
north wind be-gins to blow, Keep your head to-

think of me and soon I will be there, to bright-en up
geth - er and soon call my name out loud, Soon you'll hear me

e - ven your dark - est night. _____
knock - in' at your door. _____

You just call out my _____

© 1971 (Renewed 1999) COLGEMS-EMI MUSIC INC.
All Rights Reserved International Copyright Secured Used by Permission

name, and you know wher-ev-er I am, I'll come ___ run-nin'

to see you a - gain. ___

Win - ter, Spring, Sum - mer or Fall, ___ all you have to do is call; ___

___ and I'll be there. ___ You've got a

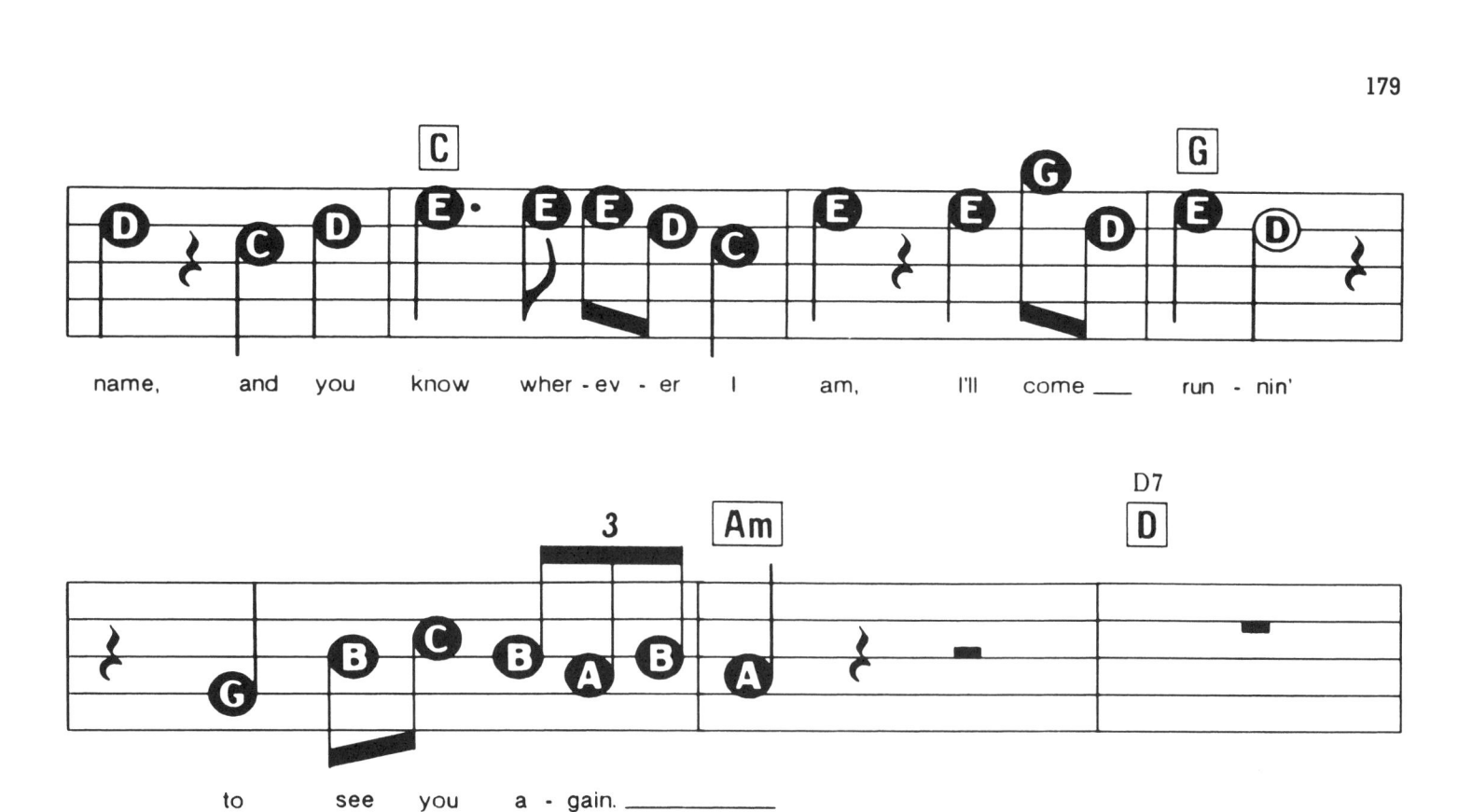

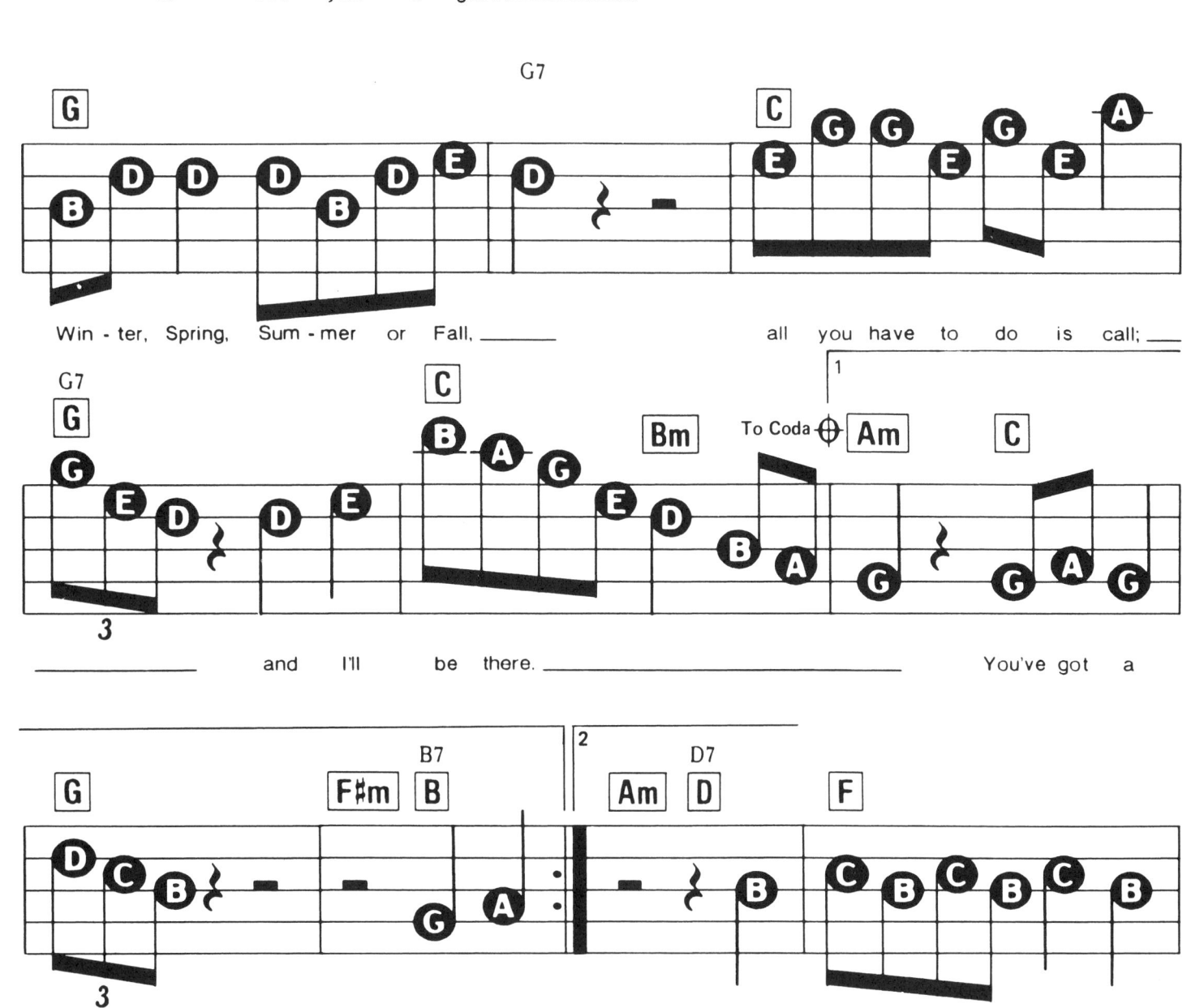

friend. ___ If the Now ain't it good to know that

you've got a friend when peo-ple can be so cold? _____ They hurt you, yes, and de-sert _____ you And take your soul if you let them. Oh, but don't you let them. You just _____ You've got a friend. _____ You've got a friend. _____ Ain't it good to know you've got a

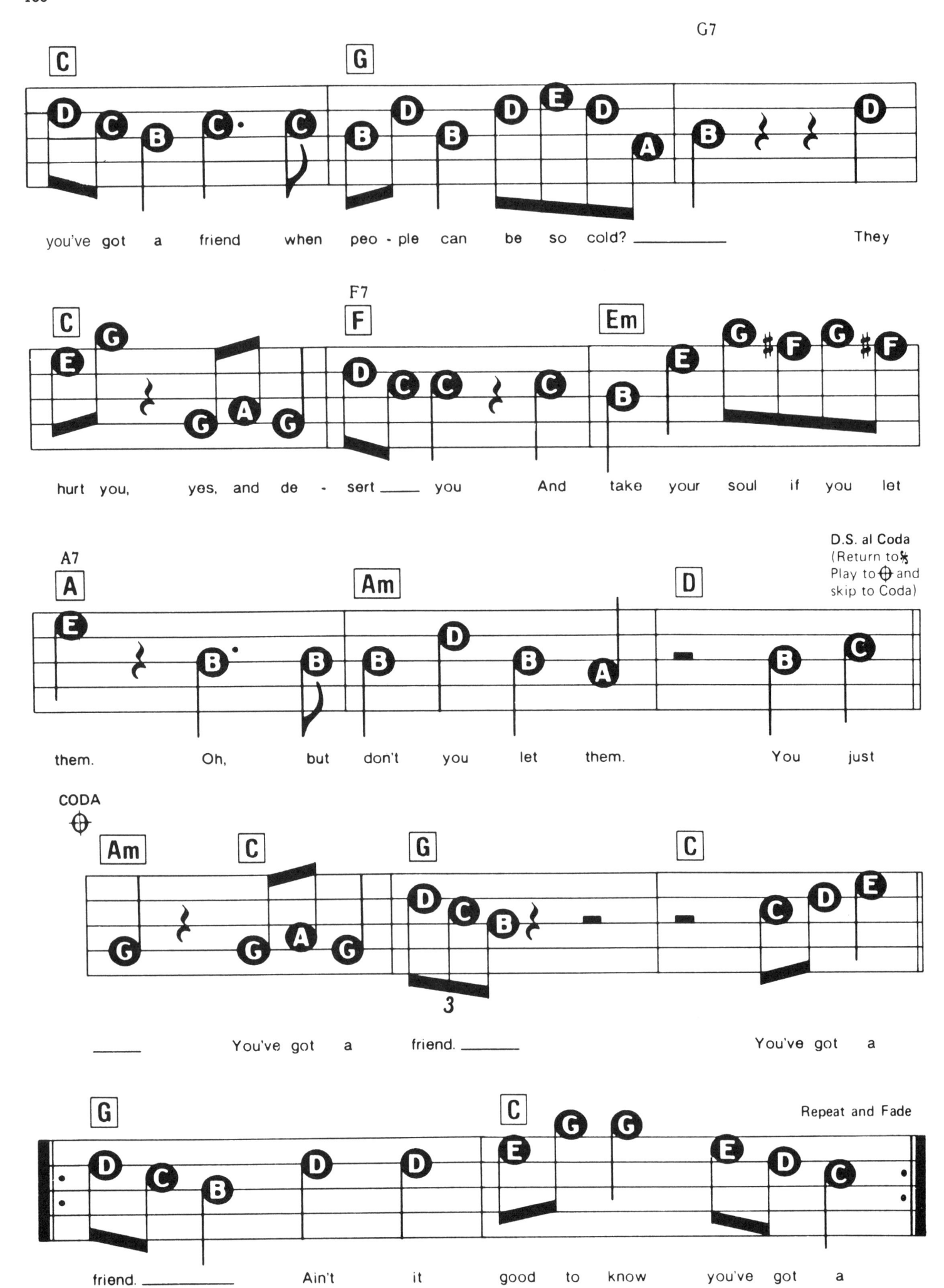

E-Z Play Today Registration Guide

- Match the Registration number on the song to the corresponding numbered category below. Select and activate an instrumental sound available on your instrument.

- Choose an automatic rhythm appropriate to the mood and style of the song. (Consult your Owner's Guide for proper operation of automatic rhythm features.)

- Adjust the tempo and volume controls to comfortable settings.

Registration

1	Mellow	Flutes, Clarinet, Oboe, Flugel Horn, Trombone, French Horn, Organ Flutes
2	Ensemble	Brass Section, Sax Section, Wind Ensemble, Full Organ, Theater Organ
3	Strings	Violin, Viola, Cello, Fiddle, String Ensemble, Pizzicato, Organ Strings
4	Guitars	Acoustic/Electric Guitars, Banjo, Mandolin, Dulcimer, Ukulele, Hawaiian Guitar
5	Mallets	Vibraphone, Marimba, Xylophone, Steel Drums, Bells, Celesta, Chimes
6	Liturgical	Pipe Organ, Hand Bells, Vocal Ensemble, Choir, Organ Flutes
7	Bright	Saxophones, Trumpet, Mute Trumpet, Synth Leads, Jazz/Gospel Organs
8	Piano	Piano, Electric Piano, Honky Tonk Piano, Harpsichord, Clavi
9	Novelty	Melodic Percussion, Wah Trumpet, Synth, Whistle, Kazoo, Perc. Organ
10	Bellows	Accordion, French Accordion, Mussette, Harmonica, Pump Organ, Bagpipes

E-Z PLAY® TODAY PUBLICATIONS

FOR ORGANS, PIANOS & ELECTRONIC KEYBOARDS

The E-Z Play® Today songbook series is the shortest distance between beginning music and playing fun! Check out this list of highlights and visit www.halleonard.com for a complete listing of all volumes and songlists.

Code	#	Title	Price
00102278	1.	Favorite Songs with 3 Chords	$7.95
00100374	2.	Country Sound	$8.95
00100167	3.	Contemporary Disney	$15.95
00100382	4.	Dance Band Greats	$7.95
00100305	5.	All-Time Standards	$7.95
00100428	6.	Songs of The Beatles	$7.95
00100442	7.	Hits from Musicals	$7.95
00100490	8.	Patriotic Songs	$7.95
00100355	9.	Christmas Time	$7.95
00100435	10.	Hawaiian Songs	$7.95
00100386	12.	Danceable Favorites	$7.95
00100345	13.	Celebrated Favorites	$7.95
00100300	14.	All-Time Requests	$7.95
00100370	15.	Country Pickin's	$7.95
00100335	16.	Broadway's Best	$7.95
00100362	18.	Classical Portraits	$6.95
00102277	20.	Hymns	$7.95
00100570	22.	Sacred Sounds	$7.95
00100214	23.	Essential Songs – The 1920s	$16.95
00100206	24.	Essential Songs – The 1930s	$16.95
00100207	25.	Essential Songs – The 1940s	$16.95
00100100	26.	Holly Season	$7.95
00001236	27.	60 of the World's Easiest to Play Songs with 3 Chords	$8.95
00101598	28.	Fifty Classical Themes	$9.95
00100135	29.	Love Songs	$7.95
00100030	30.	Country Connection	$8.95
00001289	32.	Sing-Along Favorites	$7.95
00100254	35.	Frank Sinatra – Romance	$8.95
00100122	36.	Good Ol' Songs	$10.95
00100410	37.	Favorite Latin Songs	$7.95
00100032	38.	Songs of the '90s	$12.95
00100425	41.	Songs of Gershwin, Porter & Rodgers	$7.95
00100123	42.	Baby Boomers Songbook	$9.95
00100576	43.	Sing-along Requests	$8.95
00102135	44.	Best of Willie Nelson	$8.95
00100460	45.	Love Ballads	$7.95
00100343	48.	Gospel Songs of Johnny Cash	$7.95
00100043	49.	Elvis, Elvis, Elvis	$9.95
00102114	50.	Best of Patsy Cline	$9.95
00100208	51.	Essential Songs – The 1950s	$17.95
00100209	52.	Essential Songs – The 1960s	$17.95
00100210	53.	Essential Songs – The 1970s	$19.95
00100211	54.	Essential Songs – The 1980s	$19.95
00100342	55.	Johnny Cash	$9.95
00100118	57.	More of the Best Songs Ever	$17.95
00100353	59.	Christmas Songs	$8.95
00102282	60.	Best of Eric Clapton	$10.95
00102314	61.	Jazz Standards	$10.95
00100409	62.	Favorite Hymns	$6.95
00100360	63.	Classical Music (Spanish/English)	$6.95
00100223	64.	Wicked	$9.95
00100217	65.	Hymns with 3 Chords	$7.95
00102312	66.	Torch Songs	$14.95
00100218	67.	Music from the Motion Picture *Ray*	$8.95
00100449	69.	It's Gospel	$7.95
00100432	70.	Gospel Greats	$7.95
00100117	72.	Canciones Románticas	$6.95
00100121	73.	Movie Love Songs	$7.95
00100568	75.	Sacred Moments	$6.95
00100572	76.	The Sound of Music	$8.95
00100489	77.	My Fair Lady	$6.95
00100424	81.	Frankie Yankovic – Polkas & Waltzes	$7.95
00100565	82.	Romantic Ballads & One Waltz	$7.95
00100579	86.	Songs from Musicals	$7.95
00100313	87.	The Beatles Best	$14.95
00100215	88.	The Beatles' Greatest	$16.95
00100577	89.	Songs for Children	$7.95
00290104	90.	Elton John Anthology	$12.95
00100034	91.	30 Songs for a Better World	$8.95
00100036	93.	Country Hits	$10.95
00100139	94.	Jim Croce – Greatest Hits	$8.95
00100219	95.	The Phantom of the Opera (Movie)	$10.95
00102317	97.	Elvis Presley – Songs of Inspiration	$7.95
00100125	99.	Children's Christmas Songs	$7.95
00100602	100.	Winter Wonderland	$7.95
00001309	102.	Carols of Christmas	$6.95
00100127	103.	Greatest Songs of the Last Century	$16.95
00100363	108.	Classical Themes (English/Spanish)	$6.95
00102232	109.	Motown's Greatest Hits	$12.95
00101566	110.	Neil Diamond Collection	$12.95
00100119	111.	Season's Greetings	$14.95
00101498	112.	Best of The Beatles	$17.95
00100134	113.	Country Gospel USA	$10.95
00101612	115.	The Greatest Waltzes	$8.95
00100136	118.	100 Kids' Songs	$12.95
00101990	119.	57 Super Hits	$12.95
00100433	120.	Gospel of Bill & Gloria Gaither	$14.95
00100333	121.	Boogies, Blues and Rags	$7.95
00100146	122.	Songs for Praise & Worship	$8.95
00100001	125.	Great Big Book of Children's Songs	$12.95
00101563	127.	John Denver's Greatest Hits	$8.95
00100037	129.	The Groovy Years	$12.95
00102318	131.	Doo-Wop Songbook	$10.95
00100171	135.	All Around the U.S.A.	$10.95
00001256	136.	Christmas Is for Kids	$7.95
00100144	137.	Children's Movie Hits	$7.95
00100038	138.	Nostalgia Collection	$14.95
00101732	139.	Best of Jerome Kern	$7.95
00101956	140.	Best of George Strait	$12.95
00100290	141.	All Time Latin Favorites	$7.95
00100013	144.	All Time TV Favorites	$17.95
00100597	146.	Hank Williams – His Best	$7.95
00100420	147.	Folk Songs of England, Scotland & Ireland	$6.95
00101548	150.	Best Big Band Songs Ever	$16.95
00100152	151.	Beach Boys – Greatest Hits	$8.95
00101592	152.	Fiddler on the Roof	$8.95
00100004	153.	Our God Reigns	$10.95
00101549	155.	Best of Billy Joel	$9.95
00100033	156.	Best of Rodgers & Hart	$7.95
00001264	157.	Easy Favorites	$6.95
00100049	162.	Lounge Music	$10.95
00101530	164.	Best Christmas Songbook	$9.95
00101895	165.	Rodgers & Hammerstein Songbook	$9.95
00100140	167.	Christian Children's Songbook	$10.95
00100148	169.	A Charlie Brown Christmas™	$6.95
00101900	170.	Kenny Rogers – Greatest Hits	$9.95
00101537	171.	Best of Elton John	$7.95
00100149	176.	Charlie Brown Collection™	$7.95
00100019	177.	I'll Be Seeing You – 50 Songs of World War II	$14.95
00102325	179.	Love Songs of The Beatles	$9.95
00101610	181.	Great American Country Songbook	$12.95
00001246	182.	Amazing Grace	$12.95
00100151	185.	Carpenters	$7.95
00101606	186.	40 Pop & Rock Song Classics	$12.95
00100155	187.	Ultimate Christmas	$16.95
00102276	189.	Irish Favorites	$7.95
00101939	190.	17 Super Christmas Hits	$7.95
00100053	191.	Jazz Love Songs	$8.95
00101998	192.	65 Standard Hits	$15.95
00101941	194.	67 Standard Hits	$16.95
00101609	196.	Best of George Gershwin	$7.95
00100057	198.	Songs in 3/4 Time	$9.95
00100453	199.	Jumbo Songbook	$19.95
00101539	200.	Best Songs Ever	$19.95
00101540	202.	Best Country Songs Ever	$17.95
00101541	203.	Best Broadway Songs Ever	$17.95
00101542	204.	Best Easy Listening Songs Ever	$17.95
00101543	205.	Best Love Songs Ever	$17.95
00101585	206.	Favorite Children's Songs	$7.95
00100108	208.	Easy Listening Favorites	$7.95
00100059	210.	'60s Pop Rock Hits	$12.95
00100154	212.	A Romantic Christmas	$7.95
00101546	213.	Disney Classics	$14.95
00101533	215.	Best Christmas Songs Ever	$19.95
00100156	219.	Christmas Songs with 3 Chords	$6.95
00102080	225.	Lawrence Welk Songbook	$9.95
00101482	226.	Award Winning Songs of the Country Music Association	$19.95
00101931	228.	Songs of the '20s	$12.95
00101932	229.	Songs of the '30s	$13.95
00101933	230.	Songs of the '40s	$14.95
00101934	231.	Songs of the '50s	$14.95
00101935	232.	Songs of the '60s	$14.95
00101936	233.	Songs of the '70s	$14.95
00101581	235.	Elvis Presley Anthology	$14.95
00100165	236.	Irving Berlin's God Bless America® & Other Songs for a Better Nation	$9.95
00290059	238.	25 Top Christmas Songs	$8.95
00290170	239.	Big Book of Children's Songs	$14.95
00290120	240.	Frank Sinatra	$14.95
00100158	243.	Oldies! Oldies! Oldies!	$10.95
00290242	244.	Songs of the '80s	$14.95
00100041	245.	Best of Simon & Garfunkel	$8.95
00100174	248.	O Brother, Where Art Thou?	$8.95
00100175	249.	Elv1s – 30 #1 Hits	$9.95
00102113	251.	Phantom of the Opera (Broadway)	$14.95
00100065	252.	Andy Griffith – I Love to Tell the Story	$7.95
00100064	253.	Best Movie Songs Ever	$14.95
00100176	254.	Bossa Nova	$7.95
00100203	256.	Very Best of Lionel Richie	$8.95
00100178	259.	Norah Jones – Come Away with Me	$9.95
00102306	261.	Best of Andrew Lloyd Webber	$12.95
00100063	266.	Latin Hits	$7.95
00100062	269.	Love That Latin Beat	$7.95
00100179	270.	Christian Christmas Songbook	$14.95
00100204	271.	Favorite Christmas Songs	$12.95
00101425	272.	ABBA Gold – Greatest Hits	$7.95
00102248	275.	Classical Hits – Bach, Beethoven & Brahms	$6.95
00100186	277.	Stevie Wonder – Greatest Hits	$9.95
00100237	280.	Dolly Parton	$9.95
00100068	283.	Best Jazz Standards Ever	$15.95
00100244	287.	Josh Groban	$10.95
00100022	288.	Sing-a-Long Christmas	$9.95
00100023	289.	Sing-a-Long Christmas Carols	$8.95
00100073	290.	"My Heart Will Go On" & 15 Other Top Movie Hits	$7.95
00102124	293.	Movie Classics	$9.95
00100069	294.	Old Fashioned Love Songs	$9.95
00100075	296.	Best of Cole Porter	$7.95
00102126	297.	Best TV Themes	$7.95
00102130	298.	Beautiful Love Songs	$7.95
00001102	301.	Kid's Songfest	$9.95
00100191	303.	Best Contemporary Christian Songs Ever	$16.95
00102147	306.	Irving Berlin Collection	$14.95
00102182	308.	Greatest American Songbook	$8.95
00100194	309.	3-Chord Rock 'n' Roll	$8.95
00001580	311.	The Platters Anthology	$7.95
00100195	313.	Tunes for Tots	$6.95
00100196	314.	Chicago	$8.95
00100197	315.	VH1's 100 Greatest Songs of Rock & Roll	$19.95
00100080	322.	Dixieland	$7.95
00100082	327.	Tonight at the Lounge	$7.95
00100092	333.	Great Gospel Favorites	$7.95
00100252	335.	More of the Best Broadway Songs Ever	$17.95
00102235	346.	Big Book of Christmas Songs	$14.95
00102140	350.	Best of Billboard: 1955-1959	$19.95
00100088	355.	Smoky Mountain Gospel Favorites	$8.95
00100095	359.	100 Years of Song	$17.95
00100096	360.	More 100 Years of Song	$19.95
00100103	375.	Songs of Bacharach & David	$7.95
00100107	392.	Disney Favorites	$19.95
00100108	393.	Italian Favorites	$7.95
00100111	394.	Best Gospel Songs Ever	$17.95
00100114	398.	Disney's Princess Collections	$9.95
00100115	400.	Classical Masterpieces	$10.95

FOR MORE INFORMATION, SEE YOUR LOCAL MUSIC DEALER, OR WRITE TO:

HAL•LEONARD® CORPORATION

7777 W. BLUEMOUND RD. P.O. BOX 13819 MILWAUKEE, WI 53213

Prices, contents, and availability subject to change without notice.

0708

CD PLAY-ALONG SERIES

Each book in this exciting new series comes with a CD of complete professional performances, and includes matching custom arrangements in our famous E-Z Play® Today format. With these books you can:

- Listen to complete professional performances of each of the songs
- Play the arrangements along with the recorded performances
- Sing along with the full performances; and/or play the arrangements as solos, without the disk.

SONG FAVORITES WITH 3 CHORDS • VOLUME 1
15 songs, including: Can Can Polka • For He's a Jolly Good Fellow • Kum Ba Yah • Oh! Susanna • On Top of Old Smoky • Ta-Ra-Ra-Boom-De-Ay • When the Saints Go Marching In • Yankee Doodle • and more. 00100180

CHILDREN'S SONGS • VOLUME 2
16 songs, including: Alphabet Song • Chopsticks • Frere Jacques (Are You Sleeping?) • I've Been Working on the Railroad • Jack and Jill • Looby Loo • Mary Had a Little Lamb • The Mulberry Bush • This Old Man • Three Blind Mice • and more. 00100181

HYMN FAVORITES • VOLUME 3
15 songs, including: Abide with Me • Blessed Assurance • The Church's One Foundation • Faith of Our Fathers • The Old Rugged Cross • Onward, Christian Soldiers • Rock of Ages • Sweet By and By • Were You There? • and more. 00100182

COUNTRY • VOLUME 4
14 songs, including: Crazy • Gentle on My Mind • Green Green Grass of Home • I Walk the Line • Jambalaya (On the Bayou) • King of the Road • Make the World Go Away • Son-Of-A-Preacher Man • Your Cheatin' Heart • and more. 00100183

GREAT GOSPEL FAVORITES • VOLUME 5
13 songs, including: Amazing Grace • At Calvary • Give Me That Old Time Religion • Higher Ground • His Eye Is on the Sparrow • It Is Well with My Soul • Precious Memories • Will the Circle Be Unbroken • and more. 00100184

CHRISTMAS CAROLS • VOLUME 6
15 songs, including: Deck the Hall • Go, Tell It on the Mountain • God Rest Ye Merry, Gentlemen • It Came Upon the Midnight Clear • Jingle Bells • O Come, O Come, Emmanuel • O Holy Night • Silent Night • What Child Is This? • and more. 00100185

LENNON & McCARTNEY • VOLUME 7
10 songs, including: Eleanor Rigby • Hey Jude • In My Life • The Long and Winding Road • Love Me Do • Nowhere Man • Please Please Me • Sgt. Pepper's Lonely Hearts Club Band • Strawberry Fields Forever • Yesterday. 00100240

THE SOUND OF MUSIC • VOLUME 8
10 songs, including: Climb Ev'ry Mountain • Do-Re-Mi • Edelweiss • The Lonely Goatherd • Maria • My Favorite Things • Sixteen Going on Seventeen • So Long, Farewell • Something Good • The Sound of Music. 00100241

WICKED • VOLUME 9
10 songs, including: As Long as You're Mine • Dancing Through Life • Defying Gravity • For Good • I'm Not That Girl • No One Mourns the Wicked • Popular • What Is This Feeling? • The Wizard and I • Wonderful. 00100242

LES MISÉRABLES • VOLUME 10
10 songs, including: Bring Him Home • Castle on a Cloud • Do You Hear the People Sing? • Drink with Me (To Days Gone By) • Empty Chairs at Empty Tables • A Heart Full of Love • I Dreamed a Dream • On My Own • Stars • Who Am I?. 00100243

FOR MORE INFORMATION, SEE YOUR LOCAL MUSIC DEALER, OR WRITE TO:

HAL•LEONARD® CORPORATION
7777 W. BLUEMOUND RD. P.O. BOX 13819 MILWAUKEE, WI 53213

Visit Hal Leonard Online at **www.halleonard.com**

BOOK/CD PACKAGES ONLY $12.95 EACH!

Prices, contents and availability subject to change without notice.

0608